The World
ATLAS OF WINE

SIMON AND SCHUSTER
NEW YORK

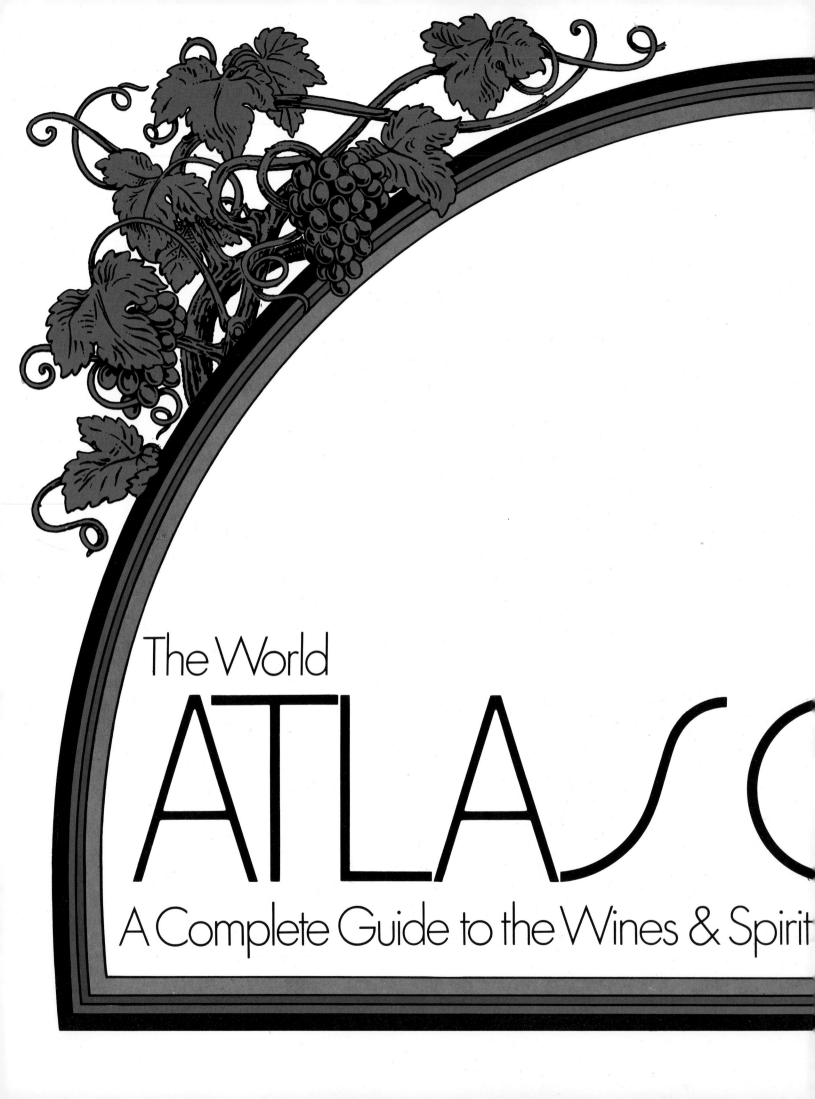

The World
ATLAS
A Complete Guide to the Wines & Spirit

OF WINE

of the World/Hugh Johnson

SIMON AND SCHUSTER
NEW YORK

The help of innumerable institutions and individuals has been vital to the completeness and authority of this book. Among them the publishers particularly wish to thank:

The Office International de la Vigne et du Vin, Paris

Institut National des Appellations d'Origine des Vins et Eaux-de-Vie, Paris

Comité National des Vins de France

Ministerium für Landwirtschaft, Weinbau und Forsten, Mainz

The Staatsdomänen of Hessen, Mosel-Saar-Ruwer, Nahe

The Istituto Nazionale per il Commercio Estero, Rome

Casa do Douro, Régua

Sindicato Nacional de la Vid, Madrid

Consejo Regulador de Denominación de Origen Jerez, Jerez de la Frontera

The Wine Institute, San Francisco

The Madeira Wines Bureau, London

The South Australian Department of Agriculture, Adelaide

The Scotch Whisky Association, London

The Bourbon Institute, New York

The Institut Technique du Vin, Paris

The regional Comités Interprofessionnels in France, Weinbauämter in Germany, Consorzi in Italy, Consejos Reguladores in Spain, the Commercial Counsellors of the London Embassies of all wine-growing countries; University Departments in France, Germany, California, Australia, and scores of wine-growers and wine-shippers all over the world.

A more complete list of sources appears on page 272

Every effort has been made to make the maps in this atlas as complete and up to date as possible. In order that future editions may be kept up to this standard the publishers will be very grateful for any information about changes of boundaries or names which should be recorded.

The World Atlas of Wine was prepared and designed under the direction and control of
Mitchell Beazley Publishers Limited
Mill House, Shaftesbury Avenue, London W1V 7AD
Published in the United States by Simon and Schuster
A Gulf + Western Company
Simon & Schuster Building, Rockefeller Center
1230 Avenue of the Americas
New York, New York 10020

First printed 1971
Enlarged and completely revised 1978
Thirteenth printing 1982
ISBN 0–671–43713–5

Library of Congress Catalog Card Number: 71–163481

Cartography by Fairey Surveys Limited
Reform Road, Maidenhead, Berkshire
Typesetting by Servis Filmsetting Limited, Manchester
Printed and bound in Italy

Contents

A detail from 'Wine-tasting in London docks' by George Cruikshank, 1821

INSTITUT NATIONAL DES APPELLATIONS D'ORIGINE
DES VINS ET EAUX-DE-VIE

PARIS (8e)
138, CHAMPS-ÉLYSÉES
TÉL. 225.54.75

Le Président

Ayant beaucoup apprécié la naissance dans la littérature viticole que constitue l'Atlas Mondial du Vin, c'est avec un vif plaisir qu'en ma double qualité de Président de l'Institut National des Appellations d'Origine des Vins et Eaux-de-Vie de France et de viticulteur, que je présente au lecteur cette seconde édition.

En réalisant cette oeuvre considérable, Monsieur Hugh JOHNSON a témoigné de son ambition et de son courage et il mérite amplement d'en être félicité. Tout d'abord parce qu'il a fort bien réussi, ainsi que le montre le succès de son ouvrage, à illustrer brillamment les vertus des terroirs propres à chaque région viticole. Ensuite parce que cet Atlas contribue à mieux faire connaître et apprécier les vins de qualité.

Or, l'INAO s'est attaché à une politique de qualité lorsque fut créée en 1935 la catégorie des appellations d'origine contrôlées.

La notion d'appellation d'origine était déjà reconnue des anciens. Beaucoup de noms de lieux furent utilisés pour désigner par des noms d'origine des objets ou des produits remarquables ou recherchés mais ce sont surtout les denrées alimentaires que l'on a désignées par des noms d'origine, et notamment des vins, car elles sont soumises presque toujours à des conditions naturelles.

Constitue, en effet, une appellation d'origine la dénomination d'un pays, d'une région, ou d'une localité servant à désigner un produit qui en est originaire et dont la qualité ou les caractères sont dûs au milieu géographique comprenant des facteurs naturels et des facteurs humains.

L'appellation d'origine atteste que le produit présente certaines qualités substancielles qui résultent d'un rapport étroit entre le terroir, c'est-à-dire les conditions naturelles, et les usages de production. Elle constitue pour les produits un titre imprescriptible inaliénable de la région et une prérogative des producteurs qui se plient aux usages traditionnels.

Aussi la précision remarquable et le soin apporté à la réalisation des cartes de cette géographie du vitis vinifira, comme à l'ensemble de l'ouvrage, sont à l'honneur de l'éditeur et ne manqueront pas d'être fort appréciés par tous les amateurs de vins ; ceux-ci auront à coeur de consulter cette oeuvre qui leur servira de guide pour une aimable promenade aux pays de la civilisation de la vigne.

Pierre PERROMAT

Introduction

MAPS, to me, since first I started on the happily absorbing study of wine, have been the vital, logical ally. Even the roughest sketch-map has always helped me, as a framework for organizing memories and impressions. With a map, distinctions and relationships become clear. Things fall into place.

This is how this atlas came into being. Bit by bit it dawned on me that maps on a large enough scale are more than aids to navigation: they are pictures of the ground and what goes on on it. That it was possible, as it were, to take a reader up into a high mountain and show him all the vineyards of the earth.

The relation between maps and wine is a very intimate one. Wine is, after all, the unique agricultural product whose price depends entirely on where it comes from. The better the wine, the more exactly it locates its origin—down, eventually, to one diminutive field in a simple village lying under what Stendhal described as 'an ugly dried-up little hill': named Romanée-Conti.

We have only to see how eerily accurate classifications of quality can remain for over a century to realize that it is the exact spot of earth which is the governing factor. Men change; techniques and fashions change; owners, machines, even the climate changes. What does not change is the soil, the elevation, the exposure. The trial and error of centuries has established where they are best—yet strange to say they have never been comprehensively mapped.

There is one classic wine atlas, Louis Larmat's *Atlas de la France Vinicole*. It was published with the help of the French wine authorities in the 1940s. It is incomplete, even of France, but some of its maps are masterpieces which will not be surpassed.

Of Germany there is nothing comparable. Nor of Italy, nor Spain, nor Portugal, nor any of the wine-growing countries of the New World. Such maps as exist tend to be preoccupied with legal boundaries rather than with topography and viticultural detail.

The emphasis of this atlas is on the consumer's point of view. Faced with the impossibility of mapping all vineyards in the same detail, I had to find a scale of priorities. The scale I have used is more or less that of one of the great wine merchants of London, New York, San Francisco or Bristol—the places in the world where the widest range of good wines is to be found. Only outside wine-growing Europe do such all-embracing, balanced selections exist: a great Moselle wine is not to be found in Paris—still less in Bordeaux.

There was no question of finding one style or one set of criteria to apply to every map. For the very fact which is most enthralling about wine is that no two regions have the same standards, or place emphasis on the same things. In Burgundy there is the most complex grading of fields ever attempted: each field, and even parts of fields, being classified in a hierarchy which is cut-and-dried. In parts of Bordeaux there is a formal grading of properties; not directly related to the land but to the estates on it. In Germany there is no land classification at all, but an ingenious hierarchy of ripeness. In Champagne whole villages are classed, in Jerez soils of certain kinds, in Italy some traditional wine zones, but not others.

Yet behind all this tangle of nomenclature and classification lies the physical fact of the hills and valleys where the vine grows. In each case I have tried to make it plain, so far as I have been able to discover, not only which corner of the countryside gives the best wine, but why; what happy accident of nature has led (in many cases) to the development of a classic taste which has become familiar—at least by name—to half the world.

If the maps succeed in portraying wine-country clearly and appealingly, as I believe they do, it is largely due to the care and vision of Harold Fullard, the cartographer, to whom I and the publishers are deeply indebted.

There are reproductions of paintings; music has scores; poems are printed; architecture can be drawn—but wine is a fleeting moment. One cannot write about wine, and stumble among the borrowed words and phrases which have to serve to describe it, without wanting to put a glass in the reader's hand and say 'Taste this'. For it is not every Nuits-St-Georges which answers the glowing terms of a general description—the corner shops of the world are awash with wine which bears little relation to the true character of the land.

This is the object of giving the most direct form of reference available: the labels of 900 producers whose wines and spirits truly represent the subject-matter of the atlas. Among the many thousands who qualify in every way to be included, the choice of which to use was almost impossible. As it stands it is partly personal, as anything to do with taste must be, and partly arbitrary, as the limitations of space ruthlessly cut out firm favourites. In the case of one or two countries, notably Russia, it was also hampered by the magnificent glue used to attach the labels to bottles.

No book like this could be attempted without the generous help of authorities in all the countries it deals with. Their enthusiasm and painstaking care have made it possible. On pages 4 and 272 there are lists of government and local offices, and some of the hundreds of others, growers, merchants and scholars, who have so kindly helped, and to whom I owe the great volume of information embodied both in the maps and the text. The facts are theirs; unless I quote a source, on the other hand, I must be held responsible for the opinions.

There is only room here to thank by name the Director, the Chef Technique Pierre Bréjoux, and the staff of the Institut National des Appellations d'Origine des Vins et Eaux-de-Vie in Paris who checked all the French maps; Dr Renz and his assistant Dr Hämmerling of the Statistisches Landesamt Rheinland-Pfalz who guided me through the shoals of the new German wine laws, and Peter Hasslacher, of Deinhard's, who accompanied me on numerous trips to Germany while the laws were in preparation; the Wine Institute in San Francisco and the KWV in South Africa who undertook extensive original map research for the atlas; and my diplomatic, patient, gay and indefatigable assistant, Colette Lebreton.

Introduction for the Second Edition

IN MOLIERE'S words, 'Nous avons changé tout cela.' Every reference book is out of date as soon as it is printed. But the energy which the grape-growers and the law-givers of the world have put into making the maps, labels and commentary of our first edition out of date has me lost in admiration.

In many places they have indeed changed all that. France seems calm, but a steady seething below the surface has constantly interesting results, which need recording. Germany, after the great upheaval of legislation in 1971, has finally, in the last two years, settled her new boundaries. Italy has made more than one hundred new controlled wine regions in the last five years. Spain has brought in a national system of controlled regions for the first time. Austria has a new wine law. So has Yugoslavia. The Soviet Union has planted another half-million acres (but they won't say where). South Africa has a new law defining and controlling 'wines of origin'. As for California, the planting of new valleys and the opening of new wineries need a television station rather than paper and ink to keep up with them.

All this change, and growth, has quickened public interest in wine to a level it has never reached before. The language of wine, the sort of questions people ask about it, have advanced from the simple, almost sentimental, to the precise, knowledgeable, not-to-be-fooled. To be sure it is easier to know the rules, even to understand the chemistry, than it is to learn to taste and remember. But the new generation of wine-lovers wants to know it all—including how to be critical.

It seems right, therefore, in this second edition to include new pages of more detailed information about how wine is being made today, as well as giving more space to regions that may have been under-mapped before, or are now emerging for the first time.

I have to acknowledge the help of more friends than ever in collecting and checking my information. Many of them are listed on the Acknowledgements page—but many more are not: every wine-grower I talk to, indeed every wine-lover, teaches me something more about this inexhaustible subject.

Right: the cellar of the 12th-century Cistercian abbey of Eberbach in the Rheingau has sheltered the wines of the Steinberg for 700 years. Today it is also the headquarters of the German Wine Academy.

The World of Wine

ONE HUMAN BEING in a hundred is a wine-grower, a wine-maker or a wine-merchant. The world wine harvest is enough to supply every one of the 4,000 million inhabitants of the globe with eight bottles a year. There are 25 million acres of vineyards—about one acre in every 130 cultivated in the world.

And yet wine is far from being a universal phenomenon. It is part of a cultural and agricultural pattern which is peculiar to the temperate zones of the earth where Mediterranean, or 'Western', man has flourished. Wine-growing and wine-drinking are attached at the roots to the most widespread and longest-lived civilization the earth has known.

The maps on this page show the distribution of vineyards, of wine-production and of wine-drinking round the world. France and Italy are far and away the biggest producers and consumers of wine. France has long been not only the biggest grower but the biggest importer in the world. At one time she accounted for two-thirds of the entire international wine trade. Now, however, Italy challenges her both in production and consumption and has become the world's biggest exporter—mainly to France.

Though growing and drinking go hand in hand in most places, there are exceptions. Muslim Algeria, for example, is still eighth in the world in production, with about 6 million hectolitres, but drinks only half a litre a head a year.

Non-wine-growing countries traditionally make a very poor showing as consumers. Britain, for example, though long famous for the quality of the wine she buys, drinks only seven bottles a head. French-speaking Belgium, drinking four times as much wine as the Flemish-speaking part of the country, does best of the non-growers.

Russia and the other Communist bloc countries, Argentina and the United States are the vineyards which have expanded most in the last decade. In Russia and America at least the popular acceptance of wine is new. Such vast newcomers to wine-drinking are bound to affect the world market radically. At present Americans only drink nine bottles a year, but their consumption is growing fast: the figure may double in the next decade.

The world-wide trend in wine-growing is towards more and more reliable wine from smaller acreages. Better kinds of grapes and better farming can take most of the credit. But there is also a tendency to abandon good but difficult old vineyards for flat and fertile ones which make more but worse wine. There is danger of a world glut of ordinary wine. Of good wine there can never be enough.

The distribution of the world's vineyards by countries, in thousands of hectares

Wine-growing is mainly confined to the temperate zones (shaded on map)

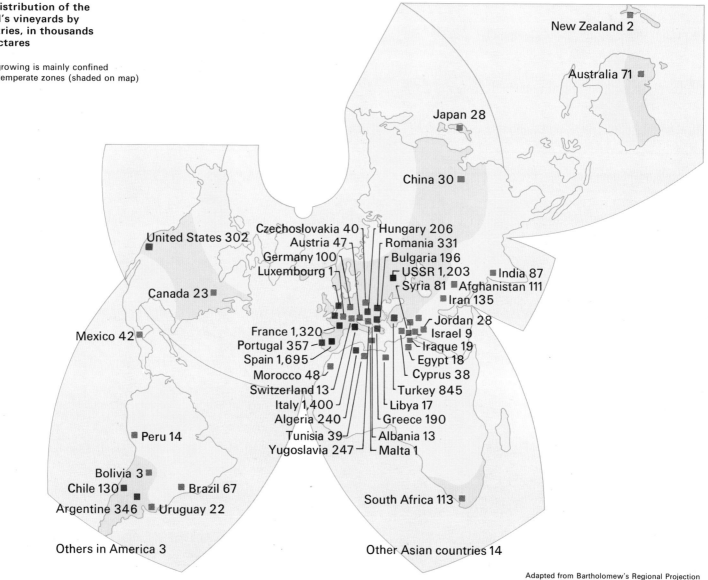

New Zealand 2
Australia 71
Japan 28
China 30
United States 302
Czechoslovakia 40
Hungary 206
Austria 47
Romania 331
Germany 100
Bulgaria 196
Luxembourg 1
USSR 1,203
India 87
Syria 81
Afghanistan 111
Iran 135
Canada 23
Jordan 28
France 1,320
Israel 9
Portugal 357
Iraque 19
Spain 1,695
Egypt 18
Morocco 48
Cyprus 38
Switzerland 13
Turkey 845
Italy 1,400
Libya 17
Algeria 240
Greece 190
Tunisia 39
Albania 13
Yugoslavia 247
Malta 1
Mexico 42
Peru 14
Bolivia 3
Chile 130
Brazil 67
Argentine 346
Uruguay 22
South Africa 113
Others in America 3
Other Asian countries 14

Adapted from Bartholomew's Regional Projection

World wine consumption
Shown in horizontal bars : in litres per head of population
☐ 1969 figures ☐ 1974/75 figures

Country	1969	1974/75
France	112	103.70
Italy	114.2	107.5
Portugal	93.2	120
Argentina	87.5	85.7
Spain	62.5	76
Chile	48.9	40
Switzerland	38.6	43.9
Austria	32	35.1
Hungary	34.8	37
Luxembourg	31	41.3
Yugoslavia	26.3	28.6
Uruguay	25	25.1
Romania	25	33
Bulgaria	21:7	19.98
Czechoslovakia	20	15
West Germany	15.9	23.2
Belgium	12.1	17.2
South Africa	9.4	10.41
Australia	8.2	11.2

Country	1969	1974/75
Cyprus	8	6.2
USSR	8.9	16
Sweden	5.8	8.25
Denmark	5.1	11.48
Netherlands	4.9	10.25
New Zealand	4.4	11.8
USA	4.5	6.53
Israel	3.9	3.75
Finland	3.7	8.86

Country	1969	1974/75
Canada	3.4	6.68
Great Britain	2.8	5.21
Lebanon	2.6	2
Morocco	2.5	2
Norway	2.2	3.34
Brazil	1.7	2
Algeria	1.5	0.5
Peru	1.1	1
Turkey	0.9	.55

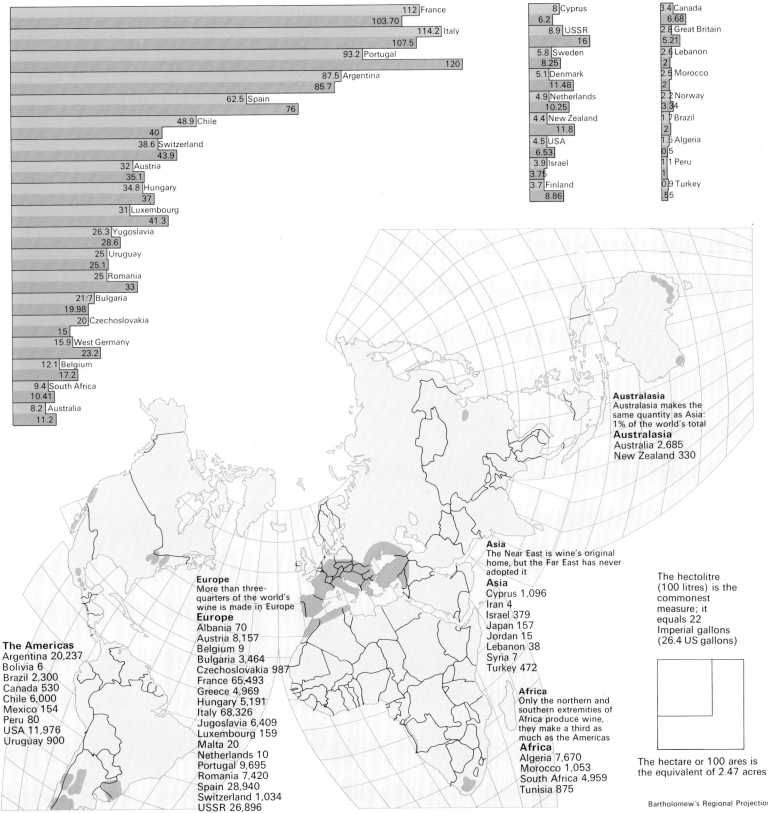

Australasia
Australasia makes the same quantity as Asia: 1% of the world's total
Australasia
Australia 2,685
New Zealand 330

Asia
The Near East is wine's original home, but the Far East has never adopted it
Asia
Cyprus 1,096
Iran 4
Israel 379
Japan 157
Jordan 15
Lebanon 38
Syria 7
Turkey 472

Africa
Only the northern and southern extremities of Africa produce wine, they make a third as much as the Americas
Africa
Algeria 7,670
Morocco 1,053
South Africa 4,959
Tunisia 875

Europe
More than three-quarters of the world's wine is made in Europe
Europe
Albania 70
Austria 8,157
Belgium 9
Bulgaria 3,464
Czechoslovakia 987
France 65,493
Greece 4,969
Hungary 5,191
Italy 68,326
Jugoslavia 6,409
Luxembourg 159
Malta 20
Netherlands 10
Portugal 9,695
Romania 7,420
Spain 28,940
Switzerland 1,034
USSR 26,896
West Germany 8,157

The Americas
Argentina 20,237
Bolivia 6
Brazil 2,300
Canada 530
Chile 6,000
Mexico 154
Peru 80
USA 11,976
Uruguay 900

The hectolitre (100 litres) is the commonest measure; it equals 22 Imperial gallons (26.4 US gallons)

The hectare or 100 ares is the equivalent of 2.47 acres

Bartholomew's Regional Projection

The Ancient World

THE HISTORY of wine runs back before our knowledge. It emerges with civilization itself from the East. The evidence from tablets and papyri and tombs can—and does—fill volumes. Man as we know him, working and worrying man, comes on the scene with the support of a jug of wine.

Historical evidence gets closer to our experience with the expansion of the Greek empire, starting a thousand years before Christ. It was then that wine first met the countries it was to make its real home: Italy and France. The Greeks called Italy the Land of Vines, just as the Vikings called America Vinland from the profusion of its native vines 2,000 years later. It seems probable that North Africa, Andalusia, Provence, Sicily and the Italian mainland had their first vineyards in the time of the Greek Empire.

The wines of Greece herself, no great matter today, were lavishly praised and generously documented by her poets. There was even a fashionable after-dinner game in Athens which consisted of throwing the last inch or so of wine in your cup into the air, to hit a delicately balanced dish on a pole. Smart young things took coaching in the finer points of 'kottabos'. But such treatment of the wine, and the knowledge that jugs of hot water for diluting it were on every table, makes it seem improbable that the wine was very good. What would have been nectar to Homer, or even to Jove, would probably seem to us like an oversweet vin rosé, possibly with a flavour of muscat, possibly

Above right: this Egyptian painting of treaders under an arbour of vines comes from the tomb of Nakht, a Theban official who died in the 15th century BC.
Below: feast scenes are one of the favourite motifs of Greek vase-painting. On a wine-vase of about 480 BC (in the British Museum) the left-hand guest is playing the fashionable after-dinner game of kottabos, which consisted of throwing the last of the wine in the cup at a special mark, a dish balanced on a pole

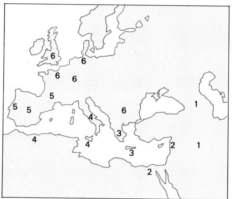

tasting of resin, and possibly concentrated by cooking, and needing dilution before drinking.

So much was written about wine and wine-making in ancient Rome that it is possible to make a rough map (right) of the wines of the early Roman Empire. The greatest writers, even Virgil, wrote instructions to wine-growers. One sentence of his—'Vines love an open hill'—might be called the best single piece of advice which can be given to a wine-grower.

There has been much speculation about the quality of Roman wine. It apparently had extraordinary powers of keeping, which in itself suggests that it was good. The great vintages were discussed and even drunk for longer than seems possible; the famous Opimian—from the year of the consulship of Opimius, 121 BC—was being drunk even when it was 125 years old.

Certainly the Romans had all that is necessary for ageing wine. They were not limited to earthenware amphoras like the Greeks—although they too used them. They had barrels just like modern barrels and bottles not unlike modern bottles. It is reasonable to suppose that most Italians of 2,000 years ago drank wine very like their descendants today; young, rather roughly made, sharp or strong according to the summer weather. The Roman method of cultivation of the vine on trees, in the festoons which became the friezes on classical buildings, is still practised, particularly in the south of Italy and northern Portugal.

But the move of most consequence for history

Left: the early movements of the vine. Starting in Caucasia or Mesopotamia **1** in perhaps 6000 BC it was cultivated in Egypt and Phoenicia **2** in about 3000 BC. By 2000 BC it was in Greece **3** and by 1000 BC it was in Italy, Sicily and North Africa **4**. In the next 500 years it reached at least Spain, Portugal, and the south of France **5**, and probably southern Russia as well. Finally (see map on opposite page) it spread with the Romans into northern Europe **6**, getting as far as Britain

Below: the wines the Romans drank; a reconstruction of wine-growing Italy in AD 100. Names of modern cities are given in italics; wine names in Roman type

1 Labicanum
2 Albanum
3 Praenestinum
4 Formianum
5 Trebellicanum
6 Gauranum
7 Beneventanum

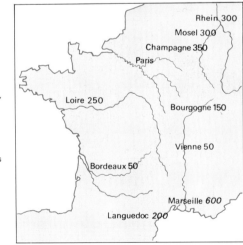

that the Romans made with their vines was to take them to Gaul. By the time they withdrew from what is now France in the fifth century they had laid the foundations for almost all the greatest vineyards of the modern world.

Starting in Provence, which had had vineyards already for centuries, they moved up the Rhône valley, and across (or by sea?) to Bordeaux in the time of Caesar. All the early developments were in the river valleys, the natural lines of communication, which the Romans cleared of forest and cultivated. They found that vineyards had a settling and civilizing effect on the population. Besides, boats were the only way of moving anything so heavy as wine. But they must also have found, as we still do, what a beneficent effect a nearby river has on vines.

By the second century they had vines in Burgundy; by the third on the Loire; and by the fourth at Paris (not such a good idea), in Champagne, and on the Moselle and the Rhine. Languedoc and the Auvergne also had vineyards. It seems that Alsace is the only major French wine region not to have Roman origins at least in part. It had to wait until about the ninth century.

Above: the Romans interpreted the graceful Greek wine god Dionysus as a more fleshly creature; in a mosaic from Pompeii, now in the Museo Nazionale, Naples, he rides his traditional mount, a lion, but boozes from a monstrous pot.
Left and below: barrels were used by the Romans. These were found being used as the linings of wells at Silchester in southern England, and are now in Reading Museum

Above: the vineyards of France and Germany at the fall of the Roman Empire. The dates of their founding are mainly conjectural. Vineyards in the Languedoc and Marseille (BC dates in italics) were founded by the Greeks; the rest by the Romans in the heyday of Roman Gaul. The history of all these vineyards has been continuous; Alsace—which does not appear here—was probably founded in about AD 800

The Middle Ages

UT OF the Dark Ages which followed the fall of the Roman Empire we emerge into the illumination of the mediaeval period, to see in its lovely painted pages an entirely familiar scene; one which was not to change in its essentials until this century. The Church had been the repository of the skills of civilization in the Dark Ages. As expansionist monasteries cleared hillsides and walled round fields of cuttings, as dying wine-growers bequeathed it their land, the Church came to be identified with wine—not only as the Blood of Christ, but as luxury and comfort in this world. For centuries it owned many of the greatest vineyards of Europe. Within this stable framework, in which tools and terms and techniques seemed to stand still, the styles of wine familiar to us now slowly came into being.

Above: tying up the vines; see opposite page. Below: in the Bayeux tapestry, Bishop Odo blesses wine before the invasion of England

Above: wine had an important place in medieval life as part of both Jewish and Christian observance. This picture of a Jewish Passover comes from an early-14th-century haggadah from northern Spain or Provence

The illuminated capital at the top of this page is from a northern French manuscript of about 1320

Left: picking the grapes. The crisp and expressive little woodcuts which illustrated the 1493 Speyer edition of Piero Crescentio's *Opus Ruralium Commodorum* have been reprinted constantly ever since (this and opposite page)

Below: in 1497 the Royal Exchequer of England laid down that eight gallons make one Winchester bushel; and 'too pottelys maketh one gallon'. The Winchester bushel is still a legal measure in the USA

Left: a late-15th-century tapestry in the Musée de Cluny in Paris shows the court happily obstructing the vintagers in their work on the banks of the Loire

Right: English wine measures of 1497 included a hogshead (63 gallons), a pipe (two hogsheads) and a tonne (two pipes). The size of ships was measured by the number of tonnes they could carry

Above: the most sumptuous of all the famous prayer-books of the Middle Ages was the Très Riches Heures painted for Jean, Duc de Berry by Pol Limbourg and his brothers about 1416. The month of September is represented by the homely scene of the vintage, under the splendid battlements of Saumur

The Evolution of Modern Wine

IT IS POSSIBLE to piece together, from the first enthusiastic mentions of particular growths in the 17th century, the rise of reputations and the evolution of our modern wines. For none of the familiar types sprang fully grown from the head of Bacchus. Nor is their evolution complete today: change continues. Burgundy, within the last 15 years, has seen a swing to much lighter wines, paler, with less depth of flavour and less able to mature—and the start of a swing back to the old style of dark and deep.

It is hard to have confidence in the descriptions of wine which survive from before about 1700. With the exception of Shakespeare's graphic tasting notes: 'a marvellous searching wine, and it perfumes the blood ere one can say "What's this?"', they tend to refer to royal recommendations or miraculous cures rather than to taste and characteristics.

Burgundy comes into focus in the 18th century: white wines 'spirity, faintly bubbly, fine and clear as spring water'; 'delicate pink wine' from Savigny. Nuits is 'wine to keep for the following year', in contrast to all the others, which were wines to drink as soon as the winter weather had cleared them. There was no call for strong, firm burgundy to lay down. Nobody knew what marvellous searching stuff it could be. Among the *vins de primeur* the first choice was Volnay.

But by the early 19th century there had been a complete revolution. Suddenly the vin rosés went out of fashion; the demand was for long-fermented, dark-coloured wine. In the Côte de Beaune, whose wines are naturally light, prices dropped. Demand moved to the Côte de Nuits, whose wines are naturally *vins de garde*—wines to keep and mature.

The explanation of the change was the discovery of the effect on wine of storing it in bottles. Since Roman times it had spent all its life in a barrel. If bottles were used they were simply carafes for serving at table. But late in the 17th century someone discovered the cork. Bit by bit it became clear that wine kept in a

A famous but anonymous English print of 1778 is the first known illustration of the corkscrew, the instrument which with the bottle and the cork brought in the age of great long-matured wines in the 18th century

tightly corked bottle lasted much longer than wine kept in a barrel, which was likely to go off at any time after the barrel was broached. It also aged in a different way; acquiring what is known as a 'bouquet'.

The wine that benefited most from this treatment was the fiery port the English had started to drink in the late 17th century. They had doubts about it at first, but as the century, and their bottles, grew older, their opinion of it rose sharply.

The trend is graphically illustrated by the way the port bottle changed shape from a carafe within a hundred years. The old model would not lie down, so its cork dried out. The slimmer bottle is easy to 'bin' horizontally in heaps.

Before long the benefits of bottle-age were beginning to change the style of all the best wines of Europe.

In 1866 A. Jullien published the figures for the alcoholic strengths of recent vintages. By today's standards the burgundies are formidable: Corton 1858, 15.6%; Montrachet 1858, 14.3%; Clos de Bèze 1858, 14.3%; Volnay 1859, 14.9%; Richebourg 1859, 14.3%. In contrast the wines of Bordeaux in the same two years ranged from 11.3% (St-Emilion Supérieur) to 8.9% (Château Lafite).

The low natural strength of the Bordeaux wines explains what seems today a curious habit of the old wine trade. Up to the mid-century the Bordeaux wines for England—which was most of the best of them—were subjected to what was known as *le travail à l'anglaise*. The recipe called for 30 litres of Spanish wine (Alicante or Benicarlo), 2 litres of unfermented white must and a bottle of brandy to each barrel of claret. The summer after the vintage the wine was set to ferment again with these additives, then treated as other wines and kept several years in wood before shipping. The result was strong wine with a good flavour, but 'heady and not suitable for all stomachs'. It fetched more than natural wine.

Today's preoccupation with authenticity, even at the expense of quality, makes these practices seem abusive. But it is rather as though someone revealed as a shocking instance of fraud the fact that brandy is added to port. We like Douro wine with brandy in it; our ancestors liked Lafite with Alicante in it.

German wines of the last century would be scarcely more familiar to us. It is doubtful whether any of today's pale, rather sweet, intensely perfumed wines were made. Grapes picked earlier gave more acid wine which needed longer to mature in cask. People liked the flavour of oak—or even the flavour of oxidation from too much contact with the air. 'Old brown hock' was a recommendation, whereas today it would be as rude a

Below: the evolution of the port bottle in the century from 1708 when it was a carafe to 1812 when it had reached its modern proportions is the vivid record of the emergence of vintage wine. As it was discovered that bottled and corked wine improved immeasurably with keeping, bottles began to be designed to be 'laid down' on their sides. This collection of bottles is at Berry Bros & Rudd, the London wine merchants

1708   1719   1739   1741   1753

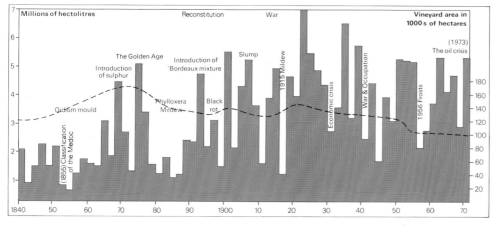

The evolution of Bordeaux's production from 1840–1975 has been plotted by Philippe Roudié of Bordeaux University in relation to wars, diseases, pests, slumps and the weather. The introduction of two great vineyard chemical aids, sulphur (against oidium mould) and 'Bordeaux mixture' (copper sulphate and lime) against mildew, can be seen to have had immediate results

remark as you could write on a tasting card.

Champagne too was fuller in colour and flavour—though otherwise very like it is today. Port and sherry had both been perfected. There was much more strong sweet wine from the Mediterranean to be seen: Malaga and Marsala were in their heydays. Madeira, Constantia and Tokay were all as highly regarded as the Trockenbeerenausleses of modern Germany.

The wine trade was booming. In the wine-growing countries an unhealthy amount of the economy rested on wine: in Italy in 1880 it was calculated that no less than 80% of the population more or less relied on wine for a living. This was the world phylloxera struck like a plague.

The methods of this little bug are described on pages 18–19. At the time, when he had succeeded in destroying or causing the pulling up of almost every vine in Europe, it seemed like the end of the world of wine.

The last 80 years have seen wine's Industrial Revolution. More particularly in the last 20 years, the scientific background to wine-making has become so much clearer that many things which were thought impossible before have become easy. Thoroughly bad wine anywhere is now almost a rarity. The New World has wine as good as any but the best of the old.

At the same time have come temptations to lower the standards of the best, to make more wine at the expense of quality.

But worse by far is the insidious trend towards making neutral, safe wine, without character, to please every taste. Wine-growers are anxious for a new market, and technology has shown them how to control what they make. It is essential for wine-drinkers at this point in history to demand unblended, individual wines with all their local character intact. It is up to us to see that the most enthralling thing about wine—its endless variety—survives.

Right: it is interesting to compare A. Jullien's classification of the great wines of the world a hundred years ago, in 1866, with the wines of today. His list in *Topographie de Tous les Vignobles Connus* (in its original spelling) ran:

Red
A Châteaux Margaux, Laffitte, Latour, Haut-Brion, Rauzan, Lascombes, Léoville, Larose-Balguerie, Gorce (Cantenac), Branne-Mouton, Pichon-Longueville
B Romanée-Conti, Chambertin, Richebourg, Clos Vougeot, Romanée-St-Vivant, La Tâche, Clos St-Georges, Le Corton, Clos de Prémeaux, Musigny, Clos de Tart, Bonnes-Mares, Clos de la Roche, Les Véroilles, Clos Morjot, Clos St-Jean, La Perrière

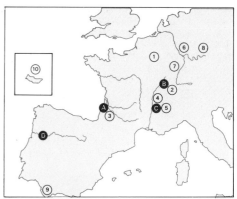

C (Hermitage) Méal, Gréfieux, Beaume, Raucoule, Muret, Guoignière, Les Bessas, Les Burges, Les Lauds
D High Douro
White
1 Sillery, Ay, Mareuil, Dizy, Hautvillers, Pierry, Le Clozet
2 Mont Rachet
3 First growths of Barsac, Preignac, Sauternes,
Bommes; dry wine of Villenave-d'Ornon
4 Château Grillet
5 Hermitage Blanc
6 Schloss Johannisberg, Rüdesheim, Steinberg, Graffenberg, Hochheim, Kiedrich
7 Liebfrauenmilch
8 Leist, Stein
9 Sherry from the white soil, Paxarete
10 Sercial

17

The Vine

As early as the beginning of April in northern Europe (or September in the southern hemisphere) the gnarled wood of the vine sports tender shoots

Within ten days of budding the stalk, leaves and tendrils are all obvious — and also vulnerable to nights of frost, which can come in late May

In late May or early June the vine forms its flower buds; looking like tiny bunches of grapes in the place where the grapes will eventually be

Early in June comes the vital flowering, which must go on for ten to 14 days for good grapes to form. Heavy rain now is fatal to the vintage

If the flowers escape rain and frost, their place is taken by baby grapes in June. In August the grapes 'set': turn colour from green to red or

translucent yellow; at this point the ripening process begins. From flowering to harvest in September or October is about 100 days (see the chart on page 26)

WINE IS the juice of grapes. Every drop of wine is rain recovered from the ground by the mechanism of the grape-bearing plant, the vine. For the first four or five years of its life the vine is too busy creating a root-system and building a strong woody stalk to bear a crop of grapes. Thereafter, left to nature, it would rampage away, bearing fruit but spending much more of its energy on making new shoots and putting out long wandering branches of leafy wood, until it covered as much as an acre of ground, with new root-systems forming wherever the branches lay along the ground.

This natural form, known as *provignage*, was used as a vineyard in ancient times. To prevent the grapes rotting or the mice getting them, since they lay on the ground, little props were pushed under the stem to support each bunch. If the vine grew near trees, it used its tendrils to climb them to dizzy heights. The Romans planted elms specially for the purpose.

In modern vineyards, however, the vine is not allowed to waste its precious sap on making long branches. Better-quality grapes grow on a vine which is regularly cut back almost to its main stem. The annual pruning is done in mid-winter when the vine is empty of sap.

Vines like most other plants will reproduce from seed. Sowing grape pips would be much the easiest and cheapest way of getting new vines. But like many highly bred plants its seeds rarely turn out like their parents. Pips are used for experimenting with new crosses between different varieties. For planting a new vineyard, though, every vine has to be a cutting —either planted to take root on its own or grafted to a rooted cutting of another species.

Great care is taken to see that the parent vine is healthy before cuttings are taken. The little 'slips' are put in sand in a nursery for a season until they form roots. They then go out into rows, in traditional vineyards one metre apart but often today one and a half, two or even three metres apart. Oddly enough experiments have found that the total yield of the vineyard in wine remains the same with half as many vines exploiting the same volume of soil.

As a vine grows older its roots penetrate

Pests which threaten the vine include, top left, the grub of the cochylis moth, seen here eating the flower buds; top right, the tiny red spider, which sucks the sap from the undersides of leaves; lower left, mildew, which attacks anything green. Mildewed grapes never ripen properly and have a peculiar taste. Copper sulphate sprays are effective against it. Lower right: oidium, or powdery mildew, is often more serious; its attack on Madeira in 1852, just before phylloxera hit the island, began the decline in Madeira's fortunes. It rots the stalks, shrivels the leaves and splits the grapes, ruining the wine and finally killing the vine

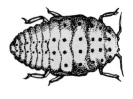
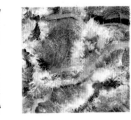

Left and below: the vine's deadliest enemy. Phylloxera vastatrix, in its root-eating form and its flying form. Below right: larvae and eggs. A century ago this American bug almost destroyed the vineyards of Europe Right: every European vine is now grafted on to American roots, which resist its attack. There used to be fierce debate as to whether European wine has suffered, but few now remember 'pre-phylloxera' wine

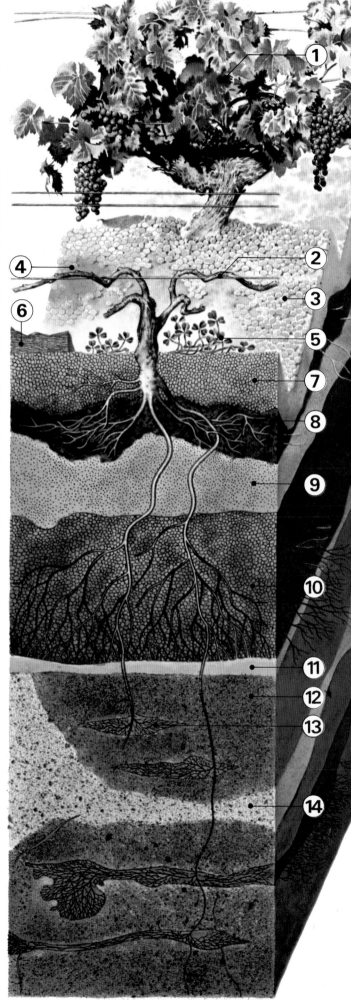

deeper into the earth. While it is young and they are near the surface they are quickly affected by drought or floods or the spreading of manure (which put on the land too liberally can affect the taste of the wine); the vine has little stability; its wine will never be first-class. But if the soil near the surface does not provide enough food it will send its roots down and down. This optimism, or curiosity, often results in its discovering valuable resources far from the surface (see right).

Unfortunately, being a pampered plant, the vine is subject to all manner of diseases. Some varieties fall sick of one particular disease (e.g. oidium or mildew) so readily that they are gradually being abandoned altogether. The best combine reasonable hardiness with fine fruit (though rarely with a very generous yield).

One insect pest is disastrous; the phylloxera. This little creature lives on the roots of the vine and kills it. In the seventies of the last century it almost destroyed the entire European vineyard, until it was discovered that the roots of the native American vine (phylloxera came from America) are immune. Virtually every vine in Europe had to be pulled up and replaced with a European cutting grafted on to a rooted cutting from an American vine.

Red spiders, the grubs of the cochylis and eudemis moths, various sorts of beetles, bugs and mites all feed on the upper works of the vine. Most of them however are taken care of by the sulphur sprays to which the vine is subjected summer-long, or by DDT.

Various moulds attack the vine as well. Oidium and mildew are the two worst in Europe; white, black and grey rot are among the others. All have to be prevented or at least treated by regular sprayings with a copper sulphate solution (known as Bordeaux mixture) and sulphur powder for as long as the vine has leaves and green wood which they can attack.

Below: the map plots the progress through France of phylloxera, starting in the département of Gard in the south in 1864 and not finishing its destruction for 30 years. France regained her production by 1920, but never her pre-phylloxera vineyard area

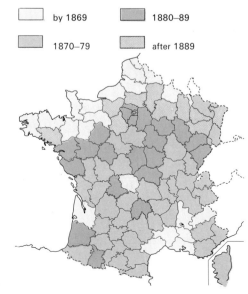

☐ by 1869		▨ 1880–89	
▨ 1870–79		▨ after 1889	

Wine has its origin as water in the soil. This cross-section of the vineyard of a riverside château in St-Julien in the Médoc shows how a vine finds enough moisture and food in poor soil by exploiting a deep and wide area. Gravel and sand are here plus-factors for quality. They make the ground permeable to a great depth, let the rain run through, and encourage the vine to go deep. In the background a 50-year-old Cabernet vine 1, trained on wires, bears fruit. In the foreground a 20-year-old vine 2 is in its winter state; pruned and with the earth banked up round it for protection. Pebbles 3 on the surface are stained with copper sulphate 4: so much is sprayed on the vines that traces of copper are analysable in the soil. Clover 5 or other crops are often ploughed in as fertilizer. Pressed skins 6 (marc—see page 30) are also spread on the ground.

The top 12 inches 7 is pebbly and sandy with few roots. Then comes a layer of marl 8 brought from elsewhere and spread by hand years ago; possibly when the vines were planted. Roots and rootlets spread horizontally in it. The next foot 9 is sandy but compacted hard and has nothing to offer. There are no feeding rootlets but only main roots descending to another thicker layer 10 like the surface, gravelly and sandy, but slightly richer in organic matter (possibly from manuring years ago) where roots abound. These roots are again brought up short by a compacted layer 11 of sand at 4 feet deep. Below this different colours of sand, rusty 12 and yellow 14, lie in clearly defined layers, with odd horizontal patches of grey sand 13 among them.

The grey is evidently where the water drains; it is filled with rootlets, which are nowhere else in the area. A 50-year-old vine still has roots an inch thick here, going down to deeper layers of grey sand and gravel. Roots can only find so much of the minerals they seek in a form they can use (i.e. in solution). The more grapes a vine bears, therefore, the less of these flavouring elements there will be per grape; the argument for restricting the crop to achieve maximum intensity of flavour. In St-Julien one vine produces enough juice for only half a bottle of wine

Based on investigations by Gérard Seguin published in his *Etude de Quelques Profils de Sols du Vignoble Bordelais* (Bordeaux 1965)

The ModernVineyard

THE LAST few years have seen the study of viticulture, the science of growing grapes for wine, advance by leaps and bounds. Until very recently planting was mainly a question of replacing old vineyards in the same fashion as before. Although the amount of wine was growing, the world's vineyard area was contracting: healthier plants and more fertilizers accounted for the bigger yield.

But in the last decade the demand for more good wine has started a planting boom, and at the same time set wine-growers to questioning traditional forms of vineyard. The questions they ask are not just 'what vines?', but 'on what roots?', 'how far apart?', 'trained high or low?', 'up the slope or across it?'. New vineyards (and there are a lot in this Atlas) embody the latest thinking about what makes grapes ripen in good health.

One of the latest and most radical studies of the subject has been going on for some years at the viticultural research station at Geisenheim in the Rheingau. The result of one of their earlier surveys of their own region appears on page 137. Since then more detailed and elaborate research has continued. A paper published by Dr G. Horney of the Agrarian Meteorological Department of the German weather service at Geisenheim sums up part of the findings.

Dr Horney begins by asking basic questions about the vine. What sort of plant is it in nature, and what are its needs? He described it as a climber of lowland woods in the Mediterranean region. As such it needs a great deal of light (its reason for climbing), a warm climate, plenty of water (it is confined in nature to low land with a relatively high water table) and relatively humid air.

The immediately interesting thing is that the last two points clash completely with the classic formula for successful wine-growing: Virgil's 'vines love an open hill'. High-quality wine seems to come from dry (or at least well-drained) ground where humidity is relatively low.

Dr Horney examines each point as it applies to conditions in the Rheingau, starting with sunlight. Vines in a vineyard can be proved to receive as much sunlight as they can assimilate, even in a cloudy year. Therefore the importance of sunshine is a question of heat, not light.

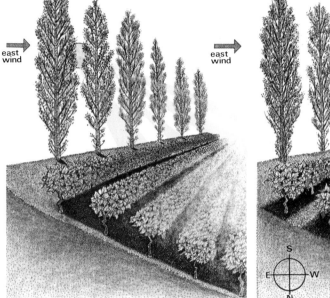

The two illustrations above show an ideal vineyard in the Rheingau (see the text on the opposite page) in early morning (above left) and at noon at the end of September—the crucial ripening season. It lies on a western slope, with a wind-break to the east to prevent the prevailing summer wind blowing a warm

microclimate out from between the rows. The rows run north-south for the same reason (see the diagrams below). In the morning mist envelops the vines—the low sun with long shadows does little good—but at noon when the mist clears and the sun is warmest it floods the vines with warmth and light

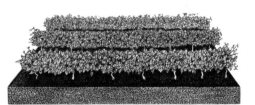

The direction of vine-rows is important, affecting the time of day when the sun reaches and warms the ground. In the vineyard above left the rows run north-south. At noon in September the maximum heat of the sun falls on the soil and vine-leaves; the grapes are

shaded. The soil will retain heat all afternoon. In the right-hand vineyard with east-west rows the 'hedges' are fully in the sun at noon but the ground is in shade and stays several degrees cooler all day. The grapes will not be so ripe

Vines can be trained to any shape or size. Different methods have evolved for different soils and climates, ranging from isolated low bushes where water is scarce to tree-high climbers where it is land which is in limited supply. The sequence of vines on the right show some of the principal variations

A Mosel vine after pruning. Two vigorous young canes are tied down to form a 'goblet' supported by an individual stake. New growth breaks from the topmost buds

A traditional system on the scattered plots and terraces of the northern Rhône. New growth from a low base is tied to light stakes known as 'échallas'

The principal system of Bordeaux and Burgundy is to train the vine on two wires; the lower for the main fruiting cane and the upper for the young shoots and luxuriant foliage

The high-wire system was developed in Austria by Lenz Moser. It encourages a big leafy canopy over the grapes; good in hot sunshine and easily cultivated by tractor

The temperature is all-important. The flowering of the vine starts in the spring as soon as the air starts to warm the ground (rather than vice versa as it does in winter). In autumn the reverse moment triggers the colouring of the leaves. Growth and every other function of the plant is linked to ground temperatures above 10°C (50°F). Assimilation and transpiration (the process of drawing up moisture and nourishment from the ground and 'breathing' through the leaves) proceeds more efficiently with rising temperatures up to a certain point. But at 28°C (82°F) evaporation overtakes assimilation: the vine demands more of its roots than they can draw from the ground—even damp ground. The growth (and ripening) process slows and stops. There is therefore an optimum temperature for vines—in the region of 25–28°C.

Turning to ground moisture, Dr Horney describes the very deep roots vines can make as evidence that the plant must have extensive water supplies and will go to any length to get them. If there is water near the surface a vine roots shallowly; nor does flooding, at least for a while, harm it. Drought, on the other hand, stops the ripening process as the leaves flag. For this reason the autumnal dews and mists after a hot summer are vital; the vine can absorb enough water through the leaves to keep the foliage healthy.

(Other aspects of drainage are discussed on pages 70–71. Well-drained land is warmer, and temperature can be more decisive than water supply.)

As to humidity, the vine is apparently happiest with a relative humidity of 60–80% or even more, were it not for the diseases which flourish in damp air.

As far as the Rheingau is concerned all the above conditions for success are met with the exception of temperature: it rarely reaches 25–28°C—or indeed above 20°C—in the Rheingau for very long. Therefore the ability of particular sites to heat up and stay warm must be a crucial factor for quality. 'Local climates' in vineyards are created above all by shelter from the wind: the vines sheltering each other, or a hedge or a hill sheltering the vineyard. For vines in the cool north mutual shelter is therefore vital. In the south, of course, where

it is often *too* hot, the determining factor is the water supply: hence the widely spaced low bushes in Mediterranean vineyards.

Dr Horney concludes by discussing how a northern vineyard can be given the best chance of being warmer than the prevailing temperatures. The first rule is to plant the rows across the direction of the prevailing wind in the warmest weather—in the Rheingau, the east wind. Rows planted north–south will avoid having their precious microclimate blown away. Another point in their favour is that the ground in the north–south alleys is warmed by the midday sun, whereas the lower leaves and grapes are shaded from it by the upper foliage: the ideal arrangement.

Best of all is a western slope, where not only is the east wind excluded but the afternoon sun of autumn can have most effect. For Dr Horney points out that it is just in the still, sunny, autumn weather which can do most good that morning mists are most common. An eastern slope can miss the best part of the day for ripening.

These conclusions, in favour of close rows of vines running north–south, preferably on western slopes and sheltered by wind-breaks, are of course only a recipe for the Rheingau and similar vineyards. The ecological factors, on the other hand, are the same in different combinations for every vineyard.

A new development in grafting technique. A simple stamping machine cuts a mortice and tenon in the root-stock and the scion of the variety to be grown. The two lock together and form a new plant almost immediately. Compare the old method on page 18 which involved knife-work and binding-up

Pergolas are widely used in northern Italy, and in Portugal for vinho verde. They give cool ripening conditions by shading the ground but make machine cultivation difficult

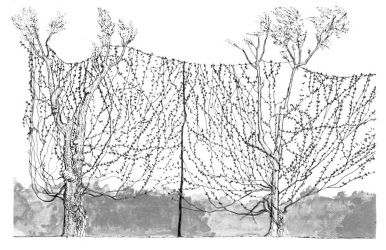

Vines have been grown up trees in Italy since earliest times. The Romans planted elms specially for the purpose. Standing a vineyard on end releases the ground for other crops—but never makes good wine, since hard pruning is impossible

The Choice of a Grape 1

THE WINE VINE is only one species of one genus of a vast family of plants, which ranges from a huge decorative Japanese climber to the familiar Virginia creeper.

Its name is Vitis vinifera. Its varieties can be numbered in thousands—as many as 5,000 are named. Those which concern a wine-lover, however, are probably not many more than about 50, of which we show 25 on these and the next pages, and in addition a few varieties from two or three other related species of vitis which produce the characteristic American wine.

All over the Old World of wine-growing, the natural selection of the variety which does best, and gives the best quality combined with reasonable quantity and a reasonable resistance to disease, has taken place gradually over centuries. In many places (the port country, for example, Chianti, Bordeaux, Châteauneuf-du-Pape) no one grape provides exactly what is needed: the tradition is either to grow a number together, or grow them separately and blend the resulting wines.

It is not the traditional practice in the main wine districts of Europe even to mention the kind of grape which goes into a wine. For one thing the choice is so old it can be assumed: for another modern laws normally make the traditional variety a condition of using the traditional wine name. White burgundy, for example, to be called white burgundy must be made entirely of Chardonnay grapes.

Thus there are very many important grapes few people have ever heard of: the Palomino and the Pedro Ximénez of sherry; the Tintas of port; the Furmint of Tokay; the Syrah of the Rhône or the brilliant white Viognier; the splendid Nebbiolo of northern Italy; the Schiava of the Adige and the Sangiovese of Chianti; the Gamay of Beaujolais; the Melon of Muscadet; the Folle Blanche and Ugni Blanc of Cognac; the Chasselas of Switzerland; the Merlot and Malbec and Petit Verdot of Bordeaux; the Savagnin of the Jura; the Arinto of Portugal.

On the other hand, there are some, like the Sercial and Verdelho of Madeira, the Barbera of Piemonte or the Gewürztraminer of Alsace, which have become the names of their wines.

Ampelography—the study of grapes—is one of the most delicate and difficult studies connected with wine. Experts often disagree about the identities of grapes: their relationships remain far beyond lay comment. There are traditions that certain well-known grapes are 'really' something else. Several grapes in Portugal and Spain, for example, are said to be German Riesling, possibly brought by pilgrims to the shrine of Santiago. The Alvarinho of Galicia and the Minho, the Sercial of Madeira and the Pedro Ximénez of Andalucia all make this claim.

In the New World of wine-growing the choice of grapes is not a question of tradition but of judgement: a realistic balance of quality, quantity and hardiness. Hence the best wines of the New World use the grape names to specify the character of the wine. And hence the curious fact that to an ordinary Californian the words Cabernet Sauvignon are more familiar than they are to a Parisian gourmet.

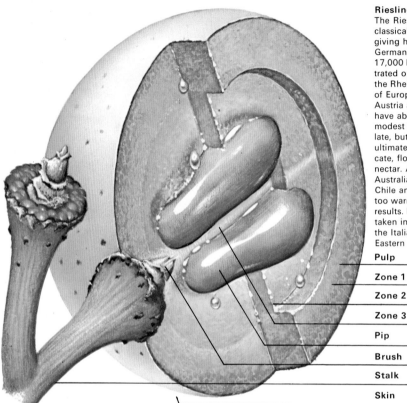

Riesling

The Riesling, left, is the classical German grape, giving her best wine. Germany has about 17,000 hectares, concentrated on the Mosel and the Rheingau; about 80% of Europe's plantation. Austria and Alsace each have about 1,000. It is a modest bearer and ripens late, but can make the ultimate honeyed, delicate, flower-scented nectar. Also planted in Australia, South Africa, Chile and California, all too warm for the greatest results. Its name is widely taken in vain; chiefly by the Italian Riesling in Eastern Europe

Pulp

Zone 1

Zone 2

Zone 3

Pip

Brush

Stalk

Skin

Above: an enlargement of a Riesling grape one month before the vintage. It is still green, and about half its final size. Ripening, it grows translucent gold with distinctive dark speckles on the skin (see the photograph of ripe Rieslings on page 111)

The stalk is normally torn off before the grapes are pressed in modern wine-making. Formerly they were left on, but they made the wine watery and could make it bitter. In red wine they also absorbed valuable colouring matter

The pulp divides naturally into three zones. Zone 2 gives up its juice in the press first, before the two zones in contact with pips and skin. The first juice from the press has long been held to make the best wine; perhaps for this reason

The pips should come through the press unscathed. If they are crushed they make the wine bitter. The skin is removed from the juice as quickly as possible for white wine; for red wine it is left in until the juice has taken its colour

The distribution of ten important grape varieties in France

Red
- Cabernet Sauvignon
- Carignan
- Gamay
- Grenache
- Pinot Noir

White
- Chardonnay
- Sauvignon Blanc
- Chenin Blanc
- Riesling
- Ugni Blanc

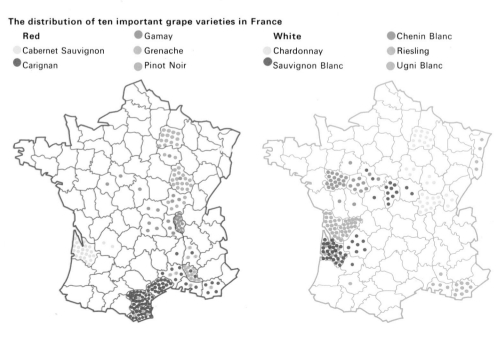

Gamay
Only makes first-class wine on the granite hills of Beaujolais; in the rest of Burgundy an inferior variety and elsewhere dull (except perhaps in California for rosé). At its best incomparably light and fruity and gulpable, though often over-sugared in Beaujolais today, with the result that it is too strong and dry

Chardonnay
The grape of white burgundy (Chablis, Montrachet, Meursault, Pouilly-Fuissé) and champagne.
Gives firm, full, strong wine with scent and character, on chalky soils becoming almost luscious without being sweet. Ages well. Also used in Bulgaria, and very successful in northern California

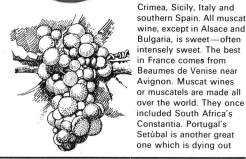

Muscat
Easy to recognize by its taste and smell, like a hothouse table grape's. Can be black or white. Some of France's first vineyards were muscat, planted by the Greeks. It spread from the Aegean with civilization, to the Crimea, Sicily, Italy and southern Spain. All muscat wine, except in Alsace and Bulgaria, is sweet—often intensely sweet. The best in France comes from Beaumes de Venise near Avignon. Muscat wines or muscatels are made all over the world. They once included South Africa's Constantia. Portugal's Setúbal is another great one which is dying out

Semillon
This grape has the great gift, shared with the Riesling, of rotting nobly. Under certain conditions of warmth and humidity a normally undesirable fungus softens the skin and lets the juice evaporate, concentrating the sugar and flavouring elements and producing luscious, creamy wine. The great golden wines of Sauternes are made like this, with a proportion of Sauvignon, not so subject to 'Pourriture noble'. Semillon is extensively used in Australia to make white wines which can be labelled anything from Riesling to Chablis

Cabernet Sauvignon
Small tough-skinned grape which gives the distinction to the red wines of Bordeaux, though always blended with Merlot and sometimes Malbec. The best Médoc vineyards have up to 80% Cabernet, but in St-Emilion and Pomerol the Cabernet's slightly lesser cousin, the Cabernet Franc, is used. Cabernet Sauvignon is widely planted in Australia, where its wine is tough and black until a great age, in Chile where it is excellent, like a light Bordeaux, in South Africa and in California, where it is dull to very fine. All Cabernet wines gain by age in bottle as well as wood

Sauvignon Blanc
The chief white Bordeaux grape, used with Semillon and a little Muscadelle to make dry Graves and sweet Sauternes. Makes interesting, clean, lighter wine on its own elsewhere: at Pouilly and Sancerre on the upper Loire (though one authority believes the Pouilly Fumé grape to be the Savagnin of the Jura, not the Sauvignon); in the Dordogne, near Chablis; in Chile, and in the Livermore and Santa Clara valleys of California, where its wine is dry, gold and of great character

Chenin Blanc
The white grape of Anjou and Touraine on the Loire. Gives nervy, intense wine, honey-like when very ripe but always with high acidity, so it ages well. Its finest wines are Vouvray, Côteaux du Layon, Savennières; at Vouvray it also makes sparkling wine. Often called Pineau de la Loire and in California (where it is successful), mistakenly, White Pinot

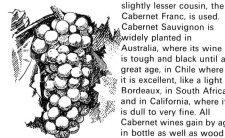

Pinot Noir
The single red grape of the Côte d'Or in Burgundy (Chambertin, Romanée, Corton, Beaune), i.e. the world's best red-wine grape, in the right place. In Champagne it is pressed before fermentation, to make white wine, which becomes the greater part of the best champagnes. At its best the scent, flavour, body, texture of its wine are all profound pleasures. It transplants from France less well than the Cabernet, makes light wines in Germany and Eastern Europe, where it goes by various names, and, with exceptions, not very exciting wines in California

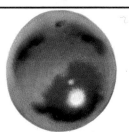

Grenache
A sweet grape with character but not much colour, used in a blend to make Châteauneuf-du-Pape and on its own to make Tavel, the best rosé of the Rhône. Known as Garnacha in Rioja, where it is the most important red variety. Used for dessert wines at Banyuls near the Franco-Spanish frontier. In Australia and California it makes the best rosés, which usually bear its name

The Choice of a Grape 2

THE WINE world has become steadily more grape-variety-conscious over the last decade.

Probably the first reason was that the New World started giving 'varietal' names pride of place on its best wines. Equally important were the successful breeding of new varieties and selections of exceptional 'clones' of old ones in research establishments around the world, but especially at Geisenheim in Germany and Davis in California.

A pioneering and most helpful discussion of the variety of grapes was published in 1965 by Doctors Amerine and Singleton in *Wine—An Introduction for Americans*. They divided wine-grape varieties into four categories. The largest (in volume grown) is of grapes which give no special flavour or character to their wine. By and large these are the grapes of the Mediterranean basin: the Carignan of the south of France is a good example; it is widely planted under local names in both Italy and Spain, but is nowhere outstanding. The wine of these grapes is not necessarily bad; it simply has no distinctive taste. For certain purposes (making sherry for example) this can be an advantage. The Swiss say each Chasselas (a non-Mediterranean example) is a 'picture postcard' of where it is grown—being so neutral in itself. On the other hand the movement to improve Midi wine consists largely of replacing Carignan and the like with grapes of character.

Grapes with distinctive flavour (whose homes, on the whole, are the cooler vineyards of northern Europe) include all those whose names appear on 'varietal' labels, from Cabernet Sauvignon to Riesling. It may well be that the long process of selection for harder conditions has improved flavour as well as performance.

The degree of flavour depends more than anything on the quantity the vine is allowed to carry. Other things being equal five tons of grapes from one acre contain as much flavour as ten tons in half as much fruit. There is little doubt that the surprising concentration and lasting-power of very old wine is at least partly due to much smaller crops.

Muscat-flavoured grapes are given a category of their own; so different is the muscat taste.

The fourth category is American: the wild vines of North America and their descendants, all of which are more or less 'foxy' in taste (see page 226).

Grape-breeders are constantly trying to find new varieties to improve on the old. The main centres of interest at present are hybrids between European and American vines, new developments in Germany to improve on the classic but difficult Riesling, and new crosses in California designed to make good table wine in very hot conditions.

The original object of crossing American vines with French was to achieve a plant with built-in resistance to phylloxera (which American vines have) but with European-tasting grapes. These French-American hybrids, first developed in France by such breeders as Seyve-Villard, Baco and Seibel, are scorned in their native land, referred to as P.Ds (*producteurs directs*, since they are not grafted) and banned from all Appellation Contrôlée areas—though widely grown outside them. They have been welcomed, however, in many other countries for their hardiness and apparent potential for good, if not fine, wine. They are steadily gaining ground in the eastern States.

German breeders have been at work on the Riesling for a century. Müller-Thurgau made the first famous cross between the light-cropping, late-ripening Riesling and the early and prolific Sylvaner. Today there is a growing catalogue of crosses of crosses, often between two or more selected clones of Riesling—even red Rieslings have been produced.

Some of the best of these are the Reichensteiner (which has French blood also), Ehrenfelser (another Riesling × Sylvaner; an improvement on Müller-Thurgau), Kerner (Riesling × the pale red Trollinger, giving fragrant and tasty wine), Bacchus and Optima (both Riesling × Sylvaner × Müller-Thurgau; Optima being the better).

Dr Helmut Becker at Geisenheim is also developing red-juice varieties to give colour to normally pallid German red wine. He is convinced both quantity and quality can be improved by propagating virus-free vines. 'There should be no red leaves in a vineyard in autumn,' he says. 'Only yellow. Red means disease.' Most of France, in other words, needs replanting. Is there evidence, though, that the greatest wine comes from the healthiest vines?

Meanwhile at Davis Dr Harold Olmo has developed several important new vines. His Emerald Riesling and Ruby Cabernet are already well established as giving good balancing acidity in the hot San Joaquin valley. His latest successful crosses use Cabernet Sauvignon × Carignan (the same as Ruby Cabernet) as a base and cross it with Grenache ('Carnelian' and 'Centurion') or Merlot ('Carmine'). The first two make huge quantities (11 or 12 tons to the acre). Carnelian is light wine; Centurion very heavy. Carmine is said to give wine like Cabernet Sauvignon, only twice as much of it.

It is easy to forget that a variety like the Pinot Noir, which has been in cultivation for centuries, has already naturally divided into many different 'clones'; some with more vigour, some ripening earlier; some with more flavour and aroma. When a wine-grower goes to a nurseryman, therefore, for new plants, a good deal of the quality of his eventual wine is decided by the particular Pinot he chooses.

Measurements of sugar-content														
Specific Gravity	1.060	1.065	1.070	1.075	1.080	1.085	1.090	1.095	1.100	1.105	1.110	1.115	1.120	1.125
°Oechsle	60	65	70	75	80	85	90	95	100	105	110	115	120	125
Baumé	8.2	8.8	9.4	10.1	10.7	11.3	11.9	12.5	13.1	13.7	14.3	14.9	15.5	16.0
Brix	14.7	15.8	17.0	18.1	19.3	20.4	21.5	22.5	23.7	24.8	25.8	26.9	28.0	29.0
% Potential Alcohol v/v	7.5	8.1	8.8	9.4	10.0	10.6	11.3	11.9	12.5	13.1	13.8	14.4	15.0	15.6

Each country has its own system for measuring the ripeness of grapes (or 'must-weight'). This chart relates the three principal ones (German, French and American) to each other, to specific gravity, and to the potential alcohol of the resulting wine if all the sugar is fermented out.

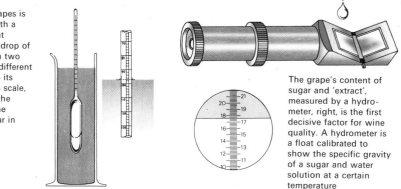

The ripeness of grapes is often measured with a refractometer. Light passing through a drop of juice held between two prisms bends at a different angle according to its sugar content. The scale, left, read through the eye-piece, gives the percentage of sugar in the juice

The grape's content of sugar and 'extract', measured by a hydrometer, right, is the first decisive factor for wine quality. A hydrometer is a float calibrated to show the specific gravity of a sugar and water solution at a certain temperature

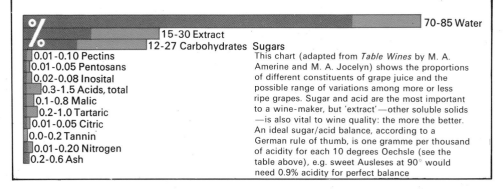

70-85 Water
15-30 Extract
12-27 Carbohydrates Sugars
0.01-0.10 Pectins
0.01-0.05 Pentosans
0.02-0.08 Inosital
0.3-1.5 Acids, total
0.1-0.8 Malic
0.2-1.0 Tartaric
0.01-0.05 Citric
0.0-0.2 Tannin
0.01-0.20 Nitrogen
0.2-0.6 Ash

This chart (adapted from *Table Wines* by M. A. Amerine and M. A. Jocelyn) shows the proportions of different constituents of grape juice and the possible range of variations among more or less ripe grapes. Sugar and acid are the most important to a wine-maker, but 'extract'—other soluble solids —is also vital to wine quality: the more the better. An ideal sugar/acid balance, according to a German rule of thumb, is one gramme per thousand of acidity for each 10 degrees Oechsle (see the table above), e.g. sweet Ausleses at 90° would need 0.9% acidity for perfect balance

Sylvaner Germany's second grape and the chief grape of Rheinhessen. Ripens early with big crops but only slight flavour, lacking Riesling's acidity. At its best in Franconia's dry Steinwein. Also grown in Alsace, northern Italy and central Europe, and in California, where it is often called Riesling

Sangiovese (or Sangioveto) is the principal red grape of Tuscany, and hence of Chianti. Only a moderate producer, rather late to ripen and without deep colour, but with good acid balance and pleasant flavour. One strain, the Brunello, is used alone to make the legendary Brunello di Montalcino, which ages, it seems, almost for ever

Müller-Thurgau The historic forerunner of many crosses of Riesling with other grapes (here the Sylvaner) and still one of the best German varieties. Widely grown in Rheinhessen, the Palatinate, S. Germany and Austria. Its plentiful wine is highly aromatic, rather soft for lack of acid, rarely of Riesling standard, but at its best (usually in sweet wines) can be superb

Syrah (or Sérine) is the best red grape of the Rhône, making dark, tannic, long-lived Hermitage. As Shiraz it succeeds admirably in Australia, which has the largest planting (18,000 acres) and uses it for both table and dessert wines, blended or alone. Some of California's Petite Syrah may be the same, in which case it should have a great future

Pinot Blanc A near relation to Chardonnay, grown with it in Burgundy and Champagne, but making wine with less character. Also much grown in N. Italy (where it makes the best dry sparkling wine) and central Europe. Its cousin Pinot Gris (Tokay in Alsace, Ruländer in Germany) has more personality, giving low-acid, blunt but pungent wine

Merlot The noble cousin of the Cabernet grown in St-Emilion and Pomerol, ripening earlier than the Cabernet and giving softer, fleshier wine, which matures sooner. Used in the Médoc in a blend (up to 75%) with Cabernet and other grapes. Makes excellent wine in N.E. Italy and good light wine in Italian Switzerland. Good in cooler California

Traminer (or Gewürztraminer) is the spicy speciality of Alsace (where it occupies 17% of the vineyard). The most pungent table-wine grape, with rather small crops ripening early in the season. Called Savagnin in the Jura and used for *Vin Jaune*. Germany has a little, central Europe more. In California it can be excellent, but tends to lack acidity

Palomino (or Listan) the great sherry grape, gives big quantities of rather neutral wine with low acidity which oxidizes easily. Widely grown in Australia, S. Africa (where it is called White French) and California for sherry-making, as well as Jerez (where it occupies 90% of the vineyard)

Folle Blanche A workhorse grape, the third most widely grown white in France (after Semillon and Ugni Blanc) with 30,000 acres. Its aliases include Gros Plant (in Brittany) and Picpoul (in Armagnac and the Midi). Historically the great grape of Cognac, having ideal high acidity and little flavour, but now supplanted by Ugni Blanc. Promising in California

Zinfandel Excellent red-wine grape peculiar to California, though it may be the same as the Primitivo of Puglia. Makes good lively fruity wine for drinking young, and can make top-quality, highly concentrated wine for long ageing, which at 50 years can taste like great Bordeaux. Likes a dry climate and gives best quality in cool areas (not the Central valley)

Welschriesling (or Wälschriesling, or Italian Riesling). The 'Riesling' of Austria, Yugoslavia, N. Italy and central Europe, giving good standard wine but never approaching real Riesling in quality. An early ripener and moderate cropper. The curious name 'Welsch' means 'foreign'. EEC law will soon ban the name 'Riesling', unqualified, for its wine

Carignan By far the commonest grape in France, where there are over 400,000 acres, largely in the Midi. Makes huge quantities of harmless but dull red wine, low in acidity, extract and tannin, but useful for blending. Rots easily in wet weather, but much planted in Algeria, Spain and California. 'Ruby Cabernet' is a Carignan × Cabernet cross

Kerner One of the new generation of German grapes produced by the Wine School at Geisenheim, a cross between Riesling and red Trollinger. Makes spicy, very fruity wine with good acidity, a bit blatant beside Riesling, but a healthy reliable vine, increasingly used in Rheinhessen to make more exciting wine than the usual Sylvaner

Seyval Blanc (alias Seyve-Villard 5/276). One of the most successful of hybrids between French and American vines made by the contemporary French breeder Seyve-Villard. The vine is very hardy and the wine attractively fruity, without a 'foxy' flavour. Banned from French Appellation areas, but winning converts to hybrids both in the eastern States and England

Catawba Perhaps the most famous native American wine-grape, a chance cross of *Vitis labrusca*, which gives abundance of fruity, though strongly 'foxy', wine, either white or pale red. The mainstay of the mid-19th-century Ohio industry, whose Sparkling Catawba was world famous. Still popular in New York for sparkling wine; only the infamous Concord has more acres

Wine and the Weather

THE WEATHER is the great variable in wine-growing. Every other major influence is more or less constant, and known in advance. But in the end it is the weather which makes or breaks a vintage—so it receives constant study.

The vine is dormant from November to March in the northern hemisphere. Only an abnormally deep frost can harm it then. From the time it buds to the vintage in September or October, however, every drop of rain, hour of sunshine and degree of heat has its eventual effect on the quality and character of the crop.

The fine wines of northern Europe are those most affected by irregular weather. In the south and in the New World, vintages tend to be much more consistent. On these pages we look at some of the factors affecting France.

The chart at the bottom of this page shows the chief events in a vine's life cycle over 19 years in Burgundy. There is a 35-day maximum variation in the starting and finishing of this cycle, and infinite variations in between, as the weather hurries it on or holds it back.

On the opposite page are isopleth graphs showing the average rainfall, temperature and sunshine for four wine regions of France. They prove nothing; but they provide a fascinating field of speculation into just what weather in what moment in a vine's cycle will result in a good or great vintage.

A thorough study of this question in Burgundy was done by Rolande Gadille in her great book *Le Vignoble de la Côte Bourguignonne*, to which this atlas owes a considerable debt. The two lower graphs opposite show her plotting of the difference in reality over 17 years between good vintages, mediocre vintages and the average; just where the weather changed to the benefit or detriment of the wine.

Frost in late spring and hail at any time are the grower's nightmares. Hail tends to be localized; one reason why growers like to have little holdings scattered all over the parish. A bad storm can not only wreck a vintage, but bruise the wood so as to affect next year's wine.

The determining factor for the quality of a northern vintage (in Burgundy for instance) is the ripeness of the grapes. As a grape ripens its acidity decreases and its sugar increases. The primitive way of judging when to pick was to crush grapes in your hands; if they were sticky it was time. In the past the danger of a change in the weather (September rain bringing mildew) made growers often pick too soon, whereas today with chemicals and knowledge the vintage gets later and later.

It almost goes without saying that dry years are normally best. But the exact balance of importance between rain, sun, temperature and humidity has never been determined. What gives character to each individual vintage is the interaction between them: bright sunlight causing early ripening; overcast skies slowing growth but sometimes enriching the grapes with minerals which give the wine long life and complexity; high temperatures reducing acidity.

Even given exactly the same ripeness at picking, grapes reflect the year they have been through: scorching by sun or wind; too much vegetation (leaves and stems) or too little;

Hail and frost are the two most serious sudden weather hazards for wine-growers. Dramatic methods are used to combat them. Right: giant flame throwers heat the air on a frosty night in May (the tender new shoots of the vines can be seen). Below: an Australian grower prepares to fire a rocket into hail-bearing clouds to bring the hail down away from his vines

	April			May			June			July			August			September			October		
	1	10	20	1	10	20	1	10	20	1	10	20	1	10	20	1	10	20	1	10	20
1945																					
1946																					
1947																					
1948																					
1949																					
1950																					
1951																					
1952																					
1953																					
1954																					
1955																					
1956																					
1957																					
1958																					
1959																					
1960																					
1961																					
1962																					
1963																					

Left: the chart shows the dates of the main events in the annual life cycle of a Burgundy Pinot Noir vine over a 19-year period. In April the buds break; in late May or early June the flowers form; about the beginning of August the grapes 'set'; change from green to be either translucent or red. A hundred days after flowering the grapes should be ripe. Flowering should take about two weeks. But the chart shows how widely the dates can vary. Of the years shown, 1945, 1947, '52, '53 and '61, all early flowering years, produced outstandingly good vintages. 1951, '54, '56, '58 and '63, mostly late, were bad

mould resulting from damp ground or bruises from hail all eventually have a bearing on the wine. No two years are ever the same.

A grower can give a fair guess at vintage time at what the quality of his wine will be, weighing its ripeness against past experience. But there is always a good chance that weather factors he is unaware of have played a part. Two or three times in ten the spring after the vintage will bring him a surprise.

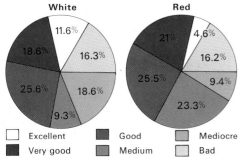

White   Red

11.6%		16.3%
18.6%		18.6%
25.6%		9.3%

21%		4.6%
25.5%		16.2%
	23.3%	9.4%

☐ Excellent   ■ Good   ▨ Mediocre
■ Very good   ▨ Medium   ▨ Bad

Above: white burgundy seems less affected by weather than red. Out of 43 vintages the white wines were outstandingly good or bad in only half; the reds divided almost equally into outstandingly good, bad or medium
Below: the temperature and sunshine month by month in Burgundy are shown in relation to good, average and bad vintages. The important differences seem to be in midsummer temperature and spring sunshine. Bad vintages suffer cold at flowering time and never catch up

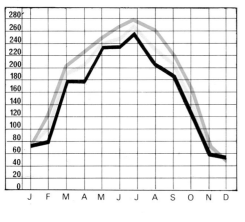

☐ Good
☐ Medium
■ Bad

Above: monthly average sunshine in hours
Below: average temperature in degrees Centigrade

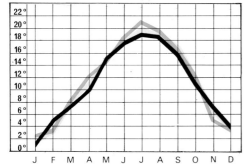

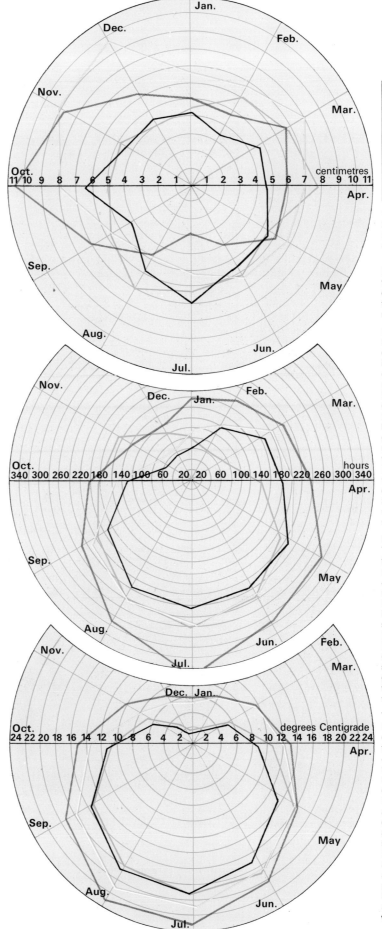

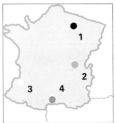

1 Champagne
2 Burgundy
3 Bordeaux
4 Montpellier

Left: isopleth graphs show the year's weather as a continuous process in the four French wine regions marked on the map above

Rainfall (top graph)
Sunshine and temperature come to a peak everywhere in midsummer; rainfall comes and goes more unpredictably. Bordeaux has a very wet winter, a comparatively rainy spring (flowering is in late May), but a long dry summer, growing wetter again, unfortunately for the vintage, in late September. Burgundy is dry in spring, wetter in summer but as dry as Bordeaux in early September. Champagne is wet in July but dry at vintage time

Sunshine (left)
The graph shows that all the regions get their maximum sunshine in July: the south by far the most all the year round. Bordeaux and Burgundy have curiously similar summer patterns from May to August, then Bordeaux has a distinctly sunnier end of season. Champagne has a good May, which is useful for the flowering of the vines

Temperature (left)
Latitude is clearly the chief factor in deciding temperature. Only in June is Burgundy as warm as Bordeaux. By September it is getting cool in Champagne; by November both Burgundy and Champagne are really cold. Bordeaux stays almost as mild as the south all the winter. Regional temperature averages are the least accurate for any particular vineyard, since local conditions of altitude and exposure make wide variations, known as 'micro-climates'

27

A Wine-Maker's Calendar

There is a job indoors in the cellar, and a job outdoors in the vines, for every day of a wine-maker's year. Every district has different methods, and a different time-table, besides modern innovations. But this is the life of a typical traditional vigneron, somewhere in the heart of France . . .

JANUARY

Pruning. Traditionally pruning started on St Vincent's Day, January 22nd. Nowadays it starts in December. If there is no snow the ground is often frozen. Vines will survive temperatures down to about −18°C

Barrels of new wine must be kept full to the top and their bungs wiped every other day with a solution of sulphur dioxide. In fine dry weather bottling of older wine can be done. Labelling and packing in boxes for shipment

FEBRUARY

Finish pruning and take cuttings for grafting. Make grafts on to root-stock and put them in sand indoors. Prepare machines for the outdoor work of the new season. Remember to order copper sulphate for spraying

Racking. In fine weather with a new moon and a north wind (i.e. when there is high atmospheric pressure), start 'racking' the new wine into clean barrels to clear it. 'Assemble' the new wine in a vat to equalize the casks

MARCH

Ploughing About mid-month the vine begins to emerge from dormancy; sap begins to rise; brown sheaths on buds fall off. Finish pruning. First working of the soil, deeply, to aerate it and uncover the bases of the vines

Finish first racking before the end of the month. Some mysterious sympathy between vine and wine is supposed to start the second fermentation when the sap rises. Keep the casks topped up. Finish bottling

JULY

Spray the vines regularly with Bordeaux mixture (copper sulphate, slaked lime and water). Third cultivation of the soil against weeds. Trim long shoots so that vines spend their energy on making fruit

No shipping in hot weather. All efforts to keep cellar cool. In heat-waves, when close weather makes it necessary to shut doors at night, burn a sulphur candle. Vine-growth slows down; bottling can start again

AUGUST

Keep the vineyards weeded and the vines trimmed. Black grapes turn colour. General upkeep and preparation of gear which will be needed for the vintage

Inspect and clean vats and casks to be used for the vintage. Vine-growth (and fermentation) starts again about mid-month so bottling must stop. Low-strength wine (being less stable) can turn in warm weather, so it must be carefully watched

SEPTEMBER

Vintage. Keep small boys and birds out of the vineyard. Keep vines trimmed, pray for sunshine. About the third week the grapes are ripe; the vintage begins

Before the vintage scour out the cuvier where the wine will be made. Put anti-rust varnish on all metal parts of presses, etc. Fill fermenting vats with water to swell the wood

APRIL

Finish ploughing. Clear up vineyard, burning any remaining prunings and replacing any rotten stakes. Plant one-year-old cuttings from the nursery. Pray for late vegetation, as frosts are frequent and hail possible

Topping up must still go on. There must never be any ullage (empty space) in the cask. Five per cent of the wine evaporates through the wooden sides of the barrel every year

MAY

Frost danger at its height. On clear nights stoves may be needed among the vines, which means sitting up to fuel them. Second working of the soil to kill weeds. Spray against oidium and mildew. Every ten days remove any suckers to encourage the sap to rise in the vines

Send off orders to customers. Towards the end of May, just before vines flower, begin the second racking off the lees into clean barrels

JUNE

The vines flower at the beginning of June when the temperature reaches 18–20°C. Weather is critical; the warmer and calmer the better. After flowering, thin the shoots, tying the best ones to the wires. Spray for oidium with powdered sulphur

Finish second racking of new wine and rack all old wines in the cellar. Evaporation is naturally accelerated by the warm weather; check all the casks for any weeping

OCTOBER

The vintage continues (see page 36) for perhaps two weeks. When it is over, spread manure (pressed grape skins are good) and fertilizer on the vineyard. Deep-plough the land for new plantations

The new wine is fermenting. Year-old wine should be given a final racking, the barrels bunged tightly and rolled a quarter-turn so the bung is at the side. Move barrels to second-year cellar to make room for new wine

NOVEMBER

Cut off long vine shoots and collect them for fuel. Finish manuring. Plough the vineyard to move soil over the bases of the vines to protect them from frost

Bottling. Rack and 'fine' (filter by pouring in whisked egg-white which sinks to the bottom) wine to be bottled. In rich and ripe vintages rack new wine now; in poor ones leave it on the lees another month

DECEMBER

If soil has been washed down slopes by rain it must be carried back up and redistributed. Pruning the vines can start before Christmas, on about December 15th

Casks must be topped up frequently. More bottling of older wine can be done. Start tasting the new wine with old friends

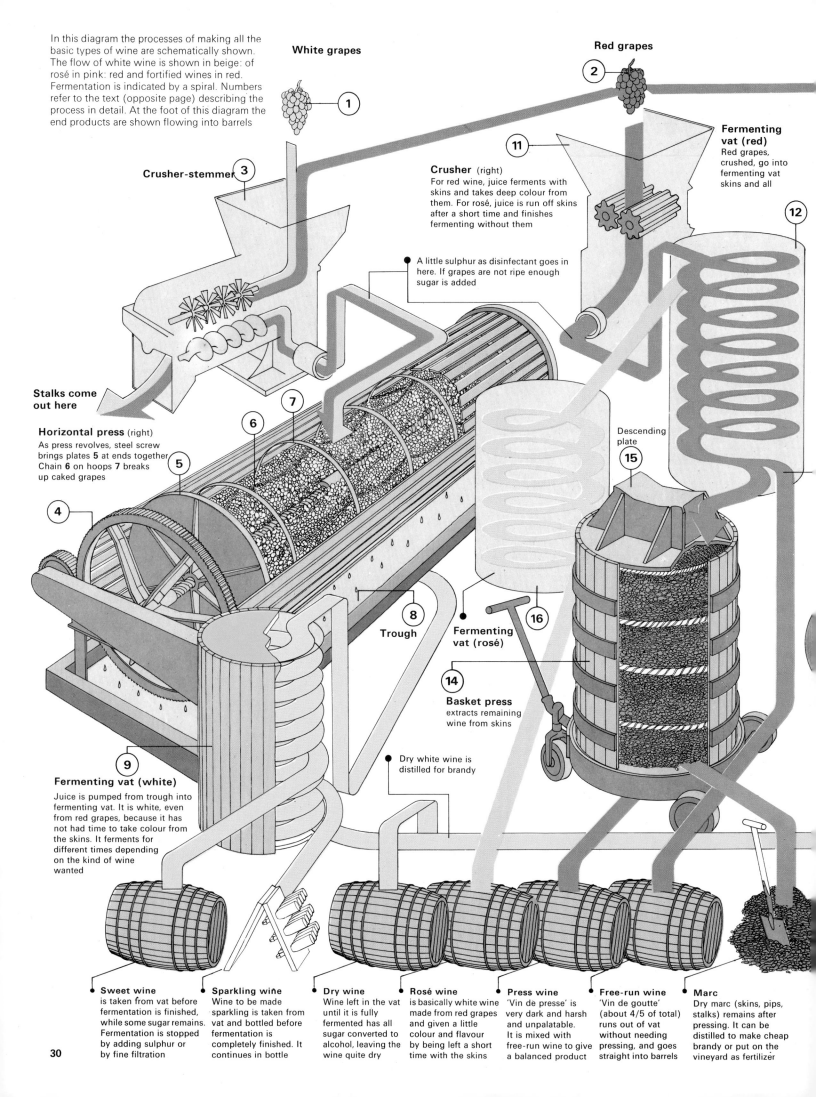

In this diagram the processes of making all the basic types of wine are schematically shown. The flow of white wine is shown in beige: of rosé in pink: red and fortified wines in red. Fermentation is indicated by a spiral. Numbers refer to the text (opposite page) describing the process in detail. At the foot of this diagram the end products are shown flowing into barrels

White grapes

1

Red grapes

2

Crusher-stemmer 3

11

Crusher (right)
For red wine, juice ferments with skins and takes deep colour from them. For rosé, juice is run off skins after a short time and finishes fermenting without them

Fermenting vat (red)
Red grapes, crushed, go into fermenting vat skins and all

• A little sulphur as disinfectant goes in here. If grapes are not ripe enough sugar is added

12

Stalks come out here

Horizontal press (right)
As press revolves, steel screw brings plates 5 at ends together Chain 6 on hoops 7 breaks up caked grapes

7

6

5

4

8

Trough

Descending plate

15

16

Fermenting vat (rosé)

14

Basket press extracts remaining wine from skins

9

Fermenting vat (white)
Juice is pumped from trough into fermenting vat. It is white, even from red grapes, because it has not had time to take colour from the skins. It ferments for different times depending on the kind of wine wanted

• Dry white wine is distilled for brandy

• **Sweet wine** is taken from vat before fermentation is finished, while some sugar remains. Fermentation is stopped by adding sulphur or by fine filtration

• **Sparkling wine** Wine to be made sparkling is taken from vat and bottled before fermentation is completely finished. It continues in bottle

• **Dry wine** Wine left in the vat until it is fully fermented has all sugar converted to alcohol, leaving the wine quite dry

• **Rosé wine** is basically white wine made from red grapes and given a little colour and flavour by being left a short time with the skins

• **Press wine** 'Vin de presse' is very dark and harsh and unpalatable. It is mixed with free-run wine to give a balanced product

• **Free-run wine** 'Vin de goutte' (about 4/5 of total) runs out of vat without needing pressing, and goes straight into barrels

• **Marc** Dry marc (skins, pips, stalks) remains after pressing. It can be distilled to make cheap brandy or put on the vineyard as fertilizer

How Wine is Made

Treading trough
(17) Grapes for port are trodden to extract colour from skins

Fermenting vat (port)
(18) Juice ferments until half its sugar is alcohol

(13) Free-run wine comes out without pressing

Brandy is added to stun the yeast and stop fermentation

(10)

Brandy
The product of distilling (see page 256) wine is brandy. If grape skins (marc) are distilled the product is called marc

Port
and most fortified wines and 'vins doux naturels' have their fermentation arrested with alcohol. They need ageing to 'marry' their different elements

Above: an ingenious 17th-century project for the mechanization of wine-making on a massive scale foreshadows the modern developments of the industry

ALL that is needed to turn grape juice into wine is the simple, entirely natural process of fermentation. Fermentation is the chemical change of sugar into alcohol and carbon dioxide gas brought about by yeasts—micro-organisms which live (among other places) on grape skins. They need only to have the grape skin broken to go to work on the sugar which comprises about 30% of the pulp. And in an instant there is wine.

Under normal conditions the yeast will go on working until all the sugar in the grapes is converted into alcohol, or until the alcohol level in the wine reaches about 15% of the volume—on the rare occasions when the grapes are so sweet that this happens naturally the yeast is overcome and fermentation stops.

Left to nature, therefore, almost all wine would be dry.

But it is possible to stop the fermentation before all the sugar is used up; either by adding alcohol to raise the level up to 15%, or by adding sulphur—both these anaesthetize the yeast, or by filtering the wine through a very fine filter to take the yeast out. These are the

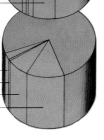

Moselle

Colour, flavour and other substances 1.2%
Acid 0.8%
Sugar 1%
Alcohol 8%
(by volume, 10%)
Water 89%

Claret

Colour, flavour and other substances 2%
Acid 0.45%
Sugar 0.2%
Alcohol 9.5%
(by volume, 12%)
Water 87.85%

Port

Colour, flavour and other substances 3%
Acid 0.35%
Sugar 10%
Alcohol 17%
(by volume, 20%)
Water 69.65%

Above: these three diagrams show the proportions of constituents in wines of three different types. The Moselle is an almost-dry white wine; a little sugar has been kept in it, probably by filtering the yeast out. The claret is a totally natural red wine. The brandy added to the port has increased its strength to 17°. Analytical strengths are measured by weight. The % of alcohol by volume (the normal measure) is given in brackets

methods which are used to make sweet wine.

One wine differs from another first and foremost because of differences in the raw material, the grapes.

But various ways of arranging the fermentation can produce all the other differences; between red, white, rosé, sweet, dry or sparkling. The diagram opposite shows how, starting with one basic material—red grapes—six quite distinct kinds of wine can be made.

White
Either white **1** or red **2** grapes are fed into a crusher-stemmer (or égrappoir) **3** which tears off the stalks and pumps the broken grapes into a horizontal press **4**. The press revolves as the steel screw brings the plates **5** at the ends together. Chains **6** and hoops **7** break up the caked grapes. The skins (marc) are left behind as the must (fresh juice) falls into a trough **8** from which it is pumped into a fermenting vat **9**, after which several courses are open to it. It may be made into sweet wine by having its fermentation stopped while it still contains sugar, or bottled before fermentation is finished, to make sparkling wine. Or it may

be fermented until all its sugar is used up, to make dry wine. And finally, the dry wine may be distilled **10** to make brandy

Red
Red grapes **2** are fed through a crusher **11** (or often a crusher-stemmer) and pumped into a vat **12** where they ferment with their skins. Traditionally the stalks go in too but they are usually removed today. The wine gradually draws out the colour and tannin from the skin. Fermentation is allowed to go on until all sugar is gone (up to 14 days). Then the tap is opened and the 'free-run' wine **13** is run off. For lighter quicker-maturing wine the modern practice is to take the wine off the skins

after a few days to finish fermenting separately. The skins are pressed in a hydraulic basket press **14** by a descending plate **15** which forces the juice out through slatted sides. Layers of matting help juice run out. This press wine, deeply coloured and tannic, is usually mixed with the free-run wine. The 'marc' left in the press is used as fertilizer or distilled to make cheap brandy

Rosé
Red grapes **2** are fed through a crusher **11** and straight into a vat **12** complete with their skins to begin fermentation. The juice for rosé wine takes a light pink colour from the skins but almost immediately it is run off

into another vat **16** to ferment without them. Normally it is allowed to finish fermentation naturally, and is thus completely dry

Port
(the process is similar for other fortified wines) Red grapes **2** are put in a stone trough **17** where they are continuously trodden with bare feet for 12 hours to make the juice take the colour of the skins. The juice is run into a vat **18** to ferment until half its sugar is converted to alcohol, when it is mixed with brandy from the still **10** to raise the alcohol level to above 15%. This stuns the yeast and stops fermentation, so the wine is both strong and sweet

The Art of the Wine-Maker

THE LAST two pages showed the simple steps common to all wine-making. Twenty years ago there was not much else to be done: you made your wine, more or less carefully and skilfully with better or worse grapes, and waited to see how it would turn out.

The best wines of the classical French and German regions are still, on the whole, made in the same spirit. One of the reasons for the emergence of these very regions is that natural conditions (autumn and winter temperatures, for example) provide natural controls. The wine-maker in such cases sees himself more as midwife than parent.

What has changed radically is the making of wine in warmer regions, where however good the grapes it was rarely possible in the past to make outstanding wine. Italy, the south of France, California, Australia, much of Spain, Chile and Argentina are all examples.

With modern knowledge the wine-maker no longer merely watches—he controls. Technology supplies him with a vast range of alternatives. And as he controls, so at every stage of the process he must decide.

His decisions start with the fruit in the vineyard. When to pick it. Hazards of weather apart, as it ripens its balance of sugar, acids, extracts and water alters daily. *Force majeure* may make him take grapes when he can get them, but a wine-maker who can afford to can take his idea of the wine he wants to make into the vineyard with him, analyse the grapes as they hang on the vine, and calculate how the wine will be if he picks today—or tomorrow.

Having chosen his moment, even his time of day to pick (early morning picking in hot weather gets the grapes into the vat cooler, which can make a difference to freshness and aroma), the wine-maker will inspect the grapes as they come in. If he finds many of them underripe, overripe or rotten he must decide whether to include them or throw them out (an expensive operation). Whichever he decides will affect the character of the wine.

For white wine he may believe in separating the juice from the skins immediately; or he may think it is better to let them separate gently and naturally; or he may want to leave them in contact for a while.

In the first case he can press the grapes straight away (with or without their stalks; the stalks make pressing easier but can give the wine a stalky flavour) and then use a centrifuge, which separates the clear liquid from the remaining suspended solids instantly, expensively, and some say too violently. Another alternative is to dispense with the press and use a 'drag-screen', which pulls the crushed grapes over a mesh, letting the liquid drop through.

In the second case he can again crush the grapes but not press them, leave them in a vat with a draining vent at the bottom while the liquid runs out naturally, then press the remaining solids. Some think this 'free-run' wine is always better. Certainly it is lighter, more limpid, quicker-maturing. But it lacks the tannin which gives pressed wine a more stable structure, more resistance to oxidation and a longer life . . . hence more opportunity to grow complex and interesting.

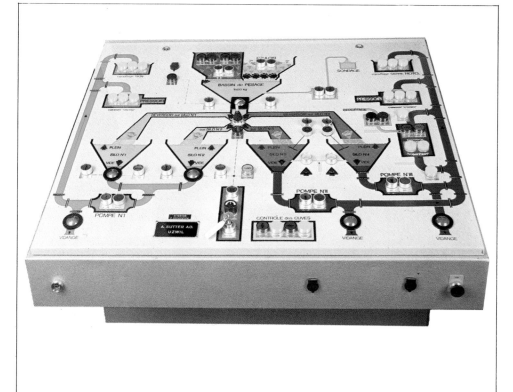

Right: the photograph of naked men breaking up the 'cap' of skins in a fermenting vat (from the Musée des Arts et Traditions Populaires) was taken in Burgundy as recently as the 1950s
Above: A control panel which allows one man to operate a whole Swiss winery at vintage time simply by pressing buttons. This is the degree of change that has overtaken the wine industry in the last twenty years

The third method is traditional in hot areas where the grapes lack acid: by macerating in the juice (even in some places briefly fermenting in the juice) the skins give tannin and aroma to wine which would otherwise be too soft and oxidize too easily. This treatment gives certain Italian wines—Frascati for example—their peculiar grape-skin character.

The next stage is fermentation. Traditionally for certain strong high-flavoured wines (white burgundy, for example) this is done in small oak barrels, which give a noticeable taste of oak to the wine. Modern practice is almost always to ferment in concrete, stainless steel or glass- or tile-lined vats. The first decision here is what yeast to use. Modern wineries almost always prevent any natural yeasts on the grapes

from starting the fermentation (a strong dose of sulphur dioxide, wine's all-purpose antiseptic, does this). Instead they choose a pure yeast culture. For California Chardonnays they use a yeast from Montrachet, which may contribute to the uncanny resemblance some of these wines have to whites from the Côte de Beaune.

The second decision is the temperature of the fermentation. In a warm climate without control fermenting wine will get hotter and hotter until the yeasts can no longer multiply and the fermentation 'sticks'—which can easily lead to vinegar. Modern practice is to ferment white wine very cool (about 60°F, or 15.5°C). Cold fermentation takes a long time—four to six weeks and even more. Some wine-makers take it faster and warmer, others even slower.

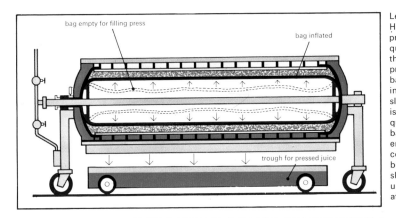

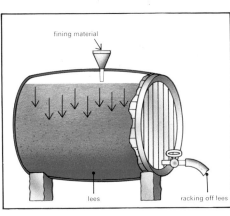

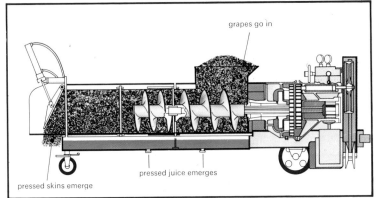

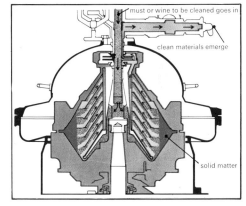

Left and below left: How the grapes are pressed affects both the quality and quantity of the wine. The air-bag press, in which a huge balloon is inflated, squeezing the grapes against the slatted sides of a cylinder, is gentle but slow. The quality is high, but each batch must be filled and emptied by hand. The continuous press is faster, but can be brutal, grinding skins and crushing pips, unless it is run slowly and at low pressure

(labels, top-left diagram:) bag empty for filling press · bag inflated · trough for pressed juice

(labels, bottom-left diagram:) grapes go in · pressed juice emerges · pressed skins emerge

(labels, top-right diagram:) fining material · lees · racking off lees

(labels, bottom-right diagram:) must or wine to be cleaned goes in · clean materials emerge · solid matter

Right and above right: Good wine 'falls bright' (i.e. clarifies itself) naturally. The traditional way of giving it a final polish is by 'fining' and 'racking'. Fining consists of pouring beaten egg-whites, ox-blood or isinglass into the barrel: as it sinks it carries all suspended solids with it. The clear wine is then 'racked' off the residue at the bottom. The centrifuge, right, is a modern method of separating solids using centrifugal force

If the wine-maker wants a very delicate grapy wine he will take every precaution to keep oxygen away from it at every stage. For example, he will fill a tank with carbon dioxide gas before he pumps the wine in and keep a 'blanket' of the gas in the space at the head of the vat all the time. This has the added advantage of preventing the natural carbon dioxide, dissolved in the wine after fermentation, from escaping into the air. A little carbon dioxide gives white wine a pleasant freshness, a faint prickle on the tongue, especially valuable when it is low in acid.

It is common practice today to adjust the acidity in warm areas by adding either tartaric acid before fermentation or citric acid after. It would be nice if it were not necessary, but since both these acids are natural components of wine no one can object to their being boosted. Sugar, after all, is often added in France.

As soon as fermentation is finished the wine must be syphoned ('racked') off the lees, the dead yeast cells and other solids at the bottom of the container. There is a natural tendency in most wines to start fermenting again soon after. This 'secondary' or 'malo-lactic' fermentation is in fact the action of bacteria which feed on the malic (apple) acid and convert it to lactic (milk) acid, which is less sharp to taste. In cool areas with acid wines malo-lactic fermentation is a boon: it softens the sharpness of the wine, and also contributes in ways which are not fully understood to its general complexity and distinction. Low-acid, hot-country wines, however, need to keep all the acidity they have. The wine-maker must therefore decide whether he wants secondary fermentation or not. If not he can stop it by keeping the sulphur dioxide level in the wine high (it constantly drops as the SO_2 combines with other elements and needs replenishing) and by frequent racking (or rapid sterile bottling).

Does the wine-maker want a freshly grapy pale wine? He must keep it protected from air until it is bottled. Does the wine have the strength and potential to mature into something rich and deep? He has a choice of containers to keep it in, allowing just enough interaction with the air for it to mature. California wine-makers have recently made remarkable discoveries about the different ways different oak barrels act on wine. They have tried oak of various French forests, traditionally used in Bordeaux and Burgundy, as well as Balkan and American white oak. Each has a subtly different effect on the taste and texture of the wine. This is another decision the wine-maker can take.

I have not mentioned the choice of whether the white wine is to be dry or sweet. If sweet wine is wanted there is a choice of ways of stopping the fermentation from using up all the sugar. There is also the regrettable alternative of adding sweet unfermented grape juice to a dry wine.

Nor have I discussed the similar range of alternatives in making red wine—of which perhaps the most crucial is the length of the fermentation of juice and skins together. The modern tendency is to try to get as much colour from the skins as possible with as little tannin. Tannin is the awkward element, the natural preservative which tastes hard and harsh itself but without which no red wine can keep long enough to mature. In the last decade very short fermentations have been in vogue. Wine-makers have felt that the public does not understand the hard taste of new red wine and has no patience to keep it for maturing. But they are beginning to realize that there is no short-cut: two or three days may be long enough to give a fine red tint to the juice (there is even a 'heat-treatment' practised to extract the colour quickly), but ten days' slow fermenting (at about 75°F) is what is needed for deep colour and long-lasting, satisfying wine.

One interesting alternative method of fermenting red wine has long been practised in Beaujolais and is currently under discussion elsewhere, particularly in the south of France. It is to put the whole bunches of grapes, uncrushed, stalks and all, into a closed vat full of carbon dioxide. A different sort of fermentation starts inside each grape, extracting the skin colour internally and eventually bursting the berry. Carbonic maceration, as the method is called, makes well-coloured, very aromatic, soft-flavoured wine, but with limited possibilities for maturing.

Even when the wine is ready for bottling there are decisions to make. The safe course to ensure shining and brilliant wine is to filter it through a fine filter. But filters remove flavour as well as specks and motes. Ideal wine eventually 'falls bright' in the barrel without special treatment. At this stage as at every other the less the wine can be manipulated the better. The ultimate art of the oenologist is to know when to do nothing.

Anatomy of a Winery

MOST modern wine is made in what amounts to a wine-factory: in western Europe most commonly a co-operative owned by the farmers (and their bank); in eastern Europe by the State; in the New World more often by a public or private company.

The term winery is not appealing, and the idea of barrels in caves has much more allure, but mass-production methods are the only practicable ways of making the huge quantities of reliable wine the world demands.

The essence of a modern winery is flexibility. It must be able to handle different grapes from different sources and turn them into different kinds of wine. In contrast to the château on the next pages, which follows a single-minded course year after year, a winery must keep all its options open to adapt to the market.

To be efficient it must have the longest possible wine-making season, using its presses and fermenting vats continually from the arrival of 'precocious' grapes in early autumn to the latest-ripeners, after the first frosts. Ideally its sources of grapes, therefore, include farmers growing many different kinds, or with widely different ripening conditions. At least one new winery saves fermenting capacity by chilling the whole crop and fermenting it in batches all the year round.

The winery on this page is based on one of California's most up-to-date and successful: the Robert Mondavi winery in the Napa valley. In essence it buys (or grows) grapes and sells finished wine, bottled and packed: all the processes between happen under its roof. Many such wineries also buy wine in bulk from others to blend, or 'finish', and sell.

Grapes are delivered from local vineyards by tractor and 'gondola', or distant ones by trucks hauling 25 tons. They are tipped into a pit and carried by an Archimedean screw to the de-stemmer and crusher

From the crusher a pipe carries the juice and broken grapes for red wine straight to the fermenting vat. White 'pomace' may be settled in a drainer-tank before pressing, or pressed straight away

Offices and reception and tasting-rooms occupy a wing. Visitors are encouraged to tour the winery and taste. Most wineries sell direct to private buyers as well as wholesale. Appearances are important

Stainless steel tanks can be used for both fermentation and storage, which increases the winery's capacity. The Mondavi winery stores well over a million gallons, yet is still among the smaller ones

Most wineries own at least some vines, but for many they produce a small proportion of the grapes they use: the rest are bought from specialist farmers. The propeller device is to keep the air moving on still nights of potential frost in late spring

Wine often changes hands in bulk between modern wineries. It may be bought for 'finishing' and bottling under the brand name, or blending with the home product, or even for resale in bulk. In this sense such a business is the *négociant* of the old world as well as the *château*

The barrel-room holds French and American oak barrels, stacked six-high, for ageing red wines, fortified wines and the few whites that are not sold young

Tanks can be made of steel, oak, redwood, concrete or fibreglass. A vast variety of sizes gives flexibility for handling big or small lots of wine

A laboratory and computer-room control the condition and whereabouts of hundreds of different batches of wine from fermentation to bottling and dispatch. Record-keeping is a vast but essential task

The bottling-line can handle up to 55 bottles a minute. Bottles arrive already in cartons, are taken out, filled and put back, then stacked on palettes ready for dispatch

The filter area. Most wine is fine-filtered before bottling. A little unfiltered wine is sometimes kept for wine-lovers who value flavour more than perfect clarity

Many modern wineries dispense with roofs and build stainless steel tanks for fermentation and storage in the open air. Their great bulk and a jacket of circulating cooling fluid keep them at the ideal temperature in any weather

Anatomy of a Château

COMPARED WITH modern industrial wine-making, the routine at a Bordeaux château, reasonably typical of the whole of France, seems as natural and uncomplicated as any traditional harvest scene. The grapes are simply picked, destalked, crushed; the rest is nature . . . but nature kept under a careful watch, with discreet adjustments where necessary.

In a typical small château such as the one shown (Château Malescasse in the Médoc), the wine is made in oak *cuves* in the *cuvier*. It ferments for about ten days before it is run off the skins and the skins are pressed. If the weather is hot and the fermentation generates too much heat it must be cooled by hosing down the *cuves* with water, or even packing blocks of ice round them.

From the *cuvier* the wine is pumped into a cement tank for two weeks before it is *débourbé* —pumped off its heaviest sediment into another tank. In this it spends the winter, going through its gentle secondary or malolactic fermentation which rids it of malic acid, making it less harsh. Traditionally secondary fermentation does not start till March, when the sap rises in the vines, but modern practice brings it forward. In February the wine is pumped into *barriques* (hogsheads) in the first-year *chai*.

It stays here for a year, being constantly topped up and occasionally 'racked' into a fresh barrel; in some years going on fermenting slightly through the summer.

In the following year it is moved into the second-year *chai*, where it is bunged tight and

left to mature until, after two years, it is ready for bottling. Some bottling is done here with a hand machine; some casks are sold for bottling by merchants. But the bottle cellar has an important role as well: for no good red Bordeaux is ready to drink before it has been in bottle for at least two years.

Château Malescasse at Lamarque is a typical small Cru Bourgeois; a modest specialized farm. Its methods (on which the drawing is broadly based) are up-to-date without being unusually modern. The château was built in about 1830. Like many in the Médoc it was given an air of importance above its station as an ordinary family house

In the kitchen a midday meal of pot au feu or cassoulet is cooked for the pickers. Their breakfast consisted of sardines, bread and red wine

The proprietor's office: on the wall hang large-scale plans of the château and the vineyard which show every barrel and vine

The first-year *chai*. New wine is pumped into oak hogsheads, and stoppered with loose glass bungs. At some châteaux wine goes straight into barrels; here it waits till the following February

Cement *cuves* hold the new wine over the winter while it undergoes secondary fermentation and rids itself of heavy sediment

Hydraulic press will press the skins to extract remaining one-fifth of the wine after the rest has been run off (see pages 30–31). The deeply coloured vin de presse is mixed with the rest

Remontage. Every morning and evening the fermenting wine is pumped up and sprayed over the floating 'cap' of skins. In fine years it is pumped via an open tub for aeration

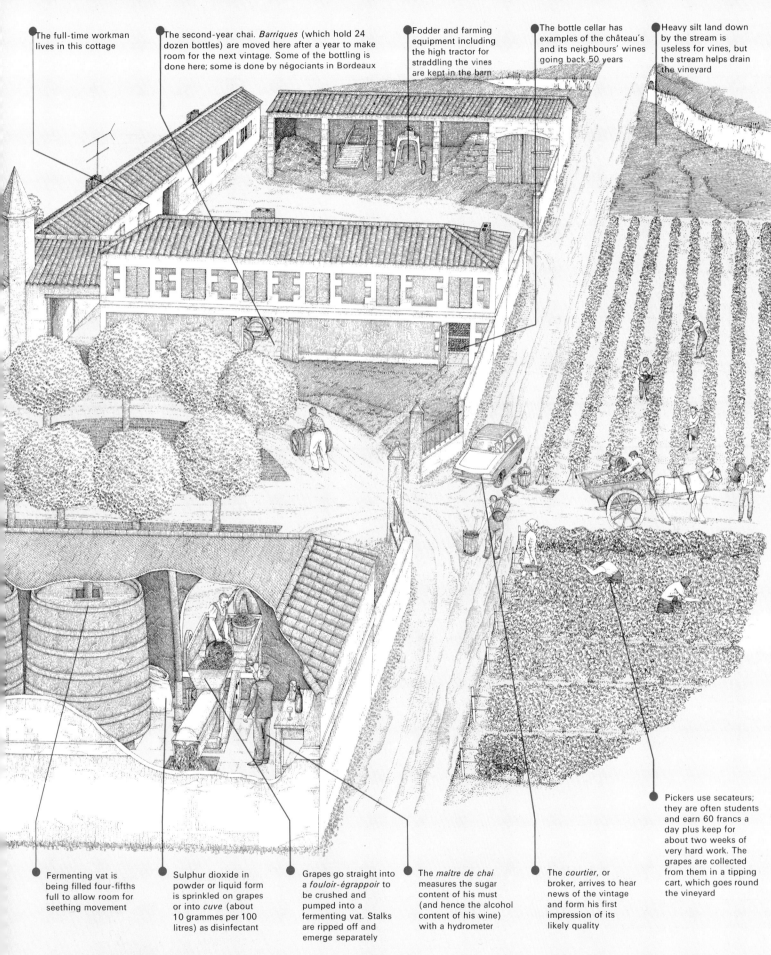

The full-time workman lives in this cottage

The second-year chai. *Barriques* (which hold 24 dozen bottles) are moved here after a year to make room for the next vintage. Some of the bottling is done here; some is done by négociants in Bordeaux

Fodder and farming equipment including the high tractor for straddling the vines are kept in the barn

The bottle cellar has examples of the château's and its neighbours' wines going back 50 years

Heavy silt land down by the stream is useless for vines, but the stream helps drain the vineyard

Fermenting vat is being filled four-fifths full to allow room for seething movement

Sulphur dioxide in powder or liquid form is sprinkled on grapes or into *cuve* (about 10 grammes per 100 litres) as disinfectant

Grapes go straight into a *fouloir-égrappoir* to be crushed and pumped into a fermenting vat. Stalks are ripped off and emerge separately

The *maître de chai* measures the sugar content of his must (and hence the alcohol content of his wine) with a hydrometer

The *courtier*, or broker, arrives to hear news of the vintage and form his first impression of its likely quality

Pickers use secateurs; they are often students and earn 60 francs a day plus keep for about two weeks of very hard work. The grapes are collected from them in a tipping cart, which goes round the vineyard

Wine and Time

Above: Louis Pasteur, born at Dôle in the Jura in 1822, was the first scientist to turn his mind to wine. He discovered that yeast causes fermentation, as well as other facts of enormous importance to wine-makers

In these hand-coloured illustrations from his *Etudes sur le Vin*, Pasteur recorded the effect of time and oxygen on red and white wine

Far left: Pasteur found that red wine without air did not change colour
Left: with air it faded

Left: white wine without air was unchanged
Right: with air it grew brown

SOME WINES are ready to drink as soon as they are made. Others improve immeasurably by being kept for even as much as 50 years. As a general rule these *vins de garde* are the better. But why? And why is it that such a mystique attaches to an old bottle of wine?

Most white wines, rosé wines and such light reds as Beaujolais and Valpolicella are at their best young. The pleasure in them is a matter of grapiness and freshness. We want them to be close to fresh fruit; direct in scent and flavour.

The great white wines and most of the best reds, however, are grown to be as full of their own particular character, extracted from their particular soil, as possible. There resides in them when young an unresolved complex of principles: of acids and sugars, minerals and pigments, esters and aldehydes and tannins. Good wines have more of these things than ordinary wines, and great wines than good wines. Which is why, in the end, they have more flavour.

But it takes time for these elements to resolve themselves into a harmonious whole and for the distinct scent of maturity, called (by analogy with flowers) the bouquet, to form. Time, and oxygen.

It was not till Louis Pasteur was asked by Napoleon III in 1863 to find out why so much wine went bad on its way to the consumer, to the great harm of French trade, that the role of oxygen was discovered. Pasteur established that too much contact with the air allows the growth of vinegar bacteria. On the other hand he found that it was very slight amounts of oxygen that makes wine mature; that the oxygen's action is not 'brusque', but gradual, and that there is enough of it dissolved in a bottle of wine to account for an ageing process lasting for years.

He showed, by sealing up wine in test-tubes, alternately full and half-full, that the oxygen in the air of the half-full tube caused the same

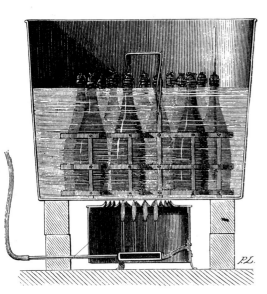

Above: Pasteur's original diagram of his method of 'pasteurizing' wine by heating it in hot water
Right: A Roman bottle of Roman wine, now in Speyer museum. Air is kept from the wine by a layer of oil on top

deposit in a few weeks as is found in very old bottles, that it faded red wine and darkened white wine, affecting their colour in exactly the same way as extreme old age.

In fact he immensely speeded up the process that happens in a bottle: the oxygen in the wine acts on its constituents to mature them, but beyond the period of maturity it continues to act; from then on the wine deteriorates.

Pasteur found that even wine which is carefully kept from the air has opportunities to absorb oxygen: when it is being racked from one barrel to another; even through the staves of the barrel (so that their thickness, whether or not they are encrusted with tartrate crystals, the capacity of the barrel, whether it stood in a draught, all become relevant). He told the story of a painted cask at the Clos de Vougeot whose wine always tasted a year or two younger than the others which were unpainted.

If wine in barrels is more subject to the action of oxygen it also has the wood itself as an agent for change. It picks up certain characteristics—extra tannin, and vanillin, which gives a vanilla flavour, particularly to spirits—from the oak. Oxygen and oak together age wine far faster than it will age in bottle.

Left too long in a barrel a light wine fades rapidly; its colour goes; its fruitiness disappears; it starts to taste dry, flat and insipid. The same wine bottled after a year or less will keep the colour, the fruit and the acidity, and last (and perhaps improve) for several more years.

Every wine and every vintage has its own time-scale. The riper the grapes, the more flavouring matter and strength there will be in the wine. Given the right amount of acidity, to prevent it becoming soft and flat, wine of good years with plenty of 'fruit' repays keeping far more than wine of average ones.

The vintage charts on pages 53–56 are some degree of guide as to how long the wines of recent vintages will benefit by being kept.

The Price of Wine

WHEN the brokers of Bordeaux set out to establish the famous 1855 classification of the Médoc they took as their guide the prices fetched by the different châteaux over the previous hundred or so years. They were safe in assuming that something for which the world is consistently prepared to pay more for so long must be better.

Things are more confused today. The 'great' wines are bought more for their reputations than for their quality. Their high price, in fact, has become the reason for buying them.

The advertising of brands similarly distorts prices: so much is for the wine in the bottle, so much for the feeling of confidence because it has been on television.

Recently the cost of the non-wine elements attaching themselves to a bottle (that is the bottle itself, the cork, label, handling and shipping, not to mention financing) have risen much faster than the price of the almost insignificant commodity inside. When taxes are taken into account a tiny proportion of the cost (to the consumer) of a bottle of ordinary wine is for the actual wine—a prima facie case for buying better wine.

Information about the price of wine is scattered in relevant places throughout the atlas. On this page are some examples of the fluctuations of wine prices over recent years.

The graphs plot the retail prices of ten representative wines over the last 17 years at one of the world's most famous wine retailers—Berry Bros & Rudd of St James's St., London. Customs duties, the only factor which would make them different from prices in comparable shops anywhere in the world, have been subtracted. Although inflation is the keynote, one can see in them the influence of fashion and the quality of vintages. Most revealing of all is to compare them with the British retail prices index; the last graph. It can be seen that in relation to most other goods the prices of several wines have actually come down considerably in the last few years.

The first-growth Bordeaux (Lafite) and the first white burgundy (Corton-Charlemagne) need charts on a different scale from the rest. Lafite doubled in price between 1962 and '68, again between '68 and '74, again between '74 and '76. Corton-Charlemagne caught up later, doubling between '68 and '70, '70 and '74, '74 and '76.

The second-growth Bordeaux climbed only slowly until '73. The second white burgundy, Meursault, was steady until 1970, but is now three times that price. The red burgundy, London-bottled Corton, has only doubled over the same period. Port (the latest vintage) has caught up with second-growth Bordeaux, from a much lower start.

Champagne (a non-vintage famous brand) has taken 16 years to treble its price, which is relatively slow. But by far the steadiest are the modest Rhine and Moselle wines and the Alsace—which is still not double its 1960 price.

There are of course German wines whose graphs would be more like that of Lafite. But who would have suspected the steadiness of price of good everyday German wine? Or, indeed, of Scotch whisky.

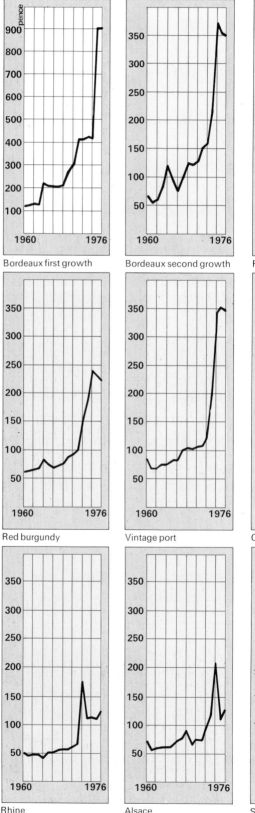

Bordeaux first growth

Bordeaux second growth

First white burgundy

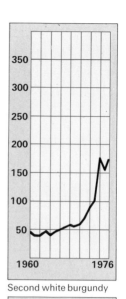

Second white burgundy

Red burgundy

Vintage port

Champagne

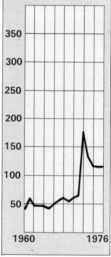

Moselle

Rhine

Alsace

Scotch whisky

GB retail price index

Prices per bottle without customs duties
100 pence = £1 = US $1.66 (on January 1st, 1977)

Far right: Prices at June 17th 1962 = 100

40

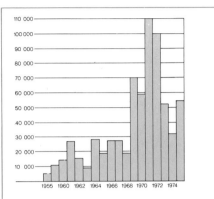

The graphs above and below vividly illustrate the boom in Bordeaux prices in the late 1960s and the reaction that followed. Above are the prices at the château (given in francs per tonneau: four hogsheads or about 1150 bottles) for the first-growth Château Lafite. Below are the prices for a first-class Cru Bourgeois (the Cru Exceptionnel Château d'Angludet at Cantenac in the Médoc). The price of Lafite in 1955 was 5000 francs. By 1959 it had doubled. The small and excellent 1961 vintage was the first real landmark—the price leapt to 27,000 francs, a level it held remarkably steadily through the later 1960s, until the failure of the 1968s and the small size of the 1969 vintage coincided with growing American demand. In 1970, the economics of scarcity took over. Lafite demanded and got 70,000 francs for the mediocre 1969s. There was so much of the superb 1970 that the price fell back to 59,000 francs at first, but the wine-investment boom had started and 1970s were changing hands later at twice the château price. The boom reached a peak with the small 1971 vintage and the plentiful 1972, poor though it was. Then in 1973 came the October war. Suddenly everyone wondered who was actually going to drink all this wine which was leaving the château at £10 a bottle. The prices of the big vintages of 1973 and 1974 tell their own story.

In contrast, Cru Bourgeois prices (below) have found and held a realistic level. In 1955 Angludet was a quarter of the price of Lafite. At the height of the boom it was one-fourteenth. In 1975 it is back to one-fifth.

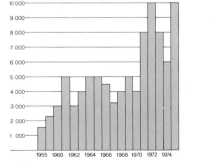

AUCTION prices give the clearest idea of the relative values put on wine on the open market. In 1966 Christie's, the London fine art auction house, restarted the practice of auctioning wine (which they originally began in the 18th century). The tables below give the results of their first ten years of wine sales, expressed as average lot values for four classes of sale: finest wines (which include old and rare wines of all sorts); claret; vintage port and burgundy.

The tables clearly show a steady climb up to the 1971–72 season, then a dramatic leap in the silly season of 1972–73, when wine suddenly became a fashionable commodity for investment (there was even talk of 'holding portfolios' of wine; a perversion which was mercifully short-lived). A flood of wine from overstocked speculators brought prices (except that of vintage port) down to their 1971–72 levels in 1974–75. 1975–76 has seen them climbing back, but mainly, one may suppose, as a result of the cheapness of the pound sterling, attracting buyers from overseas. Converted into dollars the levels show little change.

What did change during the period was the level of activity. In 1976 Christie's turnover of wine (over two-thirds of the London auction total) was double that of 1975, amounting to a million bottles, valued at five and a half million US dollars. More than half of this wine was lying overseas when it was sold. In addition, important cellars of old wines were sent to London for sale from all over the world. Since the majority of buyers are overseas as well, London has a unique situation in the world of wine as the place where values are established.

Claret and vintage port are always the most popular wines at auction for at least two reasons. First because they mature more slowly than any other wines, and therefore have a longer life in which they can safely be bought and sold. Secondly because they are clearly identifiable and easily understood: almost, in fact, a negotiable currency. There is only one Château Latour 1961 or Croft 1963. In contrast there are a dozen different growers of Chambertin and no accepted touchstone for distinguishing between them. Moreover modern burgundy cannot be relied on to keep for long in bottle.

One might hazard that German wines (except the very finest and rarest) suffer from similar disadvantages. Certainly their average lot values (not shown) follow the same pattern as burgundy rather than claret. Their bottle-life is considered—often wrongly—to be short, and the sheer complications of their naming system deters the majority of potential bidders. Beerenausleses fetch high prices, but the price-gap between these and Ausleses is exaggerated. There are no greater German wines than the finest Ausleses—only sweeter ones.

Burgundy and Germany are therefore two of the areas to explore for bargains.

Others are white Bordeaux, old champagne, and the infrequently seen lots of non-French wines (with the exception of Tokay Essence, which always fetch fantastic prices). Sauternes (Château Yquem apart) is consistently undervalued for one of the world's great wines. It can still be bought for less than many banal commercial productions.

Seasons October–July
Fine wine
£

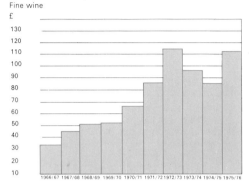

Seasons October–July
Claret
£

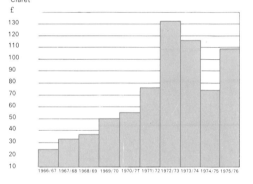

Seasons October–July
Vintage Port
£

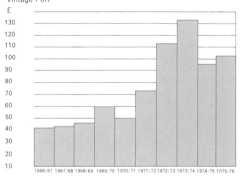

Seasons October–July
Burgundy
£

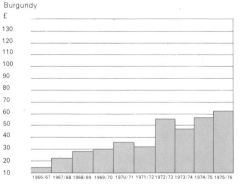

The Literature of Wine

BOOKS on wine and wine-growing have been appearing since Roman times. A gentleman farmer in the days of the Empire would have had wine books in his library by several of the greatest writers, including Virgil, Horace, Cato, Varro and Martial.

The first known farming manual was written by Mago of Carthage (in modern Tunisia) at the end of the 4th century BC. Columella, who was born in Cadiz in the sherry country, wrote his classic *De Re Rustica* in about AD 65. Both these books treated wine-growing as an important part of general agriculture, and showed that long study had already been given to factors governing the quality of wine, as well as the economics of vine husbandry . . . largely in those days a matter of how hard you could drive your slaves.

Since the 18th century a great library of technical works has accumulated. In France, particularly, some of them are treated with reverence as classics, so that modern writers still quote what Lavalle, Rodier, Roupnel, Guyot had to say about the character of a certain wine, like 18th-century parliamentarians solemnly quoting Thucydides.

Some of these books have as much value today as they ever did. The place of others has been taken by fresh works. The list which follows is a personal selection of current wine-books, along with a few irreplaceable classics.

General

H. Warner Allen
A History of Wine (London, 1961)

Maynard A. Amerine and Vernon L. Singleton
Wine, An Introduction for Americans (Berkeley & Los Angeles, 1965)

Maynard A. Amerine and M. A. Joslyn
Table Wines—the Technology of their Production (Berkeley & Los Angeles, 1970)

J. M. Broadbent
Wine Tasting (London, 1968)

Ernest Hornickel
Die Spitzenweine Europas (Stuttgart, 1963)

Edward Hyams
Dionysus, A Social History of the Wine Vine (London, 1965)

A. Jullien
Topographie de Tous les Vignobles Connus (Paris, 1866)

Alexis Lichine
Encyclopaedia of Wines and Spirits (London, 1967, 1975)

Salvatore P. Lucia
A History of Wine as Therapy (Philadelphia, 1963)

Lenz Moser
Un Nouveau Vignoble (Translated from the German, Cadillac-sur-Garonne, 1960)

Louis Pasteur
Etudes sur le Vin (Paris, 1866)

J. Ribéreau-Gayon and Emile Peynaud
Traité d'Oenologie (Paris, 1960)

George Saintsbury
Notes on a Cellarbook (London, 1920)

Frank Schoonmaker
Encyclopaedia of Wine (London, 1967)

G. Siloret
Encyclopédie des Connaissances Agricoles: Le Vin (Paris, 1963)

André L. Simon
Bottlescrew Days (London, 1926)

Philip M. Wagner
Grapes into Wine (New York, 1974)

Harry Waugh
The Changing Face of Wine (London, 1968)
Pick of the Bunch (London, 1970)
Diary of a Wine-taster (New York, 1972 and later volumes)

Albert J. Winkler
General Viticulture (Berkeley & Los Angeles, 1962)

William Younger
Gods, Men & Wine (London, 1966)

France

John Arlott and Christopher Fielden
Burgundy: Vines & Wines (London, 1976)

Pierre Bréjoux
Les Vins de la Loire (Paris, 1956)
Les Vins de Bourgogne (Paris, 1967)

Cocks et Féret
Bordeaux et ses Vins (Bordeaux, 1970: 12th edition)

Paul de Cassagnac
French Wines (Translated by Guy Knowles, London, 1930)

Hubrecht Duijker
The Great Wine Châteaux of Bordeaux (Amsterdam and London, 1975)

Patrick Forbes
Champagne (London, 1969)

Rolande Gadille
Le Vignoble de la Côte Bourguignonne (Paris, 1967)

Louis Jacquelin and René Poulain
The Wines and Vineyards of France (Translated by T. A. Layton, London, 1962)

Louis Larmat
Les Vins des Côtes du Rhône (Paris, 1943)
Les Vins de Bordeaux (1944)
Les Vins de Champagne (1944)
Les Vins des Coteaux de la Loire; Touraine et Centre (1946)
Le Cognac (1947)
Les Vins de Bourgogne (1953)

Louis Orizet
Mon Beaujolais (Villefranche, 1959)

Edmund Penning-Rowsell
The Wines of Bordeaux (London, 1969)

Pierre Poupon and Pierre Forgeot
Les Vins de Bourgogne (Paris, 1969: revised edition)

Cyril Ray
Cognac (London, 1971)

Camille Rodier
Le Vin de Bourgogne (Dijon, 1948)

V. R. Roger
The Wines of Bordeaux (London, 1960)

Philippe Roudié
Le Vignoble Bordelais (Toulouse, 1973)

Gérard Seguin
Les Sols des Vignobles du Haut-Médoc. Influences sur l'Alimentation en Eau de la Vigne et sur la Maturation du Raisin (Bordeaux, 1970)

P. Morton Shand
A Book of French Wines (London, 1928)

Allan Sichel
The Penguin Book of Wines (London, 1965)

André L. Simon
Champagne (London, 1962)

Germany

Hans Ambrosi
Wo Grosse Weine Wachsen (Munich, 1973)
Deutsche Weinatlas (Bielefeld, 1973)

H. Becker, H. Zakosek and others
Die Standortkartierung der Hessischen Weinbaugebiete (Wiesbaden, 1967)

S. F. Hallgarten
Rhineland Wineland (London, 1951)

Frank Schoonmaker
The Wines of Germany (New York, 1956, 1969)

Australia

Len Evans
Australia and New Zealand—The Complete Book of Wine (Sydney, 1973)

André L. Simon
The Wines, Vineyards and Vignerons of Australia (Melbourne, 1966)

Central Europe

R. E. H. Gunyon
The Wines of Central and South-East Europe (London, 1971)

Zoltan Halasz
Hungarian Wine through the Ages (Budapest, 1962)

Italy

Charles G. Bode
Wines of Italy (London, New York, 1956)

Cyril Ray
The Wines of Italy (London, 1966)

Bruno Roncarati
Viva Vino (London, 1976)

Luigi Veronelli
The Wines of Italy (Rome, 1966)

Morocco

Michèle Mathez
L'Arboriculture et Viticulture au Maroc (Rabat, 1968)

Scotland

R. J. S. McDowall
The Whiskies of Scotland (London, 1967)

South Africa

Gordon Bagnall
Wine of South Africa (Paarl, 1961)

K. W. V. (ed)
Wines of Origin (Paarl, 1974)

Spain & Portugal

Sarah Bradford
The Englishman's Wine (Port) (London, 1969)

Julian Jeffs
Sherry (London, 1961)

George Rainbird
Sherry and the Wines of Spain (London, 1966)

Jan Read
The Wines of Spain and Portugal (London, 1973)

Dan Stanislawski
Landscapes of Bacchus (Austin, Texas, 1970)

Switzerland

Editions Générales (publishers)
Les Vins Suisses (Geneva, 1968)

USA

Leon Adams
The Wines of America (Boston, 1973)

Hurst Hannum and Robert Blumberg
The Fine Wines of California (New York, 1971, Revised 1973)

Robert Gorman
Gorman on California Premium Wines (Berkeley, 1975)

Bob Thompson and Hugh Johnson
The California Wine Book (New York, 1976)

Choosing and Serving Wine

A Burgundy wine-grower tastes from the barrel; 'thief' in one hand, silver 'tastevin' in the other

Tasting and Talking about Wine

MOST GOOD, even most great wine is wasted. It flows over tongues and down throats of people who are not attuned to it; not receptive of what it has to offer. They are preoccupied or deep in conversation; they have just drunk strong spirits which numb the sense of taste, or taken a mouthful of vinegary salad which overwhelms it; they have a cold; or they are simply unaware of where the difference between plain wine and great wine lies. Nothing the winemaker can do dispenses with the need for a sensitive and interested drinker.

If the sense of taste were located in the mouth (where our impulses tell us it is), anyone swallowing a mouthful of wine would get all the sensations it has to offer. But as this model of Bacchus shows, the nerves which receive anything more distinctive than the basic sensations of sweet, sour, salt and bitter are higher in the head and deeper in the brain.

In fact we smell tastes, rather than tasting them with our lips and tongues and palates. The real organ of discrimination is in the upper nasal cavity, where in normal breathing the air never goes. And the only sensations that can reach it are the vapours of volatile substances. To reach the brain the vapours of wine need to be inhaled (either through nose or mouth) into the upper part of the nasal cavity, where they are dissolved in moisture. From the moisture long thin nerve processes (vacilli) take the sensations to the olfactory bulb, above the nasal cavity and right in the brain.

It is often remarked how smells stir memories more rapidly and vividly than other sensations. From the position of the olfactory bulb, nearest neighbour to the temporal lobe where memories are stored, it seems that smell, the most primitive of our senses, has a privileged position of instant access to the memory-bank. Experienced tasters often rely on the immediate reaction of their memory to the first sniff of a wine. If they cannot relate it straight away to wines they have tasted in the past they must fall back on their powers of analysis, located in the parietal lobe. In the frontal lobe their judgement of the wine is formed (to be stored in turn in the temporal lobe for future reference).

The range of reference available is the great difference between an experienced taster and a beginner. There is little meaning in an isolated sensation—though it may be very pleasant. Where the real pleasures of wine-tasting lie are in the cross-references, the stirring of memories, the comparisons between similar and yet subtly different products of the same or neighbouring ground.

Wines differ from one another in colour, texture, strength and 'body', as well as smell or 'taste'. A taster takes all these into account. His approach is shown in the pictures opposite.

What is much harder than appreciating wine is communicating its sensations. There is no notation of taste, as there is of sound or colour; apart from the words sweet, salt, sour and bitter every word in the language of taste is borrowed from the other senses. And yet words by giving an identity to sensations help to clarify them. Some of the most helpful of the many words tasters use are listed opposite.

Left: Michelangelo's head of Bacchus the wine god, with grapes entwined in his hair, has been remodelled to show the organs of taste and smell used in appreciating wine in their relation to the judgement and memory in the brain.
The tongue perceives only whether the wine is sweet (at the tip **1A**), sour (at the sides **C**), salt (at the front sides **B**), or bitter (at the back **D**). But the volatile components of the wine (principally esters and aldehydes) rise as vapour through the nostrils and from behind the soft palate **2** into the upper part of the nasal cavity **3**. Moisture in the cavity dissolves the vapours and fine nerves carry them to the olfactory bulb **4** in the brain. Just behind the olfactory bulb is the temporal lobe **5**, the storehouse of memory. Sensations of smell easily awake memories. The experience is analysed in the parietal lobe **6**. In the frontal lobe **7** judgement is passed. The alcohol in wine at first releases the mechanism of the brain and facilitates the awakening of memories. But it rapidly goes too far and upsets the delicate balance of the brain's functions. Professional tasters, therefore, always spit out a wine after they have drawn from it all the information they need

The colour of the wine at the rim of the glass, tipped against a white background, gives the taster his first information. Is it clear? Is red purplish (young) or turning to brick with age? Great wines have strikingly deep and fresh colour. Is white very light and touched with youthful green (chlorophyll) or turning to gold?

The wine's appearance

Blackish—young red, perhaps very tannic, will take a long time to mature
Brick-red—colour of mature claret
Brilliant—completely clear
Brown—except in sherry or madeira brown wine is too old
Cloudy—something is wrong; all wine should be bright
Gris—very pale rosé, the speciality of some parts of France
Intense—a useful but undefinable word for colour
Maderized—brown or going brown with the effect of oxygen and age
Pelure d'oignon—'onion skin'; the tawny-pink of Provençal rosés or the signs of browning in an aging wine
Perlant—'pearling' (or *pétillant*); wine with natural fine bubbles which stick to the glass
Purple—a young colour; translucent in young Beaujolais; deep in red wine which will take time to mature
Rosé—pink; neither red nor white; a term of abuse for red wine
Ruby (of port in particular)—the full red of young wine
Tawny (of port in particular)—the faded dark amber of old wine

The smell of wine

Acetic—wine which is 'pricked' or gone irredeemably sour through contact with the air smells of acetic acid or vinegar
Aroma—the simple grape-smell of young wine
Bouquet—the complex smell arising with maturity in good wine
Complex—the scents-within-scents; suggestions of many different analogies with fruits, flowers, etc
Corky—the smell of the (very rare) bottle which has had a mouldy cork

Foxy—the characteristic smell of the native American grape; not like foxes
Heady—attractively high in alcohol
Lively—an indefinable good sign; a fresh, frank, good smell from wine which is young and will last
Musty—unpleasant smell, probably from a barrel with a rotten stave
Rancio—the smell of oxidized fortified wine, the speciality of south-west France and Catalonia
Sappy—translation of the French 'sève'; the lively forthright style of a fine young wine, especially burgundy
Sulphury—the hot and nose-tickling smell often given by cheap white wine in which sulphur is used as a preservative. It will go off if the wine gets enough air
Yeasty—the smell of yeast can be attractive in young wine, though it usually means it has been fermenting slightly in the bottle and is unstable

Describing wine

Many words are borrowed to describe the qualities of their originals; flavours which can be conveyed in no other way, appearing in wine in traces of the same chemical constituents as the fruit (or whatever) in question. Such are:
Apples—malic acid is common in good young wine. In Moselles it is very apparent

Almost everything about a wine is revealed by its scent. The taster inhales deeply. The first impression is the most telling. Is there any 'foreign' or 'wrong' smell? Does it smell of fresh grapes or have a complex 'bouquet' from age in barrel and bottle? Is the grape identifiable (as Riesling, Pinot, Muscat, Cabernet)?

Blackcurrants—smell and flavour in many red wines
Earthy—a virtue or fault depending on the context. A common quality of Italian wines
Flowery—used generally for an attractive and forthcoming scent
Grapy—a great wine has more than grapiness, but a fresh-grape smell is always a good sign

Gun-flint—scent of flint-sparks in some white wine—e.g. Pouilly Fumé
Honey—associated particularly with 'noble rot' in great sweet wines
Nuts—nuttiness is usually found in well-aged wines. It is very marked in good old sherry

The taste in the mouth confirms the information given by the nose. The taster takes a good mouthful, not a sip, and lets it reach every part of his mouth. The body or wineyness now makes its impact. Is it generous or meagre? Is it harsh with tannin as young reds should be? Is it soft and flat or well balanced with acidity?

Oak—the character given to wine by the barrel, important and attractive as it is, should not be obvious enough to be identified as oak
Peaches—associated with a certain fruity acidity, e.g. in some Loire wines
Raspberries—a common flavour in very good red wine, particularly of Bordeaux and the Rhône valley
Smoke—smokiness is claimed for many white wines
Spice—very pronounced in the Traminer and Gewürztraminer grapes
Stalks—a green-wood smell which can arise in an under-ripe vintage
Truffles—the most elusive of all scents, found by Burgundians in Burgundy, Barolans in Barolo, hermits in Hermitage
Vanilla—scent given to wine and (much more) brandy by a component of the oak of the cask
Violets—another elusive scent found by people in their favourite wine

The list could be much extended; many tasters play the free-association game and jot down 'rubber', 'pear-drops', 'wool', etc. on their tasting cards

General terms of appreciation

Baked—flavour resulting from very hot sun on grapes
Big—strong, round and satisfying
Body—the 'volume' of a wine, partly due to alcoholic strength

Breed—balance of qualities in good wine due to grapes, soil and skill
Clean—refreshing; free from defects
Coarse—tasting crudely made
Complete—mature, balanced and satisfying
Distinctive—having its own character
Dry—the opposite of sweet
Dumb—not offering its full quality (wine is too young or too cold)
Elegant—as of a woman; indefinable
Fat—as of a man, well fleshed. Not a desirable characteristic in itself
Fiery—a good quality, in moderation
Finesse—literally, fine-ness
Finish—aftertaste; in great wine the exact flavour remains in the mouth for a considerable period after swallowing
Firm—young with a decisive style
Flat—the opposite of firm
Fruity—ripe-tasting
Hard—tannin makes young reds hard
Long—what the finish should be
Nervy—vigorous and fine; good in wine as in horses
Noble—the ultimate combination of breed, body, maturity; use with care
Old—by itself often means too old
Racy—from French *race*, meaning breed; or vital and exciting
Rough—poor, cheap, badly made
Séché—'dried up'—too-old red wine
Short—what the finish should not be
Silky—accurate word for a certain texture (found in good Beaujolais)
Stiff—similar to dumb
Stuffing—the body and character of certain red wines (Côte de Nuits, St-Emilion)
Supple—opposite of hard, but not pejorative as soft would be
Unresolved—not old enough for components to have harmonized
Vigorous—young and lively

Holding the wine in his mouth the taster draws air between his lips. The warmth of his mouth helps to volatilize the wine; a more positive impression of the taste materializes at the very back of the mouth as vapours rise to the nasal cavity from behind. After swallowing (or spitting) is the flavour short-lived or lingering?

Taking Notes

FROM TALKING about wine to writing about it is but a step—which few wine-tasters ever take. Yet there is a strong case for keeping tasting notes in a more or less organized way. In the first place having to commit something to paper makes you concentrate; the prime requirement for being able to taste wine properly at all. In the second it makes you analyse and pin labels on the sensations passing across your palate. In the third it is an *aide-mémoire*: when somebody asks you what a wine is like you can look it up and say something definite. In the fourth it allows you to extend comparisons between wines over time—either the same wine a year later, or different but related wines on different occasions.

In short, keeping tasting notes is like keeping a diary: obviously a good idea, but hard to get off the ground.

For this reason I asked Michael Broadbent, Director of the Wine Department of Christie's, London, whose book *Wine Tasting* is the standard work on the subject, to collaborate with me in compiling a suitable tasting card for keen amateurs to use.

There have been many studies (notably at the University of California) of what they call Sensory Methods of Evaluating Wine. Most depend on a scoring system of points (for clarity, colour, aroma and the rest) which lends a slightly inappropriate air of indoor games to what is really an analytical exercise.

The Broadbent-Johnson card, reproduced below, does encompass a way of scoring with points if this is what you want to do. It can be used perfectly well without them. On the other hand they do force you to make up your mind.

The notes at the bottom right of the card explain its use. The left-hand column divides each of the three basic aspects of wine (sight, smell and taste) into facets which can be isolated and examined. One of the listed descriptions of these facets in the first column should fit every wine.

The centre column is simply a list of suggested adjectives for what you may find in the glass before you. These are the words (see page 45) which are most often used in discussing wine. None of them may apply to any given wine—which is the purpose of the right-hand column: to record your own impressions, again analytically, by sight, smell and taste.

After the analysis, the judgement. The space for Overall Quality allows your general feelings of pleasure or dislike to override your objective assessment, as in the end it will, and should, do.

Left: a pre-auction tasting at Christie's Restell auction rooms, London. Concentration is difficult at crowded tastings: note-taking is essential

Below: a form to fill. A consistent analytical approach is the best way to learn about, judge and remember wine. Scoring is for amusement only

Name of Wine		Vintage	
District/type		Date purchased	
Merchant/bottler		Price	

SIGHT Score (Maximum 4)		Comments
CLARITY cloudy, bitty, dull, clear, brilliant DEPTH OF COLOUR watery, pale, medium, deep, dark COLOUR (White wines) green tinge, pale yellow, yellow, gold, brown (Red wines) purple, purple/red, red, red/brown VISCOSITY slight sparkle, watery, normal, heavy, oily	starbright, tuilé, straw, amber, tawny, ruby, garnet, oeil de perdrix, hazy, opaque	
SMELL Score (Maximum 4)		
GENERAL APPEAL neutral, clean, attractive, outstanding off (eg. yeasty, acetic, oxidized, woody, etc.) FRUIT AROMA none, slight, positive, identifiable eg. riesling BOUQUET none, pleasant, complex, powerful	cedarwood, corky, woody, dumb, flowery, smoky, honeyed, lemony, spicy, mouldy, peardrops, sulphury	
TASTE Score (Maximum 9)		
SWEETNESS (white wines) bone dry, dry, medium dry, medium sweet, very sweet TANNIN (red wines) astringent, hard, dry, soft ACIDITY flat, refreshing, marked, tart BODY very light and thin, light, medium, full bodied, heavy LENGTH short, acceptable, extended, lingering BALANCE unbalanced, good, very well balanced, perfect	appley, bitter, burning, blackcurrants, caramel, dumb, earthy, fat, flinty, green, heady, inky, flabby, mellow, metallic, mouldy, nutty, salty, sappy, silky, spicy, fleshy, woody, watery	
OVERALL QUALITY Score (Maximum 3)		HOW TO USE THIS CHART Wine appeals to three senses: sight, smell and taste. This card is a guide to analyzing its appeal and an aide-memoire on each wine you taste. Tick one word for each factor in the left-hand column and any of the descriptive terms which fit your impressions. Then award points according to the pleasure the wine gives you. Use the right-hand column for your comments.
Coarse, poor, acceptable, fine, outstanding	supple, finesse, breed, elegance, harmonious, rich, delicate	
SCORING Total Score (out of 20)	DATE OF TASTING	

Compiled by Hugh Johnson and Michael Broadbent M.W. © 1975

Choosing Wine

THE FRENCH have an inimitable way of expressing the character of a wine in terms of the perfect dish to accompany it. '. . . sur un foie gras' they say with relish: one immediately has a useful idea of the kind of wine and its appropriate place at table. With the thousands of wines in this atlas such an approach is impossible. Here we put forward some suggestions for the choosing of wine by the sort of occasion when it will be drunk, with the object of guiding the reader who is looking for (for example) an after-dinner wine, a wine to order for everyday use or an attractive wine to take on a picnic. Each suggestion is followed by the number of the atlas page where a major reference to it will be found.

Aperitifs
The ideal aperitif stimulates the appetite as well as the wits. It is brisk and dry, with either a sparkle or a tang. Cocktails leave the palate unable to appreciate good wine with the meal.

Sparkling wines Champagne, page *106*; Anjou-Saumur, *116*; Vouvray, *118*; St-Péray or Die, *120*; burgundy, *60*; Savoie, *127*; Limoux, *124*; Sekt, *135*; Asti Spumante, *164*; Neuchâtel, *196*; Spanish, *174*; California, *228*; New York, *238*; Australian, *240*.

Fortified wines Sherry, *176*; madeira, *184*; white port, *190*; Marsala, *173*; vermouth, *160*.

Natural wines Mâcon blanc, *75*; dry white Graves, *94*; Alsace Sylvaner or Riesling, *110*; Muscadet, *114*; Anjou, *116*; Sancerre or Pouilly, *119*; vin jaune or Apremont, *127*; Luxembourg Moselle, *142*; German Kabinett wines, *134*; Hungarian Riesling, *202, 204*; Tokay Szamarodni, *203*; Jugoslav Riesling, *206*; Romanian Cotnari or Riesling, *208*; Bulgarian Riesling, *210*; vinho verde, *189*; Alella, *182*; Soave, *167*; Frascati, *168*; Californian Johannisberg Riesling, *228*.

Family Meals
This big category includes the good but not the great wines of the world, perfect for leisurely but not grand meals. Sunday lunch with the family or entertaining friends. These wines have real character and quality; they are worth taking note of and discussing, without demanding attention and respect. For most formal occasions as well such wines as these are the perfect choice. Unless the company has gathered to discuss wine it is a pity to serve anything which is terribly expensive, rare and irreplaceable.

Red Côte d'Or commune wines and some Premier Crus of Santenay, Volnay, Pommard, Nuits. etc., *64*; Grand Cru Beaujolais, *76*; good Cru Bourgeois and lesser classed growths of the Médoc, *84–92*; similar wines from Graves, Pomerol and St-Emilion, *94, 98, 100*; Châteauneuf-du-Pape, *123*; Cahors, *128*; Chinon, Bourgueil, *117*; Bandol, *126*; Barolo, Barbaresco, *162*; Chianti Riserva, *170*; Alto Adige Cabernet, *166*; Lambrusco, *164*; Rioja Reserva, *180*; Colares, *188*; Dão Reserva, *189*; Australian Private Bin type clarets from Hunter, Coonawarra, etc., *240*; Californian Cabernet Sauvignon or Pinot Noir, *228*; Chilean Cabernet, *250*.

Rosé Tavel, *120*; Marsannay, *73*; Cabernet Rosé d'Anjou, *116*; Chiaretto del Garda, *164*.

White Graves Crus Classés, *94*; Chablis Premier Cru, *78*; Côte de Beaune commune wines, *65*; estate-bottled Muscadet, *114*; Vouvray, *118*; Sancerre, Pouilly Fumé, *119*; Pouilly-Fuissé, *75*; Mâcon Viré, *75*; Côte Chalonnaise, *74*; Alsace Riesling, Traminer, *110*; Middle Mosel, *142*; Nahe, *146*; Rheingau, *148*; Rheinpfalz, *152*; Rheinhessen, *154*; Franconian and Baden Kabinett wines, *156, 158*, and Spätleses of lighter vintages from these German areas; Soave, *167*; Frascati, *168*; Alvarinho, *189*; Fendant de Sion and Dorin of Vaud, *194*; Rheinriesling from Burgenland and Wachau, *198, 201*; Balatoni Szürkebarát and Kéknyelü, *204*; Californian Chardonnay or Johannisberg Riesling, *228*; Barossa Riesling, *244*.

Everyday wine
Wine for everyday, for meals in the kitchen, can be plain vin ordinaire—or something a little more interesting: the wine of a specific region.

Red Côteaux du Languedoc, *124*; Fronsac, *102*; Bourg, Blaye, *104*; Bordeaux Supérieur, *81*; Mâcon rouge, *75*; Côtes du Rhône, *120*; commune Bordeaux wines, *81*; Algerian, Tunisian, Moroccan, *218*; Corvo red, *178*; Sardinian, *173*; Klevner, *197*; Valdepeñas, *174*; Rioja Clarete, *180*; Dão Tinto, *189*; Portuguese branded wine, *186*; Argentine red, *250*; Gamza, *210*; Demestica, *214*; South African Hermitage, *248*; Kadarka, *202*; Australian Claret, *240*; Cyprus red, *217*; Californian Burgundy, *228*;

White Edelzwicker, *110*; Gros Plant du Pays Nantais, *114*; Clairette de Bellegarde or Languedoc, *124*; Entre-Deux-Mers, *81*; Hungarian or Jugoslav Riesling, *202* or *206*; Austrian Schluck, *201*; German Tafelwein, *134*; Bulgarian Chardonnay, *210*; Verdicchio, *168*; Lacrima Christi, *173*; Capri, *172*; Gallo or Italian Swiss Colony 'Chablis' or many wineries' 'mountain white', *228*.

Great wines
The great wines should never be served except to wine-lovers under ideal conditions—when there is time to appreciate their qualities, to compare them with lesser wines or their own peers, and when they can be partnered with well-chosen and well-prepared, not too highly seasoned, dishes. They should have the best glasses, and candlelight —a certain formality enhances their enjoyment. Uninhibited discussion of their qualities is essential—or they are wasted.

The qualities of a great wine stand out much more sharply if it is compared with another of the same family—perhaps a neighbour or a lesser vintage of the same vineyard. The lesser wine may well be fine in its own right; the great wine will be all the more memorable coming after it and capping its qualities. Too many magnificent wines served on one occasion, on the other hand, tend to cancel each other out so that none remains a distinct and vivid memory.

The greatest German wines are best drunk without (or after) food; all are sweet, but complete in themselves so that any sweet dish only detracts from them. They need not be thought of in conjunction with a meal at all, their low alcohol content makes them a perfect drink at any time of day when there is time to give them the attention they deserve. They are never better than when served in a garden.

Red Grands Crus and outstanding Premiers Crus of the Côte d'Or, *64*; the best classed growths of the Médoc, *84–92*; Graves, *94*; Pomerol, *98*; St-Emilion, *100*; Côte Rôtie, *121*; Hermitage, *122*.

White The Montrachets, *65*; outstanding Premier Cru Meursaults, *66*; Grand Cru Chablis, *78*; Corton-Charlemagne, *68*; exceptional Alsace Rieslings or Gewürztraminers, *112*; exceptional Vouvrays, *118*; Quarts de Chaume, Savennières, *116*; Château Grillet, *121*; Spätleses and Ausleses of the Saar, *138*; Ruwer, *140*; Middel Mosel, *142*; Nahe, *146*; Rheingau, *148*; Rheinpfalz, *152*.

Alfresco wine
The wine for a picnic or a meal in the garden should be something lighter, better and with more character than your everyday wine. The ideal has been said to be champagne, taken to the picnic spot the day before and buried under a turf in the cool ground. A stream or, more prosaically, damp newspaper is usually effective in cooling a bottle.

Red Beaujolais-Villages, *76*; Chinon, Bourgueil, *117*; Cabernet d'Anjou, *116*; Bergerac, *105*; local VDQS red, *130*; Chianti in fiaschi, *170*; Barbera or Dolcetto, *162*; Lago di Caldaro, *166*; Valpolicella, *167*; Valdepeñas, *174*; Zinfandel, *228*; Dôle, *194*.

Rosé Marsannay, *73*; Cabernet rosé d'Anjou, *116*; Provençal, *126*; Jura vin gris, *127*; Chiaretto del Garda, *164*; Ravello, *173*; California Grenache, *228*.

White Bourgogne Aligoté, *66*; Alsace Sylvaner or Traminer, *110*; Muscadet, *114*; dry Vouvray, *118*; vinho verde, *189*; Grüner Veltliner, *198*; Bernkasteler Riesling, *144*; Steinwein, *158*; retsina, *214*; Californian Riesling, *228*; Steen or Riesling, *246*; English white, *252*.

The end of the meal
Natural (or sparkling) sweet wines go admirably with a sweet course at the end of the meal—though there are certain dishes, particularly chocolate ones or those containing citrus fruits, which do not agree with them—or equally well as after-dinner drinks on their own. Their sugar and their velvety texture make them soothing and satisfying; they have the opposite effect to aperitifs, leading to contemplation rather than action. Few people drink them in any but small quantities; one glass of Sauternes goes as far as two or three of white burgundy. It is worth remembering the port-merchant's rule-of-thumb in choosing after-dinner wine. He 'buys on an apple and sells on cheese'—knowing that cheese is kind to wine, making it taste better than it is, while fruit is the opposite—only very good wine comes through the ordeal.

The strong dessert wines containing brandy (port, madeira, Tokay and the rest) go well with cheese, apples (if they are good) or nuts, but less well with sweet dishes, except quite plain and cake-like ones.

The world's great spirits find their place after dinner, when they can be drunk undiluted in small sips and there is time to enjoy their perfume.

Natural wines Sauternes, *96*; exceptional Vouvrays, *118*; Quarts de Chaume, etc., *116*; Monbazillac, *105*; Jurançon, *128*; German Ausleses, Beerenausleses and Trockenbeerenausleses, *134*; sweet muscat wines—Beaumes de Venise, *120*; Setúbal, *186*; Sicilian, *173*; Russian, *212*.

Sparkling wines Sweet champagne, *108*; Asti Spumante, *163*.

Dessert wines Port, *190*; Tokay, *203*; Malmsey or Bual madeira, *184*; cream sherry, *178*; Commandaria, *216*; vin santo, *160*; Marsala, *173*; Tarragona, *182*; Malaga, *174*.

Spirits Cognac, *258*; Armagnac, *260*; alcools blancs, *270*; Calvados, *271*; marc, *20*; malt or the finest blends of whisky, *262, 264*; rum, *266*, etc.

Looking after Wine

To BUY good wine and not to look after it properly is like hanging a masterpiece in a dark corner, or not exercising a race-horse, or not polishing your Rolls-Royce. If good wine was ever worth paying extra for it is worth keeping, and above all serving, in good condition.

There is nothing mysterious or difficult about handling wine. But doing it well can add vastly to the pleasure of drinking it—and doing it badly can make the best bottle taste frankly ordinary.

Wine only asks for two things: to be kept lying quietly in a dark cool place, and to be served generously, not hurriedly, with plenty of time and room to breathe the air.

Storage is a problem to almost everyone. Cellars like the one opposite, the perfect place for keeping a collection of wine, are no longer built. Most people have to make shift with a cupboard. But even a cupboard can have the simple requirements of darkness, freedom from vibration, and—if not the ideal coolness—at least an even temperature. Wine is not over-fussy about temperature. Anything from 45 to about 70°F will do. What matters more is that it stays the same. No wine will stand alternate boiling and freezing. In high temperatures it tends to age quicker—and there is the danger of it seeping round the cork—but if coolness is impracticable, steady warmth will do.

No special equipment is needed in cellar or cupboard. Bottles are always kept lying down to prevent the cork from drying and shrinking and letting in air. They can be stacked in a pile if they are all the same; but if they are all different it is better to keep them in a rack so that bottles can easily be taken from the bottom. Failing a wooden or metal rack, cardboard delivery boxes on their sides are satisfactory until they sag—which in a damp cellar does not take long.

Given the space, there is every argument for buying wine young, at its opening price, and

The bell, book and candle of a wine-collector's cellar: some of the elegant extras which accumulate where there is good wine. Wine with a very heavy sediment, such as vintage port or old Hermitage, is sometimes filtered into a decanter through a fine muslin cloth placed over a funnel made of glass or silver

'laying it down' in cellar or cupboard until it reaches perfect maturity. Wine merchants are not slow to point out that it may appreciate in monetary, as well as gastronomic, value out of all proportion to the outlay. While at the top end of the market with château- or domaine-bottled wines this can mean making a fortune, at the bottom it can mean that even cheap red wines become very pleasant after six months or a year longer in bottles than the shop gives them. The probable ages of maturity of recent vintages are given in charts on pages 53 to 56.

It was Pasteur who discovered (see pages 38–39) the effects on wine of exposing it to the air. The same effects lie behind the custom of decanting, or pouring wine from its original bottle into another—more often a glass carafe—before serving it. Decanting is little understood and not much practised today . . . strangely, because there is no better way of getting the most out of wine.

There is a mistaken idea that it is something you only do to ancient bottles with lots of sediment—a sort of precautionary measure to get a clean glass of wine. In reality it is young wines which benefit most. The oxygen they contain has had little chance to take effect. But the air in the decanter works rapidly and effectively. In a matter of a few hours it produces the full flowering of what was only in bud. This can mean literally twice as much of the scent and flavour that you paid for. Some strong young wines can benefit by even as much as 24 hours in a decanter. An hour makes all the difference to others. The more full-bodied the wine the longer it needs.

The technique of decanting is illustrated below. The only essential equipment is a carafe (or decanter) and a corkscrew. But a basket is a good way of keeping the bottle in almost the same position as in the rack where it was lying—so that any sediment remains along the lower side. And a corkscrew which pulls against the rim of the bottle—either a double-screw or the lever-type—makes it easy to avoid jerking.

Cut the lead capsule and take it off completely. Take the cork out gently. Wipe the lip of the bottle. Hold the bottle (with or without the basket) in one hand and the decanter in the other, and pour steadily until you see the sediment (if any) moving into the shoulder of the bottle. Then stop. Having a light—a candle-flame is ideal—behind or below the neck of the bottle makes it easier to see when the dregs start to move—besides adding to what should be a pleasantly sensuous ritual.

A wine basket should never appear on the table, but using one is the best means of keeping a bottle on its side and steady while the cork is drawn

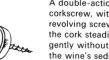
A double-action corkscrew, with counter-revolving screws, draws the cork steadily and gently without disturbing the wine's sediment

A candle below the neck of the bottle makes it easier to see when the sediment in the wine comes to the neck: the time to stop pouring

A small private wine-cellar, beneath a house, has a brick floor and brick 'bins' where the wine is laid, either on the floor or on a shelf. In the bins in this cellar, which can contain about 500 bottles, are, top row; left to right: white burgundies and German Ausleses laid down for maturing; bottles in racks (red, white and champagne) where they can easily be removed without disturbing others. These are ready for drinking. Then two more bins of red wines laid down for maturing, labels uppermost and capsules (with their names) facing out

Bottom row: claret stored in original cases from the château. Magnums of red burgundy and Bordeaux. Vintage port binned for long ageing. Red burgundy newly bought and not yet laid down. The table with candles and a funnel is for opening bottles and decanting

Another decanting technique to avoid disturbing the wine: a silver funnel with the bottom curved to make the wine run down the side of the decanter

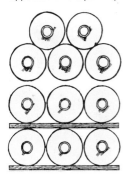

Left: professional cellar-men 'bin' bottles as much as 40 deep; by placing laths between rows they can take one bottle from the bottom of the pile. A simpler method (top) is to lay them directly on top of each other

Right: racks are most convenient for small collections, whether kept in a cupboard or cellar

Right: a personal cellar-book is a wine-collector's essential record of prices, judgements, and stock. The one shown has entries for: **1** name of wine; **2** name of shippers; **3** where and when bought; **4** vintage; **5** quantity bought; **6** price; **7** date of drinking; **8** number of bottles left; **9** comments on the wine; **10** the food; **11** the guests

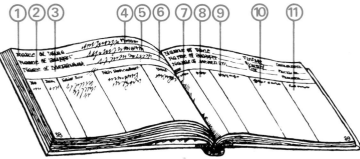

Serving Wine

THE CARE we take in serving wine and the little customs and courtesies of the table cannot do much to change its virtues or vices. But they can add tenfold to its enjoyment. If there are different glasses, decanters, even rituals for different wines it is not out of any physical necessity, but as an expression of the varying sensuous pleasures they give. In helping to emphasize the different characters of wine—and reminding us of their origins—they add to the experience and make it memorable.

These pages show a number of the more practical, as well as pretty, forms of glass which have been evolved to put each kind of wine in its best light. What they have in common are the essentials of reasonably generous size (so that a good measure fills them only a half to two-thirds full), clear uncoloured glass so that the colour of the wine is undimmed, and a rim which cups in slightly towards the top, which makes it possible to swirl the wine in the glass to release its scent without spilling it. The exception in the last case is the champagne flute: but then champagne comes up to greet you—you don't need to swirl it.

The only cut glasses in the picture are those for German wine. Some purists scorn all cut glass, but there is no doubt that the Treviris glass used on the Mosel reflects flashes of light into the pale green wine and gives it brilliance. Nor does it seem inappropriate to gaze at your hock through etched bunches of grapes—not, of course, in a clinical tasting-room but out on the terrace where the wine is meant to be enjoyed.

It may seem too obvious to mention, but wine glasses should be clean, which means polished and untainted with smells of detergents or cupboards. Ideally they should be rinsed

The champagne 'flûte': the traditional and most beautiful sparkling-wine glass. Slow to fill, as the bubbles rise like a rocket. 'Tulips' are also good for champagne: flat, shallow glasses are not

A spirit decanter; heavy cut crystal made in Poland. There is no practical reason for using a decanter for spirits. They neither improve nor deteriorate for several weeks after opening the bottle. But as an elegant extra, decanting makes whisky, brandy, gin or rum or any spirit look its best

Many wine regions have their own style of wine glass, designed to show off the local wine. The vintners of Anjou on the Loire use this original design for their fresh white wine. The long stem to hold prevents hands from warming the bowl. The clear glass allows the colour to be seen and the sloping sides concentrate the bouquet

The sherry copita: one of the world's best-designed tasting glasses, funnelling the scent of the wine to the nostrils; also the perfect size for drinking sherry, filled half-full

A wine decanter. Apart from looking magnificent on the table in a decanter, any good red wine benefits from the air (see page 48). This Georgian magnum holds a double bottle but is perfect for allowing a single one plenty of air

A Burgundian silver tastevin. Professional tasters in Burgundy keep one in their pockets. Its gleam through the wine in a dark cellar is a surer judge of colour and clarity than a glass would be; and it is unbreakable. This one is 200 years old

The traditional white-wine glass of Alsace is designed on the same principles as that of Anjou. The green stem reflects a pretty green gleam into the wine

with hot water and polished by hand. They are much easier to polish while they are still hot. No wisps of towel should stick to them. Cupboard smells usually come from keeping glasses upside down. On open shelves this may be necessary, but it is better to keep them right-way-up in a clean and airy cupboard. Sniff them before putting them on the table.

Some of the attentions paid to wine are frivolous. Others (notably decanting, for which see page 48) can make all the difference between mere satisfaction and real delight.

Any good wine benefits by comparison with another. It is no affectation, but simply making the most of a good thing, to serve more than one wine at a meal. A young wine served first shows off the qualities of an older one; a white wine (usually) shows off a red one; a light wine a massive one; a dry wine a sweet one. But any of these combinations played the other way round would be disastrous for the second wine. In the same way a really good wine puts in the shade a lesser wine served after it, and the same thing happens to a dry white wine served after a red.

The question of how much to serve is more difficult. There are six good glasses of wine (which means big glasses filled half-full, not small ones filled to the brim) in a normal bottle. At a quick lunch one glass a person might be enough, whereas at a long dinner five or six might not be too much. A total of half a bottle a person (perhaps one glass of white wine and two of red) is a reasonable average allowance for most people and occasions—but the circumstances and mood of the meal, and above all how long it goes on, are the deciding factors. There is a golden rule for hosts; be generous, but never pressing.

- Champagne or any white wine is at its best thoroughly cooled. The ideal way is in a deep ice-bucket full of cold water, with ice-cubes in the water. This more elegant but less conventional ice-bucket is an English silver punch-bowl engraved with the royal arms of George III. Ideally it should be deeper. Most ice-buckets are too shallow, so it is necessary to stand the bottle on its head in them for a few minutes to cool the top of the bottle as well as the bottom

- An 18th-century cordial glass is perfect for vodka, which is served filled to the brim, but useless for any wine, which should never more than half-fill a glass

- A useful glass for port, sherry or madeira; not a classical design but well-balanced and good for tasting

- The traditional Rhine-wine or hock glass has a stout knobbed stem of brown glass; again to reflect the desired colour into the wine. Although today the fashion is for pale wine its use continues

- A 'tulip' glass filled with red Bordeaux. One of the perfect all-purpose glasses—ideal for champagne or any white wine as well as red. The in-turned rim helps to collect the scent

- Decanter for sherry, port or madeira. For vintage port decanting is necessary, for the rest a luxury

- The pretty engraved Trier or Treviris glass for Mosel. Even small cafés on the Mosel use this graceful glass to make their pale delicate white wine catch the light and seem more inviting than ever

- Silver or gold labels for decanters are a practical old custom which is being revived. A London firm made the reproductions of famous examples used in the picture. They are suitable for any wine or spirit which is served or kept in a decanter

- Stands for decanters or bottles to prevent them from making rings on the table are known as 'coasters'. They used to be made of silver or gold, or wood, or papier mâché. Another adjunct to the serving of wine which should be revived

- A red wine glass ideal for burgundy or Bordeaux, known as a Paris goblet. Big enough to be filled only one-third full—the perfect amount for appreciating the wine

- A cognac glass from the great Baccarat factory. Designed for cupping in the hand to warm the spirit; the vapour is caught and held in the bowl. Monster balloon glasses are never used by experts in Cognac

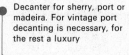

Serving Wine: Temperature

NOTHING makes more difference to the enjoyment of wine than its temperature. Stone-cold claret and lukewarn Rhine-wines are abominations. And there are good reasons why this should be so.

Our sense of smell (and hence the greater part of our sense of taste) is only susceptible to vapours. Red wine has a higher molecular weight—and is thus less volatile—than white. The object of serving red wine at room temperature, or 'chambré', is to warm it to the point where its aromatic elements begin to vaporize—which is at a progressively higher temperature for more solid and substantial wines. A light Beaujolais can be treated as a white wine; even cold its volatility is almost overwhelming. But a full-scale red wine needs the warmth of the room, of the cupped hand round the glass, and of the mouth itself to volatilize its complex constituents.

As an apparent exception to this rule the French tend to serve red burgundy cooler than red Bordeaux. Some grapes make wine that is inherently more volatile than others: Burgundy's Pinot Noir is one of the 'showy' grapes —the reason why young red burgundy is much more attractive than young Bordeaux.

Cold is also necessary to provide a sense of balance to the richness of very sweet wines, even if in doing so it masks some of their flavours. On the chart on this page all the sweetest white wines are entered at the coldest point. It is a good idea to pour them very cold and let them warm up slightly while you sip them: the process seems to release all their aroma and bouquet. Extreme cold has also been used to make overaged white wine presentable . . . there are many experiments to be made.

The chart below sets out in some detail the wide range of temperatures that bring out the best in different wines. It is based on personal experience, often modified in discussions (not to mention arguments) with many wine-lovers. Personal taste and habits vary widely from individual to individual: also from country to country. Americans tend to extremes of temperature, often serving champagne, for example, so cold that it has no flavour, or taking 'room temperature' for red wine literally in a room at 75° or 80°F. The French, by contrast, can sometimes be accused of serving all wine at the same temperature. But it is worth remembering that when the term 'chambré' was invented the prevailing temperature in French dining-rooms was unlikely to have been above 60°F.

It is easier to serve white wine at the right temperature than red: a refrigerator can so simply make the necessary adjustments. The

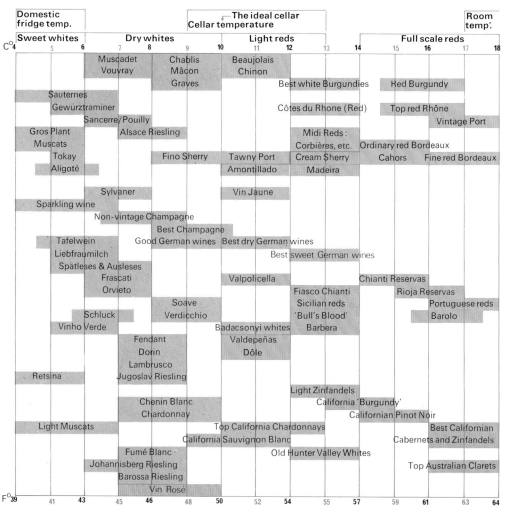

	Domestic fridge temp.				Cellar temperature / The ideal cellar							Room temp.		
C°	Sweet whites		Dry whites				Light reds			Full scale reds					
	4	5	6	7	8	9	10	11	12	13	14	15	16	17	18

Muscadet · Vouvray · Chablis · Mâcon · Graves · Beaujolais · Chinon · Best white Burgundies · Red Burgundy
Sauternes · Gewürztraminer · Côtes du Rhone (Red) · Top red Rhône · Vintage Port
Sancerre/Pouilly · Gros Plant · Alsace Riesling · Midi Reds: Corbières, etc. · Ordinary red Bordeaux
Muscats · Tokay · Fino Sherry · Tawny Port · Cream Sherry · Cahors · Fine red Bordeaux
Aligoté · Amontillado · Madeira
Sylvaner · Vin Jaune
Sparkling wine
Non-vintage Champagne
Best Champagne · Good German wines · Best dry German wines
Tafelwein · Best sweet German wines
Liebfraumilch
Spätleses & Ausleses · Frascati · Valpolicella · Chianti Reservas
Orvieto · Fiasco Chianti · Rioja Reservas
Soave · Sicilian reds · Portuguese reds
Schluck · Verdicchio · 'Bull's Blood' · Barolo
Vinho Verde · Badacsonyi whites · Barbera
Fendant · Valdepeñas
Dorin · Dôle
Lambrusco
Jugoslav Riesling
Retsina · Light Zinfandels · California 'Burgundy'
Chenin Blanc · Californian Pinot Noir
Chardonnay
Light Muscats · Top California Chardonnays · Best Californian Cabernets and Zinfandels
California Sauvignon Blanc
Fumé Blanc · Old Hunter Valley Whites
Johannisberg Riesling
Barossa Riesling · Top Australian Clarets
Vin Rosé

F°	39	41	43	45	46	48	50	52	54	55	57	59	61	63	64

The chart above suggests ideal temperatures for serving a wide range of wines. 'Room temperature' is low by modern standards: all the better for fine wine

quickest way to cool a bottle is to put it in a bucket of ice and water (not ice alone). In a very warm room (and especially a hot garden) it is a good idea to keep the bottle in the bucket between pourings, even if it means pouring the wine a bit too cold: it warms up all too quickly in the glass. A useful tip for large quantities (several bottles in a big bucket) is to make a monster block of ice by putting a polythene bag of water in the deep-freeze: the bigger the block the slower it thaws. Tall German bottles should be put in the water upside-down for a few minutes first to cool the wine in the neck.

Persuading red wine to the right temperature is harder. If it starts at cellar temperature it takes several hours in a normal room to raise it

10 or 12 degrees. The kitchen is the logical place to put it to warm up—the day before if possible —but many kitchens are well over 65°F, especially while dinner is cooking. At temperatures over 65° any red wine is thrown out of balance; the alcohol starts to vaporize and produces a heady smell, which masks its character. Red wine hurriedly dipped in hot water or stood in front of the fire is distorted out of recognition. Gentle warming in a pan of warm water, on the other hand, is better than serving the wine ice-cold.

Right: A bottle thermometer marked in degrees Centigrade which glow according to the temperature of the bottle, here the traditional shape used in Bordeaux, easily stacked for ageing. Left, are a typical sherry bottle and the slope-shouldered Burgundy model; the 'flute' of Germany, brown for Rhine wine, green for Mosel (and Alsace); the sturdy champagne bottle, built for repeated handling and a pressure of five atmospheres; the Loire variant of the Burgundy shape and Chianti's litre *fiasco*

Recent Vintages

LOCAL weather conditions (and growers' reactions to them) vary so much that any vintage chart is only a broad generalization. Moreover, vintages vary not only in quality but in style; there are years of fruity tender wines and years of firm wines full of tannin and lasting-power: the latter ultimately make the best wine—for those with patience.

In these detailed charts the following information is given:

The size of the vintage where it varies much from the average. The greatest vintages are almost always small ones: the fewer grapes on the vine the more flavour is in each grape.

The general standard and particular style of the wine of each area for each year. Dates when the wine will probably be at its best. The first date is for the lightest—which would normally be the cheapest—wine and the last for the best of the area and year. The last is impossible to calculate with precision, since the development of wine in bottle often produces surprises.

Other factors which affect ageing should also be taken into account. Half-bottles age quicker than bottles, and bottles than magnums. Warm cellars age wine faster than cold ones. Wine brought slowly to maturity in a magnum in a cold cellar is as good as it can be.

France

Red Burgundy

Côte d'Or Côte de Beaune reds generally mature sooner than the bigger wines of the Côte de Nuits. Earliest drinking dates are for lighter commune wines: Volnay, Beaune, etc. Latest for the biggest wines of Chambertin, Romanée, etc. Different growers make wines of different styles, for longer or shorter maturing, but even the best burgundies are much more attractive young than the equivalent red Bordeaux.

Year	Côte d'Or	When to drink
1981	Hail damage in July reduced the crop. A hot August and September ripened it well but rain set in at vintage time. Another light, quick-maturing vintage.	
1980	A difficult wet year. Only very conscientious growers avoided rot. In the Cote de Nuits the best wines look remarkably promising.	
1979	Big vintage, healthy and ripe but with rather low concentration and acidity. Many wines will be soft and early-maturing. The best (especially in the Cote de Beaune) may be very good.	Now–?'90
1978	An outstanding, very attractive and probably long-lasting vintage, saved by the exceptional autumn. Record prices.	Now–'95
1977	Very wet summer, fine autumn. Overall light, many poor wines, a few good.	Now–'85
1976	Hot summer, excellent vintage. Will be a classic, with some wines taking a decade to mature.	Early '80s–1990
1975	Hot summer, small wet vintage. Rot was rife, particularly in the Côte de Beaune. Mostly very poor. A few good wines from the northern Côte de Nuits with careful vinification.	Avoid
1974	Another big wet vintage; mostly poor, even the best light and lean. Drink young.	Now
1973	Again, vintage rain stretched the crop. Light wines, but many fruity and delicate. Now fading.	Now
1972	High acidity posed problems, but the wines are firm and full of character. Have aged well.	Now–1985
1971	Exceptional, splendid, powerful wines; fruity and well balanced. Small crop.	Now–1985
1970	Attractive soft fruity wines, but few will develop much further and many are fading. Big crop.	Now
1969	A magnificent vintage with very few exceptions. Small crop. Most now ready: keep only the best.	Now–mid-'80s
1968	A disaster.	Never
1967	Not a good vintage, but not a bad one either. The best have finesse, the worst are thin and over-sugared.	Now
1966	Excellent, well-rounded and vigorous, but the best are now mature. Big crop.	Now
1965	Very poor.	Avoid
1964	Big and very good, but some have more power than fruit and have dried out with age.	Now
1963	Poor; very few presentable wines.	Avoid
1962	Very fine and well-balanced; impressive for elegance rather than weight.	Now
1961	A great year. Small crop. The best are set for a long and famous life as their great concentration of taste develops.	Now–mid '80s

Older fine vintages: '59, '57, '55, '53, '52, '49, '47, '45.

Beaujolais Beaujolais is made in two ways: 'nouveau' or 'primeur' is for drinking immediately. Beaujolais-Villages and named Crus gain from one to five years in bottle. Exceptional Moulin-à-Vent vintages improve for as long as ten years.

Year	Beaujolais
1981	A healthy crop, but disappointing as 'nouveau'. The cru wines for keeping are much better, with good colour and structure.
1980	Very respectable, light, fruity and typical.
1979	Big vintage, delicious en primeur. The best very good. Drink soon.
1978	Big vintage of average quality or better. Drink soon.
1977	Fair quality in the best villages. Should be drunk.
1976	Superb: even primeurs are rich and fine. The Crus will last.

With very few exceptions older Beaujolais is too old.

White Burgundy

Côte de Beaune Well-made wines of good vintages with plenty of acidity as well as fruit will improve and gain depth and richness for some years—anything up to ten. Lesser wines from lighter years are ready for drinking after two or three years.

Year	Côte de Beaune whites	When to drink
1981	Crop reduced by hail but picked in perfect conditions. Much better than the red. The Mâconnais had a minute harvest.	
1980	More successful than the red, but a wide range of qualities.	Now–'86
1979	A big crop; quality good but not as high as quantity.	Now–'86
1978	Excellent, but quantities small and prices high.	Now–'90
1977	Pleasant light wines on the whole; some better than that.	Now
1976	Hot summer; very fine wines, some lacking acidity.	Now–late '80s
1975	Hot summer, then vintage rain. Whites did much better than reds. Rot reduced quantity, but the grapes were ripe and the wine can be good.	Now–mid-'80s
1974	Spring frosts reduced the crop. The hot summer made good wines, but they have aged disappointingly.	Now
1973	Very attractive, fruity, typical and plentiful, but not wines to keep.	Drink soon.
1972	Awkward wines to make with high acidity, even greenness, but plenty of character. The best have developed into classical wines.	Soon
1971	Great power and style; some almost too rich, but the best have good balance. Small crop.	Soon
1970	Large and very good. Attractive soft gentle style, which matured quickly.	Now
1969	An excellent all-round vintage, strong, tasty and well balanced. Small crop.	Now
1968	On the whole poor, but some drinkable light wines.	Avoid

The white wines of the Mâconnais (Pouilly-Fuissé, St-Véran, Mâcon-Villages) follow a similar pattern, but do not last as long. They are more appreciated for their freshness than their richness.

Chablis Grand Cru Chablis of vintages with both strength and acidity can age superbly for up to ten years. Premier Crus proportionally less, but too many growers are stressing quantity, which results in wines that fade away without ever achieving the classic chablis flavour. Only buy Petit Chablis of ripe years, and drink it young.

Year	Chablis	
1981	A small crop after hail and a cold flowering season means concentrated wine full of character and—rare in recent Chablis—fit to mature.	
	Pleasant fragrant and fruity wine for drinking fairly young.	
1979	Too big a crop. Wines may be pleasant but cannot be truly first class.	Now–'84
1978	Fine, firm, typical.	Now–'85
1977	Good average in Grands and Premiers Crus; elsewhere badly frosted. Keeping well.	Now
1976	A great vintage but rather heavy, soft wines.	Soon
1975	Very good; most ready now.	Now
1974	A trifle sharp at first, but lively, attractive and typical.	Now
1973	Very good ripe and plentiful vintage for drinking young.	Now
1972	Poor and sharp. Some have improved in bottle.	Now
1971	Excellent, if not classic; some as rich as Côte d'Or.	Soon
1970	Round, flowery; soft for Chablis.	Now

Older fine vintages: '67, '64, '61, '59, '57, '55, '53, '49.

Recent Vintages

Red Bordeaux

For some wines bottle-age is optional; for these it is indispensable. Minor châteaux from light vintages need only two or three years, but even modest wines of great years can improve for fifteen years or so, and the great châteaux of these years need double that time.

Year	Médoc/red Graves	When to drink
1981	After three late harvests a normal one, fully ripe and healthy but picked in late-September rain. Certainly good; in many cases very good.	'85–2000
1980	Difficult and patchy; the best good, if rather lean and tannic.	'83–'90
1979	Wet spring, moderate summer, fine autumn. A big crop, at least useful: at best probably very good.	Now–'95
1978	An excellent vintage: deep-coloured and tannic; destined for long life.	'84–2000
1977	Very wet summer. At best pleasant light wines.	Early eighties
1976	Excessively hot, dry summer; rain just before the vintage. Looks rather early-maturing, except for the best wines.	Now–?'95
1975	A splendid summer and very fine vintage, with deep colour, high sugar content and tannin. For long keeping.	Mid-'80s to 2000 and on
1974	Diluting vintage rain ruined hopes of a really good vintage. Oceans of disappointing light wines, though the best have good colour and may yet develop character.	Early '80s–'90s
1973	Again, last-minute rain turned quality into quantity. A huge vintage, attractive young but lacking acidity and tannin.	Now–mid-'80s
1972	High acidity from unripe grapes. Unripe wines, though the best will soften with age. Do not pay much for '72s.	Now–mid-'80s
1971	Small crop. Less fruity than '70 and less consistent. Some top châteaux made fine wine. Others are already drying out disappointingly.	Now–mid '80s
1970	Abundance *and* uniform quality. Big fruity wines with elegance and attractive suppleness. Although not tannic they are developing great distinction.	Now–late '90s
1969	Heavy September rain after a good summer. Mean wines lacking fruit and colour. Some pleasant now, a few improving in bottle. But a year to avoid.	Avoid
1968	This time a wet August was the culprit. Very few wine-makers made wine worth drinking.	Now, if ever
1967	Large; first judged to be light and for early drinking, has developed well in bottle and gained body and interest.	Now
1966	A very fine vintage with depth, fruit and tannin. Still needs time to open out. Classic claret.	Now–1990
1965	Rain and rot. A disaster. Very few passable wines.	Avoid
1964	A hot summer, then rain for the vintage affecting the northern Médoc most. Some excellent wines, especially in Graves. But be careful.	Now
1962	Delicious middle-weight wines, overlooked after the great '61s. Fruity, balanced and harmonious.	Now
1961	One of *the* great years, like '29 and '45. Very small crop. Concentration and power, character and class.	Now–?2000

Year	St-Emilion/Pomerol	When to drink
1981	Mostly picked before rain began; an excellent vintage—possibly a great one.	'85–2000
1980	Merlot crop very low, quality very variable. Wait and see.	
1979	A good year for Merlot. Some very good wines, some even better than the preceding year.	'83–?'94
1978	Very good; outstanding in Pomerol and neighbouring St-Emilion Crus.	Now–'95
1977	Terrible summer. Mediocre with few exceptions.	Avoid
1976	Very hot, dry summer and early vintage, but vintage rain made complications. Some excellent wines, if not very 'big'.	Early '80s on
1975	Most St-Emilions good, the best superb. Frost in Pomerol reduced crops and made splendid concentrated wine.	Mid-'80s–late '90s
1974	Vintage rain again. Mainly disappointing light wines.	Early '80s
1973	Good summer, big wet vintage. Pleasant; wines to drink young while the fruit is there.	Now or soon
1972	Poor summer but fine for the late vintage. Many unripe wines, but some will improve with time. Choose carefully.	Now–mid-'80s
1971	Small crop; fine wines with length and depth; many with more charm than Médocs.	Now–mid '80s
1970	Glorious weather and beautiful wines with great fruit and strength throughout the district. Very big crop.	Now–'90s
1969	Fine summer, small wet vintage. At best agreeable.	Now–late
1968	A disaster. Endless rain.	Never
1967	Large and generally very good; on the whole better than Médoc and Graves. Some good buys here.	Now–mid-'80s
1966	Ripe, powerful, round. Maturing well.	Now–late '80s
1965	A wash-out. Rot everywhere.	Never
1964	Generally excellent. The Merlot (predominant here) ripens earlier and therefore missed the rain.	Now
1962	Not as good as Médoc and Graves. Light. Drink soon.	Now
1961	Great wines for a long life. The first vintage of real quality here since the terrible 1956 frost.	In the '80s

Older fine Bordeaux vintages: '59, '55, '53, '52, '50, '49, '48, '47, '45, '43, '29, '28.

Sweet White Wines

Good vintages of Sauternes/Barsac and the luscious Chenin wines of Anjou (notably Coteaux du Layon) and Touraine (mostly Vouvray) are among the longest-lived white wines, improving for up to 25 years. Even moderate vintages are often worth keeping for the added depth of flavour that comes in bottle.

Year	Sauternes/Barsac
1981	A good crop with plenty of 'noble rot', but a number of châteaux had trouble with volatile acidity. Some excellent wine but be careful.
1980	Good conditions in November for a small crop with 'noble rot'. Results variable.
1979	Light in alcohol but full of 'noble rot'. Many good wines to keep.
1978	Small crop. High alcohol but no 'noble rot'.
1977	Very small crop with no good sweet wines.
1976	Superb summer; damp autumn; excellent wines. Drink Now–'95.
1975	Glorious October weather, rich wines. Drink now–1990.
1974	Rain ruined the crop.
1973	The same sad story.
1972	Poor; this time a poor summer was to blame.
1971	Fine vintage weather. Very good, elegant wine. Drink now.
1970	The rare combination, a hot summer and a fine autumn; opulent wines in abundance, but maturing quickly.
1969	Good, rather light and delicate of flavour. Drink soon.

Older fine vintages: '59, '53, '49, '45, '21.

Year	Anjou/Touraine
1981	A small crop hampered by rain.
1980	Not a sweet-wine vintage.
1979	Big vintage, at least average quality. Keep.
1978	Small quantities of fine wine. Keep.
1977	Very limited crop: little sweet wine.
1976	A splendid year. Keep.
1975	Excellent, especially in Anjou. Worth keeping.
1974	Some good wine, but a difficult cool vintage.
1973	A perfect October produced fine ripe wines, now ready.
1972	Great acidity, but a few good sweet wines for keeping.
1971	Good in Anjou, great in Touraine. For long keeping.
1970	Very good, perhaps not as long-lasting as the '71s. Drink soon.
1969	Big, sweet but well-balanced wines, will mature into the '80s.

Older fine vintages: '64, '61, '59, '55, '49, '43, '34.

Dry White Wines

White Graves and other dry white Bordeaux and Dordogne wines, the Sauvignon wines of the upper Loire (Sancerre/Pouilly Fumé) and Muscadet are all wines to drink young, though good white Graves can age well for up to ten years. Muscadet drinks best the year after the vintage, Sancerre/Pouilly Fumé up to three years later.

Year	Bordeaux
1981	Deliciously round gentle wines—not for laying down.
1980	Problems with rot and unripeness. Needed sugar. But some successes.
1979	A difficult big vintage with low natural sugar. Some good delicate wines.
1978	Extremely good well-balanced wines.
1977	Extremely good: the success of the year.
1976	Good wines if picked early; some are over-weight.
1975	Very good and typical. Now mature.
1974	Sound dry wines for early drinking.
1973	Fresh, ripe, easy-drinking wines.
1972	Not as unripe as other Sauvignon areas. Now too old.
1971	Wines of character and balance, have lasted well.
1970	Copybook weather conditions; first-class wines. Now mature.

Year	Sancerre/Pouilly Fumé
1981	A very small crop but high quality (and prices).
1980	Average quantity and quality.
1979	A big vintage of normal quality.
1978	Small quantity; average quality.
1977	Crop severely reduced but good quality.
1976	Very good, but drink soon.
1975	Good, some very good. Now mature.

Year	Muscadet
1981	Only one-third of the average crop. What there is is good or very good.
1980	Normal crop.
1979	Big yield; enjoyable light wines for immediate drinking.
1978	Small quantity; average quality. Drink up.

Avoid older Muscadet

Red Rhône

The classic wines of the Rhône valley include Côte Rôtie and Hermitage in the north, Châteauneuf-du-Pape in the south. Most Côte du Rhône-Villages are in the south.

Only the best wines are made for maturing, but those that do can achieve superlative flavour and bouquet. Châteauneuf-du-Pape is a particularly variable area: a few conservatives make wine to keep ten years; most only need four to five. Plain Côtes du Rhône matures in one to five years depending on the vintage and the maker.

Year	Northern (including Hermitage)
1981	A good-sized harvest of very good wine.
1980	A reduced crop but quality at least good.
1979	A very good vintage. Fine quality, if not as great as '78.
1978	A classic vintage, the best since '61. For long maturing.
1977	A poor light year.
1976	Excellent with big fruity wines.
1975	Poor, as in Burgundy. Rain caused rot. Avoid.
1974	The best are light and fruity, for early drinking.
1973	Attractive, but not for keeping.
1972	Superb; will keep another three years, especially Hermitage.
1971	Very good, with the strength and depth to last.
1970	Full, ripe and round. Now mature.
1969	Excellent, rich in alcohol, tannic and spicy. Will keep, especially Cote Rôtie.
1968	Unremarkable.
1967	Full and heady, now mature.
1966	Rich and strong with a good bouquet. Mostly mature.
1965	Not as bad as in other areas, but light.
1964	Strong and complete, but now mature.
1963	Very poor.
1962	Some very good, now mature.
1961	One of the greatest vintages; glorious power and flavour, now drinking splendidly, but will improve yet.

	Southern (including Châteauneuf-du-Pape)
1981	Drought resulted in a small crop of good wine; some excellent.
1980	Abundance of good, relatively light, wines.
1979	A very useful big vintage. Good quality.
1978	A classic vintage, rich and strong. For long maturing.
1977	Ripe but will mature early.
1976	Very good. Big wines to keep.
1975	Disappointing after high hopes in the summer. Avoid.
1974	Wide variation; the average is light. Some good Gigondas.
1973	Good, but now mature.
1972	Not as great as farther north, but good and maturing well.
1971	Full-bodied and well balanced. Mostly ready.
1970	Ripe, tasty vintage, but now mature.
1969	Unctuous, elegant wine, now ready to drink.

Alsace

The ordinary cheaper wines need little or no ageing. Réserves and Grands Crus of good vintages gain interest and quality in bottle for five years or more.

1981	Highly satisfactory; plenty of good wine.
1980	Small and difficult vintage with virtually no Gewürztraminer.
1979	Big, ripe vintage, successful for both Riesling and Gewürztraminer.
1978	Average or better.
1977	Useful average vintage; Gewürz and Tokay best.
1976	A stupendous vintage; many vendanges tardives (late pickings) to make beerenauslese-type wine, which keeps excellently.
1975	Very good; ripe, well-balanced wine. Now mature.
1974	Satisfactory; best for Gewürztraminers. Mature.
1973	On the light side, but fruity and typical. Mature.
1972	Poor; a few good muscats. Avoid.
1971	The best since '61. Record ripeness, especially Gewürztraminers. Only muscat failed. Still keeping well.

Older fine vintages: '70, '69, '67, '64.

Champagne

1981	A disastrously small crop, but of vintage quality.
1980	Tiny crop; good quality.
1979	Enormous harvest of remarkable quality.
1978	Very small vintage, some very good.
1977	Good non-vintage material.
1976	Drought caused difficulties. Good; maybe excellent.
1975	Very good despite late rain. Fine vintage wines.
1974	Useful non-vintage material.
1973	Very good; a vintage year of great style.
1972	Good blending stuff.
1971	An outstanding vintage, now generally mature.
1970	Soft and attractive; vintage for some houses.
1969	Beautiful vintage wines with more finesse than power. Now mature.

Older champagne is a gamble, but can be one of life's great experiences. Only risk old vintages from top shippers.
The following are relatively light; known for their finesse (and often keep better than heavier ones): 1962, 1953, 1952, 1943, 1941. 1961 and 1945 were bigger and heavier. The '45s have kept better than the '61s.

Germany

Mosel/Saar/Ruwer

Mosels (including Saar and Ruwer wines) are so attractive young that their keeping qualities are not often enough explored, and wines older than seven years or so are unusual. But well-made wines of Kabinett class gain from two or three years in bottle, Spätleses by a little longer, and Ausleses and Beerenausleses by anything from 10 to 20 years, depending on the vintage.

As a rule, in poor years the Saar and Ruwer fare worse than the Middle Mosel and make sharp, thin wines, but in the best years they can surpass the whole of Germany for elegance and 'breed'.

Year		When to drink
1981	The Middle Mosel had a bigger crop than 1980, spoilt only by heavy rain at harvest time. 30% of the wine is Kabinett and 20% Spätlese or better: a good result. The Saar and Ruwer had a very small crop.	
1980	Miserably small crop. No late-picked, higher-grade wines, but standard ones will be well-balanced.	
1979	Severe winter damaged all but Riesling. Upper Mosel devastated. In middle Mosel a good range of qualities, promising some very fine Spätleses, with excellent balance for keeping.	Now–1990
1978	Small crop of only average quality; very few Kabinett or better wines, but well balanced.	Now–1985
1977	A big crop of moderate quality, 75% of it 'Qualitätswein', only 10% in the top grades.	Soon
1976	Very good small vintage, with some superlative sweet wines and almost no dry. Keeping well.	Now–1990
1975	Very good; many Spätleses and Ausleses. Have matured faster than expected.	Now–1985
1974	Most wine needed sugaring; few Kabinetts, but some well-balanced wines which have kept well.	Now–mid-'80s
1973	Very large, attractive; but low acid and extract meant a short life. Good eiswein.	Now
1972	Large; medium to poor; few late-picked wines, many with unripe flavour.	Now
1971	Superb, with perfect balance. Many top wines will still repay keeping for years.	Now to '90s
1970	Large; good to average. Quite soft; not for keeping.	Now
1969	Some very fine wines; most merely good. Best in the Saar and Ruwer.	Now

Older fine vintages: '67, '64, '59, '53, '49, '45.

Rhine/Nahe/Palatinate

Even the best wines can be drunk with pleasure after two or three years, but Kabinett, Spätlese and Auslese wines of good vintages gain enormously in character and complexity by keeping for longer. Rheingau wines tend to be longest-lived, often improving for ten years or more, but wines from the Nahe and the Palatinate can last nearly as long. Rheinhessen wines usually mature sooner, and dry Franconian wines are best young.

The Riesling, predominant in the Rheingau, benefits most from hot summers; Palatinate wines can taste almost overripe.

1981	The Rheingau was unlucky, with scarcely any fine wines. The Nahe did better with 30 Kabinett or above; Rheinhessen was very satisfactory and the Rheinpfalz Rieslings are likely to be exceptionally good Kabinetts and Spätleses.	
1980	Rheingau and Nahe suffered badly: small disappointing harvest. Rheinpfalz made more and better.	
1979	Severe winter damage in Rheinhessen; but some good results in quality, especially from Riesling. About half 'qualitätswein', half of better qualities. The best will repay keeping.	Now–1990
1978	A disappointing year. Only 'table' or 'qualitätswein' – very little better, except in Palatinate.	Soon
1977	Useful big crop, average quality in Palatinate, below in Rheingau.	Soon
1976	The richest vintage since 1921 in places. Very few dry wines.	Now–late '90s
1975	A very good Riesling year; a high percentage of Kabinetts and Spätleses. Many now already mature.	Now–1986
1974	Variable; the best fruity and good; many Kabinetts.	Now to mid-'80s
1973	Very large, consistent and attractive, but not for keeping.	Now
1972	Excess acidity was the problem; no exciting wines, but some presentable.	Now
1971	A superlative vintage with perfect balance.	Now–1990
1970	Very pleasant wines, but no more. Huge crop. Some exceptional wines have kept remarkably.	Now
1969	All above average; the best great. Nahe and Palatinate specially good.	Soon
1968	Poor; wet summer. The Palatinate made some good light wines.	Now, if at all
1967	Marvellous; the best of the '60s; Rheinhessen made great wines.	Now

Older fine vintages: '64, '59, '57, '53, '49, '45.

Franconia
Generally follows Rhine vintages. In '79 the predominant Muller-Thürgau was badly hit by winter cold.

Recent Vintages

THE DETAILED analysis which is given to the vintages of France and Germany is not so appropriate to the way the wines of the rest of the world are made and sold. Outstanding years are worth noting everywhere, and particularly in Italy, but the concept of a vintage year is only loosely understood in Portugal, Spain, Greece and the rest of wine-growing Europe, with the exception of the peculiar case of vintage port. In these countries years with particularly good reputations become almost brand names: a bodega may go on selling '1949' because 1949 was a popular wine while it lasted. In many cases it is the practice to blend older and younger wine, not with the idea of misleading the customer, but to produce the balanced wine he will like best.

Where vintages printed on labels are most helpful in such cases is in giving an idea of the age of the bottle, which makes it easier to avoid, for example, white wines which are too old.

Italy

Exceptional years in the last decade have been:

Chianti Classico:	1968	1971	1975	1979
Piemonte (including Barolo):	1964	1968	1971	

Very Good Years:

Chianti Classico:	1964	1967	1969	1970	1978
Piemonte (including Barolo):	1965	1967	1969	1975	1980

1972 was poor, especially in Piemonte, where many Barolos were declassified into Nebbiolo. 1973 was large, but only average quality. 1974 was good, but nothing special. 1976 was wet, difficult and disappointing. 1977 was only average. 1979 was good in both regions. 1980 good in Piemonte but only adequate in Chianti. 1981 was hampered by rain in the north of Italy. Piemonte made some good wines. The centre and south of the country did very well.

Spain: Rioja

The best vintages in general of the last two decades have been 1964, '66, '68, '70, '74, '76 and '78. Degree of maturity (and indeed quality) depends entirely on the bodega. Some '76s are mature; some '64s will still improve. 1981 was a very good year in both Rioja and Penedes, where the whites were reported to be 'exceptional'.

The New World: California

In the New World vintages tend to be very much more regular than in Europe. It is not safe to assume, however, that every year has the same qualities. The following notes on recent vintages in California's Napa valley indicate some of the climatic and other factors involved.

Year	The Napa Valley
1981	A mild winter and frost-free spring, hot June and steady ripening weather brought an exceptionally early harvest, starting in late July. Extremely good whites will include many late-harvest ones. Overall a good to very good vintage.
1980	All-time record for quantity but awkward to handle; everything ripened at once. Sugar/acid balance was very good for growers who timed it right. Good reds and whites.
1979	Another record crop. Mild spring, fine summer, but hot September then cool October caused problems, especially with Cabernet Sauvignon. Uneven quality.
1978	Record crop. Wet winter, no spring frost, some early mildew, very warm autumn. Difficult conditions leading to wide variations in quality.
1977	Long drought ended at vintage time. Reduced quantity but surprising quality.
1976	Dry winter, hot flowering season and summer, extreme drought by autumn made a small crop, high in both sugar and acid. Reds variable; at best excellent, and some excellent whites.
1975	Wet spring, cool summer, late harvest into autumn rains. Good for whites and early ripening reds. Cabernet light and in some cases fine.
1974	Little frost, long cool summer, ideal ripening conditions. A big crop in perfect condition. Big-bodied healthy Cabernets; some considered great.
1973	Record vintage for quantity, quality overall fair to very good.
1972	A year of extremes: dry winter, early spring, late frost, hot July, wet harvest. Quality very mixed.
1971	Spring was late and September very hot. Quality about average overall.
1970	Bad frost year. Crop down possibly 40%. Mild ripening conditions. Good sugars with tremendous acidity. Quality excellent.
1969	Very hot weather in August; high sugar and burning in some varieties. Normal crop size. Reds big and heavy. Whites were picked early, but most were still big heavy wines.
1968	Much like 1967. Some frost damage. Picking season late, ending the last of October. Whites again better overall than reds.

Port

Long ageing in bottle is part of the process of making vintage port. Each shipper each year decides whether his wine is worthy of early bottling and 'declaring' as 'vintage' port.

Year	Port
1981	A difficult year with drought followed by rain at harvest. Unlikely to be a vintage.
1980	A very hot dry summer, made powerful wine.
1979	Big crop of average quality, not likely to be declared.
1978	Small harvest after summer drought. Declared by eight shippers.
1977	30 shippers declared. An outstanding vintage.
1976	Very dry summer, wet autumn. Not declared.
1975	Fine; declared by 24 shippers. Hot summer and autumn with just enough rain.
1974	Cool year; late harvest; good but not vintage.
1973	Wet autumn; big watery crop. Not a vintage.
1972	Hot summer, wet vintage. Early pickers did well; three shippers declared, but only just.
1971	Problems with rot. Not a vintage.
1970	Ideal weather. A very fine balanced vintage declared by 21 shippers.
1969	Not a vintage.
1968	Not a vintage.
1967	Good but delicate. Only declared by six shippers.
1966	A big and fruity vintage with a long life ahead. 22 shippers declared.
1965	One shipper (Ferreira) declared.
1964	Not a vintage.
1963	The best of the sixties; one of the best this century. Classic, rich, strong but fruitier than '45. 23 shippers declared. Becoming excellent to drink.
1962	One shipper (Offley Forrester) declared.
1961	Not a vintage.
1960	Not heavy but reliable and already delicious. 26 shippers declared. Drink from now—1990s.
1959	Not a vintage.
1958	Declared by six shippers. Delicate; some elegant. Drink soon.
1957	Not a vintage.
1956	Not a vintage.
1955	Big strapping wines, most now richly mature. 21 shippers declared.

Earlier Vintages

1950	Like 1958. Drink soon.
1948	Lovely rich wine; now ready.
1947	Good, but mature now.
1945	A great classic; huge, dark and concentrated. Now reaching its best; but there is no hurry.

Many shippers also sell 'undeclared' vintages as 'late-bottled' or 'crusted' port (partly aged in wood for quicker maturing) or under their quinta (estate) name (e.g. Taylor's Vargellas; Croft's Roeda) as a second-quality wine.

France

Champagne: in one word the sensuous elegance which is the genius of France

France

Left: France has over
1,200,000 hectares of
vineyards. Nurturing and
protecting the vines is an
unceasing task. Here, in
midsummer near Saumur
on the Loire, farmers spray
with sulphur against the
risk of mildew

FINISTÈRE ○ Brest
CÔTES-DU-NORD St-Brieuc ○
○ Quimper
MORBIHAN
Vannes ●
Nan
ATL

—·—·— International boundary

----- Département boundary

○   Chief town of département

●   Centre of VDQS area

Vins du Thouarsais   VDQS name — a guide to VDQS wines not mapped
elsewhere appears on pages 130–131

Appellation Contrôlée areas

▦   Champagne (pages 108–109)

▢   New Appellation Contrôlée areas since 1970

▨   Loire Valley (pages 114–115)

▨   Burgundy (page 60)

▢   Jura (page 127)

▨   Côtes du Rhône (page 120) and Jurançon (page 128)

▨   Cognac (page 258–259)

▨   Bergerac (page 105)

▨   Bordeaux (page 80 and Savoie (page 127)

▨   Armagnac and Madiran etc. (page 260)

▢   Gaillac (page 129) and Bellet

▨   Languedoc (page 124–125) and Cahors (page 128)

▢   Other wine-growing areas

▢   Alsace (pages 110–111) and Provence (page 126)

Proportional Circles

⬤   Area of vineyard per département
44   in thousands of hectares

WHEN the last raindrop has been counted, and no geological stone is left unturned, there will still remain the imponderable question of national character which makes France the undisputed mistress of the vine; the producer of infinitely more and more varied great wines than all the rest of the world.

France is not only sensuous and painstaking; France is methodical. She not only has good vineyards; she defines, classifies and controls them. The listing, in order, of the best sites has been going on for nearly 200 years. In the last 50 or so it has become more and more important, as the world's interest, not only in wine but also in consumer-protection, has grown.

This atlas does not attempt to reproduce the boundaries set by law to every French wine region. It has the wine-drinker rather than the lawyer in mind. There are three classes of wine with which we are concerned: Appellations Contrôlées, which are guarantees not only of origin but of a certain standard, administered by the central Institut National des Appellations d'Origine in Paris and its 'engineers' scattered round France. A second rank, for good wines of chiefly local interest, known as VDQS —Vin Délimité de Qualité Supérieure. And a third, introduced in 1973, Vins de Pays.

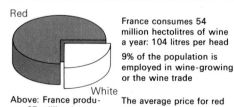

Red
White

Above: France produces 65 million hectolitres of wine a year. 68% is red. 10m is Appellation Contrôlée

France consumes 54 million hectolitres of wine a year: 104 litres per head

9% of the population is employed in wine-growing or the wine trade

The average price for red wine is 140 francs per 100 litres to the grower. (1975 figures)

Germany 32%
Belgium 14%
UK 9%
Netherlands 8%
Switzerland 7%
USA 5%

Above: France exports about 5.9m hectolitres a year. Germany is by far the biggest consumer both by volume and by value. It spends $105m a year; Britain spends $68m.
Below: France imports 3.5m hectolitres more than she exports. Most imports are blending wine

Exports
Imports

CALAIS

PAS-DE-CALAIS

Lille

BELGIQUE

NORD

Arras

SOMME

AISNE

Mézières

ARDENNES

LUXEMBOURG

DEUTSCHLAND

Amiens

Laon

SEINE-MARITIME

OISE

Reims

MARNE

Metz

Vins de Moselle

MOSELLE

BAS-

Le Havre

Rouen

Beauvais

Châlons-sur-Marne

18

Bar-le-Duc

MEUSE

MEURTHE-

Strasbourg

Caen

CALVADOS

Evreux

EURE

VAL-D'OISE

SEINE-ST-DENIS

PARIS

Versailles

HAUTS-DE-SEINE

YVE-LINES

VAL-DE-MARNE

ESSONNE

SEINE-ET MARNE

Melun

Toul

Côtes de Toul

ET-MOSELLE

Nancy

RHIN

St-Lô

ORNE

Alençon

EURE-ET-LOIR

Chartres

Troyes

AUBE

MARNE

HAUTE-

Chaumont

VOSGES

Épinal

HAUT-RHIN

Colmar

MAYENNE

SARTHE

le Mans

Laval

LOIR-ET-CHER

LOIRET

Orléans

Vins de l'Orléanais

YONNE

Auxerre

Chablis

Sauvignon de St.-Bris

CÔTE-D'OR

Dijon

HAUTE-SAÔNE

Vésoul

BELFORT

7

DOUBS

Besançon

Angers

INDRE-ET-LOIRE

Tours

Montoire-sur-le-Loir

Coteaux du Vendômois

Blois

Chambord

Mont-près-Chambord

Cour Cheverny

Cour Cheverny

23

MAINE-ET-LOIRE

Ancenis

Coteaux d'Ancenis

Nantes

CHER

Bourges

NIÈVRE

Nevers

Beaune

14

Gien

Coteaux du Giennois

3

SAÔNE-ET-LOIRE

le Creusot

JURA

Lons-le-Saunier

2

Thouars

Vins du Thouarsais

DEUX-SÈVRES

la Roche-sur-Yon

VENDÉE

9

INDRE

Châteauroux

Châteaumeillant

Coteaux de Châteaumeillant

3

ALLIER

Moulins

10

Mâcon

Bourg-en-Bresse

AIN

Geneve

HAUTE-SAVOIE

Savoie

Annecy

Poitiers

VIENNE

9

Niort

4

HAUTE-VIENNE

Guéret

CREUSE

St-Pourçain-sur-Sioule

St-Pourçain-sur-Sioule

PUY-DE-DÔME

LOIRE

Roanne

Vins de Renaison

Côte Roannaise

RHÔNE

Lyon

Vins du Bugey

Belley

Vins du Lyonnais

Chambéry

Vins de Savoie

SAVOIE

3

la Rochelle

CHARENTE-MARITIME

Cognac

CHARENTE

Angoulême

24

Limoges

Clermont-Ferrand

Côtes d'Auvergne

Vins d'Auvergne

3

Boën-sur-Lignon

Côtes du Forez

St-Étienne

ISÈRE

Grenoble

5

ITALIA

102

Périgueux

CORRÈZE

Tulle

CANTAL

Aurillac

HAUTE-LOIRE

le Puy

Tournon

Valence

20

18

le Puy

1

Gap

HAUTES-ALPES

Bordeaux

GIRONDE

Libourne

DORDOGNE

8

Entraygues

Vins d'Entraygues et du Fel

Estaing

Vins d'Estaing

Clairvaux

Vins de Marcillac

Rodez

LOT

AVEYRON

Mende

LOZÈRE

ARDÈCHE

Privas

Chatillon-en-Diois

Vins de Chatillon-en-Diois

Coteaux du Tricastin

Saint-Remèze

Côtes du Vivarais

DRÔME

Dieppe

ALPES-DE-HAUTE-PROVENCE

ALPES-MARITIMES

Marmande

Côtes du Marmandais

LOT-ET-GARONNE

Cahors

Agen

14

Buzet

Côtes de Buzet

La Villedieu-du-Temple

Vins de Lavilledieu

TARN-ET-GARONNE

Montauban

Gaillac

Albi

TARN

23

Tulette

VAUCLUSE

Avignon

Côtes du Ventoux

les Baux

Coteaux des Baux

Pierrevert

Coteaux de Pierrevert

Tour d'Aigues

Côtes du Lubéron

56

Draguignan

Nice

11

Mont-de-Marsan

LANDES

GERS

Auch

34

Côtes du Frontonnais

Villaudric

Toulouse

HAUTE-GARONNE

St Saturnin

Montpeyroux

St-Georges d'Orques

Cabrières

Faugères

Pic-St-Loup

Drézery

Vérargues

Montpellier

Coteaux du Languedoc

Nîmes

Bellegarde

Costières du Gard

GARD

St-Christol

St-Christol

25

Aix-en-Provence

Coteaux d'Aix-en-Provence

BOUCHES-DU-RHÔNE

les Arcs

Côtes de Provence

VAR

Marseille

Toulon

Puyôô

Béarn

Vins du Tursan

Geaune

PYRÉNÉES-ATLANTIQUE

Pau

Tarbes

HAUTES-PYRÉNÉES

17

Saint-Chinian

HÉRAULT

Pinet

Picpoul de Pinet

Olonzac

Minervois

Carcassonne

Narbonne

92

162

Bayonne

St-Étienne-de-Baigorry

Iroulèguy

5

Foix

ARIÈGE

3

AUDE

Lézignan-Corbières

Corbières

Corbières Supérieures

118

Perpignan

61

Corbières Supérieures du Roussillon

Roussillon dels Aspres

PYRÉNÉES-ORIENTALES

ESPAÑA

N

SUISSE

Km. 0   50   100   150 Km.

Mi. 0   50   100 Mi.

59

Burgundy

Above: Beaune is the wine capital of Burgundy; many would say of the world. The city's great landmark, the silvery roof of the medieval Hospices, gleams through the mist of an autumn evening, seen from the heights of the Montagne de Beaune to the west of the town

THE VERY name of Burgundy has a ring of richness about it. Let Paris be France's head, Champagne her soul, there is no doubt about what Burgundy is: her stomach. It is a land of long meals, well supplied with the best materials (Charolais beef to the west, Bresse chickens to the east). It is the most famous of the ancient duchies of France. But long before either, even before Christianity came to France, it was famous for its wine.

Burgundy is not one big vineyard, but the name of a province which contains at least three of France's best. By far the richest and most important is the Côte d'Or, in the centre, composed of the Côte de Nuits and the Côte de Beaune. But Chablis and Beaujolais and the Mâconnais have old reputations which owe nothing to their elder brother's.

For all her ancient fame and riches Burgundy still seems curiously simple and rustic. There is hardly a grand house from end to end of the Côte d'Or—none of the elegant country estates which stamp, say, the Médoc as a creation of leisure and wealth in the 18th and 19th centuries. Some of the few big holdings of land,

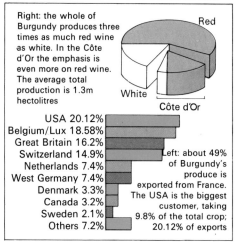

Right: the whole of Burgundy produces three times as much red wine as white. In the Côte d'Or the emphasis is even more on red wine. The average total production is 1.3m hectolitres

Red

White

Côte d'Or

USA 20.12%	
Belgium/Lux 18.58%	
Great Britain 16.2%	
Switzerland 14.9%	
Netherlands 7.4%	
West Germany 7.4%	
Denmark 3.3%	
Canada 3.2%	
Sweden 2.1%	
Others 7.2%	

Left: about 49% of Burgundy's produce is exported from France. The USA is the biggest customer, taking 9.8% of the total crop; 20.12% of exports

those of the church, were broken up by Napoleon. Now, in fact, it is one of the most fragmented of the important wine-growing districts of France.

The fragmentation of Burgundy is the cause of the one great drawback of its wine: its unpredictability. From the geographer's point of view the human factor is unmappable, and in Burgundy, more than in most places, it needs to be given the limelight. For even when you have pinned down a wine to one particular climat (field of vines) in one particular finage (village) in one particular year, it could still, in many cases, have been made by any one of six or seven men who own small parcels of the land, and reared in any one of six or seven cellars. 'Monopoles', or whole vineyards in the hands of one grower, are rare exceptions. Even the smallest grower has parcels of two or three vineyards. Bigger ones may own a total of 40 or 50 acres spread in two- or three-acre lots in a score of vineyards from one end of the Côte to the other. The Clos de Vougeot has over 60 growers in its 124 acres.

For this very reason the great majority of

burgundy is bought in barrel from the grower when it is new by négociants (or shippers), who blend it with other wines from the same area to achieve marketable quantities of a standard wine. It is offered to the world not as the product of a specific grower, whose production of that particular wine may be only a cask or two, but as the wine of a given district (be it as specific as a vineyard or as vague as a village) élevé—literally educated—by the shipper.

The reputations of these négociant-éleveurs (many of whom are also growers themselves) vary from being the touchstone of the finest burgundy to something rather more earthy.

What is certain is that all the very finest wine goes to market, as it does all over the world, with the most detailed possible description of its antecedents on its label . . . and these almost always include the name of the proprietor of the vineyard and the fact that he bottles the wine in his own cellars.

The map on this page shows the whole of wine-growing Burgundy, the relative sizes and positions of the big southern areas of Beaujolais and the Mâconnais, Chablis in the north, the tiny Côte Chalonnaise and the narrow strip of the Côte d'Or and its little-known hinterland, the Hautes Côtes de Beaune and the Hautes Côtes de Nuits. The key is an index to the large-scale maps of the areas which follow.

There are a hundred or so Appellations Contrôlées in Burgundy. Most of them refer to geographical areas and appear on the next 18 pages. Built into these geographical appel!ations is a classification by quality which is practically a work of art in itself. It is explained on page 64. However, the appellations Bourgogne, Bourgogne Aligoté (for white wine), Bourgogne Passe-Tout-Grains and Bourgogne Grand Ordinaire can be used for wine made from the appropriate grapes coming from any part of Burgundy, including the less good vineyards within famous communes which have not the right to the commune name.

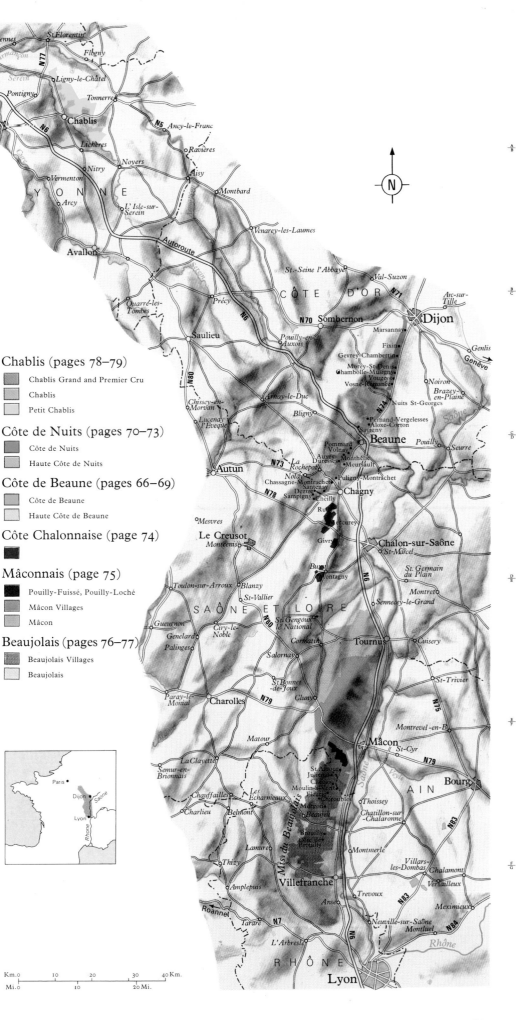

Chablis (pages 78–79)
- Chablis Grand and Premier Cru
- Chablis
- Petit Chablis

Côte de Nuits (pages 70–73)
- Côte de Nuits
- Haute Côte de Nuits

Côte de Beaune (pages 66–69)
- Côte de Beaune
- Haute Côte de Beaune

Côte Chalonnaise (page 74)

Mâconnais (page 75)
- Pouilly-Fuissé, Pouilly-Loché
- Mâcon Villages
- Mâcon

Beaujolais (pages 76–77)
- Beaujolais Villages
- Beaujolais

The Language of the Label

Climat Vineyard (individual field)
Commune or **Finage** Parish
Grand Cru or **Tête de Cuvée** A top growth with its own Appellation Contrôlée
Mise dans nos caves Bottled in our cellars (not necessarily those of the grower)
Mise (or **Mise en bouteilles**) **du** (or **au**) **Domaine** (or **à la propriété**) Bottled at the property where it is made
Mise par le propriétaire Bottled by the grower
Monopole The whole of the vineyard named belongs to the same proprietor
Négociant-Eleveur A merchant who buys wine from the grower in its first year and 'brings it up' in his own cellars
Premier Cru The second class of burgundy vineyard
Propriétaire-Récoltant Owner-manager
Récolte Vintage
Villages From selected parishes within the region named

Burgundy/the Quality Factor

A BURGUNDIAN understandably feels a certain reverence towards the commonplace-looking ridge of the Côte d'Or, as towards an unknown god. One is bound to wonder at the fact, witnessed by the tongues and palates of generation after generation, that a few small parcels of land on this hill give superlative wine, each with its own positive personality, and that others do not. Surely one can discover the facts which distinguish one parcel from another —giving to some grapes more sugar, thicker skins, a pulp more rich in minerals.

One can. And one cannot. There are millions of facts to collect and collate. Soil and subsoil have been analysed time and again. Temperature and humidity and wind-direction have been recorded; must examined under the microscope . . . yet the central mystery remains. One can only put down certain physical facts, and place beside them the reputations of the great wines. No one can prove how they are connected.

Burgundy is the northernmost area in the world which produces great red wine. Its climate pattern in summer is, in fact, curiously

like that of Bordeaux—the continental influence making up to some extent for its position farther north. Yet total failure of the vintage is a greater problem here. No overriding climatic consideration can explain the excellence of the wine—or even why a vineyard was established here in the first place. There are certain local or micro-climatic advantages: the shelter provided by the hills from west west winds; the slight elevation above the fogs of the plain; but nothing unique.

Looking farther for reasons, one turns to the soil. Here there are more clues. The ridge of the Côte d'Or is the edge of a plateau built up of various sandy limestones. Erosion, by the action of ice in the last periglacial period 18,000 years ago and since then by weather and cultivation, has broken them down into soil. Rubble and soil fall down the slope, which benefits both the nourishment and the drainage of the vine lower down. The more the soil is cultivated the greater the mixture of varied soil-types—helped also by the carting of good earth on to the better vineyards: in 1749 150 wagon-loads of turf were spread on the vine-

yard of Romanée-Conti, and the same sort of earth-moving goes on today.

The Côte de Nuits is a sharper slope than the Côte de Beaune. Along its lower part, generally about a third of the way up the slope, runs a narrow outcrop of marlstone, making limy clay soil. Marl by itself would be too rich a soil for the highest-quality wine, but in combination with the silt and scree washed down from the hard limestone higher up it is perfect. Erosion continues the blend below the actual outcrop. Above the marl, the thin light limestone soil is generally too poor for vines.

In the Côte de Beaune the marly outcrop (Argovien) is wider and higher on the hill; instead of a narrow strip of vineyard under a beetling brow of limestone there is a broad and gentle slope vineyards can climb. The vines almost reach the scrubby peak in places.

On the dramatic isolated hill of Corton the soil formed from the marlstone is the best part of the vineyard, with only a little wood-covered cap of hard limestone above it.

In Meursault the limestone reappearing below the marl on the slope forms a second and

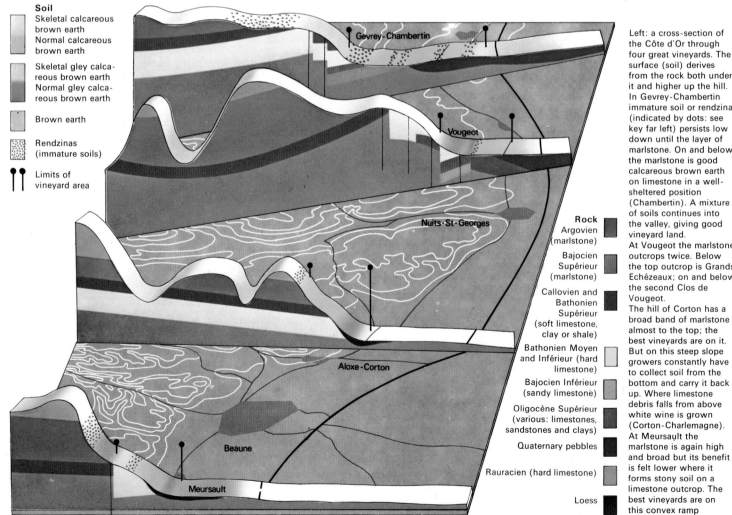

Soil

Skeletal calcareous brown earth
Normal calcareous brown earth

Skeletal gley calcareous brown earth
Normal gley calcareous brown earth

Brown earth

Rendzinas (immature soils)

Limits of vineyard area

Rock

Argovien (marlstone)

Bajocien Supérieur (marlstone)

Callovien and Bathonien Supérieur (soft limestone, clay or shale)

Bathonien Moyen and Inférieur (hard limestone)

Bajocien Inférieur (sandy limestone)

Oligocène Supérieur (various: limestones, sandstones and clays)

Quaternary pebbles

Rauracien (hard limestone)

Loess

Gevrey-Chambertin
Vougeot
Nuits-St-Georges
Aloxe-Corton
Beaune
Meursault

Left: a cross-section of the Côte d'Or through four great vineyards. The surface (soil) derives from the rock both under it and higher up the hill. In Gevrey-Chambertin immature soil or rendzinas (indicated by dots: see key far left) persists low down until the layer of marlstone. On and below the marlstone is good calcareous brown earth on limestone in a well-sheltered position (Chambertin). A mixture of soils continues into the valley, giving good vineyard land.
At Vougeot the marlstone outcrops twice. Below the top outcrop is Grands Echézeaux; on and below the second Clos de Vougeot.
The hill of Corton has a broad band of marlstone almost to the top; the best vineyards are on it. But on this steep slope growers constantly have to collect soil from the bottom and carry it back up. Where limestone debris falls from above white wine is grown (Corton-Charlemagne). At Meursault the marlstone is again high and broad but its benefit is felt lower where it forms stony soil on a limestone outcrop. The best vineyards are on this convex ramp

lower shoulder to the hill, limy and very stony; excellent for white wine.

Such illustrations are only random examples of the varied structure of the Côtes. And with each change of soil there comes a change in drainage, the soil's temperature—any one of a hundred factors which will affect the vine.

Probably it is the micro-climate, which, in combination with the physical structure, has the most decisive effect. The best vineyards of the Côtes face due east; it is the morning sun they want, to warm the ground gradually all day. They are sheltered from the south-west, the moist rain-bearing wind—but not so sheltered as to be frost pockets on still nights. What other details of their position count in the thousands of hours that the grapes are hanging on the vines it is fascinating to speculate.

The other, unmappable, quality factor is the grower's choice of vines and the way he prunes and fertilizes them. There are more or less vigorous 'clones' of the classic varieties, and a grower who chooses the most productive (or over-feeds his soil) inevitably compromises quality. Much disappointing short-lived wine is made this way.

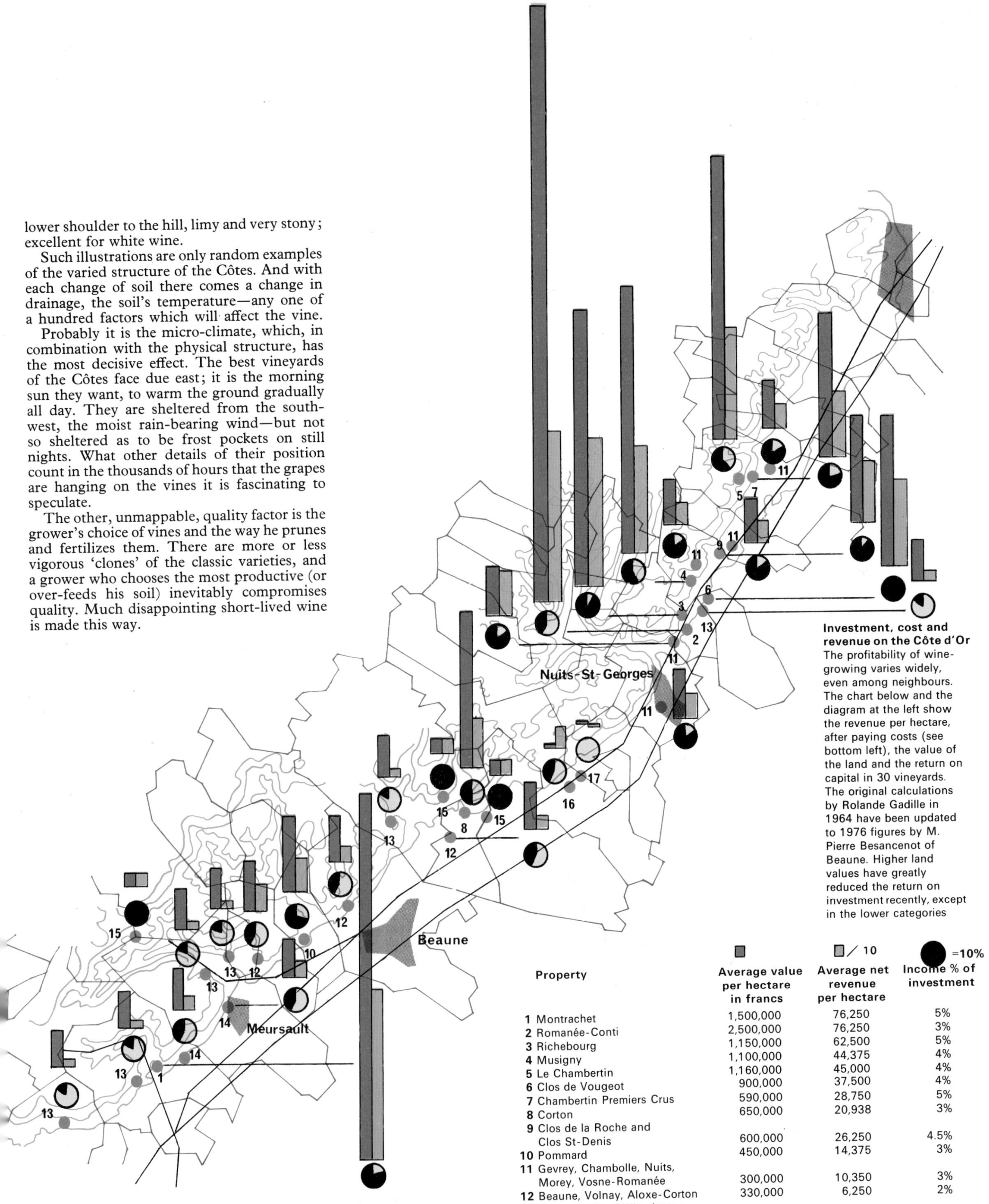

Nuits-St-Georges

Beaune

Meursault

Investment, cost and revenue on the Côte d'Or
The profitability of wine-growing varies widely, even among neighbours. The chart below and the diagram at the left show the revenue per hectare, after paying costs (see bottom left), the value of the land and the return on capital in 30 vineyards. The original calculations by Rolande Gadille in 1964 have been updated to 1976 figures by M. Pierre Besancenot of Beaune. Higher land values have greatly reduced the return on investment recently, except in the lower categories

Right: the costs of these Burgundy estates were reckoned (in 1976) at between 33,000 francs per hectare per year for Montrachet to 13,500 francs for humble properties producing Bourgogne or Aligoté, worked by the owner's family

		◼	◻ / 10	● =10%
	Property	Average value per hectare in francs	Average net revenue per hectare	Income % of investment
1	Montrachet	1,500,000	76,250	5%
2	Romanée-Conti	2,500,000	76,250	3%
3	Richebourg	1,150,000	62,500	5%
4	Musigny	1,100,000	44,375	4%
5	Le Chambertin	1,160,000	45,000	4%
6	Clos de Vougeot	900,000	37,500	4%
7	Chambertin Premiers Crus	590,000	28,750	5%
8	Corton	650,000	20,938	3%
9	Clos de la Roche and Clos St-Denis	600,000	26,250	4.5%
10	Pommard	450,000	14,375	3%
11	Gevrey, Chambolle, Nuits, Morey, Vosne-Romanée	300,000	10,350	3%
12	Beaune, Volnay, Aloxe-Corton	330,000	6,250	2%
13	Vougeot, Monthélie, Auxey, Chassagne, Santenay, Savigny	225,000	3,750	2%
14	Meursault, Puligny-Montrachet	240,000	6,250	3%
15	Côtes de Beaune-Villages, Ladoix, Pernand-Vergelesses	90,000	5,000	6%
16	Bourgogne	30,000	3,000	10%
17	Aligoté	15,000	2,400	16%

The Côte d'Or

Chancelier Nicolas Rolin & Guigone de Salins, son épouse
Fondateurs des Hospices de Beaune en 1443

THE WHOLE Côte d'Or—the Côte de Beaune and the Côte de Nuits, separated only by a few miles without vines—is an irregular escarpment 30 miles long. Its top is a wooded plateau. Its bottom is the beginning of the flat, plain-like valley of the River Saône. The width of the slope varies from a mile and a half to a few hundred yards—but all the good vineyards are limited to this narrow strip.

The classification of the qualities of the land in this strip is the most elaborate on earth.

As it stands it is the work of the Institut National des Appellations d'Origine, based on classifications going back for over 100 years. It divides the vineyards into four classes, and lays down the law about the labelling of the wine accordingly. Grands Crus (also known as Têtes de Cuvée) are the first class. There are 30 of them. Each has its own appellation. Grands Crus do not normally use the name of their commune on their labels. The single, simple vineyard name—Musigny, Corton, Montrachet or Chambertin—is the patent of Burgundy's highest nobility.

The next rank, Premiers Crus, use the name of their commune followed by the name of their vineyard (or, if the wine comes from more than one Premier Cru vineyard, the commune name followed by the words Premier Cru).

The third rank is known as Appellation Communale; that is, having the right to use the commune name. A vineyard name is permitted —though rarely used—if it is printed in letters much smaller than the name of the commune. A few such vineyards, often called Clos de . . . though not officially Premiers Crus, are in the hands of a single good grower, and can be considered in the same class.

Fourthly there are inferior vineyards, even within some famous communes, which have only the right to call their wine Bourgogne.

The system has only one drawback for the consumer. Elaborate as it seems, there remains a class of vineyards which it does not specifically recognize, but which do distinguish themselves in practice. For only in the Côte de Nuits and three communes of the Côte de Beaune are there any Grands Crus; all the rest of the finest vineyards are Premiers Crus, despite the fact that, particularly in such communes as Pommard and Volnay, some Premiers Crus consistently give better wine than the others.

Besides controlling the use of place names, INAO lays down the regulations which control quality, demanding that only the classical vines be used (Pinot Noir for red wine, Chardonnay for white); that only so much wine (from 30 hectolitres per hectare for the best, to 40 for more ordinary) be made; that it achieve a certain strength (from 12% alcohol for the best white and 11.5 for the best red down to 9% for the most ordinary red).

It remains up to the consumer to remember to make the distinction between the name of a vineyard and of a commune. Many villages (Vosne, Gevrey, Chassagne, etc.) have hyphenated their name to that of their best vineyard. The difference between a Chevalier-Montrachet (from one famous vineyard) and a Chassagne-Montrachet (from anywhere in a big commune) is not obvious; but it is vital.

Above and right: Beaune has one of the world's most famous hospitals, built in the mid-15th century and still busily in practice. The Hospices de Beaune was founded by Nicolas Rolin, Chancellor of the Duke of Burgundy, and his third wife, Guigone de Salins, in 1443, and endowed with vineyards in the surrounding country. Since then wine growers have continued to bequeath their land to the hospital (or Hôtel-Dieu). The proceeds of the annual sale of its wine maintains it with all modern equipment, tending the sick of Beaune without charge. Above is a Victorian engraving of the founder and his wife. Top right is the splendid main courtyard.
The Hospices vineyards are shown on the maps and their recent prices given on the following pages. Their prices tend to establish the level for the burgundy of that year. Right: the new wine in the cellars of the Hospices

The Hospices auction is held every November in Beaune's market hall

In the Grande Salle des Pôvres the beds are the original scarlet cubicles

The Flemish architect Jehan Wiscrere finished the block with a spire

The wine merchants of Beaune

Beaune still keeps its town walls; their turrets are often used as cellars. Many of the best merchants of Burgundy work within the old city

1 Pierre Ponnelle
2 Brocard
3 Cave du Bourgogne
4 Chanson Père & Fils
5 Bouchard Aîné & Fils
6 Patriarche Père & Fils
7 Caves de la Reine Pédauque
8 Calvet
9 Albert Morot
10 Jaffelin Frères
11 Joseph Drouhin
12 Cave des Cordeliers
13 Léon Violland
14 Louis Latour
15 Remoissenet Père & Fils
16 Bouchard Père & Fils
17 Louis Jadot

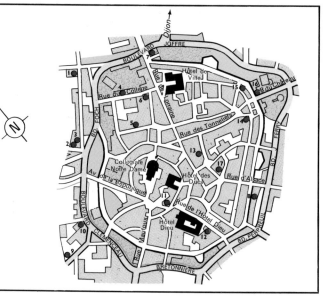

The Côte de Beaune: Santenay

THE MAPS on this and the following eight pages trace the vineyards of the Côte d'Or from south to north. The orientation of the maps has been turned through approximately 90 degrees so that what appears to be south is east-south-east.

The Côte de Beaune starts without a great explosion of famous names. It leads in gradually, from the villages of Sampigny, Dézize and Cheilly, with the one well-known cru of Les Maranges which they share (all beyond the limits of this map; see page 61), into the commune of Santenay. After the hamlet of Haut-Santenay and the little town (a spa, but not a very gay one) of Santenay, the Côte half-turns to take up its characteristic slope to the east.

This southern end of the Côte de Beaune is the most confused geologically and in many ways is untypical of the Côte as a whole. Complex faults in the structure of the hills make radical changes of soil and subsoil in Santenay. Part of the commune is analogous to parts of the Côte de Nuits, giving a deep red wine with a long life. Other parts give light wine more typical of the Côte de Beaune. Some of the highest vineyards are too stony and have been abandoned altogether.

Les Gravières (the name draws attention to the stony ground, as the name Graves does in Bordeaux) and La Comme are the best climats of Santenay. The well-known Clos de Tavannes is part of Les Gravières. As we move into Chassagne-Montrachet the character of these excellent red wine vineyards is continued. The name of Montrachet is so firmly associated with white wine that few people expect to find red here at all. But almost all the vineyards from the village of Chassagne south grow at least some red wine: Morgeot, La Boudriotte and Clos St-Jean (the last mapped on page 66) are the most famous. Their wines are solid, long-lived and deep-coloured, again unusual for the Côte de Beaune.

Indeed no one really knows why white-wine-growing took over in this district. Thomas Jefferson reported that white-wine growers here had to eat hard rye bread while red-wine men could afford it soft and white. It has been suggested that local growers were trying to ape the success of Le Montrachet (which had been famous for white wine since the 16th century). Also that the Chardonnay is a more accommodating vine in stony soil—which it certainly finds in Meursault. Whatever the answer, Chassagne-Montrachet is known to the world chiefly for its dry but succulent, golden, flower-scented white wine.

The southern end of the Côte de Beaune is known principally for its substantial red wines. Maufoux is a distinguished négociant of Santenay; the remainder are some of the good growers with vineyards on this map

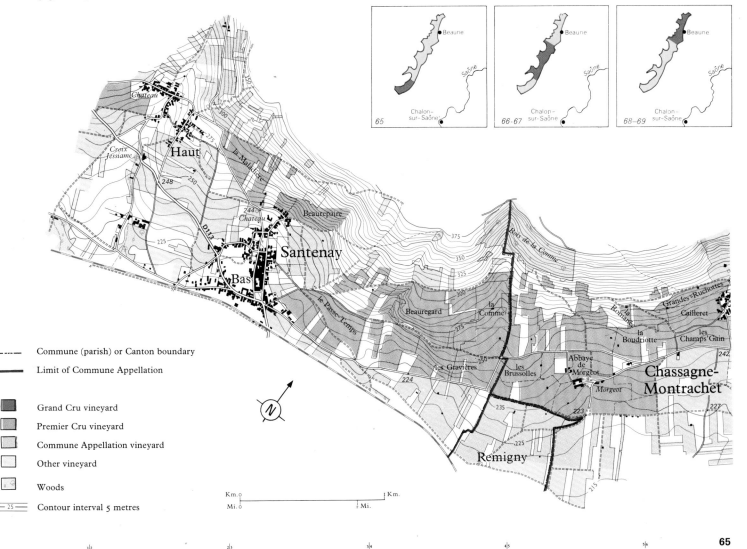

Commune (parish) or Canton boundary

Limit of Commune Appellation

Grand Cru vineyard

Premier Cru vineyard

Commune Appellation vineyard

Other vineyard

Woods

Contour interval 5 metres

The Côte de Beaune: Meursault

A SIDE VALLEY in the hills just north of Chassagne, leading up to the hamlet of Gamay (which gave its name to the Beaujolais grape in the bad old days before the Pinot came into its own), divides the vineyards of the commune in two. South of it there is excellent white wine but the emphasis is on red. North, on the border of Puligny, there is the best white wine in Burgundy, if not the world.

The Grand Cru Montrachet earns its fame by an almost unbelievable concentration of the qualities of white burgundy. It has more scent, a brighter gold, a longer flavour, more succulence and yet more definition; everything about it is intensified—the mark of truly great wine. Perfect exposure to the east, yet an angle which means the sun is still flooding down the rows of vines at nine on a summer evening; a sudden streak of very limy soil, are factors in giving it

Top: Volnay from the east
Above left: Chardonnay grapes at Meursault
Centre left: Comte Lafon in his Meursault caves
Centre right: Pinot Noir grapes at Pommard
Right: Le Montrachet at nine on a summer evening

Average price a cask (228 litres) at the 1976 Hospices de Beaune auction

Commune	Vineyard	Cuvée	francs
Auxey-Duresses	Duresses	Boillot	7,500
Monthélie	Duresses	Lebelin	5,400
Meursault	Charmes	de Bahèzre de Lanlay	8,700
Meursault	Charmes	Albert Grivault	8,000
Meursault	Genevrières	Baudot	7,700
Meursault	Genevrières	Philippe le Bon	7,500
Meursault	Poruzots	Goureau	6,500
Meursault	Poruzots	Jehan Humblot	8,900
Pommard	Epenots & Noizons	Billardet	9,700
Pommard	Epenots & Rugiens	Dames de la Charité	11,800
Volnay	Champans & Taille-Pieds	Blondeau	10,700
Volnay	Santenots	Gauvain	11,200
Volnay	Santenots	Jehan de Massol	10,300
Volnay	Village & Carelle	Général Muteau	8,300

The vineyards in which the Hospices de Beaune owns land are marked with a cross on this and the next map. Above and on page 69 are listed the 'cuvées', vineyards donated by the benefactors named, with the wines' prices in the 1976 sale, an indication of their relative reputations

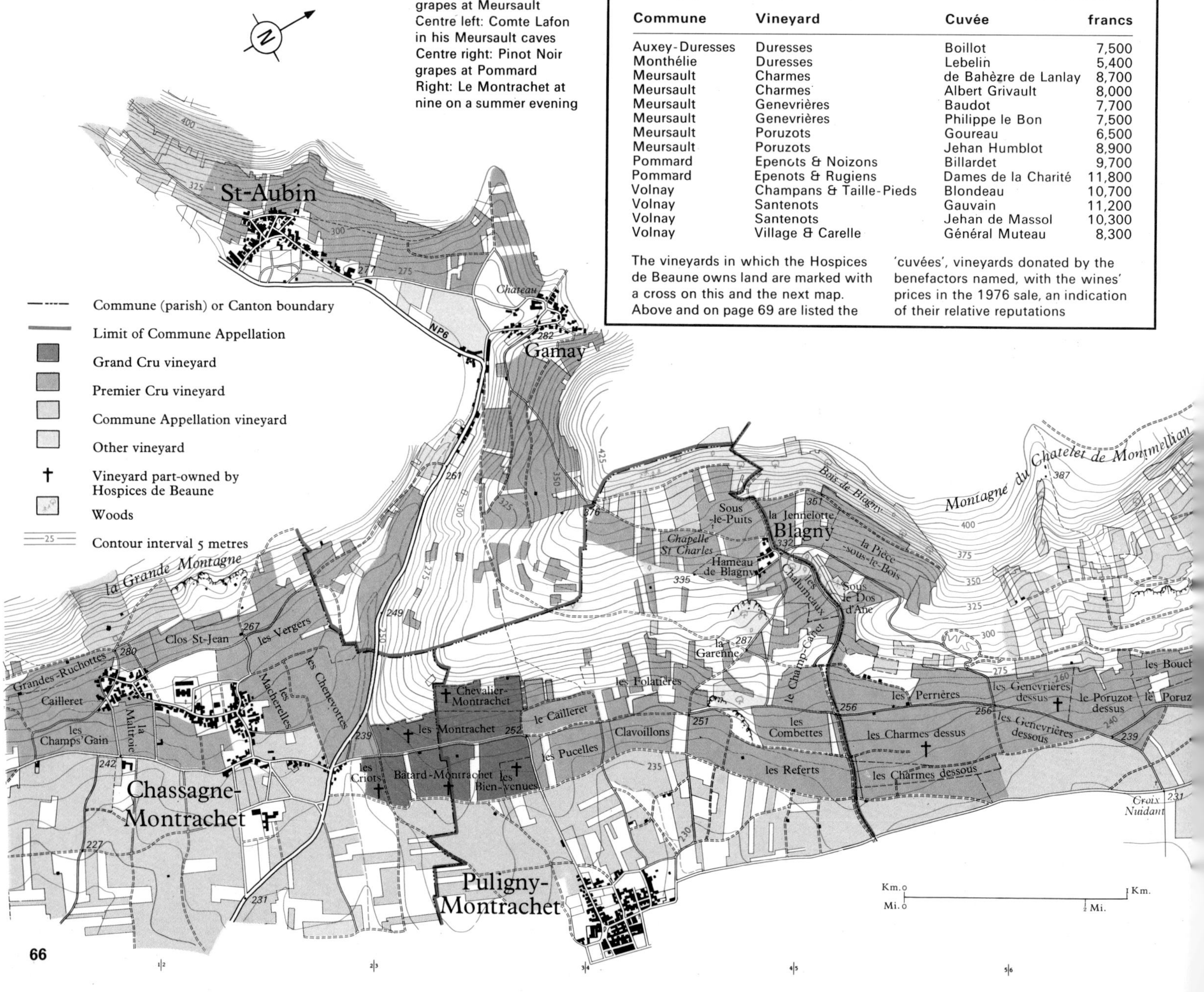

Commune (parish) or Canton boundary
Limit of Commune Appellation
Grand Cru vineyard
Premier Cru vineyard
Commune Appellation vineyard
Other vineyard
Vineyard part-owned by Hospices de Beaune
Woods
Contour interval 5 metres
St-Aubin
Gamay
Château
NP6
Blagny
Chassagne-Montrachet
Puligny-Montrachet
la Grande Montagne
Montagne du Chatelet de Montmellian
Bois de Blagny
Sous -le-Puits
la Jennelotte
Chapelle St Charles
Hameau de Blagny
la Pièce -sous-le-Bois
Sous le Dos d'Ane
les Chaumeaux
la Garenne
le Champ-Canet
Clos St-Jean
les Vergers
Grandes-Ruchottes
Cailleret
les Champs Gain
la Maltroie
les Macherelles
les Chenevottes
Chevalier-Montrachet
les Montrachet
le Cailleret
Clavoillons
les Pucelles
les Folatières
les Criots
Batard-Montrachet
les Bien-venues
les Combettes
les Referts
les Perrières
les Charmes dessus
les Charmes dessous
les Genevrières dessus
les Genevrières dessous
le Poruzot dessus
les Bouch
Croix Nuidant
Km.o
Km.
Mi.o
Mi.

an edge over its neighbours. For the other Grands Crus grouped about it come near but rarely excel it. Chevalier-Montrachet tends to be more delicate (coming from ground so stony that tilling it is barely worth while; its best soil has been used for renewing Le Montrachet). Bâtard- lies on richer ground and often—not always—fails to achieve quite the same finesse. Les Criots and Bienvenues belong in the same class—and so very often do the Puligny Premiers Crus Les Pucelles and Le Cailleret.

There is a distinction between Puligny-Montrachet and Meursault, quite clear in the minds of people who know them well, but almost impossible to define—and to account for. The vineyards of the one flow without a break into the other. In fact the hamlet of Blagny—which makes excellent wine high up on stony soil—is in both, with a classically com-plicated appellation: Premier Cru in Meur-sault, Blagny Premier Cru in Puligny-Montra-chet, and only AC Blagny when (which is rare) the wine is red.

Meursault is—to attempt the impossible—a slightly softer, drier, less fruity wine than Puligny-Montrachet. The words 'nutty' and 'mealy' are used of it; whereas Puligny is more a matter of peaches and apricots. On the whole there is less brilliant distinction (and no Grand Cru) in Meursault—but a very high and gener-ally even standard over a large area, making it a reliable and often good-value wine to buy.

The big village lies across another dip in the hills where roads lead up to Auxey-Duresses and Monthélie, both sources of very good red and white wines which tend to be over-looked beside Beaune, Pommard and Volnay.

Meursault's streets are lined with the court-yards and cellars of scores of growers, each of them owning parts of several climats.

Meursault in turn flows into Volnay. A good deal of red wine is grown on this side of the commune, but called Volnay-Santenots rather than Meursault. White Volnay can similarly call itself Meursault.

Volnay and Meursault draw as near together as red and white wines well can without being rosé; both rather soft, delicate, the red some-times rather pale yet with great personality and a long perfumed aftertaste. If Volnay makes the lightest wine of the Côte it can also be the most brilliant. Its life-span is relatively short—per-haps ten years. Caillerets is the great name in Volnay; Champans and Clos des Chênes are similar; the steep little Clos des Ducs, belong-ing to the Marquis d'Angerville, is the best climat on the other side of the village.

Right: a handful of the dozens of famous growers of this part of the Côtes; Le Montrachet has five noted owners: Laguiche, Bouchard Père, Ihénard, Calvet and the Domaine de la Romanée-Conti

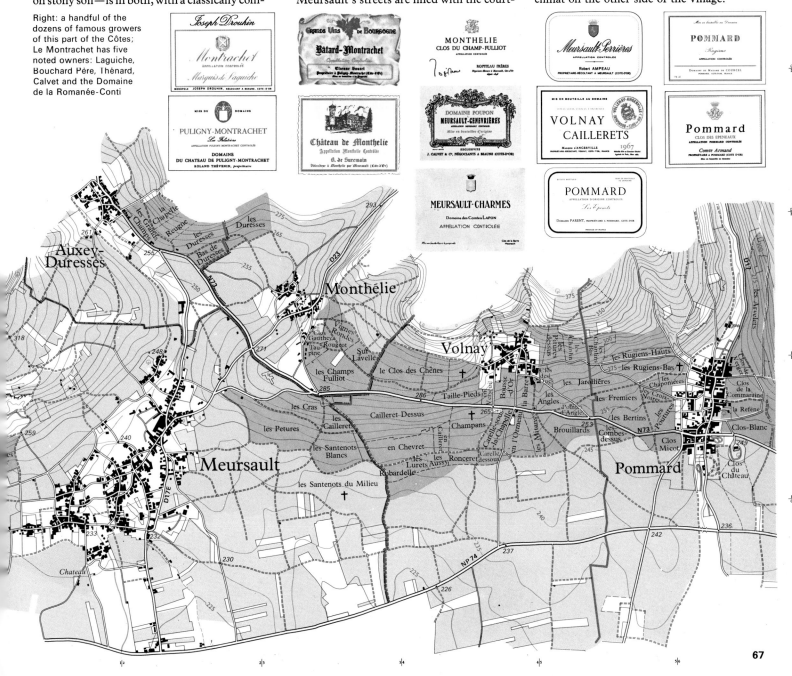

The Côte de Beaune: Beaune

POMMARD (mapped on this and the previous page) is unaccountably the best-known and most sought-after commune of the whole Côte. Unaccountably, because the commune wine is not outstanding, and there is no single vineyard with a world-wide reputation. Most critics of burgundy find Pommard the slight levelling off between the high-points of Volnay and Beaune. But what should not be ignored is the individual growers. In Burgundy the grower counts as much as the vineyard; the saying goes 'there are no great wines; only great bottles of wine'.

Pommard's most prestigious vineyard is the lower part of Les Rugiens (map page 67) above the village. One of the best cuvées of the Hospices de Beaune, Dames de la Charité, is made from Rugiens and Epenots (combined). Clos de la Commaraine is the monopole of the famous firm of Jaboulet-Vercherre. These are among the great Pommards; medium-weight wines but with the lovely savoury character of the best burgundy.

In the line of famous vineyards which occupy what the Burgundians call 'the kidney of the slope' above Beaune, a large proportion belongs to the city's négociants: Drouhin, Jadot, Bouchard Pères et Fils, Chanson, Patriarche among

them. The late Maurice Drouhin was the most recent of the centuries-old list of donors to the Hospices de Beaune. His firm's part of the Clos des Mouches is now famous; it makes a rare white Beaune there as well as a superb red one. A part of Grèves, belonging to Bouchard Père et Fils, is known as the Vigne de l'Enfant Jésus, and makes another marvellous wine. No Beaune is a Grand Cru; partly, it is said, because of the sustained high standard of so much land here. Beaune is gentle wine, lasting well but not demanding to be kept ten years or more, like a Romanée or a Chambertin.

After Beaune the road crosses a flat plain and the hills and vineyards retreat. Ahead looms the prow of Corton, the one isolated hill of the whole Côte d'Or, with a dark cap of woods. Corton breaks the spell which prevents the Côte de Beaune from having a red Grand Cru. Its massive smooth slide of hill, vineyard to the top, presents faces to east, south and west; all excellent. Indeed it has not one but two Grand Cru appellations; for white wine and red, covering a large part of the hill. The white, Corton-Charlemagne, is grown on the upper slopes, where debris from the limestone top is washed down, whitening the brown marly soil.

The red, Le Corton, is grown in a broad band all round. The map names are misleading; they record the original sites of Corton and Corton-Charlemagne rather than the present appellations. The appellations cover a much wider area; the narrow strip labelled Corton is of little account, most red Corton comes from Renardes, Clos du Roi, Bressandes and the rest. Similarly the part marked Corton-Charlemagne grows both white wine (above) and red Corton (below). There is a slight Alice in Wonderland air about the legalities, but none whatsoever about the wine; both red and white, forceful, lingering, memorable wines, are among Burgundy's very best.

The most celebrated grower of Corton is Louis Latour, whose fine press-house, known as Château Grancey, stands in an old quarry in Les Perrières. Aloxe-Corton is the appellation of the lesser wines (red or white) grown below the hill, still often excellent.

If Savigny and Pernand are slightly in the background here it is only because the foreground is so imposing. The best growers of both make wines almost up to the Beaune standard. Part of Pernand has the appellations Corton and Corton-Charlemagne.

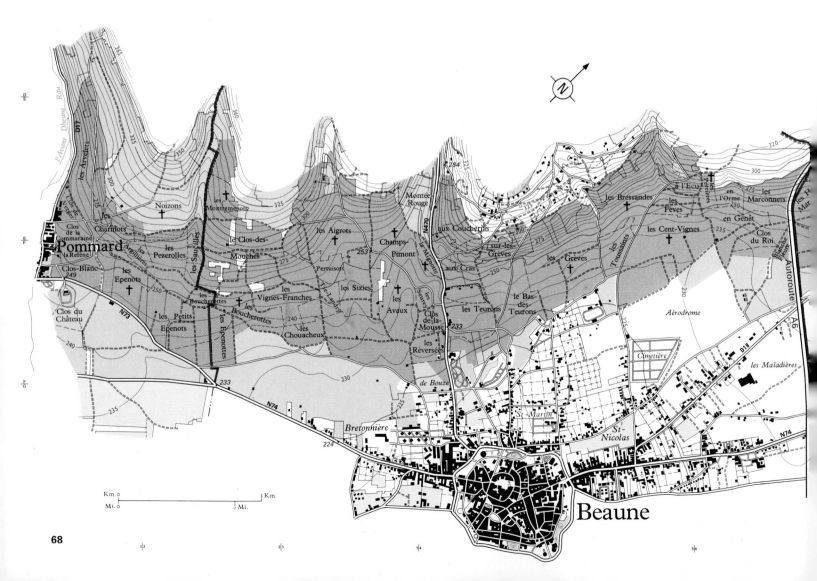

The hill of Corton from the south-east; left is the valley of Pernand-Vergelesses; centre right the village of Aloxe-Corton. High up under the woods Corton-Charlemagne is grown; lower on the right red Corton

Average price a cask (228 litres) at the 1976 Hospices de Beaune auction			
Commune	Vineyard	Cuvée	francs
Aloxe-Corton	Corton-Charlemagne (white)	François de Salins	15,100
Aloxe-Corton	Renardes & Bressandes	Charlotte Dumay	12,600
Aloxe-Corton	Bressandes & Clos du Roi	Docteur Peste	12,600
Beaune	Avaux	Clos des Avaux	11,200
Beaune	Grèves & Aigrots	Hugues & Louis Bétault	9,100
Beaune	Bressandes & Mignotte	Brunet	9,100
Beaune	Bressandes & Mignotte	Dames Hospitalières	10,100
Beaune	Avaux, Boucherottes, Champs-Pimont & Grèves	Maurice Drouhin	8,700
Beaune	Cent-Vignes & Grèves	Nicolas Rolin	12,600
Beaune	Cent-Vignes & Montremenots	Rousseau-Deslandes	10,000
Beaune	Bressandes & Champs-Pimont	Guigone de Salins	11,000
Pernand-Vergelesses	Basses Vergelesses	Rameau-Lamarosse	7,800
Savigny-les-Baune	Vergelesses & Gravains	Fouquerend	9,500
	Vergelesses & Gravains	Forneret	9,100
	Marconnets	Arthur Girard	9,000

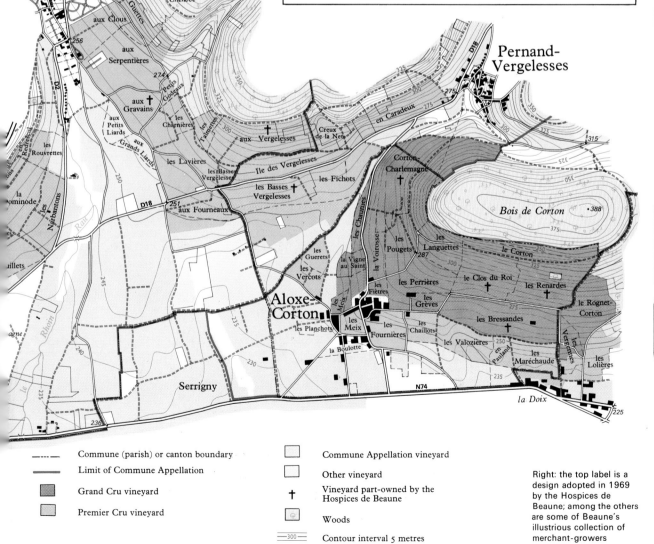

Right: the top label is a design adopted in 1969 by the Hospices de Beaune; among the others are some of Beaune's illustrious collection of merchant-growers

Commune (parish) or canton boundary

Limit of Commune Appellation

Grand Cru vineyard

Premier Cru vineyard

Commune Appellation vineyard

Other vineyard

✝ Vineyard part-owned by the Hospices de Beaune

Woods

300 Contour interval 5 metres

The Côte de Nuits: Nuits-St-Georges

The Confrérie des Chevaliers du Tastevin is Burgundy's wine fraternity and the most famous of its kind in the world. It was founded in 1933 and meets regularly for banquets with 600 guests, ceremonial (bottom right) and songs from a choir of growers (left above), the Cadets de Bourgogne. Its headquarters is the old château in the Clos de Vougeot (bottom left); there are branches in many countries and members among wine men all over the world. The Confrérie's own 'Tastevinage' label (detail above) may be used by wines which have been tasted and approved by a special committee

MORE 'stuffing', longer life, deeper colour are the signs of a Côte de Nuits wine compared with a Volnay or Beaune. Very little white is made; what there is shares the qualities of the red.

The line of Premiers Crus, wriggling its way along the hill, is threaded with clutches of Grands Crus. These are the wines which express with most intensity the inimitable sappy richness of the Pinot Noir. The line follows the outcrop of marlstone below the hard limestone hilltop, but it is where the soil has a mixture of silt and scree over the marl that the quality reaches peaks. Happily this corresponds time and again with the best shelter and most sun.

The wines of Prémeaux (the southernmost commune) go to market under the name Nuits-St-Georges. The two communes between them have over 900 acres of vines. The quality is very high and consistent: they are big strong wines, almost approaching the style of Chambertin at their best. They age well, have a particularly marked scent, and altogether deserve better than their reputation, which has suffered from 'la grande cuisine' of the blending vats. Les St-Georges is one of the best climats of the Côte; its neighbours Vaucrains, Cailles, Porets and Pruliers are comparable.

Nuits, a one-restaurant town, unlike bustling Beaune, but it is the headquarters of a number of négociants, some of whom make sparkling

Left: Nuits-St-Georges has a Hospices like a smaller version of the Hospices de Beaune; Château Gris is not strictly a Grand Cru, as it says, but the excellent domaine of a shipper, Lupé-Cholet. Among the others are growers of some of the world's greatest red wines

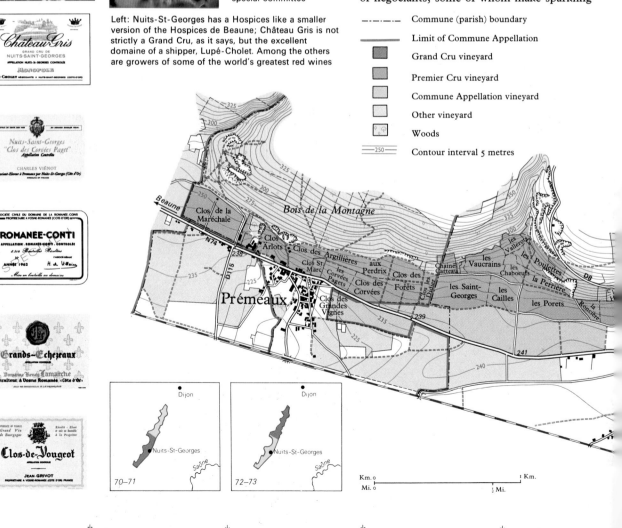

- -·-·-·- Commune (parish) boundary
- ——— Limit of Commune Appellation
- Grand Cru vineyard
- Premier Cru vineyard
- Commune Appellation vineyard
- Other vineyard
- Woods
- —250— Contour interval 5 metres

Looking straight up the hill from the track above Romanée-St-Vivant; in the foreground Romanée-Conti with its stony red earth; beyond it La Romanée. This soil gives France's most perfumed, satiny, expensive wine

burgundy out of the year's unsuccessful wine.

Vosne-Romanée is a modest little village. There is nothing to suggest that the world's most expensive wine lies beneath your feet. It stands below a long incline of reddish earth, looking up severely trimmed rows of vines, each ending with a stout post and a taut guy.

Nearest the village is Romanée-St-Vivant. The soil is deep, rich in clay and lime. The mid-slope is Romanée-Conti; poorer, shallower soil. Higher up, La Romanée tilts steeper; it seems drier and less clayey. On the right the big vine-yard of Le Richebourg curves round to face east-north-east. Up the left flank runs the nar-row strip of La Grande Rue, and beside it the long slope of La Tâche. All are among the most highly prized of all burgundies. Romanée-Conti, La Tâche, Richebourg and Romanée-St-Vivant are all owned or managed wholly or in part by the Domaine de la Romanée-Conti. For the finesse, the velvety warmth combined with a suggestion of spice, the almost oriental opulence of their wines the market will seem-ingly stand any price. Romanée-Conti is con-sidered the most perfect, but the whole group has a family likeness.

Clearly one can look among their neighbours for wines of similar character at less stupendous prices. All the other named vineyards of Vosne-Romanée are superb. One of the textbooks on

Burgundy remarks drily: 'There are no common wines in Vosne.'

The big (79 acres) climat of Echézeaux and the smaller Grands Echézeaux are really in the commune of Flagey, a village over the railway, to the south, but they can use the name Vosne-Romanée for their wine if it does not reach the statutory standards for a Grand Cru. Some very fine growers have property here, and make beautiful, delicate, so-called 'lacy' wines. They are often a bargain—people say because the name looks hard to pronounce. Grands Ech-zeaux has perhaps more regularity, more of the lingering intensity which marks the very great burgundies; certainly higher prices.

One high stone wall surrounds the 125 acres of the Clos de Vougeot; the sure sign of a monastic vineyard. Today it is so subdivided that it is anything but a reliable label on a bottle. But it is the climat *as a whole* which is a Grand Cru. The monks used to blend wine of top, middle and sometimes bottom to make what we must believe was one of the best burgundies of all . . . and one of the most consistent, since in dry years the wine from lower down would have an advantage, in wet years the top slopes. There are wines from near the top—La Perrière in particular (just outside the Clos)—which can be as great as Musigny. The name of the grower must be your guide.

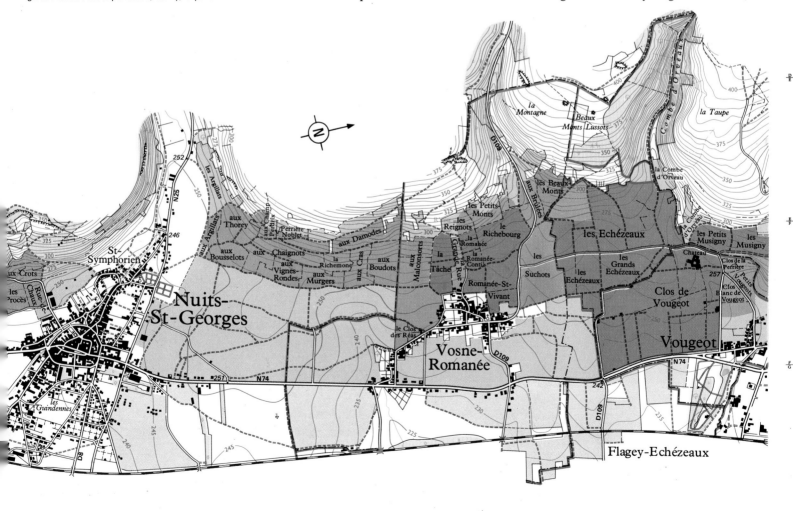

The Côte de Nuits: Gevrey-Chambertin

HERE, at the northern end of the Côte d'Or, the richest, longest-lasting red burgundies are made. Nature here adds rich soil to the perfect combination of shelter and exposure which the hills provide. The narrow marlstone outcrop, lightly overlaid with silt and scree, follows the lower slopes. From it Chambertin and the Grands Crus of Morey and Chambolle draw their power. For they are wines of body and strength, unyielding when they are young, but eventually offering more complexity and depth of flavour than any others.

Musigny, the first of the Grands Crus, stands apart, obviously related to the top of the Clos de Vougeot. There is only just room for it under the barren limestone crest. The slope is steep enough to mean the vignerons carrying the brown limy clay, heavy with pebbles, back up the hill when it collects at the bottom. This and the permeable limestone subsoil allow excellent drainage. Conditions are right for a wine with plenty of 'stuffing'.

The glory of Musigny is that it adds to its un-doubted power a lovely haunting delicacy of perfume; a uniquely sensuous savour. A great Musigny makes what is so well described as a 'peacock's tail' in your mouth, opening and be-coming more complex and seductive as you swallow it. It is not so strong as Chambertin, not so spicy as Romanée-Conti—but he must have been a great respecter of women who called it 'feminine'.

Les Bonnes-Mares, at the far side of the village, is the other Grand Cru of Chambolle-Musigny. It leads over into Morey-St-Denis, both geographically and gastronomically, for it starts as a slightly tougher wine than Musigny, and ages perhaps a little slower, but achieves a similar power and tenderness.

Les Amoureuses and Les Charmes—their beautiful names are perfectly expressive of their wine—are both among the best Premiers Crus of Burgundy. Any wine from Chambolle-Musigny, however, is likely to be very good.

The commune of Morey is overshadowed in renown by two of its Grands Crus. Clos de la Roche, with little Clos St-Denis (which gave its name to the village), like Chambertin are wines of great staying-power, strength and solidity, fed by rich soil. Clos de Tart and the Clos des Lambrays (which is the proprietor's name for the Premier Cru Les Larreys) have more in common with Bonnes-Mares. Clos de Tart, the monopole of the house of Mom-messin, has been making a remarkable light wine recently; the Domaine Dujac makes Moreys of the old style—rich and deep. Wines to keep.

In Morey the vineyards climb the hill, find-ing soil higher up than anywhere else in this area. Les Monts-Luisants, on stonier ground, makes a lighter wine than Clos de la Roche.

Gevrey-Chambertin has an amazing amount of good land. The ideal vineyard soil stretches farther out from the hill than elsewhere, so that even land beyond the main road has the appellation Gevrey-Chambertin, rather than plain Bourgogne. Its two greatest vine-yards, Chambertin and Clos de Bèze, lie under the woods on a mere gentle slope. They were acknowledged Grands Crus at a time when the citizens of Gevrey were quarrelling with the worthies of Beaune who were handing out the honours. Otherwise it is probable that the con-stellation of vineyards—Mazis, Latricières and the rest—around them would have been Grands Crus in their own right as well. Instead they have an in-between status, with the right to add -Chambertin after their names, but not (like Clos de Bèze) before. French wine law some-times becomes more subtle than theology.

— · — · —	Commune (parish) boundary
———	Limit of Commune Appellation
▨	Grand Cru vineyard
▨	Premier Cru vineyard
▢	Commune Appellation vineyard
▢	Other vineyard
▢	Woods
═250═	Contour interval 5 metres

The commune has another slope with a very good, though rather different, exposure. Here Clos St-Jacques and Les Véroilles are arguably Grands Crus in everything but name.

There are more individual vineyards known all over the world in this village than in any other in Burgundy. To many people the forceful rich wine they make *is* burgundy. Hilaire Belloc told a story about his youth, and ended dreamily: 'I forget the name of the place; I forget the name of the girl; but the wine . . . was Chambertin.'

The slopes to the north used to be known as the Côte de Dijon, and until the last century were considered among the best. But their growers were tempted to use their rich land for bulk wine for the city and planted the 'disloyal plant', the Gamay. Brochon became known as a 'well of wine' from the quantities it made. Today it has no appellation of its own: its southern edge is included in Gevrey-Chambertin; the rest has only the right to the name Côte de Nuits-Villages.

Fixin, however, has a tradition of quality. La Perrière at one time made wine 'comparable to Chambertin'. But Les Hervelets is the best-known vineyard there today.

Above: the end of the year at the end of the Côtes. A grower of Fixin burns the prunings of his vines. North of here is the Côte de Dijon, once famous but now known only for the excellent pale rosé of Marsannay

Below: Gevrey Chambertin is a big commune with over 1,000 acres of vines, one-fifth of which are Grands Crus. Many famous growers have holdings here. Others include Damoy, Ponsot, Mommessin, Pernot, Camus

The Chalonnais

As DEMAND and prices play leapfrog in the most famous wine areas of the world, the names of what used to be considered lesser regions inevitably come to the fore. The hills south of Chagny are in many ways a continuation of the Côte de Beaune, though the regular ridge is replaced here by a jumble of hillocks on which vineyards appear among orchards and crops. They take the name of the Côte Chalonnaise from the town of Chalon-sur-Saône which lies to the east.

The best of the Chalonnais wines merit comparing with standard or better, Côte de Beaune wines. Recently the names of Mercurey (for red wine) and Montagny (for white) have been heard more and more.

The map shows the east-and-south-facing slopes of the Côte Chalonnaise, with the four major communes which have appellations: Rully, Mercurey, Givry and Montagny, and some of their better-known vineyards—though at the moment only a few proprietors' wines carry vineyard names.

Bouzeron (top of map) makes sound red and a well-known Aligoté white under the simple appellation Bourgogne. Rully has a growing reputation for its light and fragrant white wine, which almost all used to be made into sparkling burgundy. Acidity can be a problem, as this implies.

Mercurey is already famous for its red wines, which are not unlike light-weight Pommards, best drunk quite young: they give of their best between about three and perhaps six or seven years. St-Martin-sous-Montaigu and the other little hamlets to the south share the appellation.

Givry becomes better and better known, principally for red wine, helped by the fact that an important grower of the Côte de Beaune, Baron Thénard, has vineyards and his cellars there.

And finally Montagny (which includes Buxy) makes white wine approaching a good Mâconvillages, but often surpassing it in price.

Km.0 ——— 1 ——— 2 ——— 3 ——— 4 ——— 5 Km.
Mi.0 ——— 1 ——— 2 ——— 3 Mi.

------- Canton boundary
------- Commune (parish) boundary
▨ Vineyards
▨ Woods
——400—— Contour interval 20 metres

Far right: Both the red and white growths of the Côte Chalonnaise, can be good value for money; the reds like scaled-down Côte de Beaune wines, the whites closer to their Mâcon neighbours to the south

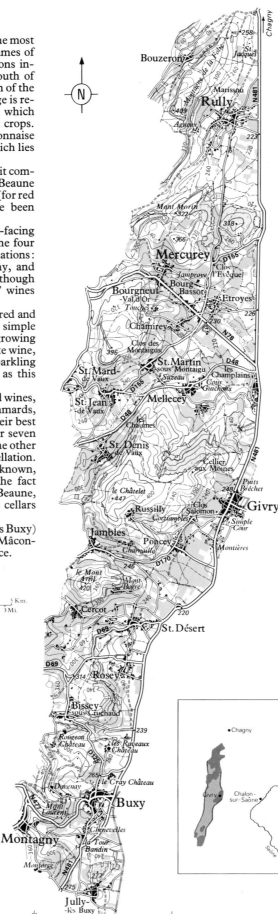

Above: a cool tank of trout gleams in the courtyard of a wine-grower's house. The light, often slightly sharp white wines of the Côte Chalonnaise are ideal for drinking with delicate fish dishes

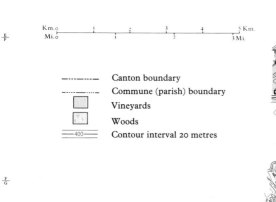

The Mâconnais

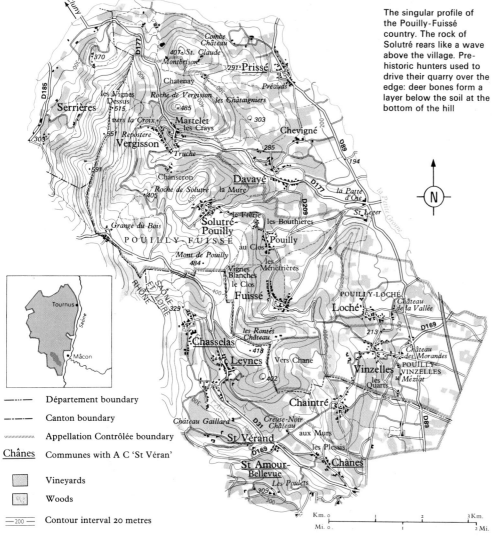

The singular profile of the Pouilly-Fuissé country. The rock of Solutré rears like a wave above the village. Prehistoric hunters used to drive their quarry over the edge: deer bones form a layer below the soil at the bottom of the hill

THE TOWN of Mâcon on the Saône, 35 miles south of Chalon, gives its name to a wide area which in general has neither the distinction of its neighbour to the north nor of Beaujolais to the south. Mâcon without qualification is good plain wine, the red only just burgundian in character, the white definitely burgundy, but without frills.

On the Beaujolais border, however, there is a pocket of white-wine growing with distinction of a different order. The Pouilly-Fuissé district is a sudden tempest of wave-shaped limestone hills, rich in the alkaline clay the Chardonnay grape loves. The map shows how the four villages of Pouilly-Fuissé—Vergisson, Solutré-Pouilly, Fuissé and Chaintré—shelter on the lower slopes.

Good Pouilly-Fuissé is a pale, refreshing, often delicate wine for a Chardonnay, without the scent of a Meursault or the style of a Chablis Grand Cru, but in its gentle way exactly what one is looking for in white burgundy, and at its best memorable.

Pouilly-Vinzelles and Pouilly-Loché are comparable, but a shade cheaper, not having the right to call themselves -Fuissé. A new appellation, St-Véran, applies to similar white wines from a handful of villages north and south of Pouilly-Fuissé. The co-operative of one of these, Prissé, has made specially good white wine of late.

Chardonnay elsewhere in the Mâconnais is often sold as what Californians would call a 'varietal'—called Pinot Chardonnay Mâcon, to distinguish it from the common white wine from the Aligoté grape. It is often very good value for everyday use.

One other part of the Mâconnais, not mapped here, must be mentioned: the village of Viré, north of Mâcon.

The growers' co-operative makes excellent white wine, and the Clos du Chapitre in particular has a long reputation of competent wine-making, as well as a lucky patch of ground.

The fresh and gentle white wines of Pouilly-Fuissé are the Mâconnais' best. The village of Viré is also famous for white Mâcon. Ordinary Mâcon Blanc from a famous shipper is good everyday wine

————— Département boundary

— - — Canton boundary

∿∿∿∿ Appellation Contrôlée boundary

Chânes Communes with A C 'St Véran'

▨ Vineyards

▨ Woods

═ 200 ═ Contour interval 20 metres

Beaujolais

Above: young Gamay vines are staked along a track leading to the village of Juliénas
Left: the lower hills sloping to south and east are almost unbroken vineyard. The Beaujolais mountains to the west, covered with pine and chestnut, rise to 3,000 feet. Their few primitive villages were immortalized in the story of Clochemerle

IF ONE single name stands for uncomplicated and satisfying red wine it is Beaujolais. The world has adopted it as a model of something deep red, fruity, lightish in body, fairly alcoholic and all too easy to drink. Merchants have never been very fussy about where it really comes from. The area is relatively big and very productive: if samples match up to a reasonable standard few questions are asked.

The Beaujolais region covers a 45-mile-long stretch of mainly granite hills south of Mâcon in south Burgundy. Most of its 60-odd villages remain obscure: the highest their wine can aspire to is the extra degree of alcohol to qualify as Beaujolais Supérieur. From this deep well about 15 million gallons of wine a year are drawn—to be drunk, in the main, before the next vintage.

The northern part of the region, however, has different standards. A group of 35 villages on steep foothills leading up to the Beaujolais mountains are classified as Beaujolais-Villages. They are expected to give wine with a shade more strength, and with the extra strength an extra touch of character and style.

Nine of the villages (the larger map) use their own names and are expected to show distinct characteristics of their own. These are the Grands Crus. The group lies just south of the Mâconnais, adjacent to Pouilly-Fuissé. Part of the best Beaujolais cru of all, in fact, Moulin-à-Vent, is actually in the Mâconnais, though to simplify things it is all regarded as Beaujolais.

The Grands Crus villages lie on spurs, outlying knolls and on the Beaujolais mountains themselves. This is much more seriously hilly country than the Côte d'Or. The road climbs and twists and climbs until vines and farms are left behind, woods thicken and upland streams tumble by. Looking behind and below, the broad band of vineyards dwindles and an immense view of the plain of the Saône expands: in clear weather Mont Blanc hangs in the far distance to the east.

The country is owned mostly by small farmers who sell their wine through négociants in Mâcon and Villefranche and Lyon, but there are a few big estates. Their wine is the grandest of Beaujolais and is often nowadays bottled on the property; but this does not change its basic nature of being a delicious easy-going drink rather than a Grand Vin.

Lightest and most luscious of all is Fleurie, with its neighbour Chiroubles. Good young Fleurie seems to epitomize the Beaujolais style: the scent is strong, the wine fruity and silky, brilliantly translucent, a joy to swallow.

'Best' in the most serious sense is Moulin-à-Vent, which now includes some of Chénas and Romanèche-Thorins. In good years this wine has darker colour, more strength and initial toughness and improves with age: not the thing Beaujolais is known for nowadays. At ten years the best Moulin-à-Vent can achieve the stature of a great red burgundy.

Local experts will distinguish between all the other crus, telling you that Morgon lasts for longer, Juliénas has more substance and vigour, St-Amour is lighter, Brouilly is grapy and rich but Côte de Brouilly grapier and richer. It would be wrong to exaggerate the differences, however: what they have in common is more important; the beautiful inviting quality given by the Gamay.

This vine which is virtually outlawed from the Côte d'Or is in its element on the granite-derived soil of Beaujolais. Its plants are almost like people, leading independent lives: after ten years they are no longer trained, but merely tied up in summer with an osier to stand free. A Gamay vine will live as long as a man.

Beaujolais is traditionally made by carbonic maceration (see page 30). The low-key fermentation preserves the characteristic flavour of fruit. But the method is slow, and the fashion today is to drink Beaujolais as young as possible, the *vin de l'année* being rushed to the eager world a few weeks after the harvest. The idea of the new wine is romantic, but wine for this purpose is never the best the country can produce. It is very quickly made, mere *vin rosé* with a purple tinge and a great surging sappy smell. The best Beaujolais has much more to it than this; but no wine of real quality was ever made overnight: it takes time in bottle as well as barrel to achieve the miracle.

The best Beaujolais is
known by the name of its
commune, and often of its
vineyard or grower's
property as well. The
Hospices de Beaujeu is a
local hospital owning
vineyards. A little dry
white Beaujolais is made
(last label)

Km. 0   1   2   3 Km.
Mi. 0   1   2 Mi.

–·–·–   Département boundary
–··–··–   Canton boundary
–––––   Commune (parish) boundary
☐   Limits of Grands Crus
☐   Vineyards
☐   Woods
200   Contour interval 20 metres

Chablis

SLEEPY little Chablis on its reedy river in the valley does not look the part of the world's most famous wine town. There is not a hoarding, not an illumination, not a whisper of the fact that round the world, every day, as much wine is drunk under its name as it often produces in a whole harvest.

While every wine-producing country of the new world, and several of the old, has appropriated the name for any dry (or even sweet) white (or even pink) wine, real Chablis continues to be produced in limited quantities, with real distinction. So distinctive is it, in fact, that it is not to everybody's taste.

Chablis sends one rummaging for descriptive phrases even more desperately than most wines. There is something there one can so nearly put a finger on. It is hard but not harsh, reminds one of stones and minerals, but at the same time of green hay; actually, when it is young it looks green, which many wines are supposed to. Grand Cru Chablis tastes important, strong, almost immortal. And indeed it does last a remarkably long time; a strange and delicious sort of sour taste enters into it at ten years or so, and its golden green eye flashes meaningfully.

Grand Cru Chablis comes only from the seven small vineyards on the hill across the river from the town. As the map shows, it faces south, giving a slight advantage in sunlight, and hence in strength, besides what the chalky soil of this particular slope has to offer.

There used to be more Premiers Crus, but the names of the better-known have recently been granted to their neighbours as well. Chief ones now are Monts de Milieu, Montée de Tonnerre, Fourchaume, Vaillons, Montmains, Mélinots, Côte de Léchet, Beauroy, Vaucoupin, Vosgros, Vaulorent and Les Fourneaux. A Premier Cru Chablis will be at least half a degree of alcohol weaker than a Grand Cru, and correspondingly less impressive and intense in scent and flavour. None the less it will be a very good wine indeed—all the better if it comes from one of the vineyards designated Premier Cru on the same (north) bank of the river as the Grands.

Chablis, without a vineyard name, is made in about the same quantity as Chablis Premier Cru, from less favoured slopes. Again it is a step down in strength and character.

And finally there is Petit Chablis, rarely exported, which is the relatively undistinguished produce of vineyards on unsuitable soils.

The scourge of the Chablis vineyards has always been frost. So prone were even the Grand Cru slopes to have their crop decimated in late spring that only a decade ago growers were going out of business, and prices were at shortage level: Grands Crus fetched the same as Corton-Charlemagne or Montrachet.

Since the mid-'60s frost-prevention (first by oil-stoves, now increasingly by sprinklers) has saved the day. Crop loss is rare, growers have replanted, enormously increasing the vineyard area and steady yields have stabilized prices remarkably. Today Grand Cru Chablis is little more than half the price of its old rivals. Yet it remains one of the classics, with all the style and character which have made it the world's most-imitated wine.

Above: in the cellars of a Chablis grower, M Simonet, a tasting-glass of wine catches the light
Above left: the Chablis landscape in spring. The vines are beginning to sprout, vulnerable to late frost. A flat vineyard like that on the left will make Chablis but not one of the Grands Crus
Above right: tools in a cooperage, for refitting barrels—one of the recurring tasks of growers

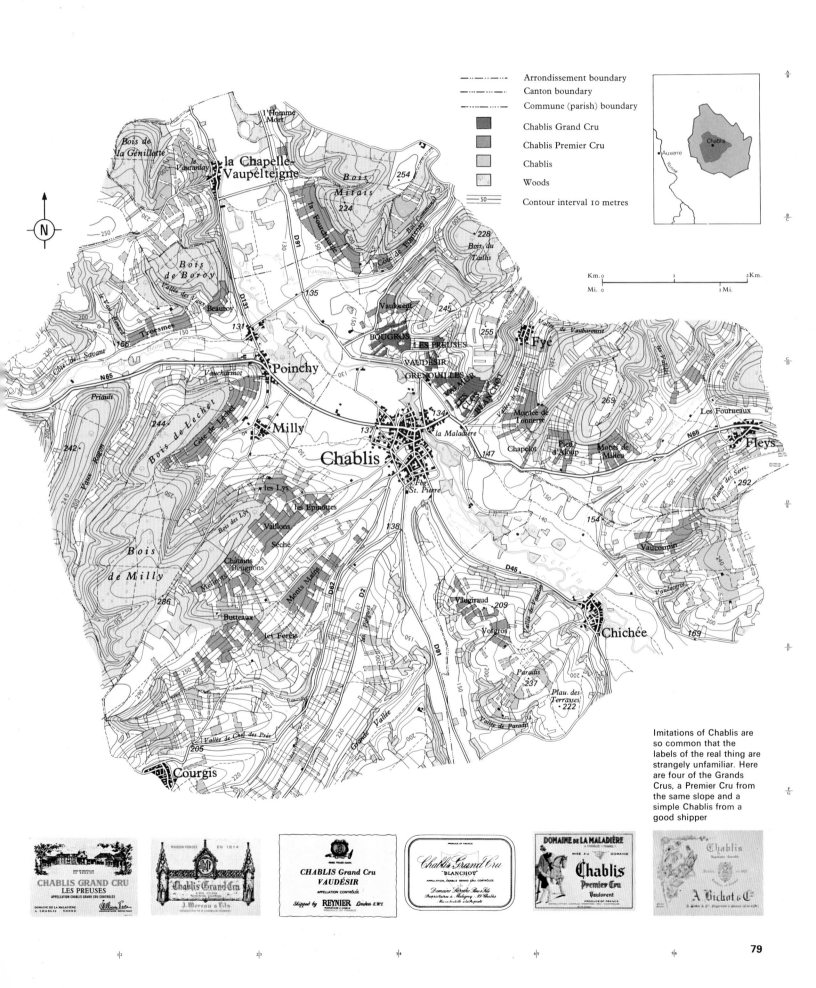

la Chapelle-
Vaupelteigne

l'Homme
Mort

Bois de
la Génillotte

le
Vaurinlay

Bois
Mitais

254

224

Côte de FONTENAY

228

Bois du
Taillis

Bois
de Boroy

Vallée des Vaux

135

Beauroy

131

Vaulorent

245

Troesmes

156

150

BOUGROS

255

Fyé

Vallée de Vauxarousse

LES PREUSES

Côte de Savant

Priault

N65

Vaucharmot

Poinchy

VAUDÉSIR
GRENOUILLES

269

Montée de
Tonnerre

Les Fourneaux

BLANCHOT

244

Bois de Léchet

Côte de Léchet

Milly

137

134

la Maladière

147

Chapelot

Pied
d'Aloup

Monts de
Milieu

N65

Fleys

242

Vaux Ragon

Chablis

les Lys

Fbg
St. Pierre

les Epinottes

138

154

292

Vaillons

Vaucoupin

Seché

Bois
de Milly

Chatains
Beugnons

Mélinots

286

Butteaux

les Foréts

Monts Mains

D62

D2

Vaugiraud

209

D45

Serein

Vaudésorce

Vaugros

Chichée

169

Paradis
237

Plau. des
Terrasses
222

Vallée de Paradis

Vallée de Chef des Prés

205

Grande Vallée

Courgis

220

Arrondissement boundary
Canton boundary
Commune (parish) boundary
Chablis Grand Cru
Chablis Premier Cru
Chablis
Woods
50
Contour interval 10 metres

Auxerre

Chablis

Yonne

Km. 0   1   2 Km.
Mi. 0   1 Mi.

Imitations of Chablis are
so common that the
labels of the real thing are
strangely unfamiliar. Here
are four of the Grands
Crus, a Premier Cru from
the same slope and a
simple Chablis from a
good shipper

CHABLIS GRAND CRU
LES PREUSES
APPELLATION CHABLIS GRAND CRU CONTRÔLÉE
DOMAINE DE LA MALADIÈRE
A CHABLIS · YONNE

MAISON FONDÉE EN 1814
Chablis Grand Cru
LES CLOS
J. Moreau & Fils
NÉGOCIANTS À CHABLIS · YONNE

CHABLIS Grand Cru
VAUDÉSIR
APPELLATION CONTRÔLÉE
Shipped by REYNIER London S.W.1
PRODUCE OF FRANCE

PRODUCE OF FRANCE
Chablis Grand Cru
"BLANCHOT"
APPELLATION CHABLIS GRAND CRU CONTRÔLÉE
Domaine Laroche Père & Fils
Propriétaires à Maligny · 89 Chablis
Mise en bouteille à la Propriété

DOMAINE DE LA MALADIÈRE
MISE AU DOMAINE
Chablis
Premier Cru
Vaulorent
PRODUCE OF FRANCE

Chablis
A. Bichot & Cie

79

Bordeaux

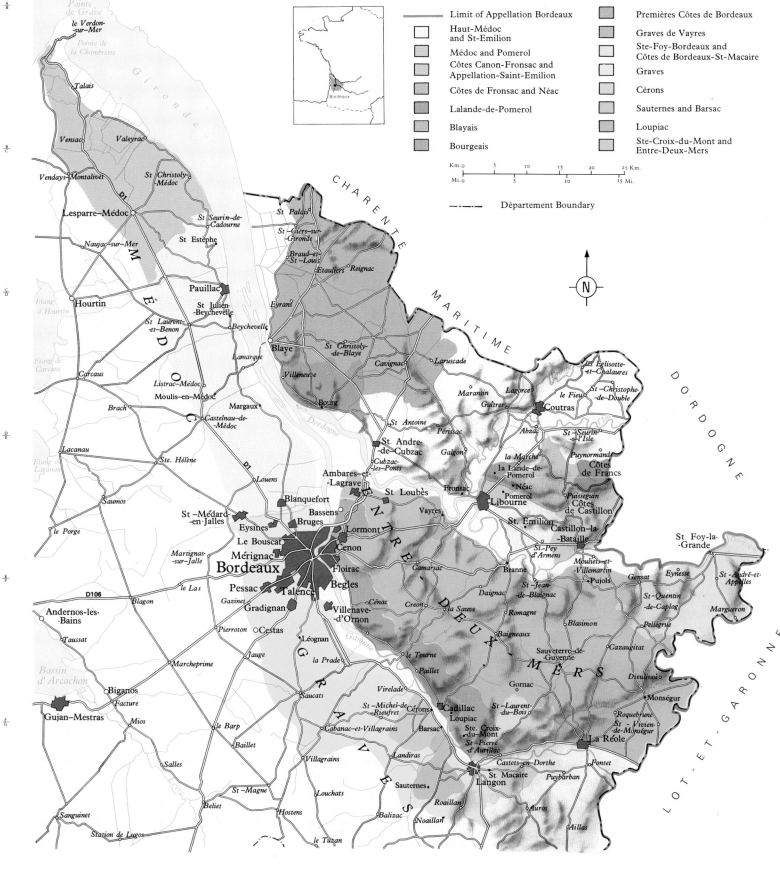

Legend:

- Limit of Appellation Bordeaux
- Haut-Médoc and St-Emilion
- Médoc and Pomerol
- Côtes Canon-Fronsac and Appellation-Saint-Emilion
- Côtes de Fronsac and Néac
- Lalande-de-Pomerol
- Blayais
- Bourgeais
- Premières Côtes de Bordeaux
- Graves de Vayres
- Ste-Foy-Bordeaux and Côtes de Bordeaux-St-Macaire
- Graves
- Cérons
- Sauternes and Barsac
- Loupiac
- Ste-Croix-du-Mont and Entre-Deux-Mers

Km.0   5   10   15   20   25 Km.
Mi.0   5   10   15 Mi.

—·—·— Département Boundary

IF THE NAME of Burgundy suggests richness and plenty, Bordeaux has more than a hint of elegance about it. In place of the plump prelate who seems to symbolize Burgundy, Bordeaux calls to mind a distinguished figure in a frock-coat. Picture him tasting pale red wine from a crystal glass. He has one thumb tucked into his waistcoat, while through the open door beyond him there is a glimpse of a turreted house, insubstantial in the pearly seaside light. He enters his moderate enthusiasms in a leather pocket-book, observing the progress of beauty across his palate like moves in a game of chess.

Aspects of Bordeaux appeal to the aesthete, as Burgundy appeals to the sensualist. One is the nature of the wine: at its best indescribably delicate in nuance and complexity. Another is the sheer intellectual challenge of so many estates in so many regions and sub-regions that no one has mastered them all.

Bordeaux is the largest fine-wine district on earth. The whole Department of the Gironde, where the waters of the Dordogne and the Garonne unite to flow into the Bay of Biscay, is dedicated to wine-growing. All its wine is Bordeaux. Its production dwarfs that of Burgundy. In 1975 it produced 92,475,416 gallons.

The total is equally divided between red wines and white. The great red wine areas lie to the north: the Médoc; the country immediately south of the city of Bordeaux; the country along the north bank of the Dordogne and facing the Médoc across the Gironde. The country between the two rivers is called Entre-Deux-Mers. Most of its wine is white, except for a fringe of villages which make red wine as well, facing Bordeaux across the Garonne. Premières Côtes de Bordeaux is the name given to their wines. All the bottom third of the map is white-wine country.

But of the white wine of this large area a relatively small proportion is notably fine. Bordeaux's great glories are its range of good to superlative red wines, and the small production of very sweet golden wine of Sauternes.

Compared with Burgundy the system of appellations in Bordeaux is simple. The map opposite shows them all. Within them it is the wine estates or châteaux which look after their own identification problem. On the other hand there is a form of classification by quality built into the system in Burgundy which is missing in Bordeaux. In its place here there are a variety of local classifications, unfortunately without a common standard.

By far the most famous of these is the classification of the châteaux of the Médoc—and one or two others—which was finalized in 1855, based on the prices the wines had fetched over the previous hundred years or more. Its first, second, third, fourth and fifth 'growths', to which were added Crus Exceptionnels, Crus Bourgeois Supérieurs, Crus Bourgeois and later Crus Artisans and Crus Paysans, are the most ambitious grading of the products of the soil ever attempted.

The overriding importance of situation in deciding quality is proved by the accuracy of the old list today. Where present standards depart from it there is usually an explanation: there was a particularly industrious proprietor

Handsome 18th-century architecture and a sensuous approach to the table are Bordeaux in a nutshell. The Allées de Tourny as it was reflected in a window of the former restaurant and food store, Dubern

in 1855, and a lazy one now . . . or vice versa.

None the less more weight is placed today on whether a château is first or fifth growth than the system really justifies. The first growths regularly fetch three times the price of the second growths . . . without necessarily being any better. The relative qualities of different châteaux really need expressing in a more subtle way than by suggesting that one is always 'better' than another. The system adopted on the maps which follow is to distinguish between classed growths and Crus Bourgeois. Many other minor growths are also marked.

Château is the word for a wine estate in Bordeaux. Its overtones of castle or stately home are rarely justified. In most cases the biggest building at the château is the *chai*—the long sheds,

often half underground, where the wine is stored—attached to the *cuvier* where it is made. (A Bordeaux château and its working routine is anatomized on pages 36–37.)

The vineyards of the château sometimes surround it in a neat plot. More often they are scattered and intermingled with their neighbours. They can produce annually anything from eight to 800 barrels of wine, each holding 300 bottles. The best vineyards make a maximum of 4,000 litres from each hectare of vines, the less good ones rather more. A hectare can have anything from 6,500 to 10,000 vines.

The *maître de chai* is an important figure at the château. At little properties it is the owner himself, at big ones an old retainer. It is he who welcomes visitors, and lets them taste the new wine, cold and dark and unpalatable, from the casks in his care. Be knowing rather than enthusiastic; the wine will not be ready to drink for two years after it has been bottled at the very least—and maybe not for twenty.

Bordeaux/the Quality Factor

THE ADVANTAGES of the Bordeaux region for wine-growing can be listed quite simply. Its position near the sea and threaded with rivers gives it a moderate and stable climate. Forests on the ocean side protect it from strong salt winds and reduce rainfall. The bed-rock is well-furnished with minerals, yet the topsoil in general is quite poor, and often very deep.

The most earnest studies have been made to decide what it is that makes one piece of land superior to its neighbour. They all start by defining exactly the geological, pedological (i.e. soil) and climatological set-up for a very fine vineyard . . . and then tend to find that exactly the same considerations seem to apply next door, where the wine is not and never has been half so good.

In Bordeaux, however, there are more variables to help explain the differences. Instead of one constant grape variety, like the Pinot Noir for all red wine on the Côte de Nuits, all Bor-

deaux is made from a mixture of three or four varieties; the proportions depending on the taste of the proprietor. To jump to the conclusion that, let us say, the soil of Château Lafite gives lighter wine than that of Château Latour would be rash, unless you have taken into account that Lafite grows a good deal of the Merlot grape while Latour is nearly all Cabernet Sauvignon . . . and Merlot wine is lighter.

Another factor is the status of the vineyard. Success breeds success, meaning more money to spend on expensive care of the land. Differences which were originally marginal can therefore be increased over the years.

Furthermore the soil of the Médoc, to speak of only part of Bordeaux, is said to 'change at every step'. No one has ever been able to isolate the wine made from a vine on one patch and compare it with that from two steps away. So nobody really knows what vines, on what kind of soil, give what kind of wine—except in the

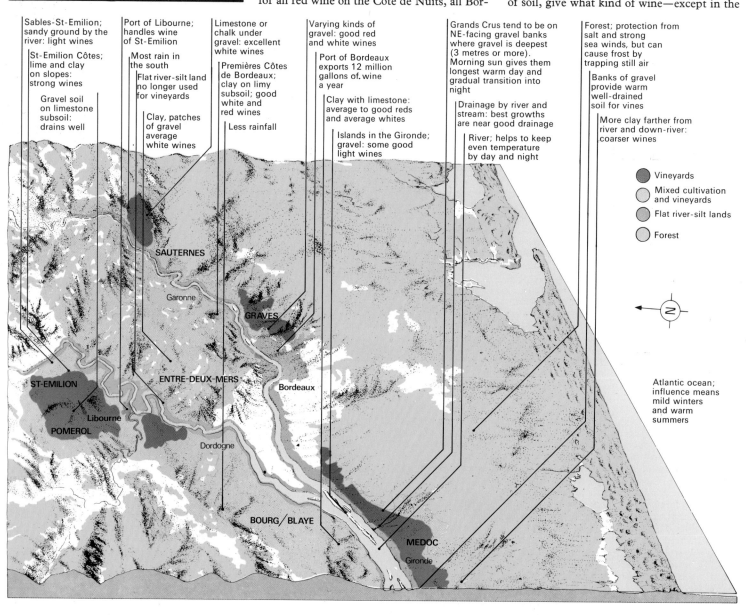

Sables-St-Emilion; sandy ground by the river: light wines

St-Emilion Côtes; lime and clay on slopes: strong wines

Gravel soil on limestone subsoil: drains well

Port of Libourne; handles wine of St-Emilion

Most rain in the south

Flat river-silt land no longer used for vineyards

Clay, patches of gravel average white wines

Limestone or chalk under gravel: excellent white wines

Premières Côtes de Bordeaux; clay on limy subsoil; good white and red wines

Less rainfall

Varying kinds of gravel: good red and white wines

Port of Bordeaux exports 12 million gallons of wine a year

Clay with limestone: average to good reds and average whites

Islands in the Gironde; gravel: some good light wines

Grands Crus tend to be on NE-facing gravel banks where gravel is deepest (3 metres or more). Morning sun gives them longest warm day and gradual transition into night

Drainage by river and stream: best growths are near good drainage

River; helps to keep even temperature by day and night

Forest; protection from salt and strong sea winds, but can cause frost by trapping still air

Banks of gravel provide warm well-drained soil for vines

More clay farther from river and down-river: coarser wines

- ● Vineyards
- ○ Mixed cultivation and vineyards
- ◑ Flat river-silt lands
- ◔ Forest

SAUTERNES

Garonne

GRAVES

ST-EMILION

ENTRE-DEUX-MERS

Bordeaux

Libourne

POMEROL

Dordogne

BOURG/BLAYE

MEDOC

Gironde

Atlantic ocean; influence means mild winters and warm summers

most general terms, and even then with many reservations.

You would not expect this to prevent the University of Bordeaux from going on trying, however. The latest theory which finds wide support is that (contrary to traditional belief) geology is scarcely a factor at all in deciding quality, at least in Bordeaux. A vine will find all the nourishment it needs almost anywhere; but the poorer the soil the deeper and wider it will root. Hence the mysterious fact that poor soil is often good for wine. Give a vine rich soil, or spread generous helpings of manure round it, and its roots will stay near the top. But plant it in stony ground, give it only the bare necessities, and it will plunge metres deep to see what it can find. For the deeper the roots go, the more constant is their environment, and the less they are subject to floods on the one hand, drought on the other, and fluctuations of food supply from manuring or lack of manuring on

the surface. Then there can be a lake around it, or total drought can parch and crack the ground, and the vine will feed normally. Provided only that the subsoil is well drained, so that the roots do not drown.

Enlarging on this idea, Dr Gérard Seguin of the University of Bordeaux suggests that the nearer a vineyard is to an effective drain, the drier the subsoil will be and the deeper the roots will go. He suggests that the first growths are vineyards nearest the drainage channels, the second growths slightly farther from them, and so on. There has always been a saying that 'the vines should look at the river'. This theory explains it. It also explains why old vines give the best wine; their roots are deepest. The theory can be examined by studying the streams on the following maps in relation to the classed and other growths.

Hence, this theory continues, it is not the chemical composition of the soil, but its phy-

sical make-up which must be taken into account. Heavy clay or sand which drains badly is the worst for wine: gravel and larger stones are best. Add to this the way stones store heat on the surface, and prevent rapid evaporation of moisture from under them, and it is easy to see that they are the best guarantee of stable conditions of temperature and humidity that a vine can have.

In the Médoc it is the deep gravel beds of Margaux and St-Julien and Pauillac which drain best. As you go north the proportion of clay increases, so that in St-Estèphe drainage is much less effective. This does not mean that all Margaux wines are first growth and all St-Estèphe fifth—though there are many more classed growths in Margaux—but it does account for higher acidity, more tannin, colour, and less scent in St-Estèphe wines. It is, after all, not only a question of quality but of the character of the wine.

Left: some of the factors affecting the varying qualities and character of Bordeaux wine are shown in this diagram of the river basin of the Gironde from the south-east. The Gironde is formed by the confluence of the rivers Dordogne (left) and the Garonne (right). Soil and subsoil have a bearing on the wine, but there is doubt about how important they are in determining its quality and character. Such factors as rainfall, and whether the sun reaches the vine in the morning or afternoon, and above all the rapid drainage of the ground, may play just as large a part.
The southern part of the area has most rainfall, the north least. White wine is grown in the south, both red and white in the centre, and more red than white in the north.
No positive link between the two facts can be proved, but it seems likely that the mists of the wetter area have been found helpful to white grapes over the years and have tended to cause rot in the red

The Language of the Label

Négociant A shipping house which often buys wine from the château a few months old and keeps it (usually in Bordeaux) until it is ready to ship or bottle. Among the most famous négociants are Calvet, Cruze, Eschenauer, Cordier, Kressmann, Moueix, Barton & Guestier, Ginestet
Château Estate
Récolte Vintage
Mis (or **Mise**) **en bouteilles au château** Bottled at the property where it is made
Grand Vin Simply 'great wine', without specific meaning
Cru Classé One of the first five official growths of the Médoc, also any classed growth of another district, however classified. The Médoc classifications are as follows—all refer to the classification of 1855:

Premier Cru First growth ⎫
Deuxième Cru Second growth ⎪ rarely
Troisième Cru Third growth ⎬ appear
Quatrième Cru Fourth growth ⎪ on labels
Cinquième Cru Fifth growth ⎭

Cru Exceptionnel In the Médoc, the second rank, below Cru Classé
Cru Bourgeois Supérieur The third rank
Cru Bourgeois The fourth rank—but often a very worthy wine—occasionally as good as most crus classés
Cru Artisan Rank below Cru Bourgeois; no longer used
Cru Paysan Rank below Cru Artisan; no longer used
Premier Grand Cru Classé The first rank of St-Emilion classed growths (1954 classification)
Grand Cru Classé The second rank of St-Emilion classed growths (1954 classification)
Supérieur (after the name of Graves or Bordeaux) Indicates wine with 1° of alcohol above the minimum allowed
Haut A mere verbal gesture, except as part of the name of Haut-Médoc

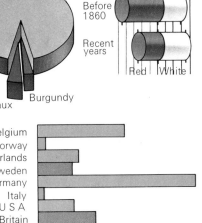

Before 1860

Recent years

Red | White

Belgium
Norway
Netherlands
Sweden
Germany
Italy
USA
Great Britain

Far left: Bordeaux produces 6% of all French wine, over twice as much as Burgundy

Left: Almost as much white wine as red is made in Bordeaux today, although the greater proportion of its AOC wines remain red. Before phylloxera, in the 1870s, red was in the majority on both counts

Left: Bordeaux exports 976,000 hectolitres (26m US gallons) a year. Germany is the biggest single customer. In 1975 she bought 310,209 hectolitres, 32% of the total volume

Bordeaux | Burgundy

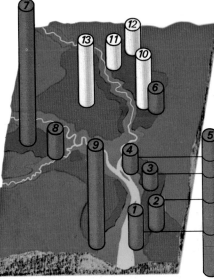

Left: the average (1971–5) production of the major red and white wines of Bordeaux
(in 1000 hectolitres)

Red
1 St-Estèphe — 46
2 Pauillac — 34
3 St-Julien — 27
4 Margaux — 30
5 All Haut-Médoc, including the above — 233
6 Graves — 40
7 St-Emilion — 224
8 Pomerol — 29
9 Bourg & Blaye — 160

White
10 Graves — 46
11 Barsac — 14
12 Sauternes — 24
13 Entre-deux-Mers — 76

St-Estèphe

Left: Château Calon-Ségur in the north of St-Estèphe has 150 acres of walled vineyard on gently rolling ground, classified in 1855 as a third growth. Its deep red wine is substantial and long-lasting

Above and right: the five Crus Classés of St-Estèphe, Château Phélan-Ségur is an example of the many Crus Bourgeois of outstanding quality in the area

THE GRAVEL banks which give the Médoc and its wines their character and quality, stretching along the shore of the river Gironde, sheltered from the ocean to the west by miles of forest, begin to peter out at St-Estèphe. It is the northernmost of the four famous communes which are the heart of the Médoc. A little *jalle* —the Médoc word for a stream—divides it from Pauillac, draining on the one hand the vineyards of Château Lafite, on the other three of the five classed growths of St-Estèphe, namely Châteaux Cos-d'Estournel, Lafon-Rochet and Cos-Labory.

There is a distinction between the soils of Pauillac and St-Estèphe: as the gravel washed down the Gironde diminishes there is a stronger mixture of clay found in it. Higher up, in Margaux, there is very little. In St-Estèphe it is heavier soil, which drains more slowly. The wines have more acidity, are fuller, solider, often have less perfume, but fairly fill your mouth with flavour. They are sturdy clarets of the kind which the British, in particular, love, and which become with age gentle but still vigorous, unfaded.

Château Cos-d'Estournel is the most spectacular of the classed growths. It is an eccentric Chinese-pagoda'ed mansion, impressively crowning the steep slope up from the Pauillac boundary (with all too good a view of the Shell refinery below). Together with Château Montrose, overlooking the river, it makes the biggest and best of St-Estèphes; strong wines with a dark colour and a long life. Montrose is an excellent château to visit to get an idea of a prosperous old-style wine estate. Its rather dark *chai*, heavily beamed, and its magnificent oak fermenting vats prepare you for the deep-coloured, deep-flavoured claret you will taste.

The other two classed growths near Cos, Châteaux Lafon-Rochet and Cos-Labory, had not distinguished themselves in recent years until Lafon-Rochet was bought by M Tesseron, a Cognac merchant, when it gained the distinction of being the first new château to be

A hundred-year-old print from Château Loudenne shows hardly-altered scenes of Médoc château life

built (or rebuilt) in Bordeaux in the 20th century. Its reputation is high today. Calon-Ségur, north of the village, has always been well known: perhaps more steady than brilliant. The Comte de Ségur, from whom it takes its name, at one time owned Châteaux Lafite and Latour into the bargain.

Above all, St-Estèphe is known for its Crus Bourgeois. There is an explosion of them on the plateau south and west of the village. Châteaux Phélan-Ségur and de Pez are both outstanding producers of very fine wine, year after year. Château Meyney, like a huge and immaculate farmyard without a farmhouse, belongs to the négociant house of Cordier and makes good

wine. Châteaux Tronquoy-Lalande, Haut-Marbuzet, Les Ormes-de-Pez . . . all the Crus Bourgeois are fountains of full-bodied, reliable, often exceptional claret.

In addition more than 200 small growers, some with named châteaux, some with just small plots of vines, send their grapes to the co-operative, whose good standard wine is sold as 'Marquis de St-Estèphe'. Co-operatives play a large and important part in the life even of such famous communes as this.

To the north of St-Estèphe the gravel bank diminishes to a promontory sticking out of the *palus*—the flat river-silt land on which no wine of quality grows. On top of the promontory the little village of St-Seurin-de-Cadourne has a dozen Crus Bourgeois. If their wine does not usually have the strength or the distinction of St-Estèphe it is still often admirable, and excellent value for money.

Where St-Seurin ends is the end of the Haut-Médoc: any wine grown beyond that point is only entitled to the appellation Médoc, plain and simple. Anchored just beyond the promontory like a ship just sailed in from Bristol lies one final gravel island in the *palus*: the British-owned Château Loudenne. In the monumental Victorian *chais* of Loudenne, Gilbey's (who bought the château in 1875) hold an imposing stock of wine from all over Bordeaux for shipment overseas. Loudenne's own wine is light, of good medium quality; a typical minor Médoc. There is also a dry white Loudenne, not at all typical of the Médoc; somewhat closer to a very dry Graves.

The country in behind St-Estèphe, farther from the river, has a scattering of Crus Bourgeois, none of them very well known. Cissac and Vertheuil lie on rather stronger and less gravelly soil on the edge of the forest. It would be fascinating to spend a day finding a favourite among their châteaux and their wine. Each has character and many have charm—yet hardly anyone except a few local brokers has investigated them in detail.

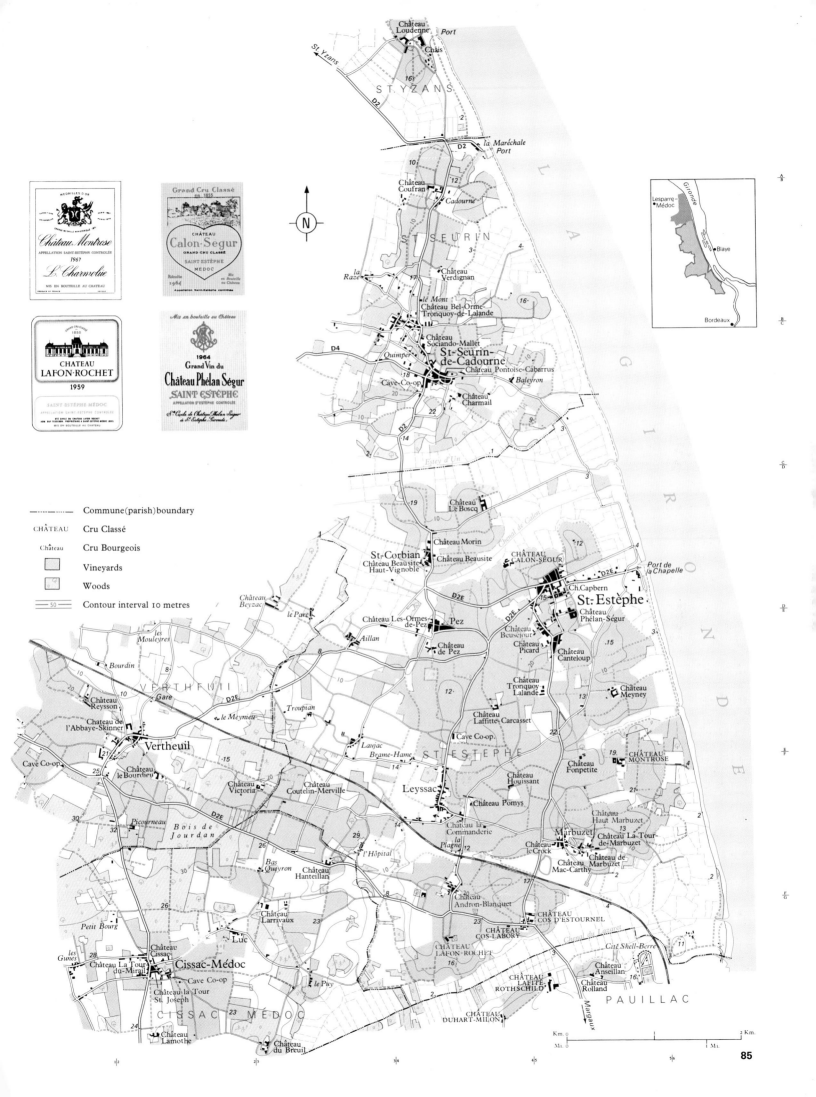

St Yzans

Port

Château
Loudenne

Chais

ST YZANS

D2

la Maréchale
Port

D2

Château
Coufran

Cadourne

ST SEURIN

la
Raze

Château
Verdignan

le Mont

Château Bel-Orme-
Tronquoy-de-Lalande

Château
Sociando-Mallet

Quimper

St-Seurin-
de-Cadourne

D4

Château Pontoise-Cabarrus

Cave-Co-op

Baleyron

Château
Charmail

D2

Château
Le Boscq

Château Morin

St-Corbian

Château Beausite

Château Beausite
Haut-Vignoble

CHÂTEAU
CALON-SÉGUR

Port de
la Chapelle

Château
Beyzac

le Parc

Château Les-Ormes-
de-Pez

Pez

D2E

D2E

Ch. Capbern

St-Estèphe

Château
Phélan-Ségur

Aillan

Château
de Pez

Château
Beauséjour

Château
Picard

Château
Canteloup

les Mouleyres

Bourdin

Château
Tronquoy
Lalande

Château
Meyney

VERTHEUIL

Gare

D2E

le Meynieu

Troupian

Château
Reysson

Château de
l'Abbaye-Skinner

Château
Laffitte-Carcasset

ST ESTEPHE

Cave Co-op.

Laujac
Brame-Hame

Château
Fonpetite

CHÂTEAU
MONTROSE

Vertheuil

Château
le Bourdieu

Cave Co-op.

Château
Victoria

Château
Coutelin-Merville

Château
Houissant

Leyssac

Picourneau

Bois de
Jourdan

D2E

Château Pomys

Château
Haut Marbuzet

Marbuzet

Château La-Tour-
de-Marbuzet

Château la
Commanderie

la
Plagne

le Crock

Bas Queyron

Château
Hanteillan

l'Hôpital

Château de
Marbuzet

Château
Mac-Carthy

Petit Bourg

Château
Larrivaux

Château
Andron-Blanquet

CHÂTEAU
COS D'ESTOURNEL

les Gunes

Luc

Château
Cissac

Cave Co-op

le Puy

CHÂTEAU
COS-LABORY

CHÂTEAU
LAFON-ROCHET

Cité Shell-Berre

Château La Tour
du-Mirail

Cissac-Médoc

Château la Tour
St-Joseph

CHÂTEAU
LAFITE-
ROTHSCHILD

Château
Anseillan

Château
Rolland

PAUILLAC

CISSAC MÉDOC

Château
Lamothe

Château
du Breuil

CHÂTEAU
DUHART-MILON

Margaux

Km. 0   1   2 Km.

Mi. 0   1 Mi.

85

Legend

— · — · — Commune(parish)boundary

CHÂTEAU   Cru Classé

Château   Cru Bourgeois

▨   Vineyards

▨   Woods

═══50═══   Contour interval 10 metres

Lesparre-
Médoc

Gironde

Blaye

Bordeaux

Pauillac

The Crus Classés of Pauillac have a sober approach to labelling. The one tearaway is Mouton-Rothschild, which commissions a different artist every year

IF ONE had to single out one commune of Bordeaux to head the list there would be no argument. It would be Pauillac. Châteaux Lafite, Latour and Mouton-Rothschild, three out of the first five of the Médoc and Graves, are its obvious claim. But many claret-lovers would tell you that the wines of Pauillac have the quintessential flavour they look for in Bordeaux—a combination of fresh soft-fruit, oak, dryness, subtlety combined with substance, a touch of cigar-box, a suggestion of sweetness. Even the lesser growths of Pauillac approach their ideal claret.

At Pauillac the gravel *croupes* of the Médoc get as near as they ever do to being hills. The highest part, with Châteaux Mouton-Rothschild and Pontet-Canet on its summit, reaches 100 feet above the sea—quite an achievement in this coastal area, where a mere swelling of the ground provides a lookout point.

The town of Pauillac is the biggest of the Médoc. Recently it has grown faster than ever before—and for a new reason. For many years it has had an oil refinery at its northern end. Now the refinery has become the centre of an expansion programme which begins to make the most illustrious piece of agricultural landscape in the world look industrial. The town's tree-shaded quay is pleasant, but there is no hotel or restaurant worth the name.

The vineyards of the châteaux of Pauillac are on the whole less subdivided than in most of the Médoc. Whereas in Margaux (for example) the châteaux are bunched together in the town, and their holdings in the country round are inextricably mixed up—a row here, a couple of rows there—in Pauillac whole slopes, mounds and plateaux belong to one proprietor. One would therefore expect greater variations between the different wines.

The three great wines of Pauillac are all very much individuals. Lafite-Rothschild and Latour stand at opposite ends of the parish; the first almost in St-Estèphe, the second almost in St-Julien. Oddly enough, though, their characters tend the opposite way: Lafite more towards the smoothness and finesse of a St-Julien, Latour more towards the strength and firmness of a St-Estèphe.

Lafite, with 200 acres one of the biggest vineyards in the Médoc, makes about 800 barrels of its fabulously expensive wine; a perfumed, polished, gentlemanly production. Formerly any lesser wine was sold as Carruades de Lafite. Lately this practice has been dropped.

The firmer and more solid Latour does not ask quite such high prices, although there are few who would say it was worth less than Lafite. It has the great merit of evenness over uneven vintages, and a superb depth of flavour. Even the château's second wine, les Forts de Latour, is first class.

Baron Philippe de Rothschild at Mouton makes a third kind of Pauillac: strong, dark, long-lasting. Given the ten or often even 20 years they need to mature (depending on the quality of the vintage), these wines reach into realms of perfection where they are rarely followed. But millionaires tend to be impatient: too much is drunk far too young.

The undoubted similarity in strength and staying-power of Latour and Mouton can apparently be put down to the unusually high proportion of Cabernet vines in their vineyards: as high as 90% at Mouton.

No visitor to Pauillac should miss the beautiful little museum of works of art connected with wine—old glass, paintings, tapestries—as well as the very fine *chais*, which make Château Mouton-Rothschild the show-place of the whole Médoc.

The two châteaux Pichon-Longueville—Baron and Lalande—face each other across the road south from Pauillac like mad old duchesses

Top: châteaux Pichon-Lalande and, left, Grand-Puy-Lacoste have the typical solid dignity of Pauillac
Right: Cabernet grapes, bloom-covered, at Lafite

in party clothes. Lalande is the bigger half of what was once one huge property—partly in St-Julien, mainly in Pauillac. It usually seems to make the better wine of the two, Baron the 'bigger'—though one thinks of it for reliability rather than sublimity.

The two best known of the remaining classified growths of Pauillac are Pontet-Canet, with the biggest production of any Cru Classé (as much as 1,600 barrels a year), and Lynch-Bages, whose rather full, heavy wine, with a most distinctive scented bouquet, is immensely popular.

Château Duhart-Milon belongs to the Rothschilds of Lafite, and Château Mouton Baron Philippe to Mouton. Both clearly benefit from the wealth and technical knowledge of their proprietors and managers. Recently Baron Philippe has added the neighbouring classed-growth Clerc-Milon to his stable.

CHÂTEAU COS
D'ESTOURNEL
CHÂTEAU
LAFON-ROCHET
CHÂTEAU
COS-LABORY
ST. ESTÈPHE
16
Canal Lazaret
3
CHÂTEAU
LAFITE-ROTHSCHILD
Château
Rolland
Château Anseillan
Cité Shell-Berre
CHÂTEAU
DUHART-MILON
Mousset
Raff de
Petrole
CHÂTEAU CLERC-
MILON-MONDON
Château la
Fleur-Milon
Loubeyres
Lhorte
CHÂTEAU
MOUTON-ROTHSCHILD
le Pouyalet
CHÂTEAU MOUTON-
BARON-PHILIPPE
Padarnac
Château
Belle-Rose
CHÂTEAU
PONTET-CANET
Lescargean
Château
Ramage-la Batisse
Château Liversan
Pibran
Château la Tour Pibran
Château Pibran
Gare
28
Guerin
Château Tourteran
Château Fonpiqueyre
Cave Coop
Château Peyrabon
ST. SAUVEUR
Château la
Rose-Pauillac
Cave Coop
CHÂTEAU
PEDESCLAUX
CHÂTEAU
GRAND-PUY-
DUCASSE
Labrousse
le Fournas
PAUILLAC
Pauillac
Port
Château
Duhart-Milon
la Naude
la Verrierie
Artiques
Château Haut-
Bages-Monpelou
CHÂTEAU HAUT-
BAGES-LIBÉRAL
Bages
Château Haut-
Bages-Avérous
CHÂTEAU GRAND-
PUY-LACOSTE
CHÂTEAU
CROIZET-BAGES
CHÂTEAU LYNCH-BAGES
Grand Moussas
Bouhoubrun
CHÂTEAU
LYNCH-MOUSSAS
Château
Haut-Madrac
Cordeillan
D2
Dauprat
St.-Lambert
Château Bellegrave
Château Balogues-
Haur-Bages
Château Fonbadet
Bois de Madrac
Daubos
CHÂTEAU
BATAILLEY
CHÂTEAU PICHON-
LONGUEVILLE-BARON
Château la Couronne
CHÂTEAU
HAUT-BATAILLEY
CHÂTEAU PICHON-
LONGUEVILLE-LALANDE
CHÂTEAU
LATOUR
ST. JULIEN

Lesparre-
Médoc
Gironde
Blaye
Bordeaux

- - - - - Canton boundary
——— Commune (parish) boundary
CHÂTEAU Cru Classé
Château Cru Bourgeois
▨ Vineyards
▢ Woods
═20═ Contour interval 10 metres

Km.0 ——— 1 Km.
Mi. 0 ——— 1 Mi.

Châteaux Batailley and Haut-Batailley, lying back in the fringe of the woods, do not spring to mind straightaway. They are relatively small (Haut-Batailley has the little Château La Couronne, classified below the Crus Classés as a Cru Exceptionnel, as neighbour and partner). One does not expect quite the same finesse from them as from the great wines nearer the river. Haut-Batailley is the finer of the two.

The two châteaux called Grand-Puy, Lacoste and Ducasse, both have high reputations, although the former is very much the bigger and more important. It is one fine continuous vineyard on high ground, surrounding its château, while Ducasse is scattered in three separ-ate parcels north and west of Pauillac, and its old château is now the Maison du Vin on the quay in the town itself.

Of the remaining classed growths, Croizet-Bages is probably the best. The wine of Haut-Bages-Libéral, next door, is made at Pontet-Canet, although its vineyard is, as the map shows, at the other end of the parish. Pédesclaux and Lynch-Moussas (recently restored) are smaller and—for the moment at least—less well-known châteaux.

Pauillac, having so many large estates, is not, like St-Estèphe, a warren of small-to-middling growers. Its one small Cru Exceptionnel, La Couronne, has already been mentioned. The Crus Bourgeois châteaux Fonbadet, Haut-Bages-Monpelou and Haut-Bages-Avérous, La Fleur-Milon, La Tour-Pibran and Anseillan are all more or less familiar names.

The local co-operative, however, is probably better known than any of them. Under the name La Rose-Pauillac around 180 small growers sell their blended wine—a reliable and distinctive, though a light-weight, product of the famous parish.

The map includes part of the next parish to the west, St-Sauveur. There are no wines of outstanding quality; the Crus Bourgeois marked, however, are respectable and useful. Château Liversan is perhaps the best known.

St-Julien

Top: Château Langoa-Barton, built in 1758, is one of the Médoc's most elegant. Its wine is a typical St-Julien—the epitome of classical claret

Above: pickers at the end of a late September day. The children still seem to have energy, although it is gruelling work and everybody joins in

St-Julien has many of the Médoc's most illustrious Crus Classés, and comparatively few but excellent Crus Bourgeois, of which Château Gloria is best known

No OTHER commune in Bordeaux has so high a proportion of classed growths as St-Julien. It is a small commune, with the smallest production of the famous four of the Médoc, but almost all of it is superlative wine-growing land; typical dunes of gravel, not as deep as in Pauillac (a cross-section of a St-Julien vine and its soil is on page 19) but very close to the river and consequently well drained.

There are few Crus Bourgeois, and those there are are very good indeed: one of them, Château Gloria, being easily on a par with the classed growths and sometimes making a wine as good as any in the district. As for spare land, or unknown little holdings to supply the very popular 'St-Julien' of the corner wine-shop, there is practically none.

If Pauillac makes the most striking and brilliant wine of the Médoc, and Margaux the most refined and exquisite, St-Julien forms the transition between the two. With one or two exceptions its châteaux make rather round and gentle wine—gentle, that is, when it is mature: it starts as tough and tannic in a good year as any.

The chief proponents of the typical smooth St-Julien style are Châteaux Gruaud-Larose and Talbot—both belonging to the négociant Cordier. There is drier, and perhaps more exciting wine made at the Italianate mansion of Ducru-Beaucaillou, and lighter, more elegant wine (in keeping with a very beautiful Louis XV château) made at Beychevelle.

The principal glory of the commune is the vast estate of Léoville, once the biggest in the Médoc, now divided into three. It lies on the Pauillac boundary, and it would be a brave man who would say that he could distinguish a Léoville from a Longueville every time (although he certainly should be able to distinguish a Château Latour, which lies equally close).

Château Léoville-Lascases has the biggest vineyard of the three, with 150-odd acres. At the moment Château Léoville-Barton has the best reputation. It belongs, together with the neighbouring Langoa, to the Bartons of Barton & Guestier, one of the best-known négociant

Daubos

CHÂTEAU PICHON-
LONGUEVILLE-BARONA

CHÂTEAU LATOUR

CHÂTEAU PICHON-
LONGUEVILLE-LALANDE

Ch. la Couronne

CHÂTEAU HAUT
BATAILLEY

Cach

CHÂTEAU
LÉOVILLE-LASCASES

St.-Julien-Beychevelle

Château Moulin-Riche

Château
Larose-Trintaudon

Château Peymartin

CHÂTEAU LÉOVILLE-
POYFERRÉ

S T   J U L I E N

Perganson

CHÂTEAU
TALBOT

CHÂTEAU
LANGOA

CHÂTEAU LÉOVILLE-
BARTON

la Mouline

le Bouscat

S T   L A U R E N T

Gare

Château
Barateau

CHÂTEAU SAINT-PIERRE-
BONTEMPS ET SEVAISTRE

Château
du Glana

CHÂTEAU
DUCRU-BEAUCAILLOU

CHÂTEAU BELGRAVE

Château Terrey
Gros - Caillou

Château Gloria

Beychevelle

LA TOUR-CARNET
CHÂTEAU

CHÂTEAU CAMÉNSAC

CHÂTEAU LAGRANGE

Château
d'Hortevie

CHÂTEAU
BRANAIRE-DUCRU

St.-Laurent-et-
Benon

CHÂTEAU
GRUAUD-LAROSE

le Bourdieu

CHÂTEAU BEYCHEVELLE

Lamothe

le Graveyron

Ysle du Nord

le Marais de Beychevelle

Château Lanessan

le Vivey

Chenal   du   Milieu

le Cul du Bosc

L A   G I R O N D E

C U S S A C

Chenal   du   Despartins

Lesparre-
Médoc

Gironde

Blaye

Bordeaux

- - - - - - -   Canton boundary

- - - - - - -   Commune (parish) boundary

CHÂTEAU   Cru Classé

Château   Cru Bourgeois

☐   Vineyards

▣   Woods

═ 50 ═   Contour interval 10 metres

Km. 0   1   2 Km.
Mi. 0   1 Mi.

houses of Bordeaux. Ronald Barton lives in the beautiful 18th-century Château Langoa, and makes his two wines side by side in the same *chai*. Langoa is usually reckoned the slightly lesser wine of the two, being fuller and more tannic, but both are among the finest clarets in a traditional manner. Such wines should be laid down for a good seven years even in lesser vintages; in great ones they will last for a generation or more.

Léoville-Lascases is seen everywhere, and has made very fine wine steadily through the sixties. Léoville-Poyferré one sees less. It sometimes seems to lack the roundness which makes St-Julien so pleasant to drink. Of course it is hard to know how much of such a characteristic is due to the techniques in use and how much to the soil and situation. A different balance of Cabernet and Merlot vines will produce different barrels from the same vineyard. On the other hand people who have tasted the wines of different grape varieties from one vineyard before they have been 'assembled' in one barrel

have often said that even while they tasted of the different grapes, each had the characterstic of the estate.

Château Ducru-Beaucaillou celebrates in its name the 'beautiful pebbles' which fill the vineyards nearest the river. They are not only large and round; they form the greater part of the topsoil. Only about two feet down does the subsoil of finer gravel and curious lumpy deposits of iron-bearing clay begin. Ducru, and Château Gloria next to it, rarely fail to produce some of the best wine of Bordeaux.

Château Beychevelle is even better known; its wine is supposed to be the height of elegance rather than power; recent vintages have been especially fine. Château Branaire-Ducru, next door, has emerged lately from relative obscurity, making wine of great flavour and style.

The group of classed growths that stand away from the river, on soil becoming slightly less outrageously stony, include the stablemates Gruaud-Larose and Talbot, which epitomize the tender, almost rich, easy-to-drink

style of St-Julien. In several vintages recently Gruaud-Larose has made one of the best wines of the parish. The united châteaux St-Pierre, Bontemps and Sevaistre, which separate them, are well known in the Low Countries: they belong to a Belgian wine-merchant.

Château du Glana, the Cru Bourgeois next door, is a property with a steady reputation which has enlarged and re-equipped lately.

The last of the classed growths, Château Lagrange, used to be better known than it is for its good, substantial wine. The 1962 was outstanding. It lies far back in the country, in a group with the three classed growths of St-Laurent—of which Belgrave, perhaps the best-known name, is now the least important. There is a world of difference between their sleepy hinterland and the exciting air of the riverside. Yet the recent restoration of no less than three properties; Latour-Carnet, Camensac and the Cru Bourgeois Larose-Trintaudon promises that we shall hear more of the commune in the future.

The Central Médoc

THIS is the bridge passage of the Médoc, the mezzo forte between the andante of St-Julien and the allegro of Margaux. Four villages pass without a single classed growth. The gravel dunes rise less proudly above the river; wood and marsh mingle with the vineyards. Many châteaux with fine great *chais* have let their vineyards dwindle to nothing. . . . And yet, as you pick your way through this less spectacular landscape, a surprising number of comfortingly familiar names appear.

Rather than dismiss the centre of the Haut-Médoc as being without interest, as so many authors do, it is worth paying attention here. Great wines are rarely made, but there is a steady flow of excellent wine for—what shall we call ourselves?—the middle classes?

At the moment Cussac, Lamarque, Arcins are not names which help to sell anything. There is a strong tradition in this region of supplying the richer neighbours to north and south with what they need for topping up, or perhaps for the insatiable public demand for 'Margaux' and 'St-Julien'.

But recently there has been more confidence to be seen, modern vinification methods have appeared, and extremely good light wines are being made. The fine old fortress of the Château de Lamarque is producing a very attractive pale red wine, fruity and ready to drink after a

mere year or two. Château Malescasse, also at Lamarque, was bought in 1969 by an American-English combine and has replanted an estate which used to be well known in Holland and Germany. Château Courant at Arcins belongs to Nicolas Barrow, an Englishman who has worked as hard as anyone to redeem the reputation of the middle-Médoc.

This is not to say that all the central Médoc shares the same obscurity. The St-Julien border boasts the very fine Cru Bourgeois Château Lanessan, which regularly makes wine of classed-growth standard (and has, besides, an entertaining carriage museum housed in the old stables).

Château La Chesnaye-Ste-Gemme stands in the same park and is part of the same estate. Château Caronne-Ste-Gemme is another big growth, rather farther inland.

The forests come towards the river for a space here, narrowing the vineyards down to a handful of Crus Bourgeois at Cussac. At Cussac also is the handsome Fort Médoc, down by the river, a 17th-century fortress which is being restored. There are plans to make it into a resort and yacht harbour.

South-west of Lamarque there is a great opening-out of vineyards as the gravel ridges fan out inland to Grand Poujeaux (which lies in the commune of Moulis) and Listrac. Château Chasse-Spleen at Grand Poujeaux is classed as a Cru Exceptionnel (in the class, that is, between Bourgeois and classé). Four châteaux with Poujeaux in their names, la Clos-

erie-Grand-Poujeaux, Dutruch-Grand-Poujeaux, Gressier-Grand-Poujeaux and Poujeaux-Theil, all have good reputations. So do the two châteaux Fourcas, -Hostein and -Dupré, among several others at Listrac.

The pattern here seems to be for solider and perhaps harsher wines to come from farther west; lighter and easier ones as you get nearer the river. So much depends, however, on the style adopted by the château—of longer or shorter fermentation, when the wine is racked and how it is looked after—that any such observation must be tentative.

Beyond the jalle de Tiquetorte, in the southeast corner of the area, we begin to enter the sphere of Margaux. The big Château Citran and the smaller Villegeorge (off the map; a Cru Exceptionnel to watch) lie in the commune of Avensan. Both are well known, and approach Margaux in style.

Soussans is among the communes whose Appellation Contrôlée is not merely Haut-Médoc but Margaux. Its Château La Tour-de-Mons might be called the Mouton of the Crus Bourgeois; a consistently excellent property. Château Paveil de Luze is also well known. Cocks and Féret's *Bordeaux et Ses Vins* says Soussans wines are 'promptement buvables'—soon ready to drink. Soon in this context means at least four years.

The hand-operated press is obsolete, but an old photograph still perfectly catches the atmosphere of many small châteaux in this part of the Médoc

Twenty or 30 Crus Bourgeois between St-Julien and Soussans, the beginning of Margaux, are well known for outstanding value in far-above-average claret

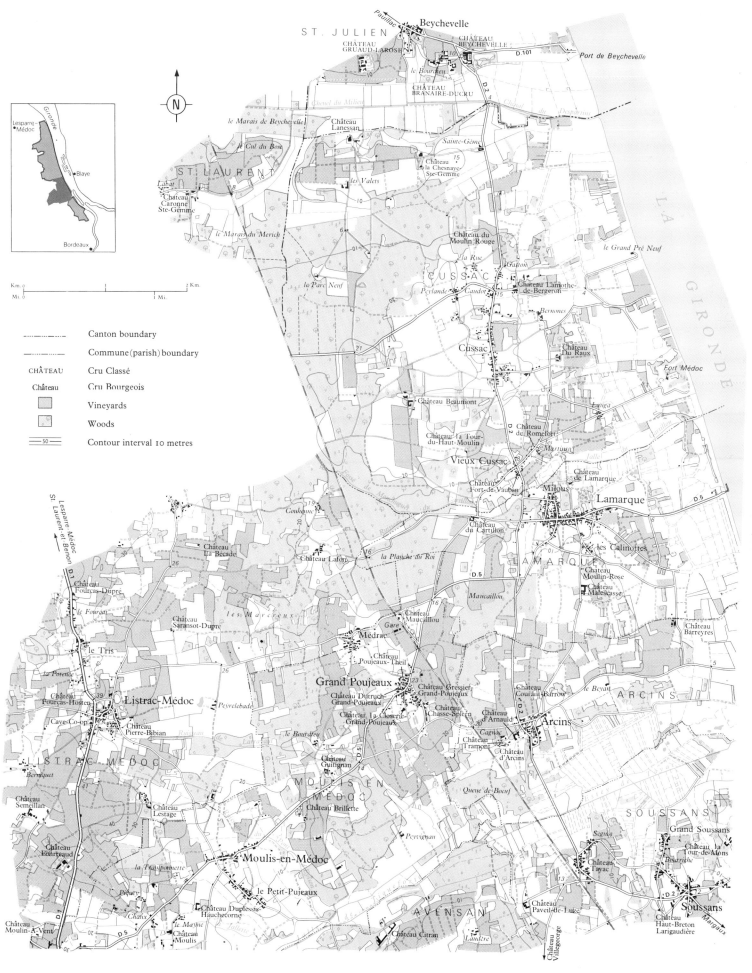

Margaux and the Southern Médoc

BY MANY accounts this, the southernmost stretch of the Haut-Médoc, makes the finest wine of all. Margaux has a tight concentration of classed growths, which continue into the hamlets of Issan, Cantenac and Labarde. The map here shows a rather different picture from Pauillac or St-Julien. Instead of the châteaux being spread out evenly over the land they are huddled together in the village. An examination of the almost unliftable volumes of commune maps in the Mairie shows a degree of intermingling of one estate with another which is far greater than in (say) Pauillac. One would therefore look to differences in technique and tradition more than changes of soil to try to explain the differences between one château and another.

In fact the soil of Margaux is the thinnest in the Médoc, with the highest proportion of rough gravel. It has the least to offer the vine in the way of nourishment, but it drains well even in rainy years. The result is wines which start life comparatively 'supple', though in poor years they can turn out thin. In good and great years, however, all the stories about the virtues of gravel are justified: there is a delicacy about good Margaux, and a sweet haunting perfume, which makes it the most exquisite claret of all.

The wines of Château Margaux and Château Palmer next door are the ones which most often reach such heights. Château Margaux is not only a first growth of the Médoc, it is the one which most looks the part: a pediment at the end of an avenue; the air of a mansion, with *chais* to match.

In great vintages its wine can justify its first-growth standing: it achieves unique finesse and subtlety. In recent vintages, however, the third-growth Palmer has often made better wine.

Château Lascombes (which was restored to glory by Alexis Lichine, and now belongs to the English brewers Bass Charrington) also often makes exceptionally good wine. Of the famous pair which used to be the big Rausan estate, as famous in the 18th century as Léoville was in St-Julien, Rausan-Ségla is today the more

important as well as the bigger of the two.

In Margaux a château name is often in truth a brand name; several châteaux are paired off under common ownership, with the label of one château apparently being used for the best wine of the property while the other goes on the less successful casks—an obvious manoeuvre where vineyards are so split up and intermingled. In this way a château which was once well known can disappear altogether as a wine-making unit and exist only as the second brand of a neighbour. Château Desmirail is an instance. It is no longer on the map; it has been swallowed by Château Palmer.

There are several distinguished pairs of châteaux in Margaux. The two second-growths Brane-Cantenac and Durfort-Vivens are jointly owned (yet make very different wine; the Brane smooth, the Durfort tough). Malescot-St-Exupéry goes with Marquis-d'Alesme-Becker —the Malescot being the better wine, often miraculously scented and one of the best of Margaux. Ferrière goes with Lascombes. Pouget is the twin of Boyd-Cantenac. Farther down the road, Siran goes with Dauzac.

Still in Margaux proper, Château Marquis de Terme, though rarely seen abroad, makes good, rather old-fashioned, wine, and Château d'Issan, which belongs to a member of the great négociant family of Cruse, is perhaps the most beautiful house in the Médoc: a 17th-century fortified manor within the complete moat of an old *château-fort*. The admirable gentle slope of its vineyard to the road is one of the best situations in Margaux.

The Crus Bourgeois include a group on the theme of Labégorce; none is world-famous, but their names stick in the mind like a nursery rhyme. Of the three, Château Labégorce-Zédé is the best known. None of the other Crus Bourgeois has a great reputation—but this does not mean that they should be ignored.

Our rather erratic path to and fro in Margaux becomes a little simpler as the châteaux thin out in Cantenac and farther south. Most of the land in the communes of Cantenac, Labarde and Arsac, as well as Soussans to the north, has

been granted the appellation Margaux, making wines of very similar style and quality. If anything, Cantenac and hamlets further south make more powerful but less fragrant wines.

In Cantenac itself Alexis Lichine's own château of Prieuré is deservedly famous for making some of Margaux's most consistently splendid claret. Château Kirwan was in eclipse, but has recently been restored and is beginning to shine.

Châteaux Cantenac-Brown and Boyd-Cantenac, which straddle the bigger and better-known Brane-Cantenac on the southern slope of Margaux's low dune of gravel, are both in capable hands. (The former belongs to the head of the famous négociant firm de Luze.) Recent vintages from both have been extremely attractive: better than for many years.

Another recent tale of restoration and renewed quality has been the lonely Château du Tertre, isolated in Arsac. Recent vintages have been excellent.

There are three more big and famous classed growths before the vineyards come to an end: Giscours, whose tall half-timbered buildings in the graceless style of Deauville or Le Touquet face a most impressive sweep of vines; Cantemerle, a perfect Sleeping Beauty château, deep in a wood of huge trees and quiet pools, and the top-flight Château La Lagune, a neat 18th-century building just off the Bordeaux road (and the nearest classed growth of the Médoc to the city). They have in common a style which is bigger and more solid than a Margaux; Giscours usually firm and La Lagune rather soft, but both full of flavour, Cantemerle a powerful, long-lasting, classical wine, generally accepted as one of the best of the whole Médoc—certainly a second growth in any new classification.

Dauzac, the fourth classed growth of this southern area, partnered by its neighbour Siran, has not shone in these last years, but the Cru Exceptionnel Château d'Angludet, admirably situated on the banks of a stream, has been in the hands of the Sichel family for 15 years and has consistently made wine of classed growth quality.

SOUSSANS

Marsac

Soussans

le Cailloux

Bessan

Richet

Château Labégorce-Zédé

L'Abbé-Gorsse de Gorsse

Château Labégorce

MARGAUX

Ile Vincent

CHÂTEAU MARQUIS-D'ALESME-BECKER

Château la Gurgue

Château Bel-Air, Marquis-d'Aligre

Château de Lamouroux

CHÂTEAU LASCOMBES

CHÂTEAU FERRIÈRE

Château Pontac-Lynch

CHÂTEAU MALESCOT ST-EXUPÉRY

Port d'Issan

CHÂTEAU MARGAUX

Vire Fougasse
D.105

Margaux

CHÂTEAU DURFORT-VIVENS

Château Canuet

Château Montbrun

CHÂTEAU Marquis DE TERME

Issan

Château Vincent

CHÂTEAU d'Issan

Lagunegrand

Mathéou

CHÂTEAU RAUZAN-GASSIES

Château Martinens

les Eyçarts

CHÂTEAU RAUSAN-SEGLA

CHÂTEAU PALMER

CHÂTEAU PRIEURE-LICHINE

Château Kirwan

Cantenac

Grange Neuve

CHÂTEAU CANTENAC-BROWN

CANTENAC

Benqueyre

CHÂTEAU BRANE-CANTENAC

Jean Faure
CHÂTEAU BOYD-CANTENAC
CHÂTEAU POUGET

la Prade

Château Siran

la Bastide

Pont de Labarde

CHÂTEAU DAUZAC

Blanchard

Château d'Angludet

Château Rosemont

la Métairie

Larrieu Terrefort

Labarde

LABARDE

Château Noton

CHÂTEAU GISCOURS

Macau

Château Ligondra

ARSAC

CHÂTEAU DU TERTRE

Bern

la Grillade

Château Cantelaude

MACAU

Les Trois Moulins

Maucamps

Château Monbrison

Ch. Priban

la Mouline

Arsac

CHÂTEAU CANTE-MERLE

Cambon la Pelouse

Ch. Felloneau

Lafon

la Houringue

Labric

Fronton

les Carrayes

Ch. d'Arche

Fontbonne

Château Palouney

Ludon-Médoc

Paloumey

Ch. Ludon-Pommies-Agassac

Bouscarrut

CHÂTEAU LA LAGUNE

les Lauriers

Feydieu

LE PIAN MÉDOC

LUDON-MÉDOC

la Taste

Peyquem

le Pian Médoc

Ch. Lafite-Canteloup

Château d'Agassac

Below: a magnificent concentration of Crus Classés distinguishes Margaux and its area. They emphasize their prestige with more gilded labels than the rest of the Médoc

Lesparre • Médoc

Gironde

• Blaye

Bordeaux •

CHATEAU KIRWAN
MARGAUX
1967
SCHRÖDER & SCHŸLER & Cⁱᵉ

CHATEAU D'ISSAN
TROISIÈME CRU CLASSÉ
APPELLATION MARGAUX CONTROLÉE
CRUSE

Château Prieuré-Lichine
GRAND CRU CLASSÉ
MARGAUX
1962
Nᵒ 4514

CHATEAU MARQUIS D'ALESME BECKER
GRAND CRU CLASSÉ EN 1855
MARGAUX
1966
APPELLATION MARGAUX CONTROLÉE

Château Dauzac
APPELLATION MARGAUX CONTROLÉE
Margaux
1967
Grand Cru Classé

GRAND CRU CLASSÉ
CHATEAU DU TERTRE
1964
APPELLATION MARGAUX CONTROLÉE

Canton boundary

Commune (parish) boundary

CHÂTEAU   Cru Classé

Château   Cru Bourgeois

Vineyards

Woods

Contour interval 5 metres

N

ILE MARGAUX

ILE DE MACAU

LA GIRONDE

ILE DES VACHES

Km. 0   1   2 Km.
Mi. 0   1 Mi.

Graves

Château Haut-Brion in the western suburbs of Bordeaux; the only first-growth château outside the Médoc

Domaine La Solitude at Martillac, like many Graves estates, is a clearing in the middle of the forest

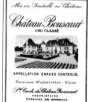

THE CHANGE from the last section of the Médoc is obvious from the map. Here the city reaches out into the pine-woods, which continue (as the Landes) from here to the Basque foot-hills of the Pyrenees. The vineyards are clearings, often isolated from one another in heavily forested and almost flat country.

The district of Graves takes its name from its gravel-and-sand soil, which it came by in just the same way as the Médoc—the spoil of the Garonne from inland hills.

Graves as a whole is known chiefly for its white wines; dry to medium sweet, pale yellow, with a peculiar faintly chemical or metallic character. They are rarely very good. Only a small part of the big region reaches distinction; the part near Bordeaux where the majority of the wines are red. They have much in common with the stouter and drier wines of the Médoc. The greatest red Graves are however in their own way the equivalent of the best wines even of Pauillac or Margaux. The fact was recognized by the authorities who classed Château Haut-Brion with three châteaux of the Médoc as a first growth. Today Haut-Brion has challengers. It is the favourite game of the millionaire wine-lover to make it defend its title against Château La Mission-Haut-Brion. La Mission, with La Tour-Haut-Brion and Laville-Haut-Brion, all in Pessac, belonged until his death in 1974 to a wine-maker of genius, Henri Woltner. With the most modern techniques of controlled fermentation he made marvellously fruity, complex, deep-scented wine. His successors still do. Which is not to say that Haut-Brion does not continue to make powerful wine with all the old distinction. The name La Tour-Haut-Brion is used for the second wine of La Mission; Laville-Haut-Brion is white, and one of the best of the white Graves.

Châteaux Pape-Clément and Les Carmes-Haut-Brion are the only other growths which survive in Pessac. The former is one of Bordeaux's oldest vineyards, named after the churchman who brought the papacy to France in the 14th century. Its wine today is as good as ever; fragrant and full of character.

Several châteaux in the next commune going south have gone out of business. It seems there is no great demand for red Graves as such; few

except the famous classed growths can survive, particularly in an area where the woods make late frosts all too frequent a danger to the crop.

It is the commune of Léognan, well into the forest, which has the next clutch of châteaux. No one would suspect its Domaine de Chevalier, which currently has the highest reputation among them, of being any such thing. It resembles a small industrial building at the end of a flat field of vines surrounded by pine-trees. None the less it succeeds in making exceedingly fine red and white wine year after year. There is something almost Californian about the little winery with its two flavours . . . both of which turn out to be brilliant.

Château Haut-Bailly is the other leading classed growth of Léognan; it is unusual in these parts for making only red wine. Haut-Bailly has always been a respected name but its last few vintages have been particularly good.

Carbonnieux and Olivier are both big properties which have exported their wines, principally white, for many years. Châteaux de Fieuzal and Malartic-Lagravière are smaller and less well known, with a higher proportion of red grapes. Château La Louvière is another big property with good white wine, though not among the classed growths. And oddly enough there is yet another Haut-Brion, Larrivet.

Three other communes, on the Bordeaux-Langon road to the east, have classed growths. In Villenave-d'Ornon there is Château Couhins, a white-wine château which also makes a vin rosé. Part of its vineyard is run separately as Château Cantebau-Couhins, and makes a very good dry white wine. The substantial châteaux Pontac-Monplaisir and Baret are not classed. In Cadaujac there is the well-known Château Bouscaut, where a great deal of money has recently been spent by new American proprietors. And finally in Martillac two excellent classed growths, Smith-Haut-Lafitte and La Tour-Martillac, make both red and white wine and an important Cru Bourgeois, Château La Garde, makes another good and full-bodied typical red Graves.

Right: Crus Classés of Graves. Seven are included in the classification for both red and white; one, Laville-Haut-Brion, for white only; the rest for red wine

les Carmes-
Haut-Brion
la Medoquine
Verthamon
CH HAUT BRION
les Echoppes
CH. LA MISSION HAUT BRION
Petit Bois
Bordeaux
CH. LA TOUR HAUT BRION
CH. LA VILLE HAUT BRION
Suzon
Bellegrave
Ch.
Côte-
Haut-Brion
Ch. Fanning-
la-Fontaine
Baraillot
Pessac
le Breuil
Talence
Plume la Poule
Chiquet
Dunoyer-
Marly
CHÂTEAU
PAPE-
CLÉMENT
Sardine
Pacaris
PESSAC
la Paillère
Château Raba
Château la
Providence
Château
Lafitte
Bénédigues
Madère
Cité Prairie
Canteloup
Brannes
Chouiney
Beaudon
Martinon
la
Mignonne
Sarcignan
Château
Pontac-
Monplaisir
Monjoux
Institut
St-François-
Xavier
le
Bruca
Pontac
**Villenave-
d'Ornon**
Gradignan
Château Baret
Château de
Terrefort-
de-Fortissan
GRADIGNAN
la Taille
Chambery
la Générale
les
Sables
Trézat
la Hontan
Branlac
VILLENAVE
Peycamin
Château Brown
Couhins
CHÂTEAU
COUHINS
Canteloup
les
Graves
Château
Lamothe-
Bouscaut
le Barbut
les
Platanes
le Bouscaut
Catoy
Chaut
Ricon
Veyres
CH. LA TOUR-
LÉOGNAN
CH. BOUSCAUT
CADAUJAC
CHÂTEAU OLIVIER
Valoux
Dussolt
les
Palomières
Domaine de
Grandmaison
CHÂTEAU
CARBONNIEUX
le Désert
la Rivière
Pirègues
le Grd
Broustey
Gascon
Lamarque
l'Oustalade
Château l'Hermitage
la Bouhume
Château
la Louvière
Château
le Thil
CH. SMITH-
HAUT-LAFITTE
CHÂTEAU
HAUT-BAILLY
Château
le Pape
Lapeyre
Château Larrivet-
Haut-Brion
les
Péaocs
la Morelle
LÉOGNAN
Château Gazin
la Salle
Château Haut-Bergey
Léognan
les Peyreyres
Château
Malleprat
CH. MALARTIC-LAGRAVIÈRE
Botte
Marquet
MARTILLAC
Bois
de
Bernin
DOMAINE
DE CHEVALIER
Mignoy
le Breyra
Château
de France
Château
Boismartin
Château-
Neuf
Mondet
Martillac
les Bouges
CHÂTEAU DE FIEUZAL
Tartarisat
Mirebeau
Château Ferran
CH. LA TOUR-MARTILLAC
Château
Haut-Gardère
Bonois
Château
la Garde
Domaine
la Solitude
Château
Haut-Nouchet

Km. 0 · · · · 1 · · · · 2 Km.
Mi. 0 · · · · 1 Mi.

	Canton boundary
	Commune (parish) boundary
CHÂTEAU	Cru Classé
Château	Cru bourgeois
	Vineyards
	Woods
50	Contour interval 5 metres

Libourne
Bordeaux
Dordogne
Garonne
GRAVES
Sauternes

Sauternes and Barsac

ALL THE other districts of Bordeaux mapped here make wines which can be compared with, and preferred to, one another. Sauternes is different. The famous white wine of Sauternes is a speciality which finds its only real rival not in France at all but in Germany. It depends on local conditions and a very unusual wine-making technique. In great years the results can be sublime; a very sweet, rich-textured, flower-scented, glittering golden liquid. In other years it can frankly fail to be Sauternes (properly so-called) at all.

Above all it is only a few châteaux of Sauternes—and in this we include Barsac—which make such wine. Ordinary Sauternes, whether called Haut or not makes no difference, is just sweet white wine. Very cold it makes a pleasant drink for serving before or after a meal.

The special technique which only the considerable châteaux can afford to employ is to pick over the vineyard as many as eight or nine times, starting in September and sometimes going on until November. This is to take full advantage of the peculiar form of mould (known as *Botrytis cinerea* to the scientist, or *pourriture noble*—'noble rot'—to the poet) which forms on the grapes in a mild misty autumn and shrivels the skins to the ugly wizened condition shown in the photograph.

Instead of affecting the blighted grapes with a flavour of rot, this botrytis engineers the escape of a proportion of the water in them, leaving the sugar and the flavouring elements in the juice more concentrated than ever. The result is wine with an intensity of taste and scent and a smooth, almost oil-like, texture which can be made no other way.

But it does mean picking the grapes as they shrivel, berry by berry—and the small proprietors of little-known châteaux have no alternative but to pick at once, and hope for as much botrytis as possible.

Production is very small, since evaporation is actually being encouraged. From each one of its 100 hectares of vineyard Château Yquem, the most famous of Sauternes, makes only about 9 hectolitres (about 1,200 bottles) of wine. A first-class Médoc vineyard would make three or four times as much.

The risk element is appalling, since bad weather in October can rob the grower of all chance of making sweet wine, and sometimes any wine at all. Costs are correspondingly high, and the low price of even the finest Sauternes (with the exception of Yquem) makes it one of the least profitable wines to the grower; to the drinker it is one of the great bargains of the wine world.

Sauternes was the only area outside the Médoc to be classed in 1855. Château Yquem was made a First Great Growth—a rank created for it alone in all Bordeaux. Eleven châteaux were made first growths and 12 more were made seconds.

Five communes, including Sauternes itself, are entitled to use the name. Barsac, the biggest of them, has the alternative of calling its wine either Sauternes or Barsac. All five communes have at least one first-growth château. The ones which today seem to make the very best wine, sometimes even on a par with the super-château, Yquem, are Suduiraut in Preignac, Rayne-Vigneau in Bommes, Rieussec in Fargues and Coutet and Climens in Barsac.

To a short list today one should add Châteaux Guiraud and Filhot in Sauternes, La Tour Blanche and Lafaurie-Peyraguey in Bommes and the two Châteaux Doisy in Barsac.

Sauternes of this quality is immensely long-lived, and repays keeping more than any other white wine. At first it is so sweet that its subtleties are masked. Gradually it takes on a warmer colour (since its bottles are clear this is easy to see) and the flavour grows deeper and more interesting. Eventually it will 'maderize'—go brown and lose some of its sugar—but this can be after as long as 30 years.

The days when Russian archdukes would drink nothing but Château Yquem—and ordered it bottled in cut-crystal decanters lettered in gold—are over. For a long time Sauternes has been banished to the end of formal banquets, and the tables of a few connoisseurs who realize that the statement it makes about the grape has no equivalent. In the sixties there was a run of bad vintages. But there is a revival on foot; the Anglo-Saxon world, Germany and Scandinavia have discovered its pleasures. Given sunshine in October before the vintage, the seventies will see Sauternes come back to the height of fashion.

Above: Sauternes labels match the glittering gold of the wine. A few châteaux make a strong dry wine as well as the famous sweet one, particularly in poor vintages
Below: The 17th-century Château de Malle at Preignac is the prettiest house in Sauternes. Its 86-acre vineyard is unusual for the district, being half red and half white. Sauternes is notoriously unprofitable to make

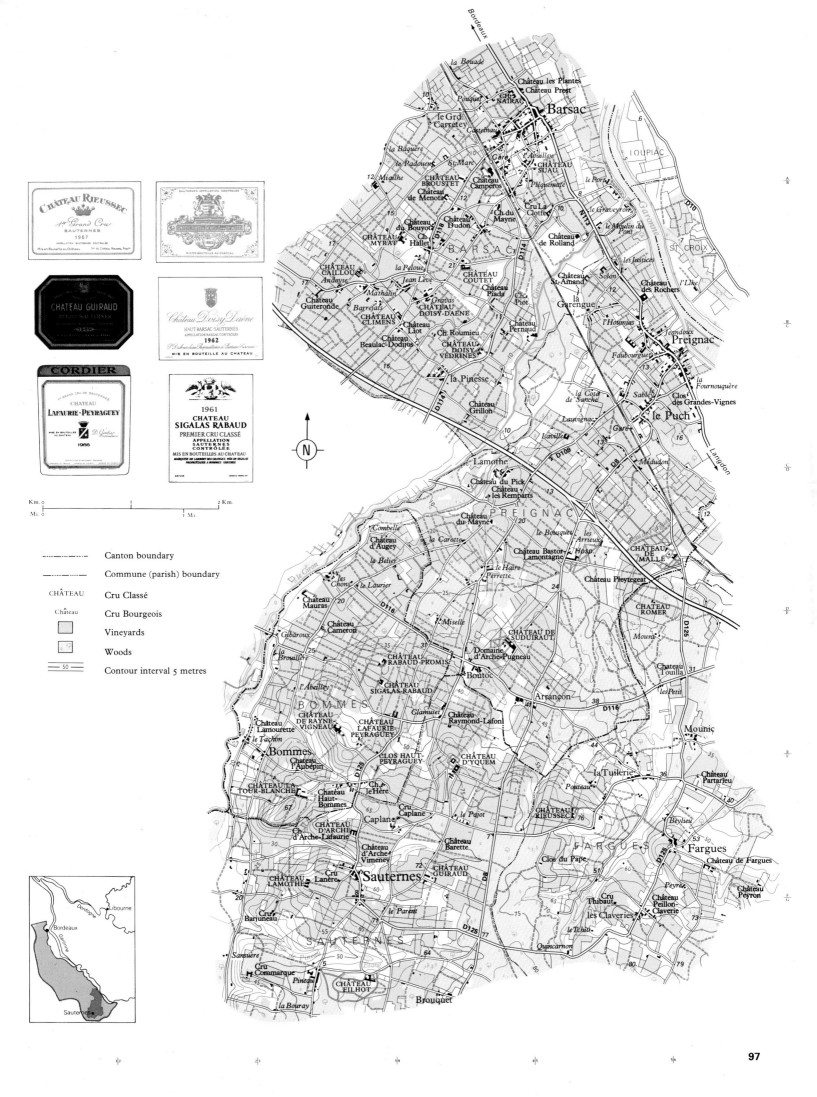

Château Rieussec
1er Grand Cru
SAUTERNES
1967

CHATEAU FILHOT
SAUTERNES APPELLATION CONTROLEE
CHÂTEAU FILHOT
1962

CHATEAU GUIRAUD
1er CRU SAUTERNES
LUTED

Château Doisy Daëne
HAUT BARSAC·SAUTERNES
APPELLATION BARSAC CONTROLÉE
1962
P. Dubourdieu Propriétaire à Barsac·Gironde
MIS EN BOUTEILLE AU CHATEAU

CORDIER
1er GRAND CRU DE SAUTERNES
CHATEAU
LAFAURIE-PEYRAGUEY
MISE EN BOUTEILLE
AU CHATEAU
1966

1961
CHATEAU
SIGALAS RABAUD
PREMIER CRU CLASSÉ
APPELLATION
SAUTERNES
CONTRÔLÉE
MIS EN BOUTEILLES AU CHATEAU
MARQUISE DE LAMBERT DES GRANGES, NÉE DE SIGALAS
PROPRIÉTAIRE A BOMMES · GIRONDE

——·— Canton boundary

——— Commune (parish) boundary

CHÂTEAU   Cru Classé

Château   Cru Bourgeois

           Vineyards

           Woods

══ 50 ══   Contour interval 5 metres

Km. 0   1   2 Km.
Mi. 0   1 Mi.

N

Bordeaux

la Bouade
Château les Plantes
Château Prost
CH. NAIRAC
Barsac
le Grd Carretey
Pouquet
Castelnau
la Bâquère
le Padouen
St Marc
Gare
CHÂTEAU SUAU
Aouilla
Miailhe
CHÂTEAU BROUSTET
Château Camperos
Pléquenade
Château de Menota
le Port
Château Dudon
Cru La Clotte
le Graveyron
le Moulin du Pont
Château du Bouyot
Ch. du Mayne
Château de Rolland
ST CROIX
CHÂTEAU MYRAT
Ch. Hallet
BARSAC
les Justices
l'Ihe
CHÂTEAU CAILLOU
Andayse
la Peloue
CHÂTEAU COUTET
Château St-Amand
Solon
la Garengue
Château des Rochers
Jean Levé
Mathalin
Château Piada
Ch. Piot
l'Houmias
Jeandoux
Preignac
Château Guiteronde
Grabas
CHÂTEAU DOISY-DAËNE
CHÂTEAU CLIMENS
Barrejats
Château Liot
Ch. Roumieu
Château Pernaud
Faubourguet
Beaulac-Dodijos
CHÂTEAU DOISY-VÉDRINES
la Côte de Sanche
Sable
la Fournouquère
Clos des Grandes-Vignes
le Puch
la Pinesse
Lauvignac
Gare
Château Grillon
Laville
Langdon
Lamothe
Médudon
Château du Pick
Château les Remparts
PREIGNAC
CHÂTEAU DE MALLE
Château du Mayné
le Bousquet
les Arrieux
Combelle
Château d'Augey
la Carotte
Château Bastor-Lamontagne
Hosp.
la Belier
le Haïre
Perrette
Château Pleytegeat
les Chons
le Laurier
CHÂTEAU ROMER
Château Mauras
Moura
Château Cameron
Miselle
la Brouillère
CHÂTEAU DE SUDUIRAUT
Château Touilla
CHÂTEAU RABAUD-PROMIS
Domaine d'Arche-Pugneau
les Petit
l'Abeilley
Boutoc
CHÂTEAU SIGALAS-RABAUD
Arrançon
Mounic
BOMMES
Clamuset
Château Raymond-Lafon
Château Lamourette
CHÂTEAU DE RAYNE-VIGNEAU
CHÂTEAU LAFAURIE-PEYRAGUEY
le Tachon
Château Partarieu
Bommes
Château l'Aubépin
CLOS HAUT-PEYRAGUEY
CHÂTEAU D'YQUEM
la Tuilerie
Pouteau
CHÂTEAU LA TOUR-BLANCHE
Château Haut-Bommes
Ch. le Hère
Cru Caplane
CHÂTEAU RIEUSSEC
Beylieu
CHÂTEAU D'ARCHE
Ch. d'Arche-Lafaurie
Caplane
le Pajot
Château Barette
FARGUES
Fargues
Château d'Arche-Vimeney
Clos du Pape
Château de Fargues
CHÂTEAU LAMOTHE
Cru Lanère
CHÂTEAU GUIRAUD
Sauternes
Peyra
Cru Barjuneau
le Parent
Cru Thibaut
Château Peillon-Claverie
Château Peyron
SAUTERNES
les Claveries
le Tchiti
Sansuère
Quincarnon
Cru Commarque
Pineau
Brana
CHÂTEAU FILHOT
Brouquet
la Bouray

97

Pomerol

Above: crimson must from Merlot grapes—the variety which gives Pomerol its softness, fruitiness and strength

The grapes are carried from the pickers to the *cuvier* in wooden tubs; each full tub makes a load for two men

Left: Vieux-Château-Certan is one of Pomerol's best vineyards and also one of the few Pomerol châteaux which looks more important than an ordinary modest house. It makes on average about 55,000 bottles a year of wine, fetching a price similar to a very good classed growth of the Médoc

IT IS strange there should be a new star in such an ancient wine country as Bordeaux. You would think it had all been known for centuries. Yet although Romans had vineyards in Pomerol, a hundred years ago it was known only for 'good common wine'. Even 40 years ago it was not considered in the top flight. Yet today its best château fetches the same price as the first growths of the Médoc, and an astonishing number of properties, for such a small area, are generally agreed to be among the best in the whole of Bordeaux.

Pomerol is such a curious corner of the world that it is hard to get your bearings. It is a good 25 miles east of Bordeaux along the Dordogne, almost in the suburbs of the sleepy old port of Libourne.

There is no real village centre in Pomerol; every family there makes wine, and every house stands apart among its vines. The landscape is evenly dotted with modest houses—each re-joicing in the name of château. The church stands oddly isolated too, like yet another little wine-estate. And that is Pomerol; there is nothing more to see.

Pomerol is another big gravel bank, or rather plateau, slightly rising and falling but remarkably flat overall. In the western part the soil tends to be sandy; to the east, where it meets St-Emilion, to be enriched with clay. It is en-tirely planted with vines, to the exclusion of all lesser plants. In the eastern part lie the best growths, so cheek by jowl with St-Emilion and under such identical conditions that it would be surprising to find any constant difference between them.

None the less the consensus is that Pomerols are the gentlest, richest, most instantly appeal-ing clarets. They have deep colour without the acidity and tannin that often goes with it, a comforting ripe smell, and sometimes great concentration of all their qualities: the striking essence of a great wine.

Pomerol is a democracy. It has no official classification, and indeed it would be very hard to devise one. There is no long tradition of steady selling to build on. Châteaux are small family affairs and subject to change as indivi-duals come and go. Furthermore a great num-ber rank together as—to keep everyone happy —'first growths'. Even to the wine merchant this is largely uncharted country. A strong tra-dition of direct supply to customers in France flourishes. Many orders that go off by train are the odd case to some doctor or lawyer in Amiens or Clermont-Ferrand.

There is a good deal of agreement, however, about which are the outstanding vineyards of Pomerol. Pétrus is allowed by all to come first. Vieux-Château-Certan, next door, is perhaps runner-up. Then in a bunch come La Fleur-Pétrus, La Conseillante, La Fleur, L'Evangile, Trotanoy, Petit-Village, Certan-de-May. It would be wrong to distinguish one group from another too clearly. Latour-à-Pomerol, L'Eglise-Clinet, Le Gay, Clos l'Eglise (how confusing the names are), La Croix-de-Gay, Clos René, Nenin and Gazin each have very high standards. On the map we distinguish the growths whose wines usually fetch the highest prices today.

Names sometimes become quite absurd. When, in eagerness to sound like some popular growth, compound names get too exuberant, we find part of the name being a claim that this is the Real and Original Château X: thus Châ-teau Vraye-Croix-de-Gay carries a picture of disagreeable neighbours which one hopes is a totally false one.

Before being overwhelmed by the complica-tions of Pomerol (and St-Emilion, where the situation is similar), it is worth knowing that the average standard is very high here. The village has a name for reliability.

Another advantage which has certainly helped Pomerol up the ladder recently is the fact that these wines are ready remarkably soon for Bordeaux. The chief grape variety here is not the tough-skinned Cabernet Sauvignon, whose wine has to live through a tannic youth to give its ultimate finesse: in Pomerol and St-Emilion the Merlot, secondary in the Médoc, is the leading vine. Great growths have about

More typical of the region, Château Moulin-à-Vent in the neighbouring commune of Lalande-de-Pomerol is a neat unit with its *chai* and *cuvier* round a yard. It produces about 40,000 bottles of red wine a year

70 or 80% Merlot, with perhaps 20% of the local Cabernet cousin, the Bouchet. Merlot wine is softer than Cabernet. Helped by rather richer soil than in the Médoc it gives the warmth and gentleness which characterize Pomerol. Even the best Pomerol has produced all its per-fume and as much finesse as it will ever achieve in 12 or 15 years, and most are already attractive at five, as against the Médoc's eight or nine.

Pomerol has no official
classification. These are
among the best growths,
but many make very
attractive reliable wine

St-Emilion

THE OLD town of St-Emilion is propped in the corner of an escarpment above the Dordogne. Behind it on the plateau vines flow steadily on into Pomerol. Beside it along the ridge they swoop down into the plain. It is the little rural gem of the Bordelais—inland and upland in spirit, Roman in origin, hollow with cellars and heady with wine.

Even the church at St-Emilion is a cellar: cut, like them all, out of solid limestone. The excellent restaurant in the town square is actually on the church roof, and you sit beside the belfry to eat your lampreys stewed in red wine à la Bordelaise.

St-Emilion makes rich red wine. Before many people can really come to terms with the dryness and delicacy of Médoc wine they love the solid tastiness of St-Emilion. The best of them in ripe and sunny seasons grow almost sweet as they mature.

On the whole St-Emilion wines take less long to reach perfection than Médoc wines, if a little longer than Pomerols: say four years for the wine of a poor vintage; eight and upwards for a good one.

There are two distinct districts of St-Emilion, not counting the lesser vineyards of the river plain and the parishes to the east and north-east which are allowed to use the name (and which are described and mapped on pages 102–103).

One group of the inner châteaux lies on the border of Pomerol, on the sandy and gravelly plateau. The most famous of this plateau district, and of the whole of St-Emilion, is Château Cheval Blanc, a trim little cream-painted house in a grove of trees which is far from suggesting the splendid red wine, some of the world's most full-blooded, which its vines produce. Like the nearby Château Pétrus in Pomerol it fetches the same colossal prices as the first growths of the Médoc.

Of Cheval Blanc's neighbours, Château Figeac comes nearest to its level, and Châteaux La Tour-du-Pin-Figeac and La Dominique are outstanding.

The other, larger group, the Côtes St-Emilion, occupies the escarpment round the town. At the abrupt edge of the plateau you can see that not very thick soil covers the soft but solid limestone in which the cellars are cut. At Château Ausone, the most famous château of the Côtes, you can walk into a cellar with vines, as it were, on the ground floor above you.

The Côtes wines may not be quite so fruity

Above: the Jurade de St-Emilion, the district's ancient association of wine-growers, processes in scarlet robes through the streets of the town
Below: Château Ausone commands a view of the Côtes to the east and of the valley of the Dordogne

as the 'Graves' wines from the plateau (the name Graves is confusingly applied to them because of their gravelly soil), but at their best they are the fullest-flavoured and most 'generous' wines of Bordeaux. They usually have 1% more alcohol than wine from the Médoc. Alkaline (i.e. chalky) soil is supposed to give wine strength; here it has the help of a full south-facing slope and in many places shelter from the west wind as well.

One other advantage the Côtes châteaux have over the Graves is their relative immunity to frost. Around Château Cheval Blanc a slight dip in the ground acts as a sump in which freezing air can collect on cloudless winter nights. On one dreadful night in February 1956 the temperature went down to $-24°$C. So many vines were killed that it took five or six years for production to pick up again.

Châteaux Canon, Magdelaine, La Gaffelière, Pavie and Clos Fourtet would certainly be on a short short list of the top Côtes wines: but the comfort of St-Emilion to the ordinary wine-lover is the number of other châteaux of moderate fame and extremely high standards providing utterly enjoyable but relatively accessible wine—the equivalent, perhaps, of the Premiers Crus vineyards of Beaune, Pommard and Volnay for value and character.

St-Emilion is not classified as the Médoc is. It merely divided its châteaux (in 1954) into Premiers Grands Crus and Grands Crus. There were 12 of the first, headed by Cheval Blanc and Ausone in a separate category of two, and 72 of the second. Some of the 72 are easily of the Médoc Cru Classé standard; others are the equivalent of Crus Bourgeois . . . but the list is alphabetical, so it is impossible to tell from it which are the best.

For consumers' purposes, if not officially, some further guide is helpful. On the map the 24 Grands Crus which normally fetch the highest prices are indicated as an intermediate category, in bigger type than the others.

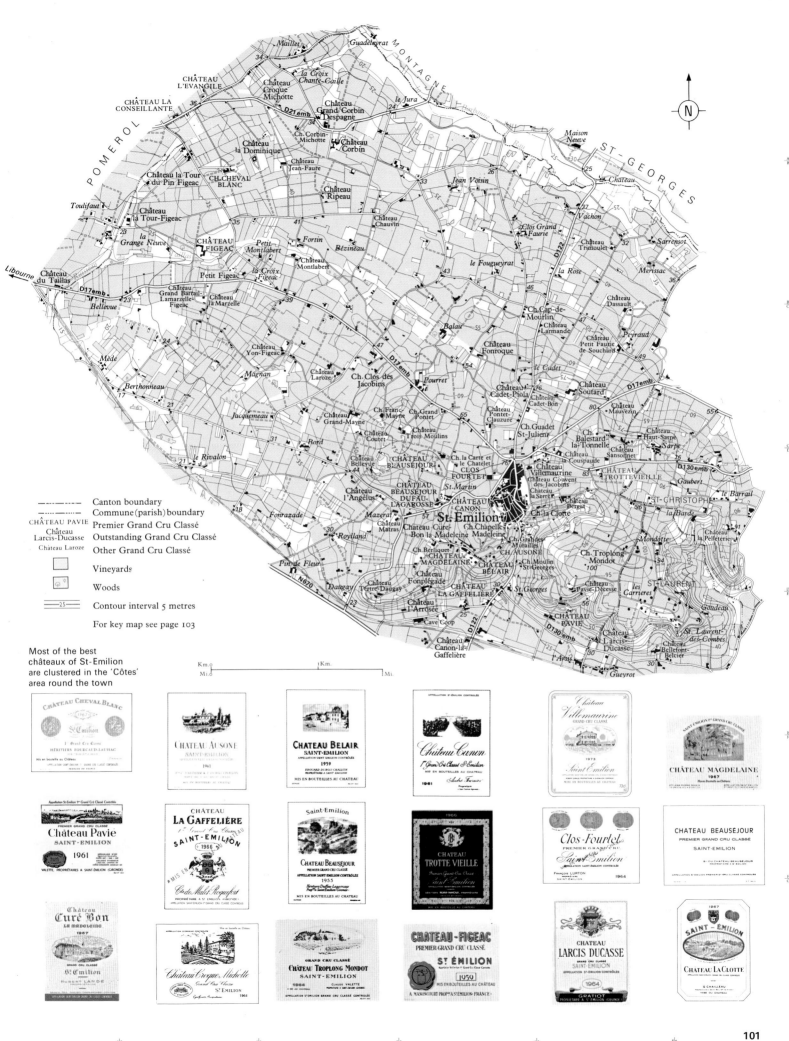

Map labels

Maillet · Guadeloupérat · MONTAGNE · ST-GEORGES

CHÂTEAU L'EVANGILE · la Croix Chante-Caille · Château Croque Michotte · le Jura · CHÂTEAU LA CONSEILLANTE · Château Grand Corbin Despagne · Ch.Corbin-Michotte · Château Corbin · Maison Neuve · Château la Dominique · Ch.Jean-Faure · Château Ripeau · Jean Voisin · Vachon · Château la Tour du Pin Figeac · CH.CHEVAL BLANC · Clos Grand Faurie · Château Trimoulet · Sarrensot · Toulifaut · Château la Tour-Figeac · la Rose · Merissac · la Grange Neuve · CHÂTEAU FIGEAC · Petit Montlabert · Fortin · Bézineau · le Fougueyrat · Château Montlabert · Château Chauvin · Château Dassault · Libourne · Château du Taillas · Château Grand Bartail-Lamarzelle-Figeac · Petit Figeac · la Croix Figeac · Château la Marzelle · Ch.Cap-de-Mourlin · Bellevue · Balau · Château Larmande · Mède · Château Yon-Figeac · Château Fonroque · Château Petit Faurie de Souchard · Peyraud · Magnan · Château Laroze · Ch.Clos des Jacobins · Pourret · le Cadet · Château Soutard · Berthonneau · Jacquemeau · Château Grand-Mayne · Ch.Franc-Mayne · Ch.Grand Pontet · Château Cadet-Piola · Château Cadet-Bon · Château Mauvezin · Château Coutet · Château Trois Moulins · Château Pontet-Clauzure · Ch.Guadet St-Julien · Ch.Balestard-la-Tonnelle · Château Haut-Sarpe · le Rivalon · Rord · Château Belleville · Ch.la Carte et le Chatelet · CLOS FOURTET · Château Couspaude · Château Sansonnet · Sarpe · CHÂTEAU BEAUSÉJOUR · CHÂTEAU BEAUSÉJOUR DUFAU-LAGAROSSE · St-Martin · Château Villemaurine · Château Couvent des Jacobins · CHÂTEAU TROTTEVIEILLE · Gaubert · ST-CHRISTOPHE · Fonrazade · Château l'Angélus · Mazerat · CHÂTEAU CANON · Château la Serre · Ch.la Clotte · Bergat · le Barral · Château Matras · Ch.Chapelle · St-Emilion · Ch.Cure-Bon la Madeleine · Madeleine · Ch.Grandes Murailles · la Barde · Château Pelleterie · Roylland · CHÂTEAU AUSONE · Mondotte · Ch.Bérliquet · CHÂTEAU MAGDELAINE · Ch.Moulin St-Georges · Ch.Troplong Mondot · ST-LAURENT · Pin de Fleur · Château Fonplégade · CHÂTEAU BELAIR · les Carrieres · Datguay · Château Tertre-Daugay · CHÂTEAU LA GAFFELIÈRE · St-Georges · Château Pavie-Décesse · Château l'Arrosée · Château Larcis-Ducasse · Goudeau · Cave Coop · CHÂTEAU PAVIE · St-Laurent-des-Combes · Château Canon-la-Gaffelière · Château Bellefont-Belcier · l'Arsis · Gueyrot · POMEROL

Legend

- - - - - Canton boundary
——— Commune (parish) boundary
CHÂTEAU PAVIE Premier Grand Cru Classé
Château Larcis-Ducasse Outstanding Grand Cru Classé
Château Laroze Other Grand Cru Classé

Vineyards

Woods

—25— Contour interval 5 metres

For key map see page 103

Most of the best châteaux of St-Emilion are clustered in the 'Côtes' area round the town

Km.0 ——— 1Km.
Mi.0 ——— 1Mi.

Wine labels

CHÂTEAU CHEVAL BLANC · St Emilion · HÉRITIERS FOURCAUD-LAUSSAC

CHÂTEAU AUSONE · SAINT-EMILION · 1961

CHATEAU BELAIR · SAINT-EMILION · 1959 · EDOUARD DUBOIS CHALLON

Château Canon · 1er Grand Cru Classé St Emilion · 1961 · André Fournier

Château Villemaurine · GRAND CRU CLASSÉ · 1973 · Saint Emilion

CHÂTEAU MAGDELAINE · 1967

Château Pavie · PREMIER GRAND CRU CLASSÉ · SAINT-EMILION · 1961 · VALETTE, PROPRIÉTAIRE A SAINT-EMILION (GIRONDE)

CHÂTEAU LA GAFFELIÈRE · 1er Grand Cru Classé · SAINT-EMILION · 1966 · Clos Malet-Roquefort

Saint-Emilion · CHATEAU BEAUSÉJOUR · PREMIER GRAND CRU CLASSÉ · APPELLATION SAINT-EMILION 1er GRAND CRU CONTRÔLÉE · 1955

CHATEAU TROTTE VIEILLE · 1966 · Premier Grand Cru Classé · Saint Emilion

Clos-Fourtet · PREMIER GRAND CRU · Saint-Emilion · François Lurton · 1964

CHATEAU BEAUSÉJOUR · PREMIER GRAND CRU CLASSÉ · SAINT-EMILION

Château Curé Bon LA MADELEINE · 1967 · GRAND CRU CLASSÉ · St Emilion · HUBERT LANDE

Château Croque Michotte · Grand Cru Classé · St Emilion · 1964

CHÂTEAU TROPLONG MONDOT · GRAND CRU CLASSÉ · SAINT-EMILION · 1964 · CLAUDE VALETTE

CHATEAU-FIGEAC · PREMIER-GRAND CRU CLASSÉ · St Emilion · 1959 · A. MANONCOURT PROP. St-EMILION-FRANCE

CHATEAU LARCIS DUCASSE · GRAND CRU CLASSÉ · SAINT-EMILION · 1964 · GRATIOT

SAINT - EMILION · 1967 · Château LaClotte · G.CHAILLEAU

Château St-Georges dominates the plateau of St-Emilion from its hilltop in the neighbouring village of St-Georges. It was built in 1774 by Victor Louis, the architect who designed Bordeaux's theatre, the finest in France

Below: Fronsac may be the next area of Bordeaux to become famous. Its wines have the classical attributes: deep colour, attractive fruitiness and long life

THE ILLUSTRIOUS parishes of Pomerol and St-Emilion are the heart of a much larger and more diffuse wine-district. St-Emilion's name is shared by seven small villages south and east, and a further five to the north-east can add the name of St-Emilion to their own. Pomerol is hemmed in by the communes of Fronsac, Néac and Lalande.

With their mixture of vines and woods and pastures and their little hills and valleys the villages east and north and west are more attractive than the monotonous vineyard of the plateau in the centre.

They are still a little-known wine-country. Even Libourne and Bordeaux négociants tend to take a local broker with them as guide when they penetrate their narrow lanes. It is almost impossible to identify the little châteaux. One wonders how their wine is distributed in a world which likes the reassurance of a famous name. Yet a network of private contacts all over France is well satisfied with their sound and solid red wine, besides what reaches 'le grand négoce' one way or another.

The châteaux shown on this map are most of the bigger and better-known of the hinterland. Fronsac, for example, has many small properties; the 11 on the map are those with more than local reputations. Fronsac as a whole is reputed the coming thing in Bordeaux; one can expect to hear more of it; its wines are splendidly fruity and full of character, and they are also still (quite) cheap.

Lalande's Château Bel-Air has long been famous. Néac also can produce some wines to compare with Pomerol.

The equivalent back-country châteaux north of St-Emilion are probably slightly less-known, with the exception of the splendid Château St-Georges, which overlooks the whole district from its hill, and makes excellent wine.

The vine is still dominant in this pretty, hilly landscape, even if there are no names to conjure with among the 'châteaux'. The co-operatives of this area, that of Lussac in particular, make very sound wine at reasonable prices. It is good country for an exploratory visit; its wines often make up in satisfying solidity what they lack in finesse.

The cluster of villages east of St-Emilion, however, are a different matter. In St-Laurent Château Larcis-Ducasse is a Grand Cru and rated among the top 15 or so wines of St-Emilion. In the same commune Château Belle-font-Belcier is also well known. To the north in St-Christophe Château Haut-Sarpe is another Grand Cru Classé, and Château Fombrauge has a certain reputation. On the outcrop of the Côtes at St-Hippolyte Châteaux Ferrand, Lassègue and Capet-Guillier make good wine and just to the east in St-Etienne Château Puy-Blanquet has a distinguished name. All these châteaux and several others in the district command prices comparable to St-Emilion Grands Crus from the central area mapped on the previous page.

Canton boundary
Commune boundary
Vineyards
Woods
Areas mapped at larger scale (pages 99 and 101)
Contour interval 20 metres

Bourg and Blaye

IT IS CURIOUS to think that Bourg and Blaye, the productive little districts the wrong side of the Gironde, were exporting wine before the mighty Médoc was ever planted. Only dire shortage of reasonably priced wine has driven people to re-explore them recently. Blaye specializes in dry white wine of moderate quality (and a little red, under the appellation Premières Côtes de Blaye): the smaller Bourg district offers principally red, from the Cabernet and Merlot grapes, Médoc style; some of it very round and fruity and good.

The country is not flat like the Médoc, which faces it across the water. Irregular soft hills give it charm. Blaye and Bourg used to be important little ports, but now almost the only activity is a useful ferry from Blaye to Lamarque near Margaux.

The best châteaux lie within a mile or so of the Gironde, as in the Médoc. Few names are well known as yet, but Châteaux du Bousquet, Rouet, de Barbe, La Croix-Millorit and Tayac in Bourg and Le Menaudat, Barbé, Sociando and Segonzac in Blaye have established reputations.

The claim has been made that the district makes the red Bordeaux most similar to burgundy. There may be some grounds for it in the limestone and clay soil, but the description does not give a true impression of the wines. They are true clarets for everyday drinking, and age excellently if anyone troubles to keep them. In the past they have reputedly been much used for underpinning Médocs of lean years. Recently they have been appearing on more and more wine lists abroad.

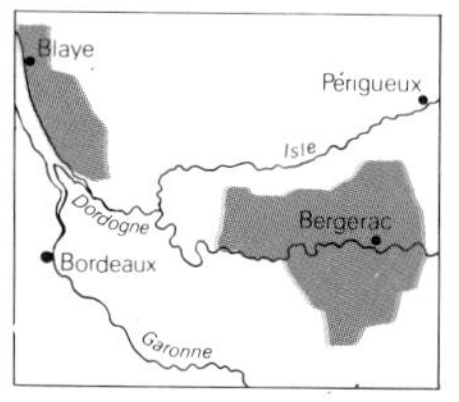

Bourg and Blaye are a reservoir of the kind of wines everyone wants: reliable, enjoyable and cheap. Their red wines are much better than their white

Arrondissement boundary
Canton boundary
Commune boundary
Vineyards
Woods
Contour interval 10 metres

Bergerac

BORDEAUX's beautiful hinterland, the Dordogne, leading back into the maze of succulent valleys cut in the stony upland of Périgord, makes simple country wine compared with Bordeaux. Yet Périgord's restaurants are famous, and their wine is the local wine. The driest (now often a Sauvignon Blanc) and the sweetest white wines of the area are good, and the red can be excellent light-weight claret. To the south, the Côtes de Duras makes similar wine.

Monbazillac is the best of the appellations within Bergerac. At one time it was a rival to Sauternes; old Château Monbazillac is supremely rich-textured, golden and intense. Now it is a co-operative and its wine, though good, is no longer made in the same laborious way. Pécharmant has the best red wine; Rosette and the Montravels better-than-average white.

Monbazillac's vineyards slope towards the north— an unusual situation. Château Monbazillac is a shade left of the centre of the skyline in this picture

Côtes de Montravel
Haut-Montravel
Montravel
Bergerac
Monbazillac
Rosette
Pécharmant
Côtes de Saussignac

For key map
see opposite page

Château Monbazillac, once a rival to the great Sauternes, is the star of Bergerac. The dry whites and everyday reds are first-rate *vins de pays*. The Côtes de Duras (label above), Bergerac's southern neighbour, makes similar red and white wines.

Département boundary — — — —

105

The Champagne Country

Immense rollers of vines stalk Champagne like the evidence of a far-off hurricane. At vintage time a gilded chill falls on the landscape; the coal-miners and their families who come to pick cannot animate the drowsy hillsides. The leaves go furiously red, and fall, and a frosty wind drives everyone indoors

THE NAME OF champagne is limited not only to a defined area, like the appellations of Bordeaux, but to a process, through which every drop of wine must go before it can claim the name. A few countries outside Europe, indeed, use the name as though it only meant the process. But it is the special qualities of this northernmost of France's great wine regions which make champagne unique.

It would be claiming too much to say that all champagne is better than any other sparkling wine in the world. There are champagnes and champagnes. But good champagne has a combination of freshness, delicacy, richness and raciness, and a gently stimulating power, which no other wine has ever quite attained.

The region whose soil and climate have so much to offer is only 90 miles north-east of Paris. It centres round a small range of hills rising from a plain of chalk and carved in two by the wanderings of the River Marne. Within this area the names of the villages do not directly concern the consumer as they do in, for example, Burgundy. For the essence of champagne is that it is a blended wine, known by the name of the maker, not the vineyard.

There are 58,000 acres in Champagne, with 17,000 proprietors. Only 13% belongs to the famous firms who make and sell two-thirds of the wine. The country is owned not by great landowners but by thousands of local, often part-time, growers, many of whom have other

jobs as well. It has been estimated that out of 18,000 men who work in the vineyards 15,500 own at least some vines: only 2,500 are employees with no vines of their own. There are 8,000 holdings of only one acre or less.

What the map shows is the heart of the region, where the grapes which the best houses buy for their best champagne are grown. Outlying districts (the small map) are still legally Champagne, but their wine is not up to the standard of the central zone. There are three distinct parts to the region shown here; some of the character of the wine of each is essential to the classical champagne blend.

The Montagne de Reims is planted with Pinot Noir vines, whose black grapes have to be pressed very rapidly to give white wine without a trace of colour. No one has quite explained how in this most northern vineyard a north slope, which some of the best of the Montagne is, can give good wine. The theory is that the air heats up on the plain below, and flows encouragingly up through the vines. . . . Montagne wines contribute to the bouquet, the headiness and what the French call the 'carpentry'—the backbone of the blend.

The Vallée de la Marne, the next area, has south and south-east slopes which trap the sun and make these the fullest, roundest and ripest wines, with plenty of bouquet. These are largely black-grape vineyards as well; here the Pinot Meunier joins the Pinot Noir. Bouzy makes the

small quantity of still red wine which the Champenois jealously keep for themselves. It can be like rather faint but exquisite burgundy.

The east-facing slope south of Epernay is the Côte des Blancs, planted with the white Chardonnay grapes which give freshness and finesse to the blend. Wine from here is sometimes sold as Blanc de Blancs, without the traditional proportion of black-grape wine. It is a question of taste, but most experienced champagne-lovers find Côte des Blancs wine on its own lacks the perfect balance—is too light. None the less Avize and Cramant are two villages with long-respected names for their (unblended) wine; Cramant, confusingly, for its *crémant*, or half-sparkling, champagne.

Today as much as a third of the crop is processed and sold by the growers themselves. Their market is mainly France. For the two-thirds that the famous 'Maisons' buy for their brands there is an unusual pricing system which expresses the quality of the different areas. At the start of the harvest, one price (per kilo of grapes) is decided on by a committee of growers and merchants. Growers in the best communes, or Grands Crus, are paid 100%, the full price. Premiers Crus receive between 90 and 99%, and so on down to 77% for some of the outlying areas.

On the maps the leading communes are shown in larger type. Most of the wine in all first-class brands comes from these villages.

Reims

Tinqueux

Cité Charbonneaux

Cormontreuil

Janvry   Gueux

Ormes

Vrigny   Les Mesneux

Bouleuse   Méry-   Coulommes   Bezannes
                  Prémecy   la Montagne
                                                    Mont Benoit   Trois
         St. Euphraise   Pargny-   Jouy-   Puits   Taissy
Aubilly et Clairizet   les-Reims   les-Reims
                                                                          Mont de   Sillery
Sarcy   Ville-   la Cuche   88
                  Bouilly   Dommange   Villers-   Puisieux
         Bligny   Sacy   aux-Nœuds   Champfleury   Montbré
                                                 Écueil   Beaumont-
Chambrecy   244   Chemin de la Barbarie   127   Chemin de la Barbarie   sur-Vesle
         135   Chaumuzy   267   Mont Trouilly   091   128
                  les Patis d'Écueil   Chamery   149   Verzenay
         140   Marfaux   148   Rilly   Verzy
                                        Pourcy   268   Chigny-   151   Mailly   208
Champlat et   Villers-   les Roses   276   283
Boujacourt   182   Courtagnon   266 Allerand   Ludes   Villers-
200   265   les Battis   Marmery
Jonquery 247   Bois de Corton   279   260
Bois de   Nanteuil   le Bois de St Remy   les Batis de Sermiers   Forêt de la Montagne de Reims
la Cohette   Cuchery   la Fosse   Bois de   Bois de Notre Dame   Ville-   208
                  Belval   263   St. Quentin   Germaine en Selve   Mont Tournant
Bois de la   sous-Chatillon   Bois de Fleury   271   Trépail
Rodemat   Cormoyeux   St. Imoges   Bois du   257   Bois des Dames   Mont Tournant
         Bois du Roi   Fleury   Romery   Bois du Gouffre   Mont St. Hubin   Louvois   112
Villers-   la Rivière   Forêt de la Montagne de Reims   Mont Hurlet   Bouzy   Vaudemanges
sous-Chatillon   234   Tauxières-   Mt.
Reuil   154   Hautvillers   Champillon   Fontaine   Mutry   Écouve   100 98   Ambonnay
Venteuil   Bois de   Bois de   sur-Ay   100
         67   St. Marc   Cumières   Charlefontaine   99   Mt
Damery   69   Dizy-   Avenay   des Plantes
         Boursault   Magenta   Val d'Or   Mont Charlier   97
Vauciennes   Mardeuil   N3   Ay   Mutigny   Bisseuil   Tours-sur-Marne   103
         91   Mareuil-sur-Ay   138   Condé-sur-Marne

Épernay   69

Chouilly   N3

Forêt d'Épernay   106   Pierry
242   178
240   Moussy
                  Vinay   88
                          Chavot   Côte des Blancs
                  Cuis   091
         Montholon   Mancy   Butte de Saran
Morangis   128
         Moslins   Granves   Cramant
                  B d'Avize   Avize   108
                                          Oger
                          Forêt d'Oger   239   116
                          Forêt du Mesnil
229   Le Mesnil-sur-Oger
                  245
         Gionges   123
                          232

Vertus

Bois de Cormont
226

Legend:
- – – – – Arrondissement boundary
- .... Canton boundary
- **MAILLY** Grand Cru commune
- VERZY Premier Cru commune
- Vineyards
- Woods
- —200— Contour interval 20 metres

Km. 0   1   2   3   4   5   6 Km.
Mi. 0   1   2   3   4 Mi.

Soissons
Reims
Château-Thierry   Châlons-sur-Marne
Paris   Épernay
         Marne
                  Aube
Seine
Troyes   Bar-sur-Aube
         Bar-sur-Seine

The Champagne Towns

Above: in 1858, bottles of champagne were (right to left) disgorged, topped up, had the cork hammered home and tied on with string
Right: today's dégorgeur uses precisely the same technique. The essential process has not changed

WHAT HAPPENS in the towns of Champagne concerns us just as much as what happens in the country. The process of champagne-making has only just begun when the grapes are picked and pressed. Without delay the opaque must is taken to the shipper's 'maison' in Reims or Epernay or Ay. There it will spend at least the next two years.

It ferments busily at first, but as it slows down the doors are thrown open to let in the wintry air. In the cold (today, of course, controlled by air-conditioning) the fermentation stops. The wine spends a chilly winter, still with the potential of more fermentation latent in it.

So it used to be shipped. England in the 17th century was an eager customer for barrels of this delicate, rather sharp wine. According to Patrick Forbes, the historian of champagne, the English bottled it on arrival; and found that they had created a sparkling wine.

Whether or not it was the English who did it first, early bottling is the vital stage in the historical process which changed the *vin du pays* of northern France into the prima donna of the world.

For the wine continued to ferment in the bottle and the gas given off by the fermentation dissolved in the wine. If the natural effect was given a little encouragement—a little more sugar, a little more yeast—what had been a slight, though very attractive, wine was found to improve immeasurably, gaining strength and character over a period of two years or more. Above all the inexhaustible bubbles gave it a miraculous liveliness.

Dom Pérignon, cellar-master of the Abbey of Hautvillers at the end of the 17th century, is credited with the next round of developments; the cork tied down with string, the stronger bottles (though still not strong enough; he lost half his wine through bottles bursting), and above all the art of blending wines from different parts of the district to achieve the best possible flavour.

The chief difference between the brands of champagne lies in this making of the cuvée, as the blending is called. All depends on the skill of the director tasting the raw young wines and peering into their future—and on how much his firm is prepared to spend on its raw materials; for the more top-quality wine goes

into the cuvée the better it will be. Each firm has a tradition of the kind of wine it makes; no difference should be noticeable in its non-vintage wine from year to year. One might instance Krug, Bollinger, Roederer, Clicquot and Pol Roger as typical of the old style, making full-flavoured, mature-tasting champagne.

Another fashion today, started by Moët et Chandon with their 'Dom Pérignon', is to make a super-luxury wine, relegating (in theory) even the best vintages to second place. Dom Ruinart, Heidsieck Diamant Bleu, Roederer Cristal and Taittinger's Comtes de Champagne are all in this bracket.

The widow Clicquot made her contribution to champagne in the early years of the 19th century. She devised a method of removing the sediment which resulted from bottle fermentation without removing the bubbles at the same time. Briefly what she invented was a desk of wood in which the mature bottles of wine could be stuck in holes upside down (*sur point*). Her cellarmen gave each bottle a gentle shake and twist (*remuage*) every day until all the sediment had dislodged from the glass and settled on the cork. Then they took out the cork with the bottle still upside down, let the eggcupful of

wine containing the sediment escape (*dégorgement*), topped up the bottle with wine from another of the same and put in a new cork. To make disgorging easier today the neck of the bottle containing the sediment is frozen first: a plug of murky ice shoots out when the bottle is opened, leaving perfectly clear wine behind.

The process which thousands of visitors go to Reims and Epernay to see remains essentially the same as ever. Not the least spectacular thing is the immense cellars where it is done. Some of them are Roman chalk pits under the city. One firm uses trains in its 15 miles of tunnel.

Every trace of sugar in champagne is used up when it is re-fermented in its bottle: it becomes totally dry—too dry for most tastes. A little wine-and-sugar is therefore added at *dégorgement*: less than 2% for wine labelled Brut; 1.5–2.5% for Extra Dry; 2–4% for Sec; 4–6% for Demi-Sec; over 6% for Doux. The last three are all properly dessert wines.

The full flavour of champagne is lost if it is served too cold. Ideally it should be thoroughly cool but not at all icy. Most important of all it should be mature. Very young champagne makes enemies. Time finds in it inimitable glorious flavours.

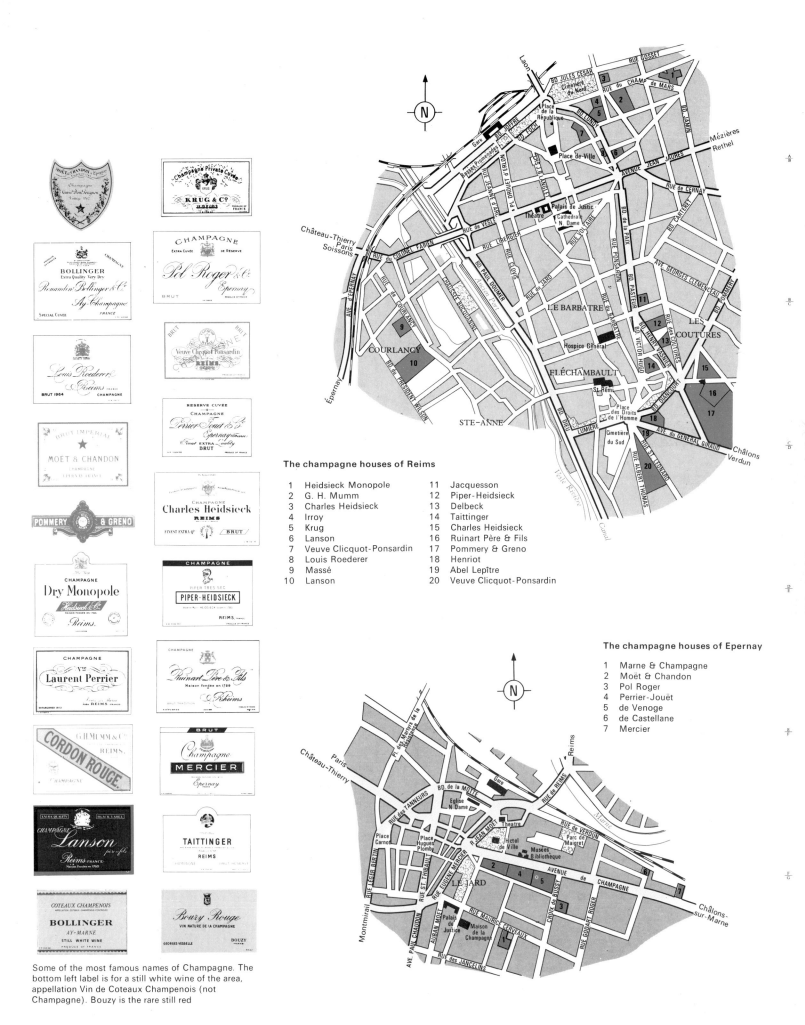

The champagne houses of Reims

1	Heidsieck Monopole	11	Jacquesson
2	G. H. Mumm	12	Piper-Heidsieck
3	Charles Heidsieck	13	Delbeck
4	Irroy	14	Taittinger
5	Krug	15	Charles Heidsieck
6	Lanson	16	Ruinart Père & Fils
7	Veuve Clicquot-Ponsardin	17	Pommery & Greno
8	Louis Roederer	18	Henriot
9	Massé	19	Abel Lepître
10	Lanson	20	Veuve Clicquot-Ponsardin

The champagne houses of Epernay

1 Marne & Champagne
2 Moët & Chandon
3 Pol Roger
4 Perrier-Jouët
5 de Venoge
6 de Castellane
7 Mercier

Some of the most famous names of Champagne. The bottom left label is for a still white wine of the area, appellation Vin de Coteaux Champenois (not Champagne). Bouzy is the rare still red

Alsace

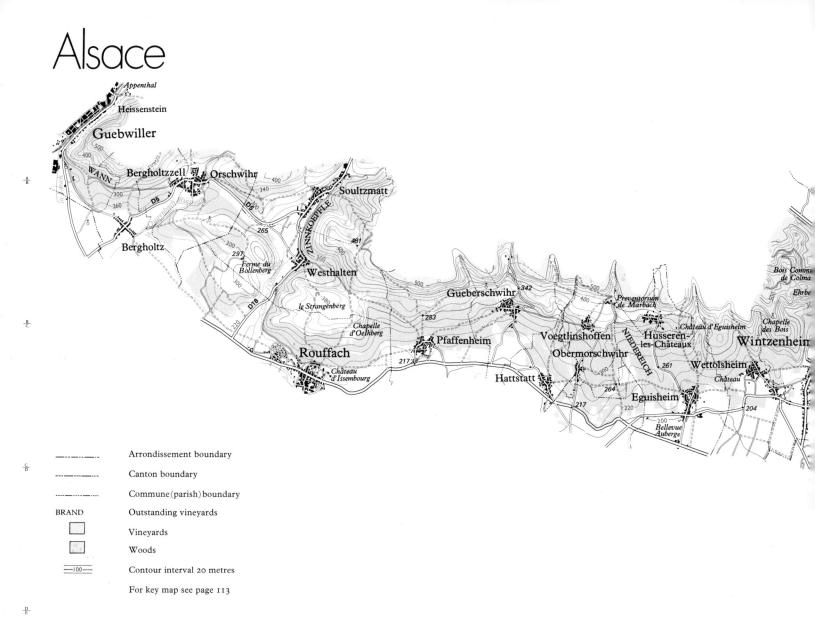

Arrondissement boundary
- - - - - - -

Canton boundary
- · - · - · -

Commune (parish) boundary
· · · · · · · ·

BRAND Outstanding vineyards

☐ Vineyards

▨ Woods

══100══ Contour interval 20 metres

For key map see page 113

THE WINE of Alsace reflects the curious situation of a border province. A traveller at the time of the French Revolution found it incredible that this land, so clearly intended by nature to be part of Germany, was actually annexed to France.

Today the Alsatians, although they still speak a sort of German, feel very differently. What has not changed is the physical barrier between them and the rest of France; for it is the Vosges, not the Rhine, which makes the great change in landscape, architecture, climate—and not least in wine.

Alsace makes Germanic wine in the French way. The tone is set by the climate, the soil and the choice of grape varieties: all comparable with the vineyards of slightly farther north, slightly farther down the Rhine valley, which are in Germany. What differs is the interpretation put on these things—because today German and Alsatian wine growers hold opposite points of view of what they want their wine to do and be.

To put the difference in a nutshell, the Germans look for sweetness, the Alsatians for strength. German wine at its best is not for the table, but the drawing-room, or the garden. Alsatian wine is the great adjunct to one of France's most splendid cuisines.

Alsace gives the flowery-scented grapes of Germany the body and authority of such table

The Confrérie St-Etienne is Alsace's red-robed wine growers' and shippers' association

wines as white burgundy, proper accompaniments to strong and savoury food.

Instead of grape-sugar lingering delicately in the wine, the grower likes a dry, firm, clean flavour. He ferments every ounce of the sugar which the long dry summers of Alsace give him, concentrating the essences of his highly-perfumed German-style grapes into a sometimes astonishingly spicy fragrance.

The Vosges Mountains are the secret of the success of these east-facing vineyards, which lie along their flank at an altitude of between 600 and 1,200 feet, in a ribbon rarely more than a mile wide. The higher the mountains are, the drier the land which they shelter from the mois-

Alsace vines are trained tall. On the wooded Vosges Eguisheim's three ruined châteaux are a landmark

ture of the west. In the north where they are lower their influence is less marked; the wines of Bas-Rhin tend to be the weaker in strength and savour. In the centre and the south of the vineyard, where the best wine villages are found, the mountains can keep the sky clear of cloud for weeks on end.

Alsace, like Champagne, is an exception to the usual French pattern of a complex structure of Appellations Contrôlées, pinning every wine down to the exact district of its birth.

The trade is based on the activities of merchant houses, most of whom are growers, but who can buy wine up and down the country for their branded blends. Instead of place names

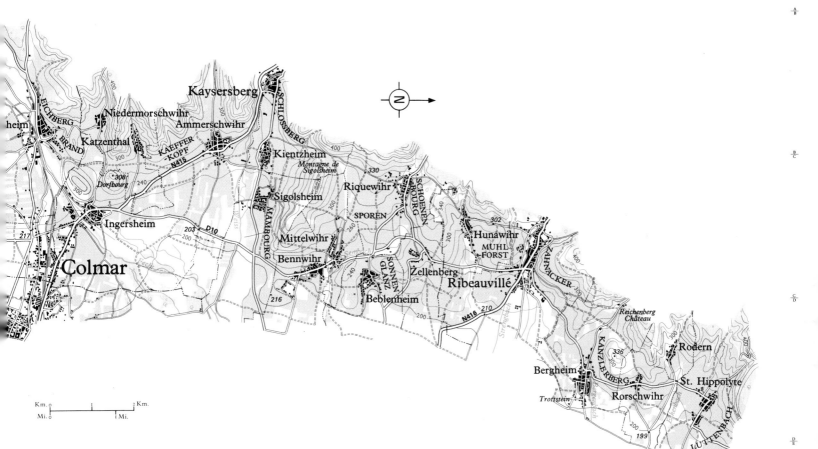

The finest of Alsace's many grapes, the Riesling of the Rhine is recognizably speckled when it is ripe

sheltered vineyards give distinctly softer and richer wine.

Up to 1975 the whole area had only one Appellation Contrôlée, local variations of sun and soil notwithstanding, In 1975 a new appellation, 'Alsace Grand Cru', was announced, to take effect in 1978. The Grands Crus will be wines from certain slopes long recognized as the best, which will have to be made exclusively from the 'noble' grapes (Riesling, Gewürztraminer, Pinot Gris or Muscat) and have to attain a certain minimum natural strength before any sugar is added.

The map on these pages shows the central and southern part of the 70-mile-long Alsace vineyard, the part which gives all the best wines and where most of the Grands Crus sites are concentrated. The vineyard names on the map will probably all be Grands Crus, though at this date only Schlössberg, between Kaysersberg and Kientzheim, has been confirmed. Many of them are already in use on the better wines of particular négociants. Other merchants have their own 'Clos' names (the Clos Ste-Hune of Trimbach, for example, or the Clos des Amandiers of Dopff & Irion), which may not be designated Grands Crus but which nevertheless guarantee some of the merchant's best wine.

A signposted Route des Vins takes visitors on a meandering course the whole length of the Alsace wine country. It calls on the way at some

The heart of Colmar, the wine capital of Alsace, is a typical superb survival from the 16th century

they market grape names. Alsace is the one part of France where you order 'a bottle of Riesling' or 'a bottle of Sylvaner', instead of specifying a vineyard, village or regional name.

The wines of the different merchants and growers, however, do tend to reflect the style and quality of the part of Alsace they come from. Barr, for example, is perhaps the best commune of the Bas-Rhin, in the north, but its wines have more acidity, are less substantial than those of Riquewihr. The region of Riquewihr, centrally placed with good south-facing slopes standing out from the Vosges, seems to have the ideal situation. At the far southern end of the region, at Guebwiller, the perfectly

of the prettiest wine towns in the world. The richest possible operatic Gothick is standard architecture here: overhanging gables and flowery courtyards and well-heads and cobbles and leaded lights and carved beams survive en masse in many of the villages. Riquewihr and Kaysersberg are the most beautiful. Colmar, the capital of Alsace wine, has a magnificent collection of timber-frame houses from the 15th century on.

Between them the high-trained vines block out the view along narrow lanes, until you reach a ridge and suddenly see the gleaming green sea rolling against the mountains before and behind, disappearing in a haze in the distance.

The Wines of Alsace

THE GRAPES which give their names and special qualities to the wines of Alsace are the Riesling of the Rhine—responsible here and in Germany for the best wine—the Sylvaner, Muscat, Pinot Gris, the lesser Chasselas and Knipperlé, and the unique and fragrant Gewürztraminer.

The Gewürztraminer is the perfect introduction to Alsace. You would not think that so fruity a scent could come from any wine so clean and dry. Gewürz means spice in German; the spice is there all the way down, and stays on your palate for two or three minutes after you have swallowed.

To the initiated a wine with so marked a character becomes dull after a while. It has its place with some of the richest of the very rich Alsatian dishes; goose or pork. But Alsatians consider the Riesling their true Grand Vin. It offers something much more elusive; a balance of hard and gentle, flowery and strong, which leads you on and never surfeits.

These two, and two more less generally known, the Pinot Gris (or Tokay d'Alsace) and the Muscat, are classed as the Noble Wines of Alsace. Only these can be used to make Grand Cru wines under the new regulations. Recently there has been renewed interest in the Tokay d'Alsace (no connection with Hungarian Tokay), which makes the fullest bodied but least perfumed wine of the region; it has obvious uses at table as an alternative to a 'big', and therefore more expensive, white burgundy. The Muscat surprises everyone who knows the wine the muscat grape makes anywhere else in the world, which is always sweet. Here it keeps all its characteristic grapy scent but makes a dry wine as clean as a whistle, a very good aperitif.

In a class above the common wines of the region, but not quite reckoned noble, comes the Sylvaner, the maid-of-all-work of the German vineyards. Alsace Sylvaner is light and sometimes nicely tart. Without the tartness it can be a little dull and coarse in flavour. It is often used as the first wine at an Alsatian dinner, to build up to the main wine, the Riesling.

The lesser grapes, the Chasselas and the Knipperlé (there are others, too), are not usually identified on the bottle—or indeed very often bottled at all. They are the open wines of cafés and restaurants. Very young, particularly in the summer after a good vintage, they are so good that visitors should not miss them by insisting on bottled wine. The term Edelzwicker (meaning 'noble mixture') is often applied to blends of more than one grape variety.

What all these wines have in common is the Alsatian style of wine-making, which is almost fanatically concerned with naturalness. To hear an Alsatian grower talking about German wines you would think they were all made by white-coated chemists on a laboratory bench. 'Once you let a chemist in your house he will make himself indispensable by frightening you with all the diseases your wine might catch', they say. They scorn refinements of fining, or anything which involves additions to the wine of any kind—except, alas, sugar: Alsace is not immune from the passion for adding sugar whether the wine needs it or not. They keep it undisturbed in huge wooden casks, racking and filtering as little as possible. They even take precautions to fill the bottle as full as possible and to use a specially long cork—all to protect the wine from the air. They achieve a remarkable balance of strength and freshness, fruit and acidity by their pains.

None the less when a really fine autumn comes on the heels of a good summer, and they find grapes ripening beautifully with no threat of bad weather, not even an Alsatian, dedicated as he is to clean dry table wines, can resist doing as the Germans do and getting the last drop of sugar out of his vines.

These late-pickings are even sometimes labelled with the German words Auslese and Beerenauslese, although the phrase Vendange Tardive is more in keeping with Alsatian feelings. They reach heights of lusciousness not far removed from the rarest and most expensive of all German wines. A late-picked Gewürztraminer or Muscat has perhaps the most exotic smell of any wine in the world, and can at the same time keep a remarkable cleanness and finesse of flavour.

At less exalted levels, the words Grand Vin, or Réserve Exceptionnelle, or any combination with the words Grand or Réserve, appearing on a bottle of Alsace wine means that it is 11% alcohol—a shade more than most fine German wines and the same as a good white burgundy. The new appellation Alsace Grand Cru (see page 111) is much more strictly delimited. In addition to achieving certain natural must-weights (equivalent to 10% alcohol for Riesling and Muscat, 11% for Gewürztraminer and Pinot Gris) the yield per hectare is controlled at 70 hectolitres (admittedly a high figure; 45 is average in Burgundy) and the grape variety must be approved for the particular site: Muscat, for example, will only be Grand Cru in very few places. And the wines of each site, each variety and each vintage must be kept separately—the idea being to encourage the same corpus of connoisseurship as Burgundy or the Moselle enjoy.

To the same end it has already been decreed that all Alsace wine must be bottled in Alsace. Champagne is the only other region with this rule.

A little red wine is made from the Pinot Noir, but it rarely gets a deeper colour than a rosé, and never a very marked or distinguished flavour. Rouge d'Alsace, and sometimes vin gris, or very pale pink wine, will be found in *brasseries* (the word for a restaurant serving Alsatian food, traditionally to go with beer) in Paris and elsewhere.

Alsace itself has two of the best restaurants in France: Gaertner's Aux Armes de France at Ammerschwihr and Haeberlin's Auberge de l'Ill at Illhaeusern. Foie gras frais (whole goose liver, as opposed to pâté de foie gras) is one of the dishes worth travelling for. In general, Alsace cooking demonstrates what a French artist can do with German ideas. Sauerkraut becomes choucroute, and suddenly delicious. Dishes which look as though they are going to be heavy turn out to be rich but light. Quiches and onion tart are almost miraculously edible. In Alsace no one looks beyond the range of white wines of the country to accompany this profusion of dishes.

Alsace labels usually feature the grape variety in type as big as the producer's name

The Language of the Label

Cuvée Blend (normal practice in Alsace)
Grand Vin Wine with over 11% alcohol
Réserve Exceptionnelle (the same)
Grand Réserve (ditto)
Grand Cru The new appellation contrôlée for wines of the best varieties from the best, designated, vineyards
Mise d'Origine All Alsace wine is now bottled in Alsace
Vendange Tardive Late-picked wine, implying more strength and/or sweetness
Spatlese, Beerenauslese, etc. These German terms are sometimes used

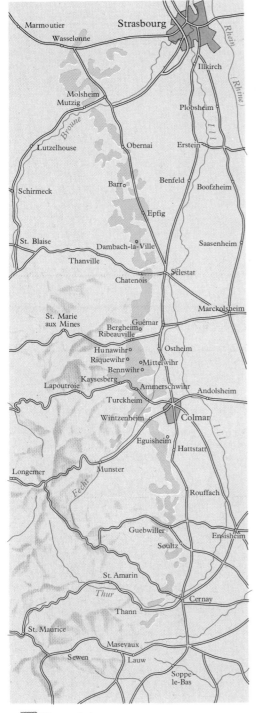

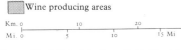

Wine producing areas

Km. 0   10   20   30 Km.
Mi. 0   5   10   15 Mi

Above: The full stretch of
the Alsace vineyards is
about 70 miles, of which
only the small central
portion (pages 110–111)
produces the very finest
wines

Right: Most famous and
unspoilt little medieval
wine town in France,
Riquewihr huddles below
the Schoenenberg in
H. Bacher's wood
engraving

The Loire Valley and Muscadet

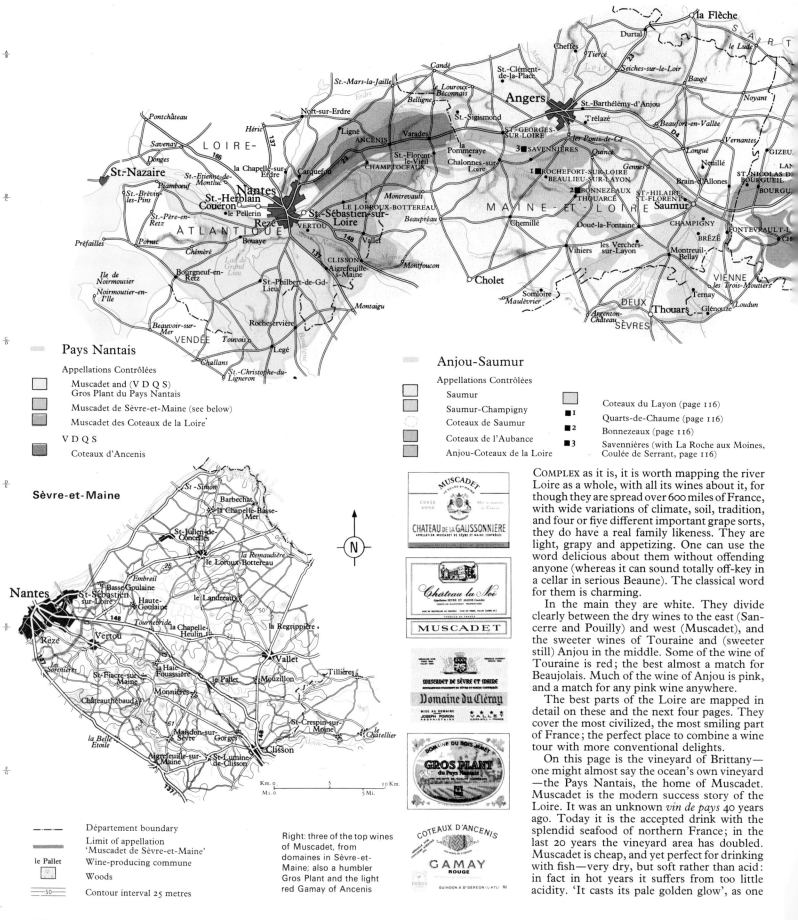

Pays Nantais

Appellations Contrôlées

Muscadet and (V D Q S)
Gros Plant du Pays Nantais

Muscadet de Sèvre-et-Maine (see below)

Muscadet des Coteaux de la Loire

V D Q S

Coteaux d'Ancenis

Anjou-Saumur

Appellations Contrôlées

Saumur

Saumur-Champigny

Coteaux de Saumur

Coteaux de l'Aubance

Anjou-Coteaux de la Loire

Coteaux du Layon (page 116)

■ I Quarts-de-Chaume (page 116)

■ 2 Bonnezeaux (page 116)

■ 3 Savennières (with La Roche aux Moines,
Coulée de Serrant, page 116)

Sèvre-et-Maine

Département boundary

Limit of appellation
'Muscadet de Sèvre-et-Maine'

le Pallet — Wine-producing commune

Woods

Contour interval 25 metres

Right: three of the top wines
of Muscadet, from
domaines in Sèvre-et-
Maine; also a humbler
Gros Plant and the light
red Gamay of Ancenis

COMPLEX as it is, it is worth mapping the river
Loire as a whole, with all its wines about it, for
though they are spread over 600 miles of France,
with wide variations of climate, soil, tradition,
and four or five different important grape sorts,
they do have a real family likeness. They are
light, grapy and appetizing. One can use the
word delicious about them without offending
anyone (whereas it can sound totally off-key in
a cellar in serious Beaune). The classical word
for them is charming.

In the main they are white. They divide
clearly between the dry wines to the east (Sancerre and Pouilly) and west (Muscadet), and
the sweeter wines of Touraine and (sweeter
still) Anjou in the middle. Some of the wine of
Touraine is red; the best almost a match for
Beaujolais. Much of the wine of Anjou is pink,
and a match for any pink wine anywhere.

The best parts of the Loire are mapped in
detail on these and the next four pages. They
cover the most civilized, the most smiling part
of France; the perfect place to combine a wine
tour with more conventional delights.

On this page is the vineyard of Brittany—
one might almost say the ocean's own vineyard
—the Pays Nantais, the home of Muscadet.
Muscadet is the modern success story of the
Loire. It was an unknown *vin de pays* 40 years
ago. Today it is the accepted drink with the
splendid seafood of northern France; in the
last 20 years the vineyard area has doubled.
Muscadet is cheap, and yet perfect for drinking
with fish—very dry, but soft rather than acid:
in fact in hot years it suffers from too little
acidity. 'It casts its pale golden glow', as one

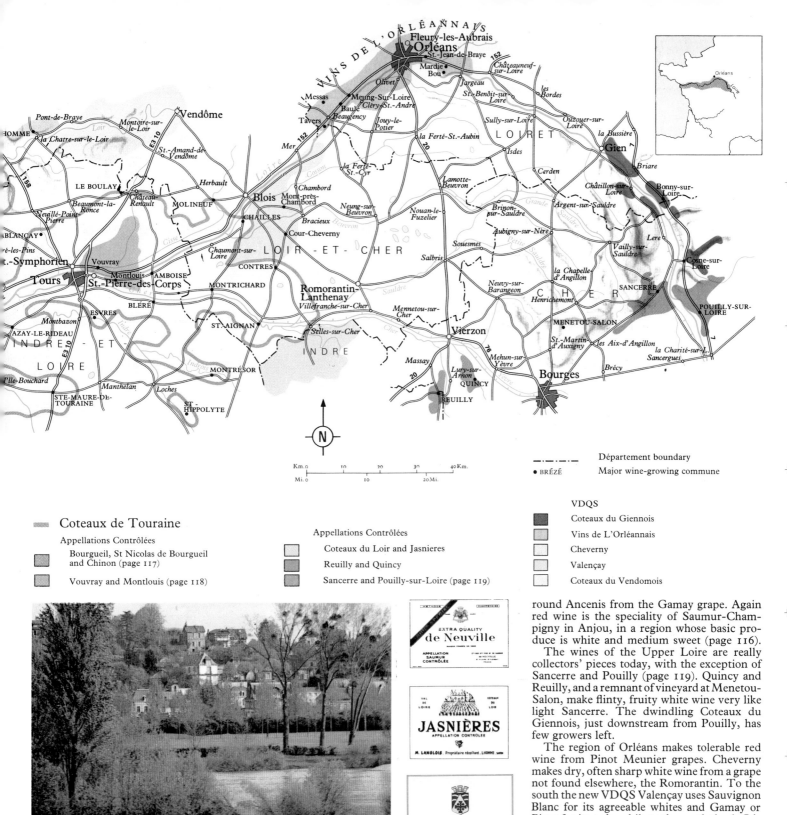

VINS DE L'ORLÉANNAIS

Département boundary
● BRÉZÉ   Major wine-growing commune

Km. 0   10   20   30   40 Km.
Mi. 0   10   20 Mi.

Coteaux de Touraine

Appellations Contrôlées

☐ Bourgueil, St Nicolas de Bourgueil and Chinon (page 117)

☐ Vouvray and Montlouis (page 118)

Appellations Contrôlées

☐ Coteaux du Loir and Jasnieres

☐ Reuilly and Quincy

☐ Sancerre and Pouilly-sur-Loire (page 119)

VDQS

☐ Coteaux du Giennois

☐ Vins de L'Orléannais

☐ Cheverny

☐ Valençay

☐ Coteaux du Vendomois

French critic has said, 'over the purple of lobsters and the pearl of oysters, the pink of shrimps and the red of mullet.'

Muscadet is the name of the vine, not of a place. The region of Sèvre-et-Maine, at far left, is the heart of the vineyard, giving the softest wines; most scented, soonest ready. Within three months of the vintage they are sold 'sur lie'—straight from the barrel, unracked. The other important area, the Coteaux de la Loire, gives better wine in hot years, with more lasting properties. The second wine of the region, Gros Plant, is also good—a minor Muscadet with more acidity. Some pleasant red wine is made

The soft watery landscape of the Loire perfectly suggests the gentle spring-like quality of its wine. Here, near Saumur in Anjou, white, pink and red wines are all light and refreshing

Right: sparkling Saumur, sweet Jasnières, obscure little Cheverny and flinty Reuilly and Quincy are among the wide variety of Loire wines

round Ancenis from the Gamay grape. Again red wine is the speciality of Saumur-Champigny in Anjou, in a region whose basic produce is white and medium sweet (page 116).

The wines of the Upper Loire are really collectors' pieces today, with the exception of Sancerre and Pouilly (page 119). Quincy and Reuilly, and a remnant of vineyard at Menetou-Salon, make flinty, fruity white wine very like light Sancerre. The dwindling Coteaux du Giennois, just downstream from Pouilly, has few growers left.

The region of Orléans makes tolerable red wine from Pinot Meunier grapes. Cheverny makes dry, often sharp white wine from a grape not found elsewhere, the Romorantin. To the south the new VDQS Valençay uses Sauvignon Blanc for its agreeable whites and Gamay or Pinot for its reds, while to the north the A.C.'s Jasnières and Coteaux du Loir make respectively good Vouvray-style white and light red of the local Chenin Noir or Pineau d'Aunis—which also gives the reds and rosés of the new VDQS zone Coteaux du Vendomois.

Irregular quality is the curse of wine-growing so far north. Many Loire growths vary so widely from one year to another that they seem hardly the same wine. A fine autumn makes it possible to gather grapes dried almost to raisins and make intensely sweet wine, but a wet one means (as in Germany) a very acid product. Hence the importance of the sparkling wine industry in Touraine and Anjou. The comparative failures of Vouvray or Saumur, fruity but acid, are ideal for transforming into sparkling wine, using the champagne method.

Anjou

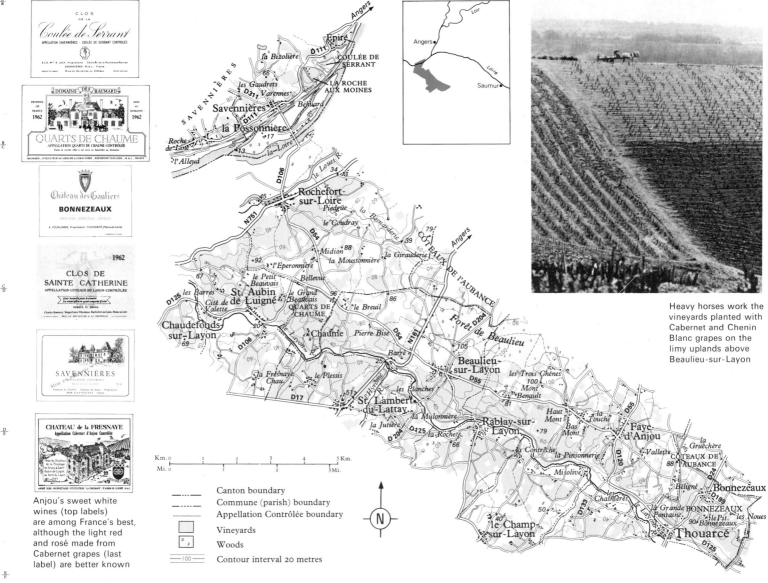

Anjou's sweet white wines (top labels) are among France's best, although the light red and rosé made from Cabernet grapes (last label) are better known

Heavy horses work the vineyards planted with Cabernet and Chenin Blanc grapes on the limy uplands above Beaulieu-sur-Layon

Canton boundary
Commune (parish) boundary
Appellation Contrôlée boundary
Vineyards
Woods
Contour interval 20 metres

Km. 0 1 2 3 4 5 Km.
Mi. 0   1   2   3 Mi.

THE WHITE wines of Anjou and Touraine have this in common with those of Germany: the better they are the sweeter they are. At their very best they are dessert wines of velvet texture, smooth with glycerine, richly and yet freshly scented, tasting of grapes, peaches, apricots, hazel-nuts, but with an underlying elusive flintiness which prevents them cloying. This is after a long warm autumn. Such wines go on improving for many years. But even in medium years they often have the balance of good German wines in which fruit and acid seem perfectly matched; the secret of making you want to sip and go on sipping.

The grape that gives us all this is the Chenin Blanc, called locally Pineau de la Loire. The area mapped on this page is where it reaches its ripest; several geographical circumstances combine to give it the dry open slopes, sheltered from north and east, which it needs. The River Layon, heading north-west to join the Loire, has cut a deep enough gulley to provide per-

fectly exposed but sheltered corners of hill.

A large part of its course has the appellation Coteaux du Layon, providing on average sweet wines notably above the general Anjou standard. But Quarts de Chaume (only 120 acres) and Bonnezeaux (about double) are outstanding enough to have appellations of their own, like Grands Crus in Burgundy. Beaulieu, Rablay, Rochefort, St-Aubin, Faye and Thouarcé are communes with particularly good wines; Rochefort is the centre for the district.

The River Aubance, parallel with the Layon to the north, makes similar wines; both also grow the red Cabernet to make good light red wine, the famous delicate Cabernet Rosé d'Anjou, and, paler still, vin gris, barely more than a blushing white.

Just south of Angers, and facing Rochefort, the north bank of the Loire has a series of small appellations which are locally important. Again it is the Chenin Blanc, though here—to confound all generalization—the wine at its best is

dry. Savennières is the general appellation for this small region (which comes within the bigger one of the Coteaux de la Loire). Within Savennières there are two Grands Crus—La Roche aux Moines (about the same size as Quarts de Chaume) and the mere 12 acres of La Coulée de Serrant.

La Coulée de Serrant epitomizes the exceptional situation which makes outstanding wine: it faces south-west in a side-valley even more sheltered than the main river bank. Its old stone press-house has an ecclesiastical air. The view over the Loire with its wooded and flowery islands is like the background to one of the medieval tapestries of Angers.

Savennières wine has a honey-and-flowers smell which makes its dryness surprising at first. It is a 'big' wine which improves for two or three years in bottle. Salmon is said to be its perfect partner, but there is such pleasure in its lingering flavour that it is a pity not to drink it on its own before a meal.

Chinon and Bourgueil

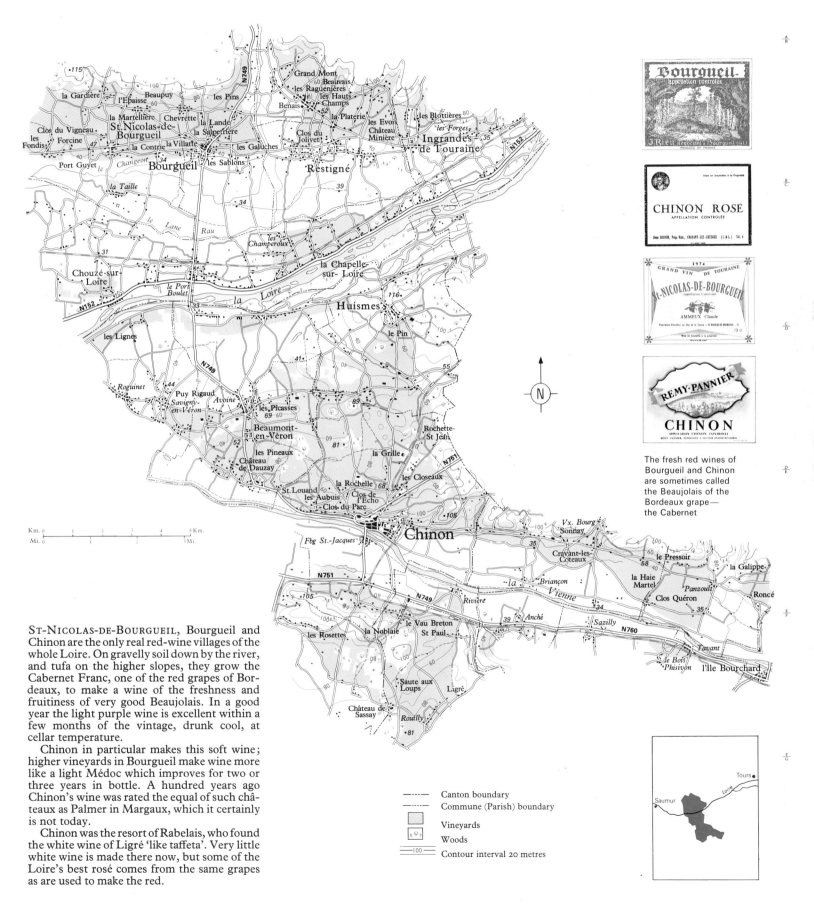

The fresh red wines of Bourgueil and Chinon are sometimes called the Beaujolais of the Bordeaux grape— the Cabernet

St-Nicolas-de-Bourgueil, Bourgueil and Chinon are the only real red-wine villages of the whole Loire. On gravelly soil down by the river, and tufa on the higher slopes, they grow the Cabernet Franc, one of the red grapes of Bordeaux, to make a wine of the freshness and fruitiness of very good Beaujolais. In a good year the light purple wine is excellent within a few months of the vintage, drunk cool, at cellar temperature.

Chinon in particular makes this soft wine; higher vineyards in Bourgueil make wine more like a light Médoc which improves for two or three years in bottle. A hundred years ago Chinon's wine was rated the equal of such châteaux as Palmer in Margaux, which it certainly is not today.

Chinon was the resort of Rabelais, who found the white wine of Ligré 'like taffeta'. Very little white wine is made there now, but some of the Loire's best rosé comes from the same grapes as are used to make the red.

Canton boundary
Commune (Parish) boundary
Vineyards
Woods
Contour interval 20 metres

Vouvray

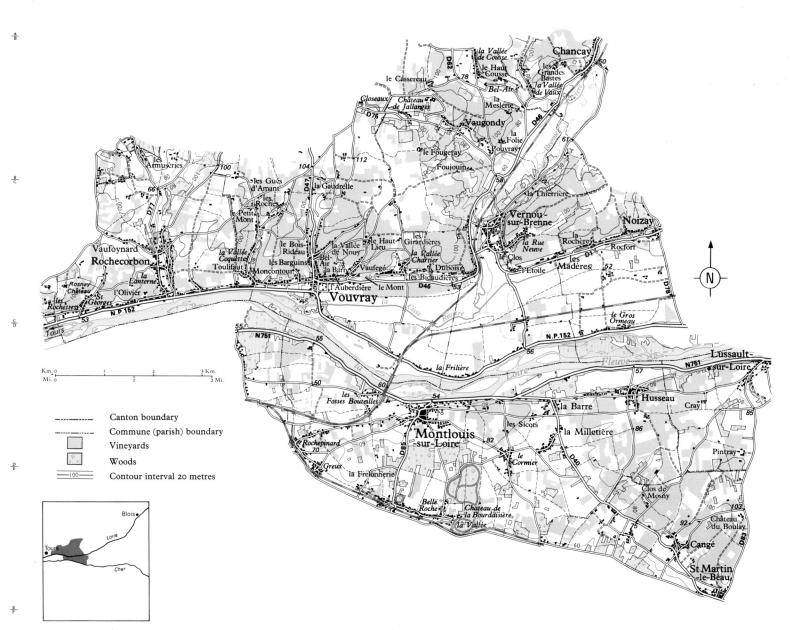

Canton boundary
Commune (parish) boundary
Vineyards
Woods
Contour interval 20 metres

JUST AS Savennières stands almost at the gates of Angers, Vouvray and Montlouis lie just outside Tours on the way to Amboise. Everything royal and romantic about France is summed up in this countryside of great châteaux and ancient towns along the gently flowing river.

Low hills of chalk flank the stream along the reach from Noizay to Rochecorbon. For centuries they have provided both cellars and dwellings in caves to the wine-growers of the district. Above the cellars, which are often great caverns extending to two acres or more, the Chenin Blanc grows in chalky soil. Its wine here, though often drier than in Anjou, at its best is honey-like and sweet. What distinguishes it more than anything, however, is its long life. For a comparatively light wine its longevity is astonishing. You may expect madeira to live for half a century, but in a pale, firm, rather delicate wine the ability to improve and go on improving for so long in bottle is very rare.

Most Vouvray today is handled by négociants, who blend the produce of one clos with another. The once-famous names of the individual sites are not often heard today. More important is the need to know whether any given bottle is dry, semi-sweet, sweet or for that matter *pétillant* or fully sparkling: Vouvray alters character radically from vintage to vintage, and its natural tendency to re-ferment in the bottle has led to an industry in converting less successful vintages into very good sparkling wine. None the less growers do triumphantly bottle their best produce and keep it for a small band of connoisseurs. To them names like Vallée Coquette are a rallying call.

Montlouis has very similar soil and conditions to Vouvray, without the perfect situation of the first rank of Vouvray's vineyards along the Loire. Montlouis tends to be slightly softer and more gently sweet, but it takes a native to tell the difference.

A dwindling number of small growers still make the great sweet wines of the Vouvray area. Another (label not shown) is Gaston Huet of Le Haut Lieu in Vouvray. Much modern Vouvray is made sparkling, either sweet or dry, using the champagne method

Pouilly and Sancerre

SANCERRE.

THE WINES of Pouilly and Sancerre on the upper Loire are perhaps the easiest to recognize in France. On these chalky hills, cut by the river, the Sauvignon grape gives a smell to the wine which is called gun-flint; it is slightly smoky, slightly green, slightly spicy and appeals to most people intensely at first. Compared with the Chenin Blanc of the middle Loire, however, the Sauvignon lacks interest after a while. Sancerre and Pouilly Fumé have strong immediate appeal as good with food, particularly shellfish. But it is only exceptional vintages which add subtlety and intriguing nuances to these wines. They are rarely wines to linger over for themselves.

Pouilly-sur-Loire is the town; its wine is only called Pouilly Fumé when made from the Sauvignon. Its second wine, from the Chasselas

and often excellent in its own way, is called Pouilly-sur-Loire. Neither have anything to do with Pouilly-Fuissé, the white wine of Mâcon.

There is not much to choose between Pouilly Fumé and Sancerre. The best of each are on the same level; the Sancerre perhaps slightly riper-tasting. In bad vintages however they can be very acid; their smell has been compared to wet wool. A year or two in bottle brings out the qualities of a good one, but they are not wines to lay down, like Vouvrays.

There is a growing fashion for Sauvignon wine, and vineyard names are more and more in evidence. Les Monts Damnés in Chavignol and Clos du Chêne Marchand in Bué are the two best-known vineyards of Sancerre; the Château du Nozet and Château de Tracy the biggest and best-known estates in Pouilly.

Above: Sancerre is still the walled town with the Loire winding by shown in this early print

Right: the best Sancerres come from Chavignol and Bué. Two big châteaux, du Nozet and de Tracy, dominate Pouilly. Only the best Pouillys are known as Fumé. The lesser (Chasselas) wines are called Pouilly-sur-Loire

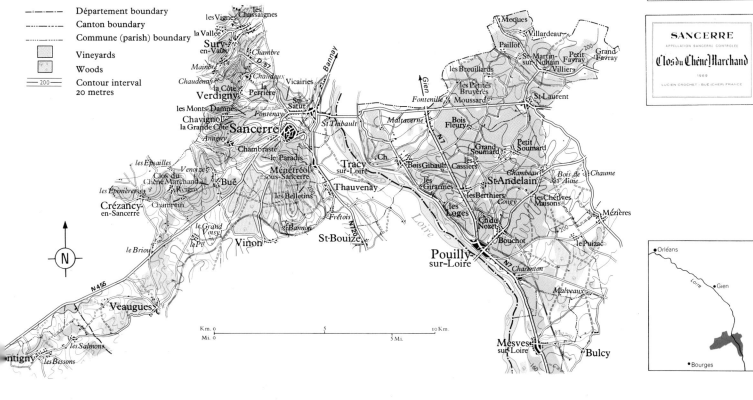

Département boundary
Canton boundary
Commune (parish) boundary
Vineyards
Woods
Contour interval 20 metres

119

The Rhône Valley

THE VALLEY of the Loire and the valley of the Rhône are two sides of the same coin. They contain respectively the best of northern and the best of southern French viticulture. Most Loire wine is white, most Rhône red. In each case there is a wide variety of styles of wine but a distinct family feeling.

Rhône red wines develop from blackness and bitterness to roundness and warmth, to a heady smell, to great softness and depth of flavour. In the north they are comparatively delicate, in the south sometimes downright enormous; but they conform to a certain pattern. Similarly the white wines are all full gold in colour and even headier than (say) white burgundy.

In the course of the Rhône the country changes from oak forest, where the vine shares the fields with peach-trees and nut-trees, to the herbal scrub and olive groves of Provence. In the north the vine perches on terraced cliffs of crumbling granite wherever the best view of the sun can be found. In the south it lies baking in broad terraces of smooth round stones where the sun is everywhere.

Rhône wines are not as a rule made from one grape variety on its own, as burgundy is, but from a blend of anything from two to 13. It is common practice to add a little of a white variety to the very dark wine of the Syrah, the classic red-wine grape of Côte Rôtie and Hermitage. Châteauneuf-du-Pape, like Chianti, is made from a whole roll-call of vines, including both red and white.

The vineyards round the Rhône fall naturally into two groups; northern and southern. The appellation Côtes du Rhône is a general one for the wine of 150-odd communes, red, white or rosé. Côtes du Rhône-Villages is applied only to 14 specific (and superior) communes in the southern part. Fifteen areas have their own separate appellations, of which all except Die are shown on the map.

A new minor appellation, Coteaux du Tricastin, is also just off the map, east of Montelimar.

On the following pages the three best areas of the Rhône are mapped in detail. Around them lie other regions of strong local character: north of Valence, St-Joseph and Cornas with excellent and undervalued red wines. To the west St-Péray with an unusual sparkling wine, full bodied and old-gold in colour. On the river Drôme to the east, Die with its pale and sparkling Clairette. North of Avignon, Tavel and Lirac with their famous strong and orange-pink rosés. Finally Rasteau and Beaumes de Venise to the east make dessert wine—the latter the best sweet muscat in France; amber, soft and only gently fortified. Drunk young and fresh it is a sheer delight.

These are the great names of the region. But its special qualities are not limited to them. Wine-growing has made great strides recently in many little-known parishes. Their wines will be lighter than the classics but can none the less be typical of the Rhône; tasty and robust.

At present the great Rhône wines like Hermitage are bargains in comparison to many grand growths of Burgundy and Bordeaux. But their vineyards are small and their price will rise when they come back into fashion—as they undoubtedly will.

The four top labels are from co-operatives in the widely varying Rhône areas of Die (sparkling wine), Gigondas (red), Beaumes de Venise (sweet muscat) and Chusclan (vin rosé)

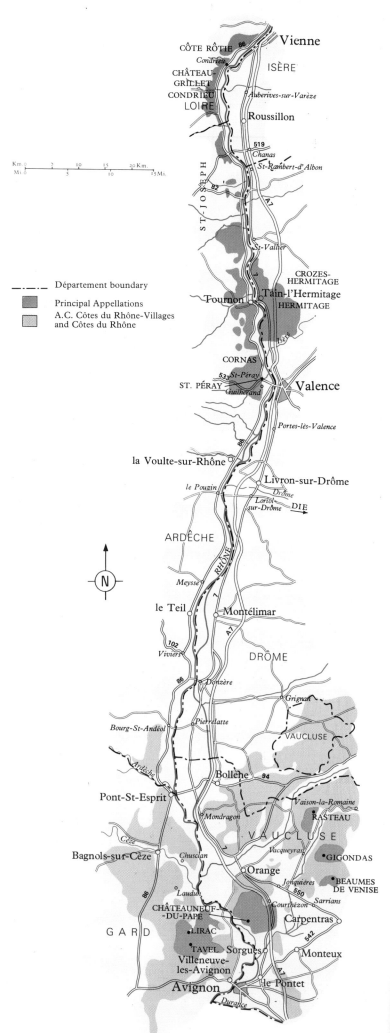

Côte Rôtie and Condrieu

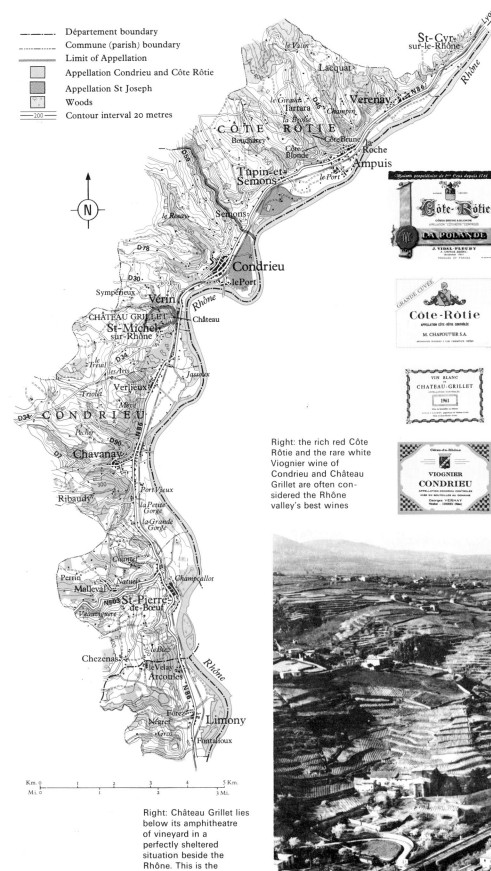

Legend:
- ─·─·─ Département boundary
- ─·─·─ Commune (parish) boundary
- ─ ─ ─ Limit of Appellation
- Appellation Condrieu and Côte Rôtie
- Appellation St Joseph
- Woods
- ═ 200 ═ Contour interval 20 metres

Km. 0   1   2   3   4   5 Km.
Mi. 0   1   2   3 Mi.

Right: the rich red Côte Rôtie and the rare white Viognier wine of Condrieu and Château Grillet are often considered the Rhône valley's best wines

CÔTE RÔTIE and Condrieu, in the northern group of vineyards round the Rhône, have nothing like the fame of Châteauneuf-du-Pape in the south. They are bound to remain collectors' wines because their vineyards are so tiny. But there is no doubt that Côte Rôtie is one of the best, if not the very best of the Rhône red wines. Those who have tasted Condrieu at the famous restaurant Pyramide at Vienne feel equally strongly about the white.

The right-hand bend of the river after Vienne provides a short stretch of very steep hill perfectly aligned for the sun. The soil varies even within the few miles of the vineyard, and there are three distinct appellations.

The northern part is called Côte Rôtie—literally 'roasted hill'—and is itself divided—though not legally—into Côte Brune and Côte Blonde; slopes with darker and lighter soil. The wines of the two are normally blended together. Côte Rôtie makes the Rhône's most complex and rewarding wine—not its strongest. With age it takes on an almost claret-like delicacy and an irresistible raspberry-like scent.

Condrieu is its white opposite number. An unusual grape, the Viognier, is the only one officially allowed within the area. It too makes a rather delicate wine for the Rhône; a dry wine with a haunting floral scent like a faint and disturbing echo from the Rhine and a very long, rather spicy after-taste. The four-acre estate of Château Grillet is the inner sanctum of Condrieu, and the smallest vineyard with its own Appellation Contrôlée in France. A perfect micro-climate gives its wine an advantage which is reflected in its strength, quality and price. Unlike most Rhône wines, the Viogniers are at their best when still young.

Right: Château Grillet lies below its amphitheatre of vineyard in a perfectly sheltered situation beside the Rhône. This is the smallest vineyard with its own Appellation Contrôlée in France

Hermitage

THE BLUE TRAIN snakes by under the stacked terraces of the hill of Hermitage, making the vineyard's magnificent stance looking down the Rhône familiar to millions.

The Romans grew wine here. A hundred years ago its 'mas'—the local name for the individual vineyards—were named beside Château Lafite and Romanée-Conti as among the best red wines of the world. A. Jullien listed them in order of merit: Méal, Gréfieux, Beaume, Raucoule, Muret, Guoignière, Bessas, Burges and Lauds. Spellings have changed: the mas remain—but today few of their names are heard, and never in the same breath as Château Lafite.

The adjective 'manly' has stuck to Hermitage ever since it was first applied to it. It has almost the qualities of port without the added brandy. Like vintage port it throws a heavy sediment in the bottle (it needs decanting) and improves for many years until its scent and flavour are almost overwhelming. Sadly, however, it is rarely kept long enough for more than its darkness and strength to become apparent.

The hill is famous for its white wine too. 'Raucoule' was named as the best by Jullien. Today Chante-Alouette is the best known. Besides being a mas, it is the trade-mark of the house of Chapoutier. The wine is golden, dry and full with a remarkably delicate and interesting flavour, and lasts, like the red Hermitage, for years.

Crozes-Hermitage is a wider appellation surrounding Hermitage—usually good, often excellent, but never with quite the same 'race'.

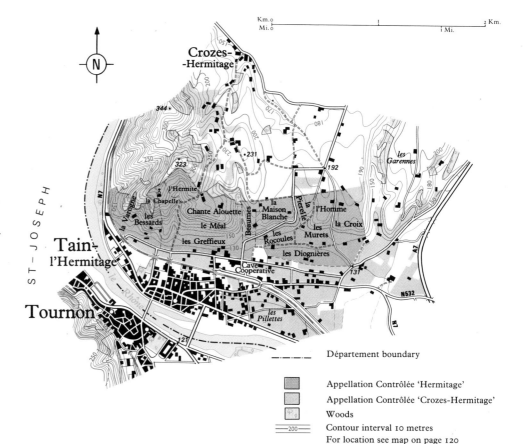

------- Département boundary

Appellation Contrôlée 'Hermitage'

Appellation Contrôlée 'Crozes-Hermitage'

Woods

—200— Contour interval 10 metres

For location see map on page 120

The hill of Hermitage, its granite terraced from top to bottom, rises above a bend of the Rhône at Tain-l'Hermitage. A hundred years ago Hermitage red wines were reckoned among the best in the world

Far right: The soil of Châteauneuf-du-Pape is completely hidden by beach-like stones which retain the day's heat far into the night. The grapes ripen to very high sugar content

Right: Chante-Alouette is the best-known white Hermitage. Crozes-Hermitage is the appellation of the vineyards not on the Hermitage hill itself

Châteauneuf-du-Pape

CHÂTEAUNEUF-DU-PAPE lies in the centre of the biggest concentration of Rhône vineyards, on hills dominated by the ruined papal summer palace. Its vines are widely spaced; low bushes in a sea of smooth stones with no earth to be seen. The deep red wine of Châteauneuf has the distinction not only of having the highest minimum strength of any French wine (12.5% alcohol) but of being the first to be so regulated. Its most famous grower, the late Baron Le Roy, initiated here what has become the national system of Appellations Contrôlées. Part of his original proposal, made in 1923, was that suitable land for fine Châteauneuf vines (there are 13 varieties) should be identified by the conjunction of lavender and thyme growing there. In addition, grape sorts, pruning, quantity and strength were to be controlled.

His foresight has been rewarded by Châteauneuf-du-Pape emerging from obscurity to become one of the world's most famous wines.

Well over a million gallons of wine a year are made here; 99% of it red. Most of it is good average; made relatively light (though not in alcohol) by increasing the proportion of Grenache grapes so that it can be drunk after a mere year or two. The neighbouring Gigondas (recently granted an appellation of its own) makes similar wine. A number of big estates, like Bordeaux châteaux, are the producers of the classical dark and deep Châteauneuf-du-Pape. But today these wines take four or five years to grow soft-flavoured and gentle as against the decade they used to need. The powerful soft-fruit scent is still there, but some of the old majesty is gone.

– – – – –	Canton boundary
– – – – –	Commune (Parish) boundary
Château	Leading growths
▢	Vineyards
⌖	Woods
—100—	Contour interval 10 metres

For location see map on page 120

Km. 0   1   2   3 Km.
Mi. 0   1   2 Mi.

Châteauneuf-du-Pape has large estates comparable to the châteaux of Bordeaux. Their impressive labels are in keeping with their strong and big-scale wine

Châteauneuf-du-Pape was traditionally aged in barrels longer than any other French wine. Modern practice makes lighter wine, maturing fast

Languedoc and Roussillon

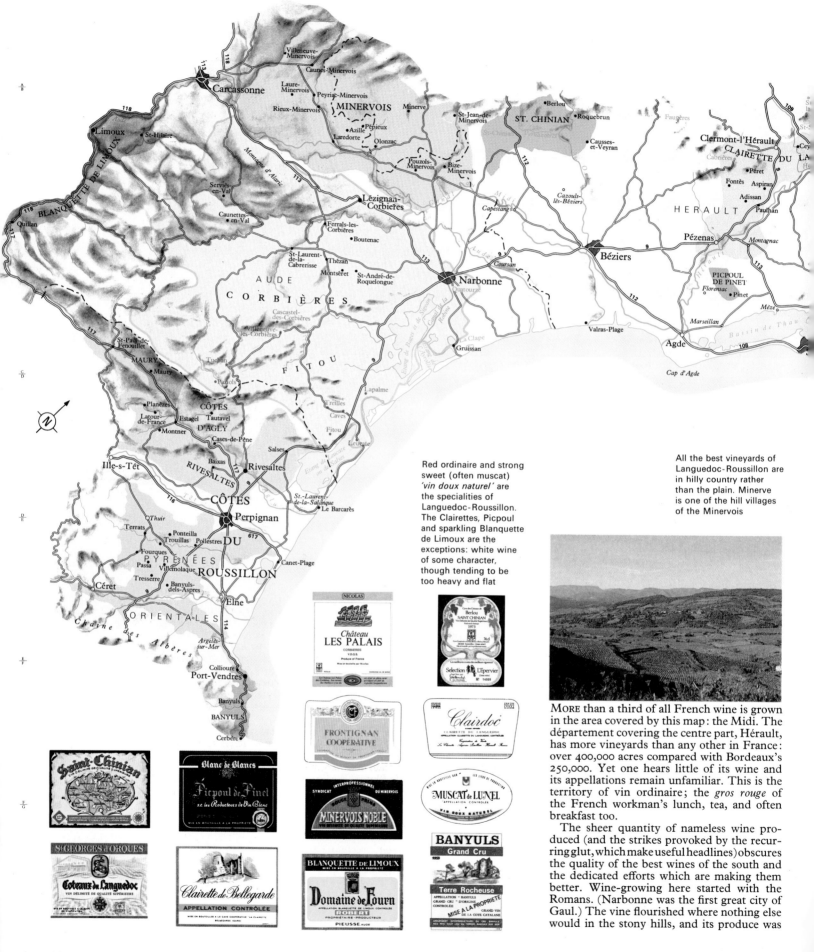

Red ordinaire and strong sweet (often muscat) *'vin doux naturel'* are the specialities of Languedoc-Roussillon. The Clairettes, Picpoul and sparkling Blanquette de Limoux are the exceptions: white wine of some character, though tending to be too heavy and flat

All the best vineyards of Languedoc-Roussillon are in hilly country rather than the plain. Minerve is one of the hill villages of the Minervois

MORE than a third of all French wine is grown in the area covered by this map: the Midi. The département covering the centre part, Hérault, has more vineyards than any other in France: over 400,000 acres compared with Bordeaux's 250,000. Yet one hears little of its wine and its appellations remain unfamiliar. This is the territory of vin ordinaire; the *gros rouge* of the French workman's lunch, tea, and often breakfast too.

The sheer quantity of nameless wine produced (and the strikes provoked by the recurring glut, which make useful headlines) obscures the quality of the best wines of the south and the dedicated efforts which are making them better. Wine-growing here started with the Romans. (Narbonne was the first great city of Gaul.) The vine flourished where nothing else would in the stony hills, and its produce was

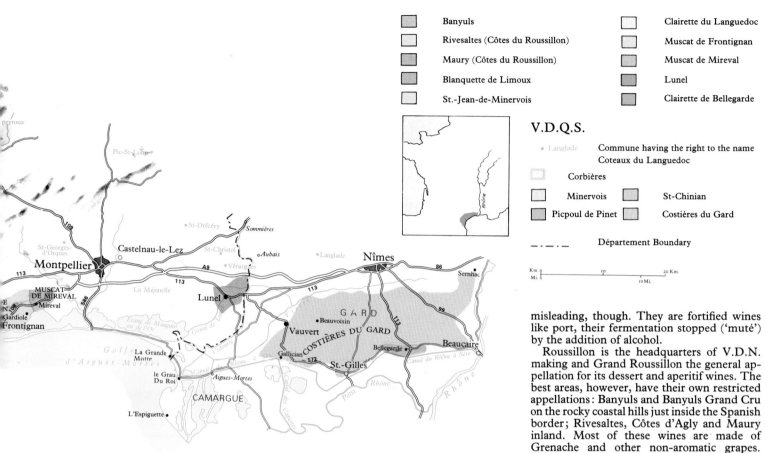

Appellations Contrôlées

• Tuchan   Commune having the right to Appellation Contrôlée Fitou

▨	Banyuls	▢	Clairette du Languedoc
▨	Rivesaltes (Côtes du Roussillon)	▨	Muscat de Frontignan
▨	Maury (Côtes du Roussillon)	▨	Muscat de Mireval
▨	Blanquette de Limoux	▨	Lunel
▢	St.-Jean-de-Minervois	▨	Clairette de Bellegarde

V.D.Q.S.

• Langlade   Commune having the right to the name Coteaux du Languedoc

▢	Corbières		
▢	Minervois	▨	St-Chinian
▨	Picpoul de Pinet	▢	Costières du Gard

– · – · –   Département Boundary

Km. 0   10   20 Km.
Mi. 0   10 Mi.

good. It was not until phylloxera crushed the hill-vignerons that the vine came down to the plain and the permanent crisis of over-production began. There are still zones of admirable soil and climate dotted among the overfertile plains; in every case on high ground where the soil is stony and well drained.

It is not easy to convince farmers that the way to prosperity is to grow less but better. Co-operatives are doing their best. They have their own research establishment with one of the most modern wineries in France at l'Espiguette in the Camargue. Tourists at the new resorts near by are used as willing guinea-pigs for experimental wines, which are well made, light and easy to drink.

The staple vine of the south is the Carignan, a big producer of dull wine. The stress is on increasing the proportion of Grenache, Cinsaut, Mourvèdre—all Midi grapes of character—but even Cabernet Sauvignon is being planted in experiments. It does well in California: why not in the Midi?

At present there are only two Appellation Contrôlée red wines in the whole of the Midi: Fitou, a group of nine communes in the Corbières, which makes solid 12° wine with a certain potential for ageing, and Collioure, a minuscule region almost on the Spanish border whose fiery reds must have caught someone's eye at some time. All the other ACs are either for dessert wines or white wines. The dessert wines have character, but the only white wine which is more than merely palatable is the

sparkling Blanquette de Limoux of the extreme west of the region.

Limoux's achievement (made possible by its altitude and the influence of the Atlantic) is to produce fresh fruity and sufficiently acid grapes to manipulate by the Méthode Champenoise into an above-average sparkling wine. The best Blanquette is very pale, very dry, with a squeeze of lemon in the taste which makes it refreshing.

Most Midi whites, including the appellations Clairette du Languedoc and de Bellegarde, lack crispness or any flavour of fruit. The Clairette is a neutral grape: its soft, heavy and rather alcoholic wine is the traditional base for French vermouth. As table wine it leaves much to be desired, although conservative growers sometimes give it a bosomy southern lusciousness. The limestone massif of La Clape on the coast near Narbonne is noted for such wine.

Picpoul de Pinet (the Picpoul is the acidic grape of Armagnac) has a certain notoriety and a VDQS label. Its 'Blanc de Blancs' is a lightweight for the Midi, but not otherwise distinguished. In the Roussillon there is a tradition of picking under-ripe Maccabeo grapes to make a 'vin vert'. Portuguese vinho verde is very much better.

For the moment the dessert wines are the best known of the region. The rich brown muscats of Frontignan, Mireval and Lunel in Hérault and Rivesaltès in the Roussillon are first-class wines of their kind: alcoholic, velvety and aromatic. The name of Vin Doux Naturel to describe these high-strength productions is

misleading, though. They are fortified wines like port, their fermentation stopped ('muté') by the addition of alcohol.

Roussillon is the headquarters of V.D.N. making and Grand Roussillon the general appellation for its dessert and aperitif wines. The best areas, however, have their own restricted appellations: Banyuls and Banyuls Grand Cru on the rocky coastal hills just inside the Spanish border; Rivesaltes, Côtes d'Agly and Maury inland. Most of these wines are made of Grenache and other non-aromatic grapes. Those (such as Muscat de Rivesaltes) which have the luscious muscat flavour say so.

Midi reds of VDQS rank, meanwhile, have a firm grip on their bootstraps and are pulling hard. Promotion is already in the wind. Work is in progress to define the better slopes which will be granted an appellation contrôlée (provided they have the right vines) before long.

The areas of most potential lie in the west. St Chinian and Minervois, Corbières and Roussillon form an arc of wild hilly country, some of it savagely beautiful, linking the Cevennes and the Pyrenees, interrupted only by the valley of the Aude.

Each of these regions is already making wine of distinct character: the St Chinians fleshy and round, the Minervois reds delicate and lively, the Corbières foursquare and solid, the Roussillons firm, muscular and perhaps potentially the most impressive of the four.

A number of producers are using Beaujolais-style vinification (carbonic maceration, see page 33) to make their wine full and fruity and immediately attractive. The standards they are reaching even with an excess of Carignan makes it certain that with better grapes they will have excellent wine to sell.

From St Chinian eastwards the VDQS Coteaux du Languedoc are much more scattered: isolated communes with ambitions for quality (and traditions, too: St-Georges-d'Orques was much appreciated by the English tourists who found themselves interned by Napoleon at Montpellier).

South of Nîmes the Costières du Gard are really the last vineyard of the Rhône. A deep deposit of pebbles in the river's former delta gives the wines of the area the advantage over their neighbours.

Provence

Key:

- ⌐‒‒ Département boundary
- ▢ V D Q S Côte de Provence and Coteaux d'Aix-en-Provence
- ▤ Appellation Contrôlée Palette, Cassis and Bandol
- • Cogolin Communes which include a Cru Classé
- • le Luc V D Q S communes

N

Bandol and Palette are Provence's best red-wine areas. Château Vignelaure near Aix has also recently been making excellent wine

Les Baux, west of Aix, is a typical rocky Provençal hill town. It has Provence's best restaurant, the famous L'Oustaou de la Baumanière

THERE ARE few areas of fully fledged Appellations Contrôlées in the south of France. Instead it is the homeland of the VDQS—the noteworthy local wine with aspirations. A whole series of VDQS areas spread from the southern Rhône both east and west. This page shows the most famous of them (partly because it surrounds the Mediterranean resorts)—the Côtes de Provence, with the Côteaux d'Aix-en-Provence to the north and three small appellations: Palette, Bandol and Cassis. It omits the similar Côtes de Luberon and Coteaux de Pierrevert farther north and the Coteaux des Baux to the west (pages 128–129).

An optimistic description of Provence wines always mentions the sun-baked pines, thyme, lavender and claims that the wine takes its character from them. This is true of some of the best of them—notably the wine of Palette, Château Simone. Others get by on a pretty colour and a good deal of alcohol. 'Tarpaulin edged with lace' is a realistic summing-up of one of the better ones. The whites are dry and can lack the acidity to be refreshing; the reds are straightforward, strong and a trifle dull; it is usually the rosés, often orange-tinted, which have most appeal. A number of the better estates are known as 'Crus Classés'.

Cassis and Bandol distinguish themselves for their white and red wines respectively. Cassis (no relation of the blackcurrant syrup) is livelier than the run of Provençal white wine, and Bandol leads the red in much the same way.

Another small appellation for red, white and rosé wines of some distinction, Bellet, lies farther east, just inland from Nice.

Savoie and the Jura

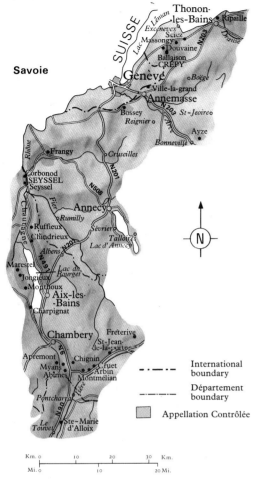

Savoie

International boundary

Département boundary

Appellation Contrôlée

Most Savoie wine is white and very dry and light. Crépy and Seyssel are Appellations Contrôlées; Varichon & Clerc make excellent sparkling wine; Chautagne is a pleasant light red

THE WINE-COUNTRY of Savoie is diffuse and its produce little known. In many ways it epitomizes the 'little local wine' which travels only in legend: its cleanness and freshness are at one with the mountain air, the lakes and streams. Savoie wine is nearly all white—as water. There is a dry softness about it like ethereal Muscadet.

The sparkling version is better known than the still: it too has this pale, elusive quality. The best is drier and more delicate than any other sparkling wine—an intriguing alternative to champagne as an aperitif.

A whole range of Savoie wines has recently (1973) been promoted to Appellation Contrôlée status. Up to then only Crépy and Seyssel were so honoured. Crépy is just across the border from Switzerland, its grape the Swiss Chasselas and its whole nature more Swiss than French. Seyssel is commonly made sparkling, but sparkling or still has delicacy and charm.

The appellation Vin de Savoie now applies to white wines of a certain strength made of the predominant local vine, the Jacquère. Of these Ayze is the best-known commune for sparkling wine, and Apremont and Abymes for still. A dwindling traditional white grape, the Altesse, carries the appellation Roussette de Savoie, sometimes qualified by such château-names as Monterminod, Frangy and Marestel.

The chief local red grape is the Mondeuse. Arbin, Montmélian and St-Jean-de-la-Porte are its best-known crus. At Chautagne the grape is the Gamay of Beaujolais. These reds also have the Appellation Contrôlée. Vin de Savoie, with or without a place name, though they are rarely as good as the whites.

A LITTLE enclave of only 1,500 acres of vines scattered among pretty woodland and meadow in what seem like France's remotest hills. . . . The Jura's production is a fraction of its old total; yet its wines are varied, good and totally original. Its three superior appellations, Arbois, Château-Chalon (a village) and L'Etoile, all count for something.

Jura wine is not only red, white and rosé, but yellow and grey. The best of it is 'yellow'; firm, strong white wine from the Savagnin (alias Traminer) which is kept for a minimum of six years in cask while it undergoes a transformation like that of sherry. The appellation Château-Chalon is limited to this odd but excellent wine, but good 'vin jaune' is also made at L'Etoile and Arbois. A special squat bottle, the *clavelin*, is used only for vin jaune.

The grey wine is simply very pale rosé, rather sharp and sometimes extremely appetising. The best Jura vin rosé, from Arbois, by contrast is more like pale red wine, unusually silky. Some of the white is made from the Chardonnay and compares well with minor Côte de Beaune wine. The red is perhaps the least interesting, though even this can be soft, smooth and enjoyable with the good local game.

In addition to all these from such a small area, Arbois is famous for its 'vin fou', pleasant cheap sparkling wine.

A large proportion of the Jura's production is controlled by one firm, Henri Maire; but one or two small growers of real quality exist.

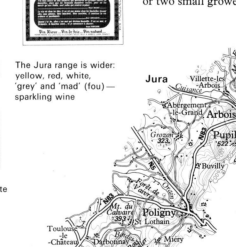

The Jura range is wider: yellow, red, white, 'grey' and 'mad' (fou)— sparkling wine

Jura

Appellation Contrôlée boundary

Vineyards

Woods

Contour interval 20 metres

Wines of the South-West

SOUTH of the great vineyard of Bordeaux, and west of the even bigger one of the Midi, the vine flourishes in scattered areas of strong local traditions.

Cahors is the senior wine of this part of France, in reputation, though not in official recognition. It was only promoted to Appellation Contrôlée in 1971, although it had long been known as the 'First of the VDQS'. In Cahors they would tell you how, centuries ago, it was their wine, not meagre Médocs, which was most in demand among foreign buyers in the port of Bordeaux.

The name given to Cahors' sturdy red wine was 'black'—and with reason. The local grapes and climate, together with old-fashioned methods of wine-making, gave it more tannin than it knew what to do with, a black-tinged 'robe' and a way of not being ready to drink for 12 or 15 years. Inevitably, these days, the tendency is to make quicker-maturing wine.

A big co-operative, Les Caves d'Olt at Parnac, handles about half the production of the area, making white and rosé as well as Vin de Cahors, which is always red. Jouffreau and Tesseydre are good growers who bottle their own wine. Leygues near Puy-l'Evêque, Prayssac and Luzech are important centres.

There are a few areas of France which are Appellation Contrôlée but which hardly make the wine they must once have made to earn the title. Gaillac is the biggest of these.

The hills round the River Tarn just below Albi, and below the magnificent gorge the river makes in the Cevennes mountains, are still lovely country with beautiful towns and villages. Seventy-three of them are contained within the appellation Gaillac, which is thus a very general name for any wine, red, white or rosé, made from a mixture of a fairly wide choice of grapes (including the Sauternes varieties, for white, but stressing the Rhône-type grapes rather than the Bordeaux ones for red).

Any white or rosé from this area which is 'champagnized'—and a little is—can be called Gaillac Mousseux.

The classical Gaillac, however, was always sweet white wine, and the inner appellation for a mere eight communes (which do not include Gaillac), Gaillac Premières Côtes, is for sweet (in reality only medium-sweet) white only.

The neighbouring appellation Côtes de Frontonais, just to the west, has a mainly local following; the citizens of Toulouse are content to absorb the production of red wine from a local variety, the Negrette, grown on the hill-sides round Fronton and Villaudric.

Westwards again the centre of the stage is held by the vineyards of Armagnac (see p. 260).

North of Armagnac on the left bank of the Garonne lies the Appellation Côtes de Buzet, whose whole production, from vineyards scattered over 27 communes of orchard and farm, is in the hands of one well-organized co-operative. To all intents and purposes the Buzet wines are minor (but not cheap) red and white Bordeaux.

The remaining wines on this map lie in the Basque province of Béarn, which has recently been given a general appellation to cover its red, white and rosé wines of a certain quality from vineyards outside its two best-known wine-centres, Madiran and Jurançon.

The Madiran vineyards lie on the hills along the left bank of the river Adour, just south of the best section of Armagnac. A local red grape, the Tannat, is well named for the dark and tannic, rude but vigorous wines it makes. Three years is the minimum barrel-ageing period, and when the wines are bottled they are still harsh. But after seven or eight years Madiran is admirable; full of flavour and life.

Jurançon remains a name to conjure with, though few people have ever tasted the reason

The ancient hillside ('coteaux') vineyards of the south-west produce all the good wine of the region. They suffered a terrible decline after phylloxera, but their reputation is growing again today

why. These steep Pyrenean foot-hills, with Pau as their market place, used to make France's best sweet wines, comparable to Sauternes or the rareties of the Loire. Descriptions of it make mention of peaches and carnations.

Today production is a fraction of what it was, and the high risk of picking grapes as late as November, necessary for *vin liquoreux*, has led most growers to make dry wine. The dry white still has richness of flavour allied to high acidity, but it is more of a historical curiosity than a gastronomic resource.

The tiny appellation of Irouléguy, with only 100 acres of vines, is the final Basque bastion, doggedly going on making red, white and rosé wines of the local grapes, the Tannat included.

The whole production of Irouléguy is made by the co-operative cellar. Most of it goes to Biarritz to irrigate Basque dishes.

The label of the rosé carries what might well be a Basque rallying cry—Hotx Hotxa Edan. Alas it only means 'Chill before serving'.

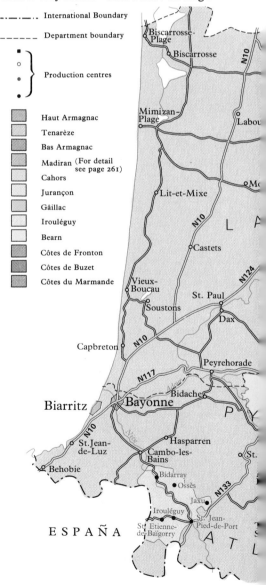

-·-—·-·-	International Boundary
- - - - - -	Department boundary
	Production centres

	Haut Armagnac
	Tenarèze
	Bas Armagnac
	Madiran (For detail see page 261)
	Cahors
	Jurançon
	Gâillac
	Irouléguy
	Bearn
	Côtes de Fronton
	Côtes de Buzet
	Côtes du Marmande

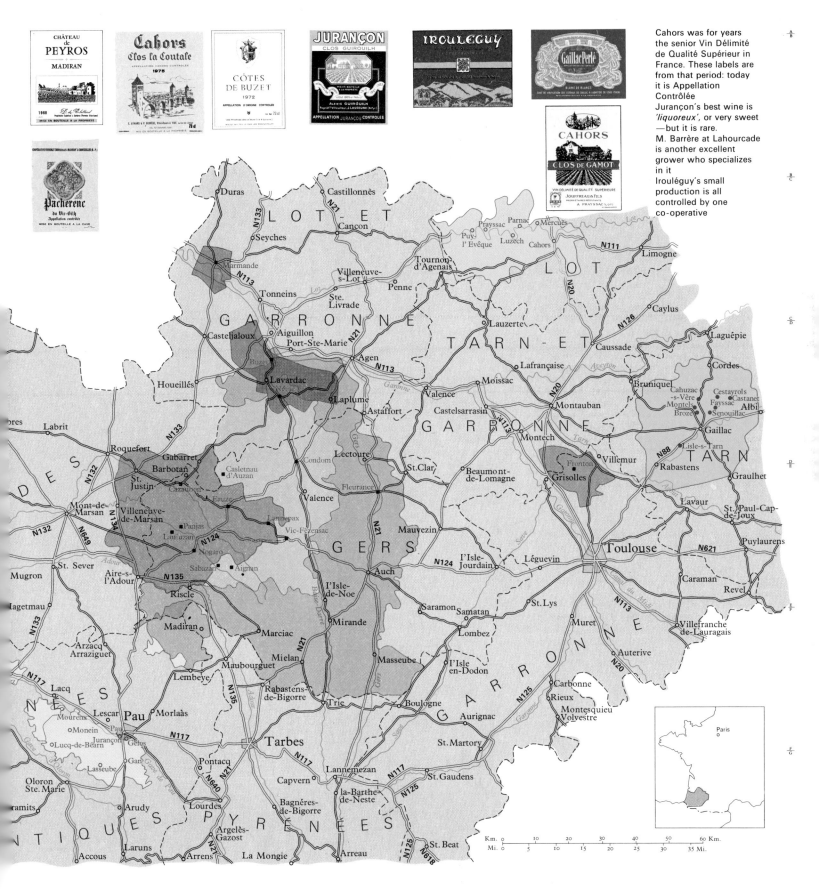

Cahors was for years
the senior Vin Délimité
de Qualité Supérieur in
France. These labels are
from that period: today
it is Appellation
Contrôlée
Jurançon's best wine is
'liquoreux', or very sweet
—but it is rare.
M. Barrère at Lahourcade
is another excellent
grower who specializes
in it
Irouléguy's small
production is all
controlled by one
co-operative

Vins de Pays

THE MAP on these pages is the first plotting of a fresh and unfamiliar list of wines: France's new class of Vins de Pays.

France has a way of producing, even in corners which have little contact with the outside world, wines which are better than any but the best from the rest of Europe. She is intensely aware of her 'little' wines, and, through the corps of inspectors of her admirably organized Institut National des Appellations d'Origine, is constantly feeling their pulses, rather like a coach keeping an eye on the colts team.

The Appellation system evolved by degrees in the 1920s and 30s. In 1949 it was followed by the creation of a second rank: Vins Delimités de Qualité Supérieure. VDQS wines have advanced steadily since their recognition. Many have already been promoted to AC. It is a fair bet that eventually almost all of them will.

Meanwhile there remained on the statute book an early version of the appellation laws known as *appellation simple*. Whereas AC regulations stipulate not only the area and the grape variety but maximum quantities, minimum strengths, methods of pruning and much else besides, A.S. wines needed only to be grown from tolerated grapes in recognized regions. An ordinary table wine could be labelled with a regional name but nobody paid much attention. No A.S. wine had enough of a reputation to command more than the basic commodity price.

The years 1973–76, however, saw a series of ordinances to give status and definition to the more identifiable of these 'table' wines, and at the same time the creation of a new authority, the Office National Interprofessionel des Vins de Table, to look after them.

In the summer of 1976 a list of 75 Vins de Pays appeared—a list which reads like poetry to anyone with a feeling for the French countryside: Vals, Coteaux and Monts, Gorges and Pays, Marches and Vicomtés, Balmes and Fiefs. Who could resist Vallée du Paradis, Cucugnan, l'Ile de Beauté, Mont Bouquet?

The ordinances list precisely which communes and parts of communes have the right to use each name.

It is frankly admitted that some of these names have more validity than others. Some, in fact, have never been used and some possibly may never be. They are, on the other hand, a challenge and a rallying point for growers who want to build on their local traditions. It is probable that the best Vins de Pays will advance to VDQS and even AC rank in time.

The controls on Vin de Pays quality have established appropriate upper and lower limits for acidity and other analysable components as well as a minimum alcoholic degree (ranging from 9.5 to 10.5% depending on the region). The wines have to be approved by a tasting panel—which is not a requirement for, for example, German tafelwein. And they have to be made from grapes mentioned in a formidable catalogue. In the south-west, (admittedly the most maverick corner of France) 61 sorts are recommended.

As to the characters and qualities of each of the wines on the map. . . . I have a lot of work to do.

ARDÈCHE
1 Coteaux de l'Ardèche
AUDE
2 Coteaux de la Cabrerisse
3 Coteaux de la Cité de Carcassonne
4 Coteaux de Miramont
5 Coteaux de Peyriac
6 Coteaux du Termenès
7 Côtes de Perignan
8 Cucugnan
9 Hauterive en Pays d'Aude (also includes 2.11.15.)

10 Haute Vallée de l'Aude
11 Val d'Orbieu
12 Val de Cesse
13 Val de Dagne
14 Val du Torgan
15 Vallée du Paradis
BOUCHES-DU-RHÔNE
16 Petite Crau
17 Sables du Golfe du Lion
DRÔME
18 Coteaux de Baronniès

GARD
19 Coteaux Cévenoles
20 Coteaux Flaviens
21 Coteaux du Pont du Gard
22 Coteaux du Salavès
23 Coteaux du Vidourle
24 Mont Bouquet
25 Sables du Golfe du Lion
26 Serre de Coiran
27 Uzège
28 Val de Montferrand
29 Vistrenque

GERS
30 Côtes du Condomois
31 Côtes de Gascogne (includes 30. 32. 33.)
32 Côtes de Montestruc
33 Côtes de Saint-Mont
HÉRAULT
34 Bessan
35 Caux
36 Cessenon
37 Collines de la Moure
38 Coteaux d'Enserune
39 Coteaux de Laurens

VDQS
◻ Vins-de-Pays
- - - - Department Areas

40 Coteaux du Libron	**ISÈRE**	**MAINE-ET-LOIRE**
41 Coteaux de Murviel	52 Balmes	60 Marches de Bretagne
42 Coteaux de Peyriac	Dauphinoises	**PYRÉNÉES-**
43 Coteaux du Salagou	53 Coteaux du	**ORIENTALES**
44 Côtes du Brian	Grésivaudan	61 Coteaux des
45 Côtes de Thau	**LOIRE-ATLANTIQUE**	Fenouillèdes
46 Côtes de Thongue	54 Pays de Retz	62 Pays Catalan
47 Gorges de l'Hérault	55 Marches de Bretagne	63 Vals d'Agly
48 Haute Vallée de	**LOT**	**SAVOIE**
l'Orb	56 Coteaux de Glanes	64 Coteaux du
49 Sables du Golfe du	57 Coteaux du Quercy	Grésivaudan
Lion	**LOT-ET-GARONNE**	65 Balmes Dauphinoises
50 Val de Montferrand	58 Côtes du Condomois	**SAVOIE ET HAUTE-**
51 Vicomté d'Aumelas	59 Agenais (includes 58.)	**SAVOIE**

66 Allobrogie		
TARN		
67 Côtes du Tarn		
TARN-ET-GARONNE		
68 Agenais		
69 Coteaux du Quercy		
70 Saint-Sardos		
VAR		
71 Les Maures		
72 Coteaux Varois		
VENDÉE		
73 Fiefs Vendéens		
74 Marches de Bretagne		

Corsica

Corsica's new vineyards in the east and south were planted by growers from Algeria in the 1960s. The old ones are starkly different: tight terraces on the rugged hills

CORSICA has only come on to the world wine map in the last 20 years. The maquis, the famous scrub-covered, bandit-haunted mountains, are scarcely suitable for wine-growing. The plains were malaria-infested. A general air of mayhem ruled. France was ready enough to forget about her largest island. But then came the split with Algeria.

In a few years the island's old total of about 8,000 hectares of rather desultory vineyards, more like the Italian variety than the French, grew to 30,000 or more. The malaria was beaten and the plains were invaded by wine-growers who had had to leave Algeria. The most modern methods rapidly made Corsica a major producer of blending wines for the French market, while improvements to the old vineyards have persuaded the authorities to grant seven of them (see the map) Appellations Contrôlées—though more as encouragement, one might think, than recognition of brilliance.

Patrimonio is known chiefly for its vin rosé made from the local Niellucio and Grenache grapes, although the appellation extends to its red and white (Vermentino) wines as well. The hillsides round Ajaccio, the capital, produce chiefly red and rosé from another native grape, the Sciacarello. Sartène has a name for its strong red wine and Cap Corse for dessert and more recently white wine. Figari and Porto Vecchio also have the right to use their names as appellations, while a general appellation Vin de Corse, not qualified by a place-name, is available to some fifty communes in less favoured situations.

In many ways Corsican wine can be compared with Provençal. The rosé in both cases is commonly the best. In both it tends to be overstrong. Both have found huge new markets waiting for their wines, eager to find in them the elusive smell of the hot herbs of the maquis.

Patrimonio was Corsica's only Appellation Contrôlée wine until recently. Its strong (12.5°) red, rosés and white are still the island's best wines. Muscat is a new introduction, not AC

Map legend

PATRIMONIO — Appellation Contrôlée

Wine-producing areas

Germany

The Riesling vine in its element: the vineyards of Bernkastel on the Mosel

The Wines of Germany

GERMANY's best vineyards lie as far north as grapes can be persuaded to ripen. They lie on land unfit for normal agriculture: if they were not there, forest and bare mountain would take their place. All in all their chances of giving the world's best white wine look slim. And yet on occasion they do, and stamp it with a style which no one, anywhere, can imitate.

Their secret is the balance of sugar against acidity. Sugar without acid would be flat; acid without sugar would be sharp. In good years, when the equation works out right, the two are so finely counterpoised that they have the inevitability of great art. They provide a stage for a mingling of essences from the grape and the ground, an ensemble customarily described in the single word 'breed'. It is all the more apparent in German wines because they are low in alcohol; there is less body in the background; nuances of flavour are brilliantly distinct; more often than not there is a great canopy of bouquet.

The best such wines are so full of character and charm, and if the word does not sound too pedantic, interest, that they are best enjoyed, unlike French wines, alone rather than with food. A bottle of a Spätlese or Auslese from the Mosel or Rheingau is a complete experience from which food, however good it may be, can only detract.

Knowing how passionately wine-lovers will follow his successes and failures, sensing vividly the drama in his battle to get the best from his grapes and from the ground he works, a German grower will treat his different barrels, from one year and one vineyard, as different wines. 'Best barrel' is not empty sales talk; cask numbers are matters for emotion. In France even Château Yquem 'equalizes' all the barrels of one year to make one standard wine —even if standard is hardly the word for it.

This is one side of the picture; the connoisseur's side. In Germany he is catered for as nowhere else in the world. On the other hand, 50% of German wine is blended if necessary, and gives uncomplicated pleasure.

Germany's vineyards lie along the river Rhine and its tributaries. They are scant in the extreme south and thickest near the French border in Rheinland-Pfalz. All the important areas are mapped on the following pages.

In addition to place names and (for the best wines) vineyards and wine qualities which appear on German labels, they often name the grape from which the wine is made.

The Riesling (see page 22) is the great grape of Germany; virtually all the best German wines are made from it and it is planted to the exclusion of almost everything else in the Mosel, Saar, Ruwer and Rheingau, and in the best sites of the lesser areas.

The price of quality, however, is quantity. The Riesling gives only half as much wine per plant as the commoner Sylvaner, which forms a large part of the vineyards of Rheinhessen, the Nahe, the Palatinate (Pfalz) and Franconia (Franken—small map). In its best sites, notably in Franconia, the Sylvaner gives very good wine, but it very rarely has the breed and balance of a good Riesling.

A new vine, called Müller-Thurgau after its propagator, has been produced by crossing the

The Great Tun of Heidelberg, built in 1663, held 37,500 gallons or 19,000 dozen bottles of wine

Sylvaner and the Riesling. It has most success in the Palatinate, Rheinhessen and Baden.

Pinot Noir (known as Spätburgunder—the late Burgundy) and the commoner Portugieser are the main sources of red wine. The valley of the Ahr near Bonn is the only district that specializes in red wine: it rarely reaches the standards of German white.

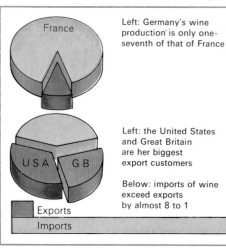

Left: Germany's wine production is only one-seventh of that of France

Left: the United States and Great Britain are her biggest export customers

Below: imports of wine exceed exports by almost 8 to 1

Exports
Imports

Germany consumed 14.4 million hectolitres of wine in 1975: 23.2 litres per head of the population

1.6% of the population is employed in wine-growing and the wine trade

Above: 85% of German wine is white. Red wine is only grown for local consumption and is often blended with imported wine

The average price for wine received by the grower varies by region from 75 to 150 DM per 100 litres

The average price to the consumer of a bottle (0.7 litre) of wine is 3.30 DM (1975 figures)

Wine Law 1971

German wine laws do not classify vineyards as the French do. Any vineyard in Germany can in theory produce top-class wine. Instead the law specifies exactly what degree of sugar the must (crushed grapes) should contain to qualify for each classification.

New laws made in 1971 lay down three basic grades of quality regardless of where in Germany the wine comes from. They are:
Deutscher Tafelwein Ordinary table wine, which need only attain 5% natural alcohol before sugaring and be made from approved grape varieties. It may use the name of a region or a village, but not a vineyard. It does not pass a test.
Qualitätswein bestimmter Anbaugebiete (*Q.b.A.*) Must come from a specified region (*Gebiet*), from certain grape varieties, attain a certain must-weight* (about 60, which would give 7½% natural alcohol), and carry a test number (*Prüfungsnummer*). It can carry a vineyard name if 85% of the grapes were grown there, a *Grosslage* name or a *Bereich* name (see below).
Qualitätswein mit Prädikat (*Q.m.P.*) The grade for the top wines which may not use sugar. Their natural must-weight has to be 73 (the equivalent of 9½% alcohol) or more depending on the region; their grapes of certain varieties; they must come from a particular area (*Bereich*), be quality-tested and carry their identifying test number.

Within the Q.m.P. grade the traditional classification by sugar content of the top wines is given precise standards. They are:
Kabinett: minimum must-weight of 73 (or more or less depending on the region).
Spätlese: minimum must-weight 85.
Auslese: minimum must-weight about 90.
Beerenauslese: minimum about 120.
Trockenbeerenauslese: minimum must-weight about 150. (Weights vary by area and grape variety.)

At the same time the 1971 law reduced the number of individual vineyards in Germany from the 20,000 in the old land register to 3,000, a bold and admirable move which has made life considerably easier for wine-lovers, provided they make themselves familiar with the new terminology and its application. There are three concepts, besides that of the individual vineyard, which must be grasped:
A *Gebiet* is simply a wine-growing region— e.g. Nahe, Rheinpfalz.
A *Bereich* is a sub-region within a *Gebiet* (see the map opposite).
A *Grosslage* is a collective site'; an area formed by a number of neighbouring vineyards (whether or not adjacent, or in the same village) and called by the name of the best known of them. It is important, though not easy, to distinguish this from a 'site' (*Einzellage*); one individual vineyard. All the best wines of the best growers carry site names.

*The number of grammes by which one litre of must is heavier than one litre of distilled water

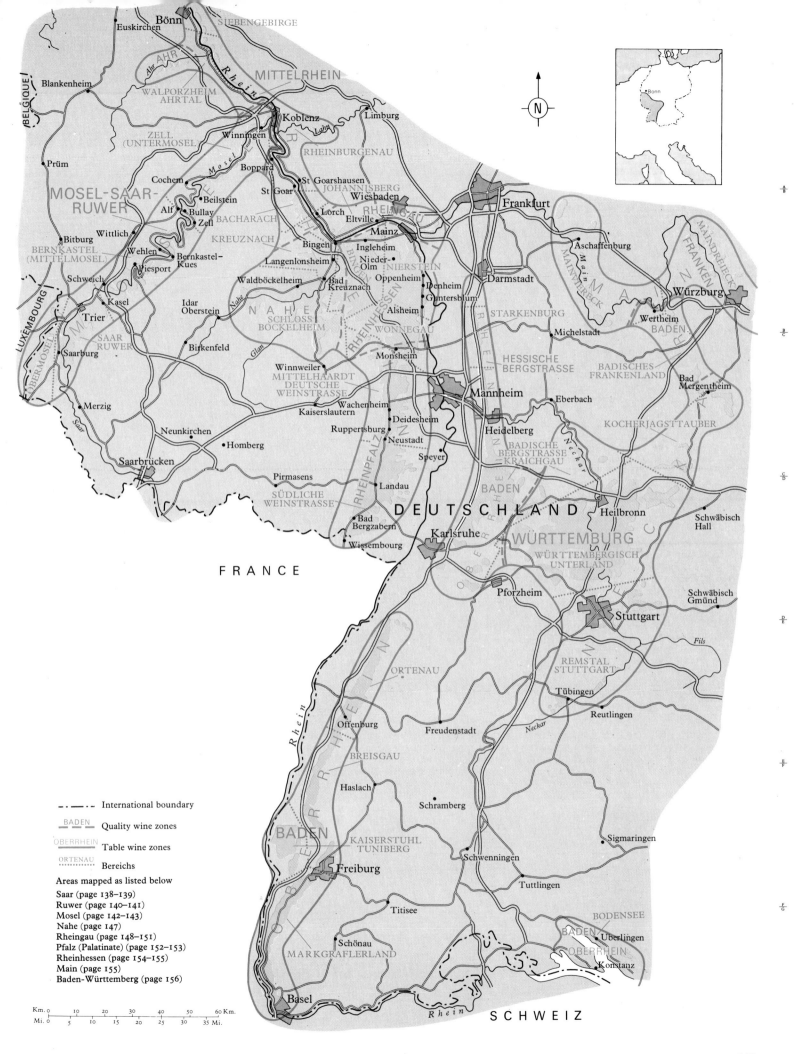

Bönn

Euskirchen

SIEBENGEBIRGE

Blankenheim

MITTELRHEIN

WALPORZHEIM AHRTAL

AHR Rhein

Prüm

ZELL (UNTERMOSEL

Koblenz

Winningen

Limburg

Lahn

RHEINBURGENAU

Boppard

MOSEL-SAAR-RUWER

Cochem

Beilstein

St Goarshausen

JOHANNISBERG

Wiesbaden

Frankfurt

St Goar

RHEINGAU

Alf Bullay

Wittlich

Bernkastel (MITTELMOSEL)

Bitburg

Wehlen

Piesport

Bernkastel-Kues

Schweich

Kasel

Idar Oberstein

Trier

Saarburg

Birkenfeld

Merzig

Neunkirchen

Homberg

Saarbrücken

Pirmasens

Zell

BACHARACH

Lorch

Eltville

KREUZNACH

Bingen

Langenlonsheim

Waldböckelheim

Bad Kreuznach

NAHE

SCHLOSS BOCKELHEIM

Glan

Winnweiler

MITTELHAARDT DEUTSCHE WEINSTRASSE

Wachenheim

Kaiserslautern

Deidesheim

Ruppertsberg

Neustadt

RHEINPFALZ

Speyer

Landau

SÜDLICHE WEINSTRASSE

Bad Bergzabern

Wissembourg

Mainz

Ingleheim

Nieder-Olm

NIERSTEIN

Oppenheim

Dienheim

Guntersblum

Alsheim

RHEINHESSEN

WONNEGAU

Monsheim

Aschaffenburg

MAINDREIECK

Darmstadt

FRANKEN

Würzburg

Wertheim

STARKENBURG

Michelstadt

BADEN

HESSISCHE BERGSTRASSE

BADISCHES FRANKENLAND

Mannheim

Eberbach

KOCHERJAGSTTAUBER

Heidelberg

Bad Mergentheim

BADISCHE BERGSTRASSE KRAICHGAU

Neckar

BADEN

DEUTSCHLAND

WÜRTTEMBURG

Karlsruhe

Heilbronn

Schwäbisch Hall

WÜRTTEMBERGISCH UNTERLAND

Pforzheim

FRANCE

Stuttgart

Schwäbisch Gmünd

ORTENAU

REMSTAL STUTTGART

Fils

Tübingen

Reutlingen

Rhein

Neckar

Offenburg

BREISGAU

Freudenstadt

Haslach

Schramberg

Sigmaringen

BADEN

Schwenningen

KAISERSTUHL TUNIBERG

Freiburg

Tuttlingen

Titisee

BODENSEE

BADEN

Schönau

Überlingen

MARKGRÄFLERLAND

OBERRHEIN

Konstanz

Basel

Rhein

SCHWEIZ

N

BELGIQUE

LUXEMBOURG

ZELL

MOSEL

SAAR RUWER

OBERMOSEL

Saar

— · — · — International boundary

BADEN Quality wine zones

OBERRHEIN Table wine zones

ORTENAU Bereichs

Areas mapped as listed below

Saar (page 138–139)
Ruwer (page 140–141)
Mosel (page 142–143)
Nahe (page 147)
Rheingau (page 148–151)
Pfalz (Palatinate) (page 152–153)
Rheinhessen (page 154–155)
Main (page 155)
Baden-Württemberg (page 156)

Km. 0   10   20   30   40   50   60 Km.
Mi. 0   5   10   15   20   25   30   35 Mi.

Germany/the Quality Factor

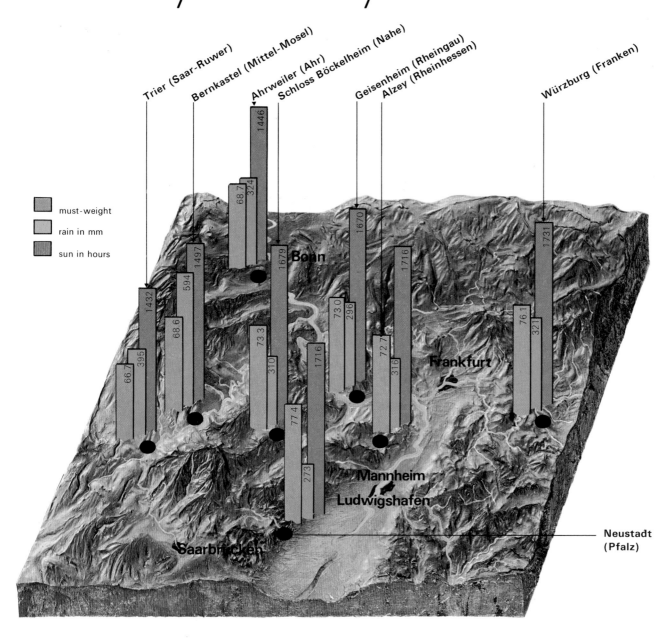

Trier (Saar-Ruwer)
Bernkastel (Mittel-Mosel)
Ahrweiler (Ahr)
Schloss Böckelheim (Nahe)
Geisenheim (Rheingau)
Alzey (Rheinhessen)
Würzburg (Franken)

must-weight
rain in mm
sun in hours

Bonn

Frankfurt

Mannheim
Ludwigshafen

Saarbrücken

Neustadt
(Pfalz)

IF IN BURGUNDY the emphasis for the study of quality is on the soil and the microclimate, and in Bordeaux on the physical make-up of the soil affecting drainage, in Germany it centres on the weather. Every conceivable aspect of weather is examined for its possible effect on the specific gravity of the grape juice, or 'must-weight': in other words on the amount of sugar in the grapes.

The map above shows sunshine and rainfall in the growing season for the principal wine regions of Germany. On the page opposite are some of the findings of perhaps the most elaborate investigation ever mounted into wine quality. The government of Hesse has spent vast sums and many years studying the Rheingau—the state's best vineyard and probably the best in Germany.

They have recorded the soil (which changes abruptly and often) in great detail, and then the amounts of sunshine, wind, late frost (in May; which can interfere with flowering) and early frost (in September; which can kill the leaves and stop the grapes ripening: map not shown) that every spot of ground could expect. Finally, with a daring all too rare among scientists, they

plotted the areas where the wine *should* be best (the last map).

Certain sites do emerge with a distinctive tint in almost every map. The Rüdesheimer Berg at the western end of the Rheingau is the only one which achieves 'excellent' in the aptitude test (map 5). But a consistent string of vineyards at a certain altitude is noticeable on each map. They happen to include most of the highest-priced of the Rheingau. The Rüdesheimer Berg, Schloss Johannisberg, Schloss Vollrads, Steinberg, the southern slopes of Kiedrich and Rauenthal are among them. And curiously the most consistently noticeable down by the river is also a very expensive vineyard—Markobrunn, between Hattenheim and Erbach. A great deal can be gleaned from these maps used in conjunction with the detailed maps of the Rheingau on pages 149–151.

Since these maps were published research has continued in even greater detail to define precise zones of soil and microclimate. The ideal vine and the ideal method of pruning, training and manuring is then recommended. A definitive map of a small part of the Rheingau

behind Mittelheim and Oestrich (including Schloss Vollrads) has been published, and the work continues. Some of the latest findings of the researchers are explored in more detail on pages 20–21.

Rainfall is comparatively light in the Rheingau. Drainage is not a big quality factor—indeed there are places (Rüdesheim is one) which suffer from drought in dry years. Since winter rain sinks right in and summer showers run off quickly the vines tend to root near the surface, and thus are particularly vulnerable to rain just before picking, water which the vine immediately pumps into the grapes. The must-weight can easily be lowered by 10° by one downpour at the last moment.

If frost and rain hold off long enough and Edelfäule (noble rot) takes a hold, the grapes go on sweetening until enormous must-weights of as much as double the normal are recorded.

As a last resort, if the grapes do freeze on the vine, which is not uncommon, the grower can pick and press them frozen. The Eiswein (ice wine) he makes will not be as good as a Trockenbeerenauslese would have been. But there are worse risks in wine-growing.

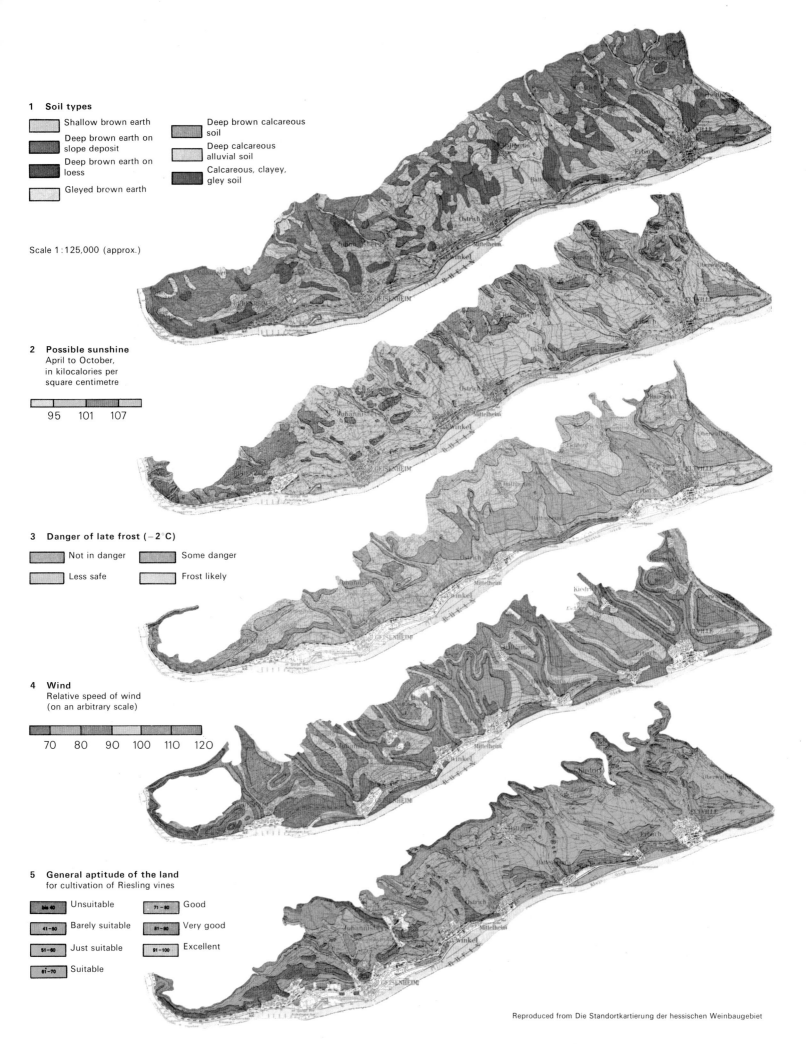

1 Soil types

	Shallow brown earth		Deep brown calcareous soil
	Deep brown earth on slope deposit		Deep calcareous alluvial soil
	Deep brown earth on loess		Calcareous, clayey, gley soil
	Gleyed brown earth		

Scale 1:125,000 (approx.)

2 Possible sunshine
April to October, in kilocalories per square centimetre

95   101   107

3 Danger of late frost (−2°C)

	Not in danger		Some danger
	Less safe		Frost likely

4 Wind
Relative speed of wind (on an arbitrary scale)

70   80   90   100   110   120

5 General aptitude of the land
for cultivation of Riesling vines

bis 40	Unsuitable	71–80	Good
41–50	Barely suitable	81–90	Very good
51–60	Just suitable	91–100	Excellent
61–70	Suitable		

Reproduced from Die Standortkartierung der hessischen Weinbaugebiet

The Saar

GERMAN wine with its problems and its triumphs is epitomized nowhere better than in the valley of the Mosel's tributary, the Saar. The battle for sugar in the grapes rages fiercest in this cold corner of the country. It is only won perhaps three or four years in ten. Yet those years give one of the world's superlative white wines; every mouthful a cause for rejoicing and wonder.

A mere 1,500 acres of vines share the valley with orchard and pasture. It is calm open agricultural country; impossible to believe that only just upstream the blast-furnaces of the industrial Saar are at work, so that even here the river is poisonous with their pollution.

The map shows clearer than any other the way south slopes—here nearly all on banks of hill sidling up to the river—offer the wine-grower his chance of enough sunshine.

As in the best part of the Mosel the soil is slate and the grape the Riesling. The qualities of Mosel wine: apple-like freshness and bite, a marvellous mingling of honey in the scent and steel in the finish, can find their apogee in Saar wine. If anything the emphasis here (again a question of weather) is more on the steel than the honey.

Unsuccessful vintages are so spectacularly unsuccessful that even the best growers can only sell their wine to the makers of sparkling Sekt, who are looking for something really acid to work on.

But when the sun shines and the Riesling ripens and goes on ripening far into October the great bosomy smell of flowers and honey which it generates would be too lush without the appley emphasis of acidity. Then the Saar comes into its own. It makes sweet wine which you can never tire of. The balance and depth make you sniff and sip and sniff again.

Some sites are better than others. Most are in the hands of rich and ancient estates which can afford to wait for good years and make the most of them. The labels of the principal ones —themselves austere compared with the flowery creations of some parts of Germany— are on this page. One of the finest of the state domains operates here, with its headquarters in the nearby old Roman wine-city of Trier. Its holdings in Ockfen (the Domäne house in the vines can be seen on the map) and in Serrig are celebrated. That at Serrig is unusual in having been created by the State from virgin woodland at the turn of the century: an optimistic move since Serrig has even more uncertain weather than the rest of the Saar. It takes a fantastic autumn . . . but then it justifies everything.

The most famous estate of the Saar is that of Egon Müller, whose house appears on the map as Scharzhof at the foot of the Scharzhofberg in Wiltingen. Among the other owners of parts of the Scharzhofberg is the cathedral of Trier ('Hohe Domkirche'), which adds the word Dom before the names of its vineyards. Egon Müller also manages the Le Gallais estate, with the famous Braune Kupp vineyard at the other end of Wiltingen. Ayler Kupp and Herrenberger, Ockfener Bockstein and Herrenberg, Wawerner Ritterpfad and the Falkensteiner Hofberg above Niedermennig are all renowned . . . for their good vintages. The new Grosslage name for the whole of the Saar is (Wiltinger) Scharzberg—not to be confused with the great Scharzhofberg.

Many of the vineyards of the Mosel, and particularly the Saar, belong to a group of religious and charitable bodies in Trier. The Friedrich Wilhelm Gymnasium (Karl Marx's old school); the Bischöfliches Konvikt (a Catholic boarding-school); the Bischöfliches Priesterseminar (a college for priests); the Vereinigte Hospitien (an almshouse) besides the cathedral are all important wine-growers. The two Bischöfliches and the cathedral operate together as the Vereinigte Bischöfliches Weingut. In their broad, dark, damp cellars in the city one has the feeling that wine is itself an act of charity rather than mere vulgar trade.

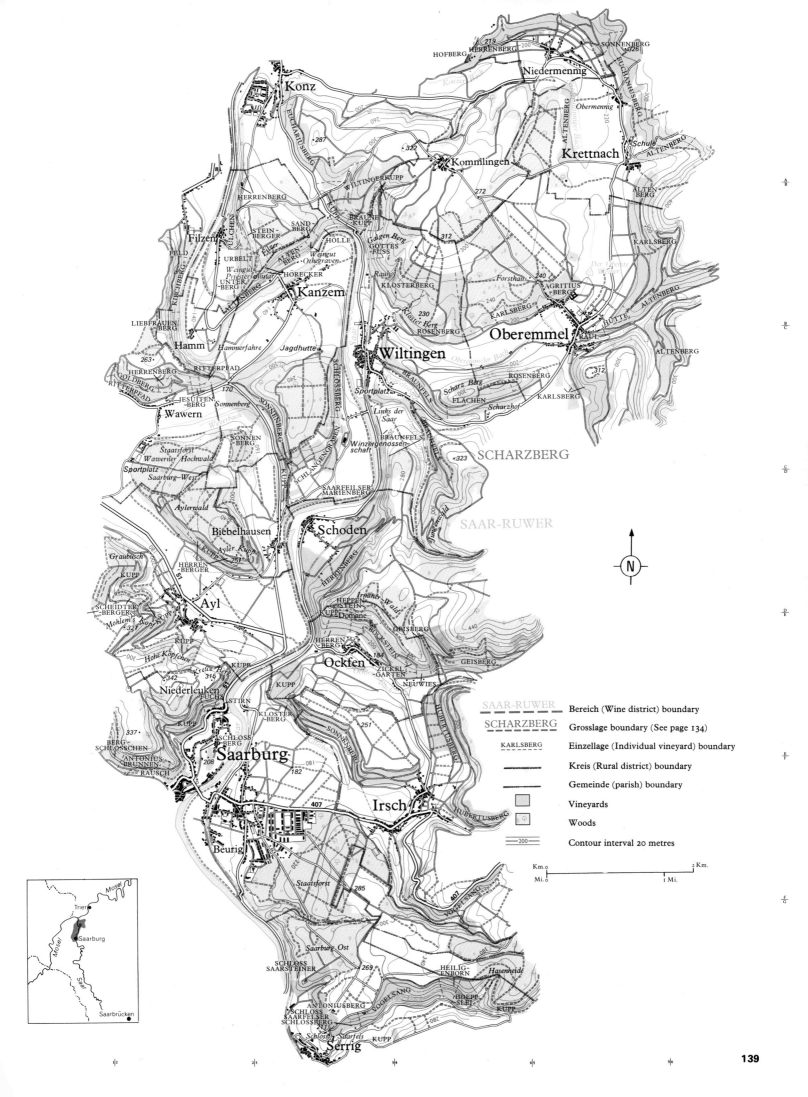

Konz

Niedermennig

SONNENBERG

HOFBERG HERRENBERG

EUCHARIUSBERG

ALTENBERG

Obermennig

Krettnach

Schule ALTENBERG

Kommlingen

WILTINGERKUPP

272

KARLSBERG

HERRENBERG

BRAUNE
KUPP

Galgen Berg

GOTTES
FUSS

312

Filzen

STEIN-
BERGER

SAND-
BERG

HÖLLE

Weingut
Othegraven

Rauhof

ALTEN
BERG

KLOSTERBERG

Forsthaus

240

AGRITIUS
BERG

Der Oberste
Weiher

FELD

URBELT

Weingut
Priesterseminar
UNTER-
BERG

HÖRECKER

Kanzem

Kloster Berg

ROSENBERG

KARLSBERG

230

Oberemmel

HÜTTE

ALTENBERG

KIRCHBERG

ALTEN
BERG

LIEBFRAUEN-
BERG

Hamm

Hammerfahre

Jagdhutte

Wiltingen

Sportplatz

BRAUNFELS

Oberemmeler Bach

Scharz Berg

ROSENBERG

KARLSBERG

ALTENBERG

312

263

HERRENBERG

GOLDBERG

RITTERPFAD

RITTERPFAD

170

JESUITEN-
BERG

Sonnenberg

Wawern

SONNEN-
BERG

SCHLOSSBERG

Links der
Saar

Winzergenossen-
schaft

FLÄCHEN

Scharzhof

SCHARZBERG

Staatsforst
Wawerner Hochwald

Sportplatz
Saarburg-West

SONNEN-
BERG

SCHLANGENGRABEN

SAARFEILSER-
MARIENBERG

323

280

SAAR-RUWER

Aylerwald

Biebelhausen

Schoden

Graubusch

KUPP

Ayler Kupp
251

HERREN-
BERGER

HERRENBERG

Irminer Wald

N

SCHEIDTER-
BERGER

Mohlem's Kopf

321

Ayl

KUPP

KUPP

HEPPEN
STEIN
KUPP

Domane

BOCKSTEIN

GEISBERG

440

400

HERREN-
BERG

Ockfen

184

GEISBERG

KUPP

Hohe Kopfchen

KUPP

ZICKEL-
GARTEN

NEUWIES

Krettz Berg
315

342

Niederleuken

FUCHS

STIRN

KUPP

KUPP

KLOSTER-
BERG

251

SONNENBERG

337

BERG-
SCHLOSSCHEN

ANTONIUS-
BRUNNEN
RAUSCH

SCHLOSS
BERG

Saarburg

208

081

182

Irsch

HUBERTUSBERG

407

Beurig

Staatsforst

285

407

SAAR-RUWER   Bereich (Wine district) boundary

SCHARZBERG   Grosslage boundary (See page 134)

KARLSBERG   Einzellage (Individual vineyard) boundary

              Kreis (Rural district) boundary

              Gemeinde (parish) boundary

              Vineyards

              Woods

─── 200 ───   Contour interval 20 metres

Km. 0   2 Km.
Mi. 0   1 Mi.

Mosel

Trier

Saarburg

Mosel

Saar

Saarbrücken

Saarburg Ost

SCHLOSS
SAARSTEINER

269

VOGELSANG

HEILIG-
ENBORN

Hasenheide

ANTONIUSBERG

SCHLOSS
SAARFELSER
SCHLOSSBERG

211

Schloss
Saarfels

HOEPP-
STEI

KUPP

VOGELSANG

Serrig

KUPP

The Ruwer

THE RUWER is a mere stream. Its vineyards add up to about half the acreage of one Côte d'Or commune. In many years its wine is unsatisfactory; faint and sharp. Yet like the Saar, when conditions are right it performs a miracle. Its wines are Germany's most delicate; gentle yet infinitely fine and full of subtlety.

Waldrach, the first wine village, makes good light wine but rarely more. Kasel is more important. The famous von Kesselstatt estate and the Bischöfliches Weingut of Trier have holdings here. There are great Kaselers in hot years.

Mertesdorf and Eitelsbach could not be called famous names; but each has one supreme vineyard, wholly owned by one of the world's best wine-growers. Mertesdorf's Maximin Grünhaus stands obliquely to the left bank of the river, with the manor-house, formerly monastic property, at its foot. The greater part of its hill of vines is called Herrenberg; the top part Abtsberg (for the abbot) and the less-well-sited part Bruderberg (for the brothers).

Across the stream Karthäuserhofberg echoes its situation, again with an old monastic building, now the manor-house, in its garden below. The subdivisions of this hill are on the map.

The town of Trier lies five miles away up the Mosel. Within the city there is one good vineyard, the Tiergarten. On the way there lies an isolated clearing belonging to the state domain and Trier cathedral; the hill of Avelsbach. Its wine is like that of the Ruwer; particularly perfumed and forthcoming.

The Grosslage name for the area is Römerlay.

Above: the beautiful old-fashioned label and (below) the manor of Maximin Grünhaus from its vineyard. In the background is Kasel and beyond, Waldrach

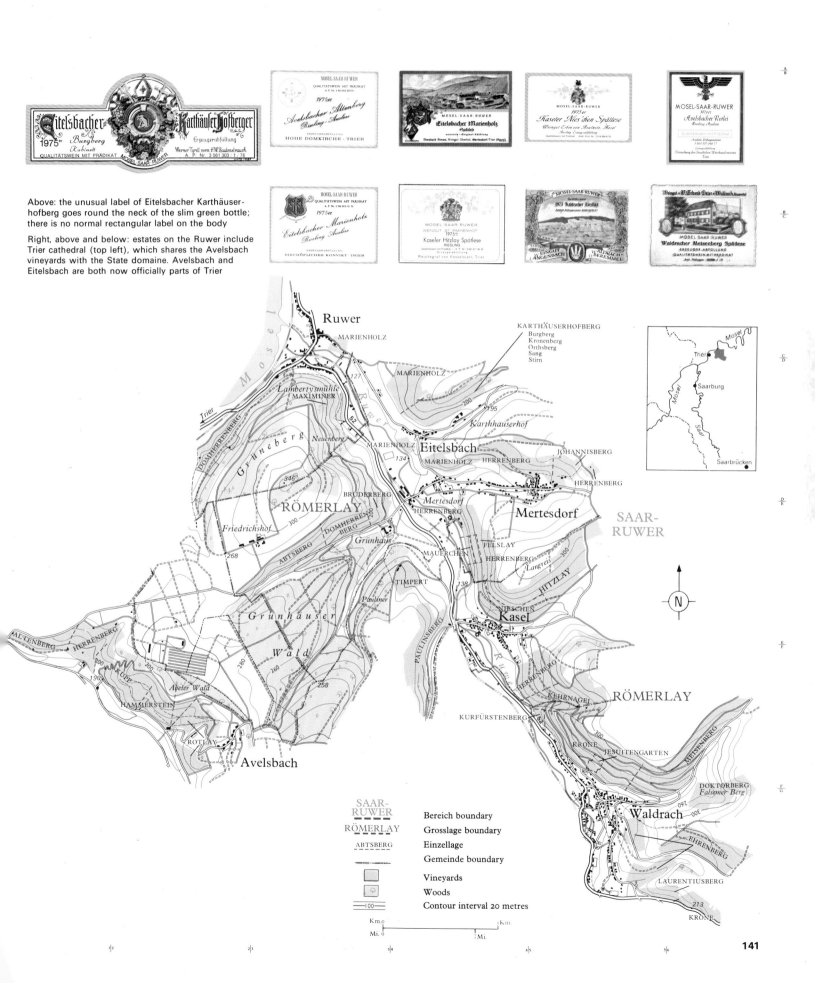

Above: the unusual label of Eitelsbacher Karthäuserhofberg goes round the neck of the slim green bottle;
there is no normal rectangular label on the body

Right, above and below: estates on the Ruwer include
Trier cathedral (top left), which shares the Avelsbach
vineyards with the State domaine. Avelsbach and
Eitelsbach are both now officially parts of Trier

Ruwer
MARIENHOLZ
MARIENHOLZ

KARTHÄUSERHOFBERG
Burgberg
Kronenberg
Orthsberg
Sang
Stirn

Lambertysmühle
MAXIMINER

Trier

Grüneberg

Neuenberg

MARIENHOLZ

Karthhäuserhof

Eitelsbach

JOHANNISBERG

MARIENHOLZ
HERRENBERG

HERRENBERG

BRUDERBERG

DOMHERRENBERG

RÖMERLAY

Mertesdorf
HERRENBERG

Mertesdorf

SAAR-
RUWER

Friedrichshof

ABTSBERG DOMHERREN-
BERG

Grünhaus

FELSLAY

HERRENBERG

Langreis

HITZLAY

MAUERCHEN

TIMPERT

Pauliner

NIESCHEN Kasel

Grünhäuser

Wald

HERRENBERG

RÖMERLAY

ALTENBERG HERRENBERG

PAULINSBERG

KEHRNAGEL

RUPP

HAMMERSTEIN

Abtei Wald

KURFÜRSTENBERG

KRONE JESUITENGARTEN

ROTLAY

MEISENBERG

Avelsbach

DOKTORBERG
Falsemer Berg

Waldrach

EHRENBERG

LAURENTIUSBERG

KRONE

SAAR-
RUWER   Bereich boundary

RÖMERLAY   Grosslage boundary

ABTSBERG   Einzellage

               Gemeinde boundary

               Vineyards

               Woods

──100──   Contour interval 20 metres

Km. 0   Km.
Mi. 0   Mi.

Mosel

Trier

Saarburg

Saarbrücken

N

The Middle Mosel: Piesport

Left: the really famous estates of the Mosel start down-river from Dhron. Dunweg and Milz, both in Neumagen, are two of the better-known growers of the upper stretch. The label of Nicola Clüsserath is a pre-1971 example, with the banned word naturrein— 'unsugared'

Above, left and right: dark grey slate and golden Riesling grapes are the elements which give Middle Mosel wine its quality. Each vine is staked independently on the vertiginous south-facing slopes above the river

THE RIVER Mosel is acquainted with the reflections of vines all the way from its rising in the Vosges mountains to its union with the Rhine at Koblenz. Light wines of little consequence grow on the French Moselle; in Luxembourg larger quantities are made, attractive but still very slight. Only in the central part of the German Mosel do the spectacular river-walls of slate, rising sometimes to 700 feet above its course, provide the perfect conditions for the Riesling vine. In the central 40 miles of the river's snake-like meandering, which only take it 18 miles as the crow flies, the Mosel's great wine is made.

The wines of the river vary along the banks even more than, say, the wines of Burgundy vary along the Côte d'Or. Given south, south-east or south-west exposure, the steeper the bank the better the wine. It is only because the thin soil here is pure slate, through which rain runs as if through a sieve, that any soil stays in place on near-precipices. The coincidence of quickly drying stable soil in vineyards which are held up to the sun like toast to a fire is the Mosel's secret.

There is no formal agreement on what constitutes the Middle Mosel. In the maps on these pages we have extended it beyond the central and most famous villages to include several whose wine is often underrated.

The first that we come to is Klüsserath. The Bruderschaft vineyard is immediately typical of a fine Mosel site: a steep bank curving from south to south-west.

The long tongue of land which ends in Trittenheim is almost a cliff where the village of Leiwen jumps the river to claim part of the vineyard of Laurentiuslay, flattening to only a gentle slope before the bend. Down to here the Grosslage name is St Michael.

Trittenheim's best-exposed sites are Apot-

heke and Altärchen, over the bridge. These are the first vineyards of the Mosel which make wine of real breed. It is always delicate, but not faint. In such a year as 1975, when the wines of the Saar and Ruwer were Germany's best, Trittenheimers come into their own.

The town of Neumagen, a Roman landing place, keeps in its little leafy square a remarkable Roman carving of a Mosel wine ship, laden with barrels and weary galley-slaves.

The wine of Dhron, its partner, is better known. Here the Mosel banks fall back as a gentle slope; it is the tributary River Dhron that has the steepest slopes and the best sites. Dhroner Hofberger is partly owned by the Bischöfliches Weingut of Trier.

Piesport has a standing far above its neighbours. It is the ideal site: an amphitheatre two miles long and 500 feet high, facing due south. The name of its magnificent Goldtröpfchen, the slope above and around the village, is world-famous for round and gently sweet wines, not with great power but with magic fragrance and breed. The vast new plantation across the river known as Piesporter Treppchen does not share Goldtröpfchen's distinction.

Michelsberg is the Grosslage name for this part of the river, from Trittenheim to Minheim.

Minheim, Wintrich and Kesten are all minor producers. There are no perfectly aligned slopes in this stretch, except for the beginning of the great ramp which rises to its full height opposite the village of Brauneberg. In Kesten it is called Paulinshofberg. In Brauneberg it is the Juffer; 100 years ago reckoned the greatest wine of the Mosel, perfectly satisfying the taste of those days for full-bodied golden wine.

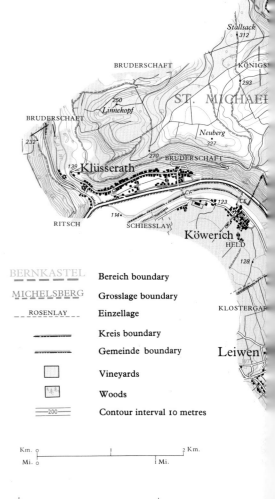

BRUDERSCHAFT

ST. MICHAEL

Linnekopf

BRUDERSCHAFT

Neuberg

BRUDERSCHAFT

Klüsserath

KÖNIGS

Stallsack

RITSCH

SCHIESSLAY

Köwerich

HELD

KLOSTERGAR

Leiwen

BERNKASTEL — Bereich boundary

MICHELSBERG — Grosslage boundary

ROSENLAY — Einzellage

Kreis boundary

Gemeinde boundary

Vineyards

Woods

200 — Contour interval 10 metres

Km. 0 . . . 1 . . . 2 Km.
Mi. 0 . . . 1 Mi.

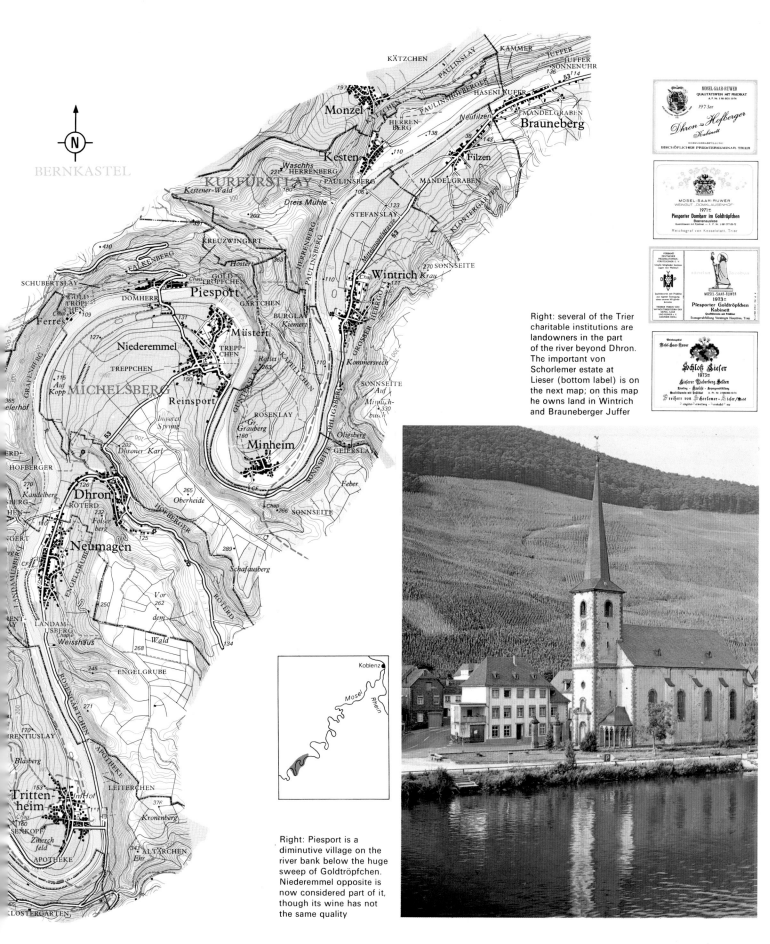

BERNKASTEL

KÄTZCHEN

PAULINSLAY

KAMMER

JUFFER
JUFFER
SONNENUHR

HASENLÄUFER

MANDELGRABEN

Monzel

HERREN-
BERG

Neufilzen

Brauneberg

KURFÜRSTLAY

Kesten

Waschhs HERRENBERG

Filzen

PAULINSBERG

MANDELGRABEN

Kestener-Wald

Dreis Mühle

STEFANSLAY

KLOSTERGARTEN

KREUZWINGERT

Wintrich

SONNSEITE

Hoster

Krau

FALKENBERG

GOLD-
TRÜPFCHEN

Piesport

GÄRTCHEN

SCHUBERTSLAY

DOMHERR

BURGLAY

GOLD-
TRÖPF-
CHEN

Müstert

Kiemert

Ferres

TREPP-
CHEN

Kommersnech

Niederemmel

SONNSEITE
Auf
Minnich-
busch

TREPPCHEN

MICHELSBERG

Reinsport

ROSENLAY

Oligsberg

Gr.
Grauberg

GEIERSLAY

Minheim

Dhroner Karl

Feber

HOFBERGER

Dhron

ROTERD

Oberheide

Folser
berg

SONNSEITE

Neumagen

Schafausberg

ENGELGRUBE

Vor
dem
Wald

LANDAM-
USBERG

Weisshaus

ENGELGRUBE

ROSENGÄRTCHEN

Kronenberg

Blasberg

LEITERCHEN

Tritten-
heim

APOTHEKE

Zinnerch
feld

ALTÄRCHEN

APOTHEKE

KLOSTERGARTEN

Koblenz

Mosel

Rhein

MOSEL-SAAR-RUWER
QUALITÄTSWEIN MIT PRÄDIKAT
1973er
Dhron-Hofberger
Kabinett
BISCHÖFLICHES PRIESTERSEMINAR, TRIER

MOSEL-SAAR-RUWER
WEINGUT „DOMKLAUSENHOF"
1971er
Piesporter Domherr im Goldtröpfchen
Beerenauslese
Reichsgraf von Kesselstatt, Trier

MOSEL-SAAR-RUWER
1973er
Piesporter Goldtröpfchen
Kabinett
Erzeugerabfüllung Vereinigte Hospitien, Trier

Mosel-Saar-Ruwer
Schloß Lieser
1973er
Lieser Niederberg Helden
Freiherr von Schorlemer Lieser/Mosel

Right: several of the Trier
charitable institutions are
landowners in the part
of the river beyond Dhron.
The important von
Schorlemer estate at
Lieser (bottom label) is on
the next map; on this map
he owns land in Wintrich
and Brauneberger Juffer

Right: Piesport is a
diminutive village on the
river bank below the huge
sweep of Goldtröpfchen.
Niederemmel opposite is
now considered part of it,
though its wine has not
the same quality

143

THE VIEW north from the bridge at Bernkastel is of a green wall of vines 700 feet high and five miles long. Only perhaps the Douro in the whole gazetteer of rivers to which the vine is wedded has any comparable sight.

From Brauneberg to Bernkastel's suburb of Kues the hills are relatively gentle. The Kirchberg in Veldenz (the village is just off the map) is one of those marginal vineyards which, like the Trittenheimers, makes beautiful wine after a hot summer. Lieser is perhaps best known for the grim great mansion of the von Schorlemers, one of the biggest estate-owners of the district, at the foot of the Rosenlay. Here again, hills at right angles to the river give good south slopes.

The Mosel's greatest vineyard starts abruptly, rising almost sheer above the gables of Bernkastel; dark slate frowning at slate. The butt of the hill, its one straight south elevation, is the Bernkasteler Doktor—perhaps the most famous vineyard in Germany. From its flank the proudest names of the Mosel follow one after another. Comparison of Bernkasteler with Graacher and Wehlener, often with wines from the same growers in each place, is a fascinating game. The trademark of Bernkastel is a touch of flint. Graachers are softer; Wehleners richer.

The least of these wines should be something of very obvious personality; almost water-white with a gleam of green and with 40 or 50 little bubbles in the bottom of the glass, smelling almost aggressively of grapes, filling and seeming to coat your mouth with sharpness, sweetness and scent. The greatest of them—long-lived, pale gold, piquant, profound as honey, frivolous as flowers—are wines that beg to be discussed in an evening garden in

Above: the town of Bernkastel and the bridge to Kues seen from the Doktor vineyard high above. Imaginative tasters detect the smoke from Bernkastel's chimneys in the flavour of Doktor, often the most expensive Mosel

Below: a charity hospital (top left) and the parish church (top right) are among famous Bernkastel growers. In Wehlen the outstanding name is Prüm; four branches of the family are all among the artists of German wine

NACKTARSCH

SCHLÖSSBERG
FALKLAY
EDELBERG
BURGLAY
MONTENEUBEL
Enkirch
STEFFENSBERG
LETTERLAYT
STEFFENSBERG
KIRCHLAY
Kröv
Wolf
Kövenig
Mont royal Feriendorf
HERREN-BERG
GOLDGRUBE
HUBERTUSLAY
Motschen-kopf
PARADIES
KIRCHLAY
230
Staustufe Enkirch
Corveyer Werth
Schlise
Kinheim
SCHATZGARTEN
WÜRZ-GARTEN
Heller Sass
Kindel
ROSENBERG
SONNENLAY
Mosel-flugplatz
Ev. Kinder-u Jugendheim
Mont Royal
Das Werth
KÖNIGSBERG
ROSENBERG
275
BATTERIE-BERG
Kaisergarten
Koppel-berg
Rissbach
Mont Royal
307
260
Greiss-Berg
SCHWARZLAY
Fieberrod
Waldschenke
Corveyer Waldchen
GAIS-PFAD
ROSEN-GARTEN
ZOLLTURM
411
KRÄUTERHAUS
Schule
Schule
102
Traben-
Starken-burg
Pferde
Kur
356
Monchhof
101
391
ABTSBERG
420
500
TALBERGHAUS
Trarbach
BURGWEG
Schloss-Berg
363
JOSEPHSHÖFER
Josephshof
DOMPROBST
SCHLOSSBERG
Graach a.d Mosel
ABTSBERG
Graacher
434
KREUZBERG
SCHLOSSBERG
Graacher Schäferei
Schanzen
403
Unheller Kuppchen
HIMMELREICH
ABTSBERG
Kaisergarten
KREUZBERG
Ungs-Berg
UNGSBERG
142
Grafssmühle
Born-miese
MATHEIS BILDCHEN
Bad
BRATENHÖFCHEN
Schule
JOHANNIS-BRÜNNCHEN
Thanischwald
BADSTUBE
267
ROSENBERG
Bernkastel-Kues
GRABEN
DOCTOR
Kues
Bernkastel
SCHLOSSBERG
CARDINALSBERG
Jugend-herberge
Das Werth
Zeltplatz
Schlossbrauerei
416
Waldschenke
Olymp
Heidesheim
STEPHANUS-ROSENGÄRTCHEN
SCHLOSSBERG
SCHLOSSBERG

BERNKASTEL — Bereich boundary
MÜNZLAY — Grosslage boundary
BURGLAY — Einzellage
— Regierungsbezirk boundary
— Kreis boundary
— Gemeinde boundary
Vineyards
Woods
—100— Contour interval 20 metres

Km. 0   2 Km.
Mi. 0   1 Mi.

shameless comparisons with music and poetry.

For this very reason the name of Bernkastel is used for very much more wine than her slopes can grow. The law allows it; Bereich Bernkastel is a possible name for any quality wine from the Middle Mosel. And Bernkastel has two Grosslage names; Badstube (exclusive to the five best sites) and Kurfurstlay, available to vineyards as far off as Brauneberg and Wintrich. The law works well only if you appreciate such niceties.

Zeltingen brings the Great Wall to an end. It is the Mosel's biggest wine commune, and certainly among the best.

At Ürzig, across the river, reddish clay mixed with slate, in rocky pockets instead of a smooth bank, gives the wines of the Würzgarten ('spice garden') a different flavour, more penetrating and 'racy' than Zeltingers.

Erden at its best is in the same rank as Ürzig. Lösnich and Kinheim begin a decline. Kröv fills cafés with tourists giggling over the label of Nacktarsch, which shows a boy with a bare bottom: the Grosslage name for the whole commune.

Traben-Trarbach is one community. Trarbach wines from steep side-valleys to the south are well known. Enkirch should be better known than it is. In its ancient inn there is round, light, slightly spicy wine with all the delicate complexity the Middle Mosel is famous for.

The Middle Mosel ends here. Downstream towards Koblenz the vineyard continues among operatic villages, some with famous names and one or two with outstanding vineyards, but the whole loses its concert pitch. Zell is the best-known town for its (Grosslage) Schwartze Katz. Bullay has wine at least as good, and Neef (its best site the Frauenberg) rather better.

Below: old-fashioned hydraulic presses like these are used alongside modern ones by Deinhard's in their Kues cellars. The latest model contains a long balloon which squeezes the grapes against the sides as it inflates

The Nahe

THE RIVER Nahe, flowing north out of the Hunsrück hills to join the Rhine at Bingen, is surrounded by scattered outbreaks of wine-growing. But at one point a sandstone barrier impedes the river's flow, a range of hills rears up along the north bank; and suddenly there are all the makings of a great vineyard.

Its wine seems to capture all the qualities one loves best in German wine. It is very clean and grapy, with all the intensity of the Riesling, like a good Mosel or Saar wine. At the same time it has some of the full flavour which in the Rheingau makes one think of the alchemist's shop; as though rare minerals were dissolved in it; possibly gold itself. The word complexity, at a pinch, might do.

Bad Kreuznach is the wine capital of the Nahe. It is a pleasant spa, beneath hanging woods, with a casino and rows of strange brushwood erections like two-dimensional barns down which salt water is poured to produce ozone for the benefit of convalescents.

Bad Kreuznach itself has some of the Nahe's best vineyards and the premises of most of the best growers. The Kauzenberg and Brückes sites, nearest the river, often make exceptional wine. In addition it gives its name to the whole Bereich, or region, of the lower Nahe, down to the Rhine at Bingen. The upper Nahe is known as Bereich Schlossböckelheim.

The fireworks really begin upstream at the Bad Münster bend. A red precipice, the Rotenfels, said to be the highest cliff in Europe north of the Alps, blocks the river's path. At the cliff-foot there is a bare hundred feet of fallen rubble, a short ramp of red earth. The vines are planted thick in the cramped space. They have ideal soil and a complete suntrap. This is the Traisener (formerly Rotenfelser) Bastei.

The degree of spice and fire in a Bastai of a good year is exceptional for such a northerly vineyard. It can remind one of great Palatinate wine, with some of the freshness and finesse of the Saar thrown in.

From this bend on upstream there is a succession of fine slopes, through the villages of Norheim and Niederhausen, to the Nahe's most illustrious vineyard of all; the Kupfergrube ('copper mine') on the eastern limit of the village of Schlossböckelheim.

The cellars where wine-making is brought to its highest peak here, if not in the whole of Germany, face the Kupfergrube from the last slope of Niederhäusen. The Nahe state domain has holdings in several Niederhäusen vineyards, including the excellent Hermannshöhle and Hermannsberg, and planted the Kupfergrube on the site of old copper-diggings. Photographs still exist of the steep hill facing the cellars when it had no vines: it is easy to picture the director observing the daylong sun on the mine workings, and forming his plan.

Many find in this domain everything they look for in white wine. The wines it makes are clean-tasting and fresh, fruity, racy and well balanced; very pale, with almost as much scent as a Bernkasteler and a long, lingering flavour in which sweetness and acidity are perfectly matched; the sign that, though the wine is so attractive new, it will take on yet more fascinating nuances as it ages.

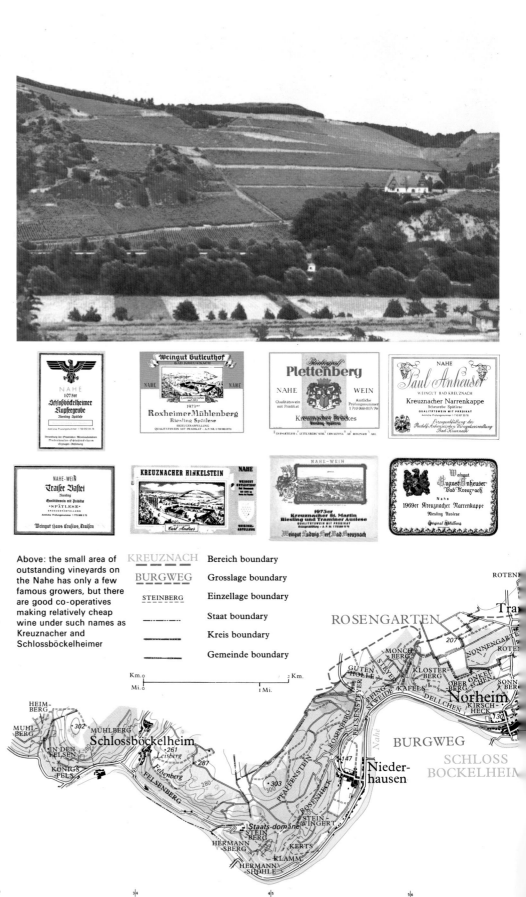

Above: the small area of outstanding vineyards on the Nahe has only a few famous growers, but there are good co-operatives making relatively cheap wine under such names as Kreuznacher and Schlossböckelheimer

KREUZNACH — Bereich boundary

BURGWEG — Grosslage boundary

STEINBERG — Einzellage boundary

——— Staat boundary

——— Kreis boundary

——— Gemeinde boundary

Left: the white building of the state domain on the end of the Hermannsberg at Niederhausen looks across a narrow defile (see map) to the most famous vineyard of the Nahe, Schlossböckelheimer Kupfergrube (in the centre). In the foreground is the little River Nahe

Right: the Rotenfels, or red mountain, on the Nahe's bend at Bad Münster, is said to be the highest cliff in Europe north of the Alps. At the foot of its 600 feet is the six-acre strip of the Traisener Bastei, admirably sheltered and facing south or south-west

	Vineyards
	Woods
—200—	Contour interval 20 metres

The Rheingau: Rüdesheim

The Rheingau is considered Germany's finest wine land, and the distinction of having owned the same Rheingau vineyard for as much as (in one case) 600 years is as great a patent of nobility as any in Europe. Among the big estates are the three shown here, and Prince Frederick of Prussia's at Erbach, Count Eltz and Baron Langwerth von Simmern at Eltville, Count von Schönborn at Hattenheim, Baron Ritter zu Groenesteyn at Rüdesheim, the Landgraf of Hessen at Johannisberg and Prince Löwenstein in Hallgarten. The biggest estates outside this aristocratic circle are the 50-acre Wegeler property, which belongs to Deinhard's, the Koblenz shippers, and the 45 acres of

Above: the magnificent 12th-century church of Kloster Eberbach in Hattenheim is the symbolic headquarters of the German state domain, which has 300-odd acres in the Rheingau, including the great Steinberg, left

the Geisenheim wine school. Some Rheingau growers, particularly the three here, distinguish between their grades of wine with a complex code of different labels, and as many as 12 different coloured lead capsules over the cork. The labels here are for their higher grade wines

Left and below: Schloss Vollrads at Winkel has been the home of the Counts Greiffenclau since the 14th century. Eighty acres produce some of Germany's most noble wines

Left and below: Schloss Johannisberg was granted to Prince Metternich by the Austrian Emperor in 1816. The present Fürst von Metternich consistently makes good wine from its 66-acre slope to the Rhine

THE RHEINGAU is the climax of the wine-growing Rhine. For almost all its length the river flows steadily north-west, except for the point just below Mainz where the high forested Taunus mountains stand in its way. It turns south-west for only 20 miles, until it reaches the Rüdesheimer Berg. There with a flurry of rocks and rapids it forces a passage northwards again. But the influence of its broad waters in that space gives Germany its most magnificent vineyard.

The best part of the Rheingau is mapped on the page opposite and the following two pages. Opposite is the downstream end, where the Rüdesheimer Berg Schlossberg is practically a terraced cliff. This is the only part of the Rheingau which is so steep. Most of it consists of stiff slopes but no more.

The Riesling is the grape of the Rheingau, as it is of the middle Mosel, but not of any except the best sites in the rest of the Rhine. The soil, which is exactly described on page 136, is a great mixture, but it comes nearer in type to the soil of Burgundy than of Germany's other Riesling areas. The climate is comparatively dry and sunny, and the river's presence makes for equable temperatures, the mists which encourage the 'noble rot' as the grapes ripen, and, they say, extra sunlight by reflection off its surface. It is half a mile wide here, a throbbing highway for slow strings of barges.

The Rheingau style of wine, at its best, is the noblest in Germany. It unites the flowery scent of the Riesling with a greater and more golden depth of flavour than the Mosel. There is a strong sense of maturity about it; with maturity comes complexity and, in a strong character (the human parallel is irresistible), balance. Soft and charming are words you should never hear in the Rheingau.

The westernmost town which is mapped opposite is Assmannshausen, round the corner from the main Rheingau and an exception to all its rules, being famous only for its red wine. The grape is the Pinot Noir; its wine is very pale here and without the power it should have, but (among others) the state domain makes much-sought-after sweet pink wine by late-gathering the grapes. Dry red Assmannshausen is Germany's most famous red wine.

The Rüdesheimer Berg is distinguished from the rest of the parish by having the word Berg before each separate vineyard name. At their best (which is not always in the hottest years, since the drainage is too good at times) these are superlative wines, full of fruit and strength and yet delicate in nuance. In hotter years the vineyards behind the town come into their own.

Among the growers of the big parish is the wine school of Geisenheim, one of the most famous centres of wine-learning in the world, which keeps, in the Fuchsberg, an experimental collection of vine varieties which may well revolutionize viticulture. Detailed soil and climate studies as well as new vine types developed here are of international importance. Some of their work is described on pages 20–21.

The entire Rheingau, confusingly enough, was given the Bereich name of Johannisberg, its most famous single parish, in 1971.

Left: growers in the big
commune of Rüdesheim
include, top, the famous
Geisenheim Research
Institute. The two lower
labels are from estates on
the Rüdesheimer Berg

Right: looking towards
the Rhine from the slope
of Schloss Johannisberg
in winter. There is a
story that Charlemagne
noticed the snow melted
first on this slope

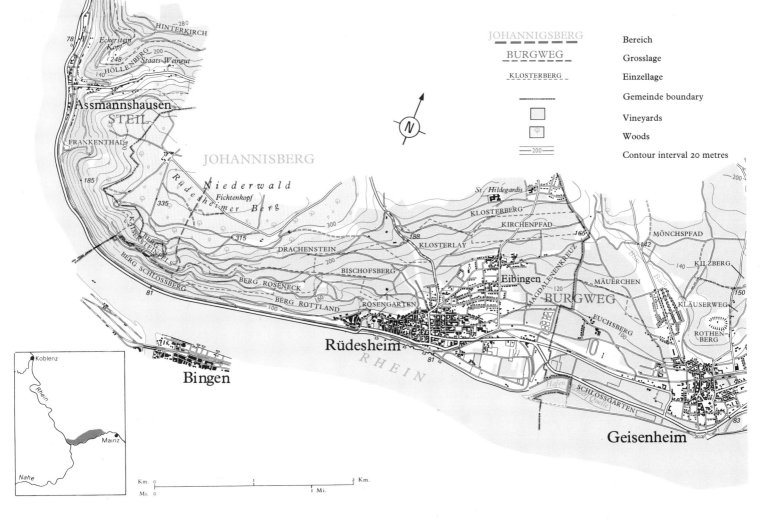

JOHANNIGSBERG   Bereich

BURGWEG   Grosslage

KLOSTERBERG   Einzellage

Gemeinde boundary

Vineyards

Woods

Contour interval 20 metres

149

The Rheingau: Eltville

SCHLOSS JOHANNISBERG, standing above a great apron of vines, dominates everything between Geisenheim and Winkel. The enormous prestige of its production, for which the wine-taster's favourite term, 'elegant', might have been invented, tends to overshadow the excellent vineyards of the rest of Johannisberg. About a third of the whole belongs to the Schloss (see page 146).

Schloss Vollrads (see page 146) stands over a mile back from Winkel and leaves the name of the town off its labels—unfortunately for Winkel, whose name would otherwise be better known than it is. Even its second-best vineyard, Hasensprung (which means hare-leap) is capable of producing superlative wine with the endless nuances which put the Rheingau in a class by itself.

Mittelheim has little identity as distinct from the more important Winkel and Oestrich. Its name does not appear on any wine of special note. There are those who say the same about Oestrich. Oestrichers have been criticized for lack of 'breed'. But character and lusciousness they certainly have. Doosberg and Lenchen are not names to be dismissed.

In Hallgarten the Rheingau vineyards reach their highest point. The Hendelberg is 1,000 feet above sea level. There is less mist and less frost up here. In the Würzgarten and Schönhell there is marly soil which gives strong wines of great lasting-power and magnificent bouquet. No single vineyard makes the village name world-famous—though the fact that a famous shipper has the same name makes it familiar.

The boundaries of Hattenheim stretch straight back into the hills to include the most illustrious of all the vineyards of the German state: the high ridge of the Steinberg, walled like the Clos de Vougeot with a Cistercian wall. Below in a wooded hollow stands the old monastery which might fairly be called the headquarters of German wine, Kloster Eberbach (see page 146). The place, the astonishing wine and the implications of continuous industry and devotion to one idea of beauty going back 600 years makes any comment seem trivial. Today Kloster Eberbach is the base of the German Wine Academy, which runs courses open to all wine-lovers.

Like Hallgarten, Hattenheim has marl in the soil. On its border with Erbach is the only vineyard which makes great wine right down by the river; in a situation which looks as though the drainage would be far from perfect. The vineyard is Marcobrunn, partly in Hattenheim but mainly in Erbach. Marcobrunner is very full flavoured, often rich, fruity and spicy. Its owners include Count Schönborn and Baron Langwerth von Simmern on the Hatten-

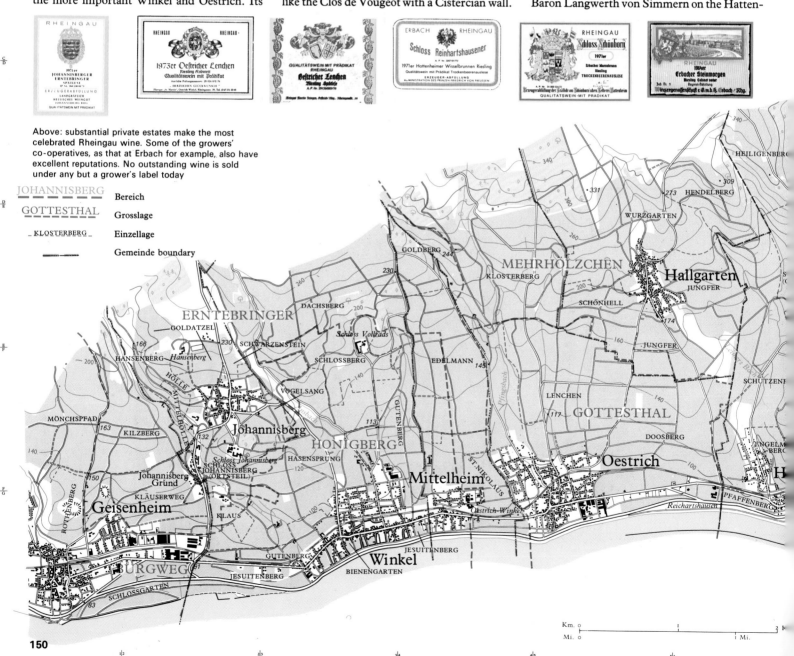

Above: substantial private estates make the most celebrated Rheingau wine. Some of the growers' co-operatives, as that at Erbach for example, also have excellent reputations. No outstanding wine is sold under any but a grower's label today

JOHANNISBERG Bereich

GOTTESTHAL Grosslage

KLOSTERBERG Einzellage

Gemeinde boundary

heim side, and the state domain and Prince Frederick of Prussia's estate in Erbach.

Again in Erbach the town's land goes back into the hills in a long narrow strip. These are good vineyards, but not the best. Steinmorgen, by the town, gives more powerful and memorable wine than Michelmark and Hönigberg.

Kiedrich's beautiful gothic church is the next landmark. The vineyards of the village make exceptionally well-balanced and delicately spicy wine. Dr Weil is the biggest Kiedrich-based grower. Gräfenberg is reckoned the best part of the vineyard, although Wasseros and Sandgrub are almost equally renowned.

Superlatives become tiring in an account of the Rheingau. Yet if the qualities of great white wine mean anything to you the peculiar sort of wine these growers make offers more to taste, consider and discuss than any other in the world. The wines which fetch the high prices, and by which the vineyards are ultimately judged, are always the late-picked, sweet and intense ones which demand to be drunk with conscious attention, and on their own rather than with food. There are better wines for any meal in other parts of Germany— and far better in Burgundy. The Rheingau's raison d'être must be understood. It is wine for wine's sake. And it does, without exaggeration, give rise to such scents and flavours that only superlatives will do.

Thus Rauenthal, the last of the hill villages and the farthest from the river, makes a different kind of superlative wine: the most expensive. Rauenthalers are the Germans' German wine. The Ausleses of the state domain and of the two lordly growers of Eltville, Baron Langwerth von Simmern and Count Eltz, as well as those of smaller growers on the Rauenthaler Berg, are prized for the combination of power and delicacy in their flowery scent and in their spicy aftertaste.

Eltville makes bigger quantities of wine without the supreme cachet. It is the headquarters of the state domain (see page 148) as well as having the beautiful old mansions of the Eltz and von Simmern families, in a group of buildings of white plaster and rosy stone, draped with vines and roses, beside the river.

Without sharing the fame of their neighbours the united Nieder- and Ober-Walluf and Martinsthal share much of their quality.

Fifteen miles farther east the Rheingau has an unexpected outpost; Hochheim. The Hochheim vineyards (which gave us the word hock) lie on gently sloping land just north of the River Main, isolated in country which has no other vines. Good Hochheimers (three labels are shown here) are on a level with the better, not the best, wines of the Rheingau.

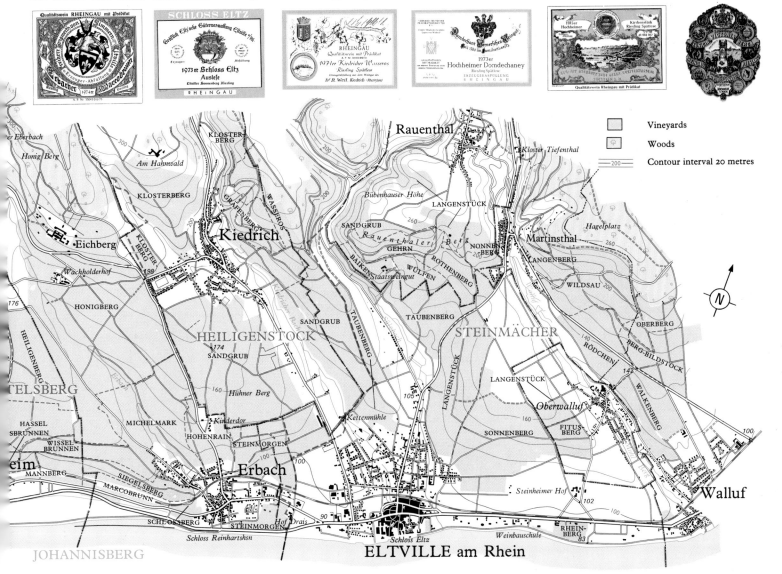

Rheinpfalz

Top: Ungstein; the lie of the land is curiously like Burgundy's Côte d'Or
Left: Deidesheim; substantial houses with arches into stone courtyards are typical of the Middle Haardt
Right: orchards surround wine-making villages along the route of the German Weinstrasse

Above: the first three labels are among the most famous designs in Germany, appearing on the cream of Palatinate wine. Senator von Buhl's estate is the biggest private wine property in the country. The growers' co-operatives of Forst (right, second from top) and Bad Durkheim (bottom left) are represented among other good growers. The Deutsche Weintor (bottom right) is the leading co-operative of the southern Pfalz

THE PALATINATE (German Pfalz) is Germany's biggest vineyard; a 50-mile stretch just north of Alsace, under the lee of the German continuation of the Vosges mountains—the Haardt.

Like Alsace, it is the sunniest and driest part of its country, and has the never-failing charm of half-timbered villages among orchards, seeming part of a better, sunlit, half fairy-tale world. A labyrinthine road, the Deutsche Weinstrasse, like the Alsatian Route du Vin, starts at the gates of Germany (literally; there is a massive gateway called the Weintor at Schweigen on the border) and winds northwards through more vines and villages than you ever hope to see. A great part of the wine of this area (Südliche Weinstrasse is its Bereich name) is made by big and efficient co-operatives

which have revolutionized casual old country methods and are making the district famous. Historically there is little Riesling here; wine tends to be low-acid, sweetish and heavy. Refrigeration and replanting are making lighter, more fragrant and better-balanced wine available at very reasonable prices.

Most of these wines are sold under Grosslage names, since few Einzellagen here have reputations of their own. Among the most important are (Rhodter) Ordensgut, (Walsheimer) Bischofskreuz, (Bergzaberner) Kloster Liebfrauenberg and (Schweigener) Guttenberg.

Ruppertsberg is the first of these villages. Hoheburg and Geisböhl, small vineyards by the village, are considered the *Spitzen*, or peak sites. The latter belongs entirely, and the former largely, to one of the district's three most famous producers: Bürklin-Wolf.

Dr Albert Bürklin-Wolf and the estates of von Bassermann-Jordan and von Buhl (the biggest private estate in Germany) between them own the most substantial part of the best

land in the Mittel-Haardt. In the next village, Deidesheim, generally reckoned the best of the whole area, besides being one of the prettiest in Germany, von Bassermann-Jordan and von Buhl have their cellars. Hohenmorgen, Kieselberg, Kalkofen, Grainhübel and Leinhöhle are Deidesheim's top Lagen.

Forst has a unique reputation, as the source of Germany's sweetest wine (not in mere sugar, but in style and character). A black basalt outcrop above the village provides dark soil, rich in potassium, which is not found elsewhere—though it is quarried and spread on other vineyards, notably in Deidesheim. Basalt here, as on Lake Balaton in Hungary, holds the heat and keeps the temperature up at night. Forst's one street is the main road. The Jesuitengarten, its most famous vineyard, and the equally fine Kirchenstück lie just behind the church. Freundstück (largely von Buhl's) and Ungeheuer above it are in the same class.

The village of Wachenheim marks the end of the best part of the Mittel-Haardt with a cluster

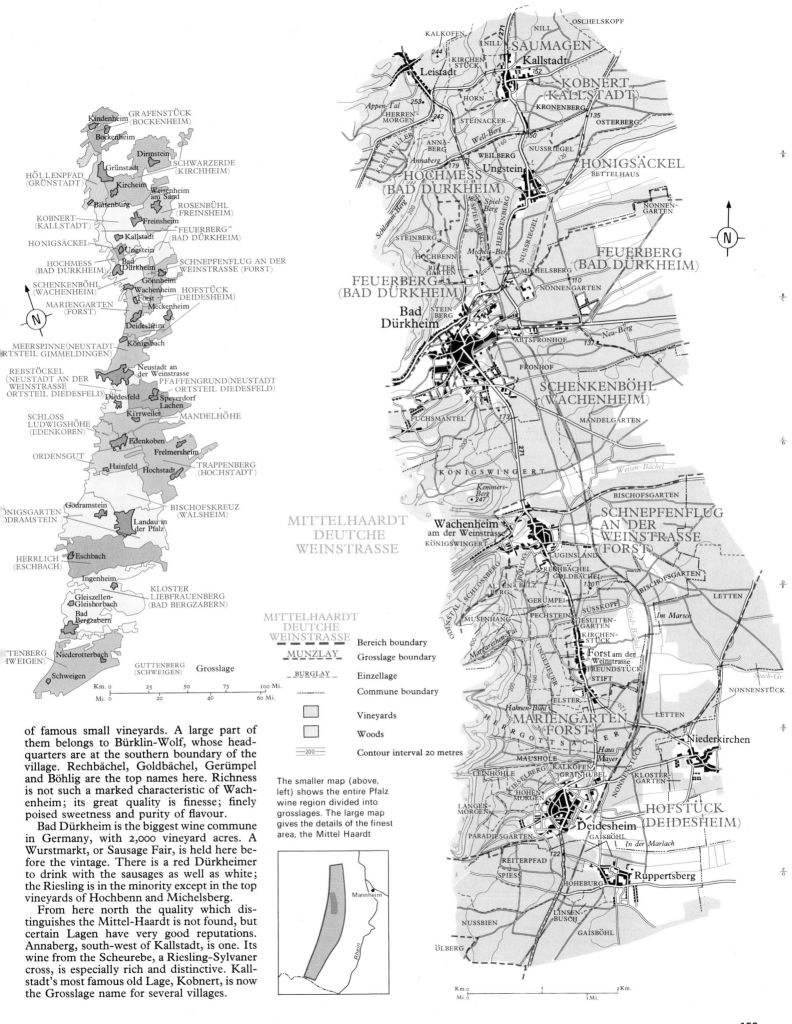

of famous small vineyards. A large part of them belongs to Bürklin-Wolf, whose head-quarters are at the southern boundary of the village. Rechbächel, Goldbächel, Gerümpel and Böhlig are the top names here. Richness is not such a marked characteristic of Wach-enheim; its great quality is finesse; finely poised sweetness and purity of flavour.

Bad Dürkheim is the biggest wine commune in Germany, with 2,000 vineyard acres. A Wurstmarkt, or Sausage Fair, is held here be-fore the vintage. There is a red Dürkheimer to drink with the sausages as well as white; the Riesling is in the minority except in the top vineyards of Hochbenn and Michelsberg.

From here north the quality which dis-tinguishes the Mittel-Haardt is not found, but certain Lagen have very good reputations. Annaberg, south-west of Kallstadt, is one. Its wine from the Scheurebe, a Riesling-Sylvaner cross, is especially rich and distinctive. Kall-stadt's most famous old Lage, Kobnert, is now the Grosslage name for several villages.

MITTELHAARDT
DEUTCHE
WEINSTRASSE

MITTELHAARDT
DEUTCHE
WEINSTRASSE

MUNZLAY   Bereich boundary

- - - - -   Grosslage boundary

BURGLAY   Einzellage

- - - - - - -   Commune boundary

Vineyards

Woods

—200—   Contour interval 20 metres

The smaller map (above, left) shows the entire Pfalz wine region divided into grosslages. The large map gives the details of the finest area, the Mittel Haardt

153

Rheinhessen

The Liebfrauenstift vineyard, origin of the name of Liebfraumilch (though long since divorced from it) lies round the Liebfrauenkirche in the city of Worms, 20 miles south of Nierstein. Nylon protects it from birds

RHEINHESSEN lies in the crook of the Rhine, hemmed in by the river on the east and north, the Nahe on the west, and the Palatinate to the south. Its 150-odd villages, spaced out over an area 20 miles by 30, grow wine as part or all of their livelihood. It is dull, undulating, fertile country, without exceptional character except where the Rhine flows by. The bulk of its wine, made from Müller-Thurgau or Silvaner grapes, is equally unexceptional; light, soft, usually sweetish, sometimes earthy, rarely vigorous enough to claim attention. It finds its outlet as Liebfraumilch, which is now legally defined as a Qualitätswein b.A. from Rheinhessen, Rheinpfalz, Nahe or Rheingau, made of Silvaner, Riesling or Müller-Thurgau grapes and 'with pleasant character'. You can expect any Liebfraumilch to be mild and semi-sweet. There are some good ones, but no wine of distinction is wasted on this kind of blend.

The map opposite shows the whole of the wine-growing Rheinhessen with its grosslage divisions—the names most commonly seen (apart from Liebfraumilch, that is) on its wine, which very seldom assumes the distinction of an einzellage name.

The vast majority of the growers, besides, have only a hectare or two of vines as part of a mixed farming operation. It is the co-operatives, therefore, that make the wine.

Three Bereich names cover the whole region: Bingen the north-west, Nierstein the north-east, and Wonnegau the south, between the principal towns of Alzey and Worms.

The town of Bingen, facing Rudesheim across the Rhine, has excellent vineyards on the steep slopes of its Scharlachberg. But by far the best and most important vineyards of Rheinhessen are concentrated in the short stretch of the Rhine-front mapped in detail on the right.

The town of Nierstein has become, partly

Left and far right: Nierstein has as many as 300 sizeable wine estates. Those of Guntrum, Balbach and Franz Karl Schmitt are the biggest. Baron Heyl zu Herrnsheim is another excellent grower. Rehbach (second label left) used to be the southern end of Pettenthal before the new law. The last label, right, is of the most important estate at Bingen to the west

through its size, and the number (about 300) of its growers, partly because its name was widely and shamelessly borrowed (usually with the site name Domthal attached) before the 1971 wine laws, but mainly because of its superb vineyards, as famous as Bernkastel. The two towns which flank it, Oppenheim and Nackenheim, have vineyards as good as most of the Nierstein, but none better than the sand-red roll of hill going north with the river at its foot. Hipping, Pettenthal and Rothenberg (which is in Nackenheim) and the small group of vineyards which share the grosslage name Rehbach, make wine as fragrant and full of character as the Rheingau, and thought by some to be a shade softer and more luxuriant.

Any true Niersteiner will use one of the lage names on the map. The best will also specify that they are made from Riesling, although some interesting wines are being made from newly introduced crosses such as Kerner.

There is no such wine as Niersteiner Domtal any longer. Niersteiner Gutes Domtal, on the other hand, is a grosslage name available to fifteen villages, but only to one part of Nierstein, and that the least distinguished.

Outside the area of this map the best villages are those just north and south: Bodenheim and Guntersblum and Alsheim.

Above: the best vineyards of Rheinhessen line the 'Rhine-front' north and south of Nierstein on 300-foot hills. Most of the Riesling in Rheinhessen is grown here

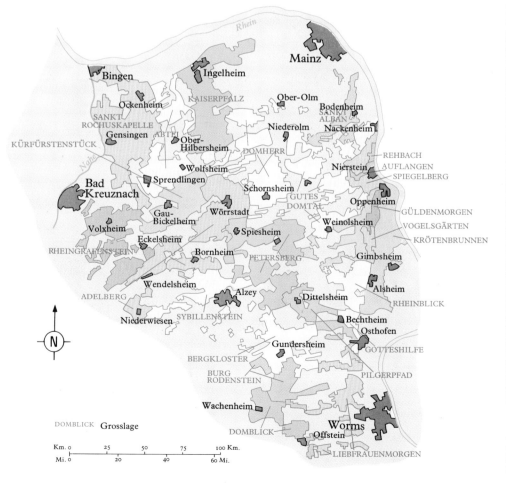

Above: A Rheinhessen grower measures the sugar content of his must with a hydrometer. Fermentation in small barrels in a cool cellar is giving way to refrigerated vats in most districts

Baden-Württemberg

YOU WOULD expect southern Germany to make more wine than the north. A hundred years ago it did. Baden was Germany's biggest producer. But the peculiar conditions of soil and climate which make wine-growing worth while in apparently unlikely spots on the Mosel and Rhine are not matched by anything in the huge state of Baden-Württemberg. The best of the wine is very good, but in tiny quantities, scattered here and there and made from a surprising number of different grapes.

The bulk of Baden's vineyards are strung out over a distance of almost 100 miles down the western edge of the Black Forest, facing Alsace across the Rhine and benefiting from a similar benevolent climate. Those of Württemberg are dotted around the river Neckar and its tributaries in country with harsher, more continental weather which takes its toll, in frosts and storms, of the unfortunate grower of grapes.

Fine wine estates are widely scattered in Baden-Württemberg. Below are the labels of six of the most famous: four lordly houses, the big cooperative of Kaiserstuhl at Breisach and the state domain of Meersburg

The Kaiserstuhl stands like an island in the flat Rhine valley with the Black Forest massif as its mainland to the east (in the background of the picture). Extensive landscaping of the Kaiserstuhl has turned awkward old patches of vines into workable modern vineyards. The local growers' co-operative is Germany's biggest

The 'Seewein' (lake wine) of the southern-most area, round Meersburg on the Bodensee, is traditionally pink-tinted Weissherbst, white wine pressed from red Spätburgunder grapes —it makes good holiday drinking.

Markgräflerland has the same grape as Switzerland; the Chasselas (here the Gutedel). It makes adequate Swiss-style wine.

The best vineyards of Baden are on a volcanic tufa outcrop in the Rhine valley, detached from the Black Forest massif: the Kaiserstuhl. Wine-growing here is dominated by one of Europe's biggest and most modern co-operatives, which has literally moved mountains in its reorganization of wearisome traditional viticulture. Armies of bulldozers have reshaped the whole landscape with spectacular results to allow mechanical cultivation. The sweetish soft and mellow wines (lack of balancing acidity is a local characteristic, particularly of wine made from the Ruländer—Alsace's Pinot Gris) satisfy the German supermarket trade. Spätburgunder reds are another Kaiserstuhl speciality.

To the north, just south of the luxurious Black Forest spa of Baden-Baden, the Ortenau is a pocket of quality wine-growing with three lordly estates, those of the Margrave of Baden (Schloss Staufenberg), Baron von Neveu and Count Wolff Metternich, whose Ruländer, Traminer and Klingelberger (the local name for Riesling) are famous. Neuweier is the centre for growing the Riesling 'Mauerwein', the excellent carafe wine of Baden-Baden. North again, the Kraichgau has few vineyards left today. Over the river Neckar in Hessen the Bergstrasse makes better-known wine; the Rheingau state domain has vineyards here.

Württemberg grows more red wine than white, largely from a poor grape called the Trollinger, which also finds itself mixed with other reds and whites to make the traditional pale pink Schillerwein. The best of the white is better than either pink or red. There is a little Riesling, much Sylvaner, some Traminer (at its best, excellent) and more and more of the new varieties being designed expressly for harsh conditions and recommended by the co-operatives to their members. The City of Stuttgart itself owns some of the best sites.

The Language of the Label

German wine-labels give more precise information about the contents of the bottle than those of any other country—but in a language that takes some mastering. Below are examples of typical labels for the three basic quality-categories of German wine, with a glossary of all the words and phrases found on labels.

Deutscher Tafelwein (= German table wine) is the lowest category. On this label Koblenz am Rhein & Mosel (Koblenz on the Rhine and Mosel) is the headquarters of the merchants, Deinhards.
Bereich = district (see the map on page 135) of Bernkastel, which covers the whole of the Middle Mosel. As an alternative to a Bereich name a Tafelwein can claim a village name, but not a vineyard.
Riesling: to name a grape variety, a Tafelwein must contain 85% of wine made of that variety.
Mosel (as opposed to Mosel-Saar-Ruwer on quality wine-labels) is the table-wine area (see page 135). No other indications of quality or origin are allowed.

Qualitätswein bestimmte Anbaugebiete is the middle category. On this label:
Erzeugerabfüllung = bottled by the grower.
Amtl. Pr. Nr. is the wine's test number (all Qualitätswein passes a tasting test).
Mosel-Saar-Ruwer is the name of the region (gebiet).
Weingut (= estate) 'Der Josephshöfer'.
Graach (alternatively Graacher) is the commune name.
1974er is the vintage.
Josephshöfer is the einzellage or individual vineyard. N.B. This wine could also legally be labelled Graacher Munzlay (the grosslage name in which Josephshöfer is included).
Reichsgraf von Kesselstatt, Trier is the name and office address of the proprietor.

Qualitätswein mit Prädikat is the category which includes all the natural, unsugared, finest wines of Germany.
On this label: 1974er is the year.
Oppenheim is the village (the suffix -er as in Londoner or New Yorker).
Krötenbrunnen is the grosslage name. (N.B. there is no way of distinguishing between a grosslage and an einzellage name without a reference book: a major fault of the 1971 law. Krötenbrunnen is a grosslage covering parts of 13 villages including Oppenheim; therefore despite every appearance this wine is possibly not an Oppenheimer at all.)
Silvaner is the grape.
Kabinett is the lowest grade for natural unsugared wine.
Q.m.P. A.P.Nr: each Qualitätswein m.P. passes an analytical and tasting test and receives a number by which it can be identified.
Rheinhessen is the region (gebiet).
Zentralkellerei is the growers' co-operative of Gau-Bickelheim.

Tafelwein ordinary table wine, not necessarily German.
Deutscher tafelwein ordinary table wine from Germany.
Qualitätswein b.A. (bestimmte Anbaugebiete = from a specified region): 'quality' wine, subject to official controls, tested and numbered.
Qualitätswein m.P. (mit Prädikat = with particular attributes): strictly controlled, unsugared, top-quality wine.
Kabinett: the basic grade of Qualitätswein m.P.; light and fairly dry.
Spätlese: wine made from later-gathered and therefore riper grapes; more full-bodied than Kabinett; usually sweeter.
Auslese: richer wine from riper bunches picked selectively; varies from medium-sweet to luscious.
Beerenauslese made from only the ripest berries, selected individually.
Trockenbeerenauslese made from grapes which have shrivelled, either from very late gathering or 'noble rot'.
Weisswein white wine.
Rotwein red wine.

Weissherbst pink wine made from red grapes.
Schillerwein pink wine made from red and white grapes mixed.
Perlwein slightly sparkling (carbonated) wine.
Schaumwein sparkling wine.
Sekt sparkling wine subject to quality controls.
Eiswein wine made of grapes which were frozen during the harvest and pressing; rare and usually very sweet.
Trocken or Diabetiker-Wein (or Für Diabetiker geeignet): fully dry wine (with a maximum of four grammes per litre of unfermented sugar) suitable for diabetics —or those who like very dry wine.
Aus eigenem Lesegut from the producer's own estate.
Eigene Abfüllung or **Erzeugerabfüllung** bottled by the producer.
Weinkellerei wine cellar or winery.
Winzergenossenschaft wine growers' co-operative.
Winzerverein the same.
Prüf. Nr. (followed by letters and figures): the wine's official test number.

Franconia

Above: Franconia is the one part of Germany which does not use the tall slim bottle. Its appetizing dry wines come in Bocksbeutels a model protected by law for Franconia

FRANCONIA (Franken) is out of the mainstream of German wine both geographically and by its quite separate traditions. It makes the only German wine not to come in flute bottles; the only great wine made of the Sylvaner instead of the Riesling. And in savour and strength it draws away from the delicate sweetness of most German and nearer to some French wines, making it one of the best of German wines to drink with food.

The name Steinwein is loosely used for all Franconian wine. Stein is in fact the name of one of the two famous vineyards of the city of Würzburg on the Main, the capital of the district. The other is Leiste. Both distinguished themselves in the past by making wines which lasted incredibly long periods. A 16th-century Stein wine (of the great vintage of 1540) was still just drinkable only a decade ago, and the Pfalz wine museum at Speyer has bottles of early 17th-century Leisten with late 19th-century labels from the royal house of Bavaria.

Such wines were Beerenauslesen at least: immensely sweet. Franconia makes few of such rarities today. The bulk of the wine in the pretty flask-shaped Bocksbeutel is decidedly dry by German standards, with something more like the size and strength of white burgundy.

Ten or twelve villages along the bends of the Main above and just below Würzburg are the producers. The most famous are Iphofen (15 miles south-east of the city), Randersacker and Escherndorf. Among the best growers are two charities, the Juliusspital and the Bürgerspital zum Heiligen Geist, with magnificent cellars in Würzburg. Vineyards occupy sites right inside the city itself, making it, together with its baroque buildings (the Residenz, built for the Prince Bishop by Balthasar Neumann in 1720, is the finest 18th-century palace in Germany), one of wine's most splendid outposts.

Right: Würzburg is the great marriage of the vine and the baroque. Vine rows are the only straight lines in this exuberant city. Below Marienberg Castle the Leiste vineyard runs down to the river Main

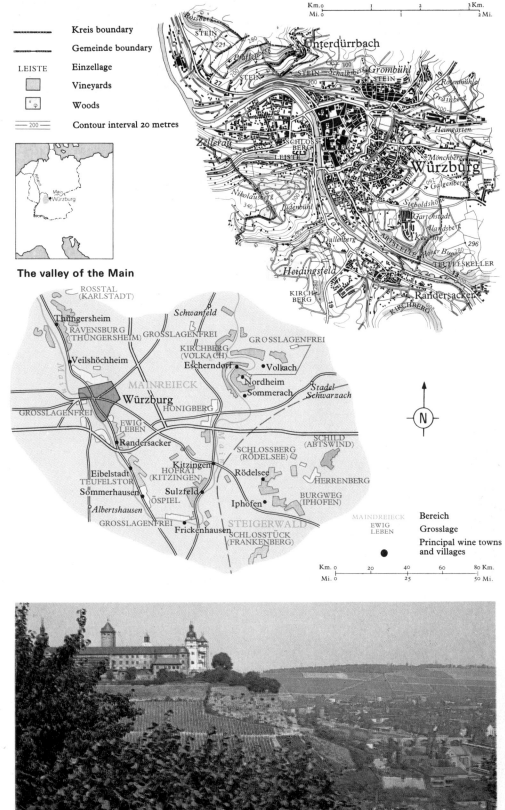

Kreis boundary
Gemeinde boundary
LEISTE — Einzellage
Vineyards
Woods
200 — Contour interval 20 metres

The valley of the Main

MAINDREIECK — Bereich
EWIG LEBEN — Grosslage
● — Principal wine towns and villages

Southern and Eastern Europe and the Mediterranean

Italian Wine

THE GREEKS called Italy Oenotria—the land of wine. The map reminds us that there is little of Italy which is not more or less wine country. Her annual production is now easily the biggest in the world. Yet what is at the same time amiable and maddening about her is her age-old insouciance about it all. With a few important exceptions, Italian wine has always been, with its delights and disappointments, enough to drive any tidy-minded wine merchant to drink.

To start with, the orderly identifying of wine by its place of origin, the method used in France and Germany, is only one of Italy's. By and large Italian wines have *names*, which may be that of the grape, or a place, or both, or pure fantasy, or pure poetry, or a historical reference, or a brand. It is not unusual for the same name to refer to red and white, sweet and dry wines equally.

Reference books in the past have had to be content with listing as many names as possible, and pinning them down as far as they could to where such wine is found. The limiting of a name to a definite area, in line with international practice, is a new idea in Italy. Without it control is impossible; exports were getting nowhere; something had to be done.

The Italian government entered the fray in 1963, with a well-conceived system of control which took inspiration from France (see Wine Law below). It had as a foundation a number of voluntary consorzi, or associations, which had been formed by growers in the more organized regions. Chianti, for example, already had an embryo wine law, which the government could learn from and adapt.

The majority of the major wine regions have now been defined and declared as DOCs. All those published up to 1975 are delimited on the maps which follow; the newest DOCs and undeclared regions appear simply as names without boundaries; the old practice.

Already the new system is reaping its rewards for Italy. The world has new confidence in her wine, and exports (and prices, too) have risen by leaps and bounds.

One should not forget, however, that the best producers have been making reliable wine for a long time, and that standards in some parts of Italy (notably Piemonte, Chianti, Verona and Trentino-Adige, the four mapped in detail in this atlas), are high.

In general in Italy the red wines are best. If they never reach the heights of a great Bordeaux or burgundy they have qualities of their own which range from the silky and fragile to the purple and potent. Above all their qualities, and the qualities of all Italian wine, must be seen in the context of the incredibly varied, simple, sensuous Italian table. The true genius of Italy lies in spreading a feast. In the Italian feast wine plays the chief supporting role.

Wine Law

The Italian wine law of 1963 lays down three standards of control. The first is:

Denominazione Semplice. It is equivalent, more or less, to the German Tafelwein; only a simple statement of the region of production is allowed; there are no set standards.

Denominazione di Origine Controllata is the next rank. A body of wine-growers may apply to have their wine registered as DOC. They must agree with Rome where it can be produced and standards of quality it must reach (e.g. specific grapes, traditional methods, limited yields, proper ageing, adequate records). DOC wines are subject to test and must wear a DOC label, in addition to their own.

Denominazione Controllata e Garantita, the top rank, is awarded only to certain wines from top-quality zones-within-zones. To be controllata e garantita a wine must be bottled and sealed with a government seal by the producer or someone who takes full responsibility for it. Eventually all the best wines of Italy will be DOCG. By 1976 none had been declared; Barolo will probably be the first.

This atlas maps the delimited areas of the 150-odd DOC wines declared up to 1975. The fact of their acceptance by that date does not prove their importance. It has been something of a band-wagon: there are far too many little DOCs for anybody's good already, and perhaps 50 more in the pipeline. Probably many minor ones, having made their gesture, will eventually amalgamate.

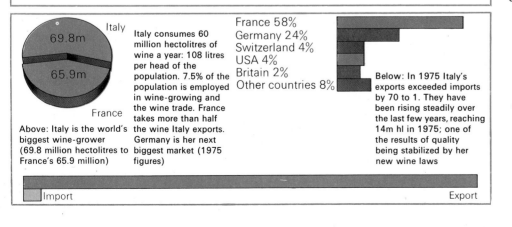

69.8m Italy
65.9m France

Italy consumes 60 million hectolitres of wine a year: 108 litres per head of the population. 7.5% of the population is employed in wine-growing and the wine trade. France takes more than half the wine Italy exports. Germany is her next biggest market (1975 figures)

Above: Italy is the world's biggest wine-grower (69.8 million hectolitres to France's 65.9 million)

France 58%
Germany 24%
Switzerland 4%
USA 4%
Britain 2%
Other countries 8%

Below: In 1975 Italy's exports exceeded imports by 70 to 1. They have been rising steadily over the last few years, reaching 14m hl in 1975; one of the results of quality being stabilized by her new wine laws

Import   Export

Below: Cinzano, Martini, Carpano, Campari, all household words for aperitifs, have their cellars round Turin. Beyond central Piemonte, however, wine districts are small and reputations mainly local. Frecciarossa, Spanna and Dolceacqua are exceptions

The North-West

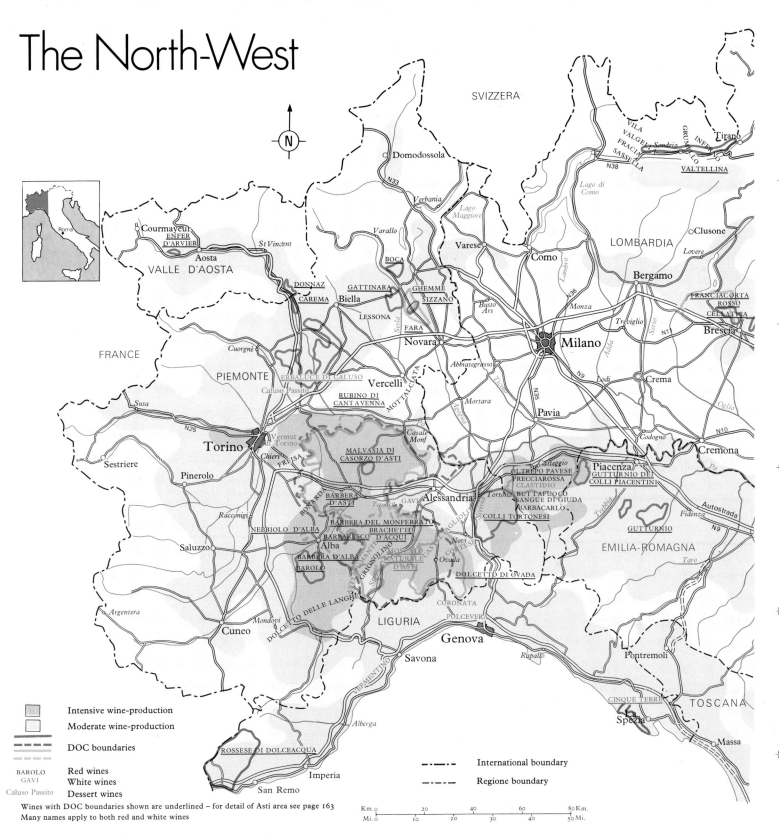

Wines with DOC boundaries shown are underlined – for detail of Asti area see page 163
Many names apply to both red and white wines

Intensive wine-production

Moderate wine-production

DOC boundaries

BAROLO — Red wines
GAVI — White wines
Caluso Passito — Dessert wines

— · — · — International boundary

— — — — Regione boundary

Km.0   20   40   60   80 Km.
Mi.0   10   20   30   40   50 Mi.

NORTH-WEST Italy means Piemonte to any wine-lover. In its bitter-sweet vermouths, its grapy spumantes, its pungent purple wines for dishes of game and cheese, it epitomizes the sensuality of gastronomic Italy. On the next two pages its heart is shown in detail.

The rest of north-western Italy has good wines, but the production is small and only locally famous. The French-speaking Valle d'Aosta has substantial Nebbiolo reds, Carema and Donnaz, and a lighter one, Enfer. Turin converts much of Piemonte's wine into its world-famous brands of vermouth. Its southern outskirts have their pleasant red Freisa— pleasant, that is, until it is made sweet and fizzy, which happens all too often.

A group of towns between Novara and Lake Maggiore grow the excellent Nebbiolo grape (though they call it Spanna) and make rather mellower, softer, even more attractive wine than Barolo. Gattinara, Ghemme, Boca, Fara, Sizzano are all local names for this wine, which scarcely varies enough to justify so many— whereas under a single name, say Spanna, it might well become famous.

The wines of Liguria are better-known by name, although the genuine article is rarely seen outside the region. Cinqueterre, the very good sweet and unusual dry white wine of five small villages on the coast north of La Spezia, is almost legendary. Polcevera and Coronata, Genoa's white wines, made of the Vermen-

tino (among other grapes) go well with fish. Dolceacqua and Rossese are the red wines of the Italian Riviera; they are pleasant but plain.

Lombardy's main wine districts fall within this map: the Oltrepo Pavese (or Pavia beyond the Po), and Brescia and the Valtellina (described on page 164). Casteggio is the main centre of the Oltrepo Pavese, which has a general DOC of Oltrepo followed by the grape name: Barbera, Pinot, Riesling, etc. The best-known wine of the district is Frecciarossa, the brand name of a good grower, whose white wine is better than his (Barbera) red.

The neighbouring DOCs of Gutturnio and Trebianino Val Trebbia, good light red and white respectively, are in Emilia-Romagna.

Piemonte

Left: Fontanafredda, under a ridge of Nebbiolo vines, is one of the finest estates of Barolo
Below: dark red wines, full of character, and sweet sparkling white wines, delicate and grapy, are the specialities of Piemonte

PIEMONTESE food and wine, like those of Burgundy, are inseparable. They are strong, rich, individual, mature, somehow autumnal. One feels it must be more than coincidence that this is the Italian province nearest to France.

Piemonte means at the foot of the mountains; the Alps. But it is on the substantial range of the Monferrato hills that the great Piemontese wines are grown. None the less the Alps have their effect, encircling the region and giving it a climate of its own, with a very hot growing season and a misty autumn.

At vintage time in Barolo the hills are half hidden. Ramps of copper and gold vines, dotted with hazel- and peach-trees, lead down to the valley of the Tanaro, lost in the fog. It is a

Torino

Casale
Monferrato

GRIGNOLINO DEL MONTEFERRATO CASELESE

Chieri

S. Salvatore
Monferrato

FREISA DI CHIERI

BARBERA D'ASTI

Alessandria

BARBERA DEI MONFERRATO

Asti

GRIGNOLINO D'ASTI

FREISA D'ASTI

MOSCATO

Acqui

NEBBIOLO D'ALBA

D'ASTI

DOLCETTO D'ACQUI

Bra

Alba

BARBERA D'ALBA

DOLCETTO DI
DIANO D'ALBA

BAROLO

- - - - - DOC Barbaresco
········· DOC Barbera d'Alba
········· DOC Barbera d'Asti
········· DOC Barbera del Monferrato
━━━━━ DOC Barolo
━━━━━ DOC Brachetto d'Acqui
━━━━━ DOC Dolcetto di Acqui
········· DOC Dolcetto d'Asti
••••••• DOC Dolcetto di Diano d'Alba
━━━━━ DOC Freisa D'Asti
━━━━━ DOC Freisa di Chieri
━━━━━ DOC Grignolino d'Asti
━━━━━ DOC Grignolino del Monteferrato Caselese
━━━━━ DOC Malvasia di Castelnuovo don Bosco
━━━━━ DOC Moscato d'Asti
- - - - - DOC Nebbiolo d'Alba

Km. 0   10 Km.
Mi. 0   10 Mi.

☐ Vineyards
☐ Woods
═══ Contour interval 100 metres
─·─·─ Provincia boundary

magical experience to visit Serralunga or La Morra and see the dark grapes coming in.

The two best red wines of Piemonte, Barolo and Barbaresco, take their names from villages. The rest have the names of their grapes— Barbera, Dolcetto, Grignolino, Freisa. If to the grape they add a district name (e.g. Barbera d'Asti) it means they come from a limited and theoretically superior area. The map shows the zones of central Piemonte—including that of the famous Moscato d'Asti spumante. The still dry white Cortese di Gavi is grown to the south-east.

Barolo is a wine on the scale of Château-neuf-du-Pape. Its minimum strength is 12%: going up to 15. It often throws a heavy sediment in its bottle, even after a minimum of three years in cask and often longer, so Barolo

bottles are traditionally kept standing up, un-like all other red wines.

The flavour of Barolo, and above all its scent, are the most memorable of any Italian wine. The Nebbiolo grape gives it a suggestion of truffles, a touch of tar, a positive note of rasp-berry. Barbaresco only differs from Barolo in coming from lower down, where fog affects the vineyard sooner, making a slightly drier, less fully ripened wine. Barolo which fails to come up to strength, sold simply as Nebbiolo, though lighter, can still be excellent. To the north, round Novara (see page 161), the same grape under the name Spanna makes equally remark-able wine.

Barbera is dark, tannic, often rather plummy and acidic; ideal wine with rich food. Freisa, the speciality of Chieri south of Turin, can be

similar—or sweet and sparkling. Dolcetto is light, faintly bitter, the carafe wine of the region. The best comes from Alba. Grignolino is also a light-weight with more character, all these are to drink relatively young.

Other specialities of this prolific region, the spaghetti-junction of denominaziones, in-clude another frothy sweet red wine, Brachetto d'Acqui, sweet pink or red Malvasia, an in-teresting yellow *passito* (made from semi-dried grapes) with the DOC Erbaluce or Caluso and an agreeable blend of Barbera and Grignolino sold as Rubino di Cantavenna.

Some of the bigger firms make a wide range of these wines; family businesses tend to make one or two, in which the characters of the grapes are likely to be more pronounced. These indi-vidual wines are worth looking for.

North-East Italy

Left: vineyards in the north-east of Italy frequently see snow, as here at Denno near Trento
Above: the wine produced is correspondingly northern and well-balanced in character

NORTH-EAST Italy owes less to tradition and more to modern development than the rest of the country. Whether it is the realism of the Venetians, the pressure of Austrian influence, the moderate climate, or all these, more wine is exported from the north-east than from elsewhere, more different grapes are grown and experimented with, and a more prosperous and professional air pervades the vineyards.

Verona and its wines—Valpolicella, Soave; Bardolino and the southern Lake Garda wines; the Alto Adige with its Lago di Caldaro and Santa Maddalena are mapped and discussed in detail on pages 166–167. The other biggest concentrations of wine-growing are due north of Venice round Conegliano, on the Jugoslav border in Friuli and in the Trentino, north of Lake Garda.

For some reason little is seen of any Lombardy wines abroad. Some are excellent. The best of all are the red wines of the Valtellina, coming from a narrow strip of vineyard which hugs the north bank of the River Adda (map on page 161). They go by the names Inferno, Grumello and Sassella, though it is hard to find anyone who knows the difference between the three. Their grape is the Nebbiolo. They are leaner and less splendidly pungent wines than Barolo and the Piemontese Nebbiolos, but they still need both barrel- and bottle-age: at least five years.

Of the other Lombardy wines on this map, the Garda-side wines are very close to the Veronese Garda wines in character. There is little to choose between Chiaretto from the Riviera del Garda (of which the best part is south of Salo, particularly round Moniga del Garda) and Bardolino. Both are reds so light as to be rosé, or rosés so dark as to be red, with a gentle flavour, soft textured and faintly sweet, made all the more appetizing by a hint of bitter-

ness, like almonds, in the taste which is common to all the best reds in this part of Italy. They should be drunk very young.

Red Botticino, Cellatica and Franciacorta are all light, too—though not often as attractive as Chiaretto. White Lugana, from the south end of Lake Garda, is good, dry, but rare.

Only one name from the flat Po valley is famous—the sparkling red Lambrusco from round Modena, above all from Sorbara. There is something appetizing about this vivid, grapy wine, despite the red bubbles, which goes well with rich Bolognese food. Unfortunately much that is exported is sweet and carbonated.

The character of the wine changes in the Veneto and eastwards. Already in the Colli Euganei (and indeed south of that, at Legnago on the excellent Quarto Vecchio estate) the red grapes are the Cabernet and Merlot of Bordeaux, above all the Merlot, which plays an increasingly dominant role all the way from Jugoslavia to the valley of the Adige north of Lake Garda, and again in Italian Switzerland.

At their best both grapes succeed admirably here; some of the Merlots can seriously be compared with St-Emilions, and the best Cabernets have considerable character and staying-power. Pinot Noir (Pinot Nero) also shows promise.

The white grapes are a mixture of the traditional—the Garganega of Soave, the versatile Prosecco, the light, sharp Verdiso and the more solid Tocai (Pinot Gris) and Verduzzo—and important new plantings of Sylvaner, Riesling, Sauvignon Blanc and Pinot Bianco.

The DOCs of the region are a series of defined areas which give their names to whole groups of red and white wines. Those known simply as (for example) Colli Euganei Rosso are standard wines made of an approved mixture of grapes. The better wines use the 'varietal' name with the DOC name—though there are also

DOCs, like Gambellara between Soave and the Colli Berici (Colli, incidentally, means hills), which are limited to a traditional grape, in this case the Garganega.

Breganze and Pramaggiore are known particularly from their Merlots and Cabernets. Farther east is traditionally white-wine country. Conegliano-Valdobbiadene specializes in Prosecco (both dry and sweetish, still and fizzy), Piave in Tocai and Verduzzo (but also Merlot and Cabernet).

The province of Friuli-Venezia-Giulia has six local DOCs: Aquileia, Collio Goriziano, Colli Orientali del Friuli, Grave del Friuli, Isonzo and Latisana; each with a full range of varietals from Cabernet to Tocai. None of them has distinguished itself so far. Standards are reasonable, but one is inclined to feel that it would be easier to build a reputation with one or two good wines with memorable identities.

Which is more or less what the Trentino has done with its full-blooded red Teroldego, from the grape of the same name grown in the cliff-hemmed, pergola-carpeted Adige valley round Trento. The best Teroldego, from north of Trento between Mezzolombardo and Mezzocorona (which appears at the south of the map on page 166), has the DOC Teroldego Rotaliano. Another Tirolese grape, the Schiava, makes the (on the whole) lighter Casteller and Sorni. The general DOC Trento covers Cabernet and Merlot (both good here, reaching very high standards at the provincial research station at San Michele all'Adige), Pinot Noir, two more Tirolese reds, the pale Lagrein and the dark Marzemino, and a range of whites including very tolerable Riesling. Trento's most distinguished white wine, however, is the *Méthode Champenoise* Ferrari Brut, made principally of Pinot Bianco; perhaps Italy's best sparkling wine.

SVIZZERA

ÖSTERREICH

N

N49 Brunico

MERANESE DI COLLINA

Merano Bressanone

S. GIUSTINA
SANTA MADDALENA

FRIULI VENEZIA GIULIA

Arabba Cortina d'Ampezzo

ALTO LAGO GUNCINA Bolzano

KALTERERSEE N13 Tarvisio

Tolmezzo

ADIGE Cles

JUGOSLAVIJA

Bormio TRAMINER

San Daniele
del Friuli Colli Orientali del Friuli

Tirano N42 PINOT
NEGRARA San Martino
di Castrozza Grave del Friuli Udine

Edolo TEROLDEGO
ROTALIANO
SORNI
MERLOT VALALAGARINA
RIESLING Belluno N51 REFOSCO PICCOLIT

VALTELLINA TRENTINO COLLIO
GORIZIANO

Clusone Trento Pordenone Gorizia

VERNACCIA N41 Feltre N13

Lovere MOSCATO RIESLING TOCAI

Trentino CASTELLER PROSECCO DI CONEGLIANO VALDOBBIADENE SAUVIGNON

Riva Rovereto
MINO Conegliano PROSECCO Monfalcone

RIVIERA
DEL
GARDA Breganze SILVANER TOCAI DI LISON
(E CLASSICO) Portogruaro N14

FRANCIACORTA VALPOLICELLA CLASSICO Bassano
del Grappa MERLOT Vini del Piave Trieste

ROSSO
CELLATICA Schio VALPANTENA VERDISO TOCAI DI LISON
&
CABERNET DI PRAMAGGIORE

Brescia BOTTICINO BARDOLINO
CLASSICO VENETO Treviso

TOCAI DI SAN MARTINO
DELLA BATTAGLIA SOAVE
SUPERIORE Vicenza Mestre

Salò LUGANA Verona SOAVE
CLASSICO GAMBELLARA Venezia

BARDOLINO
SUPERIORE Colli Berici Padova

BIANCO DI
CUSTOZA Colli
Euganei

Oglio MOSCATO Chioggia

Mantova Legnago FRIULARO

N10 Rovigo

Cremona Po

Po Porto Tolle

Autostrada Guastalla Mirandola LAMBRUSCO SALAMINO
DI SAN CROCE Ferrara

Fidenza LANCELLOTTI Sorbara

Parma FOGARINA Cento

N9 Comacchio

Taro LAMBRUSCO DI SORBARA

Reggio
Emilia Modena

LAMBRUSCO REGGIANO N64 Reno

SCANDIANO Secchia

LAMBRUSCO GRASPAROSSA
DI CASTELVETRO Bologna Ravenna

EMILIA-ROMAGNA N65

Imola Autostrada

TOSCANA N9 TREBBIANO DI ROMAGNA

Marano ALBANA DI
ROMAGNA

Forlì

SANGIOVESE
DI ROMAGNA SANGIOVESE ALBANA

International boundary
Regione boundary

Intensive wine-production

Moderate wine-production

DOC boundaries

MERLOT Red wines
ALBANA White wines
Breganze Red and White wines
Moscato Dessert wines

Wines with DOC boundaries shown are underlined
Many names apply to both red and white wines

Kms.0   20   40   60   80 Kms.
Mi.0   10   20   30   40   50 Mi.

165

Alto Adige

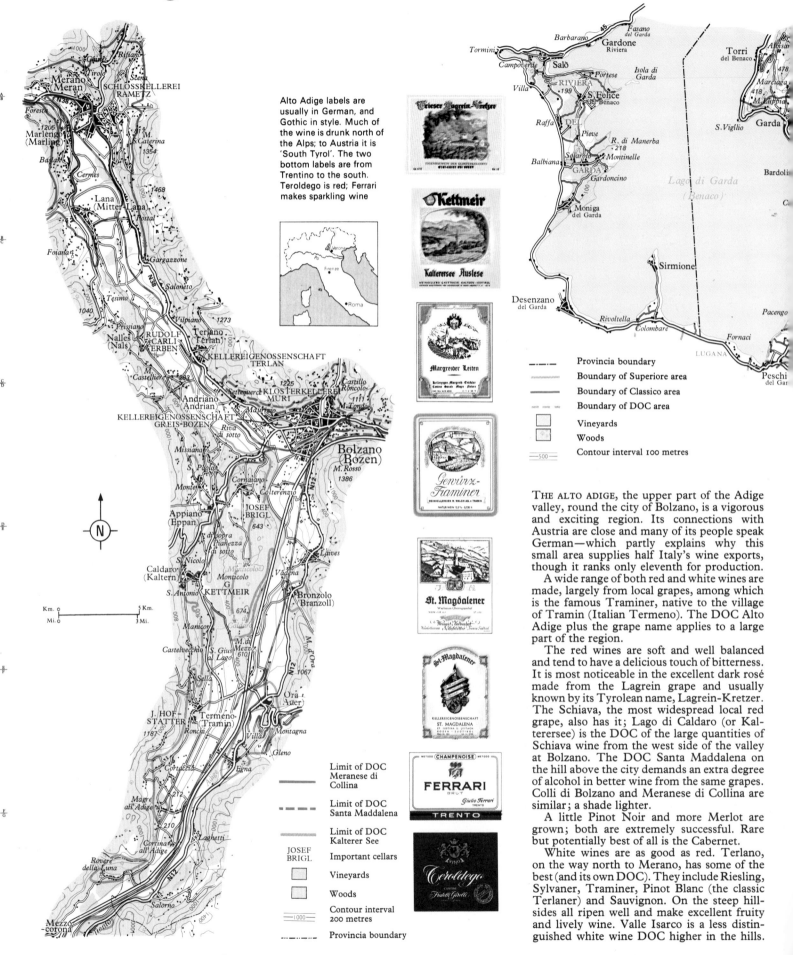

Alto Adige labels are usually in German, and Gothic in style. Much of the wine is drunk north of the Alps; to Austria it is 'South Tyrol'. The two bottom labels are from Trentino to the south. Teroldego is red; Ferrari makes sparkling wine

——— Provincia boundary

.... Boundary of Superiore area

——— Boundary of Classico area

······ Boundary of DOC area

▢ Vineyards

▢ Woods

—500— Contour interval 100 metres

——— Limit of DOC Meranese di Collina

– – – Limit of DOC Santa Maddalena

——— Limit of DOC Kalterer See

JOSEF BRIGL — Important cellars

▢ Vineyards

▢ Woods

—1000— Contour interval 200 metres

– · – Provincia boundary

THE ALTO ADIGE, the upper part of the Adige valley, round the city of Bolzano, is a vigorous and exciting region. Its connections with Austria are close and many of its people speak German—which partly explains why this small area supplies half Italy's wine exports, though it ranks only eleventh for production.

A wide range of both red and white wines are made, largely from local grapes, among which is the famous Traminer, native to the village of Tramin (Italian Termeno). The DOC Alto Adige plus the grape name applies to a large part of the region.

The red wines are soft and well balanced and tend to have a delicious touch of bitterness. It is most noticeable in the excellent dark rosé made from the Lagrein grape and usually known by its Tyrolean name, Lagrein-Kretzer. The Schiava, the most widespread local red grape, also has it; Lago di Caldaro (or Kalterersee) is the DOC of the large quantities of Schiava wine from the west side of the valley at Bolzano. The DOC Santa Maddalena on the hill above the city demands an extra degree of alcohol in better wine from the same grapes. Colli di Bolzano and Meranese di Collina are similar; a shade lighter.

A little Pinot Noir and more Merlot are grown; both are extremely successful. Rare but potentially best of all is the Cabernet.

White wines are as good as red. Terlano, on the way north to Merano, has some of the best (and its own DOC). They include Riesling, Sylvaner, Traminer, Pinot Blanc (the classic Terlaner) and Sauvignon. On the steep hillsides all ripen well and make excellent fruity and lively wine. Valle Isarco is a less distinguished white wine DOC higher in the hills.

Verona

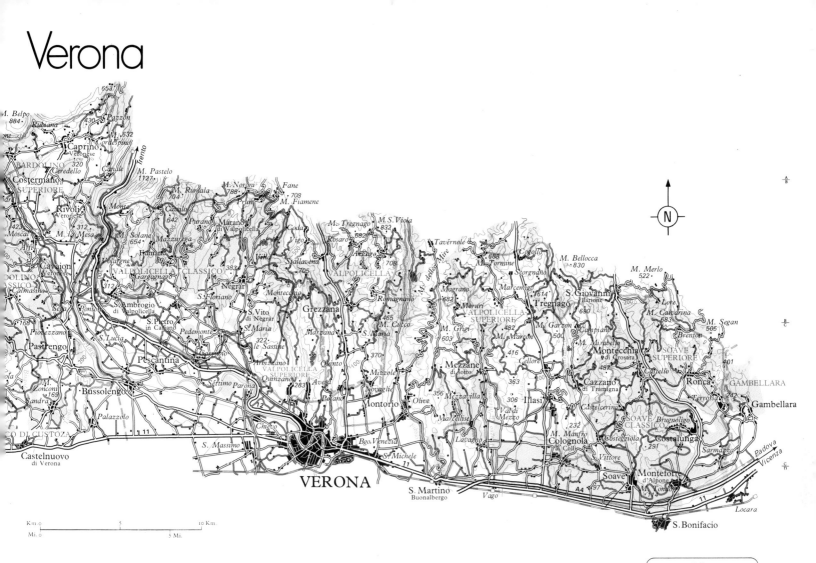

THE LOVINGLY GARDENED Verona hills, stretching from Soave, east of the city, westwards to Lake Garda, are so fertile that vegetation is uncontrollable; the vine runs riot on terrace and pergola, among villas which are the image of Italian grace.

Their Soave is probably Italy's most famous white wine. The region is tiny, and largely controlled by its cantina sociale, said to be the biggest in Europe. Considering the large-scale standardization which this involves, the wine is astonishingly good. It is relevant to wonder what the result would be if, say, all the wines of Pouilly-Fuissé were to be made together in one vat.

Soave (whether simple Soave or the slightly stronger and more expensive Classico) is a plain, dry, pale white wine. It is hard to characterize it in any more exciting way. And yet it has something—it may be a particularly soft texture—which singles it out and always makes it enjoyable. Its plainness also makes it very versatile. The thing to remember is to drink it young; even three-year-old Soave is no longer so fresh as it should be.

The same is true of the red wine of Valpolicella and its sub-district Valpantena. It has a beautiful cherry colour, a gentle sweet smell, a soft light flavour and a nice trace of bitterness as you swallow—when it is young. The best Valpolicellas (some are even kept in glass rather than wood from the start to stop them ageing) come from a few small producers in the Classico heart of the district—the prettiest imaginable hills. You may taste their wine with them, eating their bread and grilled sausage, and think you have never tasted better in the world. They will insist you go on to taste their

Above: cypresses, pale stone and leggy vines in grass like a garden: Castelnuovo di Verona in Bardolino is typical of the gentle Veronese country
Right: Verona and Garda wines are gentle, too; pale and smooth. White Soave and cherry-red Valpolicella are the best. Stronger Recioto is locally esteemed

Recioto (sweet) or Amarone (strong and dry); dark and sometimes fizzy; made of grapes dried in racks in well-ventilated lofts until after Christmas.

Almost every part of Italy makes some of its wine from grapes dried either in this way or in the sun, and prizes it highly. Verona's Reciotos are some of the best.

Bardolino is a paler, more insubstantial wine than Valpolicella—almost a rosé; drinkable as soon as it is made. Chiaretto del Garda, from the opposite side of the lake, is similar.

Central Italy

THE BEST-LOVED Italian wines, best known to travellers, most drunk in restaurants from Soho to Sydney, are encompassed by the map opposite. Above all Chianti, whose zone with its Classico heart (see next pages) occupies the better part of Tuscany. Chianti is *the* central Italian wine, and it is red. Curiously enough, though, this is the one part of Italy whose white wines outnumber the red and (Chianti aside) overshadow them in personality.

The white grape that puts its stamp on almost the whole area is the Trebbiano, known as Procanico on the Tuscan coast and the island of Elba. The same grape is grown in the Midi as Ugni Blanc and in Cognac as St-Emilion. It is a late ripener, which helps to give the coastal Procanicos (DOC Parrina) a refreshing acidity and make them ideal partners for fish.

To the north of Chianti Trebbiano is the major ingredient in the outstanding white Montecarlo. To the south it provides the bulk of Orvieto and its neighbours Est! Est!! Est!!! and Pitigliano. In the middle it performs in the agreeable mild Bianco Vergine Valdichiana. It reaches up into Verdicchio as a minor ingredient and down to Aprilia and the Abruzzi to make their respective Trebbiani. In the Roman hills it can be as much as 50 per cent of Frascati and its colleagues. There are times when one wishes such a ubiquitous fruit had more personality. All in all, however, it gives satisfaction.

Three world-famous white wines appear on this map: Umbria's Orvieto, Latium's Frascati and Verdicchio from the Marches.

Orvieto is by nature sweet, but not intended for dessert; not liquorous or lush. Various means are used for keeping it sweet or abboccato, rather than letting all the sugar ferment away. The classical one is to keep some half-dried grapes to add to the wine when it is nearly ready for bottling, and then pasteurize it in bottle. A dry version is made, which does not have the very pleasant delicacy of the sweet. Even those who will normally only drink dry white wines are seduced by the fragrant lightness which Orvieto can have, and will sit happily for hours in the restaurant facing the glittering cathedral, drinking it with fish, pasta, meat, cheese....

Roman white wines tend to be thought of, and referred to, as Frascati whether they really are or whether they come from the more broadly defined Castelli Romani or one of the group of DOCs (Cori, Velletri, Zagarolo, Montecompatri-Collona, Colli Albani) in the area. For Frascati at its best, though not easy to find, is another of Italy's most exciting wines; strong, fragrant, with a sweet flavour of ripe and golden grape skins (it is—or should be—fermented briefly on the skins) and yet finally quite dry. I sometimes fancy I can detect apricots in the flavour.

The deep cellars of Frascati date from Ancient Rome and hold more than any modern vintage has ever made. It is worth going out from Rome to taste the wine cold in a jug brought from its own cave, and to eat roast pork and bread with it in the open air: an experience to carry a romantic back 2,000 years.

More wine was made down this coast in Ancient times than is today (see map on page 13). The DOC Aprilia, for white Trebbiano and red Merlot and Sangiovese, does not correspond with the old Albanum, which grew on the hills farther from the sea. Cesanese, the (frequently sweet) red wine from south of the Castelli Romani, may be a descendant, but the hills behind Gaeta and Formia, some of Rome's most important vineyards then, no longer bear the vine.

The much-loved white wine of the east coast is the Verdicchio dei Castelli di Jesi, which appears in Italian restaurants all over the world in its amphora-shaped bottles. Verdicchio is pale, a degree or so stronger than the not dissimilar Soave, tasty without being heavy, and mercifully dry: an admirable all-purpose table wine, without leading to raptures. Its neighbour Bianchello is lighter and more fruity; Albana, Bologna's white restaurant-wine, as strong but rather neutral.

DOCs are thick on the ground along the Adriatic coast. Territory has been staked out for the red Sangiovese di Romagna and dei Colli Pesaresi, for Rosso Conero and Rosso Piceno, both made from the Montepulciano grape (Montepulciano is both a grape and a town in Tuscany), and Montepulciano di Abruzzo. Rosso Piceno can be a notable sturdy red. The Cerasuolo of the same coast is a pale 'cherry-coloured' beverage.

One lonely little DOC lies in the heart of Umbria—Torgiano. Torgiano red is a much better wine than you would expect to find on its own up in the hills; it ages well to become comparable with a distinguished Chianti Riserva.

Two other local specialities are worth trying: Aleatico, wherever you find it; an original dessert wine, sometimes fortified. Gradoli, near Lake Bolsena, is its one DOC. And the dry white Vernaccia of San Gimignano on the fringe of Chianti. Michelangelo is quoted as saying that it 'kisses, licks, bites, thrusts and stings' —such lively tasting-notes are rare.

Left: 'promiscuous cultivation' is the graphic term for the happy-go-lucky way vines are scattered among trees and crops in central Italy. Little has changed in the 50 years since this photograph was taken
Below: the famous wines of central Italy, apart from Chianti, are white: Frascati, Orvieto, Verdicchio

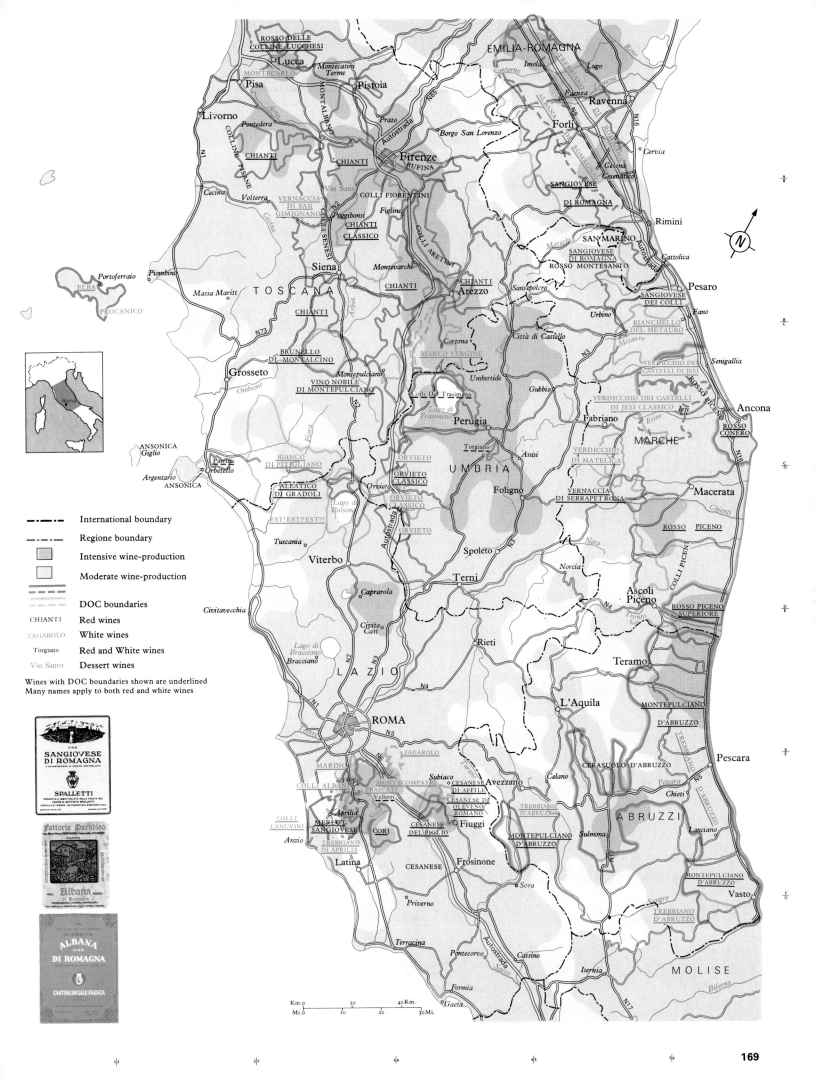

ROSSO DELLE
COLLINE LUCCHESI

MONTECARLO
Lucca
Pisa
Montecatini
Terme
Pistoia
Livorno
Pontedera
Prato
MONTALBANO
Autostrada
N65
Borgo San Lorenzo
Firenze
CHIANTI
CHIANTI
COLLINE PISANE
RUFINA
EMILIA-ROMAGNA
Reno
Imola
Lugo
TREBBIANO
Faenza
Ravenna
Forlì
N9
Cervia
N16
SANGIOVESE
DI ROMAGNA
Cesena
Cesenatico
Cecina
Volterra
Cecina
N1
N2
Vin Santo
COLLI FIORENTINI
VERNACCIA
DI SAN
GIMIGNANO
Poggibonsi
Figline
CHIANTI
CLASSICO
COLLI ARETINI
COLLI SENESI
Siena
Montevarchi
CHIANTI
Arezzo
CHIANTI
Sansepolcro
Rimini
SAN MARINO
Marecchia
SANGIOVESE
DI ROMAGNA
ROSSO MONTESANTO
SANGIOVESE
DEI COLLI
Pesaro
Cattolica
Autostrada
TOSCANA
Massa Maritt
ELBA
Portoferraio
Piombino
PROCANICO
Arbia
Cortona
Città di Castello
Urbino
Fano
BIANCHELLO
DEL METAURO
Metauro
N3
VERDICCHIO DEI
CASTELLI DI JESI
Senigallia
CHIANTI
BRUNELLO
DI MONTALCINO
Grosseto
Montepulciano
Umbertide
Gubbio
Jesi
VERDICCHIO DEI CASTELLI
DI JESI CLASSICO
Esino
Ancona
ROSSO PICENO
ROSSO
CONERO
BIANCO VERGINE
VINO NOBILE
DI MONTEPULCIANO
Ombrone
N2
Colli Del Trasimeno
Lago di
Trasimeno
Perugia
Torgiano
Assisi
Foligno
UMBRIA
Fabriano
VERDICCHIO
DI MATELICA
MARCHE
N16
Macerata
VERNACCIA
DI SERRAPETRONA
ANSONICA
Giglio
Parrina
Orbetello
Argentario
ANSONICA
BIANCO
DI PITIGLIANO
Fiora
ALEATICO
DI GRADOLI
Lago di
Bolsena
ORVIETO
ORVIETO
CLASSICO
Orvieto
ORVIETO
CLASSICO
ORVIETO
Autostrada
Spoleto
N3
Nera
Norcia
Chienti
ROSSO   PICENO
COLLI PICENI
EST! EST!! EST!!!
Tuscania
Viterbo
Terni
Ascoli
Piceno
N4
ROSSO PICENO
SUPERIORE
Tronto
Caprarola
Civitavecchia
Civita
Cast
Rieti
Teramo
MONTEPULCIANO
D'ABRUZZO
Lago di
Bracciano
Bracciano
N2
N3
N4
L'Aquila
Celano
TREBBIANO
D'ABRUZZO
Roma
SANGIOVESE
DI ROMAGNA
SPALLETTI
ZAGAROLO
MARINO
Subiaco
CESANESE
DI AFFILE
Avezzano
Pescara
Pescara
CERASUOLO D'ABRUZZO
Chieti
D'ABRUZZO
ABRUZZI
Fattoria Paradiso
Albana
DI ROMAGNA
COLLI ALBANI
FRASCATI
Velletri
MONTECOMPATRI
CESANESE DI
OLEVANO
ROMANO
Fiuggi
TREBBIANO
D'ABRUZZO
Sulmona
Lanciano
ALBANA
DI ROMAGNA
CANTINA SOCIALE FAENZA
COLLI
LANUVINI
MERLOT
SANGIOVESE
Aprilia
CORI
CESANESE
DEL PIGLIO
Frosinone
MONTEPULCIANO
D'ABRUZZO
N17
TREBBIANO
DI APRILIA
Latina
Anzio
CESANESE
Sora
Priverno
Terracina
Pontecorvo
Cassino
Sadco
Autostrada
Formia
Gaeta
Isernia
MONTEPULCIANO
D'ABRUZZO
Vasto
TREBBIANO
D'ABRUZZO
Biferno
MOLISE

International boundary
Regione boundary
Intensive wine-production
Moderate wine-production
DOC boundaries
CHIANTI   Red wines
ZAGAROLO   White wines
Torgiano   Red and White wines
Vin Santo   Dessert wines

Wines with DOC boundaries shown are underlined
Many names apply to both red and white wines

Km. 0   20   40 Km.
Mi.   10   20   30 Mi.

169

Chianti

THE HILLS between Florence and Siena come as near to the Roman poet's idea of gentlemanly country life as anywhere on earth. The blending of landscape and architecture and agriculture is ancient and profound. The villas, the cypresses, the vines, the rocks and woods compose pictures which could be Roman, Renaissance, Risorgimento . . . there is no way of telling.

In this timeless scene vineyards, in the sense of ranks of disciplined vines, are the only newcomers. Traditionally vines and olive-trees have clothed the dry gritty and sandy slopes together. On a recent agricultural map of Tuscany still not a single piece of vineyard was marked as such: the symbol everywhere was 'vines and olives'. Yet this is Chianti, and the world's entire supply (27 million gallons, of which 7 million gallons are Chianti Classico) must come from these apparently primitive plots. It is no surprise that the olives are losing, and files of vines now march up hill and down dale.

Chianti is more orderly than it seems. It was one of the first Italian wine areas to organize a consorzio of producers and discipline itself. The concept of Chianti Classico, the central and best area (mapped here), among six others with district names (Chianti Rufina, north-east of Florence, being the best of them), was established long before the present law of DOC. Not that it prevented a disgraceful amount of wine from elsewhere in Italy being sold as Chianti.

The wine is made from four grape varieties. A formula was established 100 years ago by the illustrious Baron Ricasoli, sometime Prime Minister of Italy, whose descendants still live in his castle at Brolio and make the same wine. Chianti is livened up in an unusual way by the addition of a little unfermented must of dried grapes (a trick known as 'il governo') after it has fermented; the result is a faint prickle which helps to make it refreshing.

The best Chianti, however, is aged for longer in oak before being bottled. It is distinguished by appearing in Bordeaux bottles instead of the *fiaschi* which mean Chianti to all the world. The bottle is appropriate for the nearest Italian equivalent to Bordeaux's château-wines—Chianti made and bottled on ancient private estates.

Both styles of Chianti, the current and the Riserva, are outstandingly good at their best and in their respective ways. In a trattoria in Florence the house wine to drink with the magnificently tender and tasty steaks is sometimes as compulsively drinkable as Beaujolais; faintly sweet, just frizzante, grape-smelling, with a delicious slight edge to it. A ten-year-old bottle of Riserva, on the other hand, sums up the warmth and attractiveness of Italian wine with a delicacy of its own. Its scent is powerful and it remains marvellously lively.

At Siena a unique institution, the Enoteca or Wine Library of Italy, housed in an old Medici fortress, provides an opportunity to taste not only every possible Chianti but most other Italian wines of note, with good food.

The map shows, besides the chaotic hilliness of the Chianti countryside, and the scattering of vines and olives among woods, the cellars of most of the leading producers of Chianti Classico, who all use the black cock label shown above. Non-Classico Chianti uses a cherub ('putto') for its badge. The best of these wines, such as the Nipozzano of Frescobaldi, are on Classico level. The new DOC Carmignano distinguishes a small area 15 miles north which adds Cabernet grapes to the Chianti formula, with remarkable results.

Southern Italy

International boundary
Regione boundary
Intensive wine-production
Moderate wine-production
DOC boundaries
MATINO   Red wines
ALCOMO   White wines
Solopaca   Red and White wines
Moscato   Dessert wines

Wines with DOC boundaries shown are underlined
Many names apply to both red and white wines

THERE IS ALWAYS a faint air of unreality about any complete list of Italian wines. There are indeed that many names—but are there that many identities? The question is impossible to answer. It depends on the farmer, or more often today the co-operative. Some proud local traditions, particularly here in the south, go straight into the blending vat every year to emerge as anything from Austrian wine to Beaujolais. Those wines of southern Italy which do appear in public are gaining ground, however. They used to be mere poor relations, selling (if they sold at all) on the power of association—the vine-hung terraces of Amalfi—alone. The climate coupled with old methods usually produced flat wines, deficient in acidity. But modern methods improve them every year, even as they lessen the differences.

Most famous of them are the ones tourists meet around Naples. Ischia was one of the first wines to claim a DOC, in 1966. It is easy enough for an island. Capri (not a DOC) has long been a sort of brand name for white wines; though those of the island itself are said to be much better than most 'Capri'. Lachryma Christi (not a DOC yet either) has the same status for normally inoffensive, sometimes good red and white wines from the area of Mount Vesuvius.

Ravello wines, particularly those made by the Caruso family, are well balanced; fresher than most of the south (the altitude of Ravello and its sea-mists are said to help). I cannot resist writing the name of Gran Furore Divina Costiera, which I am assured is a wine of the coast, though I have never been lucky enough to meet it.

Less known than the wines of the coast are those of inland Campania, of which Taurasi is the majestic chief; broad, dark and deep as a southern wine should be. Its grape, the Aglianico (ellenico, i.e. from Greece, like civilization itself down here), makes another good, rather lighter, red, Aglianico del Vulture, in vineyards on the inland hills of Basilicata up to 2,500 feet. The name of Greco di Tufo, a white

wine of some character from inland Campania, shares the credit between Greece and the tufa rock on which it grows. Of Basilicata the only other well-known wine (not DOC) is Asprinio, which the Potenzans manage to make mercifully unpotent, pale and crisp.

Calabria has one strong red of reputation; Ciró (there is a white Ciró as well), but recent DOCs for three others, Donnici, Savuto and Pollino. Puglia has registered a remarkable number of wines which have traditionally gone to market in bulk. It remains to be seen which of them will establish reputations. The Primitivo from round Taranto is a likely candidate; its full-bodied red is said to age very well, and in California the theory goes that it may be the origin of the estimable Zinfandel.

Both reds and whites in Puglia are being well made today, not over-strong or heavy but often rather neutral, the whites particularly, which makes them an ideal base for vermouth. The rosés of Castel del Monte are perhaps the most attractive product of the region at present: they are as good as any in Italy—or indeed France. There are good dessert wines, of Moscato and Aleatico, throughout this region.

But more than any of the wines of Puglia it is Sicilian wine which is making a name for itself today. Its treacly-dark Marsala, like a distant cousin of sherry, has been famous since Nelson's day, when he fortified the Royal Navy with it. The advent of Sicilian table wine, however, is something new. Though none has any very marked personality the general standard is high and reliable. The island has its own badge of quality, the letter Q for tested wines.

Brands rather than DOCs have made the running. The one important table wine DOC is Etna, for wines from the immensely fertile volcanic soil of that spectacular mountain. The Barone Vilagrande's red and white are typical examples; lively, well-balanced wines.

Good brands that use grapes from other parts of the island are Regaleali and the very successful Corvo, made near Palermo at Casteldaccia. Alcamo is the table wine DOC for vineyards in the north-west and Cerasuolo for light reds from Vittoria on the south coast. The rest of Sicily's DOCs are for her particular speciality; dessert wine. The moscatos of Noto and Siracusa and the little island of Pantelleria and the Malvasia of Lipari are good examples of one of Italy's oldest vinous traditions.

Most of Sardinia's DOCs, too, are for sweet wines. On Sardinia the distinction between a table wine and a dessert wine is even more blurred than in other parts of Italy; traditionally all her reds (Cannonau, Monica, Giró and Oliena are the best known) were more or less sweet. Her best wines were Vernaccia, a strong dry white which has a distinct affinity with sherry, and Nuragus, a dry white without too much alcohol and (sometimes) a firmness which makes it really appetizing. One firm in particular, however, has started making modern-style reds and whites in vast modern vineyards round Alghero in the north-west. Sella & Mosca wines are made and marketed by Piemontese and Milanese skills respectively. Attractive and reliable wines like this could come from almost anywhere in Italy.

Spain

Left: Spain's one really great wine is sherry, from Andalucia. At a *caserio*, where sherry is made, a mule fetches water from the well in the porous amphoras which keep it cool in the heat

SPAIN has the distinction of having more land under vines than any other country—even Italy. Curiously, however, she has only a third of Italy's production of wine. This anomaly is due partly to different ideas of what counts as a vineyard; mixed planting with other crops in Spain may be included, and in Italy omitted. Partly it reflects old-fashioned methods (which include not over-cropping the vine or the soil: Spanish wine is often very strong).

Only ten years ago zones, qualities and origins were casually defined in most of Spain. 1970 was the date of tightening up, with the founding of the Instituto Nacional de Denominaciónes de Origen.

In the last ten years exports have multiplied by six, while the ratio of wines exported in bottle (a rough index of quality) has gone up even faster. The world is beginning to buy Spanish wines for their character, and not just their strength.

The map opposite shows the regions which have so far been granted a Denominación de Origen—a term, be it noted, much broader than an Appellation Contrôlée. The quality wine regions (Jerez and Rioja, Montilla and Catalonia) are separately mapped on subsequent pages. What immediately emerges from the maps opposite is the huge concentration of production on the plains of La Mancha, south-east of Madrid. The town of Valdepeñas has traditionally given its name to a large part of this production; chiefly red, strong (about 13%) but light-tasting and not unpleasant vino de pasto, which is made from red and white grapes mixed and drunk with little if any ageing. Much of it is still made in huge earthenware pots (*tinajas*) like Roman amphoras ten feet high.

The next highest production, though way behind La Mancha, is in Valencia and Utiel-Requeña, and consists (in the main) of heavier and sweeter red wines than those of the inland plain. The Jumilla and Jecla regions (strong reds and strong whites), Alicante and Tarragona (also substantial reds and whites) are the same. The market for much of all this is the blending vats of France and Germany, where it makes up for the thinness of the local product.

In the scattered inland regions of the north and west, production is smaller. The name Cariñena is commonly applied to the heavy wines of Aragon, red, white or sweet, as Valdepeñas is to the wines of La Mancha. Navarre is a small producer, though the best of its red wines, from the Señorio de Sarría, is up to the best Rioja standards. In the Basque north there is a speciality called Chacolí, red or white, pétillant and with no more alcohol than a moselle—and only worth making into brandy, according to one authority.

Westwards in Castile the wine region of La Nava-Rueda makes well-balanced red and white wines, the white not unlike sherry. Toro is another red heavy-weight.

North-west Spain is largely cider country, but Ribeiro, Valdeorras and Valle de Monterey make 'green' wine like the Portuguese speciality. One area, Pontevedra, is famous for its Albariño, the best green-wine grape, said to be the Riesling, brought by pilgrims to Compostella.

More or less common wines are made round Madrid (in Méntrida) and in Extremadura (Cáceres and Almendralejo). The same is true of the reds of Huelva in Andalucia, though the good Huelva whites have long gone to market as sherry.

Andalucia's other famous name (sherry is discussed on pages 176–179) is Malaga. Malaga —once known as Mountain—is one of the great has-beens of wine, like the Sicilian Marsala. The fashion for such dark sweet wines, unless they have the finesse of port or sherry or madeira, has passed. And yet good Malaga is . . . good Malaga.

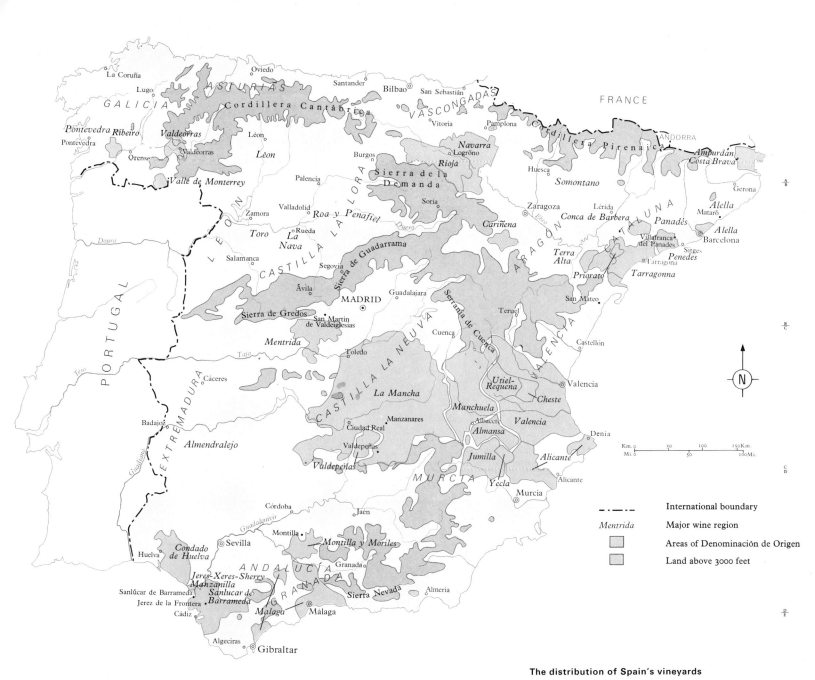

The distribution of Spain's vineyards

Below: few Spanish labels are known abroad. Most of her table wine which is not drunk locally is blended

International boundary

Mentrida Major wine region

Areas of Denominación de Origen

Land above 3000 feet

Wine-production

Over 1000 litres per hectare

100–1000 litres per hectare

10–100 litres per hectare

The Sherry Country

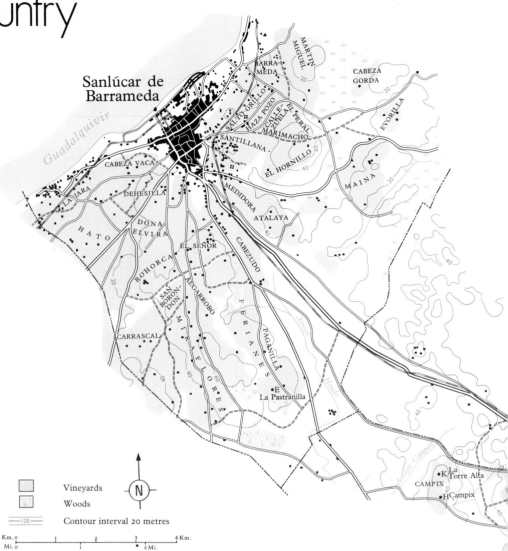

Sanlúcar de Barrameda

FINESSE—meaning fine-ness in its most literal sense, a combination of strength and delicacy —is not one of the qualities you normally find in scorched-earth wines. Where the sun fairly grills the ground, and the grapes ripen as warm as fruit in a pie, wine sometimes develops wonderful thews and sinews, power and depth. But finesse . . .

This is sherry's great distinction. It is a question of chalk; of the breed of the Palomino grape; of huge investment and long-inherited skill. Not every bottle of sherry, by a very long way, has this quality. But a real fino; the rarely shipped unstrengthened produce of the bare white chalk dunes of Macharnudo or Sanlúcar de Barrameda, is an expression of wine and wood as vivid and beautiful as any in the world.

One does not think of sherry normally in direct comparison with the other great white wines of the world—but it is, strange to say, the cheapest of them, even bodega-bottled and fully mature, ready to drink.

The sherry country, between the romantic-sounding cities of Cadiz and Seville, is almost a caricature of grandee Spain. Here are the bull ranches, the caballeros, the castles on the sky-line, the patios, the guitars, the night-turned-into-day. Jerez de la Frontera, the town that gives its name to sherry, lives and breathes sherry as Beaune does burgundy and Epernay champagne.

The comparison between sherry and champagne can be carried a long way. Both are white wines with a distinction given them by chalk soil, both needing long traditional treatment

Vineyards

Woods

Contour interval 20 metres

Km. 0   1   2   3   4 Km.
Mi. 0   1   2 Mi.

Right and below: there is a strange dazzling light reflected off the chalk in the sherry vineyards. Golden Palomino grapes almost cook in the heat; before they are pressed they are often laid out on esparto mats in the sun to sweeten even more, so that their high sugar content will give strong and stable wine. The miracle is that it is delicate as well

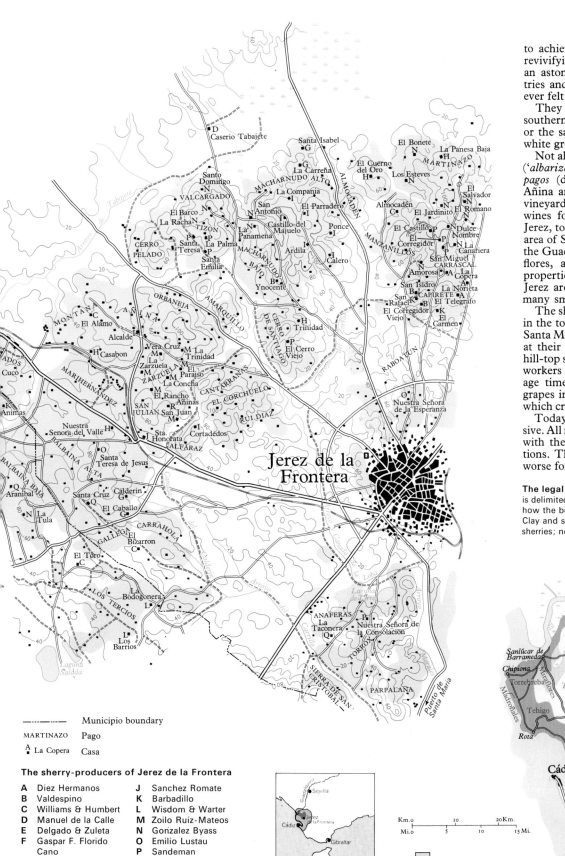

to achieve their special characters. Both are revivifying aperitifs, of which you can drink an astonishing amount in their home countries and only feel more alive than you have ever felt before.

They are the far-northern and the far-southern interpretation of the same equation, or the same poem: the white grape from the white ground.

Not all the ground is white. The chalk areas ('*albarizas*' on the map below) are best; the *pagos* (districts) of Carrascal, Macharnudo, Añina and Balbaina the most famous. Some vineyards are on sand and produce second-rank wines for blending. The main vineyards of Jerez, to the west of the town, and the distinct area of Sanlúcar de Barrameda farther west on the Guadalquivir, with its famous *pago*, Miraflores, are enlarged on the big map. The properties of most of the principal owners of Jerez are shown; Sanlúcar is divided among many smaller owners, impracticable to show.

The shippers' headquarters and bodegas are in the towns of Jerez, Sanlúcar and Puerto de Santa Maria. Traditionally they made the wine at their *caserios* among the vineyards. Every hill-top seems to have its low white house. The workers eat and sometimes sleep there at vintage time, and there they used to tread the grapes in boots with protruding rows of nails which crushed the skins but spared the pips.

Today such folklore is too slow and expensive. All modern sherry is pressed at the bodega with the latest machinery in hygienic conditions. The wine, thank goodness, is none the worse for it.

The legal area for sherry
is delimited largely in terms of the soils. This map shows how the best region falls in *albarizas* (or chalk zones). Clay and sandy soil zones make useful blending sherries; never the classical finos

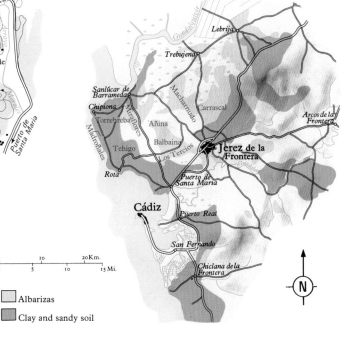

Municipio boundary

MARTINAZO   Pago

A La Copera   Casa

The sherry-producers of Jerez de la Frontera

A	Diez Hermanos	J	Sanchez Romate
B	Valdespino	K	Barbadillo
C	Williams & Humbert	L	Wisdom & Warter
D	Manuel de la Calle	M	Zoilo Ruiz-Mateos
E	Delgado & Zuleta	N	Gonzalez Byass
F	Gaspar F. Florido Cano	O	Emilio Lustau
G	José de Soto	P	Sandeman
H	Garvey	Q	Fernando A. de Terry
I	Pedro Domecq	R	Palomino & Vergara

Km.0   10   20Km.
Mi.0   5   10   15 Mi.

Albarizas

Clay and sandy soil

Jerez de la Frontera

THERE ARE little bars in Jerez where the tapas, the morsels of food without which no Jerezano puts glass to mouth, constitute a banquet. From olives and cheese to prawns, to raw ham, to peppery little sausages, to lobster claws, to miniature steaks streaked with amber onions, the path of temptation is broad and long.

Your little copita, a glass no more imposing than an opening tulip, fills and empties with a paler wine, a cooler wine, a more druggingly delicious wine than you have ever tasted. It seems at the same time dry as dust and just teasingly sweet, so that you have to sip again to trace the suggestion of grapes.

It comes in half bottles, kept on ice. A half bottle is reckoned a reasonable drink to spin out over an hour or two among the tapas. And in half bottles it stays as fresh as it was when it left the bodega—for no bottle is left half full.

The most celebrated sights of Jerez are the bodegas of the shipping houses. Their towering whitewashed aisles, dim-roofed and criss-crossed with sunbeams, are irresistibly cathedral-like. In them, in ranks of butts sometimes five tiers high, the new wine is put to mature. It will not leave until it has gone through an elaborate blending process which is known as the solera system.

The first job when the new wine has got over its fermentation is to sort it into categories; better or worse, lighter or more full-bodied. Each wine is put into the *criadera*, or nursery, appropriate to its character. Each character, or category, of wine has a traditional name.

From these *criaderas* the shipper tops up a number of soleras, consisting of perhaps 20, perhaps several hundred butts; each wine again going into the solera nearest to its character. As new wine goes into butts at one end of the solera, mature wine for blending is drawn from the other. The solera system is simply a progressive topping up of older barrels from younger of the same style, so that wine is continuously being blended, and hence always emerges tasting the same.

The solera wines are the shipper's paintbox for the blending of his brands, or for brands ordered by other wine merchants for sale under their own names. Most sherry when it is sold is a blend of several, sweetened and strengthened to the public's taste. The few 'straight solera' sherries which are sold tend to be unsweetened and therefore wines for the connoisseur.

The categories into which all young sherry is classified begin with fino. Finos are the best sherries: delicate and distinctive wines which will need a minimum of blending and sweetening. They will age excellently, but they also have the qualities which make them perfect young. Their strong individuality comes from an unusual form of yeast, flor, which forms on their surface. Tasted from the butt, when the *capataz* of the bodega thrusts his long cane-handled *venencia* through the flor into the pale wine to bring out a sample, they have a magical new-bread freshness and vitality; they

The solera system in action: sherry from younger butts, higher in the pile, is siphoned into jugs and poured from a height into an older, lower butt. The pouring allows air to mix with the wine

The sherry bodegas of Jerez de la Frontera

1	Williams & Humbert	6	Garvey
2	Zoilo Ruiz-Mateos	7	Valdespino
3	Gonzalez Byass	8	Pedro Domecq
4	Sandeman	9	Le Riva
5	Diez Hermanos	10	Agustin Blazquez

are, beyond question, Spain's finest wine of all.

Amontillado—a softer, darker wine—comes next. The best amontillados are old finos, finos which did not quite have the right freshness to be drunk young, though the name is often used in commerce for middle-character blends of no real distinction. Great amontillado soleras (for only from the solera can you taste the real individuality of the wine) are dry and almost stingingly powerful of flavour, with a dark, fat, rich tang—but words fall short.

Oloroso is the third principal class. Wines which have great possibilities for ageing, but which seem a little heavy at first, go into this solera. They are the basis for the best sweet sherries—often known as milk or cream, which suggests their silky fatness.

Sweetening wines and colouring wines for blending are specially made from sun-dried grapes and kept in their own soleras. Lesser wines which go into cheaper blends are known as *rayas*, and a final rare character, something between fino and oloroso, as *palo cortado*.

In addition there are the wines of Sanlúcar de Barrameda, known as manzanillas. Manzanilla finos are some of the most delicate and lovely of all, always with a faintly salty tang which is held to come from the sea. A manzanilla amontillado is rare, but can be exquisite, salty and brown as burnt butter.

No blend, medium-sweet or sweet as most blends are, can compare with these astonishing natural sherries. They are as much collectors' pieces as great domaine-bottled burgundies.

Right: a trade directory lists over 600 brands of sherry. Many of them, including some famous ones, belong to wine merchants who have no establishment in Spain. They order wine to their own specifications, for sale under their own name, from one of the big shipping houses. Most of the best sherries, however, come from bodegas, large or small, who bottle their own style of wine themselves. All have a wide range from dry to sweet; these labels are a representative selection

The most famous fino of all does not mention fino on the label. Extremely dry, fresh and young with real delicacy

Tres Palmas is the conventional sign on the butt for a superlative fino. La Riva bottles some very old sherries as well

Excellent light fino from Valdespino's Ynocente vineyard in Macharnudo; the only sherry vineyard named on a label

A very pale and dry manzanilla, from one of the bigger shippers in Sanlúcar de Barrameda, where big ones are few

The Carlos y Javier de Terry bodegas are in Puerto de Santa Maria, the second town of the Jerez area

The Garvey family came to Jerez from Ireland originally. They have called their best fino after Ireland's patron saint

Dos Cortados is the sign for very dry oloroso with great distinction. Williams & Humbert's is one of the best sherries sold

Varela is another of the shippers with bodegas in Puerto de Santa Maria. A typical popular, middle-ranking fino

An old, unsweetened (*al natural*) wine from a good small shipper. Amontillado character, though it does not say so

The firm of Duff Gordon is owned by Bodegas Osborne. El Cid is their most popular wine. It is a medium-sweet amontillado

A magnificent old dry oloroso from Macharnudo, one of the best wines from one of the biggest and best shippers

No type is mentioned. It is hard to know what to expect from this bottle; in fact the wine is a pungent, dark, dry oloroso

Old oloroso is the basis for good sweet sherries; the cream style is very sweet but should not mask the nuttiness of the base

The most famous of all Creams comes from a British firm in Bristol, made by them or to their requirements in Jerez

The old English firm of Sandeman is famous for both port and sherry. Their fino, 'Apitiv', is also excellent

Rioja

Left: much of Rioja
outside the river valley
has a bare highland
feeling emphasized by
the Sierra de Cantabria
in the distance,
often snow-covered.
Vineyards, crops and
pasture alternate on
the stony ground. The
vines grow as low bushes
without posts or wires

RIOJA has long had a virtual monopoly of the wine lists of good restaurants in Spain. They offer local wine, often free, in carafes. But if you want bottled wine, especially red wine, Rioja is the Bordeaux and the burgundy of Spain. You will get Rioja.

It is partly a question of human geography, as well as the physical kind. Rioja is not far from the French frontier; not far from Bordeaux. When the phylloxera arrived in the 1870s many wine-growers took off for Spain They found in Rioja rather different conditions, but an opportunity to make good wine all the same. Then the phylloxera caught up with them, and they went home. But they left French methods and ideas.

Rioja is distinctly mountainous in atmosphere. It lies in the shelter of the Sierra de Cantabria to the north, but its best vineyards are still 1500 feet above sea level. They get plenty of rain and long springs and autumns, rather than endless parching summers. The wine is correspondingly less hearty and more interesting than other Spanish wine: well-made and at the right age exceedingly delicate and fine, yet with a faintly toasted sweet warmth, which seems to proclaim it Spanish.

The area is divided into three by terrain and altitude. The areas farther up-river, Rioja Alta and Rioja Alavesa (in the province of Alava, whereas the rest is in Logroño) are cooler and wetter. Rioja Alta (the high Rioja) has the lightest and best wines; Alavesa slightly stronger but still excellent reds. Rioja Baja (the low Rioja) has a more Mediterranean climate. Its wines are more alcoholic and only

used for the cheaper blends of Rioja, or as vino corriente on their own. The division comes around the town of Logroño, one of the two main centres of the wine trade.

The chief wine centre is Haro. The rather insignificant town is dwarfed by its outskirts, which contain 13 large bodegas—a third of the total of Rioja. The country round is beautiful in an upland way: tall poplars and eucalyptus trees line the roads; orchards cover slopes along with tilting fields of vines, each vine an individual bush without posts or wires. In the rocky valley bottom the infant river Ebro, draining the Sierra de Cantabria eastwards towards the Mediterranean, is joined by the little Rio Oja, whose shortened name the region has adopted.

There are few wine estates, large or small, in Rioja which grow, make and bottle their own wine. In many matters of technique the Bordelais left their mark, but châteaux (with the single exception of Castillo Ygay) are not among them. To qualify for a Rioja Certificate of Origin a bodega has to be big enough, and most bodegas operate as sherry houses do, or the wineries of California. They buy grapes from farmers to supplement those they grow themselves, and make a blend of wine of their own house style. Vineyard names appear frequently on Rioja bottles: Viña Tondonia, Zaco, Paceta, Pomal are all well known. But they have no direct relation to the plot of land in question. They are used as brand names for the better wines by the shippers.

The best Rioja wine is red. It is made from a mixture of grapes, of which only the Garnacha (the pale red Grenache of the Rhône) is familiar.

Bordeaux- and burgundy-shaped bottles are used for, respectively, the drier and the fuller wines. Very pale red is called Clarete.

By and large these wines are made as Bordeaux was in the last century; with the idea that they should be aged for several years in barrels (two or three for ordinary wine; up to ten for Reservas) until their darkness and fruitiness has been tamed and replaced with the almost tawny colour and soft vanilla flavour which comes from oak. In Spain (where most red wine is inky) they are much appreciated light and smooth as a long time in wood makes them. By modern French standards they should be bottled earlier, so they can develop a bouquet in bottle, still with much of their fruitiness in them. It is a question of taste, but certainly many Rioja wines are older than would seem necessary; whereas the French usually err the other way.

Even white Rioja wines are often given four or five years in barrel; when they have grown round, golden and rather flat from oxidation they are reckoned at their prime, whereas earlier, sometimes marvellously stony and up to Rhône white-wine standards, they are considered too young. The dry whites are better than the sweet, which have no *pourriture noble* to concentrate their sugar and tend to be medium- rather than honey-sweet.

Vintage years are treated lightly. If a vintage is stated it is a good one, even if there is no guarantee that all the wine in the bottle was made that year. Among white wines look for the youngest, among red wines look for one ten years old or even more.

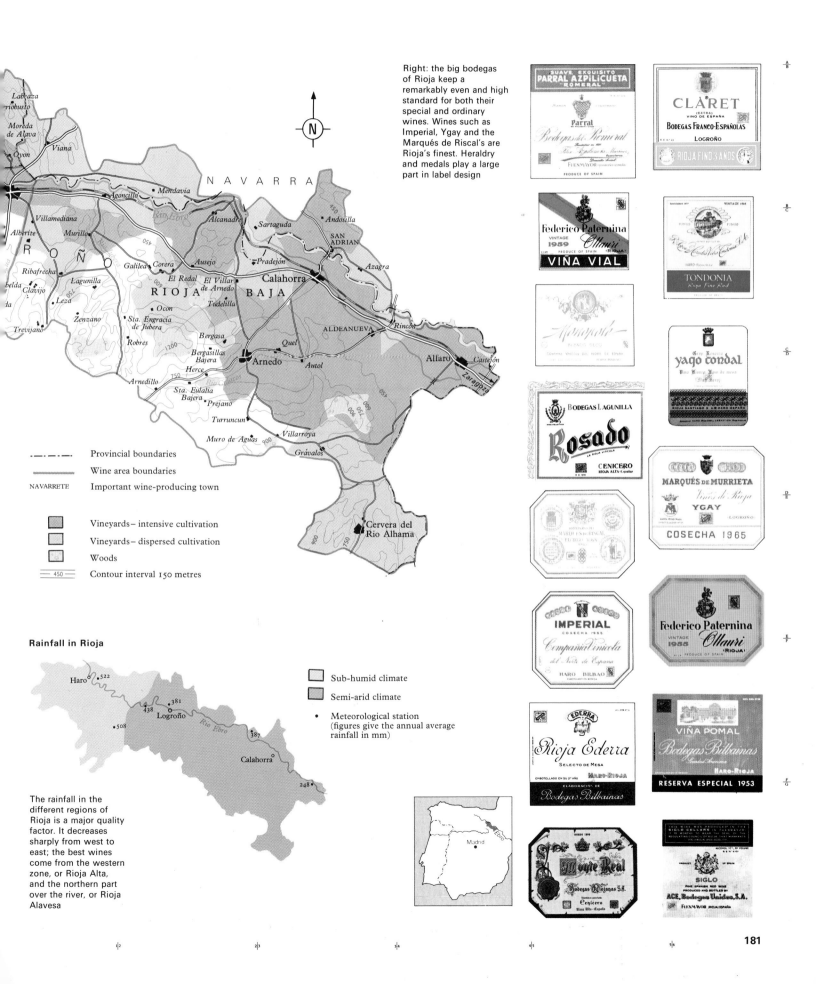

N

Right: the big bodegas
of Rioja keep a
remarkably even and high
standard for both their
special and ordinary
wines. Wines such as
Imperial, Ygay and the
Marqués de Riscal's are
Rioja's finest. Heraldry
and medals play a large
part in label design

NAVARRA

Labraza
riobusto
Moreda
de Alava
Oyon
Viana
Villamediana
Alberite
Murillo
Ribafrecha
Lagunilla
belda
Clavijo
Leza
Zenzano
Trevijano
Mendavia
Agoncillo
Rio Ebro
Alcanadre
Sartaguda
Andosilla
SAN
ADRIAN
Galilea
Corera
Ausejo
Pradejón
Azagra
El Redal
El Villar
de Arnedo
Calahorra
RIOJA
BAJA
Ocon
Tudelilla
Sta. Engracia
de Jubera
Bergasa
Robres
Quel
ALDEANUEVA
Rincón
Bergasillas
Bajera
Arnedo
Autol
Alfaro
Castejón
Herce
Zaragoza
Arnedillo
Sta. Eulalia
Bajera
Prejano
Turruncun
Villarroya
Muro de Aguas
Grávalos
Cervera del
Rio Alhama

Provincial boundaries

Wine area boundaries

NAVARRETE   Important wine-producing town

Vineyards – intensive cultivation

Vineyards – dispersed cultivation

Woods

450   Contour interval 150 metres

Rainfall in Rioja

Haro
•522
438
Logroño
•381
•508
Rio Ebro
387
Calahorra
248•

Sub-humid climate

Semi-arid climate

•   Meteorological station
(figures give the annual average
rainfall in mm)

The rainfall in the
different regions of
Rioja is a major quality
factor. It decreases
sharply from west to
east; the best wines
come from the western
zone, or Rioja Alta,
and the northern part
over the river, or Rioja
Alavesa

Madrid

Ebro

Catalonia

ON A COAST whose production is nearly all heavy and dark red wine for the world's blending vats it is a surprise to come across the world's biggest cellars for sparkling wine. But Catalonia is different from the rest of Mediterranean Spain. The Catalans have more vitality; are more demanding, destructive, creative. Several of their Denominaciónes de Origen are building international reputations today.

The Panadés sparkling wine (the centre of the industry is San Sadurní de Noya and the big cellars those of Codorníu) is extremely good. The export quality at least is well-matured, clean and very dry—without champagne's richness and finesse, it is true.

Some of the other white wines of the coast are also remarkably light and well-balanced. The Viña Sol of Bodegas Torres in Panadés is an outstanding example. Alella Marfil (the word means ivory—a fair image for the rather soft wine) can also be good. There is however a tendency to go too far in the treatments which make wine pale and light—some of it is colourless and almost tasteless, robbed of all its natural gold.

Torres is the leading table-wine brand of the coast: an old family firm with new ideas whose reds are among the best in Spain: complex wines, rich but not over-rich or over-strong. Tres Coronas and Sangre de Toro are two of their red brands. The region that can produce them has a great future.

The name of Tarragona can only be used for sweet fortified wine. Priorato is a small area within it which specializes in strong dry reds of promising quality. Sitges in Panadés also has its own denominación for its traditional dessert wines made of (white) Sumoll and Malvasia grapes.

Above: the best of Catalan wine (which includes good sparkling wine) is surprisingly dry and delicate compared with the heavy sweet produce of Tarragona
Left: a Roman aqueduct runs through vineyards and olive-groves near Tarragona

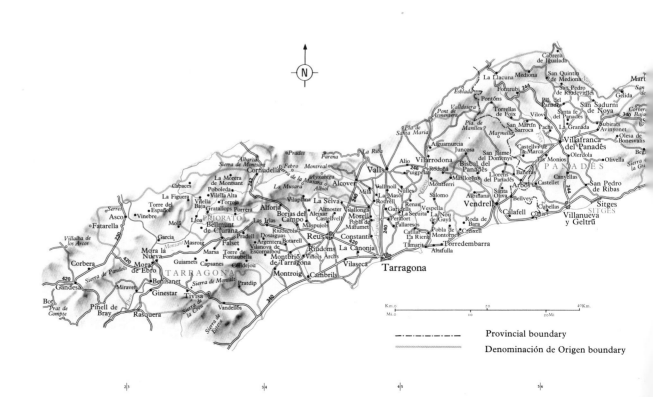

Provincial boundary

Denominación de Origen boundary

Montilla

Sherry has a shadow in Montilla. The very same chalk that gives rise to the marvellous finos of Jerez and Sanlúcar down on the coast recurs a hundred miles inland near Córdoba. In fact only comparatively recently, with the drawing up of boundaries, has real distinction been made between the wines of the Jerez zone and those of the similar but hotter hill area where Montilla is made.

Montilla is still little heard of abroad, though it is one of the most popular wines in Spain, with a production almost two-thirds that of Jerez. Its special attraction lies in its very high natural strength, which allows it to be shipped without fortification, in contrast to sherry, which is nearly always strengthened slightly. It seems strange to speak of delicacy in a wine with a natural strength of 16% alcohol—but this is in fact the characteristic which distinguishes all finos, and in a really good Montilla it is easy to appreciate.

The Montilla grape is the Pedro Ximénez—the one which in Jerez is kept for the sweetest wine. The even hotter inland climate of Montilla gives it an even higher sugar content which ferments rapidly (fermentation is done in open earthenware jars). The flor yeast also comes quickly. Within a year or two the wine is ready, with all the finesse of a fino, but more softness than, for example, a manzanilla, which always has a characteristic bite. Montillas make deceptively perfect aperitifs, slipping down like table wines despite their high strength. People claim to find in them the scent of black olives (which are of course their perfect partners).

Since they are shipped unfortified they have the advantage over most sherries of being exactly the wine which brings back such vivid memories of the south of Spain.

Above: the strong wines of Montilla ferment furiously in open earthenware tinajas which look like the amphoras used in the ancient world

Montilla and Moriles are the two centres of the Montilla trade, still largely confined to Spain. Their most popular wines are their aperitif finos, but like Jerez they also produce old, dark and sweet wines, using the same terms—oloroso, amontillado and the rest

Madeira

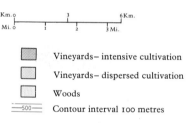

Km. 0   3   6 Km.
Mi. 0   1   2   3 Mi.

    Vineyards – intensive cultivation

    Vineyards – dispersed cultivation

    Woods

—500— Contour interval 100 metres

THE CLUSTER of volcanic islands 400 miles off the coast of Morocco which the ancients knew as the Enchanted Isles are known to us as Madeira, Porto Santo and the Desertas. Madeira is the largest island of the little archipelago and one of the prettiest in the world, as steep as an iceberg and as green as a glade. For over 500 years it has been considered by the Portuguese as part of Portugal. Now, since the 1974 Revolution, it is autonomous with its own parliament.

The story goes that when the Portuguese landed on the island (at Machico in the southeast) they set fire to the dense woods covering the mountain slopes. The fire burned for seven years, leaving the already fertile soil enriched with the ashes of an entire forest.

Certainly it is fertile today. From the water's edge to over half-way up the 6,000-foot peak it is steadily terraced to make room for patches of vines, patches of sugar-cane, little flower gardens. As in northern Portugal the vines are grown above head-height in arbours, making room for yet more cultivation beneath.

Wine has been the principal product of the island for 400 years. Its natural wine, however, is not all that its beautiful vineyards seem to promise. It has a bite of acidity which makes it

a taste not easy to acquire. Like port, it had to wait for a blender of genius to make it suitable for export, except as the ballast of sailing ships, to be drunk only in emergencies.

It was brandy (to stop it fermenting and keep it sweet) and travelling as ballast that made madeira. A long sea voyage, including a double crossing of the equator, would finish off any lesser wine, but it was found to hasten madeira's awkwardly long maturing process to a gallop.

Instead of long sea voyages madeira today is subjected to ordeal by fire. A similar effect to the tropical heat is produced by warming the wine over a long period to a temperature of 120°F or more. It stays in the hot stores (*estufas*) where this is done for four or five months. When it comes out it has the characteristic caramel tang by which all madeiras can be recognized.

The shippers of Madeira use the solera system of Jerez to blend their wine into consistent brands. Very old soleras are common, though the law no longer allows them to carry the date (e.g. Solera 1853) when the first wine was put in.

At the peak of their prosperity in the 19th century madeira shippers used to declare vintages, as port shippers still do—but the double disaster of oidium in the 1850s and phylloxera

Above left: the breakneck slopes of Madeira are terraced for vineyards from near sea level up to 3,250 feet

Right: most madeira is labelled with the name of the shipper and the grape variety: Sercial Verdelho, Bual or Malmsey, in ascending order of richness and sweetness. The only place name used today is Cama de Lobos, famous for its sweet wines blended from Malmsey and other grapes

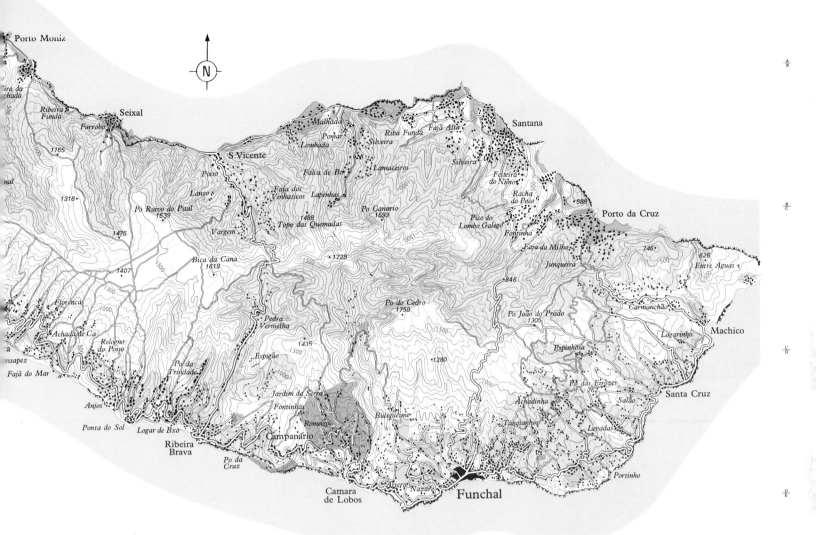

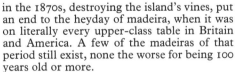

in the 1870s, destroying the island's vines, put an end to the heyday of madeira, when it was on literally every upper-class table in Britain and America. A few of the madeiras of that period still exist, none the worse for being 100 years old or more.

Today's madeira is known by the principal grape varieties used in its making. There are four, corresponding approximately to degrees of sweetness, though the sweetness is controlled not by the grape but by the amount of brandy and when it is added to the wine.

The sweetest of them all, and probably the best, is Malmsey; dark brown wine, very fragrant and rich, soft-textured and almost fatty, but with the tang of sharpness which all madeiras have. It is as good an after-dinner wine as any but excellent vintage port.

Bual madeira is lighter and slightly less sweet than Malmsey—but still distinctly a dessert wine. A good Bual is about the equivalent of a Bristol Milk-type sherry.

Verdelho is a shade less sweet than Bual; a peculiarly soft and sippable wine; the faint honey and distinct smoke of its flavour make it good either before or after meals. A light Verdelho is sold under the name Rainwater.

Sercial, the driest wine of Madeira, is grown on the upper vineyards and harvested last. The grape is none other than the Riesling of the Rhine. Like the Riesling in Germany it is a late ripener, not a big cropper, and gives uncommonly good wine. Sercial wine is light, fragrant, slightly sharp—it has all these things in common with Riesling, but with the madeira tang. It is more substantial than a fino sherry, but still a perfect aperitif.

Each of the shippers of madeira sells all of these wines, as brands at various price levels. Neither age nor a specific place name is normally mentioned on the label. Though it is possible that one day early 20th-century vintages will be offered on the market.

Funchal is the biggest wine-growing district, as well as the headquarters of the trade, where the shippers' 'lodges' are. Names which used to occur on labels and which may occasionally still be seen include Camara (or Cama) de Lobos and Campanário; both famous wine villages along the south coast.

Today the market for madeira has spread from America and Britain to Scandinavia, France and Germany. The French long ago discovered its unique value in cookery; its sharpness makes it the perfect wine in sauces. It is, after all, accustomed to heat.

Portugal

PORTUGAL is the place for wine romantics. Even more than Italy it is the country of groaning ox-carts, of dappled sunlight through arbours of vines, of treading the purple must, of maidens bearing pitchers, of songs handed down for centuries.

Fifteen per cent of the population lives by making or selling wine, and this despite the fact that a good third of the country, south of the Tagus (the Tejo), is almost wineless. In some places it must be more like 50%.

The climate of Portugal is ideal for grapes. The wine-growing northern half of the country has ample rain, except in the high Douro beyond the mountains, and a long, bright rather than blazing, summer; Atlantic characteristics which make it rather like a more southerly Bordeaux. The general standard, even of vinho de consumo, is as high as any country's, and if the best wines (apart from port) cannot compete with those of France or even Italy the run-of-the-mill produce is at least as good.

Portugal's best wine is port. It is treated in detail on pages 190–193. Besides the port area the government distinguishes two major table-wine areas and a handful of minor ones in rather the same way as the French Appellations Contrôlées. Indeed the French words have been seen on Portuguese bottles. Wine from these areas bottled in Portugal carry a government seal, *selo de origem*, as witness to their authenticity—a praiseworthy idea; but by no means all Portugal's best wines come from these areas, nor are all their wines very good.

The two biggest and three famous minor areas round Lisbon are mapped overleaf. While exports from the former—Minho and Dão—are booming, little is left of the smaller areas which used to stamp their wine with local character. The importance has shifted to the very good non-regional wines of a number of big firms, who may buy their wine for blending all over the country. The big vineyards which supply them are little known by name, and not distinguished with seals of origin. They are on the Tagus north of Lisbon, the Ribatejo; between the Tagus and the sea, centred round Torres Vedras and Alcobaça; Bairrada, between Coimbra and Oporto, Lafoes, adjoining the vinho verde country to the south; the upper Douro (famous only for port) and the country both north and south of it. A very large part of northern Portugal, in fact.

The most famous Portuguese table wine of all, Mateus rosé, does not come from a delimited area, but from Vila Real, on the fringes of both the port and the vinho verde country. The rare red Ferreirinha, probably Portugal's finest table wine, comes from the same area. Clearly it is the demarcation system, not the wine, which is at fault.

Among the merchants who market good wine from outside the official areas, known by brand names, as well as *selo de origem* wines, are Sogrape, Real Companhia Vinicola do Norte de Portugal, José Maria da Fonseca, Borges & Irmão, Arealva, J. C. Alves, J. F. Pinto Basto, João T. Barbosa. Often it is possible to deduce from the label where the wine comes from—but it is not sold as such; simply as the shipper's brand.

There are two wine regions south of the Tagus, one of real historical importance, the other of rising reputation.

Moscatel de Setúbal is the demarcated zone just south of Lisbon where one of the world's very best muscat dessert wines is made. It is fortified, though not as much as port, and the grape skins, which in muscats contain much of the flavouring elements, are steeped in it to intensify the scent. Unlike the equivalent muscats of the south of France, Setúbal improves with age. Ancient Setúbal can be exquisite.

Lagoa is quite different—a hot-country wine, profiting by the touristic development of the Algarve to improve its standards.

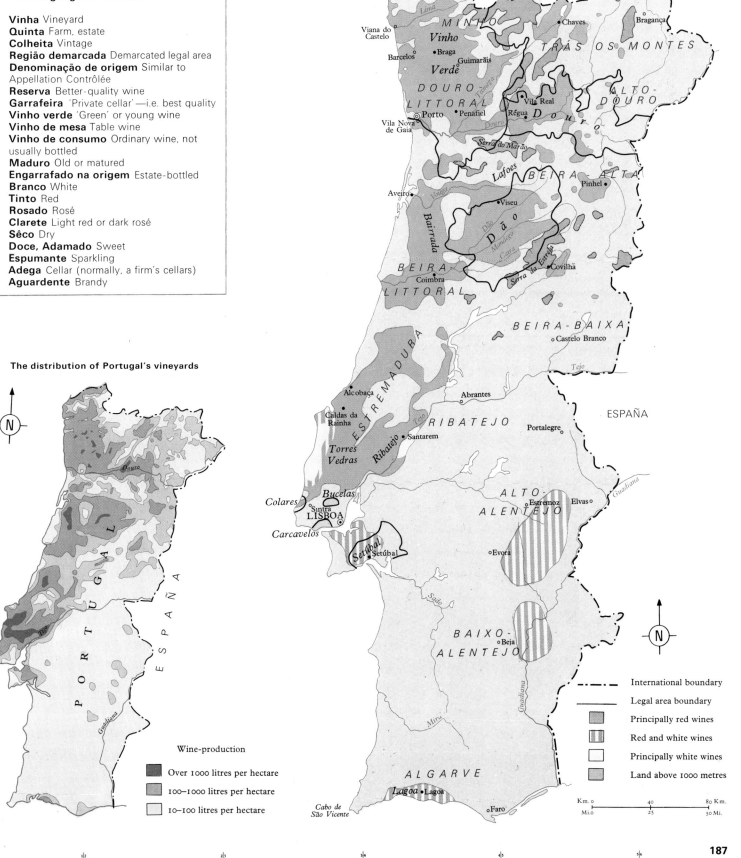

The Language of the Label

Vinha Vineyard
Quinta Farm, estate
Colheita Vintage
Região demarcada Demarcated legal area
Denominação de origem Similar to Appellation Contrôlée
Reserva Better-quality wine
Garrafeira 'Private cellar'—i.e. best quality
Vinho verde 'Green' or young wine
Vinho de mesa Table wine
Vinho de consumo Ordinary wine, not usually bottled
Maduro Old or matured
Engarrafado na origem Estate-bottled
Branco White
Tinto Red
Rosado Rosé
Clarete Light red or dark rosé
Sêco Dry
Doce, Adamado Sweet
Espumante Sparkling
Adega Cellar (normally, a firm's cellars)
Aguardente Brandy

The distribution of Portugal's vineyards

N

PORTUGAL
ESPAÑA
Douro
Guadiana

Wine-production

Over 1000 litres per hectare
100–1000 litres per hectare
10–100 litres per hectare

Valença
ESPAÑA
MINHO
Chaves
Bragança
Viana do Castelo
Vinho
TRÁS OS MONTES
Barcelos
Braga
Guimarãis
ALTO-DOURO
Verde
DOURO-LITTORAL
Vila Real
Porto
Penafiel
Régua
Douro
Vila Nova de Gaia
Serra do Marão
Lafões
BEIRA-ALTA
Pinhel
Aveiro
Viseu
Dão
Bairrada
Dão
Mondego
Serra da Estrela
Covilhã
BEIRA-LITTORAL
Coimbra
BEIRA-BAIXA
Castelo Branco
Tejo
ESTREMADURA
Alcobaça
Abrantes
ESPAÑA
Caldas da Rainha
RIBATEJO
Portalegre
Tejo
Santarem
Ribatejo
Torres Vedras
Guadiana
Colares
Bucelas
ALTO-ALENTEJO
Estremoz
Elvas
Sintra
LISBOA
Carcavelos
Évora
Setúbal
Setúbal
Sado
BAIXO-ALENTEJO
Beja
Guadiana
Mira
ALGARVE
Lagoa
Lagoa
Cabo de São Vicente
Faro

N

International boundary
Legal area boundary
Principally red wines
Red and white wines
Principally white wines
Land above 1000 metres

Km. 0   40   80 Km.
Mi. 0   25   50 Mi.

Lisbon

Above: vines trained over a little stream on wires are typical of the lush vinho verde country
Left: the village of Azenhas do Mar, north of Colares

Right and below: Colares deep red and Bucellas (from Bucelas) lively white are the only survivors of the Lisbon wine area. Many consider them Portugal's best red and white wines, but they are hard to find today.

IN KEEPING with Portugal's reputation as a maritime nation she brings vines as near as they ever get to the sea. At Colares, on the Atlantic coast, the vines grow on the beach in the sort of place where wind-beaten tamarisk and gorse are usually the only growing things.

The phylloxera cannot live in sand, so the vines are safe from him here. They creep low along the ground, their old limbs like driftwood bearing small bunches of intensely blue grapes. Low stone walls or plaited cane fences for shelter wander among them; one old vine, straggling here and there, may fill a whole little pen of its own, for instead of pruning the growers go in for the old Roman method of layering their vines—making them reroot their long branches in the sand where they will.

The small, dark, thick-skinned Ramisco is the Colares grape. Its wine is correspondingly black and tannic and needs as long to mature as claret needed a hundred years ago. It has always been esteemed Portugal's best red table wine, though little is made today, at least in the sandy soil where it is best, and even less is exported.

Carcavelos, another demarcated wine region, has been virtually swamped by Estoril. The remaining vineyards are in neighbouring villages. The wine they make is sweet and amber. During the 18th century there was a vogue for Carcavelos, and the early 20th saw an attempt to revive it, but there are more profitable investments today round Lisbon than vineyards.

Of Lisbon's local wines the one in best shape is probably Bucellas. The wine is pleasant, fresh, white and dry, but not necessarily much better than some of Portugal's branded white wines without a geographical description.

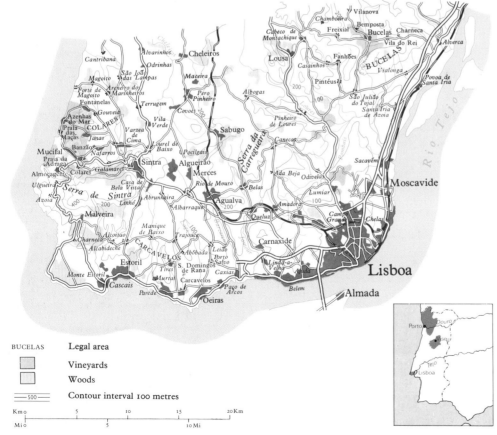

BUCELAS Legal area

Vineyards

Woods

— 500 — Contour interval 100 metres

Km 0   5   10   15   20 Km
Mi 0   5   10 Mi

Minho and Dão

Right: sharp and fizzy vinho verde comes in infinite variety. Good Dãos, the complete contrast, smooth and solid, are made by relatively few producers

PORTUGAL'S MOST distinctive and best contribution in the way of table wines is the speciality of her northern counties; their vinho verde. The name green wine describes its fresh, slightly under-ripe style, not its colour, which is red (three-quarters of it) or almost water-white.

Partly as a result of land shortage in the Minho, this most densely populated (though still utterly rural) part of the country, the vines are grown high up trees and on pergolas round the little fields. In late summer the sight of the grape-bearing garlands along every road gives almost pagan pleasure.

The grapes are picked early and fermented briefly—the object being wine with a low alcohol content and a decided tartness. Secondary fermentation is encouraged to convert the excess malic acid to lactic. The red wines tend to be cloudy, but both they and the whites (which foreigners prefer) have a scintillating little bubble about them which is marvellously refreshing. It is all too easy to gulp them like beer on a hot day.

Unfortunately, like sherry, they are usually sweetened for export, which hides their true freshness. They are best from the barrel in the spirited little taverns of Monção and Barcelos and Penafiel.

A superior sort of vinho verde is made from the white Alvarinho grape round Monção. It is bottled, and will even keep, developing a freesia-like scent but losing its bubbles. It is almost certainly Portugal's best white wine.

Basto and Amarante are considered the next best areas of the Minho for wine, followed by the more productive Braga and Penafiel. Lima makes a slightly stronger and deeper-coloured red wine than the others. But officially it is all vinho verde, and wines from the different regions are often blended together.

Dão is to Portugal what Rioja is to Spain. It does not have Rioja's tradition or range, or number of distinguished growers and merchants. But well-aged bottles suggest that given the right conditions—above all a demanding and discriminating public—the soil and the climate are right for fine wine.

Dão is granite hill country, where bare rocks show through the sandy soil. It is well inland, with a hotter and drier climate than down on the coast. Vineyards seem to have little part in the landscape, only cropping up here and there in clearings in the sweet-scented pine forests.

There are both red and white Dãos. While they are young the whites can be firm and fragrant, good value and attractive as everyday table wine. The red as it is usually sold—a blend from a big merchant perhaps four years old—is a clean, smooth and well-made wine, but hard and without attractive sweetness. On the other hand a Reserva from the same merchant 15 years old had developed a very fine scent like good Bordeaux and was gentle and interesting to drink. Such Reservas are not easy to find, and there are as yet no estate wines.

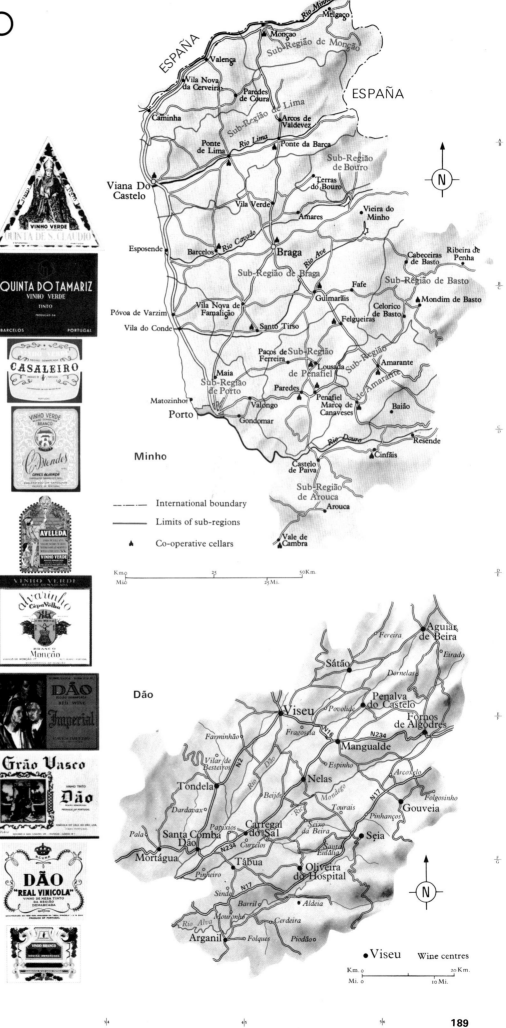

Minho

.... International boundary

———— Limits of sub-regions

▲ Co-operative cellars

Dão

● Viseu Wine centres

The Alto Douro

The little town of Pinhão is the centre of the best port-growing area. Its main street is on the left of the picture; the little tributary river Pinhão in the centre flows into the Douro in the background. In the foreground a terraced vineyard steps down typically steeply towards the town centre

——————	District boundary
—·—·—·—	Parish boundary
QTA. DA FOZ	Quinta
▢	Vineyards
▢	Woods
══500══	Contour interval 100 metres

OF ALL THE PLACES where men have planted vineyards the upper Douro is the most improbable. To begin with there was not even soil: only 60° slopes of slate and granite, flaking and unstable, baked in a 100° sun. It was a land of utter desolation.

The vine, however, is the one useful plant which is not quite deterred by these conditions. The Mediterranean-type climate of this region suits it. What was needed was simply the engineering feat of putting soil on the Douro slopes and keeping it there. Which meant building walls along the mountain-sides, thousands of them, like contour lines, to hold up patches of ground (one could hardly call it soil) where vines could be planted.

Once the ground was stabilized and rainwater no longer ran straight off, it began to form soil, and plants began to add organic matter. Now olives, oranges, cork oaks and pines flourish, and villages are surrounded with vegetable and flower gardens. But before this could happen anywhere men had to blast and chip away at the slate, piling chunks of it into terrace walls often 15 feet high. The old Douro terraces are like the earthworks of a titanic fortress more than 50 miles long.

The Douro reaches Portugal from Spain in a wilderness which is still inaccessible except by mule or canoe. It has carved a canyon 1,500 to 2,000 feet deep through the layered rock uplands of eastern Portugal. This is the port country. The 4,600-foot Serra do Marão to the west prevents the Atlantic rain-clouds of summer from reaching it.

Many of the original terraces dating from the 17th century survive in the mountains above Regua, in the original port-wine zone, given its first official limits (the first such limits ever given to any wine) in 1756. Today it remains the biggest producer, but the search for quality has led farther and farther up-river. The modern zone is 20 times the size it was in the 18th century, and all the best part is comparatively new. Below the tributary Corgo the wine is reckoned definitely inferior. The best vineyards of all today are those round Pinhão, including the tributary valleys of the Távora, Torto, Pinhão and Tua rivers.

Steps are the nightmare of workers in these

vineyards. Every grape must be carried off the hill on the back of a man. New vineyards today are contoured with dynamite and bulldozers as far as possible to eliminate steps and walls.

Vintage-time anywhere is the climax of the year, but on the Douro, perhaps because of the hardship of life, it is almost Dionysiac. There is an antique frenzy about the ritual, the songs, the music of drum and pipe, the long nights of treading by the light of hurricane lamps while the women and girls dance together.

The famous shipping firms have their own quintas up in the hills, where they go to supervise the vintage. They are rambling white houses, vine-arboured, tile-floored and cool in a world of dust and glare. Most of the famous quintas are shown on the map on these pages. Quinta names however rarely appear as wine names. Only three or four of the whole valley, of which by far the most famous is Quinta do Noval above Pinhão, sell their wine unblended. For the essence of port, as it is of champagne and sherry, is blending, and the main source of grapes and wine is not big shipper-owned estates but a multitude of small farmers.

Top left: workers carry the grapes out of the port vineyards in baskets on their shoulders
Lower left: new wide and old narrow terraces contrast at the corner of a hill
Above right: graceful *barcos rabelos* are still used for fishing on the Douro, but rarely now for carrying wine

Port/the Quality Factor

Factor	%
Low yield	21%
Altitude	21%
Nature of land	14%
Locality	13%
Training of vines	12%
Grape varieties	6%
Degree of slope	4%
Exposure	3%
Spacing of vines	2%
Type of soil	2%
Age of vines	1%
Shelter	1%

The port vineyards are graded into six classes. The quantity of wine they can sell as port is regulated by their standing. The factors by which they are judged are the same as in Burgundy, say, or Germany, but the emphasis is different. The diagram shows how here small production (as little as 600 litres per 1,000 vines) and the altitude of the vineyard (it should be below 1,500 feet) are considered of primary importance (brown) in the marking. Grape varieties are secondary factors (blue) and exposure (north or south) only tertiary (green)—though both those things would be vital in Burgundy

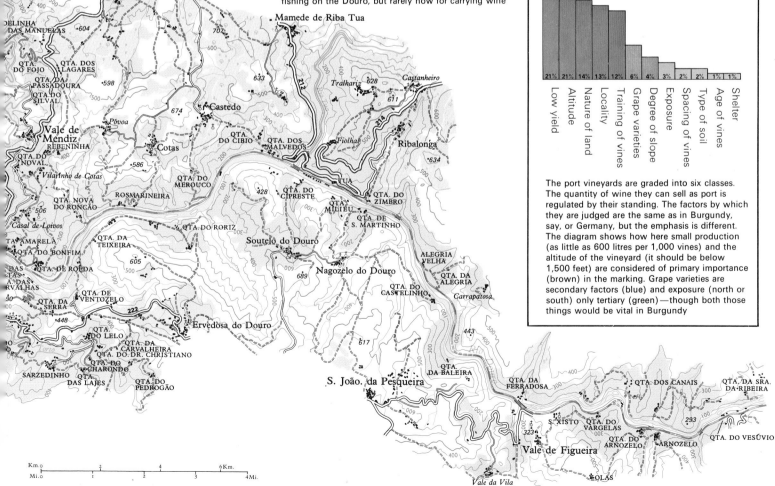

The Port Lodges

A trough made of great granite blocks, set up like a stage beneath the low roof of a farmer's outhouse, is the *lagar* where the grapes for port are trodden. There are girls treading with the men in this picture, taken in the remote village of Ribalonga; a revolutionary innovation in this superstitious country. Huge barrels like the one in the foreground are used for fermentation. The shipper who intends to buy the farmer's wine makes an inspection of every barrel before it is used, in case it is musty or vinegary and could spoil the wine

PORT is made by running off the partially fermented red wine into a barrel a quarter full of brandy, while it still contains at least half of its grape sugar. The brandy stops the fermentation so that the mixture is both strong and sweet.

The wine also needs the pigmentation of the grape skins to colour it, and their tannin to preserve it. In normal wines these are extracted during the course of fermentation. But since with port the fermentation is unnaturally short they have to be procured some other way—which traditionally in the Douro means by treading.

Treading is a means of macerating the grape skins in their juice so as to extract all their essences. The naked foot is the perfect instrument for this, being warm and doing no damage to the pips, which would make the juice bitter if they were crushed. A dozen men for a dozen hours (they work in four-hour shifts), rhythmically stamping thigh-deep in the mixture of juice and skins in a broad stone trough (a *lagar*) are the traditional means of giving port its colour, its grapiness, and its ability to last and improve for many years, instead of being a pale and uninteresting liquid.

A mechanical substitute for treading has now been introduced on a large scale. It consists of a closed fermenting vat in which the carbon dioxide pressure makes the juice circulate up a pipe from the bottom to the top, where it pours over the 'cap' of floating skins. In several days this continuous churning has the same effect as the more expensive man-hours in the *lagar*. The majority of port is now made in this modern way. But there are still shippers who feel that treading is best, and still many quintas where it goes on, particularly in the best area, above the Corgo (the area mapped

on the previous pages).

Port which is kept up the Douro is rare. It is said to take on a character known as 'the Douro burn'—a faintly roasted flavour. Virtually all port is taken down the river soon after it is made, to complete its processing in the port suburb of Oporto, Vila Nova de Gaia.

The journey down-river used to be made in high-prowed sailing boats like Viking longships, which had to be controlled through the rapids by eight men working long sweeps in the bows. Now the port is taken by truck.

The shippers' warehouses in Vila Nova de Gaia are known as lodges. They have much in common with the sherry bodegas. In the lodges the port is kept in pipes, 115-gallon barrels, for anything from two to 50 years.

Perhaps three years out of ten conditions are near perfect for port-making. The wine of these years needs no blending; nothing can be done to improve it except wait. It is bottled at two years just like claret, and labelled simply with its shipper's name and the date. This is vintage port, and there is never enough of it. Eventually, perhaps after 20 years, it will have a fatness and fragrance, richness and delicacy which is incomparable.

A great vintage port is incontestably among the world's very best wines. Other port, from near vintage standard to merely moderate, goes through a blending process, to emerge as an unvarying branded wine of a given character. This wine, aged in wood, matures much faster than vintage port and loses some of its sugar in the process. A very old wood port is comparatively pale and dry, but particularly smooth. This sort of wine is called Tawny from its colour. Expensive tawnies cost as much as vintage port and many people prefer their

mellowness and moderated sweetness to the full, fat and flowery flavour which a good vintage port keeps.

Run-of-the-mill wood ports are not kept for nearly so long, nor would such age find any great qualities in them to reveal. They taste best while they are still fruity with youth, and often fiery, too, with perhaps five years as the average age of a blend. France is the great market for these wines. They used to be the staple winter drink in British pubs, where they were kept in a barrel in the bar.

Vintage port has disadvantages. It needs keeping for a very long time. And it needs handling with great care. As the making of the wine does not reach its end until after bottling, the sediment forms a 'crust' on the side of the bottle; a thin, delicate, dirty-looking veil. If the bottle is moved, other than very gingerly, the crust will break and mix with the wine, so that it has to be filtered out again. In any case the wine must be decanted from its bottle before it is served. Which is enough to discourage many people from buying it.

As a compromise between vintage and 'wood' port, shippers now also ship Late-bottled Vintage wines—port from good years (though not always the very best) which is kept unblended but in barrel instead of being bottled at two years. After eight years or so it has rid itself of its crust and matured as far as it would in twice as long in bottle. In many ways it is the modern man's vintage port, being speeded up and cleaned up in this way. Yet there are those who argue that vintage port is not a modern man's drink, and that if you are going to indulge in an old-fashioned pastime you might as well do it properly. Certainly the old method makes the one port which deserves to be called great wine.

The port lodges of Vila Nova de Gaia

1 Fonseca
2 Graham
3 Diez Hermanos
4 Ferreira
5 Companhia Velha
6 Delaforce
7 Nie Poort
8 Martinez Gassiot
9 Cockburn
10 Barros
11 Junta Nacional dos Vinhos
12 Dow
13 Burmester
14 Mackenzie
15 Ramos Pinto
16 Sandeman
17 Hunt Roope
18 Rozés
19 Kopke
20 Wiese & Krohn
21 Gonzalez Byass
22 Rainha Santa
23 Croft
24 Taylor
25 Offley Forrester
26 Warre
27 Noval
28 Borges
29 Calem

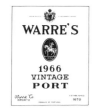

Above: the cooperage where barrels are made and repaired is a vital part of a port lodge; most port is kept in wood until it is ready to drink; from three to as many as 50 years. Good oak is the only material which allows its steady development

Left: traditionally, vintage port bottles had no labels; a stencilled name in white paint, more durable than paper, is still used by one shipper, Quinta do Noval. Many of the best names in the port trade are British; a reminder that it was the British taste for sweet wine that built up the industry in the 18th century. Today France is the biggest customer

The Language of the Label

Vintage The wine of a single exceptional year bottled early for laying down
Late-bottled vintage Similar wine bottled when mature, lighter than vintage
Crusted Good but not vintage port bottled early for laying down
Vintage character Similar to crusted
Tawny Port kept many years in wood until it fades to a tawny colour; smooth and lighter than any of the foregoing
Ruby Port aged in wood comparatively briefly; darker and rougher
White port From white grapes; often much drier than red and sold as an aperitif

Switzerland-Valais and Vaud

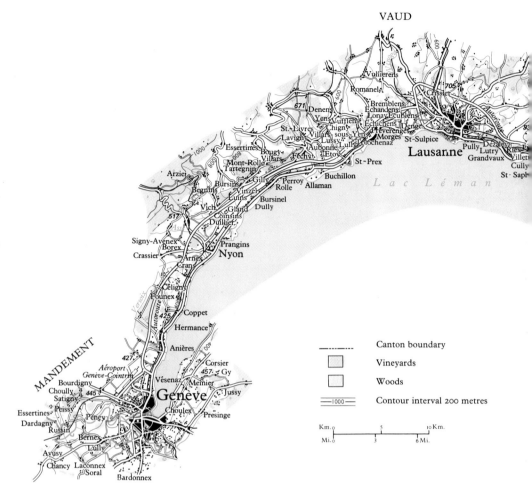

THE STEEP sides of the valley which the young river Rhône has carved through the Alps are followed by gentler slopes where it broadens into Lake Geneva. An almost continuous band of vines hugs the river's sunny north bank all the way.

In the higher valley peculiarly Alpine conditions, dry and sunny, and by the lake the mildness brought about by a great body of water both favour the vine in different ways. The Valais and the Vaud, as the two regions are called, are Switzerland's biggest and best vineyards. Including the production of Geneva's vineyards the Rhône valley gives more than three-quarters of the national total.

Four-fifths of this is white wine. The proportion used to be even higher, but Swiss growers have recently planted the Pinot Noir on a large scale and the Gamay of Beaujolais on an even larger.

The great grape of both the Valais and the Vaud is the white Chasselas. In the Valais it is called Fendant, in the Vaud Dorin. It is not reckoned a fine-wine grape in France, but the best of it in Switzerland is extremely pleasant.

In the Valais the centre of Fendant-growing is Sion and the villages just to the west, Conthey, Vétroz and Ardon. There is little rain (Sierre is the driest place in Switzerland) and endless sun. If the vines escape spring frosts they make a powerful wine with as much as 13% alcohol. Irrigation, formerly done by wooden channels called *bisses* coming breakneck down the mountain-side, is essential.

The 50-acre Domaine du Mont d'Or has the best site of all: a 600-foot southern slope protected at the foot by an outlying hill. The Sylvaner ('Johannisberg') excels itself here, shrivelling on the vine to make splendid rich wines. Even Chasselas wine puts on flesh and stiffens its sinews. Notes on the vines of the Valais and their wines will be found in the Glossary on page 196.

The best red wine of the Valais is known as Dôle. In the Vaud, Dôle-type wine is called Salvagnin. Chablais, the district between Valais and Vaud, between Martigny and Montreux, though in the canton of Vaud, is transitional in character. Aigle and Yvorne and Bex are its best-known villages. Their white wine is strong, but drier and less full than Fendant. With each step westwards the Chasselas makes more delicate wine.

The central part of the Vaud between Montreux and Lausanne is confusingly called Lavaux. Switzerland's most appealing Chasselas wines, dry, gentle and fruity, are grown in the villages of Lutry, Villette, Epesses, St-Saphorin, Chardonne and Vevey and sold as Dorin with the village name. Dézaley and Dézaley-Marsens are the exceptions; the best wines of the lake, lively and long, with their own appellations.

After Lausanne, La Côte has lighter and less distinguished wines; 40% of the Vaud total. The best is at Féchy. Nyon, the commercial centre, sees more and more light Gamay reds. The same is true of the Geneva vineyards: Gamay is the success story. Mandement Chasselas, known as Perlan, is very dry and pallid: a far cry from the Fendant of Sion.

The castle of Aigle stands out in the Rhône valley where it begins to broaden out to Lake Geneva. The centre and south-facing slopes of the valley are thickly planted with vines; where it faces north they are bare

194

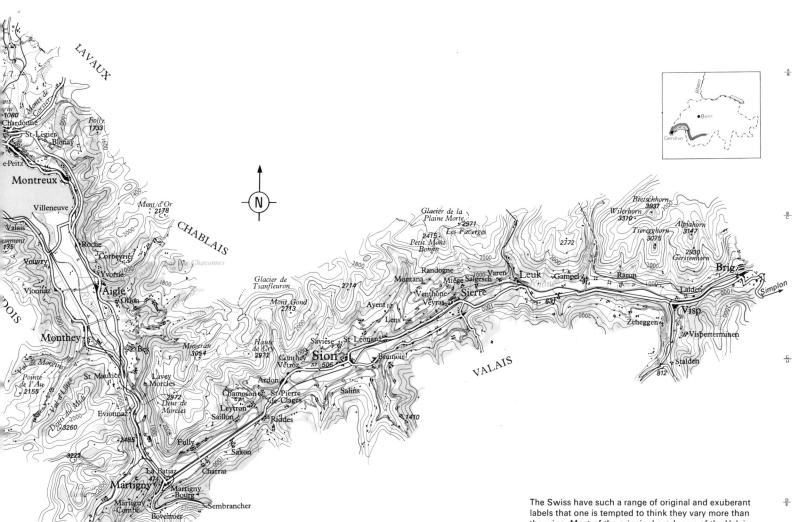

The Swiss have such a range of original and exuberant labels that one is tempted to think they vary more than the wine. Most of the principal producers of the Valais and the Vaud are represented in the selection here

Switzerland

SWITZERLAND is an intensely wine-conscious, insatiably wine-importing country as well as an important producer. She comes between France, the natural land of wine, and Germany, the land where wine is an extra, worth every bit of effort it demands. The Swiss are loyal to their own local wines, without pretending that better things do not happen in France. They are the world's biggest importers of burgundy; Beaujolais is almost their national drink.

The Swiss wine industry is in evolution, as rising costs make it a problem to many growers whether or not to persevere. The inevitable result is that poor vineyards are abandoned as not paying their way. Studies are made as to how to run the remainder, the better ones, more profitably and with less labour—which often means a change to better varieties of grapes, and more modern ways of training them.

The Swiss are efficient, if sometimes unromantic, wine-makers. By scrupulous care of their vines, using fertilizers and irrigation, they achieve yields twice as high as those in French appellation areas. They take sugaring for granted: there are no German-style indications of natural unsugared wine. By such big quantities, assisted by sugar when necessary, they make grape-growing pay in difficult terrain with a high standard of living.

At the same time the long near-monopoly of white wine in Switzerland has been broken. Red wine is in fashion, a development of the last 20 years. There has been an enormous increase in the planting of the Burgundian varieties of red grapes, Pinot Noir and Gamay, in the most important areas: Vaud, Valais and Geneva. The Ticino has concentrated on the Merlot, introduced from Bordeaux. It remains to be seen whether the fashion comes soon enough to save the dwindling vineyards of German Switzerland, which have long specialized in Blauburgunder or Pinot Noir, without making of it any more than a decent light wine.

Almost every canton in Switzerland makes a little wine. Two areas apart from the Rhône valley and Lake Geneva have important industries: the Ticino and Neuchâtel.

Italian Switzerland, the Ticino, has not long been an exporter of wine. The local tradition is a peasant one, and only 50 years ago hardship was still sending emigrants to America. (The famous Italian Swiss Colony vineyards near Santa Rosa in California are one result.) The typical local red wine, called Nostrano, is no great matter. But the Merlot is growing well there, as it does in north-east Italy and northern Jugoslavia, making a strongish but rather soft red wine. Better Ticino Merlots, attaining 12% alcohol, now use the name Viti to distinguish themselves from the rest.

Neuchâtel is equally famous for its red wine and its white—though the white is three-quarters of the crop. Without doubt the simplicity of the whole area calling its wine by the famous name of its capital has been a help. The north shore of the lake is temperate and well sheltered by the Jura. The Pinot Noir grows well (there is little or no Gamay here), giving a pale and light wine but with character and definition. The village of Cortaillod, south of Neuchâtel, is said to make the best.

White Neuchâtel is made from the Chasselas, like Fendant and Dorin wines from Valais and Vaud. It is lighter than either and encouraged to fizz faintly by being bottled *sur lie*—without being separated from its yeasty sediment. In some cases the process is carried further to making fully sparkling wines of real quality.

Lake Bienne (the Bieler See) just to the north-east has similar wines which fetch high prices in the cantonal capital of Bern.

The wines of other cantons do not travel much. The Bundner Herrschaft, a little district on the borders of Austria and Liechtenstein which has the distinction of being the

Swiss wines are known by regional names relating to grape varieties and qualities as well as geographical origins. The following names occur on their labels:

Amigne: a local Valais white grape giving heavy, tasty, normally dry, wine.
Arvine or **Petite Arvine:** another similar; if anything, better.
Blauburgunder: Pinot Noir from a German-speaking canton.
Klevner: the same.
Dôle: red Valais wine of Pinot Noir or Gamay or both, of tested quality.
Dorin: white Vaud wine of Chasselas, the equivalent of Fendant from the Valais.
Ermitage: white Marsanne vines from the French Rhône grown in the Valais: rich concentrated heavy wine, usually dry.

Fendant: White Valais wine of Chasselas; Switzerland's most famous.
Gamay: the Beaujolais grape, largely grown around Geneva and in La Côte.
Goron: red Valais wine; Dôle that failed the test.
Humagne: rare red or white Valais wine of rustic character.
Johannisberg: Sylvaner from the Valais.
Malvoisie: heavy white Pinot Gris from the Valais; often made sweet from dried ('*flétri*') grapes.
Merlot: red Bordeaux grape grown for the best Ticino wine.
Nostrano: ordinary Ticino wine from a variety of French and Italian grapes.
Oeil de Perdrix: term used for light rosé from Pinot Noir, particularly in Neuchâtel and Geneva.

Perlan: white Geneva (or Mandement) wine from Chasselas.
Premier Cru: any wine from the maker's own domaine.
Rèze: rare grape traditionally used for 'glacier' wine.
Riesling-Sylvaner: Müller-Thurgau wine, common in eastern Switzerland.
Salvagnin: red Vaud wine of tested quality; the equivalent of Dôle from the Valais.
Schafizer or Twanner: the light but expensive wine of Lake Bienne in the canton of Bern, red or white.
Viti: red Merlot wine of a certain standard from Ticino.
Any Swiss wine which is not completely dry must by law carry the words 'légèrement doux' or 'avec sucre residuel'.

first wine region of the infant Rhine, grows Blauburgunder (or Klevner) almost exclusively; the best are dear and are said to be excellent, benefiting from the warm autumn wind, the *foehn*. The Herrschaft also grows the otherwise-unknown Completer, which is picked in November to give a sort of Beerenauslese . . . though the early-ripening Müller-Thurgau is the commonest white grape in the German-speaking cantons.

Zurich, Schaffhausen, St Gallen, Basel, even Luzern maintain diminutive wine industries based predominantly on the Blauburgunder. All agree that their wine is expensive, and some that it has charm and delicacy. Certainly the evidence disappears promptly enough: none is available for export—even as far as Geneva.

Right: red and white wine labels from Neuchâtel, Merlot from Ticino and Klevner (or Pinot Noir) from north-east Switzerland. The red and white wines of Neuchâtel are both light; the white, which has a tendency to bubbles, is often made fully sparkling. The city of Neuchâtel (first label) is a top grower
Left: Europe's highest vineyards are 3,700 feet up at Visperterminen, high above the railway which takes skiers and climbers to Zermatt

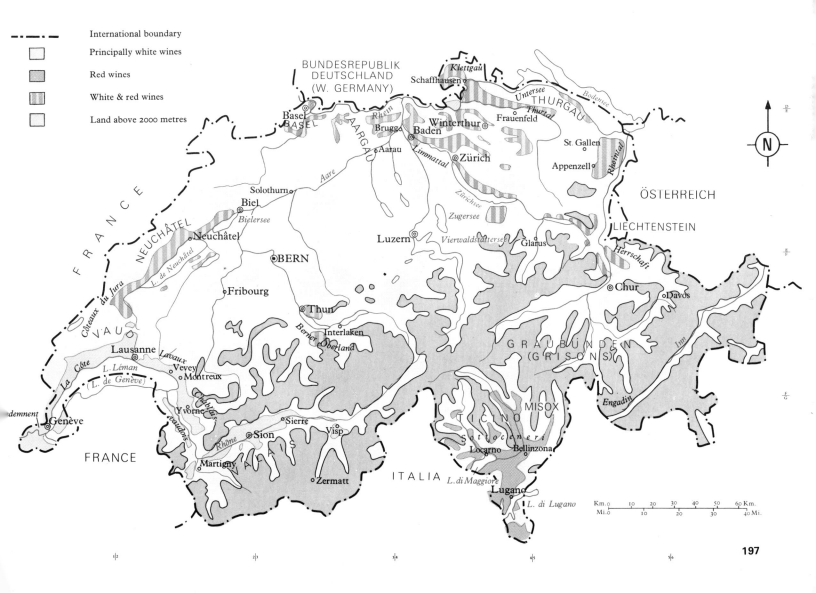

International boundary

Principally white wines

Red wines

White & red wines

Land above 2000 metres

Austria

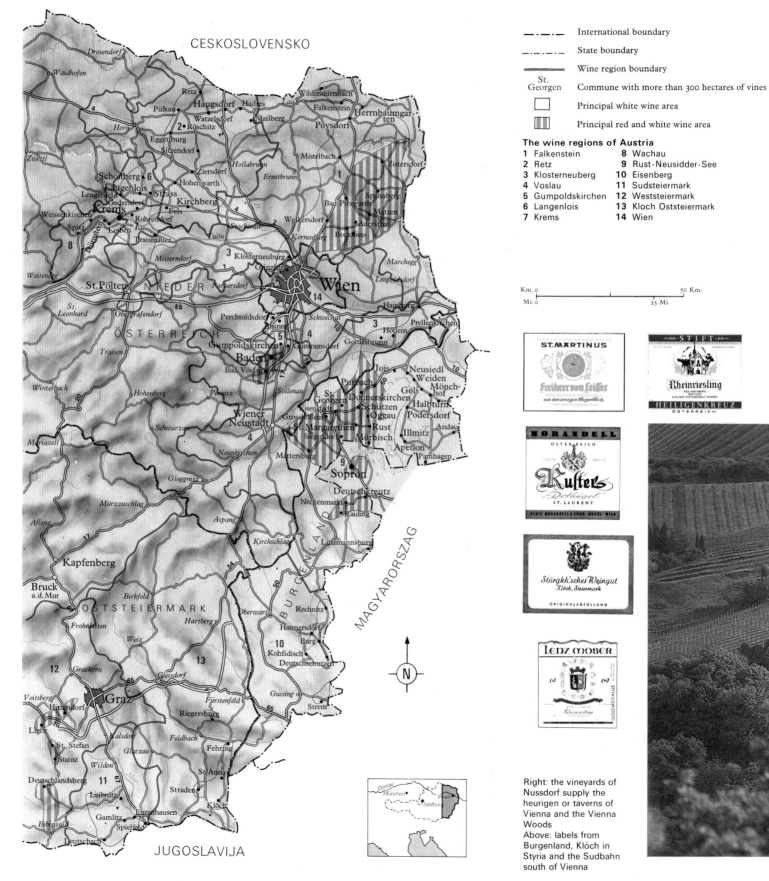

CESKOSLOVENSKO

Drosendorf

Waidhofen

Retz
Haugsdorf
Pulkau
Watzelsdorf
Hadres
Mailberg
Wildendürnbach
Falkenstein
Herrnbaumgar-
ten
Poysdorf

Horn

Zwettl

Eggenburg
Sitzendorf
Röschitz
2
Hohenwarth
Hollabrunn
Mistelbach
Ernstbrunn
1
Zistersdorf

Schönberg
Langenlois **6**
Ziersdorf
Strass
Kirchberg
Spinnberg
Matzen
Bad Pirawarth

Lengenfeld
Gedersdorf
Krems
Fels
Rohrendorf
Stockerau
Wolkersdorf
Auersthal
Bockfliess

Weissenkirchen
Spitz
Loiben
Traismauer
Tulln
Korneuburg

8
Klosterneuburg
Grinzing
Marchegg

Weitenegg
Mitterndorf
3
Leopoldsdorf

St.Pölten
NIEDER
Burgersdorf
Wien
14
Hainburg

St.
Leonhard
Obergrafendorf
Perchtoldsdorf
Schwechat
3
Prellenkirchen

ÖSTERREICH
E5
Brunn
5
4
10
Höflein

Traisen
Gumpoldskirchen
Guntramsdorf
Gottlesbrunn
10

Winterbach
Baden
Bad Vöslau
Jois
Neusiedl
Weiden
Mönch-
hof

Hohenberg
Pernitz
Sollenau
Purbach
Gols
Halbturn
10

Mariazell
Schwarzau
St.
Georgen
Donnerskirchen
Schützen
Oggau
Podersdorf

Wiener
Neustadt
Eisenstadt
Grosshöflein
Rust
Illmitz
Andau

Neunkirchen
St.Margarethen
Siegendorf
Mörbisch
Apetlon
Pamhagen

4
Mattersburg
9
Sopron

Gloggnitz
Deutschkreutz

Mürzzuschlag
Neckenmarkt
Raiding

Aflenz
Aspang
Kirchschlag
Lutzmannsburg

Kapfenberg
17
BURGENLAND

Bruck
a.d.Mur
Birkfeld
54

OSTSTEIERMARK
Oberwart
Rechnitz

Frohnleiten
Hartberg
Hannersdorf

Weiz
50
Burg
10
Kohfidisch

12
13
Gratkorn
Gleisdorf
Deutschschützen

Voitsberg
Graz
Fürstenfeld
Gussing
Strem

Lhgis
Hitzendorf
Kalsdorf
Riegersburg
65

70
St.Stefan
Glatzau
Feldbach
Fehring

Stainz
Wildon
St.Anna

Deutschlandsberg
11
Straden
Klöch
Leibnitz

Eibiswald
Gamlitz
Ehrenhausen
Spielfeld

Deutschach

JUGOSLAVIJA

MAGYARORSZAG

Legend:

— · · — International boundary

— · — State boundary

—— Wine region boundary

St.
Georgen   Commune with more than 300 hectares of vines

☐ Principal white wine area

▥ Principal red and white wine area

The wine regions of Austria

1	Falkenstein	8	Wachau
2	Retz	9	Rust-Neusidder-See
3	Klosterneuberg	10	Eisenberg
4	Voslau	11	Sudsteiermark
5	Gumpoldskirchen	12	Weststeiermark
6	Langenlois	13	Kloch Oststeiermark
7	Krems	14	Wien

Km. 0 ———————— 50 Km.
Mi. 0 ———————— 25 Mi.

N

Right: the vineyards of
Nussdorf supply the
heurigen or taverns of
Vienna and the Vienna
Woods
Above: labels from
Burgenland, Klöch in
Styria and the Sudbahn
south of Vienna

AUSTRIA has such a famous and flourishing tradition of making light wine for local consumption that the world has been misled into thinking that that is all she does. Granted that her 'open' wines are as good as any on earth, they are almost impossible to bottle and export with their character intact. Ten years ago Austria had virtually no wine exports, and her small proportion of top-quality wines went ignored by the world along with the rest.

In the last ten years her exports have multiplied fifteenfold. New technology has revived old traditions all over Austria. Today she offers under still-unfamiliar names some of Europe's most exciting white wines.

New wine laws, passed in 1973, have been a big factor. Austria now has a system of Qualitätswein, Kabinetts and the rest parallel to the German. The chief difference is that all German quality wines are tested for their 'prüfungsnummer', while in Austria only those with the 'Austrian Wine Seal' are officially approved—also that standards of ripeness, in this southern climate, are higher: an Austrian Spätlese has the (potential) alcohol of a German Auslese.

Red wine is only of local significance. All Austria's best wine, like Germany's, is white. Her central position among Europe's northern and eastern vineyards shows in the character of the wine she makes. There is something of the freshness of the Rhine in it—but more of the fieriness and high flavour of the Danube.

Only eastern Austria makes wine. The vineyards are concentrated north and east of Vienna. Styria (Steiermark) in the south, bordering on Jugoslavia's principal vineyard region, Slovenia, is of minor importance, though the Traminers of Klöch, grown on volcanic soil, are good. The regions which are flourishing, and of which we are likely to hear more, are the Wachau and Vienna with its Südbahn (both mapped in detail overleaf), Burgenland round the Neusiedler See south-east of the capital, and the Weinviertel in the north-east.

Burgenland lies on the Hungarian border—indeed the Hungarian wine district of Sopron is carved out of it. Like Hungary, it specializes in sweet wines. The country is flat and sandy round the lake (an extraordinary pool, 20 miles long and only four feet deep) and mists envelope it through its long warm autumns, making the noble rot a regular occurrence.

The most historically famous wine of Burgenland comes from Rust. Ruster Ausbruch (the local term for a wine between a Beeren- and a Trockenbeerenauslese) was formerly compared with Tokay. Today vineyards on both sides of the lake produce luscious wines of real quality. The Esterhazy estate at Eisenstadt wins gold medals regularly, and Lenz Moser at Apetlon (among others) makes superb Ausleses.

The grapes include Riesling, Müller-Thurgau, Muskat-Ottonel (one of the many varieties of this ubiquitous grape), Bouvier, Ruländer and Traminer. Where the name Riesling is used alone it means the inferior Italian Riesling; real Riesling is always called Rheinriesling.

The red wines, made of Pinot Noir (Blauburgunder), Blaufränkisch, St-Laurent and Portugieser, are not up to the standard of the whites.

In contrast to those of Burgenland the wines of the Weinviertel (the name means 'wine quarter') are in the main light and dry. The great grape here is Austria's favourite, the Grüner Veltliner. Veltliner wine when it is well-made and young is marvellously fresh and fruity, with plenty of acidity and an almost spicy flavour. To compare it with Rhine Riesling is like comparing a wild flower with a finely bred garden variety in which scent and colour and size and form have been studied and improved for many years.

There are times, when Grüner Veltliner wine is drawn straight from the barrel into a tumbler, frothing and gleaming a piercing greeny gold, when it seems like the quintessence of all that a wine should be. Drink it then, with a sandwich on the terrace. It will never taste like that under any other conditions; certainly not when it has been bottled.

In the past one reason for the disappointing quality of some Austrian wines shipped abroad was that they did not come from Austria at all. Austria used to be free and easy about labelling, both of her own and other countries' products. Unfortunately, the practice of using her name on the labels of wine from Eastern Europe and Italy helped to obscure the emerging quality of some of the wine she really makes.

Monasteries still produce many of Austria's best wines.
Above: Baroque angels embellish the vineyards of Stift Heiligenkreuz at Gumpoldskirchen
Right: the monastery of Gottweig has vineyards by the Danube opposite Krems

Vienna

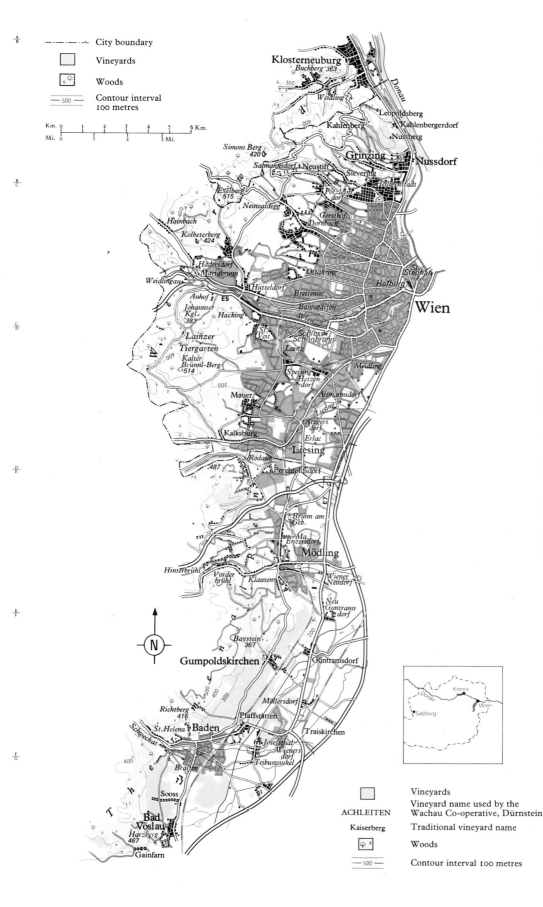

Klosterneuburg
Buchberg *363*

Weidling

300

Leopoldsberg
Kahlenberg
Kahlenbergerdorf
Nussberg

Simons Berg
420

Salmannsdorf Neustift
Sievering
Grinzing
Nussdorf

Exelberg
515

Neuwaldegg
*Pötzleins-
dorf*
Heiligenstadt

Hainbach

Gersthof
Dornbach

Kolbeterberg
424

Hadersdorf
Mariabrunn

Ottakring

Stephan
Hofburg

Weidlingau

Hütteldorf
Breitensee

E5

Auhof

Baumgarten

Wien

Wien

*Johannser
Kgl.*
383
Hacking

Veit
*Schloss
Schönbrunn*
Lainz

*Lainzer
Tiergarten*

Meidling

*Kalter
Brünnl-Berg*
514

300

Speising
*Hetzen-
dorf*

Mauer

Altmannsdorf

Liesing

*Atzers-
dorf*
Erlac

Kalksburg

Liesing

Rodaun

487

Perchtoldsdorf

*Brunn am
Geb.*

*Ma.
Enzersdorf*

Mödling

Hinterbrühl
*Vorder
brühl*
Klausen
*Wiener
Neudorf*

*Neu
Guntrams
dorf*

200

Baystein
367

N

Gumpoldskirchen
Guntramsdorf

Müllersdorf

Richtberg
416
Pfaffstätten

St.Helena **Baden**
Traiskirchen

400

Josefsthal
*Wieners
dorf*
Tribuswinkel

Schwechat

Braiten

Sooss

**Bad
Vöslau**

Harzberg
467

Gainfarn

Salzburg · Donau · Krems · Wien

Tiefental
Schildhütten

500   600

Weitenberg
Achleiten
511   Achleiten

Grubbach

ACHLEITEN

Seiberer

Rührs

Weissenkirchen

Ritzingbach

Ritzling

St.Lorenzen

200

Joching

Donau

THERE IS no capital city which is so identified
with wine as Vienna. New wine seems to be its
life-blood. Vineyards hold their ground within
the heart of the residential districts and surge
up the side of the surrounding hills into the
Vienna woods. North, east and south, where
the line of hills circles and protects the city,
there are vines. To the south they continue
along the Südbahn—the southern railway—
flanking the last crinkle of the Alpine foot-hills
facing the Hungarian plain.

Most of their wine is drunk as Heurige, in
Heurigen—for this untranslatable word means
both the new wine and the tavern where it is
drunk. Every vintner seems to be a tavern-
keeper as well, and chalks up on a board the
wines he has and the (very low) prices he wants
for them, by jug or litre bottle, label-less, to be
drunk on the spot or carried away. When
Heurige is good it is sensational; spirited,
sprightly stuff which goes straight to your head.
Most of it is Veltliner or Müller-Thurgau,
some is Riesling, some is Traminer. The best
of the new wines are not too dry.

Viennese connoisseurs know every grower in
Neustift, Grinzing, Sievering, Nussdorf and
Kahlenberg, the wine-villages of Vienna. The
atmosphere varies in their leafy taverns from
idyllic to hilarious. In most of them Beet-
hoven wrote at least a concerto. The region is
dominated by the splendid monastic cellars and
wine-school at Klosterneuburg.

The Südbahn wines are better known to the
outside world. Gumpoldskirchen, above all, for
its fine late-gathered wines made from the
lively Zierfändler, the heavier Rotgipfler or the
soft Ruländer, and Baden and Bad Voslau for
their reds. The red wine is dark, dry and
pleasant, appetizing and heady without having
particular character. Some of the best wines of
the area, including fine Rheinrieslings, come
from the Heiligenstift monastery at Thallern,
whose famous 'ried' of Wiege overlooks Gumpoldskirchen from the hill.

The Wachau

Dürnstein in the Wachau, from a 19th-century drawing by Sir David Wilkie. The castle on the crag, where Richard Coeur de Lion was imprisoned, is a total ruin today; that by the church on the Danube is a first-class hotel called after the captive king

Above: this is almost the only part of Austria with vineyard names known abroad. The co-operative (top) is the biggest bottler

THE WACHAU is Austria's best-known wine area. It lies only 40 miles west of Vienna, at a point where the Danube broaches a range of 1,600-foot hills. For a short stretch the craggy north bank of the river, as steep as some of the Mosel slopes, is patchworked with vines on ledges and outcrops, along narrow paths up from the river to the crowning woods.

There are patches of deep soil and others where a mere scratching finds rock, patches with daylong sunlight and others which always seem to be in shade. There is no grand sweep of vines here; no big estates and no unique vine variety. The Wachau is a pattern of small growers with mixed vineyards—who make good wine.

The principal export from the Wachau is the dry wine known as Schluck, made from a variety of grapes. Much of it also comes from the Kamp valley, an important vineyard area running south from Langenlois to Krems on strange soft 'loess'; half soil, half rock. The real character of the region, though, is better seen in its Grüner Veltliner—often a marvellously high-spirited and fiery, almost peppery, performance. Best of all, though rarer, is the Rhine Riesling. In the long, dry autumns of the Wachau it can make great wine.

The whole area is overshadowed by its efficient growers' co-operative. A thousand growers belong to it. It has even rearranged the names of the vineyards to simplify the marketing of its wines. (The map shows the names it uses for the different 'Rieds', or sections of the hills.)

The co-operative is at Dürnstein, the scenic climax of the valley. A very good hotel by the river is named after Richard the Lionheart, who was imprisoned here. The baroque steeple, the ruined castle and the tilting vineyards of Dürnstein are irresistibly pretty and suggestive.

Near by, to the east of the Wachau, beyond Krems (and off the map), the hills slant away from the Danube to the north-east, are lower and become sandy. Just round this corner is the village of Rohrendorf, where Austria's most famous grower, Lenz Moser, has his cellars.

Lenz Moser is the originator of a method of training vines on wires at twice the usual height which has been adopted by many progressive growers all over the world. He achieves higher yields, better quality and lower labour costs, he says, with his 'high culture' system. Certainly his own wines, made from the produce of his vineyards in several parts of Austria, are a good advertisement for it.

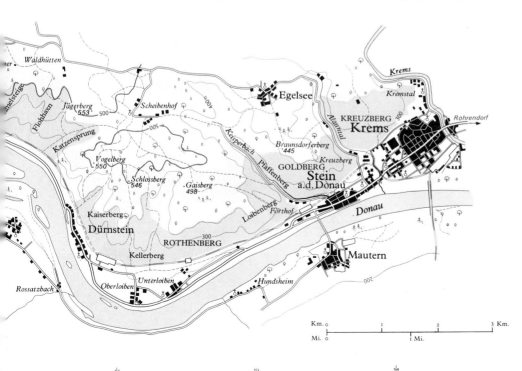

The Language of the Label

Many of the words that used to appear on German labels before the new wine law are still seen on Austrian ones, including
Naturwein Wine without added sugar
Reinsortig Only this particular type
Originalabfüllung Estate-bottled
Eigenbaugewächs From the maker's own vineyard
Weingarten, Weingut Wine estate
Ried Vineyard (as in French clos)

Hungary

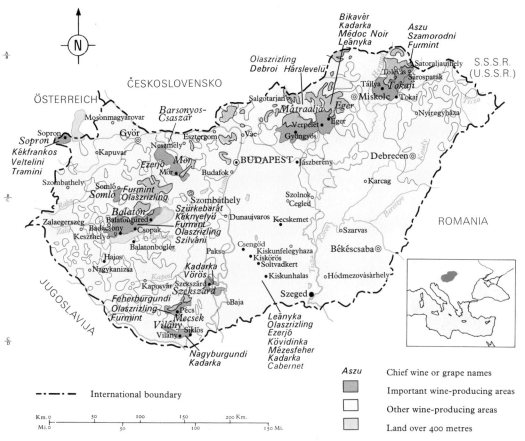

ČESKOSLOVENSKO

ÖSTERREICH

S.S.S.R.
(U.S.S.R.)

ROMANIA

JUGOSLAVIJA

Bikavér
Kadarka
Médoc Noir
Leányka

Aszu
Szamorodni
Furmint

Olaszrizling
Debroi Hárslevelü

Sopron
Kékfrankos
Veltelini
Tramini

Barsonyos-
Császár

Mátraalja   Eger

Ezerjó   Mór

Somló
Furmint   Olaszrizling
Balaton
Szürkebarát
Kéknyelyü
Furmint
Olaszrizling
Szilváni

Kadarka
Vörös
Szekszárd

Feherburgundi
Olaszrizling
Furmint
Vilány
Mecsek

Nagyburgundi
Kadarka

Leányka
Olaszrizling
Ezerjó
Kövidinka
Mézesfeher
Kadarka
Cabernet

– · – · – International boundary

Km. 0   50   100   150   200 Km.
Mi. 0   50   100   150 Mi.

Aszu — Chief wine or grape names
☐ Important wine-producing areas
☐ Other wine-producing areas
☐ Land over 400 metres

HARDLY ANY country has a national character so pronounced in its wine—and food—as Hungary. The characteristic Hungarian wine is white—or rather warmly gold. It smells more of a pâtisserie than a greengrocer, if one can so distinguish between ripe yeasty smells and the green ones of fresh fruit. It tastes, if it is a good one, distinctly sweet, but full of fire and even a shade fierce. It is not dessert wine; far from it. It is wine for meals cooked with more spice and pepper and fat than a light wine could stand.

Like Germany, Hungary treasures her sweet wines most. Tokay (opposite page) is her pride and joy. But most of the country makes wine and there are dry ones and good reds as well.

On the map the chief wine types are listed where they grow. They bear the names of their districts followed by those of their grapes.

Over half Hungary's vineyards (¼ million acres) are on the Great Plain of the Danube (Duna) in the southern centre of the country, on sandy soil which is little use for anything but vines. The vine, indeed, has been used for reclaiming sand dunes which used to shift in storms, as they do in the Sahara. Great Plain wine, about half of it red Kadarka, and much of it the white Italian (known as Olasz) Riesling, is light and soft—the vin ordinaire of Hungary.

The other half is scattered among the hills which cross the country from south-west to north-east, culminating in the Tokajhegyelja—Tokay hills. In the south the districts of Szekszárd, Vilány and Mecsek grow both red and white wines, but here the red are coming to the fore. Kadarka is the traditional grape; Pinot Noir and Cabernet the rising stars, making fruity lightish wine of good quality.

Round Lake Balaton (see next pages) some of Hungary's best table wines are made. The small isolated hill-districts of Somló to the west, growing Furmint and Riesling, and Mór to the north, growing Ezerjó grapes, also both have very distinct characters: Somló for gentler, Mór for drier and more highly flavoured wine. Both are among what Hungary calls its 'historical wine regions'.

Sopron, almost on the Austrian border, is a red wine outpost, growing Kékfrankos, a lively wine but hardly a great one. Barsonyos-Császár to the east of Sopron makes dry white wine; unlike the other named 'historical' districts it was formed by law in 1959.

Then along the south of the Mátra range to Eger comes the second biggest of Hungary's vineyards, formed by combining (again in 1959) the old districts of Gyöngyös-Visonta and Debrö. The sweet white Hárslevelü of Debrö (that is the villages of Aldebro, Feldebro and Verpelét) is its best-known wine, but Olasz Riesling and Kadarka, Hungary's commonest grapes, are also grown.

Best known, perhaps, of all Hungary's table wines is Eger's Bikavér, or Bull's Blood. The fine old town of Eger is one of Hungary's most important wine-centres, with huge State cellars, magnificent caverns cut in the soft dark tufa of the hills. Hundreds of time-blackened oak casks, ten feet in diameter and bound with bright red iron hoops, line their galleries.

Not only Bikavér, which ages well and at ten years is not unlike a good old Chianti, but 'Médoc Noir' (or Merlot) is made in the district. Once Eger was a red-wine centre exclusively. Today her Leányka (one of Hungary's lesser grapes, here giving very good light white wine) is thought by some to be her best product.

The place name, ending in 'i' (which is equivalent to the German 'er') is usually followed by the grape variety in Hungary. Most bottled wines come from state cellars

Tokay

PAINTED yellow four-in-hand gigs overtake grey old wagons of barrels on the road into Tokay. The cobbles are covered in mud and straw. A mist steams up from the Bodrog river, wreathing the coppery vines on the hill. From the door of the Halászcsárda comes a great smell of pike and paprika and bacon and dumplings and sour cream and coffee.

Tokay is like one of the provincial towns in Russian novels which burn themselves into the memory by their very plainness. And indeed Russia is only 40 miles away.

The Tokay hills are ancient volcanoes, lava covered with sandy loam—perfect soil for vines. From the plain to the south come warm summer winds and from the river moisture, while the hills themselves give shelter.

The same grapes as grow in other parts of Hungary, the Furmint and Hárslevelü, ripen perfectly here. Better still, they undergo the same 'noble rot' as the grapes of Sauternes, concentrating their sugar and flavours into quintessential-grapiness. They ferment slowly but give strong and intensely flavoured wine.

The Tokay custom is to keep the most nobly rotten (or 'Aszu') grapes to one side and crush them into a pulp in tubs called puttonyok. A number of seven-gallon puttonyok of pulp is added to barrels of one-year-old wine. Tokay barrels, called Gönci, only hold 35 gallons, so if five puttonyok are added the wine is entirely Aszu—like a German Beerenauslese.

The qualities of Tokay are known by the number of 'putts' in the Gönci barrel. If none have been added the wine is 'Szamorodni'—rather heavy and harsh but not sweet.

The most luxurious Tokay of all is made only from the juice which Aszu berries naturally exude as they are waiting to be crushed. This 'essencia' is as much as 60% sugar and will hardly ferment at all. Its normal use today is for sweetening Aszu wines—but formerly it was very slowly fermented and kept for the deathbeds of monarchs, where it was supposed to have miraculous powers. The State cellars at Tállya have only 60 barrels of essencia; none is bottled, but a persuasive visitor might be allowed a taste. Of all the essences of the grape it is the most velvety, peach-like and penetrating. Its flavour stays in the mouth for half an hour. What it is like at 200 years old (some of the great Polish cellars kept it that long) only the Tsars can tell.

Even today Tokay is kept for six or seven years in narrow, pitch-black tunnels cut in the lava. With their single files of small barrels, their thickly moss-covered vaults and the only light from flickering candles, they are some of the world's most romantic cellars.

Modern Tokay is stabilized by pasteurization, which may account partly for its faintly madeira-like or cooked flavour. Anciently brandy was added instead. The few bottles which survive of wines from the famous old private cellars of Erdöbénye, Sárospatak, Tállya and Tarcal suggest that the old wine was, at its best, finer than today's. But even today an Aszu of four or five puttonyok has a silky texture, a haunting fragrance and flavour of mingled fruit and butter and caramel and the breath of the Bodrog among October vines.

Above: Tokay labels in order of sweetness and quality, culminating in Aszu. The little neck label indicates the number of sweetening puttonyok added (the adjective is puttonyos, or puttonos) Right: the wine market in the village of Tokay on a typical misty autumn day

Lake Balaton

LAKE BALATON, besides being the biggest lake in Europe, has a special significance for Hungarians. In a country with few landmarks and no coast it is the sea and the chief beauty spot. Its shores are thick with summer villas and holiday resorts, fragrant with admirable cooking. It has good weather and a happy social life. These things, rather than anything intrinsically unusual about the lake, are its attractions.

The north shore of Lake Balaton has all the advantages of good exposure and shelter, as well as the air-conditioning effect of a big body of water. It is inevitably a vineyard. In late summer the hot moist air is said to make monster leaves on vines, which in turn hasten the ripening of the grapes.

Its special qualities come not only from the climate, but from the combination of a sandy soil and curious extinct volcano stumps, of which Mount Badacsony is the most famous, dotted around among otherwise flat land. The steep slopes of basalt-rich sand drain well and absorb and hold the heat. Grape vines are in their element.

At one time many of the noble families of the Austro-Hungarian Empire kept vineyards here. The Esterhazy farm, with a modest brick villa, stands in an ideal position half-way up the south side of Mount Badacsony, below that of the poet Kisfaludy, which is now a restaurant. In

Top left: the coffin shape of Mount Badacsony with the lake behind, from Mount St George (Szt György). The basalt outcrop makes the soil for Hungary's best table wines, light gold, lively and fiery
Left: the commoner Balaton wines are shipped abroad in cask. The superior Kéknylü and Szürkebarat from Badacsony have Monimpex labels

Vineyards
Woods
Contour interval 50 metres

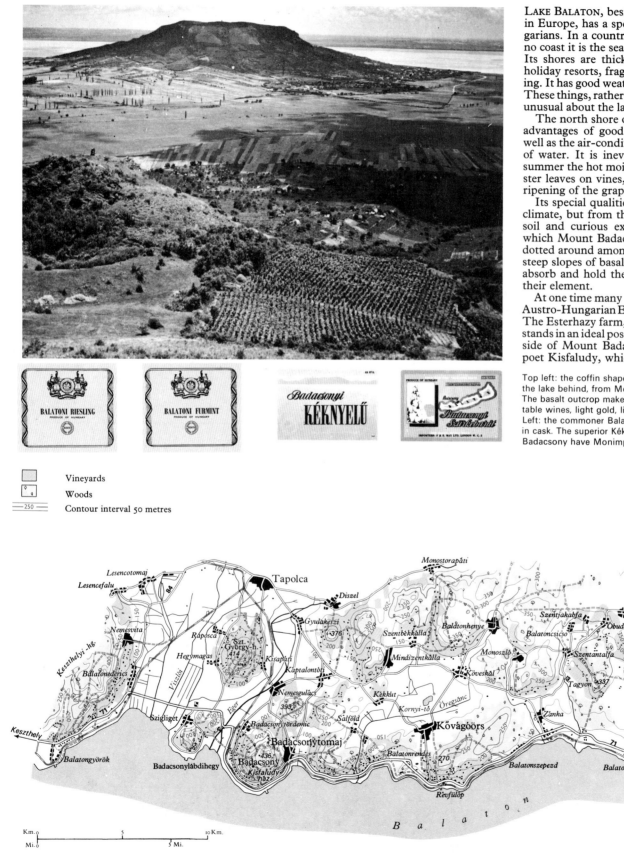

Czechoslovakia

its plain cellars, with no equipment dating from later than about 1900, the character of Hungarian wine is easy to grasp. It is strong and simple and fresh, and often has the beauty of things which are young and belong to the country.

Olasz (Italian) Riesling is the common white grape. Its wine is very good when it is only a year old; dry but fresh and clean and not too strong. The real specialities, however, are the grapes which make powerful, honey-scented wine; the Hungarian white varieties Furmint, Szürkebarát and Kéknyelü.

Even at a year old, tasted from the barrel, a Szürkebarát can still be as white as milk and prickly and fierce with fermentation. In two or three years these wines—of which the Kéknyelü is reckoned the 'stiffest' and best—have remarkable presence. They are aromatic and fiery; not exactly dessert wines but very much the wines for the sort of spiced and pungent food the Hungarians love.

The whole north shore of the lake produces them. Csopak, Balatonfüred and Badacsony are the main centres. Normally the ordinary district wine will carry the simple name Balatoni, with the name of the grape. The name Badacsonyi on a label implies a stronger, sweeter, and to the Hungarian way of thinking altogether better wine.

International Boundary
District Boundary
Wine Area Towns
Vineyards
Land above 1000 metres

Km. 0 — 100 Km.
Mi. 0 — 50 Mi.

The Castle wine cellar with young wine from the state farm at Roudnice, Northern Bohemia

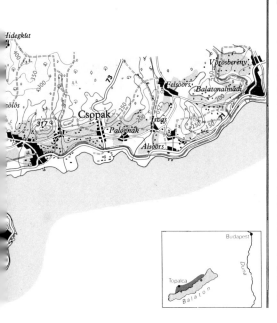

LYING along the northern borders of such incorrigibly vinous countries as Austria and Hungary it would be strange if Czechoslovakia did not make good wine too. How good it is remains almost a secret, however, for virtually none is exported: all 20 million gallons are drunk at home. Delegates to the regular international wine fair at Bratislava (where the Soviet Union wins more Golds than at the Olympic games) report very favourably.

Of the three sections of Czechoslovakia, Slovakia is by far the biggest wine-maker, with about two-thirds of the acreage and production. Moravia makes most of the rest. Bohemia has only 1,000 acres of vineyards along the right bank of the river Elbe north of Prague—though her best wine is said to be comparable to a German Palatinate.

There are predictable parallels between the wines of the three regions and those of their neighbours in, respectively, Hungary, Austria and Germany. The south-eastern corner of the Slovakia is only just across the border from Tokay and includes a small part of the classic

Tokay vineyard, growing the Tokay grapes, the Furmint and others, and apparently making very creditable wine in the same manner.

Slovakia's, and the whole country's, biggest vineyards lie north of Bratislava round Modra and Pezinok and scattered eastwards from there along the Hungarian border. They grow typical central European wine, mostly white, using much the same grapes as northern Hungary: Italian Riesling, Müller-Thurgau, Leanyka, Muscat Ottonel, Ezerjó and Veltliner. Most of the wine is made in co-operatives and sold under brand names, not necessarily indicating the grape variety or the precise origin. Malokarpatské Zlato (Little Carpathian Gold) is an example. Examples sold in the west have been dry and full of character.

Moravia's vineyards, south of Brnó, are so close to Austria's Weinwiertel (a district so given to vineyards that 'Wine quarter' became its name), sharing its strange soil, the soft wind-blown loess of the Danube valley, that its wines—all white—have what one thinks of as Austrian characteristics.

205

Jugoslavia

Above: Jerusalem, the best-known vineyard of Ljutomer
Left: barrels are cleaned out with sea water before the vintage on the island of Hvar in Dalmatia

JUGOSLAVIA has its feet in the Balkans, its head in the Alps, and leans towards Italy. The conundrum is not a bad way of visualizing Jugoslav wine, even if it is politically 50 years out of date. The range of Jugoslav wine is exceptionally wide—from relatively northern, light and fruity white wine to profoundly southern, strong, soft red. She is the tenth-biggest producer in the world, with a history of wine-making since ancient times.

The simplest way to think of the wine regions is as those of the north, Slovenia and parts of Croatia, which are the best; the coast from Rijeka south to Dubrovnik and beyond, which are the least predictable, and the eastern and inland areas—Vojvodina on the Great Plain, the Fruška Gora hills above the Danube (the Dunav), central Serbia, Kosovo and Macedonia, which are developing fast.

The map shows the main regions of production with the names of their most widely grown wines. EEC-style legal controls are now in force to define qualities and origins. Exports (12% of production) are reliable and good value. The inevitable tendency is for the 300-odd traditional grapes to give way to modern standards.

Slovenian white wines are the biggest export. The Riesling she grows is the Italian Riesling (also known as the Graševina)—not such a temperamental or distinguished plant as the Rhine Riesling, but performing at its best here under the combined influence of the Alps, the Adriatic, and the central European plain. It gives well-balanced, full-bodied yet reasonably fresh wines lacking only the vitality of fruity acidity which German wine can achieve. Cold fermentation, widely used, has improved its balance and freshness. The best examples come from Ljutomer and Maribor in Slovenia; soft but stately spätleses of real quality.

Croatia and Serbia, between them making three-quarters of the country's wine, are beginning to compete with Slovenia in quality. The Fruska Gora hills of Vojvodina have recently produced very attractive whites, Sauvignon Blanc and Traminer in particular.

Of the traditional varieties Slovenia's most interesting whites are Šipon (Hungary's Fur-mint), Tocai, Malvasia and Ranina (Austria's Bouvier); her reds a strong Teran and a pale Cviček. Serbia and Croatia include in their repertoire such kinds as Hungarian Kadarka and Romanian Ottonel.

Other grape names become familiar as one travels the country . . . for few are exported. Žilavka makes its best wine round the pretty old Turkish town of Mostar, north of Dubrovnik. Žilavka is dry and pungent and memorably fruity white wine—very often the best to be found in Jugoslav restaurants. Another is the red Prokupac, whose wine is the standard in southern Serbia and Macedonia. Between Smederevo and Svetozarevo, in Župa and Kruševac and south into Macedonia it forms about 85% of the production. It makes good rosé, firm and with plenty of flavour, and a red wine varying from dark and bitter to pleasantly fruity and drinkable. Often it is blended with the milder Plovdina and given local names (e.g. in Župa, Župsko crno). But it is slowly being ousted by such imported vines as Cabernet and Gamay, planted by co-operatives with their eye on an international market. Germany is a big customer for the red Burgundac of Kosovo, for example, under the name Amselfelder.

The biggest contrast to the massive co-operatives of the north and east is on the Dalmatian coast. A number of wines of strong personality are made on the islands, often from little rocky patches under fig-trees, pressed by an antique press and hoarded as a treasure which is none of the government's business. The dry brown Grk of Korčula, the pale and sometimes even perfumed Bogdanuša of Hvar and the similar Vugava of Vis, the thick sweetish Dingač and Postup of the Pelješac peninsula and the mighty Prošek, which can (occasionally) make a fair substitute for port, are all the specialities of small communities. Plavina, Plavac and Opol are their lighter reds, Maraština and Pošip their (none too light) whites.

With Dalmatian food—tiny oysters, raw ham, grilled fish, smoky and oniony kebabs and mounds of sweet grapes—the fire and flavour of such local wines can seem ambrosial.

The Language of the Label

Visokokvalitetno High quality
Čuveno vino Selected wine
Stolno vino Table wine
Punjeno u . . . Bottled at . . .
Proizvedeno u vinariji . . . Produced at . . .
Proizvedeno u vlastitoj vinariji poljoprivredne zadruge . . . Made in the co-operative cellars of the place named
Prirodno Natural
Bijelo White
Crno Red
Ružica Rosé
Biser (literally, pearl) Sparkling
Suho Dry
Polsuho Medium dry
Slatko Sweet
Desertno vino Dessert wine
Vinjak Brandy

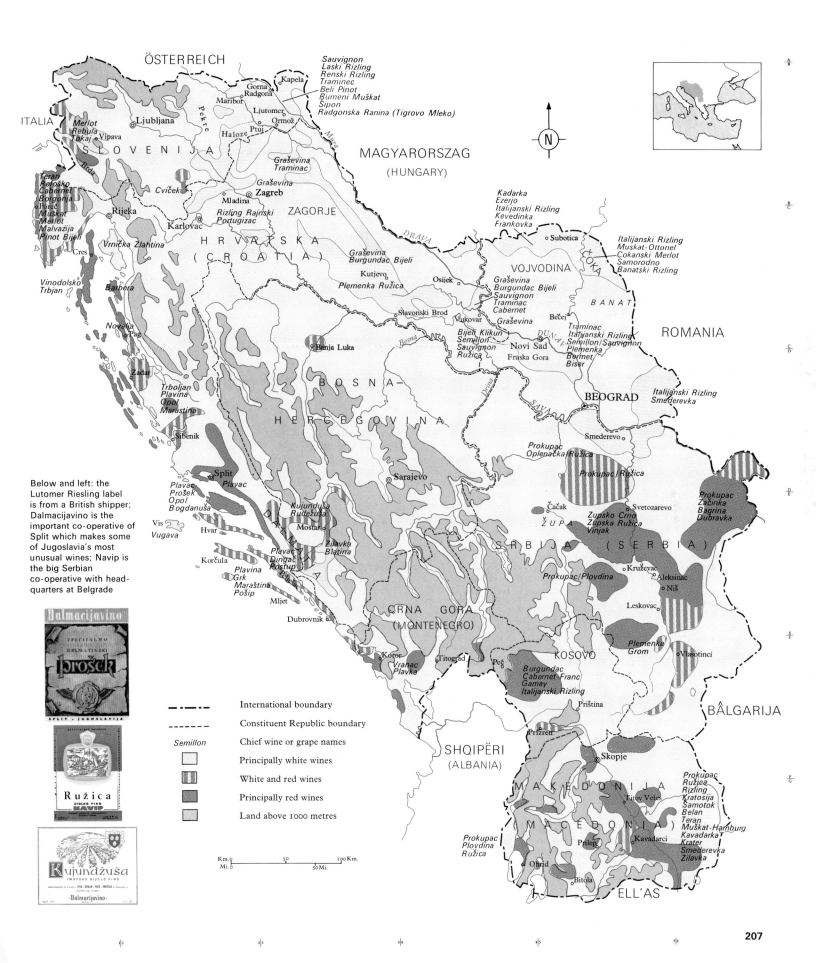

Below and left: the Lutomer Riesling label is from a British shipper; Dalmacijavino is the important co-operative of Split which makes some of Jugoslavia's most unusual wines; Navip is the big Serbian co-operative with headquarters at Belgrade

Romania

OF THE rapidly expanding wine country of the Black Sea and the Balkans, Romania almost certainly has the greatest potential for quality. It is not only a matter of situation—though Romania lies on the same latitude as France—but of temperament. There seems to be a natural affinity for the culture of France in Romania. Romanian wine literature shares the sort of hard-headed lyricism of much of French gastronomic writing. There is a great difference between the Atlantic influence which makes France moist and mild, and the continental influence which gives Romania blazing summers. But it is the more temperate conditions of the coast and the north of the country which give Romania's best wine.

The Carpathian mountains curl like a snail in the middle of Romania. They occupy almost half the country, rising from the surrounding plain to about 8,000 feet at their peaks, and enclosing the Transylvanian plateau, which is still about 2,000 feet above sea level. Across the south of the country the Danube (the Dunărea) flows through a sandy plain. Here, and in the southern and eastern foot-hills of the Carpathians, is Romania's biggest vineyard.

In Romania, as in Russia, though not to the same extent, a great planting programme has increased the national vineyard by 51% in 15 years, making her at present the sixth largest wine-producer in Europe. It is interesting to see, however, that even now only 16% of the land under vines belongs to the state. Fifty per cent belongs to the big local co-operatives and the rest, 34%, is still private property.

Like Hungary, Romania has one wine whose name was once famous all over Europe. But Tokay, though shorn of its imperial glory, soldiers on in the wine-lists of the world, whereas Cotnari, which used to appear in Paris restaurants as 'Perle de la Moldavie', has faded into obscurity. Cotnari is a natural white dessert wine like Tokay, only with rather more delicacy and less intensity. There is no doubt, in tasting it, that one is tasting something of unusual quality and character.

Cotnari comes from the part of Moldavia, in north-east Romania, which was left to the Romanians after Russia had annexed a large slice of the country. The part the Russians took, anciently known as Bessarabia, contained a large proportion of Romania's vineyards. The great concentration of vineyards south of the Carpathians dates from since that time.

All the best of Romania's wine today is white. Both old-fashioned indigenous grape varieties with such names as Fetească, Grasă and Tămîioasă are used, and the international Rieslings and Pinots and Aligotés. The most widely planted sorts are the Italian Riesling and one called the Fetească regală.

Apart from Cotnari, two areas produce white wines of a quality worth exporting: Tîrnave in Transylvania, which makes an adequate Riesling and a light, slightly sweet local speciality known as Perla, and Murfatlar near the coast on the plateau of Dobrogea Murfatlar's best-known wine is a sweet pale golden-brown muscat; although Chardonnay and other French grapes are also successfully grown. It is possible that the muscat tradition here goes back to

ancient times, for the Greeks are supposed to have taken the muscat grape as far north as the Crimea, and where the port of Constanţa now stands stood the ancient city of Tomis.

The biggest wine region of modern Romania is Focşani, east of the Carpathians, including three wine-towns with lilting names: Coteşti, Odobeşti and Nicoreşti. The terrain varies but much of it is sand, which has only recently been mastered, here as in the great plain of Hungary, for vines. The vines have to be planted in pockets dug deep enough for their roots to reach the subsoil; sometimes as much as three metres below the surface. It seems a desperate expedient, especially as it takes the vine some time to grow up to ground level and come into bearing. But in fact good light wines are being made where nothing would grow before, here and in places along the Danube.

The red Băbească of Nicoreşti is a good example of the character of the country; it is pleasantly acidic with a clove-like taste; fresh, original and enjoyable.

Following the curve of the Carpathians the next vineyard is Dealul Mare, where Romania's biggest state experimental vineyard, Valea Călugărească, lies in the foot-hills. The Cabernet is grown here with great pride, but with not always fortunate results. Like many Romanian red wines it can be sweet, heavy and without grace: possibly the result of the very hot late summer on these south-facing slopes.

Farther west the vineyards continue with both red and white wines round Piteşti and Drăgăşani. From the south on the plain near the Danube Segarcea Cabernet and Sadova rosé are exported. Both suffer from the customary sweetness. One wonders whether it is entirely traditional or whether it is in the belief that the foreign market demands it.

In the western corner of Romania the Hungarian influence makes itself felt; many of the red wines of Banat are made from the Kadarka (here spelt Cadarca) of the Hungarian plain.

The Language of the Label

Vie Vine
Viile Vineyard
Strugure Grape
Recolta Vintage
Vin superior Superior wine
Vin de masă Table wine
Vin uşor Light wine
GAS (Gospodariile Agricole de Stat) State agricultural enterprise
IAS (Intreprinderile Agricole de Stat) More up-to-date name for the same
Imbuteliat Bottled
Vin alb White wine
Vin roşu Red wine
Vin rose Rosé
Sec Dry
Dulce Sweet
Spumos Sparkling
Pivniţă (pl pivniţele) Cellar
Tuica Plum brandy
Vinexport The government exporting agency

Below: Cotnari is Romania's most distinguished white wine; a strong, dryish natural dessert wine based on the Grasă grape, which is subject like the Semillon (see page 23) to 'noble rot'. Most Romanian labels name the grape variety first and foremost; the whites (Riesling, Fetească, Furmint etc.) are best. Perla is a white wine; a speciality of Transylvania; gently sweet and pleasant. French is commonly used as the label language: German names are also adopted (last label) for wines designed for the German export market

Above: the massive maturing and bottling works of the Romanian state wine and spirit monopoly (formerly known as Romagricola, now as Vinexport) are in the capital city of Bucharest
Right: vineyards near the delta of the Danube, on sandy soil, produce Romania's traditional type of light and fruity red wine from such grapes as the Băbească. Niculitel is the best-known wine-centre of this region

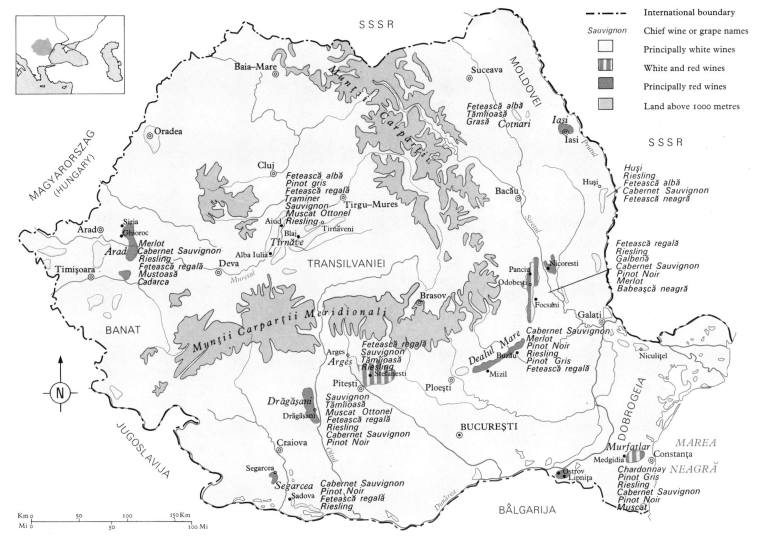

—·—·—·— International boundary

Sauvignon Chief wine or grape names

Principally white wines

White and red wines

Principally red wines

Land above 1000 metres

SSSR

MOLDOVEI

Baia–Mare

Suceava

Fetească albă
Tămîioasă
Grasă Cotnari

Iasi
Iasi

Oradea

SSSR

Cluj

Fetească albă
Pinot gris
Fetească regală
Traminer
Sauvignon
Muscat Ottonel
Aiud *Riesling*

Tirgu–Mures

Bacău

Huşi
Riesling
Fetească albă
Cabernet Sauvignon
Fetească neagră

Siria
Arad
Ghioroc
Merlot
Cabernet Sauvignon
Riesling
Fetească regală
Mustoasă
Cadarca

Arad

Tirnaveni

Blaj
Tîrnăve

Alba Iulia

Deva

Huşi

TRANSILVANIEI

Fetească regală
Riesling
Galbenă
Cabernet Sauvignon
Pinot Noir
Merlot
Babeașcă neagră

Timişoara

Mureșul

Panciu
Odobeşti

Nicoresti

BANAT

Muntii Carpatii Meridionali

Brasov

Focsani

Galati

Fetească regală
Sauvignon
Tămîioasă
Riesling

Arges
Arges
Ştefăneşti

Pitești

Buzău

Dealul Mare

Mizil

Cabernet Sauvignon
Merlot
Pinot Noir
Riesling
Pinot Gris
Fetească regală

Niculiţel

Ploeşti

DOBROGEIA

Drăgăşani

Drăgăşani

Sauvignon
Tămîioasă
Muscat Ottonel
Fetească regală
Riesling
Cabernet Sauvignon
Pinot Noir

BUCUREŞTI

Oltul

Murfatlar

MAREA

Medgidia

Constanţa

Craiova

NEAGRĂ

Segarcea

Chardonnay
Pinot Gris
Riesling
Cabernet Sauvignon
Pinot Noir
Muscat

Ostrov
Lipniţa

Segarcea

Sadova

Cabernet Sauvignon
Pinot Noir
Fetească regală
Riesling

Dunărea

BÂLGARIJA

MAGYARORSZAG
(HUNGARY)

JUGOSLAVIJA

Muntii Carpatii

N

Km 0   50   100   150 Km
Mi 0   50   100 Mi

Bulgaria

Above and right: the Bulgarian wine industry is almost entirely a creation of the 20th century. Under Turkish domination vineyards were only scattered peasant holdings. In contrast today even such timeless vintage scenes as the one above are disappearing. The vast flat vineyards are picked by automatic harvesters, which straddle a vine-row and spew the grapes into a trailer crawling alongside

The Language of the Label

Лозова пръчка (Lozova prachka) Vine or variety of vine
Лозя (Lozia) Vineyards
Винопроизводител (Vinoproizvoditel) Wine-producer
Бутилирам (Butiliram) To bottle
Натурално (Naturalno) Natural
Бяло вино (Bjalo vino) White wine
Червено вино (Cherveno vino) Red wine
Сухо вино (Suho vino) Dry wine
Сладко вино (Sladko vino) Sweet wine
Искрящо вино (Iskriashto vino) Sparkling wine
Коняк (Koniak) Brandy
С остатъчна захар (S ostatachna zahar) With residual sugar – in other words semi-sweet or sweet
Vinimpex Bulgaria's 'State Commercial Enterprise for Export and Import of Wines and Spirits', a monopoly, controls the entire wine export trade

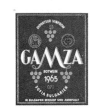

Bulgaria produces more and more Cabernet, Chardonnay, Riesling and other internationally famous grapes. These are the labels of her own sorts: Gamza, Kadarka (from Hungary), Melnik and Mavrud are red table wines; Trakia and Dimiat dry or medium white wines; Hemus sweet white, Tirnovo a sweet red and Iskra Bulgaria's semi-dry sparkling wine

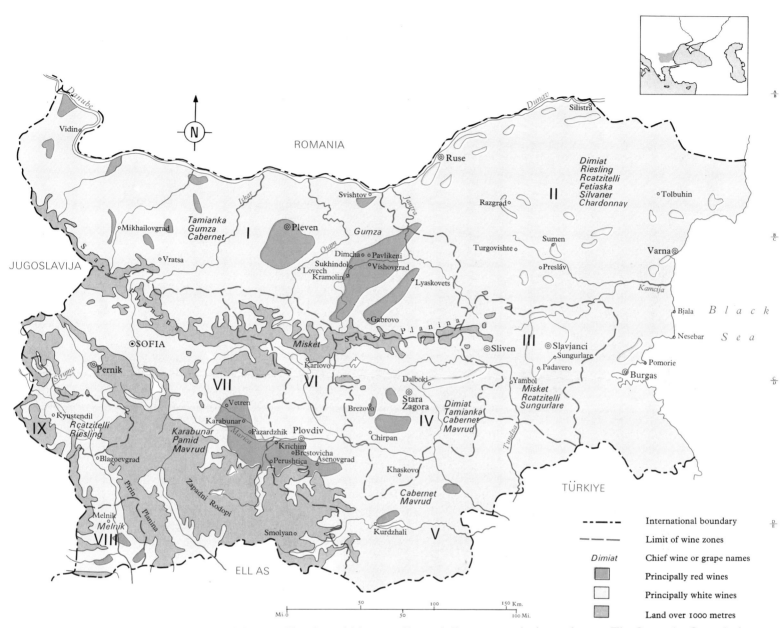

ROMANIA

Danube

Vidin

Dunav

Silistra

N

Ruse

Svishtov

JUGOSLAVIJA

Iskar

Mikhailovgrad

*Tamianka
Gumza
Cabernet*

I

Pleven

Osam

Gumza

Jantra

Razgrad

II

*Dimiat
Riesling
Rcatzitelli
Fetiaska
Silvaner
Chardonnay*

Tolbuhin

Vratsa

Dimcha Pavlikeni
Sukhindol Vishovgrad
Lovech Kramolin

Turgovishte

Sumen

Preslav

Varna

Gabrovo

Lyaskovets

Kamcija

Bjala

Black

Stara Planina

Stara Planina

Planina

SOFIA

Misket

Karlovo

Sliven

III

Slavjanci

Sungurlare

Padavero

Nesebar

Sea

Pomorie

Pernik

VII

VI

Dalboki

Struma

Yambol

*Misket
Rcatzitelli
Sungurlare*

Burgas

Kyustendil

*Rcatzitelli
Riesling*

Vetren

Karabunar

Karabunar

Pazardzhik

Plovdiv

Brezovo

Stara
Zagora

IV

*Dimiat
Tamianka
Cabernet
Mavrud*

IX

*Karabunar
Pamid
Mavrud*

Marica

Krichim
Brestovicha
Perushtica Asenovgrad

Chirpan

Blagoevgrad

Khaskovo

TÜRKIYE

Pirin
Planina

Zapadni Rodopi

*Cabernet
Mavrud*

Tundza

Melnik
Melnik

VIII

Smolyan

Kurdzhali

V

ELLAS

50   100   150 Km.

Mi. 0   50   100 Mi.

— - — - — International boundary

— — — — Limit of wine zones

Dimiat Chief wine or grape names

Principally red wines

Principally white wines

Land over 1000 metres

PERHAPS because it is in most ways a less civilized and sophisticated country than Romania, Bulgaria, once it had made up its mind to modernize its wine industry, forged ahead with complete state control at a remarkable rate. Modernization only began in 1949, and yet by 1966 Bulgaria had become the sixth-largest wine exporter in the world, following after the much older-established wine countries of Algeria, France, Italy, Spain and Portugal. Eighty per cent of the crop is exported now, mainly to Iron Curtain countries and Germany. The wine industry, in fact, is looked on as a currency earner first and foremost.

Vineyards in Bulgaria are huge blocks of flat land, which can be cultivated entirely by machinery. Wine-processing plant is modern and Bulgarian wine—at least exported wine—tends to be more stable and arrive in better condition than that of Romania. There is very little in the way of a peasant wine-making tradition, for a historical reason: the architecture, the traditional costumes and the food of the country all bear the marks of the Turkish domination, with its Muslim rules against drinking wine, which ended less than a hundred years ago.

The wines which succeed beyond all expectation in Bulgaria are those made of French grapes for western consumption—the Cabernet and the Chardonnay. The Cabernet in particular has fruit, vigour, balance—the robust qualities of red Bordeaux in a good vintage, if not its finesse.

The country is divided into nine wine regions, varying widely in size: one north of the Balkan mountains which makes mainly red wine; one to the east on the coast of the Black Sea which makes most of the best white, and the remainder in the south and west making red and heavy or sweet white, with the exception of a pleasantly scented muscat, known as Misket—which unlike all the other muscats of Eastern Europe and Russia is fully fermented to be quite a dry wine, not unlike the muscat of Alsace, though rather heavier and less elegant. It is the speciality of Karlovo, in the valley which grows musk roses for making attar of roses, and also at Sungurlare to the east.

The local-style red wines range from a quickly fermented light red ordinaire called Pamid to a darkly plummy Mavrud (Greek Mavrodaphne?) and a strong 'Alicante-style' Melnik in the south-west. The Gamza (or Gumza), the same grape as the Hungarian Kadarka, is used in the north to make a pleasant light dry red. It carries the name of its district: Pleven, Sukhindol, Pavlikeni or Kramolin.

Eastern Bulgaria, from Ruse on the Danube (the Dunav) to Burgas, grows most of the country's very drinkable dry white wines. Dimiat is the most widespread variety; the white opposite number of the Gamza, and like the Gamza attributed to a district—Varna, Preslav or Pomorie. The Riesling is the Italian version; its produce is comparable with the wine it makes in Hungary. Rcatzitelli is a grape which appears all round the Black Sea making strong white wine—in Russia it is often made sweet as well.

For the important German market, Vinimpex, the export organization, devises names like Sonnenküste for the Rcatzitelli, Klosterkeller for the full-bodied dry Sylvaner and Donau Perle for the rather neutral dry Fetiaska. The very popular white Hemus is medium-sweet, and Tamianka very sweet; these and numerous other dessert wines are made mainly in the south.

The Soviet Union

THE SOVIET UNION officially decided in favour of wine—at the expense of vodka—in the fifties. In 1950 she had one million acres of vineyard. Today she has almost three million, and the figure planned for 1980 is three and a half, which will make her second in acreage only to Spain. On the world league-table today Russia stands fourth both in acreage and volume.

This is certainly the biggest and fastest extension of the world's wine-growing capacity ever seen. Yet even this is apparently not enough: the Union is an insatiable wine-importer; the main market for Romania, Bulgaria, Algeria. . . . Surely then the vodka-drinking must have tailed off? Not a bit of it.

The industry that supplies these impressively thirsty throats has changed enormously in almost every way in recent years. A vast network of 'primary' and 'secondary' wine factories now covers the Union; the secondary plants finishing and bottling wine in consumer areas.

Wine qualities have been defined in a way not unlike the EEC three-tier system, with a dash of the USA's approach to single-variety wines (which, in Russia, must be 85% of the variety named compared with America's liberal 51%).

The three tiers are 'ordinary' (unmatured and not regionally or locally named); 'named' (matured and declaring its origin); and 'kollektsionye' (from selected areas and varieties, with at least two years' bottle-age).

Western grape varieties have now infiltrated all areas, though they are much more frequent in the northern regions (i.e. Moldavia, the Ukraine and the Russian republic) than in the conservative south.

So much is simple. The complications begin with the names, which vary from the straightforward place + variety to the romantic/fantastic: 'Black Eyes' for Russian 'port'. The map groups the principal wine names over the approximate area where they are made.

The Soviet wine belt sweeps east round the north of the Black Sea from Moldavia—which was formerly in Romania—to Armenia on the border of Turkey. Two areas, the Crimean peninsula, and Georgia on the southern slopes of the Caucasus, have been famous since ancient times for good wine and remain the best today. The Russian taste is for sweet wine; the names of port, madeira and sherry are widely taken in vain. Many of the specialities named on the map are dessert wines of between 16% and 19% alcohol and more or less sweet.

The Moldavian vineyards grow the traditional Romanian varieties alongside newcomers like Cabernet and Aligoté. The Fetjaska makes fresh dry white; Negru de Purkar is the traditional dry but fruity red. Romanesti is made with a Bordeaux-like blend of Cabernet, Merlot and Malbec. But Chumai is Cabernet made into a dessert wine. Trifesti (Pinot—or Pineau—Gris) and Gratiesti (the local Rcatzitelli) are white dessert wines.

The Ukraine is the republic with the biggest

The Language of the Label

Винозавод (Vinozavod) Wine factory
Столовое вино (Stolovoe vino) Table wine
Белое вино (Beloe vino) White wine
Красное вино (Krasnoe vino) Red wine
Розовое вино (Rozovoe vino) Rosé
Сухое вино (Sukhoe vino) Dry wine
Дессертное вино (Desertnoe vino) Dessert wine
Шампанское (Shampanskoe) 'Champagne'
Грузинское вино (Gruzinskoe vino) Georgian wine

Above: labels from Georgia (top); the Russian republic (second row); Georgian 'champagne' and dessert wine from Azerbaijan (third); Moldavia and Crimea (bottom)
Left: a state farm in Azerbaijan where sweet grape types are developed for making dessert wines
Far right: near Tbilisi (Tiflis) in Georgia a winery bottles 'champagne' under pressure

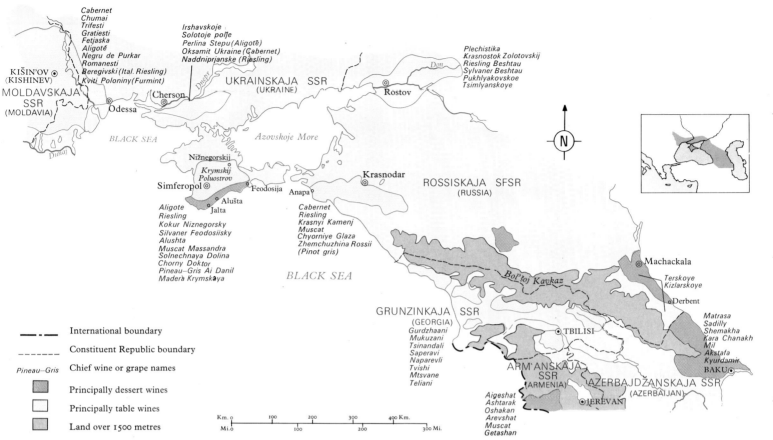

CABERNET
Chumai
Trifesti
Gratiesti
Fetjaska
Aligoté
Negru de Purkar
Romanesti
Beregivski (Ital. Riesling)
Kviti Poloniny (Furmint)

KIŠIN'OV ⊙
(KISHINEV)

MOLDAVSKAJA
SSR
(MOLDAVIA)

Odessa ⊙

Dunaj

BLACK SEA

Irshavskoje
Solotoje polje
Perlina Stepu (Aligoté)
Oksamit Ukraine (Cabernet)
Naddniprjanske (Riesling)

Dnepr

Cherson ⊙

UKRAINSKAJA SSR
(UKRAINE)

Azovskoje More

Don

Rostov ⊙

Plechistika
Krasnostok Zolotovskij
Riesling Beshtau
Sylvaner Beshtau
Pukhlyakovskoe
Tsimlyanskoye

Krasnodar ⊙

ROSSISKAJA SFSR
(RUSSIA)

Nižnegorskij ⊙
*Krymskij
Poluostrov*
Simferopol ⊙
Feodosija
Alušta
Jalta

Anapa ⊙

Aligote
Riesling
Kokur Niznegorsky
Silvaner Feodosiisky
Alushta
Muscat Massandra
Solnechnaya Dolina
Chorny Doktor
Pineau–Gris Ai Danil
Madera Krymskaya

BLACK SEA

Cabernet
Riesling
Krasnyi Kamenj
Muscat
Chyorniye Glaza
Zhemchuzhina Rossii
(Pinot gris)

Bol'šoj Kavkaz

Machackala ⊙

Terskoye
Kizlarskoye

Derbent ⊙

GRUNZINKAJA SSR
(GEORGIA)
Gurdzhaani
Mukuzani
Tsinandali
Saperavi
Naparevli
Tvishi
Mtsvane
Teliani

⊙ TBILISI

ARM'ANSKAJA
SSR
(ARMENIA)

Aigeshat
Ashtarak
Oshakan
Arevshat
Muscat
Getashan

⊙ JEREVAN

AZERBAJDŽANSKAJA SSR
(AZERBAIJAN)

Matrasa
Sadilly
Shemakha
Kara Chanakh
Mil
Akstafa
Kyurdamir
BAKU ⊙

—·—·— International boundary

——— Constituent Republic boundary

Pineau–Gris Chief wine or grape names

▨ Principally dessert wines

☐ Principally table wines

▨ Land over 1500 metres

Km. 0   100   200   300   400 Km.
Mi. 0   100   200   300 Mi.

vineyard area, including the Crimea. In the Crimea the name of the best-known estate, Massandra, the former property of Prince Woronzow, is widely used on dessert wines, which are the speciality of the south coast. Massandra muscat is full and brown, like Frontignan from the south of France. An official description of it suddenly bursts through the dull recitation of names and characteristics: 'rose and citron tones predominate in the bouquet, and the flavour is delicate with a pronounced oiliness. Plum, chocolate and balsam tones appear during maturation'. No one would be inspired like that by a routine sweet wine.

Of the others listed on the map, for the Crimea, Kokur Niznegorsky and Silvaner Feodosiisky are dry but full-bodied white wines. Alushta (from the valley behind the port) is reckoned the best red, Solnechnaya Dolina and Chorny Doktor are respectively white and red dessert wines and the Pinot Gris of Ai Danil is sweet, like Moldavian Trifesti.

The Don basin round Rostov specializes in sparkling wine. The red, sweet and sparkling Tsimlyanskoye is highly regarded. South of Krasnodar, the only Russian Riesling exported is grown at Anapa. Chyorniye Glaza ('Black Eyes') is the 'port' of the Russian republic.

Several of Georgia's traditional types have made a modest name for themselves in the world, as good dry everyday wines. In fact Tsinandali and Gurdzhaani, which are white, are comparable with good Spanish or Portuguese white wines; better than the heavy red Mukuzani, and lighter Saperavi and Napareuli.

Armenia, Azerbaijan and the area along the Caspian up to Machackala are dessert-wine country. All the types listed are sweet and strong, red, brown or white, some cooked like madeira and one quaintly named 'Kaoursky'—presumably after the 'black' wine of Cahors. The Matrasa and Sadilly of Baku, red and white table wines, are the only exceptions.

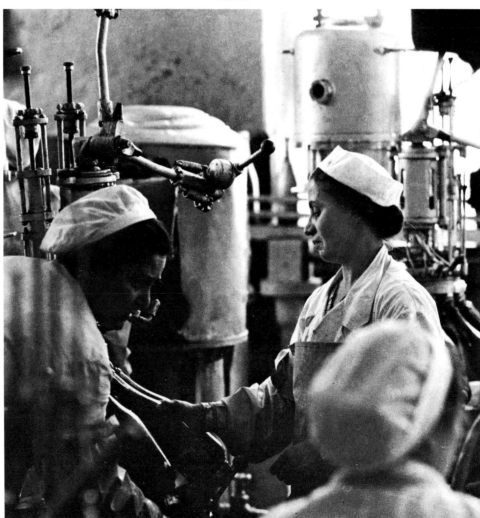

Greece

Above: the temple of Zeus near Nemea in the Peloponnese stands among vines for Nemean red wine
Right: Sifnos is typical of the rocky Aegean islands where the vine is grown casually on the hot slopes

ANCIENT and modern Greece are divided by a gulf with few bridges. The taste for resinated wine or retsina is one; perhaps the only characteristic habit of Greece which goes straight back 3,000 years and beyond, to the time when gods walked on earth.

The god of wine, Dionysus, was Zeus' son by Semele, daughter of the King of Thebes. His mother having been destroyed by Olympian intrigue, Dionysus was brought up by the nymphs of Nysa in Thrace. His tutor was the Rabelaisian old satyr Silenus, who taught him to make wine. From Thrace Dionysus set out to take the knowledge of wine to the world . . . both in legend and in fact; as the Greek Empire spread, it took the vine with it.

Traces of pine resin have been found in wine amphorae from earliest times. It is usually assumed that it was used to preserve the wine. But resinated wine does not age well. The

Right: Greek labels appear in Greek, English, French, German or mixtures. From left: a dry white wine from Marmarion at the southern tip of Euboea; a good standard red from Attica; the red of Naoussa in Macedonia; the 'Romaic' red of Crete, the best-known unresinated brand of table wine; the sweet Malvasia or Malmsey which is the speciality of Rhodes; a dark rosé from Nemea in the Peloponnese, perhaps the best branded red table wine; a strong rosé from Crete; a famous brand of retsina; the sweet red of Patras; the famous sweet muscat of Samos

real reason is surely that Greek wine is much improved by the fresh, sappy, turpentine-like flavour which resin gives if added during the fermentation. Half the wine made in Greece is so treated, and the result is one of the most individual and appetizing drinks of the world. Where peasant food is always oily (and often musty) it is also particularly effective in cancelling the flavour of a doubtful mouthful.

Attica, the region of Athens, is the home of retsina. Most of it is white, from the Savatiano grape, but some rosé or kokkineli is also made.

More than a third of the vineyards of Greece are in the Peloponnese. Both the major firms in the wine trade, Achaia-Clauss and Andrew Cambas, now have their headquarters here. The traditional speciality of the Peloponnese is sweet wine; from Monemvasia come the names Malmsey, Malvasia and Malvoisie.

Mavrodaphne, a sweetish red wine rather

in the manner of Italian Recioto, dark and strong, is reckoned the best of the region.

Mavro is the general word for red wines; its literal meaning of black is often justified; the Mavro of Naoussa in Macedonia, Nemea in the Peloponnese, Crete (where it is sometimes called Mavro Romeiko), Páros, Límnos (Kalpaki) Lefkás, Delphi's Mavroudi and Corfu's Ropa are all recognized. Few, with the exception of brands like Castel Danielis for which you pay a premium, have much appeal, but they are useful for blending, being very dark.

Dry white Greek wine is not usually remarkable. One or two brands, such as Santa Laura, Hymettus and Demestica, are pleasant; the Rombola of Cephalonia, the Verdea from Zákynthos, the Thíra of Santorin and Lindos of Rhodes are said to be above average. The sweet white muscat of Samos is, at its best, something much more individual.

214

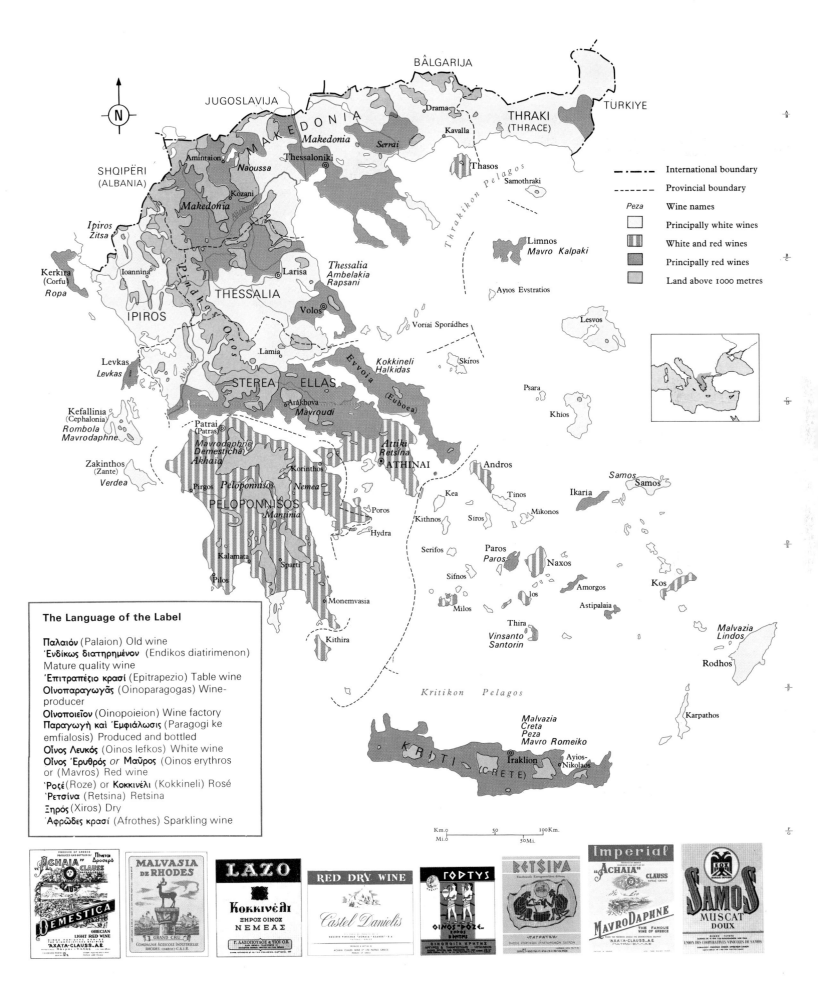

N ↑

JUGOSLAVIJA

BÂLGARIJA

SHQIPËRI (ALBANIA)

MAKEDONIA

Amintaion
Naoussa
Kozani
Thessaloniki
Makedonia

Drama
Kavalla
Serrai

THRAKI (THRACE)

TURKIYE

Thasos
Thrakikon Pelagos
Samothraki

Ipiros
Zitsa

Kerkira (Corfu)
Ropa

Ioannina

IPIROS

Pindhos Oros

Thessalia
Ambelakia
Rapsani

Larisa

THESSALIA

Volos

Limnos
Mavro Kalpaki

Ayios Evstratios

Lesvos

Akhelóos

Lamia

Voriai Sporádhes

Skíros

Psara

Khios

Levkas
Levkas

STEREA ELLAS

Arákhova
Mavroudi

Kokkineli
Halkidas

Evvoia
(Euboea)

Kefallinia (Cephalonia)
Rombola
Mavrodaphne

Patrai (Patras)

Mavrodaphne
Demestica
Akhaia

Korinthos

Nemea

Attiki
Retsina

ATHINAI

Andros

Zakinthos (Zante)
Verdea

Pirgos

Peloponnisos

PELOPONNISOS

Mantinia

Poros

Hydra

Kea

Tinos

Kithnos

Siros

Mikonos

Ikaria

Samos
Samos

Kalamata

Sparti

Serifos

Paros
Paros

Naxos

Kos

Pilos

Sifnos

Ios

Amorgos

Astipalaia

Monemvasia

Milos

Thira

Vinsanto
Santorin

Malvazia
Lindos

Kithira

Rodhos

Karpathos

Kritikon Pelagos

Malvazia
Creta
Peza
Mavro Romeiko

KRITI (CRETE)

Iraklion

Ayios-Nikolaos

Km. 0   50   100 Km.
Mi. 0   50 Mi.

—·—·—	International boundary
— — —	Provincial boundary
Peza	Wine names
☐	Principally white wines
▥	White and red wines
▨	Principally red wines
▦	Land above 1000 metres

The Language of the Label

Παλαιόν (Palaion) Old wine
Ένδίκως διατηρημένον (Endikos diatirimenon) Mature quality wine
Έπιτραπέξιο κρασί (Epitrapezio) Table wine
Οινοπαραγωγᾶς (Oinoparagogas) Wine-producer
Οινοποιεῖον (Oinopoieion) Wine factory
Παραγωγή καὶ Έμφιάλωσις (Paragogi ke emfialosis) Produced and bottled
Οἶνος Λευκός (Oinos lefkos) White wine
Οἶνος Έρυθρός or Μαῦρος (Oinos erythros or (Mavros) Red wine
Ροζέ (Roze) or Κοκκινέλι (Kokkineli) Rosé
Ρετσίνα (Retsina) Retsina
Ξηρός (Xiros) Dry
Άφρῶδες κρασί (Afrothes) Sparkling wine

215

Cyprus

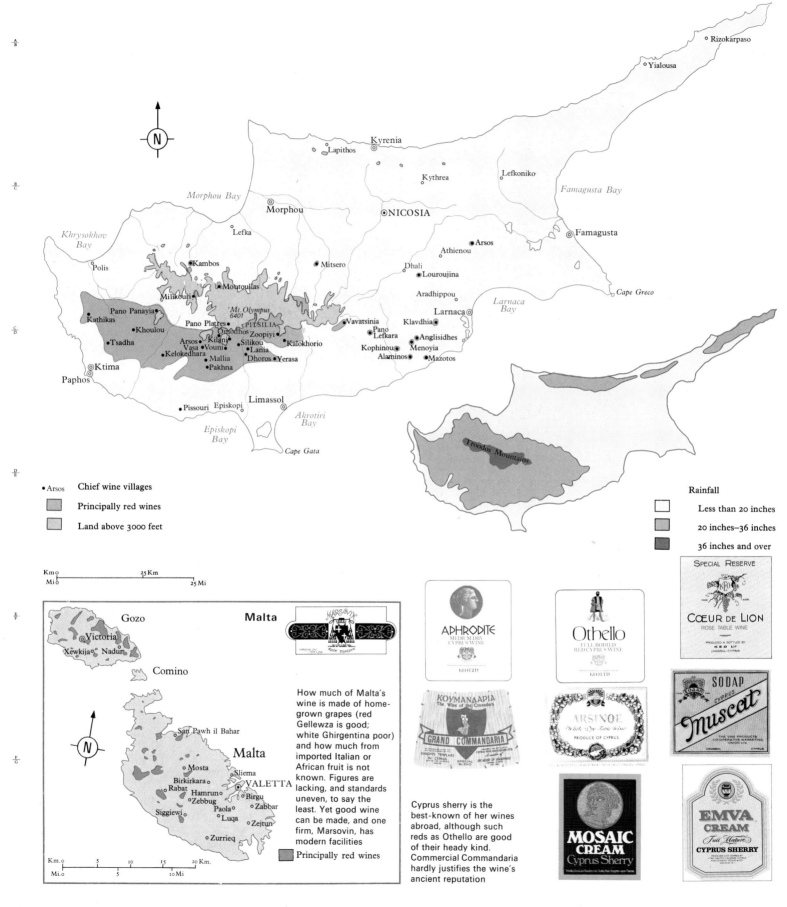

Chief wine villages • Arsos

Principally red wines

Land above 3000 feet

Rainfall

Less than 20 inches

20 inches–36 inches

36 inches and over

How much of Malta's wine is made of home-grown grapes (red Gellewza is good; white Ghirgentina poor) and how much from imported Italian or African fruit is not known. Figures are lacking, and standards uneven, to say the least. Yet good wine can be made, and one firm, Marsovin, has modern facilities

Principally red wines

Cyprus sherry is the best-known of her wines abroad, although such reds as Othello are good of their heady kind. Commercial Commandaria hardly justifies the wine's ancient reputation

In the Troodos mountains, under silver olive-trees, mules carry grapes to the press-house. Heat and drought are what give Cyprus wine its strength. Only in the Troodos, which occasionally get rain, can the vine flourish

CYPRUS not only has one of the oldest wine-growing traditions in the world. It is by far the most developed and successful of the wine countries of the eastern Mediterranean; the first (during her period of British rule starting in 1878) to restore wine to a prime place in her economy, from which Islam had toppled it.

In the last 15 years an enlightened and enquiring approach to wine-making has opened a huge export market for Cyprus wine. Her 'sherry' has made the running so far, but there is every chance that her table wine will follow. They will never be better than good ordinary wine, but they have plenty of strength and character which careful wine-making can turn into an ideal drink for rough peasant food. Excellent Cypriot restaurants all over the world serve it already as a matter of course. The more authentic their cooking the better the dark red wine tastes with it.

The Troodos mountains, attracting rain, make viticulture possible in Cyprus. The vineyards lie where the rain falls, up to nearly three thousand feet into the hills. The whole south-facing Troodos is possible wine-country. Limassol, the port on the south coast, is the entrepôt and headquarters of the three big wine firms; Keo, Sodap and Haggipavlu.

The most individual of Cyprus wines is the almost liqueur-like Commandaria which is made of dried grapes, both red and white, in the villages of Kalokhorio, Zoopiyi, Yerasa and four or five others on the lower slopes of the Troodos. Commandaria has been made at least since the crusading Knights Templar established themselves in their Grande Commanderie on the island at the end of the 12th century. Its intense sweetness (it can have four times as much sugar as port) harks back in fact far further than records go; there are references in Greek literature to such wines, which were invariably drunk diluted with water.

Commandaria is now made both as a straight commercial dessert wine of moderate age, cheap and pleasant but without interest, and by a few traditionalists as the quite alarming concentrated wine of legend. The taste and texture of an old true Commandaria are more than treacly; they have a remarkable haunting wininess.

The range of grapes grown on Cyprus is much less eclectic than in most of the developing wine countries. The island has never had phylloxera, and rather than risk it by importing new stock, growers have kept to the three traditional island grapes, the black Mavron, the white Xynisteri and the muscat of Alexandria. Platres is said to make the best red wine, and the region round about the best kokkineli; heavy alcoholic rosé. The white wine centre is round Paphos, with Pitsilia the best-known district for Xynisteri.

White wines represent only a quarter of the total. They are hard to prevent from oxidizing; until recently Cyprus sherry was in fact just fortified and sweetened oxidized white wine. Experiments have been made, however, with Spanish sherry methods, and the recent boom in exports has been partly the result.

North Africa

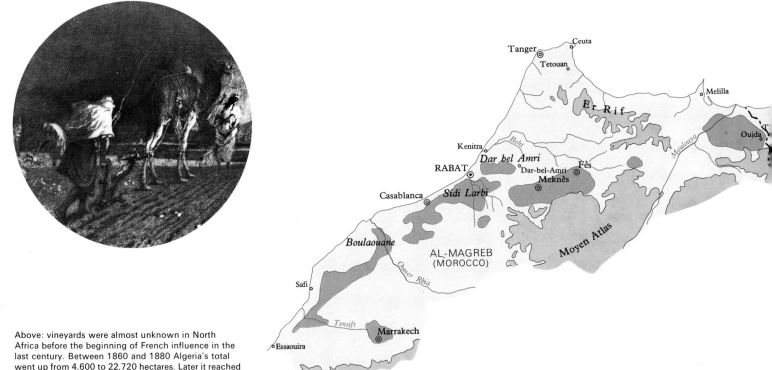

Above: vineyards were almost unknown in North Africa before the beginning of French influence in the last century. Between 1860 and 1880 Algeria's total went up from 4,600 to 22,720 hectares. Later it reached 400,000 hectares

THE NORMAL SITUATION in which the countries who grow the most wine are also those which drink most is reversed in North Africa. In the rest of the world, on an average, exports only account for 10% of wine-production; the home market for 90%. But Algeria, Morocco and Tunisia, which together grew about 10% of the world's wine, in the fifties accounted for no less than two-thirds of the entire international wine-trade. In other words they were alone in growing specifically for export— and, unfortunately for them, specifically for one market; France. Muslim prohibition meant that their home market was practically limited to the European population.

The main appeal of North African wines was to wine-growers and blenders in France, rather than consumers. Light sandy soil and a very hot summer gives them very little acidity —the preservative of northern wines. They age quickly, and naturally help to bring into balance over-acid wine. They are also between 12 and 15% alcohol, which made them vital raw material for transforming the poor under-strength wine of the Midi, often as low as 9%, into the 11% vin ordinaire which is the French workman's staple diet.

However in 1962 Algeria, by far the biggest producer in North Africa, became independent. And at about the same time measures taken in France to improve the wine of the Midi began to take effect. There was much bargaining, but the upshot was that France bought a fraction of her old total from Algeria. With the French population also greatly reduced, Algeria had far more wine than she could sell; most of it only suitable for blending.

All this is politics, but it deeply affects the

Above: Moroccan labels tend to be reticent. The second down is that of vin gris, the pale pink speciality of Boulaoune
Left: Algeria's best vineyards are all on the hills. Today their future is uncertain because of the loss of the French market

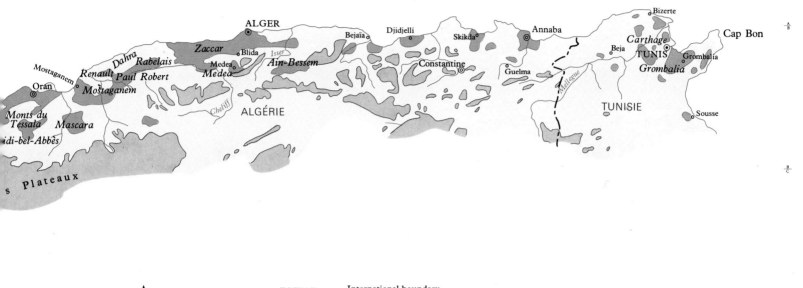

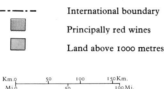

International boundary

Principally red wines

Land above 1000 metres

Km.0   50   100   150 Km.
Mi.0   50   100 Mi.

Above: Tunisian wine
harks back to the great
days of Carthage. She
makes good red ordinaire
and muscat
Left-hand column: during
the French regime a
dozen Algerian wines
were rated Vins Délimités
de Qualité Supérieure.
The technical problems of
making good red wine in
the African climate were
largely overcome. These
labels are from some of
the better estates which
may continue

future of North African wine. There are new markets: Germany and Russia are now customers, and the franc zone countries of Africa—Madagascar, Senegal, the Ivory Coast, Chad—now buy from North Africa rather than from their old supplier, France. But a world glut of vin ordinaire is an extreme danger, if not a fact already. The only sensible course is to abandon massive plains-plantations and concentrate on making better wine in the hills. Between 1966 and 1976 Algeria's vineyard was reduced by nearly a third and Morocco's and Tunisia's by 15 and 20%. But the yield dwindled to a half: from 16 to 8 thousand hectolitres.

Being the butt of endless stories about clandestine tanker-loads to Beaune, North African wines are rarely even thought of as existing in their own right. Visitors to North Africa, particularly Morocco, are invariably surprised at how good the local wine is. The fat soft red wines taste delicious with the grilled meat and the young rosés—Morocco's speciality is a very pale 'vin gris', remarkably hard, dry and refreshing—go well with the shellfish. Visitors soon learn not to try the white wines.

Morocco is the newest wine country of the three. Not until after the second world war were modern vineyards planted in place of the traditional sparse scattering of vines among trees. Her new vineyards are concentrated south and east of Rabat, the capital, stretching inland along the plain (where Sidi Larbi and Dar bel Amri make her best-known red wines) south of Meknès to Fès. Some of these vineyards are in the foot-hills of the Atlas mountains but most are on the plain. South of Casablanca, where the map shows them continuing from Boulaouane almost to Essaouira, they are much more scattered, and largely traditional in style: though Boulaouane has a modern winery.

The French planted the vineyards of Algeria in the second half of the last century. So thoroughly did they carpet the bare red hills with vines that almost 40% of the country's work force at one time were vineyard workers.

Until 1962, twelve of the Algerian hill wine regions were ranked in France as Vins Délimités de Qualité Supérieure. The best-known of them are in the hills of Tlemcen (the domaines of Lismara and Mansourah, 800 metres up and facing north-west); in the Haut-Dahra hills (the three villages with the memorable names of Rabelais, Renault and Paul Robert make red wine which is often said to be Algeria's best); Mascara (particularly the Clos de l'Emir); the hills of Zaccar west of Algiers (Château Romain) and the Domaine de la Trappe Staouëli south-east of the capital.

Seventy-two per cent of Algeria's vineyards are in the province of Oran in the west; mainly on flat land. Oran makes strong, dark-coloured, under-acid, good blending wine. Twenty-three per cent are in the province of Algiers; as they go east, the produce has less strength and character. The names on the map are those of regions of above-average quality.

Tunisia was known for its wine in ancient times; indeed Mago, the first author of a classic manual for wine-growers (and other farmers) was a native of Carthage in the fourth century BC. The muscat grape is a speciality—under the French there was an Appellation Contrôlée Muscat de Tunisie. The best of her red table wine is on a par with the best of Algeria's but the present lack of a market is causing the pulling-up of much of the Tunisian vineyard.

The Eastern Mediterranean

BÅLGARJA
(BULGARIA)

ELL'AS
(GREECE)

Kırklareli

Uzunköprü

Tekirdağ

Istanbul

III

Erdek

Çanakkale

Balıkesir

Bursa

İzmit

Adapazarı

Zonguldak

Karabük

VII

Bafra

Samsun

I

Çubuk

Kalecik

ANKARA

Keskin

Çorum

Amasya

Tokat

Sivas

VI

Akhisar

Eskişehir

Kütahya

TÜRKİYE

VIII

Bornova
İzmir

II

Usak

Afyonkarahisar

Elâzığ

Tire

Akşehir

Ürgüp
Nevşehir

Kayseri

Malatya

Soke

Denizli

Konya

IX

Niğde

Burdur

İsparta

Ereğli

Karaman

Maraş

Euphrates
(Firat)

V

Antalya

Toros Dağları

Adana

Mersin

IV

Gaziantep

İskenderun

Kilis

Antakya

Halab
(Aleppo)

Goksu

KIPROS
(CYPRUS)

Al-Lādiqīyah
(Latakia)

AS–SŬRĬYAH
(SYRIA)

Hamah

International boundary

Limit of wine zones

Red and white wines

Principally white wines

Land over 1500 metres

N

Tarābulus
(Tripoli)

Hims
(Homs)

BAYRUT
(BEIRUT)

Bekaa

Ba'labakk
(Baalbek)

Ksará

AL-LUBNAN
(LEBANON)

DIMASHQ
(DAMASCUS)

Hefa
(Haifa)

Zichron-Jacob

YISRA'EL

Tel Aviv-Yafo
Richon-le-Zion

Ram
Allah

Irbid

Az-Zarqa
(Zarqua)

AMMAN

YERUSHALAYIM
(JERUSALEM)
Gazzah

Bayt Lahm
(Bethlehem)

AL-URDUNN
(JORDAN)

Al-Iskandariyah
(Alexandria)

Bûr Sa'id
(Port Said)

Be'er Sheva

Abú Hummus

AL-JUMHURIYAH AL'ARABIYAH
AL-MUTTAHIDAH
(UNITED ARAB REPUBLIC)

Km. 0   100   200   300 Km.

Mi. 0   100   200 Mi.

Above: the top two labels are those of Turkey's two best-known wines, both red. Below them are two of Turkey's prettiest. Below them are, left, two Israeli and, right, Lebanese and Egyptian labels
Right: vineyards in the valley of Bekaa in the Lebanon

IT IS A sobering thought that some spot on this map may be the very place where man first tasted wine. Whether it was in Persia or Egypt that the first wine was made, there is no doubt that the Middle East is its home country. Noah, Naboth, Christ, St Paul, the great Roman temple at Baalbek are all evidence that the eastern Mediterranean was the France of the ancient world. And so it continued until the eighth century, until the advent of Islam.

The Prophet forbade the use of wine. How effective his teaching was has often been discussed. Some wine-growing went on, but it was not until the end of the last century that wine began to come back to its homeland in earnest. As phylloxera destroyed Europe's vineyards Asia leapt into the breach. In 1857 the Jesuits founded the cellars of Ksara in the Lebanon, still the biggest winery in the Middle East. In the 1880s a Rothschild established wine-growing once more in Israel. Turkey exported nearly 15 million gallons in one year in the 90s. In 1903 Nestor Gianaclis planted the first vines of a new Egyptian wine industry, near Alexandria, whose wine in Roman times was famous.

Turkey is the biggest producer and exporter of the eastern Mediterranean. She has the fifth largest vineyard acreage in the world, but only 3% of her grapes are made into wine. The rest are eaten. The wine industry is held back by lack of a domestic market, for 99% of the population remains Muslim. Kemal Atatürk himself built a winery in 1925 in the hope of persuading Turks of the rightness of wine-drinking, but progress is slow.

The country is divided into nine ecological zones. Zones II and III, the Aegean coast and Thrace/Marmara, are by far the biggest wine-producers, making three-fifths of the total. They are followed by zone I, Ankara, and then, much smaller, IV and IX, south-east Anatolia and south-central Anatolia. The state monopoly has 17 wineries and accounts for most exports of Turkish wine. High-strength blending wine is most in demand, though the names of Trakya and Buzbağ, its lighter and darker red wines (from Thrace and south-east Anatolia, in that order) are familiar. There is also a white Trakya, made of the Semillon grape.

Of the private firms, Doluca and Kavaklidere are probably the best, the Aral the biggest. Wineries on the whole do not own their vineyards but buy their grapes from farmers. Phylloxera is now a problem; many farmers have yet to learn about grafting vines.

Ksara's big installation is the centre of Lebanese wine-growing. Its red wines, made from French ordinaire grapes—Cinsault, Carignan, Aramon—are its best. Small farmers still use biblical methods of vinification and keep their wine in amphoras, or distil it themselves to make the aniseed-flavoured arack which is the national drink.

The considerable wineries at Richon-le-Zion and Zichron-Jacob were a gift to Israel from Baron Edmond de Rothschild. They make three-quarters of Israel's wine. Most of the 14,000 acres of wine-grape vineyard is largely planted with the common French red grapes (41% is Carignan and 32% Alicante-Grenache); the white grapes are Muscat, Semillon and Clairette, also familiar from the Languedoc. Despite the hot dry climate, modern equipment allows the making of a wide range, including a good sparkling wine, 'The President's'. Recently 'varietal' Cabernet Sauvignon, Sauvignon Blanc, Semillon and Grenache rosé has been launched with considerable success. Most exports go to the USA. There is a substantial market for Kosher wine.

The Gianaclis vineyards still operate in Egypt, north-west of the Nile delta at Abu Hummus. Four times more white grapes than red are grown, but three-quarters of the white wine is distilled. The best-known whites are Cru des Ptolemées and Reine Cléopatre. One of the red wines, Omar Khayyam, is smooth and well made, with what seems an intriguing faint flavour of dates.

The Far East

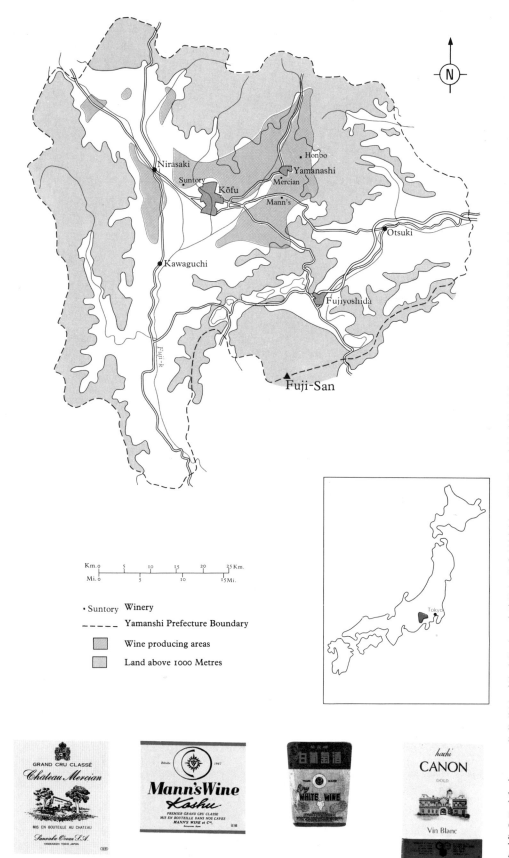

N

Km.0   5   10   15   20   25 Km.
Mi. 0   5   10   15 Mi.

• Suntory   Winery

– – – – –   Yamanshi Prefecture Boundary

▨   Wine producing areas

▨   Land above 1000 Metres

THE VINE travelled west from its earliest home, conquered the Mediterranean, and has ever since given its best performance in western Europe. But it also travelled east, across India into China. The vine was known to gardeners in China—who called one variety 'vegetable dragon pearls'. They knew how to make wine with it, and did so. Why then did it not become part of their way of life, as it has in every western country where it will grow successfully?

Mr Edward Hyams, who has studied the references to wine in oriental literature, concludes that it simply does not suit the Asiatic temperament. It clearly brings out the best in Mediterranean man—but for the Chinese it does nothing. The East is not averse to alcohol. It makes what it calls wine from rice. But wine from grapes, with its soothing, inspiring effect, has never 'taken'.

This being said, there is wine being made in modern China, and a little being exported— and it is very good. The white wine of Tsingtao (or Shantung) province—on about the latitude of Gibraltar—can be compared with a natural sherry with rather more pronounced acidity. It makes a very pleasant aperitif. Clearly there is no reason why fine wines should not grow on Chinese soil . . . yet it somehow seems unlikely that the Chinese will suddenly take to viticulture at this stage in their history.

Japan is another matter. Until the end of the last century she went even further than China in rejecting the ways of the West. But her reaction has been a wholesale trying out of western notions. Wine has taken its turn. At first it was American varieties, not the true wine grape Vitis vinifera, which were tried. There is Concord and Delaware wine made (see page 239). But only recently have true wine grapes, particularly Semillon and Cabernet, been planted with any success.

The damp climate and heavy rainfall of Japan have led to a great deal of disease, and most people who have tried their wine speak of it rather pityingly. A French wine official, however, who has tasted a Cabernet from Kofu, says that it was a perfectly respectable wine. And it is hard to believe that if the Japanese feel the inclination to grow wine in quantity, as they have felt the need to make whisky, they will not make a similar success of it.

At the moment almost all of Japan's production of about 4.8 million gallons a year is made at Kofu and Katsunuma in Yamanashi province, west of Tokyo. A little wine is also made in Osaka and Yamagata provinces. Mann's Wine Co and Sanraku Ocean are the biggest producers and a grape called Koshu (which is said to have come from Europe many years ago) and the muscat Baily A (an American hybrid) are the main grape sorts.

The few vineyards of Japan and the four principal wineries are concentrated in the fruit-growing Yamanashi prefecture between Tokyo and Osaka
Left: Japanese wine labels bear such phrases as Premier Grand Cru Classé and Mis en Bouteille au Château; and even pictures of the château itself.
The label second from right is a good dry white wine from the Shantung province in northern China

The New World

Working a labelling machine for 'sparkling burgundy' in the early days of a California winery

The New World

THE VINE was there at the foundation of the New World as it was at the emergence of the old. First in the haversacks of mission fathers, to make wine for the sacrament. Then with the governors of new colonies, to help establish European civilization on the tip of Africa or in the unpromising land round Botany Bay.

The Americas had had their first vintage by the mid-16th century. South Africa was making wine by a hundred years later. But it was not until the 19th century that the real development of the new wine countries began.

The 1840s and 50s saw wine-growing firmly established in Australia, Argentina, California. It was tentative and imitative to begin with; the wine-maker's chief aim was to make a local version of the familiar wines of Europe. It was natural to use their names for wines which he hoped would resemble them. Each wine-maker tried to make wine of all the classical kinds: red, white, sweet, dry, sparkling, in the same vineyard—and even from the same grapes.

So a tradition grew up which was to have unfortunate consequences. The names of Chablis, Sauternes, Burgundy, Champagne—all names of parts of France—became so embedded in the wine industries of far-off countries that it began to seem as though they could not move without them.

So long as viticultural knowledge and technique was limited to adapting Old World methods this was the best the wine-makers of the New World could do.

But the last 20 years have seen a revolution which may turn out to be the most important event in the history of wine. Study in universities, followed up by experiments in the fields, has so far improved the selection and cultivation of vines and the techniques of making wine, that good light table wines can be made from bulk-cropping grapes grown in country which is virtually a desert.

Above all refrigeration has come to the aid of the wine-maker. Grapes ripening late in a north-European October ferment in cold sheds gently. But in (for example) March in South Africa the run-away boiling of the must is enough to drive off all the acids and essences that go to make its character. Flat, overstrong wines tended to result.

The introduction of temperature control has meant that, for the first time, light, scented, refreshing wines can be made in the hot countries where they are wanted. Proud of making excellent wine, the vintner has taken to calling it by the name of its grape rather than a borrowed name.

The wine industries of Australia, California and South Africa at least are still only in their infancies. The years 1971–1974 saw unprecedented expansion of the acreage of the best wine grapes in California especially. As these start producing the amount of excellent wine available is bound to spread the wine-drinking habit faster than ever. Australia and South Africa present similar pictures. It seems possible, to say the least, that one day wine will be the everyday drink of the inhabitants of the New World.

Right: there are places, as here in north California, where the New World promise comes true, and a homestead clearing in the forest turns into a fruitful vineyard

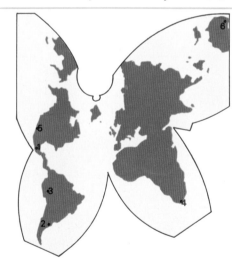

The vine moved to the New World with the early missionaries: around 1520 to Mexico **1**; 1560 to Argentina **2**; Peru **3** before the end of the century. In southern Africa, the first vines were planted by the Dutch at the Cape **4** in 1655. In 1769 missionaries had planted in California **5**. The Antipodes were the last to get vineyards: vines were brought to Australia **6** by settlers in 1788 and wine-growing was established by the first 20 years of the 19th century

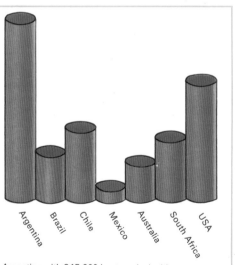

Argentina with 345,000 hectares is the biggest vineyard of the New World, and the fifth biggest in existence (in the future she may well become one of the important sources of vin ordinaire for the world). The United States comes next with 301,000 hectares (of which 85% are in California), then Chile with 130,000, South Africa with 110,000, Australia with 72,000, Brazil with 63,000, Mexico with 33,000 and New Zealand (not on the diagram) with 2,000. Modern methods have recently made such a profound difference to the quality of their wines that the years of fame for New World vineyards are only just about to begin

Wine in North America

'THE GOODLIEST SOIL under the cloak of heaven' was how one of Raleigh's men described the new-found Carolinas. One of their most impressive sights was their grape-vines, whose luscious fruit festooned the forests. The grapes were sweet, if strange to taste. It was the obvious assumption that wine would be one of the good things of the New World.

Yet 300 years of American history are a saga of the shattered hopes of would-be wine-growers. First, of those who used the wild grapes they found. 'They be fatte, and the juyce thicke. Neither doth the taste so well please when they are made into wine,' wrote Captain John Smith in 1606. Then of those who imported European vines and planted them in the new colonies. They died.

The colonists did not give up easily. Having no notion what was killing their vines they assumed it was their fault and tried different sorts and different methods. As late as the Revolution Washington tried, and Jefferson, a great amateur of wine who toured France for the purpose, had a determined attempt. Nothing came of it. The American soil was full of the European vine's deadliest enemy, phylloxera. Aided by savagely cold winters and hot humid summers such as Europe never sees, bringing with them fungus diseases, America foiled everyone who tried to make European wine.

If American wines of American grapes were bad, some were worse than others. The ancestry of grapes is almost impossible to trace, but either a chance sport of an American vine, or else a natural hybrid between an American and a European vine which had lived long enough to flower, gave its grower hope of better things. More improvements came to diligent gardeners who planted pips and tried out the results. Some of these hybrids became famous. The Catawba was born thus, and then, in 1843, the Concord—one of the healthiest, most prolific, best-looking and tastiest grapes ever introduced.

The peculiar quality of American grapes the colonists disliked only emerges fully when they are made into wine. The wine has a flavour known as 'foxy'—a distinct and easily recognized scented taste, which precludes any subtlety or complexity. There are many American species. Foxiness is most pronounced in *Vitis labrusca*. Unfortunately V. labrusca must have had its genes in Catawba and been one, if not both, of the parents of Concord. And it continued to be used by hybridizers who produced such other famous American grapes as the Delaware.

Since these were the best grapes Americans could grow, Americans grew them. Vineyards were started in New York, New Jersey, Virginia and, above all, Ohio. It was at Cincinnati, Ohio, that the first commercially successful American wine was born—Nicholas Longworth's famous Sparkling Catawba. Longworth hit on the fact that foxiness is least apparent and least objectionable in sparkling wine. By 1850 he had 1,200 acres of Catawba vineyards and was making a fortune.

It was short lived. Vine disease, the Civil War and finally Longworth's death in 1863 ended Cincinnati's challenge to Reims. But the

The Jesuit missionary Father Junípero Serra is said to have planted the first vines in California in 1769

Thomas Jefferson, wine-connoisseur and would-be wine-grower, promoted wine as the best means of combating intemperance

point was made. Longworth's champagne-makers soon found new employers: the new Pleasant Valley Wine Co of Hammondsport on New York's Finger Lakes. This time American wine had found its permanent home.

The Finger Lakes region is described more fully on pages 238–239. Here we must trace the progress of America's other wine-making tradition, which came in under Spanish colours by the back door, while the Anglo-Saxons were struggling with native vines at the front.

Jesuit fathers had taken vines with them to make sacramental wine in Mexico at the beginning of the 17th century. Their primitive vine, known as the Mission (presumably a seedling, since it is not known in Europe) flourished in Baja California. In 1767 they were expelled from Mexico and moved up the coast. Here, at the San Diego Mission, Father Junípero Serra is said to have planted the first vine in California.

There were none of the problems of the east coast here. *Vitis vinifera* had found it Promised Land. The vine moved up the coast with the

chain of mission stations, arriving at the northernmost, Sonoma, by 1805. There, though the missions declined, viticulture flourished. Jean-Louis Vignes brought better grapes than the Mission from Europe to Los Angeles. Came the Gold Rush and massive immigration. By the 1850s the redoubtable figure of Agoston Haraszthy had taken over, organizing, after a fashion, the new wine industry, and personally bringing 100,000 cuttings of innumerable varieties from Europe.

Thus by the mid-19th century America had two wine industries, poles apart. She still has. Both limped through the disastrous Prohibition period making sacramental wine (even sparkling sacramental wine) and selling grape juice with the dire warning 'Caution—do not add yeast or the contents will ferment'. They took over a decade to find their feet again after Repeal, and Americans took more than a generation to take up regular wine-drinking. But today the scene is a frenzy of activity and experiment, with vineyards being planted (in many cases replanted) not only in California

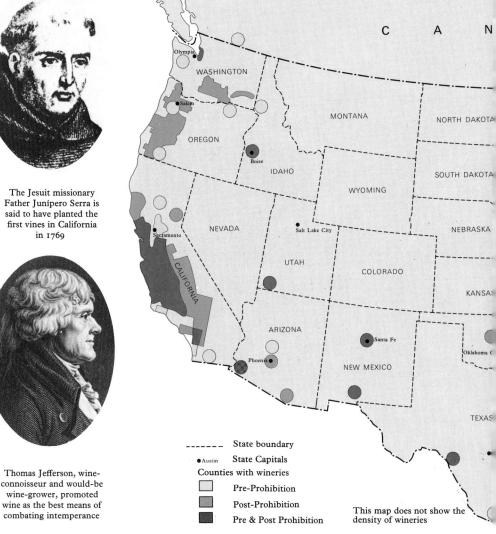

State boundary
• Austin State Capitals
Counties with wineries
Pre-Prohibition
Post-Prohibition
Pre & Post Prohibition

This map does not show the density of wineries

The Hungarian Agoston Haraszthy galvanized the California industry by introducing scores of new vine varieties in the 1840s

Frank Schoonmaker, writer and wine-merchant, influenced California to make quality wine after Prohibition by promoting 'varietal' labelling

Philip Wagner, writer and wine-maker, introduced hybrid grapes to the eastern States; a historic move in American wine-history

Eugene Hilgard, at the Agricultural Experiment Station, started in 1880 to lay the foundations of scientific viticulture in California

James D. Zellerbach pioneered the use of French oak for ageing California wine. His Chardonnays of the '50s were a turning point

Dr Konstantin Frank has proved that good wine can be made from European grapes in New York's Finger Lakes district

and New York but (as the map shows) in half the other states of the Union as well.

The South has a small wine industry of its own based on the native grape of its hot, moist woods; *Vitis rotundifolia*, the Scuppernong. The Scuppernong holds its big cherry-like grapes in clusters, not pressed together in bunches, and thus avoids the inevitable bunch-rot of normal grapes in the typical climate of Georgia and the Carolinas. Scuppernong wine is very sweet and uncompromisingly strange to vinifera-trained tongues.

Most of the other states with infant industries are planting either the well-proven American vines (of which Concord is far and away the most popular, poor though its wine is) or else the new French-American hybrids which were bred in France in the hope of solving the phylloxera problem, but are more appreciated in America as possible solutions to the riddle of the fox. The hybrids were first introduced by Philip Wagner of Boordy Vineyards in Maryland—perhaps a contribution as significant as Jean-Louis Vignes'.

It is too early yet to produce an assessment of most of the new vineyards. Ohio is back in business growing Catawbas on the shore of Lake Erie round Sandusky and on the lake's limestone islands; potentially, it seems, an excellent vineyard. Indiana, Michigan, Missouri, Wisconsin, Oklahoma, Arkansas, even Texas (round Lubbock) have wineries. In the east New Hampshire and Vermont have a hopeful little industry based (like that of Old England) mainly on hybrids. New Jersey has an old-established business. Maryland and Virginia have several wineries each (including Wagner's at Ryderwood near Baltimore) and Pennsylvania's vineyards include some flourishing Riesling.

On the west coast Washington and Oregon are both convinced of their potential for making wine at least as good as California's. Conditions, however, are more difficult. The coastal belt is rainy, probably too rainy, and the great Yakima valley in the rain-shadow of the Cascades (though so dry that irrigation is essential) has extremely cold winters. So far,

certainly, it has been planted mainly with the hardy Concord. But Ste Michelle and Boordy Vineyards have made good vinifera wines in Washington. Ste Michelle Riesling is more in the German style than any in California. And Hillcrest at Roseburg in the Umpqua valley in Oregon is making a reputation with Riesling and Chardonnay.

Canada has vineyards both in British Columbia and Ontario. The British Columbia industry is based on American vines with a few hybrids and is only of local interest. But Ontario, having long specialized in sweet sherry-type wine, has recently produced some very creditable table wines from both hybrid and vinifera vines grown in the surprisingly mild climate of the Niagara area.

The province has established a form of Appellation Contrôlée, 'Ontario Superior', for table wines from certain varieties. Bright's is the biggest company, and Château Gai and Inniskillin are others who make good light wines—particularly from the vinifera red hybrid Maréchal Foch.

California

WHAT GIVES California pre-eminence among the wine countries of the New World is largely its climatic but partly also its social conditions. France and Germany proved long ago how advanced civilizations demand and promote the improvement of viticulture. Today northern California is one of the world's great cultural centres. The concentration of intelligent demand, interest and discussion is a constant challenge to wine-makers to experiment with and to improve their wine.

The best of California's wines today are among the world's best. But more important, California has discovered how to make *good* ordinary wine cheaply and consistently. With both top-level and everyday wine outstanding in any comparison, and a rapidly growing market, California is destined to be one of the great wine countries of the future.

Her production is growing apace. Today it is already a third of that of Spain and almost a fifth of that of Italy or France. New plantings are just bearing fruit, whole new valleys just making wine for the first time.

The wine country divides very broadly into its coastal and inland parts. Inland it is very hot. Common wines used to be the whole production until new methods improved things. The coastal vineyards vary widely. An early study of the influential Viticulture and Enology Department of the University of California was to zone the state by a method known as heat-summation, adding up the number of degrees over 50°F achieved during the annual growing period of the vine. Five zones (see small map) were plotted, the coolest nearest to northern Europe in climate, the hottest most like the south of Spain or North Africa.

The constant contention of the Enology De-

partment has been that the way ahead lies in planting the right grape variety in the right place. It offers definite advice and has led to interest being concentrated on the question of grape varieties. This more than anything started the swing away from 'generic' (e.g. Chablis, Rhine) wine names. Today grape varieties are the key to California wine. It seems that when the wheel has turned full circle some of the best California wine districts will specialize in one grape, and therefore one type of wine, as, after 2,000 years, Burgundy and the Mosel have come to do.

There is a good way to go before the millennium is reached. Some big wineries (on their own admission) put 'Chablis' and 'Rhine wine' labels on wine from the same vat. And the law still only demands that 51% of the grapes in a varietal wine be of the variety named. In this respect the law lags behind the accepted practice of the most important producers.

For the moment most wineries feel it is expected of them to carry a full range of wines, which makes a visit to them a strange experience, like being in Bordeaux, Burgundy, Portugal and Champagne all at the same time.

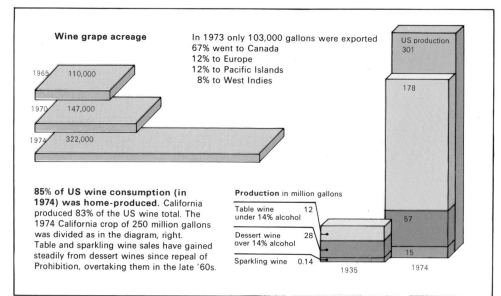

Wine grape acreage

1965 — 110,000
1970 — 147,000
1974 — 322,000

In 1973 only 103,000 gallons were exported
67% went to Canada
12% to Europe
12% to Pacific Islands
8% to West Indies

85% of US wine consumption (in 1974) was home-produced. California produced 83% of the US wine total. The 1974 California crop of 250 million gallons was divided as in the diagram, right. Table and sparkling wine sales have gained steadily from dessert wines since repeal of Prohibition, overtaking them in the late '60s.

Production in million gallons

Table wine under 14% alcohol — 12
Dessert wine over 14% alcohol — 28
Sparkling wine — 0.14

US production 301
178
57
15
1935   1974

California Grape Guide

Seventeen of the best varieties are described here, with the climate regions (see opposite) for which they are recommended by the University of California, and the normal yield per acre. One ton of grapes gives about 160 US gallons (606 litres) of wine. So 5 tons/acre = 3030 litres/acre, or approximately 73 hectolitres/hectare. Lower yields usually give higher quality. The 1975 acreage figures for the leading counties for each grape are given last.

Barbera (regions 3–4; 5–8 tons) Dark red wine with good balance of acidity even when grown in very hot conditions. Italian style. Fresno 5,694; Kern 4,313; Madera 3,751

Cabernet Sauvignon (regions 1–2; 4–6 tons) The best red wine: perfumed, fruity, dry, long-lasting. Needs ageing at least four years. Monterey 5,634; Napa 5,209; Sonoma 4,164; Santa Barbara 1,889

Chardonnay (regions 1–2; 4–6 tons) The best white wine: dry but full and sappy; perfumed; grape flavour; improved by short time in oak. Lasts well. Monterey 2,929; Napa 2,249; Sonoma 1,808

Chenin Blanc (region 1; 6–10 tons) (sometimes wrongly called White Pinot; is not Pinot Blanc). In hills sometimes makes

well-balanced, rich but tart wine. Often not very distinctive. Kern 4,844; Fresno 2,373; Merced 2,377; Monterey 2,092

French Colombard (regions 3–4; 6–10 tons) Rather neutral dry white used for blending; in cooler areas fresh and pleasant unblended. Fresno 5,835; Kern 4,995; Madera 3,365; Merced 2,509

Gamay (also known as Napa Gamay) (regions 1–2; 6–9 tons) In fact the true French Gamay, but only good for pink wine. Monterey 1,218; Napa 1,006; Kern 425; Sonoma 328

Gamay Beaujolais (regions 1–2; 3–4 tons) A form of Pinot Noir; light red wine, not comparable with French Beaujolais. Monterey 1,223; Napa 603; Mendocino 589; San Benito 518

Gewürztraminer (region 1; 4–6 tons) Gentle, often slightly sweet, distinctively spicy white wine. Monterey 795; Sonoma 473; Napa 300

Grenache (region 2; 5–9 tons) Very good for rosé; light-coloured full-bodied red used for blending. Madera 3,967; Kern 3,578; Fresno 3,041

Petite Sirah (also called Shiraz) (region 2; 4–8 tons) Dark red, strong, tannic and long-lasting. Monterey 2,234; Kern 1,887; Fresno 1,358; Sonoma 1,194

Pinot Blanc (region 1; 4–6 tons) Fruity, dry, medium to good quality white. Monterey 670; San Benito 180; Sonoma 74

Pinot Noir (region 1; 3–4 tons) Good lightish red with distinctive grape aroma; rarely absolutely first-rank in California. Monterey 2,590; Napa 2,526; Sonoma 2,523; Santa Barbara 826

Ruby Cabernet (regions 3–4; 6–8 tons) New variety makes good dry table wine in hot areas; useful not great. Kern 4,802; Fresno 4,014; Madera 2,525

Sauvignon Blanc (regions 2–3; 4–7 tons) Good to very good earthy/grapy dry white. Monterey 1,027; Napa 534; Merced 390

Semillon (regions 2–3; 4–6 tons) Medium to sweet golden-white; occasionally excellent. Kern 670; Stanislaus 504; Monterey 519

White Riesling (also called Johannisberg Riesling) (regions 1–2; 4–6 tons) Scented, fruity, ideally tart, but often soft, first-class white. Monterey 2,374; Napa 1,414; Santa Barbara 1,009; Sonoma 814

Zinfandel (region 1; 4–6 tons) 'California's Beaujolais'; raspberryish, spicy and good; also used for blending. San Joaquin 10,927; Sonoma 3,721; San Bernardino 3,303; Monterey 3,194; Napa 1,315

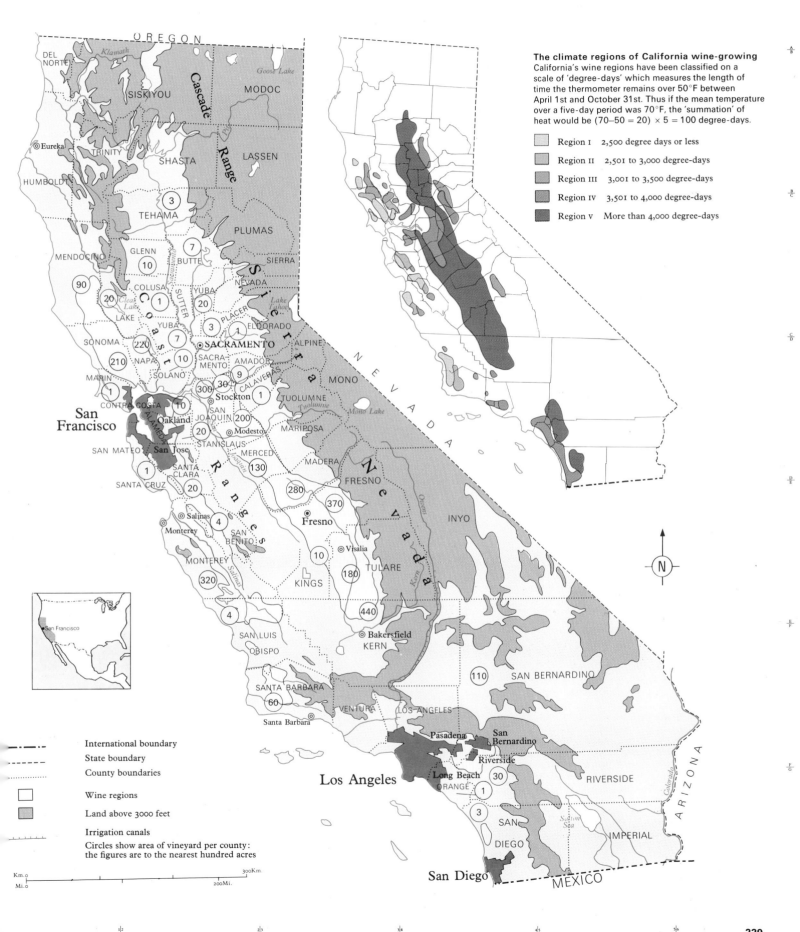

The climate regions of California wine-growing

California's wine regions have been classified on a scale of 'degree-days' which measures the length of time the thermometer remains over 50°F between April 1st and October 31st. Thus if the mean temperature over a five-day period was 70°F, the 'summation' of heat would be $(70-50=20) \times 5 = 100$ degree-days.

Region I	2,500 degree days or less
Region II	2,501 to 3,000 degree-days
Region III	3,001 to 3,500 degree-days
Region IV	3,501 to 4,000 degree-days
Region V	More than 4,000 degree-days

International boundary
State boundary
County boundaries

Wine regions
Land above 3000 feet
Irrigation canals

Circles show area of vineyard per county:
the figures are to the nearest hundred acres

Km.o   300Km.
Mi.o   200Mi.

The Russian River

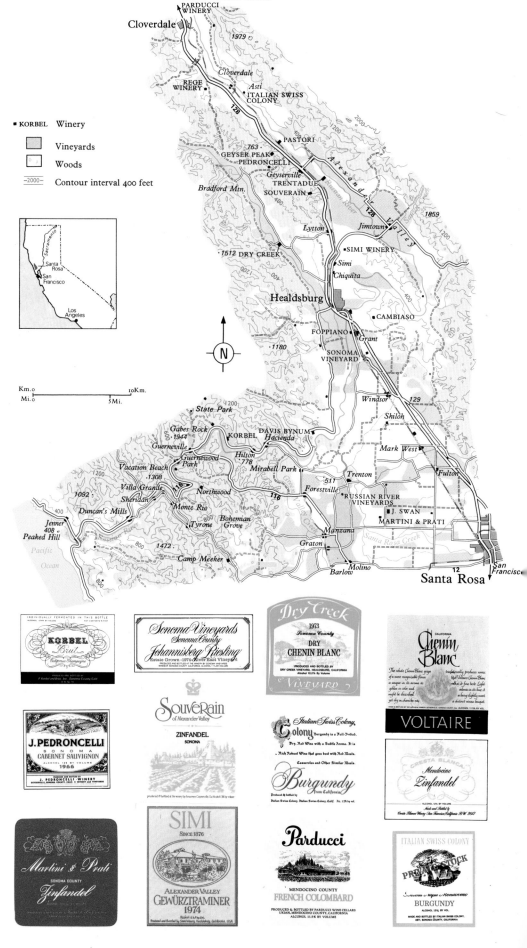

THE GREAT part of Sonoma county's vineyards lie along the Russian River (so-called from a former Russian trading post) and its tributaries, between Santa Rosa, 20 miles north of Sonoma city (page 233), and Asti, 30 miles farther on.

The California coastal climate avoids the obvious. North of the Bay it starts cool, then grows steadily warmer. At Santa Rosa it is still Region 1. By Asti it is Region 3: essentially red-wine country.

Traditionally this Russian River territory has been the source of good-quality 'bulk' wine, bought by the big firms of the Central valley for blending. It is still a major source of the excellent Gallo standard wines. Wineries have flourished here (barring the Prohibition period) for a century, but in the main anonymously. The most famous exception is Italian Swiss Colony, founded at Asti in 1881 by the Rossi family, which still produces one of California's widest ranges of wines and which pioneered fruit-flavoured wines as a way of reaching out to a wider market—with results for which the whole industry is grateful.

In a more specialized field Korbel also has an old and excellent reputation. Their vineyards are planted among the stumps of an old redwood forest along the winding course of the Russian River as it threads the Coast Range westwards to the ocean. Few, even in California, are as beautiful. Their specialities are 'champagne' and brandy. Korbel Brut is certainly among the best sparkling wines California has to offer—which is high praise.

Otherwise, until the last five years, only the small family wineries of Pedroncelli and Parducci were known outside the area.

The news of the last five years is that the sense of purposeful excitement in the wine industry has spilled north from the Napa valley and flooded the Russian River basin. Already Alexander valley, whose first quality vines are barely ten years old, is an appellation commanding respect. Simi is typical of the sleepy old stone-built wineries which have woken to a new life. Souverain by contrast typifies the luxurious new expense-no-object style. Wine technology has made such strides that clean, grapy, new-style wine is within easy reach. What follows is the fascinating part, as wine-makers discover the full potential of their new vineyards and vats.

Sonoma (formerly Windsor) Vineyards has already established a sound name in the area. Cambiaso, Foppiano and Nervo are smaller old wineries which are moving with the times. It is still too soon to say which of the half-dozen others now in their infancy will be prominent, or indeed permanent.

One which is breaking new ground to some purpose is Parducci, off the map to the north at Ukiah in Mendocino county. Ukiah is in Region 3, but the Parduccis are planting in neighbouring valleys, in a range of locations and altitudes, to discover the full range of Mendocino's possibilities. Recently they have been joined by Cresta Blanca from Livermore and Weibel from San Jose. The stress the Parduccis and others are putting on local appellations may be another stage in California's self-discovery as a great wine region.

The Napa Valley

Left: the new Joseph Phelps winery is a redwood barn built with superlative skill and imagination
Above: its neighbour, the old stone Heitz winery in Spring valley. Two of the best examples of Napa style: craftsmanship in an idyllic setting

THE NAPA valley has become the symbol as well as the centre of the top-quality wine industry in California. It does not have a monopoly, by any means. But in its wines, its wine-makers and the idyllic Golden Age atmosphere which fills it from one green hillside to another, it captures the imagination and stays in the memory.

The valley runs in an arc north-west from Napa, most of its vineyards lying on its nearly flat floor. It is realistic to consider the vineyards of the old city of Sonoma, the proclaimed capital of the Californian Republic which never was, as part of the same complex, although they lie beyond the ridge of the Mayacamas Mountains: in these mountains are some of the best of the 'Napa' vineyards, and the future is likely to see more planting both in the hills and round the southern, San Francisco Bay end of them, in the area known as Los Carneros.

Sonoma is the site of the most famous winery of the early days of California; the Buena Vista vineyard founded by Colonel Agoston Haraszthy in 1857. It was reopened in 1943 and makes good table wine today, including the Zinfandel, unique to California, which legend says was the Colonel's own contribution to his new country from his native Hungary. It is known as California's Beaujolais.

North of Sonoma the very small, super-high-quality Hanzell winery makes brilliantly rich and intense Chardonnay and Pinot Noir. Sebastiani is a full-blooded Italian family business, whose red Barbera and (white) Green Hungarian are their hallmark; racy wines for dishes made with olive oil and ham and cheese.

The typical Napa valley winery is set beside the valley road in its vines, but has more vines scattered round on the flat and in the hills. Louis Martini, for example, has five vineyards, of which the most famous is Monte Rosso, high above the Sonoma valley. Others, like the Christian Brothers at Mont la Salle, Schramsberg or Mayacamas have their vines around them in an enclave of their own in the hills.

The valley falls into two climate zones. From Napa to Rutherford is Region 1, the coolest. The northern part is in Region 2, a shade warmer. In fact a great deal depends on the altitude of the vineyard: Stony Hill and Chappellet are examples of wineries in the hills whose wines have particular finesse. The Schramsberg which Robert Louis Stevenson loved is another: the top name in California 'champagne'. So good is Napa 'champagne' that Moët & Chandon (of Champagne) have built a new winery at Yountville to make their own.

Going north from Oakville, the modernistic adobe winery of Robert Mondavi is the first essential visit. Mondavi believes passionately in temperature control and has made a study of barrel-oak, with the result that he can make his Chardonnay taste astonishingly like Meursault. Sauvignon (which he calls Fumé) Blanc, Pinot Noir and Gamay rosé are some of his other successes.

Two of the best-known wineries of the valley are next up the road. Beaulieu and Inglenook both now belong to the massive Heublein Corporation, but Beaulieu at least continues in its tradition of making the best kind of Napa wine. Its Cabernet is dark, fat and stylish.

Before St Helena there is a little showplace

for the prestigious Heitz Cellars—Joe Heitz's house and cellars are up Spring Valley Road to the east—and then the big plain hangars which house Louis M. Martini, in some ways the most distinguished winery in California. Martini is remarkable for his best wines (Cabernet and Chardonnay in particular), but also for his amazing 'jug' wines, Mountain Red and Mountain White, which must be among the best value for money in the world.

Beyond St Helena are the last two big-scale wineries of the valley; the eminent Charles Krug (with a wide range of good-average varietals) and Beringer (recently bought by the Nestlé Co) in a timbered nightmare of a building appropriately called Rhine House.

The country here where the valley narrows becomes more and more beautiful. Oaks and pines, streams, darting birds, fruit-trees, sunlit meadows stretch to the little spa of Calistoga and far beyond.

The little Freemark Abbey, new and with very high standards, and the Larkmead winery of Hanns Kornell are the only ones down in the valley here.

But above in the woods Stony Hill, Souverain and the Schramsberg which Robert Louis Stevenson loved are three of Napa's best names, with a small production which tends to be snapped up by regular customers. Higher still, on a mountain of its own to the south-east, with a staggering view over Lake Hennessey, Mount St Helena and the Napa valley, the new Chappellet winery has a remarkable amphitheatre site and a soaring modern building which is no less than a cathedral of wine.

Napa/the Quality Factor

It USED to be said that 'every year is a vintage year' in California. So far as the Central valley is concerned it is true that grapes ripen regularly and the wine of one year is much like the wine of the next. But the coastal counties' vineyards have a more wayward climate, more varying microclimates and more differing soil structures than any broad generalizations can convey. As the wine industry matures it is learning to take advantage of local conditions to produce distinctive wines by planting precisely the right grape in the right place.

At present it is still in the experimental stages. Only a few individual sites have established reputations for growing particular grapes outstandingly well. The Cabernet Sauvignon of Martha's Vineyard, regularly bought and vinified by Joe Heitz of St Helena, is perhaps the best-known example so far.

The maps on this page are a first step in plotting quality factors in detail for one small area, the northern Napa valley. They were prepared specially for this Atlas by James Lider, for many years official agricultural adviser in the area, in collaboration with his brother Lloyd Lider of the University of California, Davis.

Three variables affect the grower's decision as to what vines to plant where. Soil is the first. There are two principal soil types in the area: 'upland soil', gravelly loam, quick-draining and warm, on the lower slopes of the surrounding hills, and the heavier clay of the valley floor. The former, as a general rule, gives finer quality.

The second is the average temperature, measured in California on the scale described on page 229. Even within this small area, 17 miles by five, three different temperature zones are discernible. A larger-scale map would show innumerable local pockets of warmer or cooler conditions that in due course could create wines of particular character.

The third factor is the risk of destructive late spring frosts, worst on the valley floor where the cold air drains. Vines which come into leaf early are most at risk. After frost damage, vines are likely to replace the damaged flowers with a second flush, whose grapes will ripen later than those remaining from the first. Uneven ripeness at vintage time makes high-quality wine unlikely.

The vineyards with the highest quality potential therefore are those with upland soil and low frost risk (which usually go together) planted with the grapes indicated for that temperature zone.

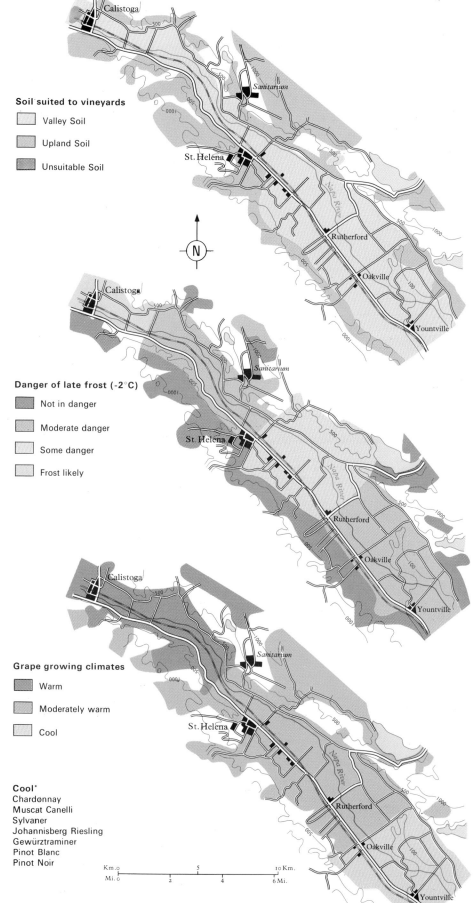

Soil suited to vineyards
- Valley Soil
- Upland Soil
- Unsuitable Soil

Danger of late frost (-2°C)
- Not in danger
- Moderate danger
- Some danger
- Frost likely

Grape growing climates
- Warm
- Moderately warm
- Cool

Some grape varieties suitable for the three temperature zones of the Napa valley

Warm*	Moderately warm*	Cool*
Petite Sirah	Cabernet Sauvignon	Chardonnay
Zinfandel	Zinfandel	Muscat Canelli
Cabernet-Sauvignon	Semillon	Sylvaner
Sauvignon Blanc	Refosco (Mondeuse)	Johannisberg Riesling
Barbera	Napa Gamay	Gewürztraminer
Grenache	Merlot	Pinot Blanc
Gamay	Gamay Beaujolais	Pinot Noir
Carignan	Chenin Blanc	
	Grey Riesling	

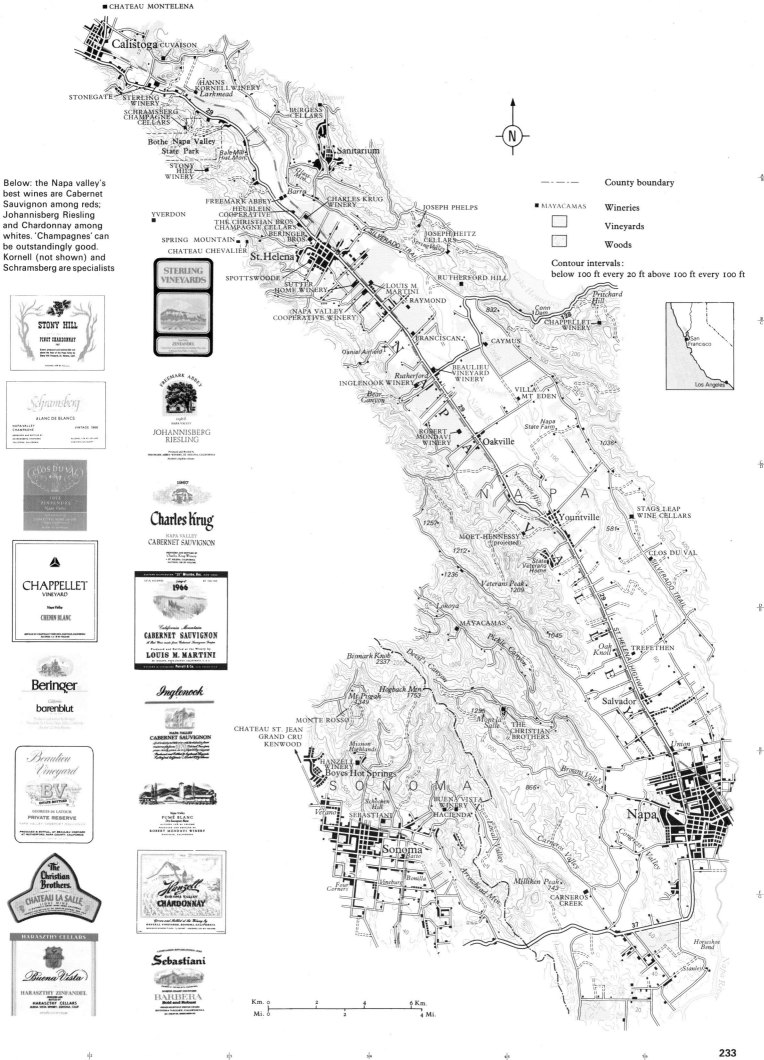

CHATEAU MONTELENA

Calistoga CUVAISON

STONEGATE
STERLING
WINERY
SCHRAMSBERG
CHAMPAGNE
CELLARS

HANNS
KORNELL WINERY
Larkmead

BURGESS
CELLARS

Bothe Napa Valley
State Park
STONY
HILL
WINERY

Bale Mill
Hist. Mon.

Sanitarium

Glass
Mtn.

Barro

Below: the Napa valley's
best wines are Cabernet
Sauvignon among reds;
Johannisberg Riesling
and Chardonnay among
whites. 'Champagnes' can
be outstandingly good.
Kornell (not shown) and
Schramsberg are specialists

FREEMARK ABBEY
HEUBLEIN
COOPERATIVE
THE CHRISTIAN BROS
CHAMPAGNE CELLARS
BERINGER
BROS.

YVERDON

SPRING MOUNTAIN
CHATEAU CHEVALIER

St. Helena

SPOTTSWOODE

CHARLES KRUG
WINERY

JOSEPH PHELPS

JOSEPH HEITZ
CELLARS

Spring Valley

County boundary

■ MAYACAMAS   Wineries

Vineyards

Woods

Contour intervals:
below 100 ft every 20 ft above 100 ft every 100 ft

STERLING
VINEYARDS

ZINFANDEL

STONY HILL
PINOT CHARDONNAY

Schramsberg
BLANC DE BLANCS
NAPA-VALLEY
CHAMPAGNE   VINTAGE 1966

FREEMARK ABBEY
1968
NAPA VALLEY
JOHANNISBERG
RIESLING

SUTTER
HOME WINERY

NAPA VALLEY
COOPERATIVE WINERY

RUTHERFORD HILL

LOUIS M.
MARTINI
RAYMOND

Daniel Airfield

FRANCISCAN

CAYMUS

832

Conn Dam
CHAPPELLET
WINERY

Pritchard
Hill

128

San
Francisco

Los Angeles

Clos du Val
1972
ZINFANDEL
Napa Valley

CHAPPELLET
VINEYARD
Napa Valley
CHENIN BLANC

Charles Krug
NAPA VALLEY
CABERNET SAUVIGNON

1966
California Mountain
CABERNET SAUVIGNON
LOUIS M. MARTINI

Rutherford

INGLENOOK WINERY

Bear
Canyon

BEAULIEU
VINEYARD
WINERY

VILLA
MT EDEN

Napa
State Farm

1200

1036

ROBERT
MONDAVI
WINERY

Oakville

NAPA

1257

Youngville Hills

Yountville

1212

MOET-HENNESSY
(projected)

State
Veterans
Home

STAGS LEAP
WINE CELLARS

581

CLOS DU VAL

Beringer
California
barenblut

Inglenook
NAPA VALLEY
CABERNET SAUVIGNON
1970

FUMÉ BLANC
Dry Sauvignon Blanc
ROBERT MONDAVI WINERY

1236

Veterans Peak
1209

Lokoya

1045

Pickle Canyon

Oak
Knoll

TREFETHEN

Beaulieu
Vineyard
BV
GEORGES DE LATOUR
PRIVATE RESERVE

Hanzell
SONOMA VALLEY
CHARDONNAY

Bismark Knob
2337

Mt. Pisgah
1349

Hogback Mtn.
1753

Devil's Canyon

1295
Mont la
Salle

THE
CHRISTIAN
BROTHERS

Salvador

Union

The Christian Brothers
CHATEAU LA SALLE
LIGHT WINE

HARASZTHY CELLARS

Buena Vista
HARASZTHY ZINFANDEL

Sebastiani
BARBERA
Bold and Robust

MONTE ROSSO

CHATEAU ST. JEAN
GRAND CRU
KENWOOD

Mission
Highlands

HANZELL
WINERY
Boyes Hot Springs

SONOMA

Verano

SEBASTIANI

Sonoma
Batto

Schocken
Hill

BUENA VISTA
WINERY
HACIENDA

866

Browns Valley

Carneros Valley

Napa

Four
Corners

Vineburg

Bonilla

100

Arrochead Mtn

Lovall Valley

Milliken Peak
743

CARNEROS
CREEK

Congress Valley

Horseshoe
Bend

Stanley

Km. 0   2   4   6 Km.
Mi. 0   2   4 Mi.

233

The Central Valley

THE SAN JOAQUIN valley, alias the Central valley, produces four bottles out of five of California wine. To put it another way, if all America's wine filled one bottle, all but one-and-a-bit glasses of it would come from this giant vineyard.

Conditions are totally different here from those among the coastal hills. You can grow anything. The soil is rich river-deposit, fertile and flat for 400 miles north-south and up to 100 miles across. Vines take their place with orchards, and among the vines table-and-raisin-grapes with wine-grapes. Many are of adaptable varieties which will do for either at a pinch.

The climate is reliably, steadily, often stupefyingly hot. For most of the length of the valley the Coast Ranges seal it off from any Pacific influence. On the University of California scale most of it is Region 5. The natural produce of such a climate is grapes with immensely high sugar content and virtually no acidity. Strong sweet wines were the best the Valley could do, until technology came to its rescue.

Fifteen years ago Americans drank 70% high-strength wine, 30% light table wine. Today the proportions are reversed. The Valley has adapted to the new demand with incredible speed and success—has indeed helped to shape the pattern of American wine-drinking by designing new kinds of light wine, making them reliably and selling them reasonably.

The University of California provided the means, in the form of new grape varieties, new ways of growing them and new wine-making techniques—not to mention new wine-makers.

Some of their new varieties, notably Emerald Riesling and Ruby Cabernet, are already established as California standards. Others such as Carmine, Centurion and Carnelian (see page 24) are reputedly even better. New varieties apart, elimination of unsuitable old ones has been an important part of the improvements.

New ways of growing them have consisted mainly of high trellising with various devices to give the maximum curtain of leaves over the grapes, of mist sprays to cool the vineyard in hot weather, and of provisions for mechanical harvesting—not yet fully in gear for political reasons, but bound to come.

In the cellar the great developments have been stainless steel and other neutral tanks, protecting the grapes, the must and wine from oxygen, various forms of presses, pumps and filters—but above all temperature control. Refrigeration more than any single factor has made good light wine possible in the Central valley.

The lead in these developments was taken and is firmly held by the brothers Ernest and Julio Gallo, whose family-owned business at Modesto is the biggest single wine-operation on earth. Its statistics are startling: a capacity of 175 million gallons; the biggest glass-factory west of the Mississippi at the start of the bottling-line; a 25-acre warehouse holding only four weeks' stock.

The figures would be impressive if it were beer they were dispensing, or even soda water. What makes them awe-inspiring is that the

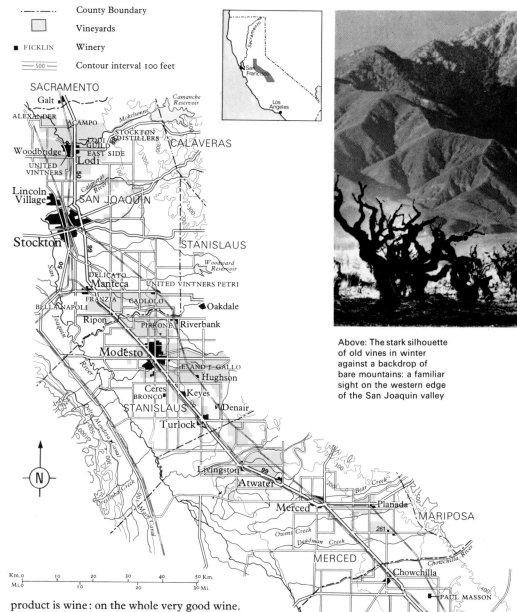

Above: The stark silhouette of old vines in winter against a backdrop of bare mountains: a familiar sight on the western edge of the San Joaquin valley

product is wine: on the whole very good wine. The Gallos have been a major influence on America's taste for wine—it could hardly be otherwise, as they make every third or fourth bottle (the figures are not available). They take the responsibility seriously, providing as it were a beginners' course from apple and other 'pop wines' by easy degrees of sweetness and fruitiness to some of the best standard 'burgundy' and 'chablis' in the business and beyond to full-dry, well-matured varietals.

They do not, and nor do the other good Valley wine-makers, necessarily limit themselves to Valley grapes. Gallo is one of the biggest buyers in the North Coast counties, including the Napa valley. But the progress of Valley viticulture means they will have to rely less on the coast in future.

The Gallos have two big colleagues in the San Joaquin valley—big enough for their wineries to remind you more of oil refineries

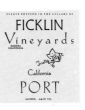

Right: The biggest winery in the world: E. & J. Gallo's headquarters at Modesto from the air. The biggest tank holds one million gallons. The warehouse in the background covers 25 acres

than of any agricultural operation.

Guild, based at Lodi, is a growers' co-operative whose Italian-style (i.e. rather sweet) Tavola brand wines are immensely popular. Winemasters' Guild is their premium brand.

United Vintners is a conglomerate company whose brands include Italian Swiss Colony, Petri, Lejon and Inglenook—the Napa winery's name now appears on an assortment of blended wines. The smaller, but still huge, Franzia Brothers winery now belongs to Coca Cola.

Besides the Valley-based wineries other well-known companies with their bases elsewhere grow or buy much of their wine there: The Christian Brothers, Paul Masson and Almaden are examples. And virtually all California 'port', 'sherry' and brandy is made from Valley grapes, wherever and by whom.

Only one section of the Valley can be said to have a different character and style from the rest: the northern end, where the San Joaquin

river curls west and flows sluggishly into San Francisco Bay. The influence of the distant Bay is still felt here in much cooler nights than farther south. Lodi, the heart of these vineyards, correspondingly has its own reputation for better table wines than the average. Three wineries at Lodi take advantage of the fact: Barengo, East-Side (whose principal brand is Royal Host) and Filice.

In the centre of the Valley at Madera the little Ficklin winery has an almost legendary name for its 'port'. Beyond Fresno at Cutler, California Growers make some of the country's best brandy under the Setrakian label.

Right in the south (off the map) near Bakersfield the Bear Mountain co-operative breaks the rules by making table wines of character in some of the hottest conditions in the State. The grapes ripen so early that they can be picked before they feel the full effect of the summer heat. M. laMont is the co-operative's label.

235

South of the Bay

THE AREA just south and east of San Francisco Bay is wine country as old as the Napa valley. Its wineries are fewer, but several of them are among California's most famous names. Recently the exploding conurbation has driven them to look for new vineyards—and hence to make a discovery of enormous importance.

Climate studies by the University of California at Davis have shown that the valleys sidling to the ocean between the parallel ranges of mountains—Salinas, Gabilan, Santa Cruz, Diablo—are cool-air corridors, benefiting from being near the sea and the Bay, but protected from the smothering Pacific fogs. That Salinas, in fact, though it is 150 miles south of St Helena, is marginally cooler, and could be even more suited to the best table-wine grape varieties. The university oenologists found that Soledad, in the Salinas valley, has the best conditions of all, possibly the best in California. . . .

Almaden winery, whose home ground at Los Gatos was rapidly being overrun by suburbs, was the pioneer in moving south, to Paicines, 1,000 feet up in San Benito county. Their initial 2,000 acres of Cabernet and Chardonnay succeeded superbly.

More recently Paul Masson from Saratoga, Mirassou from San Jose and Wente Brothers from Livermore, all pressed by suburbs, have gone farther south into the Salinas valley. The whole area now has a greater acreage than the Napa valley—and virtually all of it in very good varieties. Some of California's best wine is being made there already.

The traditional centres of wine-growing here do not stretch so far south. They are concentrated in the Livermore valley east of the Bay (gravelly and good for white wine; one of California's few compact areas with a recognizable local character); the western foot-hills of the Diablo range, where Weibel and Mirassou still have their wineries, though most of their grapes come from elsewhere; the towns south of the Bay, now built up, and along the slopes of the Santa Cruz mountains down to a cluster of family wineries round the Hecker Pass.

Their products vary from the extremely high-priced varietals of Martin Ray to very good cheap 'burgundy' from Live Oaks. Paul Masson and Almaden are the classic big two of the area. Almaden, advised by the great Frank Schoonmaker, was the pioneer of varietal labelling in the '50s. Recently Paul Masson has made the running, using the new grape varieties Emerald Riesling and Ruby Cabernet with conspicuous success.

The most startling newcomer is the mammoth Monterey Vineyards winery, the first to be built in the Salinas valley, with no less than 10,000 acres of its own land planted with top varieties. Its first wine, of the 1974 vintage, was very promising.

Perhaps the most encouraging is Chalone, 2,000 feet up in the hills just east of Soledad, where a limestone slope and a cool climate are giving Chardonnay and Pinot Noir as good as any in California, and most in France.

But the move south is not finished yet: the grapes are going in San Luis Obispo and Santa Barbara counties now.

Above: vineyards alternate with typical golden California grassland dotted with dark oaks
Below left: grape-picking machines are a revolutionary innovation for huge vineyards with a small population
Below: some of the best-known wineries of this rapidly developing area of California; the future here lies in concentrating on first-class table wine

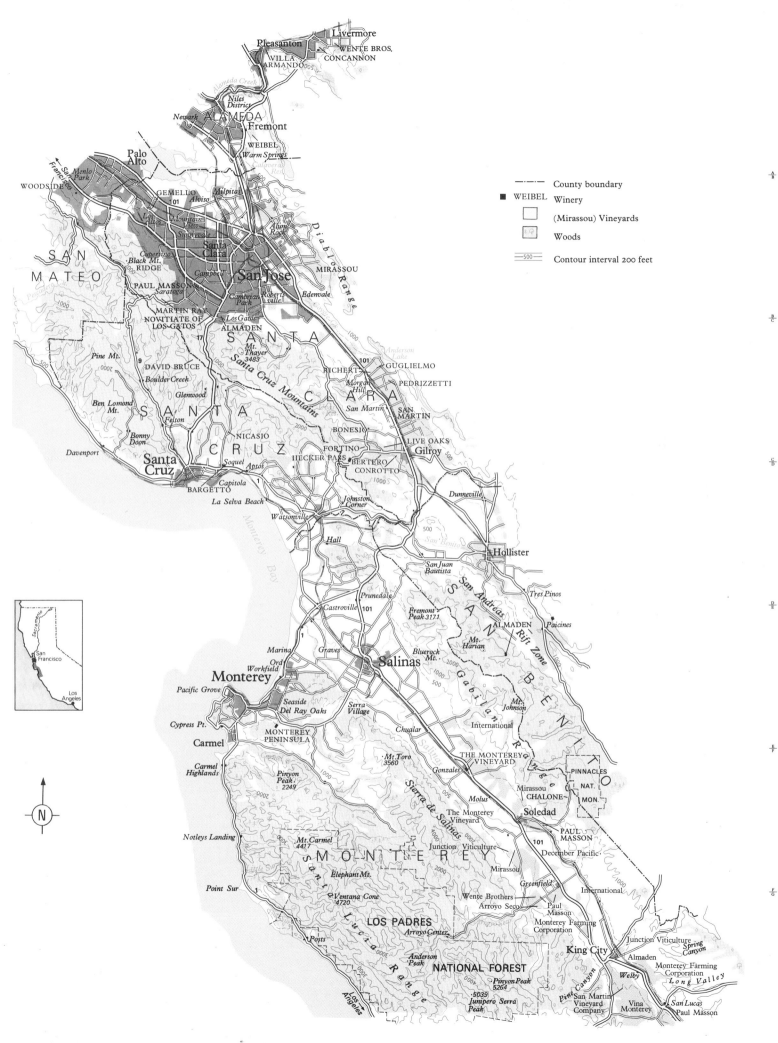

County boundary

■ WEIBEL Winery

□ (Mirassou) Vineyards

▢ Woods

—500— Contour interval 200 feet

Pleasanton Livermore
WENTE BROS.
VILLA CONCANNON
ARMANDO

Alameda Creek

Niles
District
Newark ALAMEDA Fremont
WEIBEL
Warm Springs

Palo
Alto
Menlo
Park
WOODSIDE
GEMELLO
101
Alviso
Milpitas
Los
Altos
Mountain
View
Sunnyvale
Cupertino
Black Mt.
RIDGE
Santa
Clara
Alum
Rock
San
Jose
MIRASSOU
PAUL MASSON
Saratoga
Campbell
Cambrian
Park
Roberts
ville
Edenvale
MARTIN RAY
NOVITIATE OF
LOS GATOS
Los Gatos
ALMADEN

SAN
MATEO

SANTA

Pine Mt.

Mt.
Thayer
3483

CLARA

DAVID BRUCE
Boulder Creek
Glenwood

101
RICHERT
GUGLIELMO
Morgan
Hill
PEDRIZZETTI

Ben Lomond
Mt.
Felton

SANTA

Santa Cruz Mountains

San Martin
SAN
MARTIN
BONESIO

Bonny
Doon
CRUZ
Nicasio
Soquel Aptos
FORTINO
HECKER PASS
BERTERO
CONROTTO
LIVE OAKS
Gilroy

Davenport
Santa
Cruz
BARGETTO
Capitola
La Selva Beach

Dunneville

Watsonville
500
San
Benito
Hollister

Hall
San Juan
Bautista
Tres Pinos

Monterey Bay
Prunedale
Castroville 101
Fremont
Peak 3171
ALMADEN Paicines

SAN
San Andreas Rift Zone
BENITO

Marina
Ord
Workfield
Graves
Salinas
Bluerock
Mt.
Mt.
Harlan
Mt.
Johnson

Monterey
Pacific Grove
Seaside
Del Ray Oaks
Serra
Village
International

Cypress Pt.
MONTEREY
PENINSULA
Chualar
THE MONTEREY
VINEYARD
PINNACLES
NAT.
MON.

Carmel
Mt.Toro
3560
Gonzales
Mirassou
CHALONE

Carmel
Highlands
Pinyon
Peak
2249
Molus
The Monterey
Vineyard
Soledad
PAUL
MASSON

Notleys Landing
Mt.Carmel
4417
Junction Viticulture
101
December Pacific
Mirassou

Point Sur
Elephant Mt.
Greenfield
International

Ventana Cone
4720
Wente Brothers
Arroyo Seco
Paul
Masson
Monterey Farming
Corporation

LOS PADRES
Arroyo Center
Junction Viticulture
Spring
Canyon

Posts
Anderson
Peak
NATIONAL FOREST
Pinyon Peak
5264
King City
Almaden
Monterey Farming
Corporation
Long Valley

N

5039
Junipero Serra
Peak
Los
Angeles
Pine Canyon
San Martin
Vineyard
Company
Welby
Vina
Monterey
San Lucas
Paul Masson

The Finger Lakes

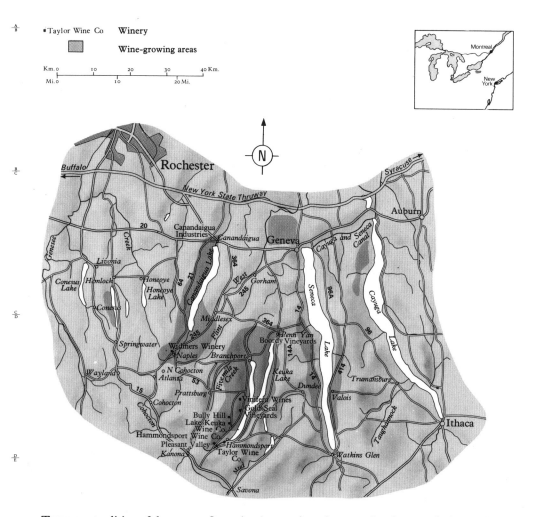

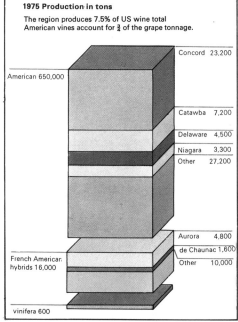

- Taylor Wine Co   **Winery**

  Wine-growing areas

Km. 0   10   20   30   40 Km.
Mi. 0   10   20 Mi.

The rambling old stone winery of the Pleasant Valley Wine Co. is the most imposing building in the little town of Hammondsport. Its principal brand name is Great Western, best known for its 'champagne'

1975 Production in tons
The region produces 7.5% of US wine total
American vines account for ¾ of the grape tonnage.

American 650,000	Concord 23,200
	Catawba 7,200
	Delaware 4,500
	Niagara 3,300
	Other 27,200
French American hybrids 16,000	Aurora 4,800
	de Chaunac 1,600
	Other 10,000
vinifera 600	

THE WINE tradition of the eastern States has its base today in upper New York State, in the area round the series of deep glacial trenches known as the Finger Lakes, just south of the great inland sea of Lake Ontario.

The sight of fields of vines comes as a shock in these distinctly northern, New-England-style surroundings, with low hills around the long blue lakes covered with birch and oak, and frame houses painted cream and blue and green like any quiet corner of the north-eastern states.

Despite the fact that the Finger Lakes and Lake Ontario help to moderate the climate it is tough and continental: there is a short growing season and a long, bitterly cold winter.

Wine-growing started here in the 1850s and 60s, while the native American vines were the only vines that could be grown in the east (see pages 226/227). The taste of the wine they make, while it is strange to anyone reared on European wine, is a long-established part of American tradition. Furthermore American vines are still the easiest and most productive to grow. Sparkling wines have been the speciality of the Finger Lakes from the start, and today about a quarter of the production is 'New York State Champagne'. Most of it is too fruity and sweet for educated tastes, but this is by design, not necessity: the best dry wines are excellent.

The inescapable discussion about New York

wines is over the future of the traditional American varieties. The bigger wineries are all broadly based on this market, yet almost all feel that it needs modifying in the light of new knowledge—particularly of the French-American hybrids introduced by Philip Wagner. Each company has its own policy, but there is a perceptible drift towards less-foxy and even non-foxy wine, suggesting that the industry will eventually move into the mainstream of wine-making.

Whether the classical European vinifera grapes will ever establish more than a toe-hold is still warmly debated. The central figure in the debate is Dr Konstantin Frank, a Russian-born German whose company, pointedly called Vinifera wines, has had startling successes with Riesling, Chardonnay and Pinot Noir. His Finger Lakes Riesling Trockenbeerenauslese caused a sensation when it appeared in 1961.

Frank's contention, which is now well proven, is that vinifera vines grafted on the right rootstocks and earthed-up for protection in winter are just as hardy as American or hybrid ones. They also ripen just as well. A considerable body of conservative opinion, however, still regards them as a risky proposition —not least because California can make vinifera wine so cheaply and well that a different product makes commercial sense.

The Finger Lakes wineries are few but famous. Hammondsport, at the south end of Lake Keuka, is the centre of the industry; Taylor's is the biggest, making mainly traditional 'generic' wines under such names as sherry, burgundy and sauternes, but also under an 'appellation' of its own coinage: Lake Country. Taylor wines are distinctly foxy, but less so than formerly as non-foxy hybrid grapes enter increasingly into the blends.

Taylor's own Pleasant Valley, whose brand name is Great Western. Great Western 'champagne' is their best-known product, but the company also makes a range of 'varietals' from such hybrids as Baco Noir, Chelois and Aurora; pleasant table wines which compromise between American and European flavours.

The Gold Seal Company, though as firmly American in its traditions as Taylor's, was the first to produce a vinifera wine in New York. It was Gold Seal's Charles Fournier (one of the company's long line of French champagne-makers) who employed Dr Frank and encouraged him to experiment with European vines. Dr Frank left to start his own company in the early '60s. Gold Seal now have 100 acres of Chardonnay and Riesling at Valois on Seneca Lake. Their best champagne carries Charles Fournier's name; popular lines are called Henri Marchant.

238

The third famous name, Widmers, has held firm with American vines—was, in fact, the pioneer in selling Delaware, Isabella, Vergennes, Niagara, Elvira and the rest under their own names. Widmers' logical approach to vinifera grapes is to grow them where there can be no doubt about it. They have planted 500 acres of them in Sonoma County, California.

Among smaller companies, Bully Hill was started in 1970 by one of the Taylors, Walter, who disagreed with family policy. Bully Hill wines are both American and hybrid, either blended or separately under varietal names.

Philip Wagner's Boordy Vineyards are established on Lake Keuka as well as in Maryland (their original home) and in Washington. But the hybrid grapes they use are grown in another New York grape belt, famous for grape-juice rather than wine: Chautauqua on the south shore of Lake Erie. Chautauqua's huge Concord production has recently been supplemented by hybrids and even experimental vinifera vines.

Two other areas of New York, Niagara and the Hudson River valley, also have substantial acreages of vineyard. The Niagara Falls Wine Cellar in the former and High Tor and Benmarl in the latter (High Tor only 28 miles from Manhattan) are energetic small enterprises of the sort which often make the running.

Most New York State wine is still made from American grape varieties. The 'champagnes' are among the best. But the label at bottom right represents a revolution

Australia

IF THE FIRST flag to flap over Australian soil in 1770 had been the white and gold of the Bourbons instead of the red, white and blue of King George . . . it is pleasant to speculate what the results would have been.

But even in Anglo-Saxon hands, wine-growing got off to a flying start. The First Fleet of 1788, bringing the first permanent settlers, carried vines among its cargo; the first Governor made wine; the first number of the *Sydney Gazette*, in 1803, carried an article (translated from the French) called 'Method of Preparing a Piece of Land for the Purpose of Forming a Vineyard', and by the 1820s the first of the present-day vineyards in New South Wales was making wine.

Doctors, brewers, seamen, labourers were among the immigrants who put their faith in wine as a way of life and scoured the empty country for suitable places to plant. They went by the natural vegetation, by stands of particular trees (peppermint gum was one, box another) and meadows of certain types of grass to find the kind of land they were looking for. As Max Lake, Hunter valley wine-grower and author,

Most of the Australian wine industry has been handed down from father to son for generations. Murray Tyrrell of Tyrrell's Vineyards, Pokolbin, in the Hunter valley, New South Wales, runs a family business that started in 1858. Australian wine-makers are proud of tradition but uninhibited about experiment: the ideal combination

points out, they were remarkably adept at choosing their sites. They sniffed out patches of good vineyard soil miles from anywhere.

All the best sites were chosen first. By the middle of the last century a powerful dynastic system, of families down to the fifth and sixth generation (to date) making wine on the same land, had begun. The majority of Australian wine today is made by people whose parents and grandparents were wine-makers. California has nothing like this continuity.

Australia's good vineyards lie between the 38th and 34th parallels. Melbourne is near the 38th, the same as Cordoba in Spain (and Sicily and San Francisco). Sydney is near the 34th, the same as Rabat, the capital of Morocco. Strong wines full of sugar but tending to lack acidity are what you would expect. Traditionally this is what Australia has produced—dessert wines and 'tonic burgundies'.

But the world-wide change of taste in favour of lighter wines, coinciding with new techniques of temperature control, is changing the pattern rapidly. All Australia's best wines being made today are table wines.

Wine production

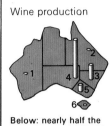

Below: nearly half the annual crop of 3.5m hl is distilled: as brandy, for fortifying wine, or (most of it) as industrial alcohol

Left: South Australia **4** has by far the greatest production; New South Wales **3** and Victoria **5** follow; Queensland **2**. Western Australia **1** and the island of Tasmania **6** only dabble in wine

Right: table wine production grows steadily (left-hand column) while fortified wines (right), traditional for Australia, fluctuate from year to year

Right: Great Britain, traditionally Australia's best customer, now buys much less of her wine than Canada. The new Japanese market has grown faster than the American

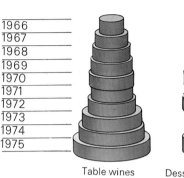

1966
1967
1968
1969
1970
1971
1972
1973
1974
1975

Table wines   Dessert wines

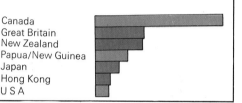

Canada
Great Britain
New Zealand
Papua/New Guinea
Japan
Hong Kong
USA

State boundaries
Fortified Wines
Table Wines
Fortified and Table Wines
Land above 1000 metres

New South Wales

NEW SOUTH WALES, the cradle of Australian wine-growing, has long since been overtaken by South Australia as the nucleus of the industry. But there remains one district 100 miles north of Sydney as famous as any in the country; the Hunter river valley round Branxton and the mining town of Cessnock.

Exceptionally, being so far north, the Hunter area is one of the few in Australia which concentrates entirely on table wines. Its production is small. Vines were planted here (at Dalwood, near the river just east of Branxton) as early as 1828, but the soil which has given the Hunter valley its reputation is found to the south in the foot-hills of the Broken Back range. Round the east side of the hills there is a strip of weathered basalt, the sign of ancient volcanoes.

The famous old wineries of the valley and several important new ones (notably Rothbury Estate, Hungerford Hill and Lake's Folly) lie on the lower slopes and the first flat land under the hills. The Hunter valley is the farthest north of Australia's first-class vineyards; the summer is very hot and the autumn often vexingly wet.

Hermitage (or Shiraz) is the classic red grape of the Hunter, and Semillon the traditional white. Rather soft and earthy but long and spicy, Hunter Hermitage lasts well and grows complex with time. Pinot Noir and Cabernet are grown too. Many think a blend of Pinot Noir and Hermitage gives the valley's best wine.

Old-style white Hunter wines were broad and golden, strong and soft; 'honey Hunters', their friends call them. Today most are being made crisper with early picking and refrigeration, and some have a little Chardonnay in the blend; a hopeful sign for the future. The Semillon is usually known on labels as the Hunter Valley Riesling, for some wry reason.

Penfold's and Lindeman are the biggest wine firms. McWilliam at Mount Pleasant, with four vineyards close together, totalling over 500 acres (Rosehill and Lovedale are their other well-known ones), is the biggest to be concentrated in New South Wales alone. For Austra-

Above right: big companies call wine after their different estates; even if (like Minchinbury) they no longer actually have any vines on them

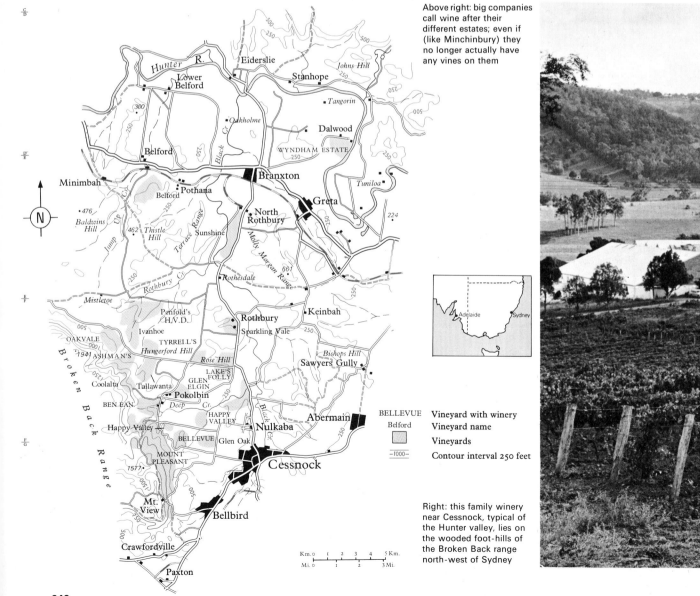

Right: this family winery near Cessnock, typical of the Hunter valley, lies on the wooded foot-hills of the Broken Back range north-west of Sydney

BELLEVUE — Vineyard with winery
Belford — Vineyard name
— Vineyards
—1000— Contour interval 250 feet

Victoria

lian wine companies have a habit of owning property in different districts and states, and often blending their wines. The practice makes it difficult to form a picture of local wine styles.

Ben Ean is the Lindeman headquarters in the district. Penfold's have moved from their old Dalwood (now renamed Wyndham's) to a new Dalwood Estate 40 miles up-river to the west at Wybong (not on the map), where they have more than 1,200 acres. Others have followed: Arrowfield, Rosemount and Hollydene among them.

Elsewhere in New South Wales the small district of Mudgee (60 miles west) is expanding, but the success story of recent years is the Riverina district round Griffith (300 miles south-west), where canalized water from the Murrumbidgee river turns desert into orchard and vineyard. After a long career making poor-quality wines, mostly fortified, the Riverina has been reborn in the era of refrigeration. McWilliams were the pioneers in making light wines of startling freshness and quality on irrigated land at Hanwood.

AT THE END of the last century Victoria had as many vineyards as New South Wales and South Australia together: 1,200, scattered over the entire state. But phylloxera, which has never reached South Australia, was appallingly destructive here; today the state's vineyards only produce 15% of Australia's total, from widely scattered regions, none of which merits a map to itself but several of which make excellent wine.

Rutherglen-Corowa on the New South Wales border and Wangaratta a few miles south specialize in dessert wines, among them Australia's finest: a 'liqueur' muscat of astonishing silky richness which may be a descendant of the once-famous Constantia of the Cape. Morris's is a first-class firm. Others are Brown's, Booth's, Bailey's (whose reds have been called 'food, wine and a good cigar'), Buller's, Smith's 'All Saints', Campbell's, Chambers and Seppelt. Old-style Rutherglen reds are burly, but age remarkably well.

Westwards along the Murray river are a number of irrigated wine districts, the most important being Mildura and Renmark (which is in S. Australia). Mildara [sic] Wines at Mildura are well known for 'sherry' (their 'George' is outstanding) and brandy.

Great Western lies 140 miles north-west of Melbourne, 1,100 feet up at the westernmost end of the Great Dividing Range. The soil is rich in lime but otherwise infertile, like that of some of Europe's best vineyards. There are two firms, Seppelt, with 650 acres, and Best, with 50. By far the most famous product is Seppelt's Great Western 'champagne', Australia's best sparkling wine, but fine red and white wines are also made.

Château Tahbilk at Tabilk [sic], 76 miles north of Melbourne on the Goulburn river, makes red wines typical of Australia's best style, needing considerable age in bottle to sort out their strong and complex flavours.

Much farther south the Drumborg area is Australia's southernmost. Seppelt's have planted there on land similar to Great Western with a cooler climate. First results are good.

Above: the enormous yield of a vintage of the 1930s was collected by teams of horses as well as tractors
Below: Victoria labels. Seppelt's Great Western is Australia's best-known sparkling wine

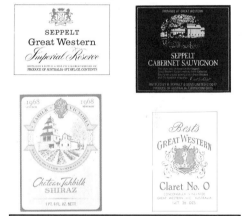

New Zealand
The young New Zealand wine industry has grown and altered significantly in the past decade. Of 5,650 acres of vines today nearly three-quarters are vinifera varieties; half of these Müller-Thurgau. Hybrids are grown in the humid north. Fifty per cent of production is table wine, with quality rapidly improving

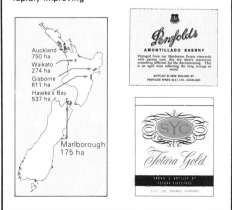

South Australia

ADELAIDE, the capital of South Australia, and hence of Australian wine-growing today, is fittingly ringed about with vineyards. A few still exist within the suburbs of the city. They have spread north to Clare and Watervale and south to Langhorne Creek (see page 240), beside the outpost of South Australian wine-making down at Coonawarra, 200 miles away.

But the most famous of them is undoubtedly the Barossa valley, only 35 miles away to the north-east: a settlement which was originally largely German, and keeps certain German characteristics to this day.

With its 22,000 acres it is Australia's biggest quality wine district. It follows the Para river for about 20 miles, and spreads eastwards into the next valley, from the 750 feet of Lyndoch to 1,800 feet in the Barossa range, where vineyards are scattered among rocky hills.

The industry here was founded on some of Australia's best 'ports' and 'sherries', which are still important. Today's star, however, is the Rhine Riesling. At its best, particularly on high ground, it gives wine of remarkable acidity and delicacy for such a hot climate. If the 'breed' of the great German wines is missing, Barossa's best Rieslings have an attractive style of their own. Yalumba's Pewsey Vale and Gramp's Steingarten, two stony vineyards high in the hills, give outstanding wine.

The most celebrated come from such wineries as Gramp's Orlando, Yalumba, Hardy's, Leo Buring's and Henschke's Keyneton. The valley's co-operative at Nuriootpa, which sells its wine under the name Kaiserstuhl, also makes excellent 'single-vineyard' Rieslings as well as good Cabernets in a big fruity style. Barossa reds (in which Cabernet and Shiraz are often blended) tend to be less tough and concentrated than many. Penfold's, Seppelt's (who blend Barossa with their Great Western wine from Victoria) and Tolley, Scott and Tolley are well known for red wines here.

Barossa Valley

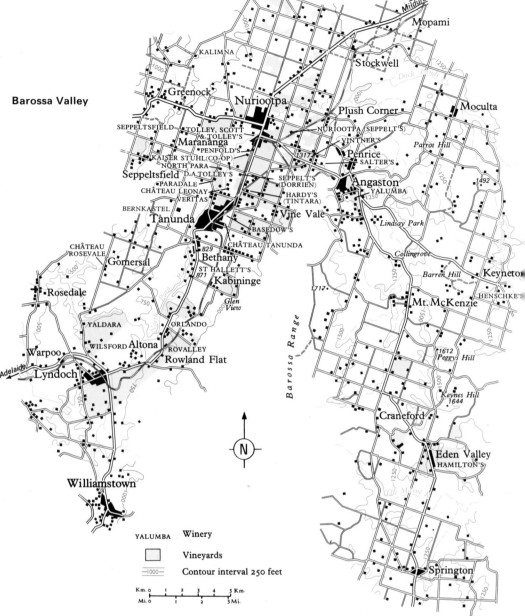

YALUMBA   Winery

Vineyards

Contour interval 250 feet

Km. 0 1 2 3 4 5 Km.
Mi. 0   1   2   3 Mi.

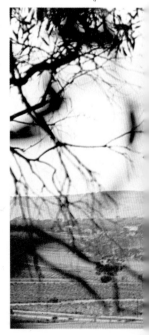

Above: 19th-century houses with graceful cast iron survive from Barossa's first German settlers, who established the Rhine Riesling as the speciality of the region. Australia's biggest quality wine district
Left: at the Barossa valley vintage fair in April a grape-treading contest draws crowds
Right: most of the vineyards are on high but comparatively flat land, but experimental plantings of vines in the hills all round them are having good results

THE SOUTHERN VALES district starts almost in the southern outskirts of Adelaide. It is South Australia's oldest: the John Reynell who gave his name to Reynella planted his vines in 1838. Today Reynella has 550 acres round the same site.

Reynella, Seaview and Tintara (Hardy's) are the important names among a score of smaller estates in Southern Vales. D'Arenberg and Coriole are also names to watch.

A few miles east of Southern Vales the 200 acres of vines at Langhorne Creek are noted for the powerful reds made by two companies—Bleasdale and Metala.

Even within Adelaide itself there are still vineyards, including the home (at least in name) of Australia's most famous red: Penfold's Grange Hermitage. The Grange was the original Penfold property on the foot-hills of the Mount Lofty Range, now in the eastern suburbs of the city. In the same area Wynn's and Stonyfell have estates, and elsewhere in Adelaide Hamilton's, Tolley's and Angove's.

Eighty miles north of the city the small (5,200 acres) district of Clare-Watervale is in some senses the Hunter valley of South Australia, with a warmer climate and making big soft wines. 'Clare Riesling' is Semillon, and Stanley's, Buring's, Lindeman's and Quelltaler Hock the best-known brands.

COONAWARRA is not mapped here, but many say this small and remote district gives the best red wines in all Australia. It lies between Naracoorte and Millicent (see page 240), and is the southernmost vineyard in South Australia; correspondingly cooler and prone to frosts. What marked out this little plot for vines was its strange red soil, a narrow strip (at its narrowest 200 yards wide), quite different from the surrounding land, poised over limestone and a good supply of water. Wynns, Lindeman ('Rouge-Homme'), Penfold's, Mildara and Brand's own the vineyards. Coonawarra claret is Australia's nearest approach to Bordeaux.

Southern Vales

EMU   Winery

    Vineyards

—1000—   Contour interval 250 feet

Km. 0   5   10 Km.
Mi. 0   5 Mi.

Below: most of the best-known Australian wines come from South Australia's three famous regions: Barossa, Southern Vales (Hardy, Seaview and Reynella labels) and Coonawarra (last two). Metala is in a fourth, Langhorne Creek

South Africa

THE SCENERY of Cape Province combines the luxuriant and the stark. Blue-shadowed crags rise from placid green pastures. Smooth rivulets of cultivation run between gaunt walls of rock. An almost perfect climate, with rare summer rain, gives the vine everything it needs.

From these Elysian fields used to come one of the very greatest wines in the world—the legendary Constantia. Constantia was bought by European courts in the early 19th century in preference to Yquem, Tokay, Madeira . . . an indication that the Cape is capable of producing wines of the very highest class.

It takes certain social conditions, however, as well as the right climate, to develop an industry in fine wines. They existed briefly with the early Dutch governors—it was the second, Van der Stel, who planted the Constantia vineyard, as well as giving his name to Stellenbosch. But in more recent times South Africa has been more of a spirit-drinking country, and only very recently has the modern trend towards wine got under way. Still something like half of the grape harvest is distilled,

but today South Africans drink some nine litres of wine a head a year.

The difficulties experienced by wine farmers in the past have left a useful legacy in the form of a constitutional body to control prices and absorb surplus. This is the KWV, a sort of national co-operative with five wineries and, at Paarl, some of the world's biggest and most modern wine-processing premises.

In 1972 the South African government introduced an elaborate system of control for 'Wines of Origin', which bears comparison with EEC regulations. It designated 14 areas or origins (which are shown on the map opposite) and at the same time put firm limits on the use of such terms as Estate or Superior, vintage dates and indications of grape variety. Now any claim as to origin, grape, vintage, estate-production or superiority has to be officially certified by a government seal on the neck of the bottle. The seal is illustrated and explained opposite.

The heart of the fine-wine region of South Africa, round the towns of Stellenbosch and

Paarl, is mapped in detail on the following pages. Prevailing westerlies make the Cape itself and the hilly country just inland cooler and wetter than farther north and east beyond the mountains, which depend on irrigation and specialize in fortified and distilling wine.

The principal red-wine grape is the Cinsaut of southern France, which makes better wine in South Africa than in Europe. It has been crossed here with the Pinot Noir to make the Pinotage; a distinct improvement, just as Cabernet and Carignan have been crossed in California to make Ruby Cabernet. Pinot Noir, Shiraz, and increasingly Cabernet are also grown.

A form of Chenin Blanc, the Loire grape, known here as Steen, is traditional and can make good light and fruity wine. Semillon (called Green Grape), the Palomino of Jerez (called French Grape!), Clairette from the Languedoc and Riesling are all successful. For sweet wines farmers in the inland areas grow red Muscadel and Muscat of Alexandria (which they call Hanepoot).

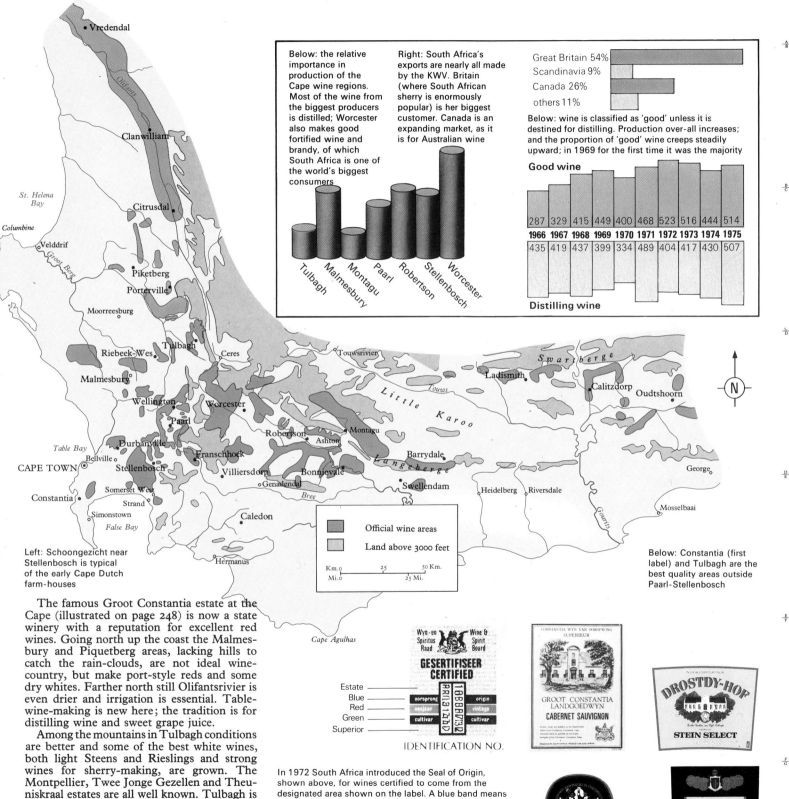

Below: the relative importance in production of the Cape wine regions. Most of the wine from the biggest producers is distilled; Worcester also makes good fortified wine and brandy, of which South Africa is one of the world's biggest consumers

Right: South Africa's exports are nearly all made by the KWV. Britain (where South African sherry is enormously popular) is her biggest customer. Canada is an expanding market, as it is for Australian wine

Great Britain 54%
Scandinavia 9%
Canada 26%
others 11%

Below: wine is classified as 'good' unless it is destined for distilling. Production over-all increases; and the proportion of 'good' wine creeps steadily upward; in 1969 for the first time it was the majority

Good wine

1966	1967	1968	1969	1970	1971	1972	1973	1974	1975
287	329	415	449	400	468	523	516	444	514
435	419	437	399	334	489	404	417	430	507

Distilling wine

Bar chart: Tulbagh · Malmesbury · Montagu · Paarl · Robertson · Stellenbosch · Worcester

Legend:
- Official wine areas
- Land above 3000 feet

Km.0 — 25 — 50 Km.
Mi.0 — 25 Mi.

Left: Schoongezicht near Stellenbosch is typical of the early Cape Dutch farm-houses

Below: Constantia (first label) and Tulbagh are the best quality areas outside Paarl-Stellenbosch

The famous Groot Constantia estate at the Cape (illustrated on page 248) is now a state winery with a reputation for excellent red wines. Going north up the coast the Malmesbury and Piquetberg areas, lacking hills to catch the rain-clouds, are not ideal wine-country, but make port-style reds and some dry whites. Farther north still Olifantsrivier is even drier and irrigation is essential. Table-wine-making is new here; the tradition is for distilling wine and sweet grape juice.

Among the mountains in Tulbagh conditions are better and some of the best white wines, both light Steens and Rieslings and strong wines for sherry-making, are grown. The Montpellier, Twee Jonge Gezellen and Theuniskraal estates are all well known. Tulbagh is included with Paarl in the demarcated origin Boberg, which is reserved for 'ports' and 'sherries'.

Worcester, Robertson, Swellendam and the Klein Karoo are specialists in dessert and distilling wines, though here too the move towards table wines is perceptible.

Wyn-en Spiritus Raad — Wine & Spirit Board

GESERTIFISEER CERTIFIED

Estate — oorsprong / origin
Blue
Red — nesjaar / vintage
Green — cultivar / cultivar
Superior

IDENTIFICATION NO.

In 1972 South Africa introduced the Seal of Origin, shown above, for wines certified to come from the designated area shown on the label. A blue band means the origin is certified. An additional red band means the vintage is also certified. With a green band the grape variety is guaranteed (80% of the wine is of the variety named). The word Estate is limited to some 40 approved and delimited properties that bottle only the wine they grow. A 'Superior' wine must be 100% of the variety named. The centre panel contains identification numbers

GROOT CONSTANTIA LANDGOEDWYN CABERNET SAUVIGNON

DROSTDY-HOF STEIN SELECT

Twee Jongegezellen Estate Wine — TJ Riesling Sec

DROSTDY Medium Cream SHERRY

Paarl and Stellenbosch

STELLENBOSCH is the centre of estate wine-making in South Africa and the seat of the country's biggest wine-company, the Stellenbosch Farmers' Winery. Paarl is the capital of the sherry and dessert-wine industry and head-quarters of the state co-operative, the KWV.

The wine-makers of Paarl do not let you forget that their vineyards lie on almost the same latitude as Jerez. The South African sherry they make, using Spanish methods, including both the solera system and flor yeast, has been their fortune since they started it in the 1930s. They do make the best imitation of Spanish sherry in the world—to most people virtually indistinguishable from the original. The chalky soil of Jerez, which gives the wine its ultimate finesse, is all they lack.

Paarl is also the centre of the industry in Tawny, Ruby and Vintage port-style wines—which again, at their best, are truly remarkable.

These are the natural kinds of wine for South Africa, even here in its cooler parts, to make. It is still a Mediterranean climate. Table wines in the past have suffered from overweight, and above all from over-rapid fermentation, leading to oxidation, darkening and lack of scent. Now with refrigeration well-balanced table wines are made, particularly in the Stellenbosch area, open to the ocean at False Bay.

The soils of Stellenbosch vary from light and sandy in the west, which is largely planted with Steen grapes, to decomposed granite at the foot of the Simonsberg and Stellenbosch mountains in the east, where Cinsaut, Pinotage and Cabernet give good solid red wines. Until recently unfortified sweet wine was prohibited by law, but a new ordinance has allowed the Nederburg winery to make some late-gathered Riesling of real quality.

Above: Groot Constantia near Cape Town once made one of the world's great wines. It is a museum today
Below: Paarl Steen, Roodeberg and Mymering are three of the brand names of the KWV, which is based at Paarl. Zonnebloem, Lanzerac and La Gratitude are from the Stellenbosch Farmers' Winery Co-operative, based at Libertas. Nederburg, Bellingham and Schoongezicht (see photograph on page 246) are private estates

Above: the floor of the Hex River Valley looking west towards Buffelshoekkloof and the peaks of Hexrievierberge

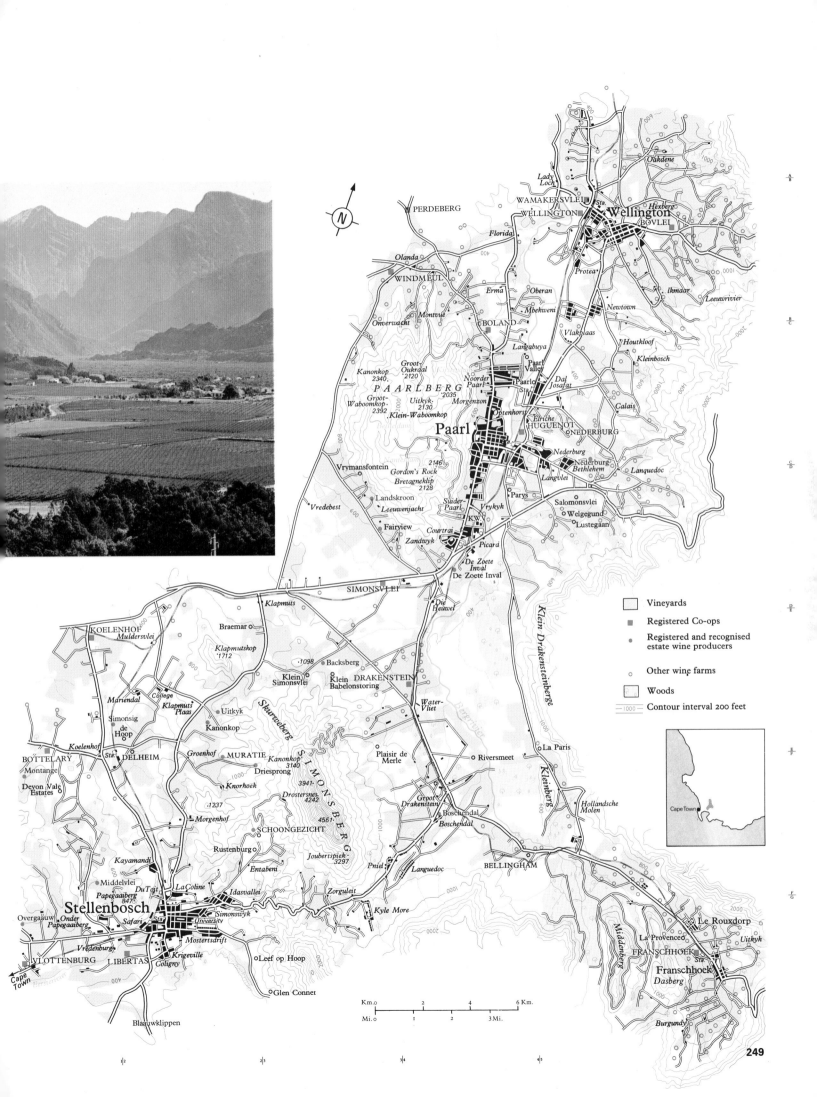

N

PERDEBERG

WAMAKERSVLEI
WELLINGTON   Sta.   Wellington
                                   Hexberg
                                   BOVLEI
Lady
Loch   Oakdene
Florida
Olanda
WINDMEUL   Erma   Oberan   Ikmaar   Leeuwrivier
              Montvlie   Mbekweni   Newtown
Onverwacht   BOLAND   Vlakplaas
              Langabuya   Houtkloof
Kanonkop   Groot-   Noorder   Kleinbosch
2340   Oukrdal   Paarl   Paarlo
              2120   Sta.   Calais
Groot-   Uitkyk-   Morgenzon   Dal Josafat
Waboomkop   2130   2035
2392   Klein-Waboomkop
              PAARLBERG   Elriche   HUGUENOT   ONEDERBURG
Paarl   Optenhorst
                                        Nederburg
Vrymansfontein 2146   Nederburg
              Gordon's Rock   Bethlehem   Lanquedoc
              Bretagneklip Langulei
              2128   Parys
Landskroon   Salomonsvlei
Vredebest   Leeuwenjacht Suider-   Welgegund
              Fairyview   Paarl   Lustegaan
              Zandwyk   Courtrai   Vrykyk
                            Picard   KWV
                            De Zoete
                            Inval
SIMONSVLEI   De Zoete Inval
                            Die Heuwel
Klapmuts   Vineyards
Braemar   Registered Co-ops
KOELENHOF   Klapmutskop   Registered and recognised
Muldersvlei   1712   estate wine producers
              1098   Backsberg
              Klein   Klein   DRAKENSTEIN   Other wine farms
Mariendal   Simonsvlei   Babelonstoring
College   Klapmuts   Water-   Woods
Simonsig   Plaas   Uitkyk   Vliet   1000 Contour interval 200 feet
de Hoop   Kanonkop
Koelenhof   Sta. DELHEIM Skuraeberg
BOTTELARY   Groenhof   MURATIE   Kanonkop   Plaisir de
Montange   Driesprong 3140   Merle   Riversmeet   La Paris
Devon Vale   Knorhoek   3941
Estates   Drostersnes 4242
              1237   4561   Groot-   Hollandsche
              Morgenhof   Drakenstein Molen
              SCHOONGEZICHT Joubertspiek   Boschendal
Kayamandi   Rustenburg   3297   Boschendal
Middelvlei   Entabeni   Pniel   Languedoc   BELLINGHAM
Papegaaiberg DuToit LaColine Idasvallei Zorguleit
847   Simonswyk   Kyle More
Overgaauw Onder Safari University
Papegaaiberg
Stellenbosch Simonswyk   Le Rouxdorp
Vredenburg   Mostertsdrift   La Provenco
VLOTTENBURG   LIBERTAS Coligny Leef op Hoop   FRANSCHHOEK
Cape Town   Krigeville   Franschhoek Sta.
                                                                 Dasberg
Blaauwklippen Glen Connet

Km.0   2   4   6 Km.
Mi.0   1   2   3 Mi.
                                                            Burgundy

Cape Town

249

South America

SOUTH AMERICA makes one bottle in eight of the world's wine. Argentina vies with Russia for fourth place in the production table. Yet we hear little more of Argentine wine than we do of Russian, and for the same reason: the domestic market is apparently insatiable: Argentinians use wine like the French and Italians. We can expect to hear more, however, for two reasons; Argentina needs exports, and her wine has reached a level of quality the world cannot ignore.

The industry is organized on a mass-production basis. There are few wines of individual interest. No Napa valley. Instead an endless stream of sound, satisfying and enjoyable standard wines from plump, ripe, healthy grapes growing under ideal conditions.

Seventy per cent of the vineyards of Argentina (or half those of South America) are in the state of Mendoza, under the Andes and on the same latitude as Morocco. San Juan to the north has the second biggest acreage. The climate is arid and the massive flat vineyards are irrigated from the Andes by canals. The same volume as Russia's is produced here on one-third of the acreage: with little disease in the dry air, on ungrafted roots and with abundant water the yields are enormous. Equipment is modern and technology sophisticated.

Apart from the traditional Criolla, now dwindling, the most widely planted grape is the Malbec, one of the less important varieties of Bordeaux. But plantings of Cabernet and Pinot Noir are on the increase, and the good Cabernets can take their place with those from Chile as wines of serious merit. Red wines are on the whole better than white, which tend towards the oxidized condition of sherry (the Spanish Pedro Ximénez is the main grape, and the name Jerez is freely used). Strangely one of the best wines of the country is a sparkling 'champagne' made by a subsidiary of Moët & Chandon and sold without a blush as Champagne.

Argentina's red 'jug' wines, sold in 5-litre flagons, are appetizing and good, inclining to sweetness in the Italian style. Those of Chile by contrast are drier and more French in feeling.

The centre of Chilean wine-growing lies only 150 miles due west of Mendoza. But in those 150 miles the Andes climb to 17,000 feet. The highest peak in the Andes, Aconcagua, reaches 23,000 feet just to the north. There is a radical change of climate here, with the arid zone which reaches into northern Chile from the Bolivian plateau crossing the Andes into Argentina. Arica in northern Chile gets one millimetre of rain a year. Santiago gets 370. Concepción, only 250 miles farther south, gets 1,320. Mendoza gets 200.

Santiago's rainfall is still not enough to grow grapes without irrigation; an astonishing network of canals and streams originated by the Incas supplies all the vineyards with water. But the oceanic climate seems to suit Bordeaux's grapes perfectly. The valleys of the Aconcagua, Maipo, Cachapoal and Maule rivers, cooled by the sea to the west and the Andes soaring in the east, are planted with Cabernet, Merlot, Sauvignon and Semillon, Bordeaux-fashion. And much of their wine is worthy of Bordeaux.

Above and right: the vineyards of Chile give South America's best wine. Most are irrigated, although such foot-hill areas as the top picture, Los Perales at Marga-Marga in the south, have enough natural rainfall. Low-paid workers are one reason why Chilean wine is remarkably cheap for its high quality

The Cabernet is fruity, tannic, balanced and long-lived. Treated like claret, bottled after two years and kept for another four or five, it develops into very fine wine.

Sauvignon Blanc, too, makes a powerful dry but mellow wine with plenty of character, as it can in California. There are round soft Semillons of good style. The Riesling, which is grown in small quantities, tends to be drier and stronger than the ideal, but can have a fine lingering flavour. On the whole, though, the red wines are more impressive than the white.

With light but fertile soil and complete control of the water supply grape-growing looks absurdly easy. Phylloxera has never reached Chile. Vines can grow on their natural roots without grafting. So a new vineyard is made by simply sticking canes of the desired vines in the ground at two-metre intervals. Within a year they are growing happily as new vines and within three years bearing their first grapes.

The best-known bodegas lie round about Santiago: Viña Cusiño at Macul almost in the eastern suburbs, Undurraga to the south, Concha y Toro south-east, Santa Rita south in the Maipo valley. Fine delicate Cabernets also come from farther south in Talca province, from Viña San Pedro and Lomas de Pulmodón. Cañepa at Valparaiso also uses grapes from Lontué in Talca.

There is no escaping the fact that politics have hampered Chilean wine-making in the last five years—throughout the period when comparable countries have been making rapid progress. Inflation and lack of foreign currency to buy new equipment (or even oak for barrels) have frustrated excellent wine-makers with

some of the world's best grapes. In the long run, however, Chile has an assured place as a very important wine country.

Brazil and Uruguay both have flourishing wine industries for the home market. The centre of Brazilian viticulture, the province of Rio Grande do Sul, lies on the same latitude as Mendoza and Santiago, just north of Buenos Aires. Rainfall here is high and the climate mild and humid. Vinifera grapes have suffered in the past, and American vines have been grown. Recently, however, a study by the University of California has encouraged new planting and such enterprises as National Distillers, Cinzano, Pedro Domecq and Moët & Chandon have taken an interest in a local supply for the growing Brazilian market. According to the San Francisco paper *Wines & Vines* Cinzano has a vineyard near Recife only ten degrees from the equator and gets two grape crops a year. The area is dry and the vines are forced to go dormant and make new buds by taking off the irrigation.

A future edition of this atlas may have some very surprising maps.

International boundary

Provincial boundary

Wine producing provinces

Principle quality wine areas

Land above 3000 metres

Mexico
Mexico is a growing wine-producer: 3½ million gallons a year and 100,000 acres planted. Missionaries planted vines in the 16th century, but quality wines were impossible before modern technology. The best-known bodega is Santo Tomas in Baja California. Others are unremarkable

International boundary

Wine regions

Land above 2000 metres

Left: the left-hand labels come from Chile, which makes South America's best wine; the second column from Argentina; the third from Brazil, and the last from Uruguay

251

England and Wales

Left: almost all modern English wine is white. There is already an elegant country-house style of label design: the Hambledon motif comes from the first cricket club, which was at Hambledon Above: a strange setting

for the vine; Sir Guy Salisbury-Jones's vineyard on the South Downs at Hambledon near Portsmouth consists of 5 acres of Seyve-Villard and Chardonnay vines. His average crop is 12,000 bottles

THE PAST few years have seen the dawn of confidence in English wine. It used to be thought that England lies too far north for the grape to ripen—and besides that there is too much rain.

The fact remains, however, that in the early Middle Ages the monastic vineyards of England were extensive and by all accounts successful. Had it not been for England's acquisition (by the marriage of Henry II to Eleanor of Aquitaine in 1152) of Bordeaux—an easily accessible source of better wine—they would probably have continued to this day. But they faded away in the later Middle Ages, and since then only spasmodic attempts at wine-growing in England and Wales were made until recently.

Now England and Wales have some 490 acres of vineyard, almost all in white grapes. Most are in the south of England. The map shows those over one hectare ($2\frac{1}{2}$ acres) in comparison with the sites of known medieval vineyards.

Müller-Thurgau and Seyval Blanc (a French hybrid) are the two most popular vines at present, being early ripeners and disease-resistant. Various German crosses, including the new Reichensteiner, show signs of promise. The wine normally needs the help of sugar, as it does in Germany and often in Burgundy. But the quality is encouraging, and it only needs a more helpful attitude by the government, who at present charge duty on English wine as though it were imported, to make possible a small but serious wine industry in England.

Right: on this map, modern English and Welsh vineyards of more than one hectare are shown in relation to known medieval vineyard sites

1   Linton, Cambridge
2   Cavendish, Suffolk
3   Inkpen, Berks.
4   Godalming, Surrey
5   Adgestone, Isle of Wight
6   Biddenden, Kent
7   Nettlestead, Kent
8   Felsted, Essex
9   Ashton Keynes, Wilts.
10 Westfield, Sussex
11 Pangbourne, Berks.
12 Goudhurst, Kent
13 Otley, Suffolk
14 Camborne, Cornwall
15 South Kilworth, Leics.
16 Diss, Norfolk
17 Dereham, Norfolk
18 Arundel, Sussex
19 Broadclyst, Devon
20 Wickhambrook, Suffolk
21 Colchester, Essex
22 North Wooton, Somerset
23 Pilton, Somerset
24 Purleigh, Essex
25 Rodmell, Sussex
26 Bradfield, Berks.
27 Wedmore, Somerset
28 Barningham, Suffolk
29 Duddenhoe End, Essex
30 Prithsden, Herts.

31 Bury St Edmunds, Suffolk
32 Lamberhurst, Tunbridge Wells, Kent
33 Ardleigh, Essex
34 Lamphey, Pembrokeshire
35 Horam, Sussex
36 Beaulieu, Hants
37 Singleton, Sussex
38 Bickleigh, Devon
39 Newent, Glos.
40 Clyro, Herefordshire
41 Cranmore, Isle of Wight
42 Bolney, Sussex
43 Sandy, Beds.
44 Thurston, Suffolk
45 Hambledon, Hants
46 Bradford on Avon, Wilts.
47 Wilburton, Camb.
48 Ashton Keynes, Wilts.
49 Cratfield, Suffolk
50 Rowlands Castle, Hants
51 Purley, Berks.
52 Llanarth, Cardiganshire
53 Finchampstead, Berks.
54 Alresford, Hants
55 Blackfield, Hants

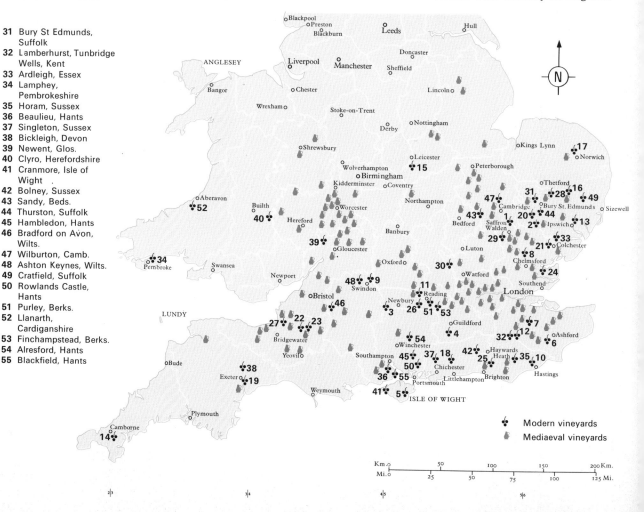

♣ Modern vineyards
🍇 Mediaeval vineyards

A whisky distillery in the austere beauty of the western islands of Scotland: Laphroaig on the island of Islay

The World of Spirits

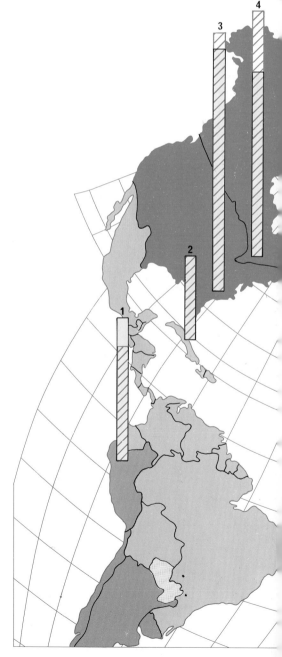

THE WINE COUNTRIES of the world are limited to the temperate zone, and to places where Mediterranean civilization has set the pattern of life. Spirits have no such climatic or cultural limits. They can be made wherever they are wanted. Distilling is not agriculture, with its roots directly in the ground, but industry. Where water runs and a truck can go you can make whisky, brandy, gin, rum or any other spirit.

But there is an élite among spirits—and for very much the same reasons as there is an élite among wines. Occasionally a complex set of natural conditions adds up to a style and quality of drink which can be imitated—but can never be reproduced. These are the spirits which bear their geographical origins like a coat of arms, and whose production, like wine-making, is partly science, mostly hard work, but also partly a creative art. International trade in spirits consists almost entirely of these superior products, and is limited to the richer nations.

Spirits can be distilled from anything which can be induced to ferment; anything containing sugar which can be turned into alcohol. Mankind has shown real ingenuity in finding fermentable and distillable supplies in the most unlikely places.

The list below shows some of his resources, from wine to milk, hogweed, potatoes and cactus. The maps also show his capacity for drinking (or at least for paying for) spirits, and the remarkable way it has fluctuated over the last decade.

Apples
Applejack	New Jersey, USA
Batzi	Switzerland
Trebern	Austria

Apricots
Barack pálinka	Hungary

Cactus
Pulque	Mexico
Tequila	Mexico

Cherries
Kirsch	Austria; Germany; Switzerland
Kirsebaerlikoer	Denmark

Cider
Calvados	Calvados, France
Eau de vie de cidre	Northern France

Coconuts
Arak, Arrack	East

Dates
Arak, Arrack	Middle East; North Africa
Zibib	Egypt; Middle East

Fruit
Alcools blancs	France
. . . Geist	Germany; Switzerland
. . . Wasser	Germany; Switzerland

Gentian
Enzian	Switzerland

Grain
Akvaviittee	Finland
Akvavit	Norway; Sweden; Denmark
Bourbon whisky	USA
Gin	England; North America
Genever	Holland
Korn	Germany
Poteen	Ireland
Schnapps	Germany
Steinhäger	Germany
Vodka	Russia; Poland
Whiskey	Ireland
Whisky	Scotland; North America

Grape skins
Aguardiente	Spain
Bagaceira	Portugal
Grappa	Italy
Komovica	Jugoslavia
Marc	France

Hogweed
Bartzch	Northern Asia

Milk
Awein	Tartar Russia
Skhou	Caucasus; Russia

Molasses
Aguardiente	Dominican Republic
Arrack	Indonesia
Basi	Philippines
Pinga	Brazil
Rum	West Indies; Mexico Central America, and S America; Madagascar; New England; Java; Philippines; Egypt

Plums
Rakia	Bulgaria
Sljivovica, slivovitz	Bulgaria; Austria
Slivowitz	Jugoslavia
Szilva	Hungary
Tuica	Romania

Potatoes
Akvaviittee	Finland
Akvavit	Norway; Sweden; Denmark
Schnapps	Germany
Vodka	Finland; Sweden

Rice
Arak, arrack	Far East

Sugar-cane
Cane spirit	South Africa
Rum	West Indies

Water-melons
Kislav	Russia

Wine
Aguardente	Portugal
Aguardiente	Spain
Arak, Arrack etc (or dates, rice, coconuts)	Africa; Middle East; Far East
Armagnac	Armagnac, France
Brandy	South Africa; Australia, New Zealand; Middle East; Italy; Germany
Cognac	Cognac, France
Coñac, Kanjak, Konjak etc	Spain; Portugal Chile; Eastern Europe Greece; Turkey; Russia
Mastika	Greece
Ouzo	Greece; Egypt; Middle East
Pisco	Peru
Rajika, Raki, Rakía	Balkans; Turkey Middle East
Vinjak	Jugoslavia

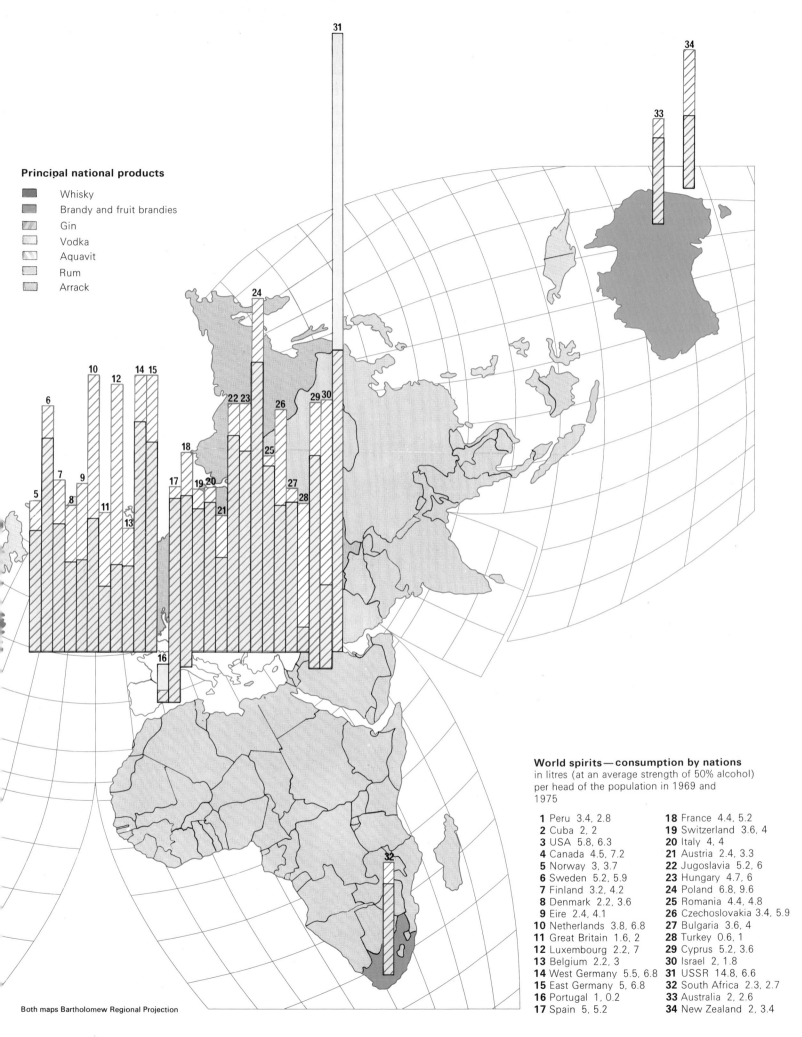

Principal national products

- Whisky
- Brandy and fruit brandies
- Gin
- Vodka
- Aquavit
- Rum
- Arrack

World spirits—consumption by nations

in litres (at an average strength of 50% alcohol) per head of the population in 1969 and 1975

1 Peru 3.4, 2.8	**18** France 4.4, 5.2
2 Cuba 2, 2	**19** Switzerland 3.6, 4
3 USA 5.8, 6.3	**20** Italy 4, 4
4 Canada 4.5, 7.2	**21** Austria 2.4, 3.3
5 Norway 3, 3.7	**22** Jugoslavia 5.2, 6
6 Sweden 5.2, 5.9	**23** Hungary 4.7, 6
7 Finland 3.2, 4.2	**24** Poland 6.8, 9.6
8 Denmark 2.2, 3.6	**25** Romania 4.4, 4.8
9 Eire 2.4, 4.1	**26** Czechoslovakia 3.4, 5.9
10 Netherlands 3.8, 6.8	**27** Bulgaria 3.6, 4
11 Great Britain 1.6, 2	**28** Turkey 0.6, 1
12 Luxembourg 2.2, 7	**29** Cyprus 5.2, 3.6
13 Belgium 2.2, 3	**30** Israel 2, 1.8
14 West Germany 5.5, 6.8	**31** USSR 14.8, 6.6
15 East Germany 5, 6.8	**32** South Africa 2.3, 2.7
16 Portugal 1, 0.2	**33** Australia 2, 2.6
17 Spain 5, 5.2	**34** New Zealand 2, 3.4

Both maps Bartholomew Regional Projection

255

How Spirits are Made

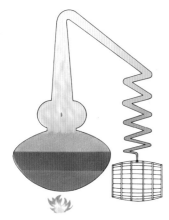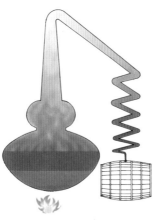

Above: the pot-still or alembic; the original design and still the best. A kettle holding 1,200 litres of white wine (in the case of cognac) sits on a fire. Highly volatile elements vaporize first. These are condensed in the copper coil (which is immersed in cold water) and collected in a barrel. They are known as headings (for whisky, foreshots). As it heats further the alcohol vaporizes and is in turn condensed and collected in another barrel. This is 'brouilli' (or in whisky 'low wines'). The less volatile part goes into a third barrel; these tailings (for whisky, feints) and the headings are added to the next kettle of wine to be distilled. Then the same process is repeated, using the brouilli in place of wine. This time the middle third is brandy

Above: brandy flows from the condenser of a pot-still in Cognac. The clear white spirit is running into a brass tray with a funnel into the oak barrel below
Below: one of the few big distilleries of Cognac has six identical pot-stills built over brick furnaces. In the smaller vase-like tanks on top (right) the wine is warmed by the vapour before it goes into the alembic

PUT AT ITS simplest, distilling is a way of concentrating the strength and flavour of any alcoholic drink by removing most of the water. It relies on the fact that alcohol is more volatile than water—which is to say that it boils at a lower temperature. If you boil wine in a saucepan it will lose all its alcohol and most of its aromatic elements into the air long before the pan is dry. So if you collect the steam and condense it you will have the alcohol and very little of the water; you will have, in fact, brandy.

This fact has been known in the East for thousands of years. It entered the western world in the 14th century, via the Arabs, whose words al embic (meaning a still) and al cohol we still use.

The original form of still, the pot-still (illustrated left), is simply a kettle on a fire, with a long spout, usually curled into a worm, in which the vapour condenses. Even now this is the best design, and used for all the highest-quality spirits. Its great advantage is that it gives total control. The distiller can choose precisely what part of the vapour he wants to keep, as containing the desirable proportion

Above: the art of distilling arrived in Europe late in the Middle Ages. This engraving of 1519 from Strasbourg is one of the earliest illustrations of a still

of alcohol and flavour. He can eliminate undesirable elements which vaporize sooner than alcohol and 'pass over' first or which are less volatile and 'pass over' later.

The pot-still's disadvantage is that it is slow, it needs a craftsman to operate it, and it needs to be cleaned out and-filled up after every operation.

Most modern distilling is done in the patent continuous still, which was invented by an Irish exciseman called Coffey. The picture on the right shows how it uses steam to vaporize the alcohol, letting the waste run away continuously, which makes it faster in operation than the pot-still and much cheaper to run. The only drawback is that you must distil at very high strength in order to get a clean enough spirit to drink; you cannot choose precisely which 'fraction' of the vapour you will keep. Continuous-still spirits therefore normally have less of the congenerics, as the flavouring elements which 'pass over' with the alcohol are called. They have less of the original taste and smell of the raw material; they also need less time in wood to mature.

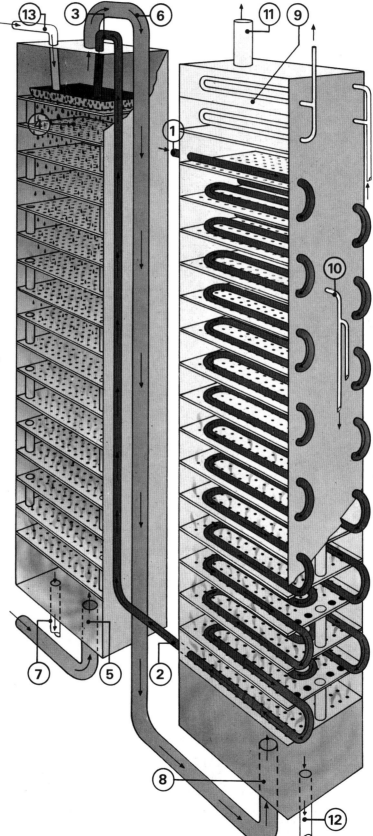

Left: most spirits are made in the continuous still. It takes in a steady stream of 'wash' (which can be wine, beer, or fermented molasses) at one end and emits a stream of spirit at the other: a more efficient and time-saving process than the pot-still on the opposite page. The continuous still consists of two columns as much as 80 feet high. Cold 'wash' goes into the 'rectifier' column at 1 and passing down twisting pipes is heated by mounting hot vapour. At 2 it emerges very hot from the rectifier and is taken to the top of the 'analyser' 3 where it flows into an open trough. The trough overflows, letting the hot wash fall on to perforated plates 4.
Meanwhile very hot steam enters at 5, rises and meets it, causing the volatile elements to boil away immediately. They pass as vapour out of the analyser at 6. Most of the water in the wash continues to fall down the column and is drained away at 7.
At 8 the spirit vapour (from 6) re-enters the rectifier. As it rises in this column, being cooled by the incoming wash pipes, less volatile elements ('feints') condense first and fall back to 12. From there they are pumped to join the fresh wash in the analyser at 13 and go through the process again. The spirit alone reaches the top. A cold-water radiator 9 there finally condenses it and it flows out of the column at 10. Only the most volatile elements (the equivalent of the foreshots of a pot-still) remain as vapour and emerge at 11.
While this method is much less laborious than the old one, there is not the nicety of control; the distiller does not choose an exact moment to separate spirits from foreshots and feints. To be safe he must treat a smaller and stronger fraction of the total as drinkable spirit and reject or redistil the rest. Hence the use of the pot-still for the fine spirits (e.g. cognac and malt whisky) which need to retain more of the congenerics which give flavour

Cognac

Above: the River Charente among vines near Jarnac
Below: fume-blackened warehouse roofs in Cognac
Bottom: cognac matures at least two years in oak

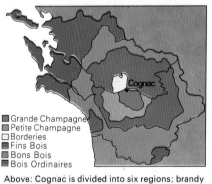

Grande Champagne
Petite Champagne
Borderies
Fins Bois
Bons Bois
Bois Ordinaires

Above: Cognac is divided into six regions; brandy
of the finest quality comes from the central zones
Below: of the five chief consumers of cognac,
Great Britain is the biggest outside France

France 24%
Great Britain 17%
USA 8%
Germany 8%

Canton boundary
Commune boundary
Vineyards
Woods
50
Contour interval 10 metres

Km. 0   1   2   3   4 Km.
Mi. 0   1   2 Mi.

The cognac houses

♣ 1 Martell
♣ 2 Hennessy
♣ 3 Remy Martin
♣ 4 Otard-Dupuy
♣ 5 Courvoisier
■ 6 Ricard-Bisquit Dubouché
■ 7 Hardy
♣ 8 J. G. Monnet
♣ 9 Camus
♣ 10 Salignac
♣ 11 Prince de Polignac
■ 12 Castillon
♣ 13 Larsen
♣ 14 Hine
♣ 15 Tiffon
♣ 16 Frapin

■ 17 Croizet-Eymard
■ 18 Dist. de Segonzac (Marte
■ 19 Dist. de Galienne (Marte
■ 20 Dist. de St-Martin (Marte
■ 21 Moulineuf (Martell)
♣ 22 Hennessy
♣ 23 Viticulteurs Réunis
♣ 24 Coop. de Cognac et
    Vins Charentais
♣ 25 Hennessy
♣ 26 Hennessy
♣ 27 Martell
■ 28 Hennessy
■ 29 Hennessy
■ 30 Hennessy
♣ 31 Delamain

■ Distillery   ♣ Warehouse

THERE IS an uncanny fresh-grape sweetness about good cognac, as though the soul of the vine has been etherealized and condensed. It makes you think not just of wine but of great wine—it has the same elusive complexity; the same raciness and excitement.

And yet the wine it comes from is not great at all. The Charente vineyards, now given over exclusively to cognac, were originally the poor pedlars of very inferior stuff to seamen from Britain and the Low Countries coming to buy salt. It was only in the 17th century that some of these immigrants began 'burning' the wine. But once the experiment had been made the word got round. A Mr Martell came from the Channel Islands, a Mr Hennessy from Ireland and a Mr Hine from Dorset. Cognac had found its métier.

The Appellation Contrôlée Cognac covers almost two whole departments just north of the Gironde estuary, the whole sparsely contoured basin of the River Charente, and even the small islands off-shore in the Bay of Biscay.

Some 50,000 farmers in this area grow white grapes, and as many as one in ten have a still of their own for distilling the wine. The variety they grow—today mainly Ugni Blanc, known locally as St-Emilion—gives wine without

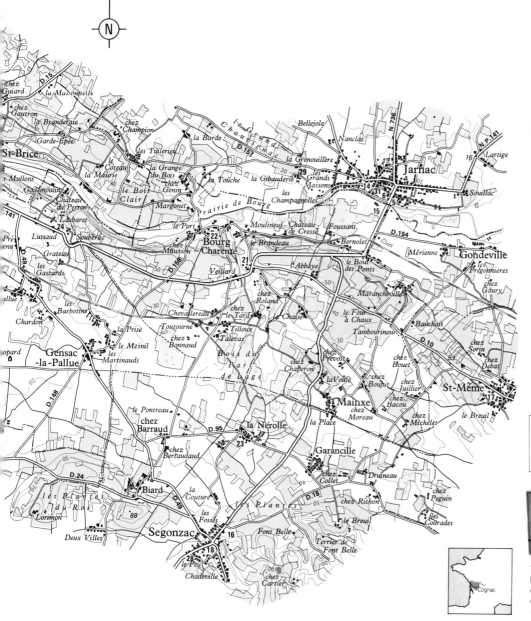

many other possibilities; only about $7\frac{1}{2}\%$ alcohol and with as much as 10 grammes per litre of acidity. Indeed they tend to pick before the grapes are fully ripe to be sure of this acidity, which makes it the perfect wine for distillation. The St-Emilion crops heavily here in the mild coastal climate with high rainfall.

The quality of the resulting brandy depends almost entirely on the soil. At its best, in the heart of the Charente (see the small map) it is as chalky as in Champagne. Hence the similarity of names between the two unrelated regions. Concentric circles of progressively less chalky and (for this purpose at least) inferior soils surround it. From a topsoil of 35% chalk, with 80–90% chalk only 20 centimetres down, to 25%, to 15% is the progression from Grande Champagne to Petite Champagne to Borderies. The corresponding progression in the cognac is from maximum finesse to a more full-bodied and high-flavoured spirit—still excellent in its way. Beyond the small and central Borderies, however, the three Bois—Fins, Bons and Ordinaires—have yellower, richer soil which results in less delicate cognac, with a distinct goût de terroir or earthiness.

Cognac is distilled in the winter months as soon as possible after the wine has stopped fermenting. The pot-still used is shown on page 256. The wine is warmed in a tank beforehand and then boiled away by a steady coal fire. Two distillations are needed to get the fraction with exactly the right amount of alcohol and congenerics: it runs from the still for the second time, white and clear, at about 70% alcohol: one barrel of brandy for every ten of wine which went in.

New cognac is harsh, overstrong, incomplete. Ageing in oak is as much part of the process as distillation. The forest of the Limousin, 80 miles to the east, supplies the perfect material; oak with a high porosity and rather low tannin content. Two years in a Limousin barrel is the legal minimum for any cognac; most good ones in practice have three and VSOPs (Very Special Old Pale) have five or more. The airy *chais* where the barrels lie are scattered throughout the region, their roofs blackened with a fungus which lives on the fumes; for the rate of evaporation is daunting: as much cognac is lost into the air every year as is drunk in the whole of France.

Five years is now the maximum age which the law allows a firm to claim on the label for its cognac, however old it may really be. The former practice of keeping unblended vintages has been outlawed as being impossible to control. One kind of certified older cognac, however, is still available; cognac which has been 'early-landed' in a foreign port in barrel and kept in the customs cellar while it matures. The London docks have long been famous for the gentle and exquisite, faintly sweet and faintly watery-tasting, very pale old cognac which has passed 20 or 30 years gradually losing alcohol and gaining finesse in their particularly damp cellars.

Normal commercial cognac is diluted to 40% alcohol with distilled water, and its sweetness and colour are adjusted with sugar and caramel. Each shipper has his house style, which he keeps constant from year to year.

The large map shows the heart of Cognac; the country between Cognac, the prosperous little capital, Jarnac and Segonzac. The area south of the Charente is in Grande Champagne, north is mainly Fins Bois and north-west, facing Cognac, is Borderies. The principal distilleries and warehouses are marked. In the well-tended but rather dull countryside the characteristic building is the *logis*; the old fortified farmhouse, high-walled and gated. Many have stills: the greater part of cognac is made by farmers and matured by shippers.

Armagnac

THE WORLD has only one other brandy which can be compared with cognac—and it too comes from western France, from an area which at its closest point is only 80 miles from the Charente. But armagnac shares only its subtlety and its very high standards with cognac; for the two brandies are poles apart in style, and in the techniques used to make them.

Armagnac is a remote country region, hilly in the south, known as Haut-Armagnac, and almost a plain in the north—Ténarèze and Bas-Armagnac, the areas which give the best-quality brandy. Bas-Armagnac might be called the Grande Champagne of the region, except that in place of chalk it has sandy soil.

Apart from the soil and Armagnac's generally warmer climate the big differences between armagnac and cognac come from the type of still and the local wood. The armagnac still is something between a pot-still and a continuous still, a sort of double boiler in which the wine is distilled once, at a much lower strength than most spirits: 53% as against cognac's 70—though recently high-strength distillation has been allowed.

The lower the strength of the distillation the more flavouring elements are left besides the alcohol in the brandy. Thus armagnac starts with a stronger flavour and scent than cognac. To this the local 'black' oak, sappy (so sappy in fact it should be hewn with an adze rather than sawn) and itself full of flavour, adds its character. In black oak brandy ages much faster than in white Limousin oak in Cognac. At eight years it is well-aged; at 20 superb.

Until 1905 Armagnac had no real identity. It sold all its good brandy to shippers in the Charente; a large part of the cognac of those days was really armagnac, for the deep blackish colour and seeming extreme age of armagnac helped young cognacs to appear older.

Comparisons of the flavours of armagnac and cognac always class armagnac as 'rustic', with the implication that it is a coarser spirit. It has been compared with hand-woven tweed in contrast with worsted. But tweed is a rough cloth, and it is armagnac's special distinction to be marvellously velvety smooth. At the same time it is dry; sugar is not normally added, as it is to cognac. Armagnac has a great pungent smell, which stays in your mouth or even in an empty glass for a long while. Its spirity, fiery quality is very similar to cognac's. The only great quality of the best cognacs it does not have is the brilliant, champagne-like finesse.

There are no great shippers like Martell and Hennessy in Armagnac. The labels here are those of some of the best of the many small houses; some of which also make liqueurs— the lower-quality brandy of Haut-Armagnac lends itself to this kind of processing.

The main centres of the industry are the little market-towns of Auch, Condom and Eauze. As in most of the wine areas of France, a good deal of private buying goes on direct from farmers.

Above left: the Armagnac pattern of still is quite different from those of Cognac and produces lower-strength spirit with more flavour-giving congenerics
Left: the rolling green countryside of Bas-Armagnac in the west of the region produces the best brandy

Two small Appellation Contrôlée areas for wine adjoin Armagnac's best area in the south. Madiran is a strong red (which must legally stay three years in cask); Pacherenc du Vic-Bilh is a sweet white. See also page 128

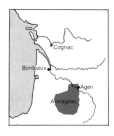

Limits of A C Madiran and Pacherenc du Vic Bilh
Département boundary
Haut-Armagnac
Ténarèze
Bas-Armagnac
•Panjas   Production centres

Km.0   10   20   30   40 Km.
Mi.0   10   20 Mi.

Below: a large number of small producers make Armagnac an interesting subject to explore. Armagnac ages more rapidly than cognac, and at ten years has a dark colour and enormously attractive scent. The traditional bottle is round and squat; labels usually conform to this shape

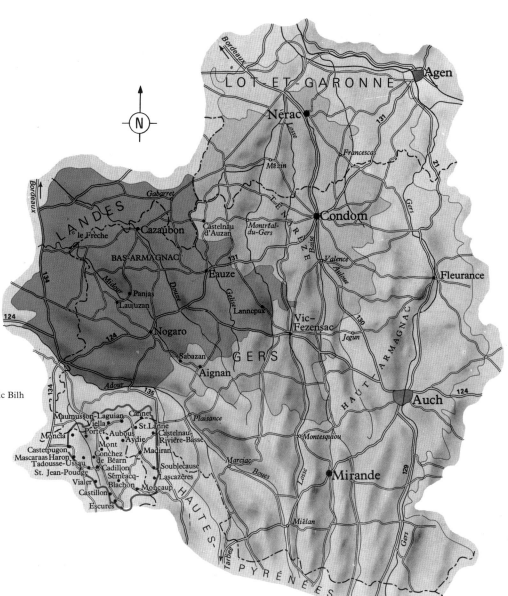

Scotland: the Highland Malts

Above: the fire and water of the Highlands; peat for drying the malt and the silver thread of the river Spey Below: some of their classic products. Less than half the malt distilleries mapped opposite sell their whisky unblended; these are among the most famous

THE 'SINGLE', or unblended, malt whiskies of the Highlands round the river Spey are to Scotch what château-bottled classed growths are to Bordeaux. The highest quality is combined in them with the maximum individuality and distinction. Each of them is superb, recognizable, consistent, and exactly like no other whisky on earth.

Most malt whisky is used to give character to the famous blends which sell all over the world. Only a little is sold 'single'. It has much more body, fragrance, texture and usually sweetness than blended whisky—but no two are alike.

On the next pages the products of the whole of Scotland are mapped. On the facing page is singled out the very heart of the whisky world; the extraordinary concentration of an industry which is also an art, miles from anywhere in barren and beautiful hills beside the Moray Firth in north-eastern Scotland.

A typical Speyside distillery is a quiet place. It seems to have the pace of farm life rather than industry. On a bright cool summer morning or in the almost permanent darkness of a Scottish winter the same simple processes are repeated by quiet men.

One long building covers the malting floor. Painted iron pillars punctuate a sea of barley, knee-deep, raked patiently this way and that while it germinates by men who do not speak.

The pointed building with the little hat contains the drying kiln, where peat from Pitsligo to the south smoulders on the red coke under a smoking hill of the germinated malt.

The next big stone barn is full of tanks and pipes and copper covers and the soothing smell of a brewery. And the next with the strange massive heads of stills, monster kettles squatting on bright points of fire, rumbling like old men who have lost touch with the world.

In this last is the first sight of whisky; a smooth little burn running a short course in a brass-bound glass case. Padlocked. And silent.

There is endless debate about the sources of quality and character in Scotch. The water is one favourite topic. There is general agreement that it should be soft, since soft water is a better solvent than hard, and extracts more proteins from the malted barley. Traditionally the best water is said to come through peat over red granite—as the burns do which flow down from the hills of the treeless deer forests past the distillery doors.

Another factor is the barley. Highland barley is not 'fat', but full of protein, which means more flavour. Another is the peat for the fire on which the barley is dried. Its smoke contributes to the taste. Another is the shape of the still; any alteration will alter its product. Another is the oak barrels in which it is matured —old sherry casks are best.

And most important is the age. Three years is the legal minimum, but at ten years or more a malt reaches its peak. Beyond 15 years or so in oak it is said to go 'slimy'.

The most famous of all the distilleries is the Glenlivet, standing on a bare slope overlooking the little river Livet where it runs down from Glenlivet forest to join the Avon, a tributary of the Spey. It was the first distillery to conform to the licensing laws which in 1823 made the hundreds of small stills of the Highlands illegal. Its fame today rests on its gently sweet, slightly smoky, marvellously delicate whisky.

No fewer than 23 other firms all over Speyside have annexed Glenlivet's name to their own at some time, among them Glen Grant, Macallan, Longmorn, Dufftown and Glenfarclas—all superb in their own right, and all bottled and sold (in small quantities) unblended.

Others in this area which can be bought 'single', each with its own character, are Glenfiddich, Balvenie and Mortlach from Dufftown, and Strathisla from Keith. The rest, with their musical, savage names, find oblivion in the blending vats of the great brands. But without them the Scotch whisky that the world knows would not exist.

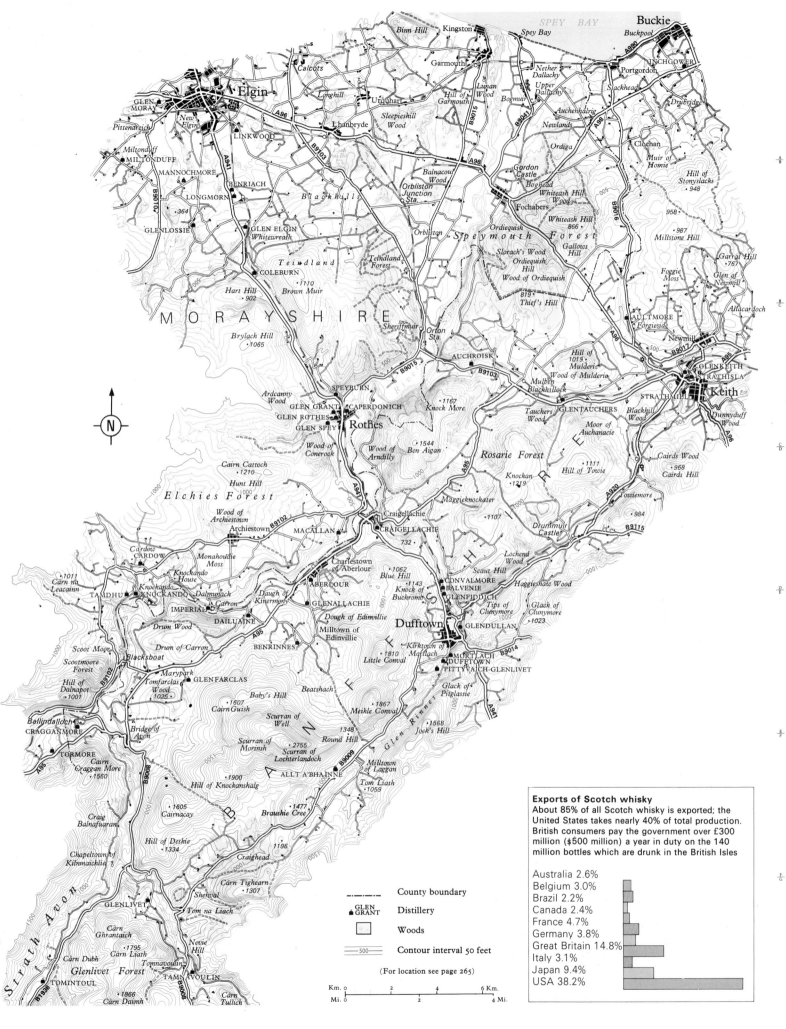

Scotch Whisky

ANY WHISKY which is made in Scotland, whether in the Highlands or the Lowlands, whether of barley or corn, whether in a pot-still or a continuous steam-still, is Scotch. The vast majority of the Scotch which is sold, in fact, is a mixture of all these different kinds of whisky, adding up to a standard drink with an unmistakable but not too pronounced flavour. There are over 2,000 of such blends. Anybody could devise a new one tomorrow. But of the individual whiskies which go into them there are only 130, from 130 different distilleries. And of these only about 40 are ever sold 'single', and known by the name of their distilleries: the rest are entirely used in blends.

Very loosely speaking, whisky is distilled beer; beer unflavoured with hops. The distiller's first job is the same as the brewer's; to make malt from barley; to dissolve it in water, and to ferment the resulting 'wash'. The brewer would add hops to the resulting 'worts'; the whisky-maker distils it, twice over. The first and last of the liquid which runs from the condenser the second time goes back to be distilled again. The middle part is whisky.

What sort of whisky it is is determined by where it is done and with what equipment and materials. Five kinds of Scotch are recognized.

The first is grain whisky, distilled from barley and maize in continuous stills—a comparative newcomer but now the bigger part of the industry. Grain whisky has little flavour or colour. Practically none of it is ever drunk unblended. But it is the vehicle for the flavours of all blended Scotch; the cheaper blends have as much as 70% of it; the best about 30%.

Being mild and light it needs less maturing than the more highly flavoured kinds.

One straight grain whisky, from Cameronbridge distillery, is sold, under the name 'Old Cameron Brig'. It is rare, but for the curious an interesting experience: a smooth, pleasant and mild-flavoured spirit.

All the other kinds of Scotch are known as malts—being made from malted barley. There are four, because four areas of Scotland make them; and each has its own particular character.

Best and most famous of all are the malts from the district of the river Spey. They are mapped and described on the previous two pages. The malts of northern Scotland come nearest to them. Some are equally fine; often with rather stronger flavours. Of the northern malts Clynelish, Dalmore, Glenmorangie and Balblair are all bottled 'single'. One particularly fragrant and full-flavoured malt from the island of Orkney, Highland Park, is considered in the top rank.

Most distinctive of all are the malts from the western islands Islay, Jura and Skye. They are known by the strong peaty smell and flavour which gives them a slightly medicinal character. One theory is that the island peat consists of ancient deposits of seaweed which contain iodine. Certainly they are the easiest malts to recognize; those who like them will drink nothing else. A little goes a long way in a blend. Laphroaig (the distillery is shown on page 253) is the most famous of the island malts. Another Islay distillery, Lagavulin, sells a little in bottle and is highly thought of. Talisker on Skye also has a following.

Just south of the islands on the promontory of Kintyre are two remaining distilleries from what was once a thriving centre; Campbeltown. Only Springbank can be bought unblended.

The rest of the malt distilleries are classed as Lowland and are reckoned to produce rather gentler, less high-flavoured Scotch. All except three, Bladnoch in the west and Rosebank and Littlemill in the centre, sell their entire production for blending.

Of the hundreds of blends of Scotch the most famous are the six classics produced by the giant Distillers Co: John Haig, Johnnie Walker, Black & White, Dewar's White Label, White Horse and Vat 69. All are irreproachable and wholly consistent. Many knowledgeable people think Haig the best of them; Johnnie Walker is the best-seller; White Horse is the maltiest. The Distillers Co owns almost half the malt distilleries in Scotland and accounts for half the exports of Scotch . . . and about 85% of the total is exported.

Their principal rivals include the favourites in America, Cutty Sark and J & B Rare, which are light in colour and flavour, and such brands as Standfast, Teacher's, Bell's, Long John, Ballantine's and Whyte & Mackay's.

Then there are some excellent smaller concerns with such blends as The Famous Grouse, Catto's, Usher's, McCallum's, Queen Anne and Spey Royal.

And finally there are a number of de luxe blends, among them Dimple Haig, Johnnie Walker Black Label, Islay Mist and Chivas Regal, which contain more and older malts and are correspondingly more expensive.

Far left: the 'worts' of barley-malt and water ferment briefly and turbulently in the 'wash-back' to reach the strength of strong beer
Left: malt whisky is distilled twice. The wash-still for the first and the spirit-still for the second distillation stand side by side over a coal furnace
Above: from the wash-still the 'safe' receives 'low wines'; then from the spirit-still whisky and finally 'feints'

Distilleries

▮	Highland Malt
▼	Lowland Malt
▲	Islay Malt
◆	Campbeltown Malt
●	Grain
▓	Speyside: larger scale map on Page 263
░	Land above 1200 feet

Some of the products of northern, island and lowland distilleries which are sold unblended: all are malts except the bottom label, which is the only straight grain whisky there is on the market

265

Rum

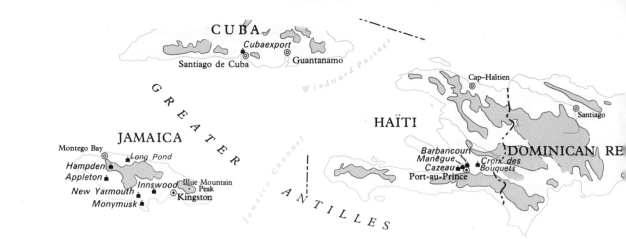

EVER SINCE the Spaniards in the 16th century took sugar-cane, which had come to Europe from China, to their colony of Santo Domingo, its pungent fiery distilled essence has been the drink of the chain of Caribbean islands which curves like a cutlass from Cuba to Venezuela.

All these islands, British, French, American, Spanish or Dutch, make at least a little rum. Sometimes it is only in a palm-thatched shelter in the cane gardens, with a decrepit old copper pot-still. In Guyana such moonshine is known as 'Bushie'; in St Kitts 'Hammond'; in St Lucia 'L'Esprit d'Amour'.

The modern rum industry, however, has little to do with such folk-lore. Its big distilleries grow bigger and fewer year by year as rum gets in line as a polite social drink. The map shows where the principal ones are today.

Rum is made of either cane juice, crushed out of fresh cane by roller mills, or molasses,

the residue after the juice has been boiled to make sugar. Distillers on the British and American islands, who use molasses almost exclusively, call it by the intimidating name of blackstrap. The French contrast their cane juice rum by calling it 'agricole'.

Either material is first fermented. Then it can be distilled in either of the two kinds of still: pot or continuous. Just as with whisky, the continuous still makes a more neutral but cheaper spirit; the pot-still, operated with skill, can give the perfect fraction, without too much or too little of the flavouring essences. Commercially the same answer has been found for rum as for whisky; most rums on the market are a blend of the two.

Different methods and tastes give different styles to the rums of various islands. Distillers also give credit for the individuality of their products to the yeasts they use, their water, their local variety of cane, the soil it grows on (in about that order). Particular attention is paid to yeasts. The modern trend is for laboratory-developed pure yeast cultures which give a quick clean fermentation, in place of the chance natural yeasts of the cane-gardens. But for what in Jamaica is known as Plummer or Wedderburn rum or in Martinique as Grand Arôme, the residue from previous distillations is stored in 'dunder pits' where it ferments slowly and continuously, a black and astonishingly pungent concentration of everything that gives rum its taste and smell. Dunder is used to start the fermentation of fresh batches, just as 'sour mash' is used in Kentucky. The result is a sort of ancestral character continuing from batch to batch.

Rum does not need nearly so much ageing as brandy. Six months in oak is enough for good light rum. Five years would be enough for any.

Fashion today is abandoning the sweet, dark,

rummy rums in favour of drier and paler sorts which impose their character less forcefully on mixed drinks. Germany and France (where it accounts for 40% of all spirits sold) still like the taste of rum, but the United States is in two minds about it. In fact the best rums today manage to keep the familiar happy pungency but in a lighter and more elegant vehicle.

Cuba, the original home of Bacardi, exports little now, but Cuban rum is apparently excellent and light.

Jamaica is by tradition the home of the heaviest rum. Some (Hampden) is still made hyper-flavoured for mixing with neutral spirit to make the German 'Rum Verschnitt', but most are of medium richness today.

Haiti. Fully flavoured rum, but being double pot-distilled like Scotch or cognac the best have real finesse. Barbancourt is the most famous.

Puerto Rico is the world's biggest producer. All

Left, from top: Bacardi moved from Cuba to Puerto Rico and is now also made in the Bahamas, Mexico and even Spain; Lemon Hart is a Jamaica blend; the three famous French rums are from Martinique; Mount Gay is from Barbados, Caroni from Trinidad and Lamb's from Guyana
Right and below: cane gardens and a farm in Guadeloupe

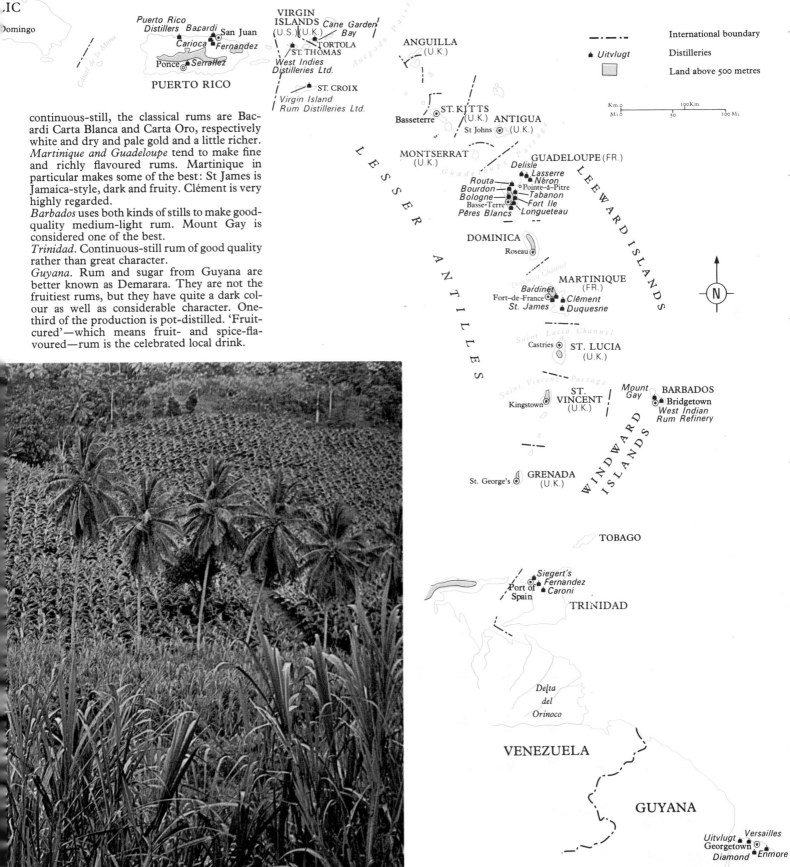

continuous-still, the classical rums are Bacardi Carta Blanca and Carta Oro, respectively white and dry and pale gold and a little richer.
Martinique and Guadeloupe tend to make fine and richly flavoured rums. Martinique in particular makes some of the best: St James is Jamaica-style, dark and fruity. Clément is very highly regarded.
Barbados uses both kinds of stills to make good-quality medium-light rum. Mount Gay is considered one of the best.
Trinidad. Continuous-still rum of good quality rather than great character.
Guyana. Rum and sugar from Guyana are better known as Demarara. They are not the fruitiest rums, but they have quite a dark colour as well as considerable character. One-third of the production is pot-distilled. 'Fruit-cured'—which means fruit- and spice-flavoured—rum is the celebrated local drink.

Domingo

Puerto Rico Distillers Bacardi San Juan
Carioca Fernandez
Ponce Serrallez
PUERTO RICO

VIRGIN ISLANDS Cane Garden
(U.S.) (U.K.) Bay
ST. THOMAS TORTOLA
West Indies Distilleries Ltd.
ST. CROIX
Virgin Island Rum Distilleries Ltd.

ANGUILLA (U.K.)

International boundary
Uitvlugt Distilleries
Land above 500 metres

Km.0   100Km.
Mi.0   50   100 Mi.

ST. KITTS (U.K.) **ANTIGUA**
Basseterre St Johns (U.K.)

MONTSERRAT (U.K.) **GUADELOUPE**(FR.)
Delisle
Lasserre
Néron
Routa Pointe-à-Pitre
Bourdon Tabanon
Bologne
Basse-Terre Fort Ile
Pères Blancs Longueteau

DOMINICA
Roseau

MARTINIQUE (FR.)
Bardinet
Fort-de-France Clément
St. James Duquesne

Castries **ST. LUCIA** (U.K.)

ST. VINCENT (U.K.) Mount Gay **BARBADOS**
Kingstown Bridgetown
West Indian Rum Refinery

St. George's **GRENADA** (U.K.)

LESSER ANTILLES

LEEWARD ISLANDS

WINDWARD ISLANDS

TOBAGO

Siegert's
Fernandez
Port of Spain Caroni
TRINIDAD

Delta del Orinoco

VENEZUELA

GUYANA

Uitvlugt Versailles
Georgetown
Diamond Enmore

Kentucky's Bourbon

BOURBON whisky, or whiskey, is defined in terms of what it is made of and how, rather than where it comes from. Kentucky has no monopoly of its production. Yet history and sentiment identify bourbon with the state where it was first made (in Bourbon County), and even today more than half of America's bourbon distilleries are in Kentucky.

United States law lays down that bourbon must be made from not less than 51% corn grain; be distilled at not over 160 US proof (or 80% alcohol); be reduced with water to 125 proof before maturing; be matured for two years or more in new barrels of white oak, charred on the inside; and be bottled at not less than 70 proof.

In more sensual terms, Bourbon is a light brown, fruity-flavoured, often rather sweet whisky, with a penetrating and unforgettable taste composed of charred oak and caramel. In practice it is made of a mixture of corn (maize), rye and barley malt fermented together with the distiller's own strain of yeast and often a little 'sour' or matured mash for continuity.

Distillers who use a higher proportion of corn get a lighter whisky. By increasing the proportion of rye they make one with more body and flavour which needs longer ageing.

Bourbon has been traced back to the still of Elijah Craig, a Baptist preacher in Georgetown, ten miles north of Lexington. He is reputed to have made the first bourbon in 1789, the year George Washington became first president. His innovation was using a mixture of grains for his mash.

It differed from the modern whisky chiefly in being made in a copper pot-still, whereas today gigantic continuous stills are used. Hence the law setting a maximum strength: a continuous still could remove all the flavouring elements and leave pure alcohol.

Bourbon is normally sold 'straight'—either just the produce of one distillery or as 'a blend of straights', the produce of several. If it is mixed with neutral spirit, as in some of the cheaper blends, it is no longer called bourbon but simply 'blended whisky'. If labelled Bottled in Bond it is stronger (50% alcohol as against the normal 43), older (at least four years) and probably fuller-flavoured and better.

There are more than 2,900 brands of bourbon. Sales of them all together make it possibly the biggest-selling spirit in the world.

Geography is not totally irrelevant to bourbon-making. What first made Kentucky a distilling centre was partly the good supply of corn, and the difficulty of moving it to market —a keg of whisky being easier to transport than 11 bushels of grain—and partly the ample supply of limestone spring water for making the mash and cooling the condenser.

Most of the bourbon distilleries outside Kentucky lie in states on the same limestone belt: Virginia makes excellent bourbon; Pennsylvania and Maryland (traditionally the centre for rye whisky) also have bourbon distilleries. And Tennessee makes, in the 'sour mash' Jack Daniels and George Dickel, Bourbon of a particular style, produced by 'leeching' the raw whisky through powdered maple charcoal, which is certainly some of the best in America.

Top: when bourbon was sold to saloons in barrels the labels were barrel-head size. This label shows an early pot-still
Above: beside a distillery, a pond of Kentucky's famous limestone water. Neighbouring states which make bourbon are on the same belt of limestone
Left: bourbon must be matured in new white oak barrels; cooperage is a thriving trade; old barrels are sold to (among others) Scotch distillers to be used again
Right: barrels are set on fire inside; the charring gives flavour and colour to bourbon

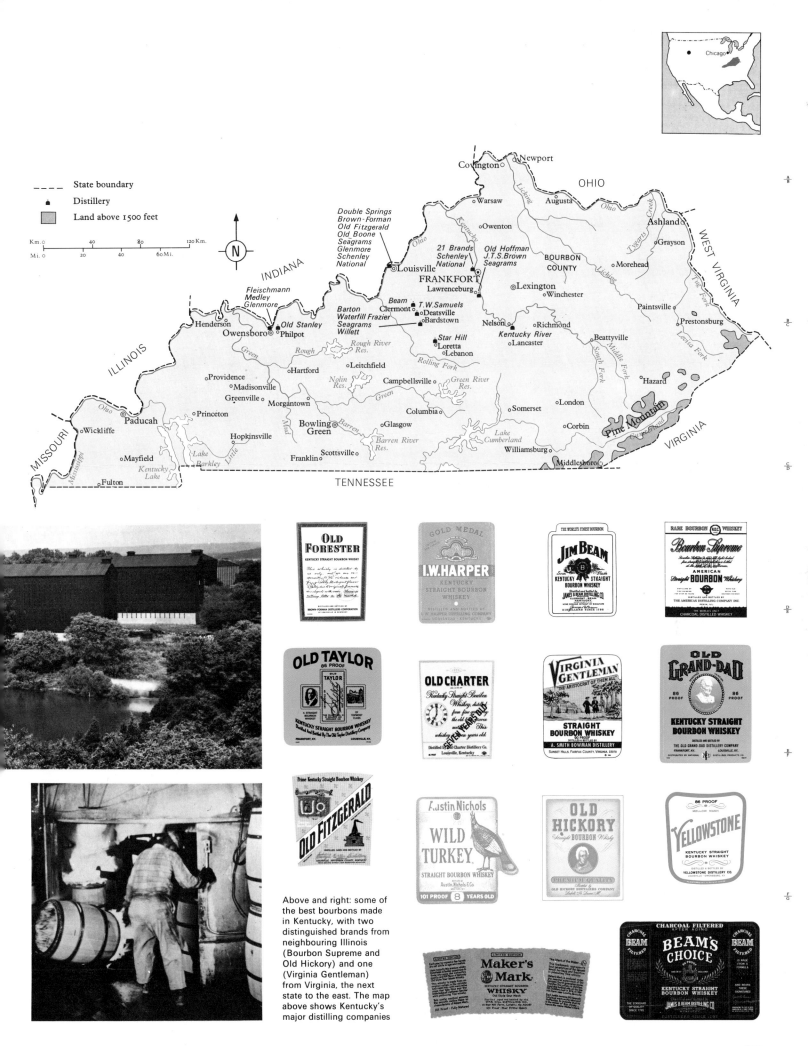

Above and right: some of the best bourbons made in Kentucky, with two distinguished brands from neighbouring Illinois (Bourbon Supreme and Old Hickory) and one (Virginia Gentleman) from Virginia, the next state to the east. The map above shows Kentucky's major distilling companies

The Kirsch Family

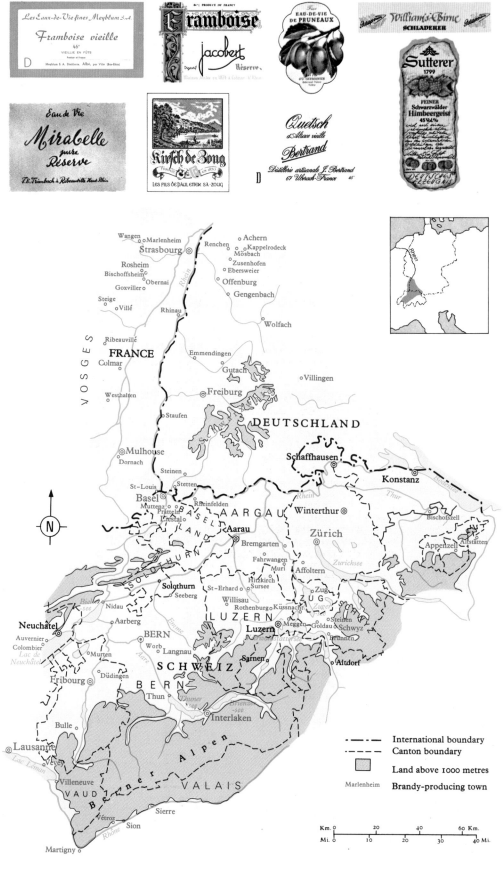

Every fruit that grows in the orchards of Switzerland, the Vosges mountains and the Black Forest is distilled to make high-strength clear white spirit of great fragrance. Above right are some of the scores of good producers

DISTILLING nowadays is nearly all big business. There are bootleggers still—probably more than most people suppose—but in most countries the old cottage industry has been taxed out of existence. Only where the results are exceptional does it still flourish. That place, above all, is the stretch of Europe east and south of the Vosges; the Black Forest and the northern half of Switzerland.

The local eau-de-vie is distilled in pot-stills from every edible fruit, and several which are not eaten. Kirsch, made of cherries, is the most common and widespread of these 'alcools blancs'—so-called because they are aged in glass or pottery rather than wood, and thus have no colour. But pears, apricots, blue plums, and more extravagantly raspberries, wild strawberries, and even holly berries (which give a fantastically pungent—and expensive—spirit) are distilled. The soft fruits and small berries are needed in huge quantities; prices for the genuine article are thus very high.

There are comparatively few big firms in the business: names such as Schladerer, Jacobert, Etter are well known, and Alsace wine-shippers sell alcools, whether they make them or buy them, under their own names. Some of the finest of all come from farm-houses in the Black Forest or the Vosges, with the still in a little room off the kitchen and a vat house no bigger than a one-car garage, lined with little tanks of the essences of the local orchards.

The French tend to distil lightly for maximum flavour; the Swiss distil further and get a more neutral spirit. The Germans distinguish between a 'Wasser', which is a spirit obtained by direct distillaton of the fermented fruit, and a 'Geist', which is partly a Wasser, but partly also made by infusing the fruit in alcohol—the method used with soft fruit.

The best fruit brandies are made of pears (called in France Poire William, in Germany Birngeist), raspberries (framboise, Himbeergeist), cherries (Kirsch), apricots (abricot, Aprikosengeist), blue plums (quetsch, Zwetschenwasser), gentian (gentiane, Enzian) and, principally in France, yellow plums (mirabelle), wild strawberries (fraise des bois), bilberries (myrtille), blackberries (mûre sauvage), rowan (alise) and holly (baie de houx).

Calvados

Right: Calvados du Pays d'Auge is the Appellation Contrôlée for the best Calvados, fiery and with a strong scent of apples when it is newly distilled, then matured in big oak casks until it grows nearer to brandy

AN ARMADA galleon, *El Calvador*, wrecked on the Normandy coast as it ran from the guns of Drake's flotilla, is supposed to have given its name to the département of Calvados, and hence to the world's most famous apple brandy. Cider is the local wine of this grapeless part of France. And the local brandy is cider 'burnt' in a still. There are records of cider-distilling going back to the 16th century on the Cotentin peninsula, west of Calvados. Now 11 regions, shown on the map above, use the name, followed by their own.

In 1946 one limited area and one method of distilling cider was given an Appellation Contrôlée: Calvados du Pays d'Auge. It must be made of cider from fruit crushed in the traditional fashion and fermented for at least a month (though in a whole month it only reaches about 4% alcohol). It must be distilled twice in a pot-still, in exactly the same way as cognac, and at about the same strength (72% alcohol). It must be sold at between 40 and 50%. It must be aged for at least a year.

Well-made Calvados is quite drinkable, though very fiery, when new, but in practice the best is aged for several years in big oak casks. Before it is sold it is slightly coloured with caramel, but not normally sweetened, so it remains a very dry spirit. In its degree of scent and flavour it is very like brandy. But good Calvados recaptures in an uncanny way the evocative smell of apples. It plays an important part in Norman cooking: terrines, tripes, creamy dishes of chicken or sole are perfumed with it, and often called Pays d'Auge. There is a famous local custom of drinking a glass of Calvados between two courses of a long meal, to make a hole, a 'trou Normand', to fill with yet more delectable dishes.

The other regions which make Calvados are not obliged to use the pot-still, but if they use a continuous still it must have devices for extracting undesirable essences from the column. This less refined Calvados is not Appellation Contrôlée but only Réglementée.

Cheaper apple brandy is permitted to be made in an ordinary continuous still, but is not allowed the name Calvados. It can call itself eau de vie de cidre (or poiré, from pears) de Normandie, Bretagne or Maine.

Acknowledgements

IN ADDITION to the bodies named on page 4, and the hundreds of wine-lovers whose help has been invaluable in making this atlas, the author particularly acknowledges the contributions in information, time and advice of the following:

France
Bureau Interprofessionnel de l'Armagnac, Eauze
Comité Interprofessionnel des Vins des Côtes de Provence, Les Arcs-sur-Argens
Comité Interprofessionnel des Vins des Côtes du Rhône, Avignon
Comité Interprofessionnel des Vins Doux Naturels et Vins de Liqueur à Appellations Contrôlées, Perpignan
Comité Interprofessionnel du Vin d'Alsace, Colmar
Conseil Interprofessionnel des Vins à Appellation Contrôlée de Touraine, Tours
Conseil Interprofessionnel des Vins de la Région de Bergerac, Bergerac
Conseil Interprofessionnel du Vin de Bordeaux
Mr Nicolas Barrow, Château Courant, Arcins
M Pierre Besancenot, Beaune
M Pierre Bouard, Colmar, Alsace
Colonel Maurice Buckmaster, London
M Roger Danglade, Château Rouet, Fronsac
M J. Dargent, Conseil Interprofessionnel du Vin de Champagne, Epernay
M. Jean-Henri Dubernet, Narbonne
M Yves Fourault of Eschenauer, Bordeaux
Fédération Nationale des Vins Délimités de Qualité Superieure, Paris
Fédération Regionale des Vins de Savoie, Bugey, Dauphiné, Chambery
Food from France, London
M Francis Gardère, Pauillac
M Pierre Gouttier, Paris
M Laurent Gaud, Institut des Vins de Table
M Jean Latour, Hospices de Beaune, Beaune
M Jean Hugel of F. E. Hugel & Fils, Riquewihr
M Louis-Noel Latour of Beaune
Mr Michael Longhurst, Château Loudenne, Médoc
Mr T. Marshall, Nuits-St-Georges
Martell & Co, Cognac
M J. C. Berrouet of J-P Moueix & Co, Libourne
M Philippe Roudié, Bordeaux
Mr Peter Sichel, Château d'Angludet, Cantenac
Syndicat du cru Corbières, Lézignan
Union Interprofessionnel de la Côte d'Or et de l'Yonne pour les Vins de Bourgogne, Beaune
Union Interprofessionnel des Vins du Beaujolais
Union Viticole Sancerroise, Sancerre

Germany
Dr Hans Ambrosi, Verwaltung der Staatsweingüter im Rheingau, Eltville am Rhein
Dr H. Becker, Geisenheim
Dr H. Breider, Bayerische Landesanstalt für Wein-, Obst-und Gartenbau
Herr Paul Bergweiler, Wehlen
Dr Albert Bürklin, Wachenheim/Pfalz
Herr Hermann Herlet of Deinhard's, Koblenz
Dr G. Horney, Deutsche Wetterdienst, Geisenheim
Dr F. W. Michele, Mainz
Dr H. G. Woschek, Deutsche Wein-Information, Mainz
Frau Marina Knobloch, Deutsche Wein-Information, Mainz
Dr Aichele, Deutscher Wetterdienst, Trier
Prof Heinrich Zakosek, Hessisches Landesamt für Bodenforschung, Wiesbaden
Hessische Lehr-und Forschungsanstalt für Wein Industrie-und Handelskammer, Baden-Baden
Dr Weiss, Industrie-und Handelskammer, Stuttgart
Herr Hoepfener of Karl Heinrich Kraus, Nierstein
Herr Breithaupt, St Nikolaus Hospitien, Kues
Dr Goedecke, Staatliche Weinbaudomänen Niederhäusen-Schlossböckelheim
Bürgermeister Schuh, Neumagen
Bürgermeister Schütz, Enkirch
Verwaltung der Bischöflichen Weingüter, Trier
Herr A. von Schubert, Maximin Grünhaus, Trier
Herr Karl-Felix Wegeler, Oestrich
Dr A. Krayer, Weinbauamt, Eltville
Herr Karl Schnitzius, Weinbauamt, Kröv
Olr. F. Rath, Weinbauschule, Bad Kreuznach
Georg Westermann Verlag, Braunschweig

Algeria
Office de Commercialisation des Produits Viti-Vinicoles, Algiers

Argentina
Vinos Argentinos S.A. Exportadora, Buenos Aires

Australia
Mr Stuart Foulds, Australian Wine Centre, London
Mr George Kolarovitch, Barossa Co-operative Winery
Federal Wine and Brandy Producers, Adelaide
Hamilton Ewell Vineyard Prop., Adelaide
Thomas Hardy & Sons, Mile End, South Australia

Austria
Herr Lorenz Möser, Rohrendorf bei Krems
Österreichisches Weininstitut
Winzergenossenschaft Wachau, Dürnstein

Bulgaria
Vinimpex, Sofia

Chile
Anglo-Chilean Society, London
Asociación Nacional de Viticultores, Santiago

Corsica
Groupement Interprofessionnel des Vins de l'Ile de Corse

Cyprus
Keo, Limassol
Vine Products Commission SAP, Limassol

Czechoslovakia
Dr Erich Minárik, Bratislava

Greece
Ministry of Agriculture, Athens

Hungary
Mr I. Toporczy, Commercial Secretary, London Embassy
Monimpex, Budapest
Mr Edward Roche, London

Israel
Israel Wine Institute, Rehovot

Italy
Consorzi di Vini di Asti, di Verona, di Alto Adige
Italian Institute for Foreign Trade, London
Rivista di Viticoltura e di Enologia, Conegliano, Treviso
Dr Bruno Roncarati, London
Unione Italiana Vini, Milan

Japan
Japan Spirits & Liquors Makers Association, Tokyo
Mr Robert Mendelsohn, London

Jugoslavia
Mr E. C. Burgess, Teltscher Brothers, London

Lebanon
Caves de Ksara, Ksara
Vins Musar, Beirut

Luxembourg
Fédération des Associations Viticoles de Luxembourg, Grevenmacher
Station Viticole, Remich

Madeira
Mr Noel Cossart, Cossart Gordon
Mr A. Jardim of Henriques & Henriques

Mexico
Mr Dimitri Tchelistcheff, Bodegas de Santo Tomas

Morocco
Comité National de Géographie du Maroc, Rabat

New Zealand
Viticultural Advisory Committee, Department of Agriculture, Wellington

Portugal
Casa de Portugal, London
Comissão de Viticultura da Região dos Vinhos Verdes, Porto
Mr Jorge Dias, J. Turner & Co, London
Instituto do Vinho do Porto, Porto
Mr Alistair Robertson of Taylor, Fladgate & Yeatman, Vila Nova de Gaia

Romania
Institutul de Cercetari Pentru Viticultura si Vinificatie Romagricola, Bucharest
Mr L. Lin, London

Scotland
Distillers Co Ltd, London

South Africa
KWV, Cape
Mr Henry Damant of SAWFA, London
Mr Peter Finlayson, Groot Drakenstein

South America
Mr David Stevens, Matthew Clark & Sons, London

Spain
Mr Brian Buckingham, London
Mr John Lockwood of Sandeman Bros, Jerez de la Frontera
Mr Derrick Palengat of Williams & Humbert, London
Mr Jan Read, London

Switzerland
M Philippe Orsat, Martigny
Société des Exportateurs de Vins Suisses, Lausanne
Société Suisse des Liquoristes, Berne

Tunisia
Union Centrale des Cooperatives Viticoles, Tunis

Turkey
Turkish State Monopolies, Istanbul

USA
Brother Timothy, The Christian Brothers, California
Professor Maynard A. Amerine, California
Mr Leon Adams, Sausalito
Prof H. W. Berg, Davis
Mr Gary Hicks, Hammondsport
Dr Mark Kliewer, Davis
Mr James Lider, St Helena
Mr Robert Mondavi, Oakville
Dr Harold Olmo, Davis
Mr Brian St Pierre, Wine Institute, San Francisco
Mr Robert Thompson, St Helena

USSR
Ministry of Food Production, Moscow
Sojuzplodoimport, Moscow

West Indies
Mr Ben Cross de Chavannes of Booker Brothers McConnell, London
Mr Robert Engelhard, Comité Français du Rhum
United Rum Merchants, London
West Indies Rum Committee, Barbados

General
Mr Gerald Asher
The late Mr Ronald Avery of Avery's, Bristol
Mrs I. M. Barrett, Felsted
Mr Michael Broadbent MW of Christie's, London
Dr Peter Hallgarten of S. F. & O. Hallgarten, London
Mr Tony Laithwaite, Windsor
Mr George Bull and Mr James Long of International Distillers & Vintners, London
Mr Anthony Goldthorpe of O. W. Loeb, London
Mr David Peppercorn MW, London
Mr Edmund Penning-Rowsell, London
Mr Peter Reynier of J. B. Reynier, London
Dr James Rose, Birkbeck College, London
The late André L. Simon
Mr Robin Yapp, Mere
Miss Serena Sutcliffe MW, London

Index

Alphabetization is word by word ignoring de, du, etc.
Asterisks indicate the main entry on the subject
(All château names appear under *Châteaux*)

Gazetteer

This 7,000 entry gazetteer includes place name references of all vineyards, châteaux, general wine areas and other information appearing on the maps in the Atlas, with the exception of minor place names which appear as background information in italic type. All châteaux are listed under C (e.g. Château Palmer) in the gazetteer. All place names, vineyards etc beginning with le, la or les (e.g. la Perrière) are indexed under L. Names of wine or spirit producers appearing on the maps are also listed.

A
Aarau 197 E3, 270 E4
Aarberg 270 F3
Aare 197 B3, 270 F4
Aargau 197 E3, 270 E4
Abacus 190 E3
Abaújszántó 203 B3
Abbaye de Morgeot 65 F5
Abel, Lepître 109 C5
Aberdeen 265 D6
Aberfeldy 265 E4
Abergement-le-Grand 127 E5
Aberlour 263 D3
Abermain 242 F3
Abîmes 127 D1
Abrantes 187 D4
Abruzzi 172 B2
Abtei 144 D5, 155 E2
Abtsberg 145 E1
Abtsfronhof 153 C4
Abtsleite 158 F5
Abû Hummus 220 G2
Abymes 127 D1
Achern 156 E2
Achkarren 156 F1
Achleiten 200 F6
Aconcagua 250 C1, 251 A3
Acqui 163 D5
Adana 220 D4
Adapazari 220 B3
Adelaide 245 A4, 240 E5
Adelaide Metropolitan 240 E6
Adgestone 252 G5
Adissan 125 C6
Adorigo 190 G5
Affoltern 270 E5
Afyonkarahisar 220 C3
Agde 124 D6
Agen 59 F2, 261 B6, 129 D3
Aglianico del Vulture 172 C4
Agricoltori del Chianti Geografico 171 F4
Agrigento 172 G2
Agritiusberg 139 B5
Agualva 188 F2
Aguascalientes 251 F2
Agueux 74 B4
Aguiar de Beira 189 E6
Aguilar 183 F4
Ahr 135 A2
Ahrweiler 135 A3
Aigeshat 213 C4
Aigle 195 C1
Aignan 261 D4, 129 F2
Aigrefeuille-sur-Maine 114 C3, F2
Aiguamurcia 182 F5
Aigues-Mortes 125 D9
Aiguillon 129 D3
Ain 59 D4, 61 F6
Ain-Bessem 219 B3
Airdrie 265 F4
Aire-s-l'Adour 129 F2
Aisne 59 A3
Aiud 209 E3
Aix-en-Provence 59 F5, 126 B1
Aix-les-Baines 127 C1
Ajaccio 132 F4
Akhaia 215 D2
Akhisar 220 C2
Aksehir 220 C3
Akstafa 213 C6
Alameda 229 D2, 237 A2
Alaminos 216 D3
Alba 161 D3, 163 D3
Albacete 175 C4
Albaida 175 C4
Alba Iulia 209 E3
Albana 165 G4
Albana di Romagna 165 G3, 169 A5
Albanello 172 G3
Albas 128 B4
Alberto, Crastan 166 A2
Albertshausen 158 E3
Albi 59 F3, 129 D6
Albiñana 182 F5
Albo 132 D5
Albury 241 F3
Alcalde 177 D2
Alcamo 172 F1
Alcobaça 187 D3
Alcover 182 E4
Aldeanueva 181 C3
Aldinga 245 D3
Aldinga Beach 245 D3
Aleatico 169 C2, D3
à l'Ecu 68 E5
Alegria Velha 191 F4
Aleixar 182 F4
Aleksinac 207 E5
Alella 183 E1, 175 B6
Alençon 59 C1, 271 B2
Alep (Halab) 220 D5
Aleppo (Halab) 220 D5
Aléria 132 E6
Alessandria 161 D4, 163 B6
Alexander 234 B3
Alexandria (Al-Iskandariyah) 220 G2
Alexandrie (Alessandria) 161 D4, 163 B6
Alf 135 B2
Alfaraz 177 D2
Alfaro 181 D4
Alforja 182 F4
Algarrobo 176 C4
Algarve 187 G4
Algeciras 175 E2
Alger 219 B2
Algeria (Algérie) 219 B2
Alghero 172 D1
Algueirao 188 E2
Alicante 175 D5
Aligoté 213 A1, B2
Alio 182 F5
Al-Iskandariyah 220 G2
Al-Jumhuriyah Al'Arabiyah Al-Muttahidah 220 G3
Al-Lādiqīyah 220 E5
Allaman 194 B5
Allauch 126 C2
Allemagne (Deutschland) 135
Allier 59 D3
Alloa 265 E4
Al-Lubnan 220 F4
Allt A'Bhainne 263 F3
Almada 188 F3
Almadén 237 C2, E4, G5
Almaden 235 G1
Al-Magreb 218 C4
Almansa 175 C4
Almendralejo 175 C2
Almeria 175 D4
Almocaden 177 C3, C4
Almoçageme 188 F1
Almoster 182 F4
Aloxe-Corton 61 C5, 69 F3
Alpes-Maritimes 59 F6
Alsace 59 B5
Alsheim 135 B4
Alstätten 270 E6
Altafulla 182 C5
Alta Loma 230 G4
Altärchen 143 G1
Altdorf 270 F5
Altenberg 139 B3, B5, C5, A5
Altenburg 153 D4
Alto Adige 165 C2, 166
Alto-Altentejo 187 E5
Alto-Douro 187 B5
Altona 244 C4
Altsheim 155 F3
Al-Urdunn 220 F5
Alushta 213 B2
Alušta 213 B2
Alvações do Corgo 190 F2
Alzey 135 C6, 155 F2
Amador 229 D2
Amalfi 172 C3
Amarante 189 C5
Amares 189 B5
Amarquillo 177 C2
Amasya 220 C5
Ambares-et-Lagrave 80 E3
Ambelakia 215 C3
Amboise 115 B2
Ambonnay 107 D5
Amery 245 C4
Amiens 59 A3
Amintaion 215 B2
Amman 220 F5
Ammerschwihr 111 B2, 113 E2
Amorgos 215 E5
Amorosa 177 C4
Ampuis 121 B3
Amtsgarten 144 G5
Anaferas 177 F3
Anapa 213 B3
Ancenis 59 D1, B3
Ancône (Ancona) 169 C6
Andalucia 175 D3
Andau 198 D4
Andel 144 G6
Andernos-les-Bains 80 F1
Andolsheim 113 E2
Andriano 166 D2
Andros 215 D4
Angaston 245 B5
Angers 59 C1, 114 B5
Anglisidhes 216 D4
Angoulême 59 E2, 130 C5
Anguilla 267 B4
Anières 194 C4
Animas 177 D1
Añina 177 C2
Añinas 177 D2
Ankara 220 C3
Annaba 219 B4
Annaberg 153 A4
Annecy 59 D5, 127 B1
Annemasse 127 B2
Ansonica 169 C2
Antakya 220 D4
Antalya 220 D3
Antigua 267 B4
Antinori 171 B2
Antioch (Antakya) 220 D4
Antofagasta 250 C1
Antonius Brunnen 139 E1
Aosta 161 B2
Apetlon 198 D4
Apotheke 143 G1
Appenzell 197 E5, 270 E6
Appiano 166 D2
Appleton 266 A3
Apremont 127 C1
Arad 209 E1, E2
Aradhippou 216 C4
Aragón 175 C4
Arákhova 215 C3
Aranibal 177 E1
Ararat 241 G1
Arbin 127 D1
Arbois 127 E5
Arbos 182 F5
Arbus 128 F4
Arcambal 128 B6
Archiestown 263 D2
Arcins 91 F5
Arcos de Valdevez 189 A5
Arcoules 189 F2
Ardbeg 265 F3
Ardèche 59 E4, 120 D5
Ardennes 59 A4
Ardila 177 C3
Ardleigh 252 F6
Ardmore 265 C5
Ardon 195 D3
Arevshat 213 D4
Arezzo 169 B4
Arganil 189 G4
Argentera 182 G3
Argentina 251 C2
Arges 209 F3
Ariège 59 G3
Arlay 127 F4
Alresford 252 G5
Armagnac 59 F2, 261
Arm'anskaja 213 C5
Armenia (Arm'anskaja) 213 C5
Armijo 176 C4
Arnedo 181 D3
Arnex 194 C4
Arnozelo 191 G5
Arouca 189 D5
Arrancon 97 E5
Arras 59 A3
Arsac 93 D3, E2
Arsos 216 C4, D2
Artiguelouve 128 F4
Arundel 252 G5
Arzie 194 B4
Aschaffenburg 135 B5
Asco 182 G2, 132 E5
Ascoli Piceno 169 D5
Asenovgrad 211 D3
Ashland 269 B6
Ashman's 242 F1
Ashtarak 213 C4
Ashton 247 D3
Ashton Keynes 252 F5
Aspiran 125 C6
Asprinto 172 C4
Assmannshausen 149 E2
As-Sūrīyah 220 E5
Asti 161 D3, 163 C4, 230 A4
Astipalaia 215 E5
Asti Spumante 161 D3
Asturias 175 A2
Asuncion 251 A3
Aszu 202 A4
Atacama 250 C1
Atalaya 176 B5
Athens (Athinai) 215 D3
Athienou 216 C4
Attiki 215 D3
Attilafelsen 156 F1
Atwater 234 E5
Aube 59 C4
Aubonne 199 B5
Aubous 261 D3
Auburn 238 C4
Auch 59 G2, 261 D6, 129 F3
Auchentoshan 265 F4
Auchroisk 263 C4
Au Clos, 'Pouilly' 75 E3
Aude 59 G3, 124 C2
Auersthal 198 C3
Auf der Heide 145 B3
Auflangen 154 E4, 155 E4
Auggen 156 G3
Augusta 269 B5
Aultmore 263 C5
Aurillac 59 F3, 130 D6
Australia (Australie) 240, 241
Austria (Österreich) 198
Autriche (Österreich) 198
Autun 61 D4
Auvernier 270 F3
aux Argillats 71 F2
aux Boudots 71 F3
aux Bousselots 71 F2
aux Chaignots 71 F3
aux Champ-Perdrix 71 F3
aux Charmes 72 F5
aux Cheusots 73 E3
aux Clous 69 D1
aux Combottes 72 F5
aux Coucherias 68 E4
aux Cras, Beaune 68 F4
aux Cras, Nuits-St-Georges 71 F3
aux Crots 71 F1
aux Brûlées 71 E4
aux Damodes 71 F3
Auxerre 61 A3, 59 C3
Auxey-Duresses 67 E1, 61 D5
aux Fourneaux 69 E2
aux Grands Liards 69 E1-2
aux Gravains 69 D2
aux Guettes 69 D2
aux Malconsorts 71 F4
aux Murgers 71 F3
aux Murs 75 G3
aux Perdrix 70 F5
aux Petits Liards 69 D1
aux Quatre Vents 77 C4
aux Serpentières 69 D1
aux Thorey 71 F2
aux Vergelesses 69 E2
aux Vignes-Rondes 71 F3
Avallon 61 B3
Aveiro 187 C4
Avellino 172 C3
Avelsbach 141 F3
Avenay-Val d'Or 107 D4
Avensan 91 G4
Aveyron 59 F3
Avezzano 169 F4
Avignon 59 F4, 120 G5
Ávila 175 B3
Avinyonet 182 B6
Avize 107 F3
Avusy 194 D3
Ay 107 D3
Aydie 201 D3
Ayent 195 C3
Ayios Evstratios 215 C4
Ayios Nikolaos 215 F5
Ayl 139 D2
Ayr 265 F4
Ayze 127 B2
Azay-le-Rideau 115 C1
Azen do Mar 188 E1
Azerbaijan (Azerbajdžanskaja) 213 C5
Azerbajdžanskaja 213 C5
Azille 124 B3
Azov, Sea of (Azovskoje More) 213 B3
Az-Zarga 220 F5
B
Baalbek (Ba'labakk) 220 F5
Băbească neagră 209 F5
Bacardi 267 A2
Bacău 209 E4
Bacharach 135 B2
Backsberg 249 E3
Badascony 202 C1, 204 G3
Badacsonylábdihegy 204 G2
Badacsonytomaj 204 G3
Badajoz 175 C2
Bad Bergzabern 135 D3, 153 E1
Bad Cannstatt 156 D4
Bad Dürkheim 153 C4
Baden, Österreich 198 D3, 200 F2
Baden, Suisse 197 E4
Baden-Baden 156 D2
Badenweiler 156 F1
Baden-Württemberg 135 D5, 156 E4
Badia a Coltibuono 171 E5
Bad Kreuznach 135 B3, 155 E1, 147 E1
Bad Mergentheim 135 C6
Bad Münster 147 F1
Bad Pirawarth 198 C3
Bad Vöslau 198 D3, 200 G2
Baena 183 F4
Bagno a Ripoli 171 A4
Bagnols-en-Forêt 126 B5
Bagnols-sur-Cèze 120 F4
Bagrina 207 D6
Bafra 220 B5
Bahia Blanca 251 D3
Baia-Mare 209 D3
Baião 189 C6
Baiken 151 E3
Bairrada 187 C4
Bairro 190 F2
Bairnsdale 241 G3
Baixas 124 E2
Baixo-Alentejo 187 F4
Baja 202 C2
Baja California 251 F1
Bakersfield 229 F3
Bakers Gully 245 B5
Baku 213 C6
Ba'labakk 220 F5
Balagne 132 D5
Balaton 202 C2, 204
Balatonboglár 202 C2
Balatonfüred 202 C2, 204 F6
Balatonudvari 204 G6
Balbaina 177 F5
Balbaina Alta 177 D1
Balbaina Baja 177 E1
Balblair 265 C4
Bâle (Basel) 156 G3, 197 B3, 270 E4
Bālgarija 211
Balikesir 220 B2
Ballaison 127 A2
Ballarat 241 G2
Balmenach 265 C9
Balranald 241 E2
Balvenie 263 D4
Banat 209 F2
Banatski Rizling 207 C5
Bandol 126 C2
Bañeras 182 F5
Banff 205 C5
Banja Luka 207 C3
Banska Bystrica 205 B5
Banyuls 124 F2
Banyuls-dels-Aspres 124 E2
Banzão 164 E1
Baraillot 95 A1
Barbacarlo 161 D5
Barbados 267 D5
Barbadillo 176 D6, 177 C4, D1
Barbancourt 266 A5
Barbaresco 161 D3, 163 D3
Barbechat 114 E2
Barbera 207 C1
Barbera d'Alba 163 E3, 161 D3
Barbera d'Asti 161 D3, 163 B4
Barbera del Monferrato 161 D3, 163 C3
Barbotan 129 E2
Barcelona 175 B6, 183 F1
Barcelos 187 B4, 189 B4
Bardinet 267 C5
Bardolino 165 E2, 166 B6, 167 A1, C1
Bardolino Classico 167 B1
Bardonnex 194 D4
Bardstown 269 C4
Bari 172 B5
Bar-le-Duc 59 B4
Barletta 172 B4
Barningham 252 F6
Barolo 161 D3, 163 E2
Barr 113 C2
Barone Ricasoli 171 F5
Barossa Valley 240 E6, 244
Barrameda 176 A5
Barros 193 D3
Barrydale 247 D4
Barsac 80 G4, 97 A5, B4
Barsonyos-Császár 202 B2
Barton 269 B3
Bas-Armagnac 261 C3
Bas de Duresses 62 E2
Basedow's 244 B5
Basel 197 D3, G3, 270 E4
Basel-Land 270 E4
Basilicata 172 C4
Basle (Basel) 156 G3, 197 B3, 270 E4
Bas-Morgon 77 E4
Bas-Rhin 59 B5
Bassano di Grappa 165 D4
Basse-Goulaine 114 E1
Bassens 80 E3
Basses-Alpes 59 F5
Basses-Pyrénées 59 G1
Basse-Terre 267 C4
Basseterre 267 B4
Bastelica 132 F5
Bastia 132 D6
Bâtard-Montrachet 66 G3
Bathurst 241 E4
Battenburg 153 B1
Baule 115 A3
Bayern 135 C2
Bayon 104 F2
Bayonne 59 G1, 128 F5
Bayrūt 220 F4
Bayt Laym 220 G4
Beam 269 B4
Beattyville 269 C5
Beaucaire 125 D10
Beaujolais 61 F5, 77
Beaulieu, Hampshire 252 G5
Beaulieau-sur-Layon 114 B5, 116 D4
Beaulieu Vineyard Winery 233 C4
Beaumes 122 C4
Beaumes de Venise 120 F6
Beaumont-en-Véron 117 D2
Beaumont-sur-Vesle 107 B5
Beaune 59 C4, 61 D5, 64, 68 G5
Beaupuy 117 B2
Beauregard 65 F4
Beaurepaire 65 E3
Beauroy 79 C2
Beauvais, Oise 59 B2
Beauvais, Restigné 117 B3
Beauvoisin 125 C9
Beaux Bruns 72 F3
Beaux Monts 125 E5
Beblenheim 111 C3
Bečej 207 C5
Bechtheim 155 F3
Beersheba (Be'er Sheva) 220 G4
Be'er Sheva 220 G4
Begas 183 F6
Begles 80 F3
Begnins 194 B4
Beilstein, Baden-Württemberg 156 D4
Beilstein, Rheinland-Pfalz 135 G2
Beira-Alta 187 C5
Beira-Baixa 182 D5
Beira-Littoral 187 D4
Beirut (Bayrūt) 220 F4
Beja (Bejaïa) 219 B3
Beja, Portugal 187 F5
Bekaá 220 F4
Békéscsaba 202 C3
Bel-Air, Chiroubles 77 D3
Bel-Air, Gevrey-Chambertin 72 F6
Bel-Air, Pomerol 99 A3
Bel-Air, Vouvray 118 C3
Belan 207 G6
Belford 242 D2
Belfort 59 C5
Belgrade (Beograd) 207 D5
Beli Pinot 207 B3
Bella Napoli 234 D3
Bellbird 242 G2
Bellegarde 59 F4, 125 D10
Bellet 59 F6
Bellevue 242 F2
Belley 59 E5, 131 C2
Bellingham 249 F4
Bellinzona 197 G4
Bellmunt de Ciurana 182 G3
Belluno 165 C4
Bellvey 182 F5
Bellville 247 D2
Belz 153 D4
Berner Alpen 270 G4
Bemposta 186 E3
Benais 117 B3
Benalla 241 F3
Bendigo 241 F2
Ben Ean 242 F1
Benevento 172 B3
Benfeld 113 C2
Benisanet 182 G3
Ben Nevis 265 D3
Bennwihr 111 C3
Benriach 203 B2, 113 D2
Benrinnes 263 E3
Benromach 265 C4
Bensheimo 156 B3
Ben Wyvis 265 C4
Beregivski 213 A1
Bergamo 161 B5
Bergerac 59 F2, 105 E5
Bergheim 111 D5, 113 D2
Bergholtz 110 B2
Bergholtzzell 110 A2
Berg Kaisersteinfels 149 F2
Bergkirche 154 D5
Bergkloster 155 G3
Berglichteneck 156 F1
Bergrivier 249 E4
Berg Roseneck 149 F3
Berg Rottland 149 F3
Berg Schlossberg 149 F2
Bergschlossen 139 F1
Bergstrasse 156 B3, 135 C4
Beringer Bros 233 B3
Berlou 124 B5
Bermet 202 C5
Bern 197 F3, 270 F3
Berner Oberland 197 C3
Bernex 194 D3
Bernkastel 135 B2, 244 B4
Bernkastel-Kues 145 F2, 135 B2
Berri 240 E6
Berson 104 D3
Bertero 237 C3
Bertineau 103 C3
Besançon 59 C5, 131 A3
Beshtau 213 A4
Besigheim 156 D4
Bessay 77 A4
Besse-sur-Issole 126 C4
Bethany 244 C4
Bethlehem (Bayt Laym) 220 G4
Bettelhaus 153 B5
Beugnons 79 E2
Beurig 139 F2
Beychevelle 89 D5, 91 A4
Beyrouth (Bayrūt) 220 F4
Bex 195 C2
Béziers 124 C5
Bianchello 169 C5
Bianco Vergine 169 C4
Biard 259 D2
Bibbiano 171 F3
Bickleigh 252 G4
Bidarray 128 G6
Biddenden 252 G6
Biebelhausen 139 D2
Biel 197 E2
Bieler See 270 F3
Biella 161 B3
Bienne (Biel) 197 B2
Biganos 80 F1
Bijeli Klikun 207 C4
Bikavér 202 A3
Bilbao 175 A3
Bildstock, Rheingau 151 F5
Bildstock, Rheinhessen 154 F4
Bingen 135 B3, 149 G2, 155 E2
Bio-Bio 250 C1
Birgu 216 G2
Birkenfeld 135 C2
Birkirkara 216 G2
Bisbal del Panadés 182 F5
Bischoffsheim 270 C4

Bischofs Berg 149 F3
Bischofsgarten 153 D5
Bischofskreuz 153 D2
Bischofszell 270 E6
Biser 207 C5
Bisseuil 107 D4
Bissey-sous-Cruchaud 74 F3
Bitburg 135 B1
Bitola 202 G5
Bize-Minervois 124 B4
Bizerte 219 A5
Bjala 211 C6
Blackfield 252 G5
Bladnoch 265 G4
Blagny 66 F4
Blagoevgrad 211 D2
Blair Athol 265 D4
Blaj 209 E3
Blanche Fleur 68 F6
Blanchot 79 D4
Blankenheim 135 A1
Blanquefort 80 E3
Blanquette-de-Limoux 124 C1
Blatina 207 E3
Blayais 80 D3
Blaye 80 D3, 104 D1
Bléré 115 B2
Blewitt Springs 245 C4
Blida 219 B2
Blois 59 C2, 115 B2
Blonay 195 B1
Bloomington 230 G5
Blue Mountain 260 B3
Boca 161 B4
Bockenheim 153 A1
Bockfliess 198 C3
Bockstein 139 E4
Bocognano 132 F5
Bodenheim 156 G4, 155 E3
Boden See 156 G6, 197 B5, 270 E6, 135 G5
Bodrogkeresztúr 203 C4
Bodrogolaszi 203 B5
Bodrogszegi 203 C4
Boën-sur-Lignon 59 E4, 131 C2
Bogdanuša 207 E2
Bogotá 250 B1
Böhlig 153 D4
Bohorca 126 B4
Bois Fleury 119 F4
Bois Gibault 119 F4
Boisse 105 F6
Boland, Co-op 249 B4
Bolivia (Bolivie) 250 C2
Bollène 120 F5
Bolney 252 G5
Bologna 165 G3
Bologne 267 C4
Bol'šoj Kavkaz 213 C5
Bolzano 165 C3, 166 D3
Bommes 97 E3
Bonarda 161 D3
Bône (Annaba) 219 B4
Bonesio 237 C3
Bonifacio 132 G5
Bonn 135 C1
Bonnanarg 172 D1
Bonneville-et-St-Avit-de-Fumadières 105 E2
Bonnezeaux 114 B5, 116 E6
Bonnievale 247 D3
Bonny-sur-Loire 115 B5
Boofzheim 113 C2
Boordy Vineyards 238 D3
Boppard 135 A3
Bordeaux 59 F1, 80 E3, 95 A4
Borex 194 C4
Borges 193 D5
Borgonja 207 B1
Borjas del Campo 182 C4
Bormes 126 C4
Bornheim 155 F2
Bornovo 220 C1
Bosa 172 D1
Bosna-Hercegovina 207 D3
Bosset 105 D4
Bossey 127 B2
Botarell 182 G4
Bottelary, Co-op 249 E1
Botticino 165 D2
Bou 115 A4
Bouaye 114 C2
Bouc-Bel-Air 126 B1
Boucharey 121 B3
Bouches-du-Rhône 59 F5, 126 B1
Bouchot 119 F4
Bougie (Bejaïa) 219 B3
Bougros 79 C3
Bougy-Villars 194 B5
Boulaouane 218 C3
Bouniagues 105 F5
Bourbon County 269 B5
Bourdigny 194 C3
Bourdon 267 C4
Bourg 80 D3, 104 G4
Bourg-Bassot 85 C4
Bourg-Charenté 259 B2
Bourgeais 80 D3
Bourg-en-Bresse 59 D4, 61 F6
Bourges 59 D3, 114 C5
Bourgneuf-en-Retz 114 C2
Bourgneuf-Val-d'Or 85 C3
Bourgogne 59 D4, 61
Bourgueil 114 B6, 117 B2
Bousse-d'Or 67 F4
Boutenac 124 C3
Boutiers-St-Trojan 258 A6
Boutoc 97 E4
Bouzeron 74 B4
Bouzy 107 D5
Bovernier 195 E2
Bovlei, Co-op 249 B6
Bowen 251 D6
Bowling Green 269 C3
Bowmore 265 F2
Boyes Hot Springs 233 F3
Bra 163 D2
Brachetto 161 D4
Brachetto d'Acqui 103 E4
Bradfield 252 F5
Bradford on Avon 252 F4
Braemar, Scotland 265 D5
Braemar, South Africa 249 D3
Braga 187 B4, 189 B5
Bragança 187 B6
Brain-sur-Allones 114 C6
Bramois 195 D3
Brand 111 B1
Brando 132 D6
Branne 80 E4
Branxton 242 E2
Brasil 250 B2
Brasilia 250 B2
Brasov 209 F4
Braten 145 F2
Bratislava 205 C5
Brauneberg, Konz 139 A3
Brauneberg, Mosel 143 B4, 144 G5
Braune-Kupp 139 B3
Braunfels 139 C4
Brazil (Brasil) 251 A4
Brda 207 B1
Brechin 265 D5
Břeclav 205 B4
Bredasdorp 247 E3
Breganze 165 D3
Breisgau 135 F3
Breitenweg 147 D1
Bremblens 194 A5
Bremgarten 270 E4
Brenec 205 B5
Bréry 189 F4
Brescia 161 C6, 165 E1
Brésil (Brasil) 251 B4
Bressanone 165 B3
Brest 58 C5
Brestovicha 211 D3
Brezanky 205 A3
Brézé 114 C6
Brezovo 211 D3
Bridgetown 267 D5
Brienzer See 270 F4
Brig 195 C6
Brighton, Australia 254 A4
Brindisi 172 C5
British Guyana (Guyana) 250 B2
Broad Clyst 252 G4
Brno 205 B4
Brochon 73 E2
Broken Back Range 242 F1
Bronco 234 D4
Bronzolo 166 E3
Brookside 230 G5
Brookside Vineyards 230 G4
Brora 265 B4
Brouillards 67 F5
Brouilly 61 F5, 77 G3
Brouquet 97 G4
Brown, J. T. S. 269 B4
Brown-Forman 269 B3
Broze 129 D6
Bruce, David 237 C2
Bruchsal 156 C3
Bruck a. d. Mur 198 E1
Brückchen 154 F4
Brückes 147 C2
Brudersberg 154 C4
Brüderschaft 142 E6
Bruges 80 E3
Brugg 197 E3
Bruichladdich 265 F2
Brunello di Montalcino 169 C3
Brunico 165 B4
Bruniquel 129 D5
Brunn 198 D3
Brunnen 270 F5
Bucelas 187 E3, 188 E3
Bucharest (București) 209 G4
Bucherots 77 B5
Buchillon 194 B5
Buckie 265 A6
București 209 G4
Budafok 202 B2
Budapest 202 B2
Budduso 172 D2
Bué 119 F2
Buenos Aires 251 C3, D3
Buenaventura 250 B1
Buena Vista Winery 233 F4
Bühl 156 D4
Bühlertal 156 D4
Bulcy 119 G5
Bulgaria (Bâlgarija) 211
Bullay 135 B2
Bulle 270 F3
Bully Hill 238 D2
Bunnahabhain 265 F2
Burdur 220 D2
Burg 198 F3
Burgas 211 C5
Burgberg, Mosel 139 F2
Burgberg, Saar 145 C1
Burgenland 198 E3
Burgess Cellars 233 A3
Burglay 143 C3, 145 B3
Burgos 175 A3, 180 B4
Burg Nevenfels 156 G1
Burg Rodenstein 155 G3
Burgundac 207 F5
Burgundac Bijeli 207 C3, C4
Burgundy 59 D4, 207
Burgweg (Iphofen) 158 E5
Burg Zähringen 156 F2
Bürkheim 156 F1
Burmester 193 D4
Burra 240 E5
Bursa 220 B2
Būr Sa'id 220 G3
Bursinel 194 B5
Bursins 194 B4
Bury St. Edmunds 252 F6
Busque 129 G3
Bussières 77 G3
Bussolengo 167 C1
Buttafuoco 161 D5
Butteaux 79 E2
Buvilly 127 E5
Buxy 61 D5, 75 G3
Buzău 209 F4
Buzet 59 F2, 130 D5

C

Cabaces 182 F3
Cabasse 126 B4
Cabeceiras de Basto 289 B6
Cabernet 165 D4, 207 B1, C4, 211 B2, D4, 213 A1, B3
Cabernet-Franc 207 F5
Cabernet Sauvignon 209 E2, E5, F5, G3, G5
Cabeza Gorda 176 A5
Cabeza Vaca 176 B4
Cabezudo 176 B5
Cabo de São Vicente 187 G3
Cabra 183 F4
Cabras 172 D1
Cabrières, Châteauneuf-du-Pape 123 B4
Cabrières, Herault 59 G4, 125 B6
Cabrils 183 E2
Cabrera de Igualada 182 E6
Cacchiano 171 F4
Čačak 207 E5
Cáceres 175 C2
Cachapoal 251 C2
Cadarca 209 F2
Cadaujac 95 E5
Cadillac 80 F4
Cadillon 261 D3
Cádiz 175 E2, 177 G5
Cadlolo 234 D4
Caen 59 B1, 271 B1
Cagliari 169 G2, 172 E2
Cahors 59 F2, 129 C5
Cahuzac-sur-Vère 129 D6
Cailleret 65 F6, 66 F1
Cailleret-Dessus 67 F3
Cairngorm Mountains 265 D5
Calabria 172 F4
Calafell 182 F5
Calahorra 181 C3
Calaveras 234 B4
Calcinaia Vicchiomaggio 171 D3
Caldaro 166 E2
Caldas da Rainha 187 E3
Calderin 177 E2
Caledonian 265 F5
Caledon 247 D3
Calem 193 B5
Calero 177 C3
California 229
California Growers 235 G2
California Wine Association 234 C1
Calistoga 233 A2
Calitzdorp 247 C5
Calheta 185 D1
Callas 126 A5
Callezuela 176 A5
Caloueres-les-Chaffots 72 E4
Caltagirone 172 G3
Caltanissetta 172 F2
Caluso Passito 161 C3
Calvados 59 B1, 271
Calvados du Cotenin 271 B1
Calvados de la Vallée de l'Orne 271 B2
Calvados de l'Avranchin 271 B1
Calvados du Calvados 271 B1
Calvados du Domfrontais 271 B1
Calvados du Mortainais 271 C1
Calvados du Pays d'Auge 271 B2
Calvados du Pays de Bray 271 B2
Calvados du Pays de la Risle 271 B2
Calvados du Pays du Merlerault 271 B2
Calvi 132 D4
Camara de Lobos 185 E3
Cambiaso 230 C5
Cambo-les-Bains 128 G5
Cambon-la-Pelouse 93 E4
Camborne 252 G3
Cambres 190 G2
Cambrils 182 G4
Cambus 265 E4
Cameronbridge 265 E5
Caminha 189 A4
Campalli 171 F3
Campanário 185 D3
Campania 172 C3
Campbellsville 269 C4
Campbeltown 265 F3
Campidano 169 G2, 172 E2
Campix 176 D6
Campobasso 172 B3
Campomaggio 171 E4
Camus 258 A5
Cañada Seca 251 D5
Canakkale 220 B1
Canandaigua Industries 238 C2
Canandaigua Lake 238 C2
Canberra 241 F4
Cane Garden Bay 267 A3
Canelli 163 D4
Canelones 251 C4
Cangé 118 E6
Cannet 261 D4
Cannonau 169 G2, 172 E2
Cannonau di Sardegna 172 D2
Canon Fronsac 102 C6
Cantal 59 E3
Cantarranas 177 D2
Canteloup, Gradignan 95 D2
Canteloup, Villénave 95 C4
Cantenac 93 C4
Cantina Sociale 167 D5
Canyellas 182 F6
Caol Ila 265 F2
Cap Corse 132 A3
Caperdonich 263 C3
Cape Town 247 D2
Cap-Haïtien 266 A5
Capirete 177 C4
Caplane 97 F3
Capo Bianco 172 F4
Capri 172 C2
Caprino Veronese 167 A1
Capsanes 182 G3
Caracas 250 B1
Carcassonne 59 G3, 124 B2, 130 E6
Carcavelos 187 F3
Carcès 126 B4
Cardesse 128 F4
Cardow 263 D2
Carelle dessous 67 F4
Carelle-sous-la-Chapelle 67 F4
Carema 161 B3
Cariñena 175 B4
Carioca 267 B2
Carmel 237 F2
Carnaxide 188 F3
Carneros Valley 233 F5
Carnoules 126 C4
Caroni 267 E5
Carpathian Mountains (Munții Carparții) 209 D3
Carpentras 120 G6
Carqueiranne 126 D3
Carquefou 114 B3
Carrahola 177 E2
Carrascal 177 C4
Carrascal 176 C4, 177 C4
Carregal do Sal 189 F5
Carrieres 72 F2
Cars 104 D2
Carsac-de-Gurçon 105 D2
Carsebridge 265 E5
Carthage 219 B5
Casablanca 218 C4
Casabon 177 D1
Casale Monferrato 163 A5
Casalino 171 F4
Casamozza 132 D6
Cascatel-des-Corbières 124 D3
Casenuove 171 D3
Caserta 172 C3
Cases-de-Pène 124 D2
Casletnau d'Auzan 129 E2
Casorzo d'Asti 163 B5
Cassa 237 C3
Cassino 172 B2
Cassis 126 C2
Castanet 129 D6
Castedo 191 E2
Castel del Monte 172 B4
Castelfranc 128 B4
Castell Acquaro 172 C5
Castellammere 172 C2
Casteller 165 C2
Castellet 182 F5
Castelli Grevepesa 171 C3
Castellina in Chianti 171 E3
Castell' in Villa 171 G5
Castelli Romani 169 F3
Castello di Brolio 171 F5
Castello di Cerreto 171 G4
Castello di Montefioralle 171 D3
Castello di Rencine 171 F3
Castello di Volpaia 171 F4
Castello di Uzzano 171 C4
Castellón 175 C5
Castellvell 182 G4
Castellvi de la Marca 182 F5
Castelnau d'Auzan 261 C4
Castelnau-le-Lez 125 C8
Castelnau-Rivière-Basse 261 D4
Castelnuovo Barardenga 171 G5
Castelnuovo di Verona 167 C1
Castelo Branco 187 D5
Castelo de Paiva 189 D5
Castelot 103 E3
Casteltagliolo 161 D4
Castetpugon 261 D3
Castile, New (Castilla la Nueva) 175 C3
Castile, Old (Castilla la Lora) 175 B3
Castilla la Lora 175 B3
Castilla la Nueva 175 C3
Castillo del Majuelo 177 C3
Castillon, Basse Pyrénées 261 E3
Castillon, Cognac 258 A5
Castillon-la-Bataille 80 E5
Castlemaine 241 F2
Castries 267 D5
Castro del Rio 183 F4
Castrovillari 172 D4
Catalonia (Cataluña) 175 B5, 182
Cataluña 175 B5, 182
Catamarca 251 B2
Catánia 172 F3
Catanzaro 172 E5
Catignano 171 G4
Catllar 182 G5
Catusseau 99 C4, 103 D2
Caucasus (Bol'šoj Kavkaz) 213 C5
Caunes-Minervois 124 B3
Caunettes-en-Val 124 C2
Cauro 132 F5
Causses-et-Veyran 124 B5
Cavalaire-sur-Mer 126 C5
Cavaion Veronese 167 B1
Cave Co-op, Cissac-Médoc 85 G2
Cave Co-op, Leyssac 85 E4
Cave Co-op, Listrac-Médoc 91 F1
Cave Co-op, St-Emilion 101 E4
Cave Co-op, St-Sauveur 87 C2
Cave Co-op, St-Seurin-de-Cadourne 85 C4
Cave Co-op, Vertheuil 85 F1
Cavendish 252 F6
Caves 124 D3
Cavriglia 171 D5
Cayenne 250 B2
Caymus 233 C4
Cayuga Lake 238 C3
Cazaubon 261 C4, 129 E2
Cazeau 266 A5
Cazzano di Tramigna 167 C5
Cebreros 175 C3
Cegled 202 B3
Celeiros 190 D6, E6
Celigny 194 C4
Cellatica 165 D1
Cellier aux Moines 74 E4
Celorico de Basto 127 C5
Cenon 80 E3
Cenicero 180 B6
Cephalonia (Kefallinia) 215 D1
Cerasuolo 172 G3
Cerasuolo di Abruzzo 169 F5
Cerbère 124 G2
Cercié 77 F3
Cercot 74 F3
Ceres 234 D4, 247 C3
Céret 124 E1
Cerignola 172 B4
Cerna 171 F3
Cernay 113 F2
Cérons 80 F4
Cerro Pelado 177 C2
Cerro de Santiago 177 D3
Certaldo 171 D1
Cervera del Rio Alhama 181 E3
Cervione 132 E6
Cesanese 169 F4
České Budějovice 205 B4
Cessnock 241 D5, 242 G3
Cestas 80 F3
Cestayrols 129 D6
Ceuta 218 B5
Ceyras 125 B6
Ceyreste 126 C2
Chabiots 72 F2, F4
Chablais 195 C2, 197 D2
Chablis 59 C4, 61 A3, 79 D3 131 A1
Chagny 61 D5
Chailles 115 B2
Chaines Carteau 70 F5
Chaintré 75 F3
Chais 85 A4
Chalone 237 F5
Chalonnais 61 D5, 74
Chalonnes-sur-Loire 114 B4
Châlons-sur-Marne 59 B4
Chalon-sur-Saône 61 D6
Chambéry, Savoie 127 E5, 59 C1, 131 C3
Chambéry, Villenave 95 D3
Chambertin 72 F6
Chambolle-Musigny 61 C5, 72 E2
Chambord 59 C2, 130 A6
Chambraste 119 F2
Chamirey 74 D4
Chamoson 195 D2
Champagne 59 B3, 106, 107
Champans 67 F4
Champillon 107 D3
Champigny 114 C6
Champ Lévrier 77 E4
Champs-Pimont 68 F3
Champtin 119 F2
Champtocaux 114 B3
Chancay 118 B5
Chanceleiros 190 F6
Chancy 194 D3
Chandlers Hill 245 B5
Chânes 75 G3, 77 A6
Chanseron 75 E2
Chante Alouette 122 C4
Chapelle Chamb 72 F6
Chapelot 79 D4
Chappellet Winery 233 C5
Chardonnay 209 G5
Chardonne 195 B1
Charentay 77 G4
Charente 59 E1
Charente Maritime 59 E1, 80 C3
Charles Krug Winery 233 B3
Charlestown of Aberlour 263 D3
Charmes-Chambertin 72 F5
Charneca 188 E4
Charolles 61 E4
Charpignat 127 C1
Charrat 195 D2
Charrières 72 F4
Chartres 59 C2
Chassagne-Montrachet 61 D5, 66 G2
Chasselas 75 F2
Châtain 103 C3
Châtains 79 E2
Château
Andron-Blanquet 85 G4
Anseillan 85 G5, 87 A5
Ausone 101 D4
Badon 103 E3
Balestard-la-Tonnelle 101 C5
Baloques-Haut-Bages 87 E5
Barbé 104 D2
Barbe-Blanche 103 B5
Baret 95 D4
Barette 87 F4
Barreyres 91 E6
Bastor-Lamontagne 97 D5
Batailley 87 E4
Bayard 103 D5
Beaulac-Dodijos 97 C3
Beaulieu 104 F4
Beaumont 91 D4
Beauregard 99 D4
Beauséjour, Puisseguin 103 D5
Beauséjour, St-Emilion 101 D4
Beauséjour, St-Estèphe 85 E4
Beauséjour Dufau-Lagarosse 101 D4
Beausite 85 D4
Beausite-Haut-Vignoble 85 D4
Bel-Air, Bourg 104 F3
Bel-Air, Lalande-de-Pomerol 103 C2
Bel-Air, Lussac 103 B5
Bel-Air, Pomerol 99 B3
Bel-Air, St-Emilion 101 D4
Bel-Air Marquis-d'Aligre 93 B1
Belgrave 89 C3
Bellefont-Belcier 101 E5, 103 E3
Bellgrave 87 E5
Belle-Rose 87 B5
Belles-Graves 103 C2
Bellevue, Lussac 103 C5
Bellevue, St-Emilion 101 D3
Bergat 101 D5
Berliquet 101 D4
Berthou 104 F3
Beychevelle 89 D5, 91 A4
Bidou 104 E2
Binet 103 D5
Blissa 104 F3
Boismartin 95 G3
Château
Boissac 103 C5
Bonneau 103 D5
Bourseau 103 C1
Bouscaut 95 E5
Boyd-Cantenac 93 C4
Branaire-Ducru 89 D5, 91 A4
Brane-Cantenac 93 C3
Brillette 91 F3
Brousseau 103 F4
Broustet 97 B4
Brule-Sécailles 104 F4
Cadet-Bon 101 C4
Cadet-Piola 101 C4
Caillou 97 B3
Calon-Ségur 85 D4
Camensac 89 D3
Cameron 97 E3
Camperos 97 A4
Canon, Canon-Fronsac 102 D6
Canon, St-Emilion 101 D4
Canon-Chaigneau 103 C3
Canon-de-Brem 102 D6
Canon-la-Gaffelière 101 E4
Cantelaude 93 D4
Canteloup 85 E5
Cante-Merle 93 E5
Cantenac-Brown 93 C2
Cantereau 99 C2
Cantin 103 E5
Canuet 93 B2
Capbern 85 D5
Cap-de-Mourlin 101 C4
Capet-Guillier 103 F4
Carbonnieux 95 E4
Caronne Ste-Gemme 91 B2
Caruel 104 F3
Cassat 103 D5
Castel Viaud 103 C1
Certan-de-May 99 C5
Certan Giraud 91 C5
Chalon 127 F4
Chantegrive 103 E3
Chapelle-Madeleine 101 D4
Chardonnay 211 B5
Charmail 85 C4
Charron 104 C2
Chasse-Spleen 91 F4
Chauvin 101 B3
Chêne-Liège 99 B4
Cheval Blanc 99 D5, 101 B2
Chevalier 233 B3
Chevrol Bel-Air 103 C3
Christoly 104 G5
Cissac 85 G2
Citran 91 G4
Clerc-Milton-Mondon 87 B5
Climens 97 B3
Clinet 99 B4
Clos des Jacobins 101 C3
Corbin-Michotte 101 A3
Corbin, Montagne-St-Georges 103 C4
Corbin, St-Emilion 101 A3
Cos d'Estournel 85 G5, 87 A4
Cos-Labory 85 G4, 87 A4
Coubet 104 E2
Coucy 103 D5
Coufran 85 B4
Couhins 95 D5
Courant-Barrow 91 F5
Courpon 104 G4
Coustolle 102 C6
Coutelin-Merville 85 F3
Coutet, Barsac 97 B4
Coutet, St-Emilion 101 C3
Couvent-des-Jacobins 101 D5
Croizet-Bages 87 D5
Croque-Michotte 99 C6, 101 A3
Croute-Charlus 104 G4
Cruzeau 103 D1
Cure-Bon la Madeleine 101 D4
d'Agassac 93 G6
d'Angludet 93 D3
d'Arche 97 F3
d'Arche-Lafaurie 97 F3
d'Arche-Vimeney 97 F3
d'Arcins 91 F4
d'Arnauld 91 F4
Dassault 101 B5
d'Augey 97 D3
Dauzac 93 C5
de Barbe 104 E2
de Carles 102 B6
de Dauzay 117 D2
de Fargues 97 F6
de Fieuzal 95 G2
de Franc 95 G2
de la Commanderie 103 B2
de la Croix-Millorit 104 F2
de Lamarque 91 D5
de Lamouroux 93 B2
de la Nerthe 123 C5
de la Nouvelle Eglise 99 B4
de la Vallée 75 F4
de Malle 97 D5
de Marbuzet 85 F5
de Mille-Secousses 104 G4
Montelena 233 A2

Cortina d'Ampezzo 165 C4
Corton Charlemagne 69 E3
Corum 220 B4
Corunna (La Coruna) 175
Corvo 172 F2
Cosne-sur-Loire 115 B6
Costalunga 167 C5
Costermano 167 B1
Costières du Gard 125 D9, 131 E2
Cotas 191 E2
Côte d'Or 61 C5
Coteaux d'Aix-en-Provence 59 F5, 126, 131 E3
Coteaux d'Ajaccio 132 C2
Coteaux d'Ancenis 59 D1, 112 D3
Coteaux de Châteaumeillant 130 B6
Coteaux de la Loire 114 B3, B4
Coteaux de l'Aubance 114 B5, 116 C4, E6
Coteaux de Pierrevert 131 E3
Coteaux de Saumur 114 C6
Coteaux de Tricastin 131 D2
Coteaux des Baux 59 F5
Coteaux du Giennois 59 C3, 115 A5, 131 A1
Coteaux du Jura 197 C2
Coteaux du Languedoc 131 E2
Coteaux du Layon 114 B5, C5
Coteaux du Loir/Jasnières 105 A1
Coteaux du Vendômois 115 A2, 130 A5
Côte Blonde 121 B3
Côte Brune 121 B3
Côte Beaune 61 C5, D5
Côte de Beaune: Beaune 68, 69
Mersault 66, 77
Santenay 65
Côte de Brouilly 77 F3
Côte de Fontenay 79 C3
Côte de Léchet 79 D2
Côte de Nuits C6, 70, 71, 72, 73
Côte d'Or 64-73
Côte-Rôtie, Chiroubles 77 D3
Côte-Rôtie, Côtes du Rhône 120 A5, 121 B3
Côte-Rôtie, Morey-St-Denis 72 E4
Côtes Canon-Fronsac 80 E4
Côtes d'Agly 124 D2
Côtes d'Auvergne 131 C1
Côtes de Bordeaux-Saint-Macaire 80 F6
Côtes de Castillon 80 E5
Côtes de Francs 80 E5
Côtes de Fronsac 80 E4
Côtes de Néac 80 E4
Côtes de Provence 131 E3
Côtes du Forez 131 C2
Côtes du Frontonnais 59 G2
Côtes du Luberon 131 E3
Côtes du Marmandais 130 D5
Côtes-du-Nord 58 C6
Côtes Roannaise 131 C2
Côtes-du-Rhone 59 E4, F4, 120
Côtes-du-Roussillon 124 E2,
Côtes du Roussillon 131 F1
Côtes du Ventoux 59 F5, 131 E2
Côtes-Fronsac 102 C5
Cotignac 126 B4
Cotnari 209 F4
Coulée de Serrant 116 B3
Cour-Cheverny 115 B3, 59 C2, 130 A6
Courgis 79 F2
Courmayeur 161 B2
Cours-de-Piles 105 E5
Courvoisier 259 B3
Coutras 80 D5
Covelinhas 190 G4
Covilhã 187 C5
Covington 269 A4
Cowra 241 E4
Cragganmore 263 E1
Craigellachie 263 D4
Craiova 209 G3
Cramant 107 F3
Craneford 244 D5
Cranmore 252 E6
Crans 194 C4
Crassier 194 C4
Cratfield 252 F6
Cravant-les-Coteaux 117 E5
Crawfordville 242 G1
Cray 118 D6
Creixell 182 G5
Crema 161 C5
Cremona 161 C6, 165 E1
Crémone (Cremona) 165 E1
Crépy 127 A2
Cres 207 C1
Cresta Blanca 237 A3
Cresta Blanca Winery 230 A4
Crestview 235 G1
Creta 215 F4
Crete (Kriti) 215 F4
Creuse 59 E3
Creux de la Net 69 D3
Creysse 105 E5
Crézancy-en-Sancerre 119 F2
Crieff 265 E4
Crissier 194 A6
Crna Gora (Montenegro) 207 F4
Croft 193 C5
Crouin 258 B5
Croix des Bouquets 266 A6
Croizet-Eymard 259 C4
Crotone 172 E5
Crozes-Hermitage 120 B6, 122 B4
Cru Barjuneau 97 G3
Cru Caplane 97 F4
Cru Commarque 97 G3
Cruet 127 D1
Cru la Clotte 97 B5
Cru Lanère 97 F3
Cru Thibaut 97 F5
Csengöd 220 C2
Csopak 202 C2, 205 F1
Cuba 266 A4
Cubaexport 266 A4
Cubellas 182 F6
Cuenca 175 C4
Cubuk 220 C4
Cucamonga Vineyard Co 230 G4
Cucamonga Winery 230 G5
Cuers 126 C3
Ciudad Real 175 C3
Cuis 107 E3
Cully 194 B6
Cumières 107 D2
Cunèges 105 F4
Cuneo 161 E2
Cunit 182 F5
Cuges-les-Pins 126 C2
Cuqueron 128 F4
Curicó 250 C1, 251 D2
Cussac 91 C4
Cutler 235 G2
Cuvaison 233 A2
Cviček 207 B2
Cyprus (Kipros) 216 E3, 220

D

Dachsberg 150 F3
Dahra 219 B1
Dailuaine 263 E2
Dallas Dhu 265 C5
Dalboki 211 C4
Dallenberg 158 F5
Dalmatia 207 E3
Dalmore 265 C4
Dalwhinnie 265 D4
Dalwood 242 D3
Damas (Dimashq) 220 F5
Damascus (Dimashq) 220 F5
Dambach-la-Ville 113 D2
Damery 107 D2
Dão 187 C4, 189
Dar bel Amri 218 C4
Darbonnay 127 F4
Dardagny 194 D3
D'arenberg 245 C4
Darlington 245 A4
Darmstadt 135 B4
Daub-Haus 154 G5
Daubos 87 E5, 89 A4
Davayé 75 E3
Davis Bynum 230 D5
Davos 197 F5
Dealul Mare 209 F4
Deanston 265 E4
Deatsville 269 B4
Debrecen 202 B4
Debroi Hárslevelü 202 B3
de Castellane 109 F5
Dehesilla 176 B4
de Hoop 249 E2
Deidesheim 135 C4, 153 F5
Deinheim 154 G5
Delaforce 193 C3
Delamain 259 B3
Delgado and Zuleta 176 C5
Delheim 249 G2
Delicato 234 C3
Delisle 267 B4
Dellchen 146 F6
Del Rey 235 G1
Demesticha 215 D2
Denair 234 D4
Denens 194 A5
Denges 194 B6
Denheim 135 B4
Denia 175 C5
Deniliquin 241 F2
Denizli 220 D2
Derbent 213 C6
Dereham, Norfolk 252 E6
Derriere-le-Grange 72 F3
Desenzano del Garda 166 C5
Deutschherrenberg 144 C5
Deutschkreutz 198 E3
Deutschlandsberg 198 G1
Deutschschutzen 198 F3
Deux-Sèvres 59 D1, 114 C5
Deva 209 F2
de Venoge 109 G5
Devesas 190 G2
Devon Vale Estates 249 F1
Dézaley 194 B6
Dezize 61 D5
De Zoete Inval 249 D4
Dhali 216 C4
Dhoros 216 D2
Dhron 143 D1
Diamond 267 G6
Diedesfeld 153 C2
Dienheim 135 B4, 154 G5
Diez Hermanos, Jerez 177 C4
Diez Hermanos, Vila Nova de Gaia 193 B3
Digne 59 F5, 131 D3
Dijon 59 C4, 61 C6
Dimashq 220 F5
Dimcha 211 C3
Dimiát 211 B5, D4
Dingač 207 E3
Dinuba 235 G2
Dirmstein 153 B2
Diss 252 E6
Dittelsheim 155 F3
Dizy-Magenta 107 D3
Djidjelli 219 B3
Dobrogeia 209 G5
Doktor 145 F2
Doktorberg 141 G6
Dolceacqua Rossese 161 F3
Dolcetto d'Asti 163 D4
Dolcetto delle Langhe 161 E3
Dolcetto di Acqui 163 D5
Dolcetto d'Ovada 161 D4
Domaine d'Arche-Pugneau 97 E4
Domaine de Chevalier 95 G2
Domaine de Grandmaison 95 E4
Domaine-de-la-Combe 99 A4
Domaine-de-l'Eglise 99 B5
Domaine la Solitude 95 G5
Domäne 139 E3
Domblans 127 F4
Domblick 155 G3
Domherr 155 E3, 314 C1
Domherrenberg 141 D2, E3
Dominica 267 C4
Dominican Republic 266 A6
Domodossola 161 A4
Domprobst 145 E1
Don 265 D6
Doña Elvira 176 B4
Doña Mencia 183 F4
Donauland 198 D3
Donnaz 161 B3
Donnerskirchen 198 D3
Doosberg 150 F5
Dordogne 59 E2, 80 D6
Dorgali 172 D2
Dornach 270 E4
Dornoch 265 C4
Dosaiguas 182 C3
Double Springs 269 B3
Doubs 59 C5
Douby 77 D4
Doué-la-Fontaine 114 C5
Douelle 128 B5
Douro (Duero) 175 B2, 187 B5
Douro-Littoral 187 B4
Douvaine 127 A2
Douville 105 D5
Dow 193 D4
Drachenstein 149 F3
Drăgășani 209 G3
Draguignan 59 B4, 126 F6
Drakenstein (co-op) 249 E4
Drama 215 A4
Driesprong 249 F3
Dhronhofberger 143 D2
Drôme 59 F5, 120 D5
Drumborg 241 G1
Dry Creek 230 B4
Dubbo 241 D4
Dubois 118 C4
Dubrvaka 207 E6
Dubrovnik 207 E3
Duddenhoe 252 F5
Düdingen 270 F3
Duero 175 B2
Dufftown 263 E4, 265 C5
Duillier 194 B4
Dulce Nombre 177 C4
Dully 194 B4
Dumbarton 265 F4
Dumfries 265 G5
Dunajska Streda 205 C5
Dunaujvaros 98 C2
Dundee 265 E5
Duquesne 267 C5
Duravel 128 B5
Durbach 156 E2
Durbanville 247 D2
Dürnstein 198 C1, 201 G1
Durtal 114 A5

E

East Side 234 B3
Eauze 261 C4, 129 E2
Eberbach 135 C5
Ebersberg 154 E3
Eberweier 270 C4
Ebro 175 B5
Echandens 194 B5
Echichens 194 B5
Echuca 241 F2
Eckelsheim 155 F2
Ecuador 250 B1
Ecublens 194 B5
Ecueil 107 B3
Edelberg 145 B3
Edelmann 150 F4
Edenkoben 153 D2
Eden Valley 244 D6
Edinburgh 265 E5
Edradour 265 D5
Egelsee 201 F3
Eger 202 B3
Eggenburg 198 B2
Eguisheim 110 C5, 113 E2
Ehrenberg 141 G6
Ehrenhausen 198 G2
Ehrenstetten 156 F3
Eibelstadt 158 E3
Eibingen 149 F4
Eichberg, Alsace 111 B1
Eichberg, Eltville 151 E1
Einzellagenfrei 147 D2
Eisenberg 198 F3
Eisenstadt 198 D3
Eitelsbach 141 D4
El Alamo 177 C1
Elâzig 220 C6
Elba 169 B1
El Barco 177 C2
El Bizarron 177 E2
El Bonete 177 B4
El Caballo 177 E1
El Carmen 177 C4
El Castillo 177 C4
El Cerro Viejo 177 D3
El Ciego 180 B6
El Condado 175 D2
El Corchvelo 177 D2
El Corvegidor 177 C4
El Corregidor Viejo 177 C4
El Cuco 177 D1
El Cuerno del Oro 177 B3
Elderslie 242 D2
Elgin 263 A2, 265 C5
El Hornillo 176 B5
Elizabeth 240 E5
El Jardinito 177 C4
Ellas 215
Ellergrab 145 C4
Elne 124 F2
Eloro 172 G3
El Paraiso 177 D2
El Parradero 177 C3
El Peral 176 A5
El Pollero 176 D6
El Rancho 177 D2
El Ribiero 175 A2
El Romano 177 C4
El Salvador 177 C4
El Señor 176 B4
Els Monjos 182 F6
Elster 153 E5
El Telegrafo 177 C4
El Toro 177 E1
Eltville 135 B3
Eltville-am-Rhein 151 G3
Elvas 187 E5
Emeringes 77 B3
Emilia-Romagna 161 D5, 165 G2, 169 A4
Emilio Lustau 177 D1, D4
Emme 270 F4
Emmendingen 270 D4
Emu 245 B4
en Cailleret 67 F4
en Caradeux 69 D3
en Chevret 67 F3
Endingen 156 F1
Enfer 161 B2
Engadin 197 D5
Engelgrube 143 E1
Engelsberg 154 B5
Engelsmann's Berg 150 G6
en Genêt 68 E6
England and Wales 252
en Guinelay 77 B5
Enkirch 145 B4
en l'Orme 68 E6
en l'Ormeau 67 F4
Enmore 267 G6
Enna 172 F3
en Paulaud 69 F4
en Redescul 69 E1
Ensisheim 113 F2
Entraygues 59 F3, 130 D6
Entrecasteux 126 B4
Entre-Deux-Mers 80 F4
en Verseuil 67 F4
Epernay 107 E3, 109
Epesses 194 B6
Epfig 113 C2
Epinal 59 B5
Epiré 116 B3
Epirus (Ipiros) 215 C2
Episkopi 216 D2
Equateur (Ecuador) 250 B1
Erbach 151 F2
Erbaluce 161 C3
Erdek 220 B2
Erden 144 C6
Erdöbénye 203 B4
Erdöhorváti 203 B4
Ereğli 220 D4
Erlenbach 156 C4
Erstein 113 C2
Ervedosa do Douro 191 F2
Eschbach 153 D1
Escherndorf 158 D4
Escurès 261 E3
Eskisehir 220 C3
España (Espagne) 175
Espejo 183 F4
Espinho 190 G6
Esposende 189 B4
Essaouira 218 D3
Essertines 194 B4, D3
Essonne 59 B3
Estagel 124 D2
Estaing 59 F3, 131 D1
Est Est Est 169 D3
Estoril 188 F2
Estremadura 187 D4
Estremoz 187 E5
Esvres 115 B1
Esztergom 202 B2
Etournelles 73 E1
Etoy 194 B5
Etna 172 F3
Etroyes 74 C4
Euboea (Evvoia) 215 C3
Eucharisberg 139 A5
Eugenio Bustos 251 B4
Euphrates (Firat) 220 D5
Eure 59 B2
Eure-et-Loir 59 B2
Euskirchen 135 A2
Evenos 126 C3
Evionnaz 195 D1
Evisa 132 E4
Evora 187 F5
Evorilla 176 A6
Evreux 59 B2
Evvoia 215 C3
Extremadura 175 C2
Eymet 105 G4
Eyrans 104 B2
Eyrenville 105 F5
Eysines 80 E3
Ezerjó 202 B2, C3, 207 B4

F

Fabriano 169 C5
Faconnières 72 F4
Fafe 189 C5
Fahrwangen 270 E4
Fairview 249 D4
Falklay 145 B4
Falkenberg 143 C2
Falkenstein 198 B3
Falkirk 265 E4
Falqueyrat 105 G5
Falset 182 G3
Famagusta 216 C5
Fanhões 188 E3
Fara 161 C4
Fargues 97 F6
Farnesi 235 G5
Faro, Italia 172 F4
Faro, Portugal 187 G4
Farques 128 C4
Faugères 59 G3, 124 B6
Favaios 191 D2
Faye-d'Anjou 116 D5
Fayssac 129 D6
Féchy 104 B5
Feherburgundi 202 C2
Fehring 198 G2
Felgueiras 189 C5
Fels 139 B2
Fels 198 C2
Felsenberg 146 G4
Felsen Eck 147 F2
Felsen-Steyer 146 F5
Felsted, England 252 F6
Feodosija 213 B3
Ferianes 176 C5
Fernandez 267 B2, E5
Fernando A de Terry 177 E1, F3
Fernán Núñez 183 F3
Ferrals-les-Corbières 124 C3
Ferrara 165 F3
Ferreira 193 B3
Ferres 143 C1
Fès 218 C5
Feteascǎ albǎ 209 D4, E3, E5
Feteascǎ neagrǎ 209 E5
Feteascǎ regalǎ 209 E3, E5, F2, F3, G3
Fetiaska 211 B5
Fetjaska 213 A1
Fettercairn 265 D5
Feverberg 153 B2
Feydieu 93 F4
Fiano 172 C3
Ficklin 234 F6
Figanières 126 B5
Figari 132 G5
Figline 171 C5
Filippi Winery 230 G5
Filton, Gloucestershire 252 C3
Filzen 139 B2, 143 B4
Finchampstead 252 F5
Findling 154 D4
Finger Lakes 238
Finistère 58 C5
Firat (Euphrates) 220 D5
Firenze 169 A4, 171 A3
Fitusberg 151 F5
Firvida 190 F2
Fitou 124 D3
Fiuggi 169 F4
Fixin 61 C6, 73 E4
Flachen 139 C4
Flagey-Echézeaux 71 G5
Flassans-sur-Issole 126 B4
Flaugeac 105 F4
Flayosc 126 B4
Flein 156 D4
Fleischmann 269 B3
Fleurance 261 C6, 129 E3
Fleurie 61 F5, 77 C4
Fleury-les-Aubrais 115 A4
Fleys 79 D6
Flohhaxn 201 F1
Floirac 80 E3
Florence (Firenze) 169 A4, 171 A3
Florentin 129 F3
Fochabers 263 B5
Focsani 209 F5
Fogarina 165 F2
Foggia 172 B4
Foix 59 G3, 130 F6
Folgosa 190 G4
Foligno 169 D4
Fonroque 105 F4
Fonseca 193 B2
Fontalioux 121 F2
Fontana 230 G5
Fontanafredda 163 E3
Fontanelas 188 E1
Fortelo 190 G3
Fonterutoli 171 F3
Fontès 125 C6
Fontevrault-L'Abbaye 114 C6
Fontrubi 182 F5
Foppiano 230 C5
Forbes 241 E4
Forcine 117 B1
Forez 121 F2
Forlì 165 G4, 169 A5
Fornos de Algodres 189 F6
Forres 265 C5
Forst 147 D1, 153 C2
Forst a. d. Weinstrasse 153 E5
Forsterlay 145 C1
Fort-de-France 267 C4
Forth 265 E4
Fort Ile 267 C4
Fortino 237 C3
Fort William 265 D3
Fortino 237 C3
Fougueyrolles 105 E3
Foujouin 118 B4
Founex 194 C4
Fourques 124 E2
Fours 104 B2
Fousselottes 72 F2
Fowler 235 G1
Fracia 161 A5
Fraisse 105 D3
Francesco Bertolli 171 F2
Franciacorta 161 B6, 165 D1
Franciscan 233 C4
Franconia 158
Frangy 127 B1
Franken 135 B6
Frankenthal 149 E1
Frankfort, Kentucky 269 B4
Frankfurt 135 B4
Franklin 269 C3
Frankovka 207 C4
Franschhoek 247 D2, 249 G6
Franzia 234 D3
Frapin 259 D2
Frascati 169 F3
Fraserburgh 265 C6
Fratenilli 171 E2
Frauenfeld 197 D4
Frecciarossa 161 D5
Freemark Abbey 233 B3
Freiburg 135 F3, 156 F1, 270 D4
Freinsheim 153 B2
Freis d'Asti 163 C3
Freis di Chieri 163 B1
Freisa 161 C3
Freixial 188 E3
Frelmersheim 153 D2
Fréjus 126 B5
Fremont 237 A3
French Guiana (Guyane Française) 250 B2
Fresno 229 E3, 234 G6, 235 G1
Fréterive 127 C2
Freudenstadt 135 E4
Freundstück 153 E4
Fribourg 197 F2, 270 F3
Frickenhausen 158 E4
Frithsden 252 F5
Friularo 165 E4
Friuli Venezia Giulia 165 C5
Frohnhof 153 C4
Fronsac 80 E4, 102 D6
Frontignan 125 D7
Fronton 59 F2, 129 E5
Frosinone 169 F4, 172 B2
Fruska Gora 207 D4
Fuchs 139 E2
Fuchsberg 149 F5
Fuchsmantel 153 D4
Fuenmayor 180 B6
Fuissé 75 F3
Fuji-San 222 D3
Fujiyoshida 222 D3
Fully 195 D2
Fulton 269 D1
Fumane 167 B2
Funchal 185 D4
Furmint 202 A4, C2, B2
Furore Divina Costiera 172 C3
Fürsteneck 156 E2
Fye 79 C4

G

Gabarret 129 E2
Gabbiano 171 C3
Gabilan Range 237 E4
Gabrovo 211 C3
Gaeta 172 B2
Gageac-et-Rouillac 105 E4
Gaillac 59 F3, 129 E6
Gainfarn 200 G2
Gaiole in Chianti 171 E5
Galafura 190 F4
Galaţi 209 F5
Galbenǎ 209 E5
Galéria 132 E4
Gallega 177 E1
Gallicia 175 A1
Gallician 125 D9
Gallipoli 172 C6
Gallo-S. California Winery 230 G5
Gallo, W. E. & J. 234 D4
Galt 234 B3
Gamay 66 E3, 207 F5
Gambellara 165 E3, 169 C6
Gamlitz 198 G2
Gampel 195 C5
Gan 129 G1
Gandesa 183 G2
Gap 59 E5, 131 D3
Garanche 77 G3
Garancille 259 D3
Garcia 182 G3
Gard 59 F4, 120 G4, 125 C10
Garda, Lago di 166 B6
Gardone 166 A5
Gardonne 105 E4
Garidells 182 F4
Garmouth 263 A4
Garonne 59 F2
Gärtchen 143 C3
Garvey 176 D6, 177 D1, B3, B4, D3
Gaspar F. Florido Cano 176 C4
Gassin 126 C5
Gattinara 161 B3
Gau-Bickelheim 155 F2
Gauriac 104 F2
Gavá 183 F1
Gavi 161 D4
Gawler 240 E5
Gazetiers 73 E2
Gaziantep 220 D5
Gazzah 220 F4
Geaune 59 G1, 130 E5
Gedersdorf 198 C2
Geelong 243 G2
Gehrn 151 E3
Geisberg 139 E4, 147 D4, 151 E5
Geisböhl 153 G5
Geisenheim 149 G5, 150 G2
Gelida 182 F6
Gelos 129 G1
Gemeaux 72 F6
Gemello 237 B2
Genadendal 247 D3
Genders 245 C4
General Alvear 251 D6
Gengenbach 270 C4
Gênes (Genova) 161 E4
Geneva 59 D5, 127 B2, 194 C4, 197 G1
Genève 59 D5, 127 B2, 194 C4, 197 G1
Genoa (Genova) 161 E4
Genova 161 E4
Gensac-la-Pallue 259 C1
Gensingen 155 E2
George 247 D6
Georgetown 250 B1, 267 G6
Georgia (Grunzinkaja) 213 C4

Gerona 175 B6
Gers 59 G2, 261 D4
Gerümpel 153 E4
Gervide 190 F2
Getashan 213 D4
Gevrey-Chambertin 61 C5, 73 E2
Geyser Peak 230 B4
Geyserville 230 B5
Ghemme 161 B4
Ghioroc 209 E2
Ghisonaccia 132 F6
Ghisoni 132 F5
Gien 59 C3, 115 A5
Gigondas 132 F6
Gilly 194 B4
Gilly-les-Citeaux 72 G2
Gilroy 237 C4
Gimbsheim 155 F4
Ginestet 105 D4
Giretti 237 C3
Giro 169 G2, 172 E1
Gironde 80 F1
Girvan 265 G4
Givry 61 D5, 74 E4
Gizeaux 114 B6
Gland 194 B4
Glarus 197 E4
Glasgow, Kentucky 269 C3
Glasgow, Scotland 265 F4
Glen Albyn 265 C4
Glenallachie 263 E3
Glenburgie 265 C5
Glencadam 265 D5
Glen Conner 249 G3
Glendora 230 F3
Glendronach 265 C5
Glendullan 263 E4
Glen Elgin 242 F2
Glen Elgin 263 B3
Glenfarclas 263 E2
Glenfiddich 263 E4
Glen Foyle 265 E4
Glenfyne 265 E3
Glengarioch 265 C5
Glenglassaugh 265 C5
Glengoyne 265 E4
Glen Grant 263 C3
Glenkeith 263 C6
Glenkinchie 265 F5
Glenlivet 263 G2
Glenlochy 265 D3
Glenlossie 263 B2
Glenloth 245 B4
Glen Mhor 265 C4
Glenmorangie 265 C4
Glen Moray 263 A2
Glenmore 269 B3
Glen Oak 242 F2
Glénouze 114 C6
Glen Rothes 263 C3
Glenrowan/Milawa 241 F3
Glen Scotia 265 F3
Glen Spey 263 C3
Glentauchers 263 C5
Glenturret 265 E4
Glenugie 265 C6
Glenury-Royal 265 D5
Glöck 154 D5
Godalming 252 G5
Godramstein 153 D1
Godenano Secondo 171 E3
Godoy Cruz 251 B5
Goldan 270 F5
Golden Luft 154 D5
Goldatzel 150 F2
Gold-Bächel 153 D4
Goldberg 139 C2, 150 E4, 201 F3
Goldgrube 145 B3
Goldschmied 153 G5
Gold Seal Vineyards 238 D2
Goldtröpfchen 143 C1, C2
Goldwingert 144 B6
Golop 203 C3
Gols 198 D4
Gomersal 244 C3
Gonçalo 190 F2
Gondeville 259 B4
Gondomar 189 C4
Gonfaron 126 C4
Gönnheim 153 B2
Gonzalez Byass 177 B4, C2, C3, C4, E1, 193 C4
Gorges 114 F2
Gorizia 165 D6
Gornac 80 F4
Gorna Radgorna 207 A2
Gotteshilfe 155 F3
Gottlesbrunn 198 D3
Gottwaldov 205 B5
Gotzen Fels 147 F1
Goudge 251 D5
Goudhurst 252 G6
Goulburn 241 E5
Gouveia 189 F6
Gouvinhas 190 F5
Goxviller 270 C4
Gozo 216 F2
Graach a. d. Mosel 145 E1
Graacher Schäferei 145 E2
Graben 145 F2
Gradignan 80 F3, 95 C3
Grafenberg 143 D1, 151 E2
Grafenstück 153 A2
Graham 193 B2
Grainhübel 153 F5
Granada 175 D3
Grand Bigaroux 103 E3
Grand Favray 119 E5
Grandes-Ruchottes 65 F6
Grandes Ruchottes 66 F1
Grande Rue 71 F4
Grant Mont 117 B3
Grand Cru 233 E3
Grand Poujeaux 91 F3
Grands Murs 72 F2
Grand Soumard 119 F4
Grand Soussans 91 G6
Grandvaux 194 B6
Grantown 265 D5
Graša 209 E4
Graševina 207 B2, B3, C3, C4
Gratallops 182 F3
Gratiesti 213 A1
Graubunden 197 F4
Graulhet 129 E6
Gravedel Friuli 165 D5
Graves 80 F3, 95
Graves de Vayres 80 E4
Grayson 269 B5
Graz 198 F2
Greater Antilles 266
Great Western 241 G1
Greco di Gerace 172 F4
Greco di Tufo 172 C3
Greece (Ellas) 215
Greenock 244 A4
Greenville 269 C2
Grenada 267 E4
Grenoble 59 E5, 131 C3
Grenouilles 79 D4
Greta 242 E3
Greve 171 D4
Grezzana 167 B3
Griffith 241 E3
Grignolino 161 D3, 163 A4
Grignolino d'Asti 163 C4
Grimaud 126 C5
Grinzing 198 C3, 200 B3
Griotte-Chambertin 72 F6
Grisolles 129 E5
Grk 207 F2
Grom 207 F5
Grombalia 219 B5
Gros Plant du Pays Nantis 58 D6, 130 B4
Gross-Bottwar 156 D4
Grosser Hengelberg 143 D1
Grosser Herrgott 143 C3, D3
Grosseto 169 C2
Grosshöflein 198 D3
Grosslagenfrei 158 D4, E3, 156 E3
Grozon 127 E5
Gruenchers 72 F3
Grumello 161 A6, 165 C1
Grüneberg 141 D2
Grünstadt 153 B1
Grunzinkaja 213 C4
Guadalajara 251 F2, 175
Guadalquivir 175 D3
Guadeloupe 267 B5
Guadiana 175 C3
Guagno 132 F5
Guiana, Fr (Guyane Fr.) 250 B2
Guantanamo 266 A4
Guastalla 165 F2
Guasti 230 G4
Guaymallén 251 A5
Gueberschwihr 110 B4
Guebwiller 110 A1, 113 F2
Guelma 219 B4
Guémar 113 D2
Guéret 59 D2, 130 C6
Guerneville 230 D4
Guglielmo 237 C4
Guiães 190 E4
Guiamets 182 G3
Guild 234 B1
Guild Winery 230 G4
Guimarãis 187 B4, 189 C5
Gujan-Mestras 80 F1
Güldenmorgen 155 F4
Gumpoldskirchen 198 D3, 200 F2
Gumza 211 C3
Guncina 165 C3
Gundelsheim 156 C4
Gundersheim 155 G3
Guntersblum 135 B4
Gunterslay 143 C2, D1, D2
Guntramsdorf 198 D3, 200 F3
Gurdzhaani 213 C4
Gutach 270 D4
Gutenberg 150 G2
Gutental 147 C2
Gutleut-Haus 154 G6
Guttenberg 153 E1
Gutten Holle 146 F5
Gutturnio 161 D5
Guyana 250 B2, 267 G5
Guyane (Guyana) 250 B2
Guyane Fr. 250 B2
Gy 194 C4
Gyöngyos 202 B3
Györ 202 B2

H

Hackham 245 C4
Hadres 198 B3
Haifa (Hefa) 220 F4
Hainburg 198 C4
Hainfeld 153 D1
Haiti 266 A5
Hajos 202 E1
Halab 220 E5
Halbturn 198 D4
Halkidas 215 C3
Hallcrest 237 C2
Hallett Cove 245 B4
Hallgarten 150 E6
Haloze 207 B2
Haltingen 156 G1
Hamah 220 E5
Hambledon, Hampshire 252 G5
Hameau de Blagny 66 F4
Hamilton 241 G1
Hamilton's 244 D6
Hamm 139 C2
Hammerstein 141 F2
Hammondsport Wine Co. 238 D2
Hampden 266 A3
Hamrun 216 G2
Hannersdorf 198 F3
Hans Kornell Winery 233 A2
Hanzell Winery 233 F3
Happy Valley 242 F1
Thos. Hardy 245 C4
Hardy's (Tintara) 244 B5
Haro 180 B5
Hartford 269 C3
Häschen 143 E1
Hasenläufer 144 G5
Hasensprung 150 F3
Haslach 135 F3
Hato 176 B3
Hattenheim 150 F6
Hattstatt 110 C4, 113 E2
Haugsdorf 198 B2
Haut-Armagnac 261 D5
Haut-de-Bosdarros 128 G6
Haut-de-Seine 59 B2
Haute-Garonne 59 G2
Haute-Goulaine 114 E2
Haute-Loire 59 E4
Haute-Marne 59 C4
Haute-Saône 59 C5
Haute-Savoie 59 D5
Haute-Vienne 59 E2
Hautes-Alpes 59 E5
Hautes-Pyrénées 59 G2
Haut-Rhin 59 C5
Haut-Santenay 65 E2
Hauts Doix 72 F2
Hautvillers 107 D2
Haza Pozo 176 A5
Hazard 269 C5
Healdsburg 230 C5
Hecker Pass 237 D3
Hefa 220 F4
Heidelberg 247 C5, 135 C4
Heilbronn 135 D5
Heiligenbaum 154 E4
Heiligenberg 150 F6
Heiligenborn 139 G4
Heiligenhäuschen 141 G5
Heimberg 148 F3
Heissenstein 110 A1
Helenenkloster 144 G6
Hendelberg 150 D6
Henderson 269 C2
Hennessy 152 A5, A6, 153 B2, B3, D2
Henriot 109 C5
Henschke's 244 C6
Heppenheim 156 B3
Heppenstein 139 E3
Hérault 125 C6, 59 G3
Hercegkút 203 B5
Hermance 194 C4
Hermanus 247 E2
Hermitage 120 B6
Herrenberg, Franconia 158 E5
Herrenberg, Ruwer 141 D4
Herrenberg, Mosel: Piesport 143 B3
Herrenberg, Rheinhessen 154 G5
Herrenberg, Saar 139 B3, C2, D2, E3
Herrenberg, Mosel: Bernkastel 145 B4
Herrenberg, Rheinpfalz 153 B4
Herrenmorgen 153 A3
Herrgottsacker 153 E4
Herrlich 153 E1
Herrmans 146 G4
Herrmans Berg 146 G4
Herrnbaumgarten 198 B3
Herrnberg 154 G5
Herrngarten 154 F6
Herrschaft 197 C5, B5
Hessen 135 B6, C2
Heublein Co-operative 233 B3
Heuchelberg 156 D3
Hiedsieck, Charles 109 A5, C6
Hiedsieck Monopole 109 A5
Highland Park 265 A5
Highway City 234 F6
Hillside 265 D6
Himmelreich 145 D5, E1
Himmelsteige 201 F1
Hims 220 E5
Hine 259 B3
Hinkel Stein 147 D1
Hinterkirch 149 D2
Hipping 154 D5
Hitzendorf 198 F1
Hitzkirch 270 E5
Hitzlay 141 E5
Hlohovec 205 B5
Hochbenn 153 B4
Hochfelden 113 B1
Hochmess 153 B1
Hochstadt 153 D2
Hódmezovásárhely 202 C3
Hodonin 205 B5
Hoeppsel 139 G4
Höfchen 145 F2
Hofgarten 147 D1
Höflein 198 D4
Hofstatter, J. 166 F2
Hofstück 153 C2
Hoheburg 153 F5
Hohenberg 156 D3
Hohenmorgen 153 F4
Hohenneuffen 156 E4
Hohenrain 151 E1
Hohenwarth 198 C2
Hohle 146 G5
Höll 147 F1
Hölle, Saar 139 B3
Hölle, Rheingau 150 F2
Hölle, Rheinhessen 154 E5
Höllenberg 149 D2
Hollenpfad 153 B1
Hollister 237 D4
Homberg 135 C2
Homs (Hims) 220 E5
Honbo 222 C3
Honeoye Lake 214 C2
Hongrie (Magyarorszag) 202
Hönigberg 151 E1, 158 D4, 147 C1
Honigsackel 153 B1
Hopkinsville 269 C2
Horam, Sussex 252 G6
Horn 153 A4
Horndale 245 B4
Horsham, Australia 241 F1
Hourtin 81 D1
Hoy 265 A5
Hrvatska (Croatia) 207 C2-3
Hubertuslay 139 E4, 145 C1
Huelva 175 D2
Huesca 175 A4
Hughson 234 D4
Huguenot (co-op) 249 C5
Huhnerberg 145 E3
Huismes 117 C3
Hunawihr 111 C4, 113 D2
Hunter River 242
Hunter Valley 241 D5, 242
Hunt Roope 193 C4
Husi 209 E5
Husseau 118 D5
Husseren-les-Châteaux 110 C5
Hütte 139 C5
Hvar 207 E2
Hydra 215 D3
Hyères 126 C3

I

Iasi 209 E5
Ica 250 B1
Idar Oberstein 135 B2
Iglesias 172 E1
Ihringen 156 F1
Ikaria 215 D5
Ile de Macau 93 B4
Ile des Vaches 93 C5
Ile des Vergelesses 69 E2-3
Ile Margaux 85 A4
Illas 167 C4
Ille-et-Vilaine 58 C6
Ille-sur-Têt 124 E1
Illkirch 113 B2
Illmitz 198 D4
Imola 165 G3
Imperia 161 F3
Imperial 263 E2
Impruneta 171 B3
Inchgower 263 A6
Indre 59 D2, 115 C3
Indre-et-Loire 59 C2, 115 C1
Inferno 161 A6, 165 C1
Ingelheim 135 B3, 155 E2
Ingenheim 153 E1
Ingersheim 111 C1
Inglenook Winery 233 C4
Ingrandes de Touraine 117 B4
Inkpen 252 F5
Innswood 266 B3
Institut St-Francois-Xavier 95 C3
Interlaken 197 F3, 270 F4
Interleven 265 E4
Invergordon 265 C4
Inverness 265 C4
Inverurie 265 D5
Ioannina 215 C2
Ios 215 E4
Iphofen 158 E4
Ipiros 215 C2
Iraklion 215 F4
Irbid 220 F4
Iroulèguy 59 G1, 128 G6
Irroy 109 A5
Irsch 139 F3
Irshavskoje 203 A2
Ischia 172 C2
Isère 59 E5, 120 A5
Iskenderun 220 D5
Islay 265 F2
Isle of Jura 265 F3
Isparta 220 D3
Israel (Yisra'el) 265 F4
Issan 93 B3
Issigeac 105 F5
Istanbul 220 B2
Italian Swiss Colony 230 A4
Italijanski Rizling 207 C4, C5, D5, F5
Ithaca 238 D4
Ivanhoe 242 F2
Izmir 220 C1
Izmit 220 B3

J

Jacquesson 109 B5
Jaén 175 D3
Jalta 203 B2
Jamaica 266 A3
Jambles 74 E3
Jarnac 259 B4
Jászberény 202 B3
Javrezac 258 A5
Jaxu 128 G6
Jerevan 203 C5
Jerez de la Frontera 175 D2, 177 E3, 179
Jerez y Sanlúcar 175 D2
Jerusalem (Yerushalayim) 220 F4
Jesuitenberg 150 G3
Jesuitengarten 141 F5, E5
Jihlava 205 B4
Joching 200 G5
Johannisberg 185 B3, 141 D5, 150 F3
Johannisberg Grund 150 F2
Johannisbrünnchen 145 F2
Jois 198 D3
Jongieux 127 C1
Jordan (Nahr al-Urdunn) 220 F4
Jordan (Al-Urdunn) 220 F5
Jordanie (Al-Urdunn) 220 F5
Jose de Soto 177 E2, B3
Josef Brigl 166 D2
Joseph Heitz Cellars 233 B4
Joseph Phelps 233 B4
Josephshof 145 E1
J. Swan 230 D5
Juffer 143 A5, 144 F5
Jujuy 251 A2
Juliénas 61 F5, 77 A4
Jullié 77 A3
Jully-lès-Buxy 74 G3
Jumilla y Monovar 175 C4
Juncosa 182 B5
Junee 241 E3
Jungfer 150 E6
Junin 251 B5
Junta Nacional dos Vinhos 193 D4
Jura 265 D5, E3
Jurançon 129 G1
Jussy 194 C4

K

Kabininge 244 C4
Kadarka 202 A3, D3, C2, D2, 207 B4
Kadina 240 E5
Kaefferkopf 111 B2
Kafels 146 F6
Kahlenberg, Nahe 147 D1
Kahlenberg, Österreich 200 B3
Kahlenbergerdorf 200 B4
Kaiserberg 200 F6, G1
Kaiserslautern 135 C3
Kaiserpfalz 155 E2
Kaiserstuhl 156 F1
Kaiser Stuhl (co-op) 244 B4
Kaiser Stuhl Tuniberg 135 F3
Kalamata 215 E2
Kalbsflicht 151 F3
Kalecik 220 C4
Kalimna 244 A4
Kalkofen 153 A4, F4
Kalksburg 200 D2
Kallstadt 153 A4
Kalokhorio 216 D3
Kalterersee 165 C3
Kambos 216 C2
Kangarilla 245 C5
Kanonkop 249 E2, F3
Kanzem 139 B3
Kanzlerberg 111 D5
Kapela 207 B3
Kapellchen 143 D3
Kapellen Pfad 147 D2
Kapfenberg 198 E1
Kaposvár 202 C2
Kappelrodeck 156 E4, 270 C4
Kapuvar 202 B1
Karabük 220 B4
Karabunar 211 D2
Kara Chanakh 213 C6
Karaman 220 D4
Karcag 202 B3
Kardinalsberg 145 F1
Karlovac 207 B2
Karlovo 211 C3
Karlsberg 139 C4
Karlsruhe 156 D3, 135 D4
Károlyfalva 203 A5
Karpathos 215 F6
Karthäuserhofberg 141 D4
Kasel 135 B2, 141 E4
Kathikas 216 C1
Katoomba 241 E4
Kätzchen 143 A4
Katzensprung 201 F1
Katzenthal 111 B1
Kausenberg 147 E1
Kavadarci 207 G5
Kavadarka 207 G6
Kavalla 215 B4
Kawaguchi 222 C2
Kayseri 220 C5
Kaysersberg 111 B2, 113 E2
Kea 215 D4
Kecskemet 202 C3
Kefallinia 215 D1
Keinbah 242 F4
Keith 263 C6, 265 C5
Kékfrankos 202 B1
Kéknyelyü 202 C2
Kellerberg 201 G2
Kellereigenossenschaft Greis-Bozen 166 D2
Kellereigenossenschaft Terlan 166 C2
Kelokedhara 216 D2
Kenitra 218 C4
Keuka Lake 238 D2
Kentucky River 269 C4
Kerchen 156 D3
Kenwood 233 E3
Kerkira 215 C1
Kern 229 F3
Kernagel 141 F4
Kertz 146 G5
Keskin 220 C4
Kesten 143 B3
Keszthely 202 C1
Kettmeir 166 E2
Kevedinka 207 C4
Keyes 234 D4
Keyneton 244 C6
Khaskovo 211 D4
Khios 215 D5
Khoulou 216 C2
Kickels Kopf 147 F1
Kiedrich 151 E2
Kientzheim 111 B3
Kieselberg 153 F4
Kilani 216 D2
Kilis 220 D5
Kilsberg 150 F2
Kinclaith 265 F4
Kindenheim 153 A1
King City 237 G5
Kings 229 E3
Kingsburg 235 G1
Kingston 263 A4, 266 B3
Kingstown 267 D4
Kinheim 145 C1
Kipros 216, 220 E3
Kirchberg, Saar 139 B2
Kirchberg, Österreich 198 C2
Kirchberg, Mosel 144 G5
Kirchberg, Würzburg 158 D4
Kirchen 149 F4
Kirchenpfad 149 E4
Kirchenstück 153 A4, 153 E5
Kirchheck 146 F6
Kirchheim 135 D6, 153 B1
Kirchlay 145 B2
Kirchplatte 154 D3
Kirklareli 220 B1
Kirkwall 265 A5
Kirrweiler 153 C2
Kishinev (Kišin'ov) 213 A1
Kišin'ov 213 A1
Kiskörös 202 C3
Kiskunfelegyhaza 202 C3
Kiskunhalas 202 C3
Kithira 215 E3
Kithnos 215 D4
Kitingen 158 E4
Kizlarskoye 213 C6
Klamm 146 G5
Klaudhia 216 C4
Klaus 150 F3
Kläuserweg 150 G2, 149 F6
Klein Babelonstoring 249 E3
Klein Drakensteinberge 249 E5
Klett 197 B4
Klöch 198 G2
Klöch-Oststeiermark 198
Klosterberg, Kiedrich 151 E2
Klosterberg, Nahe 146 F6
Klosterberg, Oestrich 150 E4
Klosterberg, Rudesheim 149 E4
Klosterberg, Saar 139 C4, E2
Kloster Eberbach 151 D1
Klostergarten, Filzen 143 B4
Klostergarten, Leiwen 142 F6
Klostergarten, Rheinhessen 154 D4
Klostergarten, Rheinpfalz 153 F5
Klosterhofgut 144 D5
Klosterkellerei Muri 166 D3
Kloster Liebfraunenberg 153 E2
Klosterneuburg 200 B3
Klosterneuburg 198 C3
Klüsserath 142 E5
Kobnert 153 B1
Knockando 263 E2
Knockdhu 265 C5
Koblenz 135 A3
Koelenhof (co-op) 249 E1
Kofu 222 C2
Kohfidisch 198 F3
Kokkineli 215 C3
Kokur Niznegorsky 213 B2
Komarno 205 C5
Kommlingen 139 A4
Königsbach 153 C2
Königsberg 142 E6
Königsberg, Klüsserath 142 E5
Königsberg, Traben-Trarbach 145 C4
Königs Fels 146 G3
Königsgarten 153 D1
Konigswingert 153 D4
Konstanz 156 G6, 270 E6
Konya 220 D3
Konz 139 A3
Kopf 156 D4
Kophinou 216 D3
Kopke 193 C3
Korbel 230 D4
Korčula 207 E2
Korinthos 215 D3
Korro 245 C4
Kos 215 E5
Košice 205 B6
Kosovo 207 F5
Kotor 207 F3
Kövágóörs 204 G4
Kovenig 145 B3
Kövidinka 202 C3
Köwerich 142 F6
Kozani 215 B2
Kraichgau 156 C3
Kramolin 211 C3
Kranzberg 154 D5
Krasnodar 213 B3
Krasnostok Zolotovskij 213 A4
Krasnyi Kamenj 213 B3
Krater 207 G6
Kratosija 207 G6
Kräuterhaus 145 D3
Kreidkeller 153 A3
Krems 198 C2, 201 F3
Krettnach 139 A5
Kreuz 154 G5
Kreuzberg, Mosel 145 E3
Kreuzberg, Österreich 201 F3
Krichim 211 D3
Kriti 215 F4
Kröne 141 F5, F6
Kronenberg 147 D1
Krötenbrunnen 155 F4
Kroten Pfuhl 147 D2
Kröv 145 B2
Krug 109 A5
Kruževac 207 E5
Ksará 220 F5
Ktima 216 D1
Kues 135 B2
Kujunduša 207 E3
Kunkelman-Piper-Hiedsieck 109 B5
Kupfergrube 146 G4
Kupp, Saar 139 B3, D2, E2
Kupp, Ruwer 141 F2
Kurdzhali 211 E4
Kurfürstenberg 141 F4
Kurfürstenstück 155 E2
Küssnacht 270 F5
Kütahya 220 C2
Kutjevo 207 C3
Kviti Poloniny 213 A1
K.W.V. 249 D4

Kyrenia 216 B3
Kyurdamir 213 C6
Kyustendil 211 D1

L

Labarde 93 D4
la Barre, Volnay 67 F4
la Barre, Montlouis 118 C3, D5
Labastida 180 B5
la Batiaz 195 D2
L'Abbé-Gorsse de Gorsse 93 A2
la Biaune 77 C4
La Bodogonera 177 E2
la Boudriotte 65 F5
la Boulotte 69 F3
Labrousse 87 C1
la Cadière d'Azur 126 C2
la Calera 251 A2
La Canariera 177 C4
La Canonja 182 G4
La Carrena 177 B3
La Casinca 132 E6
la Chapelle, Auxey-Duresses 67 D2
la Chapelle, Hermitage 122 C4
la Chapelle-Basse-Mer 114 E2
la Chapelle des Bois 77 C4
la Chapelle-sur-Erdre 114 B3
la Chapelle de Guinchay 77 B6
la Chapelle-Heulin 114 F2
la Chapelle-sur-Loire 117 C3
la Chapelle-Vaupelteigne 79 B2
la Ciotat 126 C2
La Clape 124 D4
la Combe d'Orveau 71 E5, 72 E1-F1
la Comme 65 F4
La Compania 177 C3
La Concha 177 D2
Laconi 172 D2
Laconnex 194 D3
la Contrie 117 B2
La Copera 177 C4
La Coruña 175 A2
La Côte 194 A4, 197 C1
la Côte, Sancerre 119 E2
Lacq 129 F1
Lacquat 121 B3
la Crau 126 C3
Lacrima Christi 172 C3
la Croix 122 C5
la Croix Valmer 126 C5
Ladismith 247 C5
la Dominode 69 E1
Ladyburn 265 G4
la Farlède 126 C3
La Figuera 182 F3
la Flèche 114 A6
Lafoes 187 C5
la Folie 118 B4
la Force 105 E4
la Fourchaume 79 C3
la Frelonnerie 118 E3
la Galippe 117 E6
la Garde 126 D3
la Garde-Freinet 126 C5
la Gardière 117 B1
la Gardine 123 C4
la Garengue 97 B5
la Garenne 66 F4
la Gaudrelle 118 C3
Lagavulin 265 F2
la Gibauderie 259 B3
Lagoa 187 G4
Lago di Garda 165 D2, 166 B6
la Goutte-d'Or 66 F1
La Granada 182 F6
la Grande Côte 119 F2
la Grand Gardiole 123 A5
la Grèce (Ellas) 215
Lagrein 165 C3
la Grille 117 D3
Lagrima 172 D4
Laguardia 180 B6
la Haie Fouassière 114 F2
la Haie Martel 117 E5
La Jara 176 B3
la Jennelotte 66 F4
Lake Hennessey 233 B5
Lake Keuka Wine Co. 236 D2
Lake's Folly 242 F2
la Lande 117 B2
Lalande-de-Pomerol 99 A4, 103 C2, 80 E4
Lalden 195 C6
La Llacuna 182 E5
la Londe-les-Maures 126 C4
la Maison Blanche 122 C5
la Maladière 65 E3
la Maltroie 66 G1
La Mancha 175 C4
Lamarque 91 D5
la Martellière 117 B2
La Masó 182 F4
Lamberhurst 252 G6
Lambrusco 165 F2
la Medoquine 95 A3
la Méjanelle 125 C8
la Meslérie 118 B4
Lamia 215 C3
la Mignotte 68 F4
la Milletière 118 D5
la Môle 126 C5
Lamonzie-St-Martin 105 E4
La Morera de Montsant 182 F3
la Morra 163 E2
Lamothe 97 C4
Lamothe-Montravel 105 E2
la Motte 126 B5
la Mouline 93 E2
Lamphey, Wales 252 F3
la Mure 75 E2
Lana 166 B1
La Nava 175 B3
Lancaster 269 C4
Lancellotta 165 F2
Lancié 77 D5
Landamusberg 143 E1
Landau 135 D3
Landau inder Pfalz 153 D2
Landes 59 F1, 261 C3
la Nérolle 259 D3
Langeais 114 B6
Langenberg 151 E3, E5; F5
Langenlois 198 C2
Langenlonsheim 135 B3
Langen-Morgen 153 F4
Langenstück 151 F4
Langhorne Creek 134 F6
Langlade 125 C5
Langnau 270 F4
Langon 80 G4
Languedoc 59 G3, G4
Lania 216 D2
Lannepax 261 C4, 129 E3
la Noblaie 117 F3
La Nou de Gaya 182 G5
La Norieta 177 C4
Lanquais 105 E6
Lansac 104 F4
Lanson 109 A5, C4
Lanusei 172 D2
Laon 59 A3
La Pagliaia 171 F5
la Paillère 95 B2
La Palma 177 C2
Lapalme 124 D3
La Pampa 251 D2
La Panamena 177 C2
La Paris 249 E5
La Pastranilla 176 C5
La Paz 250 C1
la Perrière, Fixin 73 E3
la Perrière, Gevrey Chambertin 73 F1
la Pierrière, Nuits-St-Georges 70 F6
la Perrière, Sancerre 119 E3
La Pesanella 171 D4
Laphroaig 265 F3
la Pièce-sous-le-Bois 66 F5
la Pierelle 122 C5
la Pierre 77 C5
la Pinesse 97 C4
Laplume 129 D3
la Platerie 117 B3
la Pommeraye 114 B4
la Possonnière 116 B2
Lapoutroie 113 E1
La Provence 249 G5
La Quercia 171 D4
L'Aquila 169 E5
La Racha 177 C2
La Rambla 183 F3
Laredorte 124 B3
la Refène 68 F1, 67 F6
la Regrippière 114 F3
La Réole 80 G5
la Richemone 71 F3
La Riera 182 C4
La Rioja 251 B2
la Riotte 72 F4
Larisa 215 C3
Larnaca 216 C4
la Roche 121 B3
la Roche aux Moines 116 B3
la Roche-sur-Yon 59 D1, 131 B4
la Rochelle, Charente-Maritime 59 E1, 130 C4
la Rochelle, Chinon 117 E3
la Rochelle, Moulin-à-Vent 77 C4
la Rochère 118 C5
la Roilette 77 C4
la Romanée 71 F4
la Romanée 65 F5
la Romanée-Conti 71 F4
la Roncière 70 F6
Larsen 258 B5
la Salpetrière 117 B2
Lascazères 261 E4
La Secuita 182 F5
La Selva 182 F4
la Seyne-sur-Mer 126 D3
las Heras 251 A5
Las Irlas 182 G4
Laski Rizling 207 A3
la Solitude 123 C5
La Spezia 161 E5
Lasserre 267 B4
Lasseube 129 G1
Lasseubetat 128 G5
Lastra 171 A1
Las Vegas (Chile) 251 A2
la Tâche 71 F4
La Taconera 177 F3
Latakia (Al-Lādiqīyah) 220 E5
Latakie (Al-Lādiqīyah) 220 E5
la Thierrière 118 C4
Latina 169 F3, 172 B1
La Torre Alta 176 D6
la Tour du Bief 77 B5
Latour-de-France 124 D2
la Tour de Peilz 195 D1
Latricières 72 F5
La Trinidad 177 D2
la Tuilerie 97 F5
La Tula 177 E1
l'Auberdière 118 C3
Laudamusberg 143 E1
Laudun 120 G5
Lauffern 156 D4
Laujuzan 261 C3, 129 F2
Laure-Minervois 124 B3
Laurentiusberg 143 F1, 141 G6
Laurentiuslay 143 F1
Lauria 172 D4
Lausanne 194 B6, 197 F2, 270 G3
Lauw 113 G2
Laval 59 C1
la Valette-du-Var 126 C3
la Vallée 119 E2
la Vallée Chartier 118 C4
la Vallée Coquette 118 C2
la Vallée de Nouy 118 C3
la Vallée de Vaux 118 B5
Lavardac 129 D3
la Varogne 122 C3
Lavaux, Suisse 195 A1, 197 C2
Lavaux, Gevrey-Chambertin 93 E1
La Verne 230 G3
Lavey Morcles 195 D2
la Vigne au Saint 69 E3
Lavigny, Jura 127 G4
Lavigny, Suisse 194 B5
la Villatte 117 B2
La Villedieu-du-Temple 59 F2
la Voirosse 69 E3
la Voulte-sur-Rhône 120 D5
Lawrenceburg 269 B4
Lay 145 F2
La Zarzuela 177 D2
Lazio 169 E3, 172 B2
Lazise 166 C6
Leányka 202 A3, C3
le Bais Clair 259 B2
Lebanon (Al-Lubnan) 220 F4
Lebanon, Kentucky 269 C4
le Beausset 126 C3
le Bois Rideau 118 C3
le Boucou 123 C5
le Boulay 115 B1
le Bouscat 80 E3
le Bouscaut 95 E5
le Breynets 77 C5
le Cailleret 66 G3
le Cannet-des-Maures 126 B5
le Carquelin 77 C5
le Cassereau 118 B4
le Castellet 126 C2
Lecce 172 C6
le Champ-Canet 66 F5
le Champ de Cours 77 C5
le Champ-sur-Layon 116 E4
le Clos, Châteauneuf-du-Pape 123 C4
le Clos, Pouilly-Fuissé 75 F2
le Clos, Vernou-sur-Brenne 118 C4
le Clos Baulet 72 F4
le Clos des Chênes 67 F3
le Clos des Réas 71 F4
Le Corti 171 C2
le Corton 69 E4
Lectoure 129 E3
Le Creusot 61 D4, 59 D4
Ledaig 265 E3
le Désert 95 E4
Leef op Hoop 249 G3
Leeward Islands 267
le Fleix 105 E3
le Fougeray 118 B4
le Frèche 261 C3
le Frérie 75 E2
le Grand Carretey 97 A4
le Haut Cousse 118 B4
le Haut Lieu 118 C3
Le Havre 59 B1, 271 B2
Leibnitz 198 G1
Leimen 156 C5
Leinhöhle 153 F4
Leistadt 153 A4
Leiste, Würzburg 158 E5
Leitchfield 269 C3
Leiterchen 143 F1
Leiweu 142 G6
le Landreau 114 E2
Le Loroux-Bottereau 114 C3, E2
le Luc, Var 126 B4
le Luc, Cissac-Médoc 85 G2
Léman, lac 59 D5, 194 B6, 197 C2, 270 G3
le Mans 59 C1
le Mayors 126 C4
Lembras 105 E5
le Méal 122 C4
Le Mesnil-sur-Oger 107 F3
le Mont 118 C3
le Montrachet 66 G3
le Moulin 77 C4
le Moulin-à-Vent 77 C5
Le Muy 126 B5
Lenchen 150 F4
Lengenfeld 198 C1
Lens 195 C3
Léognan 80 F3, 95 F3
Léon 175 A2
Leopoldsberg 200 B3
l'Epaisse 117 B2
le Pallet 114 F2
le Paradis 119 F3
le Passe-Temps 65 F3
le Pave 77 F3
le Pellerin 114 C2
le Petit Mont 118 C2
le Petit-Pujeaux 91 G3
Le Pian-Médoc 93 G4
Le Piazze 171 F3
Le Pile e Lamole 171 D4
le Pin, Huismes 117 D3
le Pin, Jura 127 G4
le Plâtre 77 D4
le Point du Jour 77 C4
le Pontet 120 G5
le Port 121 C3
le Poruzot 66 F6
le Poruzot dessus 66 F6
le Pouyalet 87 B5
le Pradet 126 D3
le Pressoir 117 E5
le Puch 97 C5
le Puizac 119 F5
le Puy 59 E4, 131 D1
Leqé 114 D3
le Royal-Canadel 126 C5
le Richebourg 71 F4
Lérida 175 B5
le Rognet-Corton 69 F5
Le Rouxdorp 249 G6
les Aigrots 68 E3
les Amoureuses 72 F2
les Angles 67 F4
les Arcs 59 F6, 126 B5
les Argillats 71 E2
les Argillières 68 F1
les Armusèries 118 B2
les Arsures 127 E5
les Arvelets 67 E6, 68 E1, 73 E4
les Aubuis 117 E3
les Aussy 67 F4
les Avaux 68 F3
les Baraques de Gevrey Chambertin 73 F1
les Barguins 118 C3
les Bas-des-Teurous 68 F4
les Basses Vergelesses 69 E2
les Baudes 72 F3
les Baux 59 F5
les Belletins 118 F3
les Berthiers 118 F4
les Bertins 67 F5
les Bessards 122 C4
les Bidaudières 118 C4
les Bienvenues 66 G3
les Billaux 103 C1
les Blottières 117 B4
les Bonnes Mares 72 F3
les Borniques 72 F2
les Bouchères 66 F6
les Boucherottes 68 F2
les Bouchots 72 E4
les Bouthières 75 E3
les Bressandes 68 E5, F4
les Breuillards 119 E4
les Brussolles 65 F5
les Bruyères 77 E3
les Caillerets 67 F3
les Cailles 70 F6
les Calinottes 91 E5
les Capitans 77 A5
Lescar 129 G1
Les Carmes-Haut-Brion 95 A2
les Cassiers 119 F4
les Cent-Vignes 68 E5
les Chaboeufs 70 F6
les Chaillots 69 F4
les Chalumeaux 16 F4
les Champeaux 73 E2
les Champlains 74 D4
les Champonnets 73 E1
les Champs Fulliot 67 F3
les Champs' Gain 65 F6, 66 G1
les Champs Grilles 77 A5
les Chanlin 67 E5
les Chanlins Bas 67 E5
les Chanoriers 77 A4
les Chaponières 67 F5
les Charmes 72 F2
les Charmes dessous 66 G5
les Charmes dessus 66 G5
les Charmots 68 E1
les Charnières 69 D2
les Chassaignes 119 E2
Les Chatelots 72 F2
les Chaumes, Côte de Beaune 69 E3
les Chaumes, Côte Chalonnais 74 D3
les Chênes 77 D4
les Chenevottes 66 F2
les Chers 77 A4
les Chétives Maisons 110 F5
les Chouacheux 68 F3
les Claveries 97 G5
les Clos 79 D4
les-Clos-des-Mouches 68 E2
les Clos du Roi 69 F4
les Closeaux 117 E4
les Combes-dessus 67 F5
les Combettes 66 G4
les Corbeaux 73 F1
les Corvées Pagets 70 F4
les Cras, Côte de Beaune 67 F3
les Cras, Côte de Nuits 72 F2
les Crays 75 E2
les Criots 66 G2
les Croix-Noires 67 F5
les Deduits 77 C4
les Diognières 122 C5
les Duresses 67 E2
les Echézeaux 71 F5
les Echoppes 95 A2
les Epenots 68 F1
les Epenottes 68 F2
les Epinottes 79 D3
les Evois 117 B3
les Fèves 68 E5
les Fiètres 69 F3
les Fichots 69 E3
les Folatières 66 F4
les Fondis 117 B1
les Fontenys 73 E1
les Forêts 79 E3
les Fourneaux 79 D6
les Fournières 69 F3
les Fremières 72 F4
les Fremiers 67 F5
les Froichots 72 F4
les Fuées 72 F3
les Galuches 117 B2
les Garrants 77 C4
les Gaudets 77 D4
les Genevrières 72 E4
les Genevrières dessous 66 G6
les Genevrières dessus 66 F6
les Gimarets 77 C5
les Girardières 118 C4
les Girarmes 119 F4
les Goulots 73 E2
les Grandes Bastes 118 B5
les Grands Champs 67 E2
les Grands Cras 77 E4
les Grands Echézeaux 71 F5
les Gravières 65 F4
les Greffieux 122 C4
les Grèves 69 F4, 68 F5
Les Groseilles 72 F3
les Gruenchers 72 F4
les Guerets 69 E3
les Gués d'Amant 118 C2
les Guillattes 77 C5
les Hauts Champs 117 B3
les Hauts Jarrons 69 E1
les Hauts-Marconnets 68 E6
les Hauts-Pruliers 70 F6
les Hervelets 73 E4
les Jarollières 67 F5
Leskovac 207 E5
les Languettes 69 E4
les Larreys 72 F4
les Lavières 69 E2
les Lavrottes 72 F3
les Lèches 105 D4
les Lignes 117 D1
les Loges 119 F4
les Lurets 67 F4
les Lys 79 D3
les Macherelles 66 F2
les Madères 118 C5
les Marconnets 68 E6
les Maréchaude 69 F4
les Mayons 126 C4
les Meix 69 F3
les Ménétrières 75 F3
Les Mesneux 107 A3
les Millandes 72 F4
les Mitaus 67 F4
les Montremenots 68 E2
les Monts Damnés 118 F2
les Moriers 77 C4
les Murets 122 C5
les Musigny 71 F6, 72 F1
les Nabantons 69 E1
les Noirots 72 F3
les Noizons 68 E2
Lesparre-Médoc 80 C2
les Perrières 66 F5
les Perrières 68 E6, 69 F4
les Petites Bruyères 118 E4
les Petits Epenots 68 F2
les Petits-Monts 71 E4
les Petits Musigny 71 F6, 72 F1
les Petures 67 F3
les Peuillets 68 E6
les Pezerolles 68 F2
les Picasses 117 D3
les Pinchons 77 B5
les Pineaux 117 D3
les Pins 117 B2
les Pitures dessus 67 E5
les Planches-près-Arbois 127 E5
les Planchots 69 F3
les Plantes 72 F2
les Plessis 75 G3
les Porets 70 F6
les Pougets 69 E3
les Poulettes 70 F6
les Poutures 67 F5
les Preuses 79 C4
les Procès 71 F1
les Pruliers 70 F6
les Pucelles 66 G3
les Quarts 75 F3
les Raguenières 117 B3
les Referts 66 G4
les Reignots 71 F4
les Renardes 69 F4
les Réversées 68 F4
les Roches 118 C2
les Rocoules 122 C5
les Rosettes 117 F3
les Rouvrettes 69 E1
les Rugiens-Bas 67 F5
les Rugiens-Hauts 67 E5
les Ruchots 72 F3
les Sablons 117 B2
les Saint-Georges 70 F5
les Santenots Blancs 67 F3
les Santenots du Milieu 67 F3
les Saucilles 68 E2
les Saunières 65 D2
les Sentiers 72 F3
Lesser Antilles 267
les Seurey 68 F4
les Sicots 118 D4
les Sizies 68 F3
Lessona 161 B3
les Sorbés 72 F4
les Suchots 71 F4
les Talmettes 69 D2
les Teurons 68 F4
les Thorins 77 C5
les Toussaints 68 E5
les Vallerots 70 F6
les Valozières 69 F4
les Vaucrains 70 F5
les Verchers-sur-Layon 114 C5
les Vercots 69 E3
les Vergennes 69 F5
les Vergers 66 F2
les Véroilles 73 D1
les Verrillats 77 B5
les Vignes 118 E2
les Vignes Dessus 75 D2
les Vignes-Franches 68 F2
Lesvos 215 C5
le Teil 120 E5
le Tholonet 126 B2
le Thoronet 126 B4
l'Etoile, Vernou-sur-Brenne 118 C4
l'Étoile, Jura 127 G4
le Tris 91 E1
Letten 153 E5
Letterlay 145 B3
Leucate 124 D3
Leuk 195 C4
Leutschach 198 G1
le Vau Breton 117 F4
le Velay 121 F2
le Vernois 127 G4
le Vieux Télégraphe 123 C5
le Vivier 77 C5
Levice 205 C5
Levkas 215 C2
Lexington 269 B4
Leynes 75 F2
Leyssac 85 F4
Leytron 195 D2
Lézignan-Corbières 59 G3, 124 C3, 131 E1
Lhanbryde 263 A3
l'Hermite 122 C4
l'Homme, Hermitage 122 C5
l'Homme, Sarthe 115 A1
l'Homme Mort 79 B3
Liban (Al-Lubnan) 220 F4
Liberec 205 A4
Libertas 249 G2
Liberty 234 B1
Libourne 59 F1, 80 E4, 99 D1, 103 D1
Liebfrauenberg 139 C2
Liebfrauenmorgen 155 G3
Lieser 144 F6
Liesing 200 D3
Liestal 270 E4
Ligist 198 F1
Ligné 114 B3
Ligré 117 F4
Liguria 161 E4
l'Ile Bouchard 117 F6
l'Ile Rousse 132 D5
Lille 59 A3
Lilliano 171 F3
Lima 250 B1
Limassol 216 D2
Limburg 135 A3
Limmattal 197 B4
Limnos 215 D4
Limoges 59 E2, 130 C6
Limony 121 F2
Limoux 124 B1
Linares 250 C1
Lincoln, England 252 E5
Lincoln Village 234 C3
Lindos 215 E6
Linkwood 261 A3
Linsenbusch 153 G5
Linton 252 F5
Lipnita 209 G5
Lirac 120 G5
Lisbon (Lisboa) 187 E3, 188 F3
Lisbonne (Lisboa) 187 E3, 188 F3
Lisle-sur-Tarn 129 E6
Listrac-Médoc 91 F2
Lithgow 241 E5
Litoměrice 205 A4
Little Karoo 247 D4
Littlemill 265 E4
Live Oaks 237 C4
Livermore 237 A3
Liverpool, Australia 241 E5
Livingston 234 E4
Livorno 169 A2
Livron-sur-Drôme 120 D5
Ljubljana 207 B2
Ljutomer 207 B3
Llanarth 252 F3
Lloa 182 G3
Llorens del Panadés 182 F5
Lloyd Light 245 B5
Locarno 197 G4
Loché 75 F3
Lochnagar-Royal 265 D5
Lochside 265 D5
Lockeford 234 B2
Locorotondo 172 C5
Lodi 234 B3
Lodoline 171 F4
Logroño 175 A4
Logroño 180 B6
Loiben 198 C2
Loibenberg 201 G2
Loire 59 E4, 120 A5
Loire-Atlantique 58 C6, 114 B2
Loiret 59 C3, 115 A4
Loir-et-Cher 59 C2, 115 B3
Loire Valley 59 D1, D2, C2
l'Olivier 118 C1
Lombardia 161 B5
Lomond 265 E4
Lonay 194 B5
London (Kentucky) 269 C5
Long Beach 229 G4
Longemer 113 E1
Longmorn 263 B2
Long Pond 266 A3
Longueteau 267 C4
Lons-le-Saunier 59 D5, 127 G4
Lorch 135 B3
Lorenzhöfer 141 E4
Loretta 269 C4
Lorettoberg 156 F1
L'Orléannais 115 A4
Lormont 80 E3
Lorques 126 B4
Lörrach 156 G1
Los Angeles 229 G3
Los Angeles Co. 230 F3
Los Barrios 177 F2
Los Cuadrados 177 D1
Los Esteves 177 C4
Los Gatos 237 C2
Lösnich 144 C6
Los Tercios 177 E1
Lot 59 F2
Lot-et-Garonne 59 F2, 80 G6, 261 B4
Louis M. Martini 233 B4
Louisville 269 B3
Loupiac 80 F4
Loureiro 190 F1
Lousa 188 E3
Lousada 189 C5
Louvois 107 C5
Louroujina 216 C4
Lovech 211 C3
Lower Belford 242 D2
Lozère 59 F4
Lo Zucco 172 F2
Lucca 169 A3
Lucena 183 G4
Lucenec 205 B5

Ockley, Surrey 252 D4
Odenas 77 G3
Odessa 213 A2
Odobesti 209 F4
Oeiras 188 F2
Oestrich 150 F5
Offenburg 261 C4, 156 E2, 135 E3
Offley Forrester 193 C4
Offstein 155 G3
Oger 107 F3
Oggau 198 D3
O'Higgins 251 C3, 250 C1
Ohligsberg 143 D3
Ohrid 207 G4
Oise 59 B2
Oksamit Ukraine 213 A2
Olaszliszka 203 C5
Olazrizling 202 A3, C3, C2, B2
Olbia 172 C2
Ölberg 154 E4
Old Boone 269 B3
Old Fitzgerald 269 B3
Old Hoffman 269 B4
Oldmeldrum 265 D6
Old Stanley 269 C3
Olerdola 182 F6
Olesa de Bonesvalis 182 F6
Oliena 169 F2, 172 D2
Oliveira do Hospital 189 G5
Olivella 182 F6
Ollauri 180 B5
Ollon 195 C2
Olonzac 124 B3, 59 G3
Oloron Ste Marie 129 G1
Oltrepo 161 D5
Omodhos 216 D2
Ond 203 C3
Onkelchen 146 F6
Ontario, California 230 G4
Oplenačka Ružica 207 D5
Opol 207 E2
Oppenheim 135 B4, 154 F5
Ora 166 F3
Oradea 209 E2
Oran 219 B1
Orange, France 120 F5
Orange, Australia 241 E4
Orange, California 229 G4
Orange Cove 235 G2
Orbaneja 177 C2
Orbel 154 E4
Orbost 241 G4
Ord 265 C4
Ordensgut 153 D1
Orense 175 A2
Oriano 251 C3
Oristano 172 D1
Orkney Islands 265 A5
Orlando 244 C4
Orléans 115 A4, 59 C2
Ormanni 171 E2
Ormož 207 B3
Orne 59 B1
Orschwihr 110 A2
Ortenau 156 E2, 135 E3
Ortenburg 156 E2
Orthez 129 F1
Orvieto 169 D3
Orvieto Classico 169 D3
Oshakan 213 D4
Oschelskopf 153 A4
Osijek 207 C4
Ospiel 158 E4
Ossès 128 G6
Osteiermark 198 F2
Oster Höll 147 D1
Osterberg 153 A5
Osterreich 198
Ostheim 113 D2
Osthofen 155 F3
Ostrov 209 G5
Otsuki 222 C4
Ostuni 172 C5
O'Sullivan Beach 245 B3
Otard-Dupuy 258 A5
Otley 252 F6
Oudtshoorn 247 D6
Oujda 218 C6
Ouyen 241 E1
Overgaauw 249 G1
Oviedo 175 A3
Owensboro 269 C3
Owenton 269 B4
Oxted, Surrey 252 D4
Ozieri 172 D1

P

Paarl 247 D2, 249 C4, C5
Paarlberg 249 C4
Paarl Valley 249 C5
Pachs 182 F6
Pachino 172 G3
Pacos de Ferreira 189 C5
Padavero 211 C5, D5
Padoue (Padova) 165 E4
Padova 165 E4
Padthaway 240 G6
Padua (Padova) 165 E4
Paducah 269 C2
Pag 207 C2
Paganilla 176 C5
Pagliarese 171 G5
Paignton, Devon 252 D2
Paillot 119 E4
Paine 251 C3
Paintsville 269 B5
Pakhna 216 D2
Paks 202 C2
Palamino & Vergara 177 G2
Palazzo al Bosco 171 B2
Palencia 175 B3
Palermo 172 F2
Pallaresos 182 G5
Pallette 126 B1
Palmi 175 E4
Palo Alto 237 A2
Paloumey 93 F5
Pamhagen 198 D4
Pamid 211 D2
Pamplona 175 A4
Panadés 182 F6, 175
Panciu 209 F4
Paneretta 171 E2
Pangbourne 252 F5
Panjas 261 C4, 129 E2
Pano Lefkara 216 D3
Pano Panayia 216 C2
Pano Platres 216 C2
Páola 172 D4
Paola 216 G2
Papagni 234 F6
Paphos 216 D1
Para (North) 244 B4
Parada do Bispo 190 G3
Paradale 244 B4
Paradelinha 190 D6
Paradiesgarten 153 F4
Paraguay 251 A3
Paramaribo 250 B2
Parana 251 A4
Parducci Winery 230 A4
Paredes 189 C5
Paredes de Coura 189 A4
Paradies 145 C2
Paris 59 B3
Parkes 241 D4
Parlier 235 G1
Parma (Parme) 165 F2
Parnac 129 C4
Paros 215 E4
Parpalana 177 F3
Parramatta 241 E5
Parsac 103 D5
Parys 249 D4
Pasadena 229 F4
Pas-de-Calais 59 A2
Passa 124 E2
Passenans 127 F4
Pastori 230 B4
Pastrengo 167 C1
Paterberg 154 F5
Paterhof 154/155 G6
Paterno 172 F3
Patrai 215 D2
Patras (Patrai) 215 D2
Patrimonio 132 B2
Patriti 245 A4
Pau 59 G1, 129 G1
Paulhan 125 C6
Paulinsberg 141 F4, 143 C3
Paulinshofberg 143 B3
Paulinslay 143 A4
Paul Masson 237 B2, F5, G5, 234 F6
Paul Robert 219 B2
Paulsberg 144 E5, E6
Pauillac 80 C2, 85 G5, 87 C5
Pavia 161 C5
Pavlikeni 211 C3
Paxton 242 G2
Pazardzhik 211 D3
Paziols 124 D2
Peć 207 F4
Pechstein 153 E4
Pécs 202 C2
Pedrizetti 237 C4
Pedro Domecq 177 D2, C3
Pedroncelli 230 B4
Peissy 194 D3
Pekre 207 B2
Pelequen 251 C2
Pelješac 207 E3
Pellaro 172 F4
Peloponnese (Peloponnisos) 215 D2
Peloponnisos 215 D2
Pembroke, Pembrokeshire 252 F3
Penafiel 187 B4, 189 C5
Peñaflor 251 B2
Penalva do Castelo 189 E5
Peney 194 D3
Penfold's 244 B4
Penfold's H.V.D. 242 F2
Penrice 245 B5
Pépieux 124 B3
Peplina Stepu 213 A2
Perafort 182 G5
Perchtoldsdorf 198 D3, 200 D3
Perdeberg 249 B4
Pères Blancs 267 C4
Péret 125 B6
Périgueux 59 E2, 130 C5
Pernand-Vergelesses 69 D4
Pernand-Vergelesses 61 C5
Pernik 211 C2
Pérou (Péru) 250 B1
Pérouse (Perugia) 169 C4
Perpignan 59 G3, 124 E2
Perrière Noblet 71 E3
Perrier-Jouet 109 F4
Perrin 121 E1
Perroy 194 B5
Perth 265 E5
Pertuisots 68 F3
Peru 250 B1
Perugia 169 C4
Perushtica 211 D3
Pesaro 169 B6
Pescantina 167 C2
Pescara 269 F6
Peschiera del Garda 166 C6
Peso da Regua 190 G2
Pessac 80 F2, 95 A2
Pessione 163 B2
Peterborough 240 D5
Peterhead 265 C6
Petersburg 155 F2
Petit Bois 95 A4
Petite Chapelle 72 F6
Petit Favray 119 E5
Petit Figeac 161 B2
Petit Soumard 119 F4
Petits Godeaux 69 D2
Petits Vougeots 71 F6, 72 F1
Petreto-Bicchisano 132 F5
Pettenthal 154 C5
Peynier 126 B2
Peyrehorade 128 F6
Peyriac-Minervois 124 B3
Pez 85 E4
Peza 215 F4
Pézenas 125 C6
Pezinok 205 C5
Pfaffenberg 201 F3, 150 G6
Pfaffengrund 153 C2
Pfaffenheim 110 C4
Pfaffenstein 146 G5
Pfaffstätten 200 F2
Pfingstweide 146 F5
Pforzheim 156 D3, 135 D4
Phillippeville (Skikda) 219 B4
Philpot 269 C3
Piacenza 161 D5
Pian d'Albola 171 D4
Piazza Armerina 172 F3
Piccolit 165 C5
Pichetti 237 B2
Picpoul de Pinet 125 C6, 131 E1
Pic-St-Loup 59 F4, 125 B2
Pied d'Aloup 79 D5
Piedicroce 132 E5
Piemonte 162
Piemonte 161 C2
Pierrefeu-du-Var 126 C4
Pierreux 77 G5
Pierrevert 59 F5
Pierry 107 E2
Piesport 143 C2, 135 B2
Pignans 126 C4
Pignerol (Pinerolo) 161 D2
Piketberg 247 C2
Pikkara 245 D4
Pilgerpfad 155 F3
Pilos 215 E2
Pilton 252 F4
Pimpala 245 B4
Pineau-Gris Ai Danil 213 C2
Pinedale 235 F1
Pinerolo 161 D2
Pinet 59 G4, 125 C6
Pinhao 190 F6
Pinhel 189 C5
Pinot 165 C3
Pinot Bijeli 207 C1
Pinot gris 209 E3, F5, G5
Pinot Noir 209 F5, G3, G5
Pintéus 188 E3
Pintray 118 D6
Piper, Delbeck & Co. 109 C5
Pirgos 215 D2
Pirin Planina 211 D2
Pirramimma 245 D4
Pirrone 234 D4
Pisa 169 A2
Pissouri 216 D2
Pistoia 169 A3
Piteşti 209 F3
Pitigliano 169 C3
Pitlochry 265 D5
Pitsilia 216 D2
Pittyraich-Glenlivet 263 E4
Pizay 77 E4
Plaisance (Piacenza) 161 D5
Plaisir de Merle 249 E3
Planada 235 G4
Planá del Panadés 182 F5
Plan-de-la-Tour 126 C5
Planèzes 124 D2
Planoiseau 127 G4
Plantes 72 F2
Plassac 104 D1
Plavac 207 D2, E3
Plavina 207 D2, E2
Plavka 207 F4
Pleasant Valley 238 D2
Pleasanton 237 A3
Plechistika 213 A4
Plemenka 207 C5, F5
Plemenka Ružica 207 C3
Pleven 211 B3
Plobsheim 113 C2
Ploeşti 209 F4
Plovdina 207 E5, G4
Plovdiv 211 D3
Plume la Poule 95 B4
Plumpton Green, Sussex 252 D4
Plush Corner 245 B5
Plzeň 205 B3
Pobla de Mafumet 182 G4
Pobla de Montornes 182 G5
Poboleda 182 F3
Podersdorf 198 D4
Poggibonsi 171 E2
Poiares 190 F3
Poinchy 79 D3
Pointe-à-Pitre 267 C4
Pointes-d'Angles 67 F5
Poissenot 73 E1
Poitiers 59 D2, 130 B5
Pokolbin 242 F2
Polcevera 161 E4
Poligny 127 F5
Pollestres 124 E2
Pollino 172 D4
Pol Roger 118 G5
Pomerol 80 E4, 101 A1, 103 C2
Pommard 61 D5, 67 F5, 68 E1
Pommery et Greno 109 C6
Pomona 230 G3
Pomorie 211 C6
Pomport 105 F4
Ponce 267 B2
Ponce, Jerez 177 C3
Poncey 74 E4
Ponchapt 105 E3
Pontac 95 C4
Ponte da Barca 189 B5
Ponte de Lima 189 B4
Ponteilla 124 E2
Ponte-Leccia 132 E5
Pontevedra 175 A1
Pontóns 182 F5
Pontremoli 161 E5
Pont-St-Esprit 120 F5
Pordenone 165 D5
Poreč 207 B1
Poros 215 D3
Porrera 182 F3
Portacomaro 163 B4
Port Adelaide 240 E5
Portalegre 187 E5
Port Augusta 240 D5
Port-au-Prince 266 A5
Port Dundas 265 F4
Port Ellen 265 F2
Porterville 247 C2
Portet 261 D3
Portgordon 263 A5
Port Guyet 117 B1
Port Kembla 241 E5
Portland 241 G1
Port Noarlunga 245 C4
Port Noarlunga South 245 C3
Porto 187 B4, 189 C4, 132 E4
Porto Alegre 250 C2
Porto da Cruz 185 C5
Port of Spain 267 E4
Porto Moniz 185 A1
Porto Tolle 165 F4
Porto Vecchio 132 G6
Port Pirie 240 D5
Portree 265 C2
Port Said (Būr Sa'īd) 220 G3
Port-Ste-Foy-et-Ponchapt 105 E3
Portugal 187
Portugizac 103 B2
Port Valais 91 C1
Port Vendres 124 F2
Port Willunga 245 D3
Pošip 207 E2
Postup 207 E3
Potenza 172 C4
Pothana 242 E2
Pouilly 75 E3
Pouilly-Fuissé 75 E2
Pouilly-Loché 75 F3
Pouilly-sur-Loire 115 B6, 119 G4
Pouilly-Vinzelles 75 F4
Pourcleux 126 B3
Pourrières 126 B2
Pouvray 118 B4
Pouzols-Minervois 124 B4
Póvoa de Varzim 189 C4
Poysdorf 198 B3
Pradell 182 G3
Praha (Prague) 205 B4
Praia da Adraga 188 E1
Praia das Maças 188 E1
Prangins 194 B4
Prat de Llobregat 183 F1
Pratdip 182 C3
Pratteln 270 E4
Prayssac 129 C4
Preignac 97 C6, D4, D5
Prellenkirchen 198 D4
Prémeaux 70 F4
Premières Côtes de Bordeaux 80 F4
Presinge 194 D4
Preslav 211 C5
Prestonsburg 269 C6
Prestwick 265 F4
Préverenges 194 B5
Prievidza 205 B5
Prignac-et-Cazelles 104 G5
Prigonrieux 105 E4
Prilep 207 G5
Primativo 172 C5
Prince de Polignac 258 A5
Princeton 269 C2
Priorato 175 B5, 182 G3
Prissé 75 D4
Prissé D3
Priština 207 F5
Privas 59 F4, 131 D2
Prizren 207 F5
Procanico 169 B1
Prokupac 207 D6, E5, F6, G4
Prokupac Ružica 207 D5
Propriano 132 G5
Prosecco 165 D4
Prošek 207 D2
Provence 59 G5
Provesende 190 E6
Providence 209 C2
Provitaro 172 E4
Prüm 135 A1
Pruzilly 77 A4
Psara 215 C4
Ptuj 207 B3
Puente Alto 251 B2
Puente Genil 183 G3
Puerto de Santa Maria 177 F4
Puerto Rico Distillers 267 A2
Puget-sur-Argens 126 B5
Puget-Ville 126 C4
Puglia 172 C4
Puigpelat 182 F5
Puisieux 107 B4
Puisseguin 103 D5
Pujols 80 F5
Pukhlyakovskoe 213 A4
Pulchen 139 B2
Puligny-Montrachet 61 D5, 66 G3
Pulkau 198 B2
Pully 194 B6
Pulteney 265 B5
Pupillin 127 E5
Purbach 198 D3
Purleigh 252 F6, F5
Puy-de-Dôme 59 E3
Puyguilhem 105 F4
Puy-l'Evêque 129 C4
Puyloubier 126 B2
Puyoô 59 G1
Puy Rigaud 117 D2
Pyrenées Orientales 59 G3, 124 E2

Q

Quarts de Chaume 116 D3
Quartorse La Clape 131 F1
Quatourze 124 C4
Queanbeyan 241 F5
Querceto e Santa Lucia 171 C3
Queretaro 251 F2
Queyssac 105 D5
Quillan 124 C1
Quillota 251 B2
Quilpué 251 B2
Quincy 115 C4
Quinta Amarela 191 F1
Quinta da Alegria 191 F4
Quinta da Baleira 191 G4
Quinta da Boa Vista 190 F3
Quinta da Cabana 190 F3
Quinta da Cachucha 190 F6
Quinta da Carvalheira 191 F2
Quinta da Costa 191 D1
Quinta da Costa de Bo 190 F5
Quinta da Ferrad 190 G4
Quinta da Ferradosa 191 G4
Quinta da Foz 190 F6, 190 G3
Quinta da Foz de Temjlobos 190 G3
Quinta da Lagoa Alta 190 F5
Quinta da Pacheca 190 G2
Quinta da Passadoura 191 E1
Quinta da Pilarrela 190 E2
Quinta da Poca 190 F6
Quinta da Portela 190 G4
Quinta da Ribeira 190 D6
Quinta da Sapa de B. 190 F6
Quintas das Baratas 191 F1
Quinta das Carvalhas 191 F1
Quinta da Senhora da Ribeira 191 G6
Quinta da serra 191 F1
Quinta das Lajes 191 G1
Quinta das Manuelas 191 D1
Quinta da Teixeira 191 F1
Quinta da Torre 190 G3
Quinta da Vacaria 190 G2
Quinta de Bagauste 190 G3
Quinta de Campanha 190 F2
Quinta de Napoles 190 G5
Quinta de Roeda 191 F1
Quinta de Romarigo 190 F2
Quinta de Santa Barbara 190 G2
Quinta de São Martinho 191 F3
Quinta de Tourais 190 G2
Quinta de Ventozelo 191 F1
Quinta do Arnozelo 191 G5
Quinta do Barrilario 190 G4
Quinta do Bom Dia 190 F5
Quinta do Bom Retiro 191 F1
Quinta do Bonfim 191 F1
Quinta do Bragão 191 E1
Quinta do Canal 190 G3
Quinta do Carneiro 190 G2
Quinta do Castelinho 191 F3
Quinta do Castello Borges 190 G5
Quinto do Charondo 191 G1
Quinta do Cibio 191 E2
Quinta do Cipreste 191 E3
Quinta do Crasto 190 F5
Quinta do Dr. Christiano 191 G2
Quinta do Eiravelha 190 F6
Quinta do Fojo 191 D1
Quinta do Garcia 190 G2
Quinta do Junco 190 E6
Quinta do Lelo 191 F1
Quinta do Merouco 191 E2
Quinta do Mourão 190 G2
Quinta do Noval 191 E1
Quinta do Panascal 190 G6
Quinta do Pedrogão 191 G2
Quinta do Pego 190 G6
Quinta do Peso 190 F3
Quinta do Roriz 191 F2
Quinta do Sagrado 190 F6
Quinta dos Canais 191 G5
Quinta dos Currais 190 G2
Quinta do Seino 190 F6
Quinta dos Frades 190 G4
Quinta do Silval 191 E1
Quinta dos Lagares 191 D1, 190 F2
Quinta dos Malvedos 191 E2
Quinta do Sol 190 G3
Quinta do Tedo 190 G5
Quinta do Vale de Figuira 190 F6
Quinta do Vale de Sapos 190 G2
Quinta do Vargelas 191 G5
Quinta do Vesúvio 191 G6
Quinta do zambujal 190 G3
Quinta do zimbro 191 G6
Quinta Milieu 191 E3
Quinta Nova do Roncão 191 E1
Quinta Velha 190 G2
Quintigny 127 G4
Quorn 240 D5

R

Rabastens 129 E5
Rabat 216 G2, 218 C4
Rabelais 219 B2
Rablay-sur-Layon 116 D4
Raboatun 177 D4
Raboso Piave 165 D4
Rača 205 C5
Radda in Chianti 171 E4
Radgonska Ranina (Tigrovo Mleko) 207 B3
Ragusa 172 G3
Raiding 198 E3
Rainha Santa 193 C4
Rama Caida 251 D5
Ram Allah 220 F4
Ramatuelle 126 C5
Ramos Pinto 193 C4, B4
Rancagua 251 C3
Randersacker 158 E3, D5
Randogne 195 C4
Rapsani 215 C3
Raron 195 C5
Rastatt 156 D2
Rasteau 120 F6
Rátka 203 C3
Rauenthal 151 D4
Rausch 139 E2
Ravello 172 C3
Ravenna (Ravenne) 169 A5, 165 G4
Ravensburg 158 D3
Ray, Martin 237 B2
Raymond 233 B4
Razac-de-Saussignac 105 E3
Razac d'Eymet 105 F4
Razgrad 211 B4
Rcatzitelli 211 B5, D5, D1
Rebeninha 191 E1
Rebstöckel 153 C1
Rebula 207 B1
Rech-Bächel 153 D4
Rechnitz 198 F3
Recioto 165 D2
Reedley 235 G1
Refosko 207 B1
Refosco 165 D5
Rege Winery 230 A4
Reggio di Calabria 172 F4
Reggio Emilia 165 F2
Regina Grape Products 230 F5
Régua 187 B5
Reigny 119 F2
Reims 59 B4, 109 A3
Reinsport 143 D2
Reiterpfad 153 F4
Rekord 207 E6
Remigny 65 G4
Remstal Stuttgart 135 E5
Remy Martin 258 B5
Renau 182 F5
Renault 219 B1
Renchen 270 C4
Rengo 251 C2
Renmark 240 E6
Rennes 58 C6
Renski Rizling 207 A3
Requeña y Utiel 175 C4
Resende 189 D6
Restigné 117 B3
Retsina 215 D3
Retz 198 B2
Reugne 67 E2
Reuilly 115 C4
Reus 182 G4
Reutlingen 135 E5
Reynella 245 B4
Reynells 245 B4
Rezé 114 C3, F1
Rhein 197 B3, 270 C4, 135 A2
Rheinblick 155 F3
Rheinburgengau 135 A3
Rheinfelden 270 E4
Rheingau 135 B3, 149, 150, 151
Rheingrafenstein 155 F2
Rheinhessen 135, 154, 155
Rheinpfalz 152, 135 C3
Rheintal 197 B5
Rhinau 270 D4
Rhône 59 D4, 61 G5, 197 D2
Rialto 230 G6
Ribagnac 105 F5
Ribalonga 191 E3
Ribatejo 187 E4
Ribaudy 121 E1
Ribeauvillé 270 D3, 111 C4, 113 D2
Ribeira Brava 185 D2
Ribeira de Penha 189 B6
Ricard-Bisquit Dubouché 259 B3
Richert 237 C3
Richmond 269 C4
Richon-le-Zion 220 F4
Riddes 195 D3
Riebeek-Wes 247 C2
Riegersburg 198 F2
Riesling 165 C3, D6, 209 E2, E3, E5, F3, F5, G3, G5, 211 B5, D1, 213 A4, B2, B3
Rieti 169 E4
Rieux-Minervois 124 B3
Riex 194 B6
Rijeka 207 B2
Rilly 107 B4
Rimavska Sobota 205 B6
Rimini 169 B5
Rio Bom 190 G1
Rio de Janeiro 250 C2
Rio Ebro 180-1
Rio Grande do Sul 251 B4
Rioja 180
Rioja Alavesa 180 B5, B6
Rioja Alta 175 A4, 180 B5
Rioja Baja 175 A4, 181 C2
Rioja Valley 181
Rio Minho 189 A5
Rio Negro 251 D2
Ripaille 183 A2
Ripon 234 D3
Riquewihr 111 C3, 113 D2
Riscle 129 F2
Ritsch 142 F5
Rittergarten 153 B4
Ritterpfad 139 C2
Rittersberg 156 C3
Ritzling 200 G5
Riudecols 182 G4
Riudoms 182 G4
Riva 165 D2
Rivadavia 251 B5
Riverbank 234 D4
Riverina 241 E3
Riversdale 247 D5
Riverside 229 F4, G5
Riversmeet 249 E4
Riversaltes 124 G2
Riviera del Garda 165 D2, 166 B5
Rivoli Veronese 167 B1
Rizling 201 G6

Soave Classico 167 C5
Societa Esportazione Vini Affini 171 C4
Sofia 211 C2
Soïtue 251 D5
Soke 220 C1
Sokolov 205 B3
Solano 229 D2
Soledad 237 F5
Solenzara 132 F6
Solliès-Pont 126 C3
Solnechnaya Dolina 213 B2
Solopaca 172 B3
Solothurn 197 E3, 270 E4
Solotoje polje 213 A2
Soltvadkert 202 C3
Solutré-Pouilly 75 E2
Sombernon 61 C5
Somerset 269 C4
Somerset West 247 D2
Somló 202 B1
Somlóire 114 C5
Somme 59 A2
Sommerach 158 D4
Sommerhausen 158 G3
Somontano 175 A5
Sonnay 117 E5
Sonnenberg 139 A5, 139 C3, 139 E3
Sonnenberg, Ruwer 139 A5, D3
Sonnenberg Nahe 146 F6
Sonnenberg Rheingan 151 F4
Sonnenglanz 111 C3
Sonnenlay 144 G6, 145 C3
Sonnenuhr 145 D1
Sonnseite 143 C4, E3
Sonoma 229 D1, 233 F4
Sonoma Vineyard 230 C5
Sooss 200 G2
Soppe-le-Bas 113 G2
Sopron 198 E3, 202 B1
Soral 194 D3
Sorbara 165 F2
Sorgues 120 G5
Soria 175 D4
Soriano 251 C3
Sorni 165 C2
Sottocenerri 197 D4
Sotteceneri 197 D4
Soublecause 261 D4
Soultz 113 F2
Soultzmatt 110 B3
Sous le Dos d'Ane 66 F5
Sous-le-Puits 66 F4
Soussans 91 G6, 93 A2
Sousse 219 B6
Soutelo do Douro 191 F2
South Africa 247
South America 250
South Australia 240, 244
Southern Mount 245 D4
Southern Vales 240 E5, 245 A3
Southern Vales Co-op 245 D4
South Esk 245 D5
South Kilworth 252 E5
Souverain 230 B5
Spain (España) 175
Spannberg 198 C3
Sparkling Vale 242 F2
Sparti 215 E3
Spey 263 C4, 265 C5
Spey Bay 263 A5
Speyburn 263 C3
Speyer 135 C4
Speyerdorf Lachen 153 C2
Speyside 265 D4
Spiegelberg 155 E4
Spielberg 153 B4
Spielfeld 198 G2
Spiesheim 155 F2
Spitz 198 C1
Split 207 D2
Spoleto 169 D4
Sporen 111 C3
Spottswoode 233 B3
Spring Mountain 233 B2
Springbank 265 F3
Springton 244 E6
Squinzano 172 C6
Srbija (Serbia) 207 E4
Stags Leap Wine Cellars 233 D5
Stainz 198 G1
Stalden 195 C6
Stanhope 242 D3
Stanislaus 234 C4, D4, 229 D2
Stara Planina 211 C1, C2, C3, C4
Stara Zagora 211 D4
Star Hill 269 C4
Starkenburg 145 C4, 156 B3
Staufen 270 F3, D4
Staufenberg 156 C4
Stawell 241 F1
Stefanesti 209 F4
Steige 270 D3
Steiger Dell 147 F1
Steigerwald 158 E4
Steinacker 153 A4
Stein a.d. Donau 201 F3
Steinbach 156 D2
Steinberg, Saar 139 B2
Steinberg, Nahe 146 G4
Steinberg, Rheingau 150 E6
Steinberg Rheinpfalz 153 B4
Steinen 270 E4, F5
Steinmorgen 151 F2
Steinweg 147 D1
Steinwingert 146 G5
Stein, Würzburg 158 D4, D5
Steffensberg 145 B2, 145 B4
Stellenbosch 247 D2, 249 F2
Stenfanslay 143 C4
Stephan-Rosengärtchen 145 G2
Sterea Ellas 215 C3
Sterling Winery 233 A2
Stetten 156 D4, 270 E4
Stift 153 E5
Stift Heiligenkreuz 200 E3
Stiftsberg 156 C3
Stirling 265 E4
Stockbridge, Hampshire 252 D3
Stockton Distillers 234 B3
Stockton 229 D2, 234 C3
Stockwell 244 A5
Stonegate 233 A2
Stonehaven 265 D6
Stony Hill Winery 233 A2
Straden 198 G2
Strand 247 D2
Stranraer 265 G3
Strasbourg 59 B5, 270 C4, 113 B2
Strass 198 C2
Strathclyde 265 F4
Strathisla 263 C6
Strathmill 263 C6
Strem 198 F3
Stromberg 156 D3
Sturovo 205 C5
Stuttgart 135 E5, 156 D3
Subirats 182 F6
Subotica 207 C5
Suceava 209 D4
Südsteiermark 198
Suisse 197
Suisse (Schweiz) 270
Sukhindol 211 C3
Sulmona 172 B2
Sulzfeld 158 F4
Sumen 211 B5
Summerhausen 158 E3
Sungurlare 211 C5
Suni 172 D1
Sunny St Helena Winery 233 B4
Sunshine 242 E2
Suntory 222 C2
Surinam (Suriname) 250 B2
Suriname 250 B2
Sur Lavelle 67 E3
Sur-les-Gréves 68 E4
Sursee 270 E4
Sury-en-Vaux 119 E2
Sussenberg 144 F6
Süsskopf 153 E5
Sutter Home Winery 233 B3
Suzon 95 A4
Svery Peter 205 C5
Svetozarevo 207 E5
Svishtov 211 B3
Swan Hill 241 F1, 241 F2
Swellendam 247 D4
Switzerland 196, 197
Switzerland (Schweiz) 197, 270
Switzerland-Valais and Vaud 194
Sybillenstein 155 F2
Sydney 241 E5
Sylvaner 165 D4
Sympérieux 121 C2
Syracuse, Sicily 172 G4
Syria (As-Sūrīyah) 220 E5
Syrie (As-Sūrīyah) 202 E5
Szamorodni 202 A4
Szarvas 202 C3
Szeged 202 C3
Szegilong 203 C4
Szekszárd 202 C2
Szerencs 203 C3
Szigliget 204 F2
Szilváni 202 C2
Szolnok 202 B3
Szombathely 202 B1
Szürkebarát 202 C2

T

Tabajete, Caserio 177 B2
Tabanon 267 C4
Tábua 189 G4
Tacna 250 C1
Tadousse-Ussau 261 E3
Tagus (Tajo) 175 C2
Tahbilk 241 F3
Taille-Pieds 67 F4
Tain 265 C4
Tain-l'Hermitage 120 B6, 122 C3
Taittinger 109 C5
Tajo 175 C2
Talagante 251 B2
Talca 250 C1, 251 D2
Talence 80 F3
Talence 95 B3
Talisker 265 D2
Tallawanta 242 F2
Tállya 202 B3, 203 C3
Tamarit 182 G5
Tamdhu 263 E1
Tamianka 211 B2, D4
Tămîioasă 209 D4, F3
Tamnavoulin 263 G2
Tanger 218 B5
Tanunda 245 B4
Tapolca 204 E3
Tarābulus 220 E4
Taradeau 126 B4
Taranto 172 C5
Tarapaca 250 C1
Tarbes 59 G2, 129 G2
Tarcal 203 D4
Taree 241 D6
Tarn 59 F3
Tarn-et-Garonne 59 F2
Tarragona 175 B5, 182 G3, G4
Tartara 121 B3
Tartegnin 194 B4
Taubenberg 151 F3
Taubenhaus 145 E3
Taupine 67 E3
Taurasi 172 C3
Tauriac 104 F5
Taurus Mountains (Toros Daglari) 220 D3
Tauxières-Mutry 107 D4
Tavarnelle 171 D2
Tavel 120 G5
Tavers 115 A3
Tay 265 D4
Taylor 193 C4
Taylor Wine Co. 238 D2
Tbilisi 213 C5
Teaninich 265 C4
Tehigo 177 F5
Tekirdağ 220 B2
Tel Aviv-Yafo 220 F4
Teliani 213 C4
Temora 241 E3
Tempio Pausania 172 C1
Tenarèze 261 C5
Teno 251 D2
Tenuta Ricavo (Hotel) 171 E3
Teramo 169 E5
Teran 207 B1, G6
Terciona 171 C3
Terlano 165 C3, 166 C2
Termeno 166 F2
Términi 172 F2
Ternay 114 C6
Terni 169 D4
Teroldego 165 C2
Terras do Bouro 189 B5
Terrats 124 E2
Terskoye 213 C6
Teruel 175 B4
Tetouan 218 B5
Teufelskeller 158 F6
Teuillac 104 E4
Teyá 183 E2
Thallern 200 F3
Thann 113 F2
Thanvillé 113 D2
Thasos 215 B4
Thauvenay 119 F3
Thénac 105 F4
Theodorshall 147 F1
Thessalia 215 C3, 215 C2
Thessaloniki 215 B3
Thézan 124 C3
Thira 215 E4
Thomas Vineyards 230 G4
Thonon-les-Bains 127 A2
Thouarcé 114 C5, 116 E6
Thouars 59 D1, 114 C5
Thrace (Thraki) 215 A4
Thrace (Trakya) 220 B2
Thraki 215 A4
Thun 197 F3, 270 F4
Thuner See 270 F4
Thüngersheim 158 D3
Thurgau 197 D4
Thurso 265 B5
Thurston 252 F6
Thurtal 197 B4
Tiana 183 E1
Ticino 197 G4
Tie-Landry 68 F3
Tiffon 259 B3
Tihany 204 G6
Tijuana 251 E1
Tillières 114 F3
Timişoara 209 F1
Timpert 141 E4
Tinos 215 D4
Tinqueux 107 A3
Tirano 161 A6, 165 C1
Tire 220 C2
Tirgu-Mures 209 E3
Tirnăve 209 E3
Tirnăveni 209 E3
Titisee 135 G3
Titograd 207 E4
Titov Veles 207 G5
Tivisa 182 G3
Tizon 177 C2
Tlemcen 218 B6
Tobago 267 E5
Tocai, Italy 165 D6
Tokaj 202 B4, 203 D4, 207 B1
Tokat 220 C5
Tolbuhin 211 B6
Tolcsva 202 B3, 203 B5
Toledo 175 C3
Tolima 250 B1
Tolley, Scott & Tolleys 244 B4
Tolmezzo 165 C5
Tolochenaz 194 B5
Tomatin 265 C4
Tomintoul 263 G1
Tondela 189 F4
Topolcianky 205 B5
Torbato 169 G2, 172 E2
Torcolato 165 E3
Torgiano 169 C4
Torino 163 A1, 161 C2
Tormore 263 F1
Toro 175 B3
Toroja 182 F3
Toros Dağlari 220 D3
Torrebreda 177 F4
Torre de Fontaubella 182 G3
Torre del Español 182 F3
Torredembarra 182 G5
Torre Giulia 172 B4
Torrellas de Foix 182 F5
Torreón 251 F2
Torre Quarto 172 B4
Torres Vedras 187 E3
Torri del Benaco 166 A6
Torrox 177 F3
Tortola 267 B3
Toscana 161 E6, 165 G1, 169 B3
Toul 59 B4
Toulifaut 118 C2
Toulon 59 G5, 126 D3
Toulouse 59 G2, 129 E5
Toulouse-le-Château 127 F4
Tournon 59 E4, 120 B5, 122 D3
Tournon d'Agenais 129 C4
Tournus 61 E5
Tours 59 D2, 115 B1
Tour d'Aigues 59 F5, 131 E3
Tours-sur-Marne 107 D5
Touwsrivier 247 C3
Traben 145 D3
Tracy-sur-Loire 119 F3
Traisen 146 F6
Traiskirchen 200 F3
Traismauer 198 C2
Trakya 220 B2
Traminac 207 B3, C4, C5
Traminer 165 C3, 209 E3
Tramini 202 B1
Tramonti 172 C3
Trans-en-Provence 126 B5
Transilvaniei 209 F3
Trappenberg 153 D2
Trapani 172 F1
Traralgon 241 F3
Trarbach 145 D3
Trás os Montes 187 B5
Travassos 190 F2
Trbjan 207 C1
Trebbiano 165 G4, 169 A5, F3, 172 B1
Trebbiano di Abruzzi 169 E6
Trefethen 233 E5
Tregnago 167 B5
Treilles 124 D3
Trélazé 114 B5
Trencin 205 B5
Trentadue 230 B5
Trentino 165 C3
Trento 165 D3
Trépail 107 C5
Treppchen 144 B6
Tresserre 124 E2
Trets 126 B2
Treviso 165 D4
Trier 135 B1
Trieste 165 D6
Trifesti 213 A1
Trinidad 267 E5
Tripoli (Tarābulus) 220 E4
Trittenheim 143 G1
Trnava 205 B5
Troblijan 207 D2
Troesmes 79 C2
Troia 172 B3
Trois Puits 107 A4
Tronquoy-de-Lalande 85 B4
Trouillas 124 E2
Troyes 59 B4
Tsadha 216 D1
Tsimlyanskoye 213 A4
Tsinandali 213 C4
Tua 191 E3
Tübingen 135 E5
Tuchan 124 D2
Tulare 229 E3
Tulbagh 247 C2
Tulette 59 F5, 131 D2
Tulle 59 E3, 130 C6
Tullibardine 265 E4
Tunis 219 B5
Tunisia 219
Tunuyán 251 B4
Tupin-et-Semons 121 B3
Tupungato 251 B4
Turgovishte 211 C4
Turin (Torino) 161 C2, 163 A1
Turckheim 113 E2
Turkey (Türkiye) 220 C3
Turkheim 111 B1
Türkiye 220 C3
Turlock 234 D4
Turna 205 B6
Tuttlingen 135 F4
Turquie (Tükiye) 220 C3
Tvishi 213 C4
Tyrrell's 242 F2

U

Udine 165 C5
Uitkyk 249 E2
Uitvlugt 267 G6
Ukraine (Ukrainskaja) 211 A3
Ukrainskaja 211 A2
Umbria 169 D4
Ungeheuer 153 E4
Ungsberg 145 E3
Ungstein 153 B5
United Arab Republic 220 G3
United Vintners 234 C3, 235 G1
United Vintners Petri 234 C3
Unterberg 139 B2
Unterdürrbach 158 B5
Unterland 197 B4
Unterloiben 201 G2
Unter Türckheim 156 D4
Untersée 197 B4
Upland 230 G4
Urbelt 139 B2
Ürgüp 220 C4
Urquhart 263 A4
Uruguay 251 C4
Ürzig 144 B5
Usak 220 C2
Uv-Madera 234 F6
Uzunköprü 220 B1

V

Vác 202 B2
Vaillons 79 E3
Valais 197 G2, 270 G4
Valagarina 165 C3
Valcargado 177 C2
Valdadige 165 D2
Val de Loire 59 D1, D2, C2
Val de Marne 59 B3
Valdeorras 175 A2
Valdepeñas 175 C3
Valdespino 177 C3, 177 C4
Val di Chiana 169 B4
Val di Lupo 172 F3
Val-d'Oise 59 B2
Vale de Cambra 189 D5
Vale de Figueira 191 G4
Vale de Mendiz 191 E1
Valença 187 A4, 189 A4
Valença do Douro 190 G6
Valence 59 E4, 120 C5, 129 E3
Valençay 115 C3, 130 B6
Valencia 175 C5
Valetta 216 G2
Valeyrac 80 B2
Valgella 161 A5
Valladolid 175 B3
Valle d'Aosta 161 B2
Valle del Cauca 250 B1
Valle d'Oro 245 C5
Vallet 114 C3, 114 F3
Vallmoll 182 F4
Vallo della Lucania 172 C3
Vallromanas 183 E1
Valls 182 F4
Valmur 79 D4
Valongo 189 C5
Valpantena 165 E2
Valparaíso 250 C1, 251 B2
Valpolicella 165 E2, 167 C3
Valpolicella Classico 167 B2
Valpolicella Superiore 167 B4
Valtellina 161 A5, 165 C1
Vámosújfalu 203 B5
Vandellos 182 G3
Vannes 58 C6
Var 59 G5, 126 B3
Varen 195 C4
Varese 161 B4
Varna 211 C5
Vasa 216 D2
Vascongadas 175 A4
Vasto 169 G6
Vavatsinia 216 C3
Vaucluse 59 F5, 120 D5
Vaucoupin 79 E5
Vaud 279 G3, 194 A6, 197 F1
Vaudemanges 107 D6
Vaudésir 79 C4
Vaudieu 123 B4
Vaudois 197 D2
Vaufegé 118 C3
Vaufoynard 118 C1
Vaugiraud 79 E4
Vaugondy 118 B4
Vaulorent 79 C3
Vauvert 125 D9
Vayres 80 E4
Veaugues 119 G2
Veilshöchheim 158 D3
Vegardó 203 B6
Velce 205 B4
Velddrif 247 C1
Veldenz 144 G6
Vélines 105 E2
Velke Levare 205 B5
Velkev Zernoseky 205 A3
Veltelini 202 B1
Vendée 59 D1, 114 D2
Vendôme 115 A2
Vendrell 182 F5
Veneto 165 D3
Venezia 165 E4
Venezuela 267 F4, 250 B1
Venice (Venezia) 165 E4
Venise (Venezia) 165 E4
Venthône 195 C4
Ventiseri 132 F5
Vera Cruz 177 D2
Vérargues 59 F4, 125 C9
Verceil (Vercelli) 161 C4
Vercelli 161 C4
Verdea 215 D2
Verdicchio dei Castelli di Jesi 169 C5
Verdicchio di Matelica 169 C5
Verdigny 119 E2
Verdiso 165 D4
Verdon 105 E6
Verduzzo 165 C6
Verenay 121 B3
Vergisson 75 E2
Vérin 121 C2
Veritas 244 B4
Verlieux 121 D2
Vermentino 161 E3, 169 F2, 172 D1
Vermut di Torino 161 C3
Vernaccia 165 D3, 169 F2, 172 D1
Vernaccia di Oristano 172 D1
Vernaccia di Serrapetrona 169 B5
Vernaccia Gimíniano 169 B3
Vernou-sur-Brenne 118 C4
Verona 165 E3, 167 D3
Vérone (Verona) 165 E3, 167 D3
Verpelét 202 B3
Verrazzano 171 C3
Versailles 267 G6, 59 B2
Vers Chane 75 F3
Verthamon 95 A2
Vertheuil 85 E2
Vertou 114 C3, 114 F1
Vertu 107 G3
Verzenay 107 B5
Verzy 107 B5
Vésenaz 194 C4
Vésoul 59 C5
Vespella 182 F5
Vesuvio Gragnano 172 C3
Vetren 211 D2
Vétroz 195 D3
Vétroz 270 G3
Veuve Cliquot-Ponsardin 109 D5, A5
Vevey 195 B1, 197 F2, 270 G3
Véyras 195 C4
Vialer 261 E3
Viana do Castelo 187 B4, 189 B4
Vibo Valéntia 172 E4
Vicairies 119 E3
Vicenza 165 E3
Vicence (Vicenza) 165 E4
Vic Fezensac 261 C5
Vich 194 B4
Vic-la-Gardiole 125 D7
Victor Harbour 240 F5
Victoria, Australia 241 G2
Victoria 216 F1
Vidauban 126 B4
Vidin 211 B1
Vieira do Minho 189 B5
Viella 261 D3
Vienna (Wien) 198 C3, 200 C4
Vienne 59 D2, 120 A6, 114 C6
Vierwaldstätter See 197 C4, 270 F5
Vierzon 115 C4
Vieux Château Certan 99 C5
Vieux-Cussac 91 D4
Vignale 171 E4
Vignamaggio 171 D4
Vignavecchia 171 E4
Vignes Blanches 75 F2
Vignes Rondes 67 E3
Vignonet 103 G3
Vihiers 114 C5
Vila 161 A5
Viladecáns 183 F1
Vila do Conde 189 C4
Vila do Rei 188 E4
Vilallonga 182 F4
Vila Nova da Cerveira 189 A4
Vilanova de Escornalbou 182 G3
Vila Nova de Famalição 189 C4
Vila Nova de Gaia 187 B4, 193
Vilány 202 C2
Vilaplana 182 F4
Vila Real 187 B5
Vilarinho dos Freires 190 F3
Vilarrodona 182 F5
Vilaseca 182 G4
Vila Verde 189 B5
Vilella Alta 182 F3
Vilella Baja 182 F3
Villa Arceno S.p.A. 171 G5
Villa Armando 237 A3
Villa Atuel 251 D5
Villafranca del Panadés 182 F6, 175
Villa Mt Eden 233 C5
Villamblard 105 C5
Villanueva y Geltrú 182 F6
Villardeau 119 E5
Villarosa 171 E2
Villars-sous-Yens 194 B5
Villaudric 59 G2, 130 E6
Villé 270 D3
Ville-Dommange 107 A3
Villefranche 61 G5
Villefranche-de-Lonchat 105 D2
Ville-la-Grand 127 B2
Villemolaque 124 E2,
Villenave 95 D4
Villenave-d'Ornon 95 D5, 80 F3
Villeneuve (Switz) 104 E2, 195 B1, 270 G3
Villeneuve-de-Marsan 129 E2
Villeneuve-les-Avignon 120 G5
Villeneuve-les-Corbières 124 D3
Villeneuve-Minervois 124 B3
Villers-Allerand 107 B4
Villers-Marmery 107 C6
Villette 194 B6
Villette-les Arbois 127 E5
Villié-Morgon 77 D4
Villiers 119 E5
Villiersdorp 247 D3
Villingen 156 F2, 270 D5
Vilovi 182 F6
Viña del Mar 251 B2
Vinebre 182 G3
Vine Vale 245 B5
Vinho Verde 187 B4
Vinifera Wines 238 D2
Vinjak 207 E5
Vinne 205 B6
Vinodolsko 207 C1
Viñols Archs 182 G4
Vinon 119 F2
Vin Santo 169 B3
Vinsanto 215 E4
Vins de Béarn 130 E4
Vins d'Entraygues et du Fel 131 D1
Vins d'Estaing 131 D1
Vin de Lavilledieu 130 E6
Vins de Marcillac 130 D6
Vins d'Orléanais 130 A6
Vins de Savoie 131 C3
Vins du Bugey 131 C2
Vins du Haut-Poiton 130 B5
Vins du Lyonnais 131 C2
Vins du Thouarsais 130 B5
Vins du Tursan 130 E4
Vintner's 245 B5
Vinzel 194 B4
Vinzelles 75 F3
Vionnaz 195 C1
Vipava 207 B1
Virgin Islands 267 A3
Virgin Island Rum Distilleries Ltd. 267 B3
Vis 207 E2
Visalia 229 E3
Viseu 187 C5, 189 E5
Vishovgrad 211 C3
Visp 195 C6, 197 G3
Visperterminen 195 C6
Viterbo 169 D3
Vitiano 171 B4
Viticulteurs Réunis 259 D2
Vitoria 175
Vittoria 172 G3
Vivario 132 E5
Vlasotinci 207 F6
Vlottenburg (Co-op) 249 G1
Voegtlinshoffen 110 C5
Vogelsang, Nahe 147 C1
Vogelsang, Rheingau 150 F3
Vogelsang, Saar 139 F3, G3
Vogtei Rötteln 156 G1
Voiteur 127 F4
Vojvodina 207 C4
Volkach 158 D4
Volnay 61 D5, 67 E4
Volos 215 C3
Volxheim 155 F2
Voriai Sporádhes 215 C4
Vörös 202 C2
Vosges 270 D3
Vosgros 79 E4
Vöslau 198 D3
Vosne-Romanée 61 C5

Editor: Patrick Matthews
Designer: Florianne Henfield
Production: Donald Porter

Map Director: Harold Fullard
Chief Cartographer: Peter Gutteridge

Illustrators: Norman Barber, Roger Bristow, Marilyn Bruce, Ray Burrows, David Cook, Diagram, Chris Forsey, David Fryer, Gilchrist Studios, Patrick Leeson, Michael McGuinness, Vernon Mills, Peter Morter, Shirley Parfitt, Charles Pickard, Quad, Colin Rose, Rodney Shackell, Alan Suttie, Peter Wrigley.

Photographs and Pictures

Sequence from left to right, top to bottom from A:

6 Mary Evans Picture Library
9 Colin Maher
12 B Michael Holford
13 A BPC Library: B, C Reading Museum
14 A Bodleian Library, Oxford: C John Rylands Library: E Michael Holford
15 Giraudon, Paris
16 A André Simon Collection: B Richard Winslade
18 Pierre Mackiewicz
26 A Elizabeth Photo Library: B Colorific
32 A Roland Vadi: B Musée des Arts et Traditions Populaires, Paris
38 A Giraudon
39 B Historisches Museum der Pfalz
41 A Richard Winslade
43 French National Tourist Office
44 John Hedgecoe: Bacchus model by Alistair Bowtell
45 Photographs of Michael Broadbent, wine director of Christie's, by John Hedgecoe
48 Richard Winslade
49 A John Hedgecoe: B Richard Winslade
50–51 John Hedgecoe: punch bowl, N. Bloom & Son, London: decanter labels, Wyard Druitt & Co, London
57 Hugh Johnson
58 John Bulmer
60 Jean Michot
64 B, E Jean Michot: C, D, F Guy Gravett
66 A, B, D, E Hugh Johnson: C Guy Gravett
69 Hugh Johnson
70 Guy Gravett
71 Hugh Johnson
73 Guy Gravett
74 A Robert Harding Associates: B Hugh Johnson
75 Robert Harding Associates
76 A, B Picturepoint
78 Guy Gravett
81 Guy Gravett
84 A Guy Gravett: B International Distillers & Vintners, London
86 Guy Gravett
88 B Marc Riboud
90 Les Editions des Deux Coqs d'Or
94 A Grants of St James's: B Guy Gravett
96 Robert Harding Associates
98 A, B, C Guy Gravett
100 A Marc Riboud: B Guy Gravett
102 Guy Gravett
105 Aerofilms
106 Daily Telegraph Colour Library
108 B Comité Interprofessionnel du Vin de Champagne
110–111 A Ian Yeomans: B, C, D Comité Interprofessionnel du Vin d'Alsace
115 Guy Gravett
116 Guy Gravett
119 French National Tourist Office
121 Editions J. Cellard

122–123 A Editions des Deux Coqs d'Or: B Guy Gravett: C ZEFA
124 Virginia Fass
128 ZEFA
132 ZEFA
138 Bavaria Verlag
140 Bavaria Verlag
142 A Hugh Johnson: B Adam Woolfitt
143 Toni Schneiders
144–145 Deinhard & Co
146 Staatlichen Weinbaudomänen Niederhäusen-Schlossböckelheim
147 Picturepoint
148 A Peter Hallgarten: B, C Editions des Deux Coqs d'Or
149 Peter Hallgarten
152 A Editions des Deux Coqs d'Or: B, C, D Urbanus-Fotopress
154 Adam Woolfitt
155 A ZEFA: B Colin Maher
156–157 Foto Muhlbauer
158 A Rodney Todd-White: B ZEFA
159 Hugh Johnson
162 Guy Gravett
164 Italian State Tourist Department
167 Camera Press
168 Popperfoto
170 Hugh Johnson
173 ZEFA
174 Guy Gravett
176 A Guy Gravett
178 Guy Gravett
180 Picturepoint
182 Anne Bolt
183 Western Licence Suppliers
184 Picturepoint
186 Guy Gravett
188 A Hugh Johnson: B Guy Gravett
190–191 Guy Gravett
192–193 Guy Gravett
194–195 Camera Press
196 A, B Swiss National Tourist Office
198–199 A ZEFA: B Hugh Johnson: C Austrian State Tourist Department
201 Radio Times Hulton Picture Library
203 Editions des Deux Coqs d'Or
204 CTK, Czechoslovakia
206 A David Ross: B Guy Gravett
209 A Romanian Press Office: B Camera Press
210 Keystone
212 Novosti
213 Peter Keen
214 A Guy Gravett: B Greek National Tourist Office
217 Guy Gravett
218 B Paul Almasy
221 M.E. Archives
223 Wine Institute
225 Wine Institute
226–227 Portraits courtesy Wine Institute/Mansell Collection/Crown Zellerbach Corporation/D. J. Flanagan-Buffalo/Philip Wagner/Konstantin Frank
231 Harolyn Thompson
234 A Wine Institute: B Ted Streshinsky
235 Hugh Johnson
236 A Wine Institute
238–239 Taylor Wine Co
240 Colorific
242 New South Wales Government Office
243 George Rainbird
244–245 John Hedgecoe
246 KWV
248 KWV
250–251 A Anglo-Chilean Society: B Picturepoint: C Evans Brothers
252 Guy Gravett
253 Scotch Whisky Association: B Hugh Johnson
264 A, B, C Distillers Co Ltd
266–267 Yves Alexandre, Paris
268–269 Bourbon Institute
270 Swiss National Tourist Office
271 Guy Gravett